International Media C   in a Global Age

International Media Communication in a Global Age provides a thorough examination of key issues regarding global communication, with a focus on international news and strategic communication. Acknowledging the extensive breadth and scope of the international communication research field, this volume serves as an introduction to the latest trends in global communication scholarship. It addresses:

- New theoretical approaches to studying the field of international communication;
- International journalism, focusing on ways in which journalists frame the news, how credible readers perceive the news to be, and the influence of online news and blogging on the media environment;
- Key concepts of strategic global communication, such as international public relations, ethics, advertising, and global media ownership.

Unique features of this work include:

- Theoretical and practical studies that highlight the complicated nature of the international news selection process;
- Research findings on the cross-national and cross-cultural nature of media coverage of global events, presented in the interdisciplinary context of political communication, war coverage, new technologies, and online communication.

With contributions from leading international scholars doing work in this field, this collection will serve as an indispensible resource in the field of global media communication research.

Guy J. Golan is an assistant professor in the Department of Communication of Seton Hall University.

Thomas J. Johnson is the Marshall and Sharleen Formby Regents Professor in convergent media and a professor of journalism in the College of Mass Communications at Texas Tech University.

Wayne Wanta holds the Welch-Bridgewater chair at the Oklahoma State University.

COMMUNICATION SERIES

Jennings Bryant / Dolf Zillman, General Editors

Selected titles in Journalism (Maxwell McCombs, Advisory Editor) include:

Real Feature Writing
Aamidor

Communicating Uncertainty
Media Coverage of News and Controversial Science
Friedman/Dunwoody/Rogers

Professional Feature Writing, Fifth Edition
Bruce Garrison

Taking it to the Streets
Qualitative Research in Journalism
Iorio

Twilight of Press Freedom
The Rise of People's Journalism
Merrill/Gade/Blevens

Public Journalism and Public Life
Why Telling the News Is Not Enough, Second Edition
Merritt

Reviewing the Arts
Titchener

International Media
Communication in a Global Age

Edited by

Guy J. Golan, Thomas J. Johnson, and Wayne Wanta

Routledge
Taylor & Francis Group

NEW YORK AND LONDON

First published 2010
by Routledge
270 Madison Ave, New York, NY 10016

Simultaneously published in the UK
by Routledge
2 Park Square, Milton Park, Abingdon, Oxon OX14 4RN

Routledge is an imprint of the Taylor & Francis Group, an informa business

© 2010 Taylor and Francis

Typeset in Sabon and Gill Sans by EvS Communication Networx, Inc.
Printed and bound in the United States of America on acid-free paper by Edwards
Brothers, Inc.

Library of Congress Cataloging in Publication Data
International communication in a global age / edited by Guy J. Golan, Thomas Johnson
and Wayne Wanta.
p. cm.
1. Foreign news. 2. Communication, International. 3. Journalism—United States.
4. Journalism—Political aspects. I. Golan, Guy J. II. Johnson, Thomas, 1960– III. Wanta,
Wayne.
PN4784.F6I583 2009
302.2—dc22
2009010029

ISBN10: 0-415-99899-9 (hbk)
ISBN 10: 0-415-99900-6 (pbk)
ISBN 10: 0-203-88128-1 (ebk)

ISBN 13: 978-0-415-99899-4 (hbk)
ISBN 13: 978-0-415-99900-7 (pbk)
ISBN 13: 978-0-203-88128-6 (ebk)

Contents

PART I

The Determinants of International News Flow and Coverage   I

Introduction: International News Coverage and Americans' Image of the World   3
GUY J. GOLAN, THOMAS J. JOHNSON, AND WAYNE WANTA

1 Changing Global Media Landscape, Unchanging Theories?: International Communication Research and Paradigm Testing   8
TSAN-KUO CHANG

2 Determining the Scope of "International" Communication: A (Living) Systems Approach   36
SHELTON A. GUNARATNE

3 International News Determinants in U.S. News Media in the Post-Cold War Era   71
KUANG-KUO CHANG AND TIEN-TSUNG LEE

4 The Impact of Global News Coverage on International Aid   89
YON SOO LIM AND GEORGE A. BARNETT

5 Coverage of Foreign Elections in the United States: A Model of International News Flow   109
WAYNE WANTA AND GUY J. GOLAN

6 Determinants of International News Coverage   125
GUY J. GOLAN

PART II

The Language of International News   **145**

7 How Could So Much Produce So Little?: Foreign Affairs
   Reporting in the Wake of 9/11   147
   SHAHIRA FAHMY

8 Patterns of News Quality: International Stories Reported
   in American Media   160
   RENEE MARTIN-KRATZER AND ESTHER THORSON

9 The Influence of Contextual Factors on the Selection of News
   Frames: A Cross-National Approach to the News Coverage
   of Severe Acute Respiratory Syndrome (SARS)   177
   KUANG-KUO CHANG, CHARLES T. SALMON, BYOUNGKWAN LEE,
   JOUNGHWA CHOI, AND GERI ALUMIT ZELDES

10 News as Culture: A Comparative Study of Newspaper
    Coverage of the War in Iraq   200
    SALMA I. GHANEM

11 Frame Building and Media Framing of the Joint
    Counterterrorism: Comparing United States–Uganda Efforts   220
    YUSUF KALYANGO JR.

12 See No Evil, Hear No Evil, Judge as Evil?: Examining
    Whether Al-Jazeera English-Language Web Site Users
    Transfer Their Belief in Its Credibility to Its Satellite Network   241
    THOMAS J. JOHNSON AND SHAHIRA FAHMY

13 An Exploration of the Determinants of International News
    Coverage in Australia's Online Media   261
    XIAOPENG WANG

14 Blogs as Stealth Dissent?: "Eighteen Touch Dog Newspaper"
    and the Tactics, Ambiguity, and Limits of Internet Resistance
    in China   277
    WEI ZHA AND DAVID D. PERLMUTTER

PART III

Strategic Global Communication   **297**

15 Global Integration or Local Responsiveness?: Multinational
    Corporations' Public Relations Strategies and Cases   299
    JOON SOO LIM

16 Coordination and Control of Global Public Relations to
    Manage Cross-National Conflict Shifts: A Multidisciplinary
    Theoretical Perspective for Research and Practice   319
    JUAN-CARLOS MOLLEDA AND ALEXANDER LASKIN

17 Netizens Unite!: Strategic Escalation of Conflict to Manage a
    Cultural Crisis   345
    SOOYOUNG CHO AND GLEN T. CAMERON

18 Communicating with Global Publics: Building a Theoretical
    Framework for International Public Relations   366
    PAUL S. LIEBER AND COLIN HIGGINS

19 Columbia's Juan Valdez Campaign: Brand Revitalization
    through "Authenticity" and "Glocal" Strategic
    Communications   380
    JUAN-CARLOS MOLLEDA AND MARILYN S. ROBERTS

20 The Influence of Mobile Phone Advertising on Dependency:
    A Cross-Cultural Study of Mobile Phone Use between
    American and Chinese Youth   401
    RAN WEI

21 Fractured Images: Disability Advertising Effects on Filipino
    Audiences   422
    ZENY SARABIA-PANOL

22 Concentration of Ownership in European Broadcasting   442
    MARIUS DRAGOMIR

    Index   463

Part I

The Determinants of International News Flow and Coverage

Introduction

International News Coverage and Americans' Image of the World

Guy J. Golan, Thomas J. Johnson, and Wayne Wanta

Following the collapse of the Soviet Union and the subsequent end of the Cold War, the world has witnessed an unprecedented transformation of global politics and economics that was sparked by the emergence and applications of new communication technologies. As globalization redefined the basic axioms of 21st century society, scholars of international communications had to reexamine some of the very fundamental understandings of how the mass media operate in this new globalized world.

In his book, *The World is Flat* (2005), *New York Times* columnist Thomas Friedman outlined a new paradigm for understanding this so-called new flat world. He argues that globalization, along with a variety of factors, have made the world flat. In this flat world, knowledge-based industries can be assisted from any place in the world. So, for example, a software company that is based in the United States can hire software engineers from Russia and Israel for development, customer service representatives from India, accountants from Canada, and marketing firms from California and New York. Friedman argues that the flattening of the world has reshaped and redefined many of the very basic concepts of world economics, politics, and culture. Friedman identified several separate forces that led to the flattening of the world, including the fall of barriers, Internet browsers, open sourcing, out sourcing, off-shoring, supply chain logistics, the availability of information and digitalization.

One can argue that globalization has redefined international communication in several ways. First, it opened previously closed markets to conglomerate media corporations across the world. Second, the diffusion of high speed Internet and bandwidth has transformed the nature of international news content availability. Finally, the combination of globalized media conglomerates and the Internet/digital revolution has changed the very nature of the area in which global journalism and mass communication operate across the world (Pavlik, 2001).

The first proposition regarding globalization and media conglomerates was evident in the late 1990s with the fall of the Soviet Union and the emergence of free markets. As former spheres of influence, nations

Al-Jazaeera Web site have transferred their credibility judgments of the Web site to the Arab-language Al-Jazeera television network. Finally, two studies explore questions concerning convergent media technologies. Xiaopeng Wang expanded the study of international news flows to the online media environment by focusing on online media coverage in Australia. Wei Zha and David D. Perlmutter look at a popular Chinese blog "Eighteen Touch Dog Newspapers" to explore ways in which a blog supposedly devoted to canine issues can be a vehicle of dissent *without* incurring the wrath of the state.

Part III of our book deals with key concepts of strategic global communication, such as international public relations practices, ethics, international advertising, and global media ownership. Two authors suggest new theoretical approaches to improve the practice of public relations. Joon-Soo Lim introduces the integration-responsiveness grid model for optimizing multinational corporations' international public relations strategies. Juan-Carlos Molleda and Alexander Laskin provide a comprehensive review of the public relations and international business literatures to offer evidence for effective organizational structure, strategies, and actions to manage conflicts or crises that originate in one country that transfer and have consequences for the organization's headquarters or main host markets. Sooyoung Cho and Glen T. Cameron employed conflict management and crisis management strategies to examine how a South Korean company tried to communicate and manage a specific crisis in regards to nude images it was marketing through cell phones that portrayed a famous Korean actress as a "comfort woman," those women who were used by the Japanese army as sex slaves during World War II. Paul S. Lieber and Colin Higgins, on the other hand, synthesized research on international public relations ethics, examining PR ethics in Australia, New Zealand, and the United States. Juan-Carlos Molleda and Marilyn Roberts examine Colombia's strategic communication campaign to select and rebrand one of the world's most famous icons, Juan Valdez. Ran Wei studied high school students in the United States and China and examined the role of advertising in cultivating a dependency relationship with the mobile phone. Zeny Sarabia-Panol did an experiment that examined reactions of Filipinos to advertising that featured models with physical impairments and ones that did not. Finally, Marius Dragomir discusses the trend toward concentration of media ownership in Europe and the problems inherent in this trend.

Fully aware of both the extensive breadth and the scope of the international communication research field, the current book serves as an introduction rather than a summary of some of the latest trends in global communication scholarship. As the ever changing nature of international communication continues to evolve, it is our hope that this book will help advance knowledge in the field of international communication for both students and scholars alike.

References

Chan-Olmsted, S. M., & Chang, B. H. (2003). Diversification strategy of global media conglomerates: Examining its patterns and determinants. *Journal of Media Economics, 16*(4), 213–233.

Friedman, T. L (2005). *The world is flat: A brief history of the 21st century.* New York: Farrar, Straus & Giroux,

Jin, D. Y. (2007). Transformation of the world television system under neoliberal globalization, 1983–2003. *Television and New Media, 8*(3), 179–196.

Pavlik, J. V. (2001) *Journalism and new media.* New York: Columbia University Press.

Wu, H. D. (2000). Systemic determinants of international news coverage: A comparison of 38 countries. *Journal of Communication, 30*(2), 110–130.

Chapter 1

Changing Global Media Landscape, Unchanging Theories?

International Communication Research and Paradigm Testing

Tsan-Kuo Chang

On May 25, the 2008 Cannes film festival awarded the French film *Entre les Murs* ("The Class") the Palme d'Or as the best film among the 22 films in competition. This was the first time in 21 years that a French film had won the top prize at the Cannes international festival. Also, according to *The Economist* ("On-Screen Confidence," May 31, 2008, p. 89), another French film, *Bienvenue Chez les Ch'tis* ("Welcome to the Sticks"), "is set to overtake James Cameron's Hollywood blockbuster, 'Titanic,' as the country's all-time top box-office hit." Given the significance of these two historical moments, *The Economist* opened its report from Paris this way: "The French film industry is more often given to introspective agonizing about *American cultural imperialism* [italics added] or the tyranny of the market than to self-congratulation" (p. 89,). In the wake of the two milestones, it remains to be seen whether French intellectuals and critics of U.S. media practices will breathe a collective relief over the passing of American cultural imperialism in France. It is not clear whether the characterization of *American* cultural imperialism by *The Economist*, a highly respected international magazine, implies that there are types of *non-American* cultural imperialism.

Nevertheless, what is significant, both theoretically and practically, about the story is that the phrase *American cultural imperialism* continues to be used in international news discourse as a point of reference concerning the flow of cultural products between countries when globalization has increasingly become the driving force behind today's interconnected and interdependent communities of nations. *The Economist* certainly is not alone among the international news media to adopt the jargon of international communication research in their news reporting. It is hardly surprising, however, because in recent years scholarly books and journal articles on international communication have followed cultural imperialism either as a theoretical framework or as a discourse in explicating the diffusion of various cultural products across national borders in the age of digital technologies and global communication.

Although the precise origin of the idea of *cultural imperialism*[1] is difficult to trace, it has been commonly accepted that it was first proposed in the late 1960s as a theoretical formulation to tackle the structure and processes of the complex phenomenon of U.S. media domination at the international level. Since then, the world's media landscape has changed dramatically. This is especially true because the Internet and its surrounding digital technologies have since the mid-1990s created new opportunities and challenges to the traditional media regarding the production, distribution, and consumption of content. As a theoretical framework that has weathered through the end of Cold War, the collapse of communism in Eastern Europe and the former Soviet Union, the demise of the New World Information and Communication Order, and the rise of the Internet as the first true democratic medium, the thesis of cultural imperialism apparently exhibits a remarkable shelf life with no sign of abating. Any field of intellectual inquiry that has endured for more than four decades deserves close scholarly scrutiny. The purpose of this chapter is to offer a critical examination of how and why the theory of cultural imperialism has persisted over time in terms of its epistemological approaches, methodological designs, and knowledge claims as well as its relationship with other competing theories.

Against the backdrop of the sociology of knowledge (Mannheim, 1936) and using Kuhn's (1970/1996) notion of paradigm testing[2] as the conceptual framework, this chapter specifically focuses on the discourse of cultural imperialism in international communication research as an area of theoretical articulation and persuasion. Since the 1960s, the global media landscape has changed dramatically in ways that have fundamentally rearranged the media actors and reconfigured the rules of their engagement. For one thing, as *The Economist* put it ("Wrestling for Influence," July 5, 2008, p. 34), a "modern map of power and influence" should not only include *"transformational tools"* [italics added] such as the Internet, but also dozens of actors exercising different kinds of power. If the media are no longer American, as Jeremy Tunstall argued in his book *The Media Were American: U.S. Mass Media in Decline* (2008), is the thesis of cultural imperialism still theoretically relevant to international communication research? If not, why and how does it become a "dominant paradigm" (e.g., Chadha & Kavoori, 2000; Chilcote, 2002) that has been routinely accepted as a given in the literature (e.g., Kamalipour, 2007; Mody, 2003; Silverblatt & Zlobin, 2004) when the theory apparently has not solved any problems of international communication?

Although some scholars have regarded the thesis of cultural imperialism as a dominant paradigm in international communication research, it is not the intention of this chapter to extend its theoretical status in the Kuhnian sense of the word.[3] For lack of a better word, the notion of *paradigm* testing, as will be discussed later, does not necessarily imply the existence of competing paradigms in international communication research. Nor does this chapter seek to provide another review of cultural imperialism in its historical and empirical context. There have been ample discourses and extensive critiques of the conceptual and epistemological problems of cultural imperialism in various texts elsewhere (e.g., Chadha & Kavoori, 2000; Curtin, 2007; Golding & Harris, 1997; C-C. Lee, 1979; S-N.P. Lee, 1988; Roach, 1997; Salwen, 1991; Tomlinson, 1999).

This chapter departs from previous studies in two main respects. First, the advent of new information and communication technologies from the 1960s through the 1990s, especially satellites and the Internet,[4] has unequivocally created a global media environment that defies traditional conceptions and requires rethinking of what is to be seen and how to see it. The network structure—the interconnectedness and interdependence of countries as nodes in cyberspace—has conceptual and theoretical implications for international communication research. Second, given the shifting reality in international communication that has been conceived and investigated in various theoretical perspectives over time, no existing theory can be tested in isolation by itself, nor can it be assumed to progress from the previous ones. It is imperative that theories purported to describe and explain the same phenomenon in international communication be tested comparatively. Epistemologically, the validity of cultural imperialism as a theory and its knowledge claim hinges on how it stacks up against alternative explanations.

Given the increasing scholarly attention to the phenomenon of globalization in international communication research, the thesis of cultural imperialism is not, as will be discussed later, necessarily being replaced by the theoretical formulation of globalization as a general framework that appears to encompass many elements underpinning the "dominant paradigm." The fact that cultural imperialism and globalization seem to be able to explain more or less the same patterns of flow of cultural products and their consequences means that neither theory should be examined in isolation for its explication of the facts, but must be theoretically and empirically juxtaposed, if international communication researchers seek to determine in the changing global media landscape which competing theory fits the reality better.

The Changing Global Media Landscape: New Reality and Concepts

The Internet is about 40 years old, if 1969 is used as the starting point, when the U.S. ARPANET became the predecessor of today's network of networks. Coincidentally, Herbert Schiller first published his influential book *Mass Communications and American Empire* in the same year. Compared to other forms of mass media, the history of the Internet is relatively short and its future direction and development are still unpredictable. What is certain is that since the advent of the Internet, the field of international communication as we knew it some 15 years ago has changed considerably in areas of production, dissemination and consumption of news, information, and data, not to mention its form of global reach and complex structure.

Quantitatively, where local access points are available through either broadband or dial-up services, the Internet has increasingly expanded the size of daily audiences in units of millions at a speed and pace previously unthinkable. Qualitatively, the technological convergence has led to a single communication platform within which all existing forms of mass media and the emerging ones, especially those personalized vehicles such as cell phones, have merged to create the world's largest library, theater, shopping mall, bookstore, social network, information center, news outlet, public forum, and many more entities that recognize no national borders and are readily available by a click of the mouse or a touch of the screen (e.g., Castells, 2001). Not only is content the new king, its speedy delivery is also unrivaled.

Economically, the gains of the Internet have increasingly come at the expense of the conventional media forms, especially the newspaper and television. In the United States, major newspapers and the three traditional commercial networks have been losing audiences and hence advertising revenues to the Internet since the mid-1990s. The Internet, however, is not the only cause of the troubles faced by the traditional media. Cable and satellite TV, especially CNN, started the downturn of viewership for ABC, CBS, and NBC in the early 1980s. The e-commerce and new economy made possible by the Internet have made it worse since the 1990s (e.g., Castells, 2001). Consequently, reduction of staff and reorientation of the content to stay competitive in the marketplace have been a staple of traditional media's responses to the challenges of the Internet (e.g., *Star Tribune*, "Star Tribune to Cut Staff as Circulation, Revenue Fall," May 8, 2007; *New York Times*, "The Times to Cut 100 News Jobs," February 15, 2008). The trend will most likely continue for years to come. It means that the media landscape has undergone unprecedented changes in terms of its configuration and operations. In the age of the digital revolution, when the media reality has shifted beyond recognition and in the context of research through observation and explanation, the academic community has been slow to keep abreast with the changing media reality. This is especially true in the theoretical domain. If "changes in communications alter cultures—expanding, changing, and destroying them," as Greig (2002) argued, then it is theoretically important to carefully reexamine how the advent of the Internet

penetrating as they might be at the global level, still face the political powers, exercised not necessarily by the individual nation-states of the European Union, but by the authority of the EU as a regional block (e.g., Chadwick, 2006).

Explanation for the persistent domination of cultural products by a few countries cannot be reduced to a single dimension—the logic of capitalism expansion in search of more overseas markets and hence more profits. The autonomy of nation-states and the strategies they may take to protect their best interests cannot be underestimated. A recent example in South Korea is illustrative. Although not directly related to the flow of cultural products, the online protests and activism in South Korea against the import of American beef demonstrate that a strong nationalist sentiment or movement could in some way undermine or confront foreign imposition of commercial products. In other words, nationalism may rise to the challenge of imperialism, if any. This should also be true in international communication.

It is therefore difficult to imagine that the nation-state could be completely bypassed when multinational corporations decide to move cultural products from one country to another or to invest heavily in other countries. The diffusion of capital, technologies, and cultural products must end somewhere where the recipients are willing or are in a position to accept and absorb the flows on an equal basis (e.g., Creig, 2002). The nation-state might be coerced to accept unfair and unequal conditions when capital is badly needed in terms of foreign direct investment, either through the imposition of global financial organizations such as the World Bank and International Monetary Fund (IMF) or through bilateral agreements between a powerful patron and a client. As such, dissemination of cultural products is often taken in the literature to mean consumption and reception as well as internalization of foreign products and tastes (e.g., Salwen, 1991). But it is unthinkable to envision that audiences worldwide could be coerced to consume cultural products exported from multinational corporations just because they are available. In the era of the Internet, it is even more unimaginable that individual users as nodes of the network could be unwillingly compelled to expose themselves to the kinds of content that they do not choose in the first place.

As a result of globalization, is the global network a new configuration of the world media landscape or merely an extension of the old order and as such nothing more than cultural imperialism in disguise? For some, the ubiquitous Internet has provided a new vehicle to further expand American imperial influences in cyberspace. The domination of U.S. corporations among the top Web sites worldwide appears to support this observation. There is evidence that the structural imbalance and unequal flow in international communication are being reproduced through hyperlinks in the world of global digital communication where the United States stands as the center of the networks among nations (e.g., Chang, Himelboim, & Dong, in press; Himelboim, 2008). But is it indeed an *imperialistic* structure that compels countries to offer hyperlinks to Web sites located in the United States rather than the other way around? The network structure deserves to be further explored.

Open Network, Closed Flow, and the Power-Law Distribution

Since its inception, all countries have more or less been connected to the Internet, but inside cyberspace most nations appear to be disconnected to one another. As demonstrated by Chang, Himelboim, and Dong (in press) and Himelboim (2008), in the global network society, only a small number of countries, particularly the United States and the United Kingdom, are connected to many countries through either incoming or outgoing hyperlinks, while most countries have no linkages to other countries at all. This pattern is similar to the one commonly identified in the literature that involves international news flow and coverage. No existing theory in international communication research, however, seems to be able to explain why the structure of the offline world gets reproduced in cyberspace. Given the various efforts to define imperialism in ways of conceptual clarity and operational measurement in international communication research, it may be tempting to call such U.S. domination in the networks of cyberspace as *cyber*imperialism or neoimperialism. To do so, however, would be sidestepping a great scholarly opportunity for theory building and knowledge accumulation through interdisciplinary cross-fertilization. International communication research has to go beyond its own theories and look at what other fields of research have to offer.

Whether social or natural networks, a unique property of networks, especially large ones, is the power-law distribution, which in communication and social networks "reflects the existence of a few nodes with very high degree and many with low degree" and the "high connectivity nodes play the important role of hubs in communication and networking" (Adamic, Lukose, Rajan, Puniyani, & Huberman, 2001, p. 1). Simply put, in a large network, few nodes are highly connected to other nodes while many nodes are much less connected (e.g., Barabasi, 2003; Newman, 2003). For example, in their study of connections among Web pages, Barabasi and Albert (1999) found that few network nodes had many more linkages than the average node. They called those few network nodes "hubs," an idea akin to the hubs of international flights where few airports serve as the dominant destinations for many connecting flights from around the world while many airports worldwide do not. This power-law distribution has been observed in a variety of networks, including social groups, citations, communication, AT&T phone calls, and biological linkages (for a useful review of the related literature, see Himelboim, 2008). In other words, it is a structural attribute common to all relatively large networks.

Since telegraph, undersea cable, and telephone lines connected different parts of the world in the late 19th century, international communication has clearly formed a network of nations, through which each country as a node in the network is linked to other countries in some way. Because it is global, the network itself is undoubtedly huge. A growing body of literature has well documented that, as far as international flow of cultural products and coverage of foreign news are concerned, only a very few countries dominate the form and content of international communication while most countries stand at the receiving end or turn out to be largely invisible (e.g., Chang, 1998; Wu, 2000). As shown in Figure 1.1, this persistent pattern of international communication is similar to the power-law distribution of large networks. The accepted knowledge of the skewed equation in international communication (e.g.,

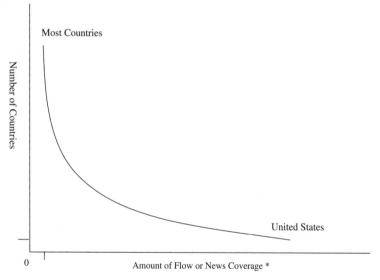

Figure 1.1 A Power-Law Distribution of International Communication

* The amount of flow or news coverage denotes the volume of international flow of cultural products (e.g., movies or TV programming) from a specific country to other countries or the volume of news coverage received by a specific country in other countries. There is not a single country around the world that never sends any cultural product to other countries or receives no coverage in international communication. Most countries are more or less covered, for example, in foreign news reporting. Also, no country ever totally dominates the international flow of cultural products or foreign news coverage. According to various findings in the literature, few countries, including the United States, command both the flow and coverage in international communication by a large amount, but not the total amount.

domination by the United States or an unequal flow) is, at least in the literature, that it is imperialism at work. An immediate question that has yet to be fully addressed is, why would an inherent structure, by default of large networks, be interpreted as imperialistic? In order to enter into a balanced state of interaction, countries should have the ability and resources to produce something equal to what is imported from other countries. Not many countries are in a position to do so in the realm of international communication, however. The imbalance is by default, not necessarily by design. Is cultural imperialism then in the eyes of beholder?

Within the perspective of the sociology of knowledge, this chapter seeks to determine the modes of thinking among scholars of international communication research to "accumulate, preserve, reformulate, and disseminate" their intellectual heritage (Wirth, cited in Mannheim, 1936, p. xxix; see also Berger & Luckmann, 1966). The organized patterns exhibited in international communication research represent what Berger, Berger, and Kellner (1974, p. 14) called "specific fields of consciousness," each of which "is a structure constituted by the modes and contents of what is consciously experienced" by the researchers. In any academic community, where publication of research is often required not only as a form of peer recognition for the privilege of remaining in the profession (e.g., tenure), but also more importantly as a venue for knowledge sharing, the modes of thinking, both individual and collective, are generally recorded in the literature. When they are summarily transferred to textbooks, they become part of what Kuhn (1970/1996) called paradigm learning. If cultural imperialism can be regarded as a paradigm, the question of its validity and knowledge claim can be best answered when it is pitted against other competing explanations. Although central to the normal science, Kuhn's idea of paradigm testing should be relevant to international communication research.

Paradigm Testing and International Communication Research

Simply put, Kuhn's paradigm testing means "comparison of theories" through a "joint verification-falsification process" (1970/1996, p. 147). It is useful to quote Kuhn extensively on the importance of paradigm testing in scientific research:

> Such a two-stage formulation has, I think, the virtue of great verisimilitude, and it may also enable us to begin explicating the role of agreement (or disagreement) between fact and theory in the verification process. To the historian, at least, it makes little sense to suggest that verification is establishing the agreement of fact with theory.

All historically significant theories have agreed with the facts, but only more or less. There is no more precise answer to the question whether or how well an individual theory fits the facts. But questions much like that can be asked when theories are taken collectively or even in pairs. It makes a great deal of sense to ask which of two actual and competing theories fits the facts *better*. (p. 147)

The last two sentences summarize the essence of paradigm testing: theories have to be compared in some way and their validity has to be judged based on which theory better explains the facts. Historically, considered in isolation, the thesis of cultural imperialism has produced impressive facts that agree with the theory. Cultural imperialism persists as a theory, not because it has solved the problems of international communication flows (e.g., unequal traffic of cultural products, external threats to indigenous culture or national identity), but because scholars and researchers continue to embrace the idea of imperialists among the media conglomerates. The global media industries, especially those of non-Western or American origin, have made significant progress toward diversity, interconnectivity, and equity (e.g., Tunstall, 2008). Yet the theory of imperialism has failed to reexamine the fixed prism used to observe the reality that has changed beyond recognition during the past few decades.

The contention of this chapter is not to deny the existence of unequal flow of cultural products at the international level, nor the fact of continuing domination of a few countries in the global media landscape. Rather, the assertion is that, given the fast changing media environment since the 1970s and 1980s, how best to explain the processes and structure of international communication requires looking at the extant theories in terms of which fits the facts better. In other words, no single theory should be considered in isolation. This is precisely the analytical weakness that is commonly found in the literature on cultural imperialism, particularly the studies that attempted to define how imperialism should be measured at the variable level. It should be safe to point out that the world international communication researchers observed is never fixed once and for all by the nature of the media landscape. The data collected in international communication research are now of different kinds: either they were not available before or they were insignificant or inconsequential.

What has not been answered compellingly is: does the theory fit the facts better than all other theories that have been proposed to explain the same facts? Theoretical orientation of international communication research can be broadly classified into two approaches: functionalist and diffusionist. The former locates the spirit and practices of international communication to internal factors while the latter traces them to external factors. As will be discussed later, the different assumptions lead to incompatible conceptualization regarding the interaction and consequences of mass communication across national borders.

In the face of increasing globalization in the media landscape, there has been an effort (e.g., Jin, 2007) to return to cultural imperialism as the theoretical framework for understanding the global flows of cultural products. The irony is that since the 1990s, there have been calls in the field of international communication research to go beyond cultural imperialism as an all-encompassing framework to examine the processes and structure of mass communication between countries (e.g., Golding & Harris, 1997; Roach, 1997; Straubhaar, 1991). The rationale has been that the audience is not passive, but autonomous; that the global media market has become more competitive as emerging economies have begun to challenge the traditional powerhouses; and that information and communication technologies have leveled the playing field for even the smallest nation-state.

In light of intellectual allegiance to conflicting theories, the strength and weakness of each theory cannot be assessed in isolation (i.e., how well the theory itself fits the facts), but rather, as Kuhn (1970/1996) argued, should be gauged, preferably in pairs (i.e., which of the competing theories fits the facts better through comparison of evidence and theoretical formulation). A recent study by Hong and Chang (2008) should be illustrative. In their study of the consumption of U.S. movies in South Korea and the United Kingdom from 1994 to 2006, they proposed to examine the interplay between culture and the flow of U.S. films in paired theoretical comparisons. Although their comparisons focused on cultural proximity, cultural discount, and globalization as competing explanations for the flow of films from the United States to the other two countries, the model can be modified to include imperialism and diffusion as two more explanations for the same phenomenon.

As outlined in Figure 1.1, they found a high degree of correlation (r = .675, p < .01) between the box offices of the same U.S. 757 movies in the United States and South Korea, indicating a strong positive relationship between the consumption of movies in the two countries. The evidence apparently does not support the thesis of cultural discount, which refers to the "diminished appeal" of cultural products rooted in one culture and not attractive in that setting to viewers elsewhere because they "find it difficult to identify with the style, values, beliefs, institutions and behavioral patterns of the material in questions" (Hoskins & Mirus, 1988, p. 500). Considering South Korea's screen quota policy that limits the import of foreign films into the country and the rejection of cultural discount as a feasible explanation for the Korean consumption, it is reasonable to attribute the flow of U.S. movies as cultural imperialism. The evidence itself appears to provide empirical support for such a conclu-

Table 1.1 Theoretical and Methodological Domains of Imperialism and Globalization

Domains	Imperialism	Globalization
Unit of Analysis	Nation-State	Non-Nation-State
Underlying Process	Diffusion	Diffusion
Direction of Flow	One-way	Two-way or Multiple ways
Major Actors	U.S. Multinational Corporations (e.g., Disney, MTV)	U.S. and Emerging National Corporations (e.g., Indian and Chinese firms)
Locus of Research	Imposition/Exploitation	Convergence/Supply and Demand
Type of Analysis	Mostly descriptive	Descriptive/Hypothesis testing
Mode of Influence	Domination/Imposition	Empowerment/Interaction
Effects on Culture	Homogenization	Homogenization, Heterogeneity, Hybridization

empirical issues that are identified through a critical review of the literature (see Chilcote, 2002 for a useful comparison of three dominant theories). Table 1.1 summarizes the competing domains of imperialism and globalization in international communication research.

Imperialism vs. Globalization in International Communication

Tunstall's (2008) proclamation that the media *were* American explicitly announces the passing of an old order of international and global communication and ushers in a new one, in which a fresh set of media organizations and arrangement of market relations has emerged that differs significantly from the decades when "the media are American" (Tunstall, 1977). It is telling that in 1977, Tunstall spent a considerable amount of space defining media imperialism and tackling its consequences; 30 years later, the word *imperialism* is not even indexed in his new book, but *globalization/global media* is. If the statement that the media were American is any indication, it means the U.S. media no longer take high command in the global media marketplace, not to mention exercising their supreme authority in the production, distribution, and consumption of cultural products.

What Tunstall observed in 2008 is that so far as information and communication technologies are concerned, the United States no longer dominates the production, distribution, and consumption of not only traditional media, but also cell phones, PDAs, and other personalized digital devices. In the age of the Internet, the digital pulses recognize no national boundaries and are not necessarily confined to specific origins. The Internet has offered opportunities and innovative means for groups and individuals to organize protests, movements, and struggles against multinational corporations. If the Internet could be used as an anti-globalization tool for all sorts of activists, ranging from antifree trade movements, human rights, labor rights, environmentalists, and so on, could it not be used against cultural imperialists? The Internet and other digital technologies have allowed media outlets worldwide to reconfigure their operations and practices in order to reach a vast number of people beyond their geographical boundaries, thus refiguring geopolitics to an extent that was unimaginable some 10 to 15 years ago. The rise of Al Jazeera as the CNN of the Islamic world is a case in point.

The proliferation of news media in various countries and on the Internet has made it possible for the organization of new alliances across diverse political spectrums and economic interests against metropolitan media and the creation of channels of wide distribution of struggles and resistance against dominant views. To some extent, theorists of cultural imperialism have failed to take note of the technological innovations and the shift of content production from corporate interests to user-generated concerns, which have largely reshaped the global media landscape. For example, the spread of viral ads on the Internet has created conflicts and ambiguities regarding the cultural significance of such texts (e.g., *Business Week*, "Raising the Bar on Viral Web Ads," July 23, 2006). Hundreds of millions of people could have access to these advertising texts that have nothing to do with corporate commercial interests. In fact, multinational corporations and mainstream media could be by-passed altogether. It is difficult to argue that in the age of Web 2.0, domination and exploitation or even imposition still rules the day in international communication. Undoubtedly, digital technologies have restructured the form and content of flows of cultural products across national borders.

The flow of cultural products from the West to the rest of the world, to use the terminology of cultural imperialism thesis, is the export of TV programming, movies, music, and other cultural forms from the center of the world capitalism system to the periphery. The other key variable is foreign ownership of media outlets in many developing and underdeveloped countries through the hands of multinational corporations. The variable-oriented approach hence leaves the nation-state out of the equation as if territorial governments worldwide are powerless and defenseless in the face of the onslaught of global media conglomerates. As powerful as Google has been in its global reach and influence, it has come to terms with the Chinese government's demand by moving its servers to China in order to serve the Chinese language users inside China. As such, it is difficult to imagine such a form of foreign direct investment as constituting cultural imperialism. Also, foreign direct investment cuts both ways: in 2007 foreign investors spent $267.8 billion "to acquire or establish American businesses"; the amount was "67% more than in 2006 and the highest level since the peak in 2000," the vast share of which was acquisitions ("Love Me, Love Me Not," *The Economist*, July 12, 2008, p. 36).

Unit of Analysis

Many key ideas, such as domination of flows, foreign ownership of media, homogenization of cultural values and tastes, appear in the thesis of both cultural imperialism and globalization. To some, globalization is simply an extension of imperialism (e.g., Vilas, 2002) or the current stage of cultural imperialism because there seems to be little theoretical effort or attempt to separate the two: it is as if they are the same just because they both refer very much to the same phenomenon. To others, globalization is qualitatively different from imperialism (e.g., Chilcote, 2002; Kellner, 2002). Although the two theories may indeed seek to make sense of the seemingly similar patterns of mass communication at the global level, their conceptual and operational departure points proceed on different units. Imperialism as a theoretical explanation for the international configuration of capitalist structure assumes the nation-states to be the unit of analysis.

Is cultural imperialism still central to the contemporary media landscape in which no one single nation-state, let alone a single conglomerate, has been able to dominate what the picture may look like? Presumably, cultural imperialism is imposed from above through multinational corporations supported by powerful nation-states in search of both profits and hegemonic influences at the international level. Globalization, in addition to imposition from above, can be configured from below, as contested at the national level. Could there be imperialism from below? The answer is obviously not if the nation-state remains the unit of analysis. The significance of Google lies not necessarily in its American-ness, that is, its identity as an American company or the location of its headquarters in the United States, but in its algorithm, a series of equations of mathematical operations consisting of abstract possibilities. In the age of digital technologies and cyberspace, scholars and researchers need to think more theoretically than empirically. Google, in its brick form, may be based in a nation-state, but in its click form, it has nothing to do with the nation-state, nor with the company itself. It is just digital pulses triggered by a touch of a mouse or a screen that run through cyberspace.

Underlying Process: Diffusion

If part of the larger phenomenon (e.g., foreign direct investment) is imperialistic, what would the whole be? Is the movement of media practitioners also imperialistic? In the conceptualization of globalization, the flow of cultural products, including films, music, TV programming and others, is part of a larger flows of products, people, ideas, services, capital, and information (e.g., Held, 2004). If the flow of cultural products is conceived as cultural imperialism in international communication research, how do we explain the flow of actors, musicians, artists and other talents in various media industries from other countries to the United States? Could this phenomenon be considered a reverse imperialism, as *Forbes* magazine argued in a commentary concerning the rise of Indian companies ("A Case of Reverse Imperialism," June 6, 2008)? A diffusionist approach would probably better explain such phenomenon. As a matter of fact, the underlying process of both imperialism and globalization has always been diffusion.

Any individual cultural product, be it a new movie, a new song, a new book or even a new advertising campaign, represents some sort of innovation. A good example is the remake of some classic movies in the United States that often outdo the previous versions. Because they embody the latest innovations, they would create lasting demand. If they remain "the same old, same old," why would audiences and consumers flock to see or make a purchase when the products become available in the market? The thesis of cultural imperialism fails to recognize that institutions, groups, individuals, and companies in any given nation-state may use the mass media and other information and communication technologies for their own purposes. The emergence of Web 2.0 again points to the new opportunities and possibilities. In the world of cyberspace, it is difficult to determine where the center is and what constitutes the periphery.

The thesis of cultural imperialism, with its root firmly grounded in the process of diffusion, has often bypassed or sidestepped the theoretical model proposed by Rogers (1971) who argued convincingly that the transfer of techniques, ideas and ways of doing things take place frequently when people share similar cultural values. At the international level, it means cultural proximity is conducive to the flows of products and services, including films, TV programming and other cultural products among nations. The acceptance of cultural imperialism as a theory is less a result of paradigm testing that rejects Rogers's diffusion of innovations than of an attempt to reinterpret well-known observations of general patterns of international flow of cultural products. Part of the inadequate conceptualization and the lack of empirical testing of competing theories is the division of labor in academic research that fails "to grips with the totality of the effects of an interaction process" (Galtung, 1971, p. 88). To be fair, it is apparently difficult, if not impossible, for scholars and researchers to see the processes and structure of international communication "in its social totality" (Galtung, 1971, p. 88). What they see mostly tends to be limited by the range of their observation, particularly the direction of flow from one country to another.

Direction of Flow

Most "new media" studies seldom question the assumptions behind existing theories that were developed when the world was very much dominated by analog communication through light and sound, rather than digital communication in bits and bytes. In the world of analog communication, the flow of messages from one place to another has to overcome physical barriers. In the world of cyberspace, the movement of messages takes on a different form. When U.S. journalists could not travel to a particular country to cover a story and when such a story was covered by local journalists, it had no way of reaching the United States; for all practical purposes, the event simply did not occur so far as American readers were concerned. And we cannot blame the U.S. media for their failure to bring it to the attention of American people or "compassion fatigue" (e.g., Moeller, 1999). In the age of the Internet, non-U.S. media have increasingly competed against their American counterparts to report world events from many different angles.

Imperialism and globalization deal with the same phenomenon that is previously known and continues to occur. As theory, they both stand at the same level; one is not necessarily higher than the other, therefore providing linkage between high and low level theories. It is doubtful that any mass communication theory is developed in a cumulative fashion. A normative theory, imperialism prescribes what should not be in international communication, but does not suggest what will likely happen. When it was first proposed in the late 1960s and early 1970s (e.g., Dorfman & Mattelart, 1971; Wells, 1972), imperialism did not even explain well the existing phenomenon, let alone those that have yet to happen (e.g., the Internet). Imperialism as a theory to explain international communication flows implies a location of origin and a direction of its traffic. Globalization may indicate both location and direction, but it underscores multiple points and multiple directions.

The Internet is the culmination of a number of media that were produced in a linear fashion throughout human history. Accordingly, scholars and researchers tend to think of the process of the Internet in a linear manner. In cyberspace, the content moves, for example, from the *New York Times* to the users. But is it indeed a form of flow at all? In the traditional notion of the concept, the flow of something implies a change of location in a physical sense, from point A to point B. Is there a location per se in the world of cyberspace? Apparently not: It is the change in equation in an abstract sense that generates the presence of that something in cyberspace.

As opposed to cultural imperialism, globalization refers to the diffusion of information, communications and cultural products around the world through open markets and free trade (e.g., Held, 2004). In international communication, globalization signals a shift of the nation-state to multinational media corporations that are not bound by any national territories. Diffusion is a form of interaction. Where there is little or no demand, there would be little or no supply at all. In international communication research, scholars have failed to take note of the multiple dimensions involved in the flows of goods and services, both tangible and intangible between nations. Diffusion as an explanatory framework cannot be ignored in international communication research. However, the diffusionist perspective has often been brushed aside as if the flow of cultural products has nothing to do with diffusion. The phenomenon of globalization in the flow of cultural products and their consumptions underscores the theoretical importance of considering the relevance of diffusionist approach.

Change in belief about the reality must take place before a new theory can emerge. If globalization is to be accepted as a plausible theory of international communication, then imperialism must be rejected as a theory in the context of new theory. As indicated by recent studies on global communication (e.g., Curtin, 2007), scholars have not been able to see the goodness of fit between the theory and the facts. They seldom question the validity of the theory when new facts have emerged that cannot be effectively explained by the theory they embrace as logical and legitimate. Imperialism as a theory appears to claim that it applies only to a certain phenomenon, not all ranges of the same phenomenon. For example, the domination of U.S. cultural products around the world would be an instance for the theory, but the spread of telenovelas or Indian films in many parts of the world would not.

In the movie industry, the United States does not produce the most number of films. Its production lags far behind that of India in terms of both number of movies and box office revenues. But Indian films have not dominated the world movie market the way the U.S. films have done. As such, the sheer quantity of films cannot feasibly explain the domination of U.S. movies around the world. The standard Marxist explanation is to argue that it is not diffusion through supply and demand per se that leads to the spread of U.S. films from country to country, but rather the practices of superior marketing strategies and the internal logic of capitalism that *imposes* U.S. films on client states in the world market. Because of its limited application, imperialism as a theory could not

In its many dimensions, globalization would require us to avoid media determinism as an extreme theoretical formulation. The literature on the network society has clearly demonstrated that the Internet and computer mediated networks have created a globalized form of interconnected and interdependent global society. Theorists of cultural imperialism have yet to take this well-established body of knowledge into account in their explication of the flows of cultural products. The theory of imperialism presented a new problem in international communication, but not a solution of that problem. If cultural imperialism is accepted as a paradigm, an immediate question has to be asked: What solution does it offer to solve the puzzle, if any, in international communication? By default, the theory of cultural imperialism contains an implicit solution: imperialists must be resisted or defeated. Neither members of the international communication research community nor global media practitioners, however, should solve the problems together. When solutions are sought outside the academic and professional communities, the issue tends to be political and ideological. A higher state authority at the global level therefore becomes attractive and logical. This is precisely why in the 1970s and the early 1980s, the New World Information and Communication Order had appealed to UNESCO to arbitrate a set of rules as solutions to the imperialistic structure of international communication (Preston, Herman, & Schiller, 1989). And yet we continue to see the world rush to embrace the cultural products provided by the imperialists.

Mode of Influence

Cultural imperialism portrays the world of international communication as a monolithic system of domination and exploitation, which is made possible by the ever penetrating multinational corporations into foreign markets without any resistance on the receiving end (Dorfman & Mattelart, 1971; Schiller, 1971; Wells, 1972). In mass communication research, at least as has been commonly accepted in the literature, imperialism is a "dependent relation" between countries through domination of one country over many others. Imperialism as a conceptual framework often implies an unequal relationship between countries, in which one, especially those in the West, tends to exploit another in the rest of the world (Schiller, 1991). In contrast, globalization as a theoretical formation leaves room for the interaction between countries, which does not necessarily lead to exploitation or domination (Chilcote, 2002).

Effects on Culture

Cultural imperialism tends to portray the flows of cultural products across national borders in ways that have damaging effects on the countries at the receiving end. Globalization, on the other hand, recognizes both the destructive and constructive impacts of global flows. Because of historical legacy and negative connotations, cultural imperialism often leaves little or no room for the nation-state to defend itself in the face of foreign intrusion. Globalization at least accepts the fact that it takes two to tango no matter how bad the dance may turn out to be.

If globalization undermines the power and authority of the nation-state, cultural imperialism tends to overstate the role of nation-state in connection to the military-industrial complex or to the primacy of the state media apparatus. Other than resistance or a complete break, cultural imperialism implies a one-way process that seeks to impose, conquer, dominate, or exploit the weaker party. Globalization, on the contrary, acknowledges the possibility for local appropriation, adaptation and hybridization of cultural products (Kraidy, 2005).

Conclusion and Discussion

Theories have their life-cycle. The thesis of cultural imperialism was first and foremost conceived by Western scholars. For whatever reasons in the 1970s, many scholars and researchers in the developing countries tended to pick up theories developed in the West, including cultural imperialism, as they slowly diffused to other parts of the world. An illuminating case is the four theories of the press. Although it has been critically challenged, if not discredited, the theory continues to be followed by scholars from many developing and underdeveloped countries. In international communication research, it has serious implications for the dissemination and accumulation of knowledge.

As Galtung (1971, p. 93) put it, "Theories, like cars and fashions, have their life-cycle, and whether the obsolescence is planned or not there will always be a time-lag in a structure with a pronounced difference between center and periphery. Thus, the tram workers in Rio de Janeiro may carry banners supporting Auguste Comte one hundred years after the center of the Center forgot who he was...." This seems to be the case with the literature in international communication research. Some 40 years after its inception, the thesis of cultural imperialism continues to be followed by scholars in Latin America (e.g., Vilas, 2002) even though the global media landscape has changed almost beyond recognition.

In the age of the Internet and digital communication, the thesis of cultural imperialism has remained well entrenched in the literature, not necessarily because it is a "dominant" school of thought as some scholars have claimed, but because it is seldom put under theoretical and methodological scrutiny in connection to another theory that may undermine its validity and knowledge claim. As theories, *cultural* imperialism and *audience* reception do not really address the same conceptual domains,

Curtin, M. (2007). *Playing to the world's biggest audience: The globalization of Chinese film and TV.* Berkeley: University of California Press.

Dorfman, A., & Mattelart, A. (1971). *How to read Donald Duck: Imperialist ideology in the Disney comic.* New York: International General.

Galtung, J. (1971). A structural theory of imperialism. *Journal of Peace Research, 8,* 81–117.

Golding, P., & Harris, P. (Eds.). (1997). *Beyond cultural imperialism: Globalization, communication and the new international order.* London: Sage.

Goldsmith, J., & Wu, T. (2008). *Who controls the Internet? Illusions of a borderless world.* New York: Oxford University Press.

Greig, J. M. (2002). The end of geography? Globalization, communications, and culture in international system. *Journal of Conflict Resolution, 46,* 225–243.

Held, D. (Ed.). (2004). *A globalizing world? Culture, economics, politics.* London: Routledge.

Himelboim, I. (2008). *Civil society versus network society: Network structures of computer-mediated social interactions.* Unpublished dissertation, University of Minnesota-Twin Cities.

Hong, Y., & Chang, T-K. (2008, August 6–9). *Culture and international flow of movies: Proximity, discount or globalization?* Paper presented at the International Communication Division of the annual conference of the Association for Education in Journalism and Mass Communication, Chicago, Illinois.

Hoskins, C., & Mirus, R. (1988). Reasons for the US dominance of the international trade in television programs. *Media, Culture, and Society, 10,* 499–515.

Iwabuchi, K. (2001). Becoming "culturally proximate": The ascent of Japanese idol dramas in Taiwan. In B. Moeran (Ed.), *Asian media productions* (pp. 54–74). Richmond, England: Curzon.

Jin, D. Y. (2007). Reinterpretation of cultural imperialism: Emerging domestic market vs. continuing US dominance. *Media, Culture & Society, 29,* 753–771.

Kalathil, S., & Boas, T. C. (2003). *Open networks, closed regimes: The impact of the Internet on authoritarian rule.* Washington, DC: Carnegie Endowment for International Peace.

Kamalipour, Y. R. (Ed.). (2007). *Global communication* (2nd ed.). Belmont, CA: Thomson Wadsworth.

Kellner, D. (2002). Theorizing globalization. *Sociological Theory, 20,* 287–305.

Kessler, C. S. (2000). Globalization: Another false universalism? *Third World Quarterly, 21,* 931–942.

Kraidy, M. M. (2005). *Hybridity or the cultural logic of globalization.* Philadelphia: Temple University Press.

Kuhn, T. S. (1996). *The structure of scientific revolutions* (Rev. ed.). Chicago: University of Chicago Press. (Original work published 1970)

La Pastina, A. C., & Straubhaar, J. D. (2005). Multiple proximities between television genres and audiences. *Gazette, 67,* 271–288.

Laing, D. (1986). The music industry and the "cultural imperialism" thesis. *Media, Culture and Society, 8,* 331–341.

Lee, C-C. (1979). *Media imperialism reconsidered: The homogenizing of television culture*. Beverly Hills, CA: Sage.

Lee, S-N. P. (1988). Communication imperialism and dependency: A conceptual clarification. *Gazette, 41*, 69–83.

Mannheim, K. (1936). *Ideology and utopia: An introduction to the sociology of knowledge*. San Diego, CA: Harcourt Brace.

Mody, B. (Ed.). (2003). *International and development communication: A 21st-century perspective*. Thousand Oaks, CA: Sage.

Moeller, S. D. (1999). *Compassion fatigue: How the media sell disease, famine, war and death*. New York: Routledge.

Newman, M. E. J. (2003). The structure and function of complex networks. *Society for Industrial and Applied Mathematics Review, 45*(2), 167–256.

Preston, W., Jr., Herman, E. S., & Schiller, H. I. (1989). *Hope and folly: The United States and UNESCO, 1945–1985*. Minneapolis: University of Minnesota Press.

Roach, C. (1997). Cultural imperialism and resistance in media theory and literary theory. *Media, Culture & Society, 19*, 47–66.

Rogers, E. M., with F. F. Shoemaker. (1971). *Communication of innovations: A cross-cultural approach*. New York: Free Press.

Salwen, M. B. (1991). Cultural imperialism: A media effects approach. *Critical Studies in Mass Communication, 8*, 29–38.

Schiller, H. I. (1971). *Mass communications and American empire*. Boston: Beacon. (Original work published 1969)

Schiller, H. I. (1991). Not yet the post-imperialist era. *Critical Studies in Mass Communication, 8*, 13–28.

Silverblatt, A., & Zlobin, N. (2004). *International communications: A media literacy approach*. Armonk, NY: M.E. Sharpe.

Straubhaar, J. D. (1991). Beyond media imperialism: Assymetrical interdependence and cultural proximity. *Critical Studies in Mass Communication, 8*, 39–59.

Tehranian, M. (1999). *Global communication and world politics: Domination, development, and discourse*. Boulder, CO: Lynne Rienner.

Tomlinson, J. (1991). *Cultural imperialism*. Baltimore: Johns Hopkins University Press.

Tomlinson, J. (1999). *Globalization and culture*. Chicago: University of Chicago Press.

Tunstall, J. (1977). *The media are American: Anglo-American media in the world*. New York: Columbia University Press.

Tunstall, J. (2008). *The media were American: U.S. mass media in decline*. New York: Oxford University Press.

Vilas, C. M. (2002). Globalization as imperialism. *Latin American Perspectives, 29*, 70–79.

Wells, A. (1972). *Picture-tube imperialism? The impact of U.S. television on Latin America*. Maryknoll, NY: Orbis Books.

Wu, H. D. (2000). Systemic determinants of international news coverage: A comparison of 38 countries. *Journal of Communication, 50*, 110–130.

Chapter 2

Determining the Scope of "International" Communication

A (Living) Systems Approach

Shelton A. Gunaratne

Glossary

Autopoiesis The pattern of life or "self-making" of a living system. It complements cognition, the process of life.

Bell's Theorem The mathematical theorem in quantum physics that supports the Eastern philosophical concept of universal interconnectedness. It is based upon correlations between paired particles similar to the pair of hypothetical particles in the Einstein-Podolsky-Rosen thought experiment. Bell's theorem (published in 1964) shows that the principle of local causes is mathematically incompatible with the assumption that the statistical predictions of quantum theory are valid. The Aspect experiment of 1982 further weakened the principle of local causes by establishing that correlated particles can communicate at speeds surpassing the speed of light.

Covering Laws Model An offshoot of the Newtonian-Cartesian paradigm, this model states that eternal rules ("predictive laws" or linear and deterministic equations), which could be stated optimally in simple formulas, governed physical phenomena.

Dependent Co-arising Paradigm The paradigm extracted from the fundamental Buddhist concept of *paticca samuppāda* (Gunaratne, 2008a, 2008b). It depicts the universe as a network of interconnected, interdependent, and interacting networks of varying size and duration. The presumption of mutual causality eliminates the positivistic reification of the so called independent variable. The DCP denies a first cause. Because each network and the co-arising elements constituting it are impermanent (i.e., undergoing constant change), it implicitly throws doubts on the validity of *reliability*. It serves as a complex systems framework for conceptualizing globalization.

Dissipative Structures Theory This theory of change, associated with Ilya Prigogine and complexity science, sees fluctuations, instability, multiple choices, and limited predictability at all system levels. It asserts that irreversibility processes give rise to both order and chaos. It sees biological and social systems as open dissipative structures far from equilibrium that exchange energy/matter/information with their environments. These structures self-organize into more complex forms after a bifurcation point engendered by nonlinear dynamics. Prigogine derived this theory by focusing on the second law of thermodynamics (the law of entropy). Autopoiesis (self-making) and cognition are two fundamental phenomena inherent to all dissipative structures (Gunaratne, 2005b), e.g., cyclones, lasers, organisms, etc.

Eastern Philosophy   The axiology, epistemology, and ontocosmology of Buddhism, Confucianism, Daoism, and Hinduism make up the lion's share of what's commonly called Eastern philosophy. Capra (1975) has highlighted the parallels between these axial philosophies and quantum physics. Islam, considered to be an Abrahamic religion just like Judaism and Christianity, is not part of axial Eastern philosophy although it has many adherents in Asia proper.

Emergence   The complexity resulting from a system self-organizing from a lower level to the next higher level at a bifurcation point is called *weak* or *transformational* emergence. Where the whole is more than the sum of a system's parts (at any level of the hierarchy), the *more* denotes the attribute called *strong* emergence.

Entropy   Used-up free energy or disorder. "Quantity specifying the amount of disorder or randomness in a system bearing energy or information. Originally defined in thermodynamics in terms of heat and temperature, entropy indicates the degree to which a given quantity of thermal energy is available for doing useful work—the greater the entropy, the less available the energy" (Columbia Electronic Encyclopedia, n.d.).

Equilibrium   In classical sociology, equilibrium meant a theoretical state of balance between interrelated components or subsystems in a social system. A social system, when disturbed, was believed to return to its original state. This concept favored maintenance of the status quo. Equilibrium, however, has varying meanings. For instance, in thermodynamics, equilibrium is reached when entropy is at its maximum, the point of "heat-death."

Homeostasis   In sociology, homeostasis meant a theoretical state of a social system that allowed its interrelated components to move away from equilibrium, but strictly within a regulated range, as in the case of a thermostat. It described the state of near-equilibrium.

Newtonian-Cartesian Paradigm   This is the classical scientific paradigm combining the thinking of Isaac Newton and Rene Descartes that prevailed from the seventeenth century. Its hallmark is Newton's reductionism (i.e.., the reduction of the complex whole into manageable parts for investigation and analysis) justified by Descartes' mind-body distinction, which enabled scientists to view the world objectively as mechanistic and materialistic since they could treat matter as inert and completely distinct from themselves. The paradigm presumed that eternal rules, which could be stated optimally in simple formulas, governed physical phenomena. These equations were linear and deterministic. Once one knew these equations and any set of so-called initial conditions, one could predict perfectly the future and track the past. Time was reversible. Whatever fluctuations occurred in the real world, largely the result of measurement errors, were swiftly tamed by a return to equilibrium (Wallerstein, 2006).

Quantum Physics   The branch of physics concerned with subatomic particles.

Social Science   The study of *people* in society and how they relate to one another and to the group to which they belong (e.g., anthropology, economics, history, political science, psychology, sociology, etc.). This definition excludes the Buddhist perspective of society, which encompasses not only people but also all interlinked elements in the environment. Therefore, social science has a Western anthropocentric bias. Moreover, Hayek (1942) has criticized the unwarranted application of the habits of thought of natural science to what is called social science, which has produced *scientistic* as distinguished from scientific outcomes. Testability is the hallmark of science.

Yijing Paradigm   An ancient Chinese analytical framework, which uses the concept of the interaction of *yin* and *yang*, the two complementary energy forces of which everything and everyone in the universe is made, to explicate how Nature and all its constituent elements converge toward harmony. It illustrates how unity produces diversity through successive bifurcations into two bigrams, eight trigrams, 64 hexagrams, *ad infinitum*; and how they are interlinked with and interdependent on one another within unity. It is a prototype of systems thinking, which scholars can use to analyze phenomena like globalization, migration, world system, etc. Gunaratne (2006, 2008a, 2008b) explains this paradigm in greater detail.

Introduction

This chapter asserts that theoretical biologist J. G. Miller's living systems theory (LST) can guide the determination of the scope of what constitutes the subject matter and the research frame of international communication, as argued later, a field that should be more accurately named *cosmopolitan communication*. Miller identified complex structures that can carry out living processes at eight nested hierarchical levels ranging from the smallest to the largest—cell, organ, organism, group, organization, community [institution], society [nation], and supranational [world] system (Figure 2.1).[1] Each system, irrespective of its hierarchical level in space-time, is an open system composed of 20 critical subsystems, which process inputs, throughputs, and outputs of various forms of matter-energy and information (Table 2.1).[2] Together they make up a living system. Notwithstanding the evolutionary process ("shred out" or "fray out"),[3] each system at each level retains the same 20 subsystems although the properties of each subsystem become more complex because of "transformational emergence" (Bailey, 1994, p. 193) at each upward level. Thus it is possible to observe, measure, and compare variables constituting a subsystem at each of the levels and across the levels. It is this feature that makes LST a general theory, which attempts to integrate applicable social, biological, and physical sciences. International communication scholars can focus on the communication dimension of the information-processing subsystems of LST—input transducer, internal transducer, channel and net, timer, decoder, associator, memory, decider, encoder, and output transducer, as well as the reproducer and

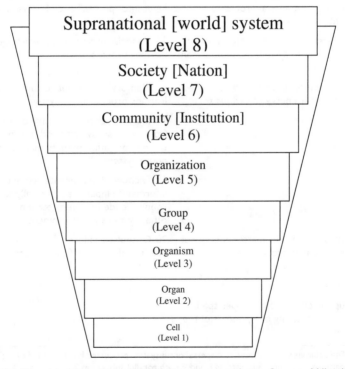

Figure 2.1 The eight hierarchies of Miller's living systems theory. Sources: Miller (1978), Miller & Miller (1992). Bailey (1994) suggested the improvements in square brackets.

Table 2.1 Critical Subsystems of a Living System

Subsystems which process both matter/energy and information	
1. Reproducer helps recreate other systems similar to its own system	
2. Boundary holds together system components and polices external inflows into system	

Matter/energy pro-cessing subsystems	*Information pro-cessing subsystems*
3. Ingestor brings matter-energy across system boundary from environment	11. Input transducer brings markers bearing information into the system
	12. Internal transducer receives markers bearing information from system components
4. Distributor carries inputs from outside or outputs from its subsystems around the system	13. Channel and net transmits markers bearing information to all parts of the system
	14. Timer synchronizes internal processes of system and coordinates system with its environment
5. Converter changes inputs into more useful forms for special processes relevant to the system	15. Decoder alters code of information input into "private" code for system's internal use
6. Producer forms stable associations among inputs to system or outputs from its converter	16. Associator carries out first stage of learning process
7. Matter-energy storage retains in the system matter-energy of various sorts	17. Memory carries out second stage of learning process in the system
	18. Decider receives information inputs from other subsystems and transmits to them information outputs that control entire system
	19. Encoder alters "private" code of information input used internally to "public" code for interpretation by other systems in environment
8. Extruder transmits matter-energy out of the system as products or wastes	20. Output transducer puts out markers bearing information from system
9. Motor moves the system or parts of it in relation to its environment	
10. Supporter maintains proper spatial relationships among components of the system	

Note: The columns show downward dispersal of subsystem processes. Blank cells indicate absence of parallels. Exception: Subsystems 8 and 9 both parallel subsystem 20.
Sources: Miller (1978), Miller and Miller (1992).

boundary, which both information processing and matter-energy processing share.

The researcher can define the communication dimension of the variables constituting each of the information-processing subsystems and develop hypotheses for comparison within the supranational [world] system level, or the society [nation] level. The researcher can also make comparisons and interconnections of these subsystems across these two levels, and go beyond them to the lower hierarchical levels.

The term *international communication* confines the scholar to the seventh hierarchical level of society [nation] with the supranational [world] system as its environment. *International* denotes the dealings between the government of one nation-state with the government of another nation-state, or of several nation-states; and *communication* denotes the sender-message-channel-receiver interaction process.[4] Thus, all information, which includes a large flow of data, is not communication. Communication is a "multidirectional phenomenon with no distinguishable beginning or end" (Ruben, 1979, p. 95) as attested by Buddhist philosophy (Macy, 1991). Because the term *international communication* excludes interactions other than overt or covert exchanges among nation-states, as well as communication across the levels below the seventh, that term is no longer appropriate to define the field. If the field were to adopt the LST model, communication researchers could collaborate with biological and physical scientists to build a general living systems theory.

This chapter will use the following steps: First, I will expand on Miller's theory in greater detail and examine its strengths and limitations, and also alert communication scholars to parallels in Buddhist and Daoist philosophy from which they can draw more ideas to enrich systems thinking, as outlined by Gunaratne (2008a).

Second, I will present a historical overview of the evolution of systems theory within social science; recognize the early communication scholars who enthusiastically embraced the philosophy of general systems theory, on which Miller based his LST. This overview, as outlined by Gunaratne (2008b), will explicate the transition of sociological approaches from equilibrium/homeostasis (as with early Parsons) to entropy/emergence.

Third, I will explicate the applicability of Miller's LST to communication science; examine the current models used for IC research, which have failed to meet the challenges of complexity science; illustrate how to derive relevant hypotheses from the variables constituting the information processing subsystems at the levels of society [nation] and supranational [world] system; and show why cosmopolitan communication would be a better rubric to identify the field, as outlined by Gunaratne (2007b).

More on Miller's Theory

James Grier Miller (1978) wrote a 1,102-page volume to present his living systems theory. He constructed a general theory of living systems by focusing on concrete systems—nonrandom accumulations of matter-energy in physical space-time organized into interacting, interrelated subsystems or components. Slightly revising the original model a dozen years later, he distinguished eight "nested" hierarchical levels in such complex structures. Each level is "nested" in the sense that each higher level contains the next lower level in a nested fashion.

Central Thesis

Miller's central thesis is that the systems in existence at all eight levels are open systems composed of 20 critical subsystems that process inputs, throughputs, and outputs of various forms of matter-energy and information. Two of these subsystems—*reproducer* and *boundary*—process both matter-energy and information. Eight of them process only matter/energy. The other 10 subsystems process information only.

> All nature is a continuum. The endless complexity of life is organized into patterns which repeat themselves—theme and variations—at each level of system. These similarities and differences are proper concerns for science. From the ceaseless streaming of protoplasm to the many-vectored activities of supranational systems, there are continuous flows through living systems as they maintain their highly organized steady states. (Miller, 1978, p. 1025)

Seppänen (1998) says that Miller "applied general systems theory on a broad scale to describe all aspects of living systems" (pp. 197–198).

> Miller considers living systems as a subset of all systems. Below the level of living systems, he defines space and time, matter and energy, information and entropy, levels of organization, and physical and conceptual factors, and above living systems ecological, planetary and solar systems, galaxies, and so forth. (Seppänen, 1998, p. 198)

Miller's theory posits that the mutual interrelationship of the components of a system extends across the hierarchical levels.[5] Examples: Cells and organs of a living system thrive on the food the organism obtains from its suprasystem; the member countries of a supranational system reap the benefits accrued from the communal activities to which each one contributes. Miller says that his eclectic theory "ties together past discoveries from many disciplines and provides an outline into which new findings can be fitted" (Miller, 1978, p. 1025).

Essential Concepts

Miller says the concepts of *space, time, matter, energy,* and *information* are essential to his theory because the living systems exist in space and are made of matter and energy organized by information. Miller's theory of living systems employs two sorts of spaces: physical or geographical space, and conceptual or abstracted spaces. *Time* is the fundamental "fourth dimension" of the physical space-time continuum/spiral. *Matter* is anything that has mass and occupies physical space. Mass and energy are equivalent as one can be converted into the other. *Information* refers to the degrees of freedom that exist in a given situation to choose among signals, symbols, messages, or patterns to be transmitted.

Other relevant concepts are *system, structure, process, type, level, echelon, suprasystem, subsystem, transmissions,* and *steady state.* A *system* can be conceptual, concrete, or abstracted. The *structure* of a system is the arrangement of the subsystems and their components in three-dimensional space at any point of time. *Process,* which can be reversible or irreversible, refers to change over time of matter/energy or information in a system. *Type* defines living systems with similar characteristics. *Level* is the position in a hierarchy of systems. Many complex living systems, at various levels, are organized into two or more *echelons.* The *suprasystem* of any living system is the next higher system in which it is a subsystem or component. The totality of all the structures in a system which carry out a particular process is a *subsystem. Transmissions* are inputs and outputs in concrete systems. Because living systems are open systems, with continually altering fluxes of matter/energy and information, many of their equilibria are dynamic—situations identified as *steady states* or *flux equilibria.*

Levels and Subsystems

Miller (1978) identifies the comparable matter-energy and information processing critical subsystems as shown in Table 2.1 and explained in Appendix 2.1. Elaborating on the eight hierarchical levels (Figure 2.1), he defines *society,* which constitutes the seventh hierarchy, as "a large, living, concrete system with [community] and lower levels of living systems as subsystems and components" (p. 747). Society may include small, primitive, totipotential (capable of carrying out all necessary activities for life) communities; ancient city-states, and kingdoms; as well as modern nation-states and empires that are not supranational systems. Miller provides general descriptions of each of the subsystems that fit all eight levels. To give the *communication science* researchers (see endnote 4) a sense of how they may interpret these subsystems to formulate LST-based hypotheses, Appendix 2.1 provides an example of a main component for each subsystem at the level of *society* [nation].

In Miller's (1978) view, a supranational system, "is composed of two or more societies, some or all of whose processes are under the control of a decider that is superordinate to their highest echelons" (p. 903). However, he contends that no supranational system with all its 20 subsystems under control of its decider exists today. The absence of a supranational decider precludes the existence of a concrete supranational system. Miller says that studying a supranational system is problematical because its subsystems

> tend to consist of few components besides the decoder. These systems do little matter-energy processing. The power of component societies [nations] today is almost always greater than the power of supranational deciders. Traditionally, theory at this level has been based upon intuition and study of history rather than data collection. Some quantitative research is now being done, and construction of global-system models and simulations is currently burgeoning. (Miller, 1978, p. 1043)

At the supranational system level, Miller's emphasis is on international organizations, associations, and groups comprising representatives of societies (nation-states). Miller identifies the subsystems at this level to suit this emphasis. Thus, for example, the *reproducer* is "any multipurpose supranational system which creates a single purpose supranational organization" (p. 914); and the *boundary* is the "supranational forces, usually located on or near supranational borders, which defend, guard, or police them" (p. 914).

LST's Strengths

Not just those specialized in international communication, but all *communication science* scholars could pay particular attention to the major contributions of LST to social systems approaches that Bailey (2006) has pointed out:

- the specification of the 20 critical subsystems in any living system;
- the specification of the eight hierarchical levels of living systems;
- the emphasis on cross-level analysis and the production of numerous cross-level hypotheses;
- cross-subsystem research (e.g., formulation and testing of hypotheses in two or more subsystems at a time).
- Cross-level, cross-subsystem research.

Bailey (2006) says that LST, perhaps the "most integrative" social systems theory, has made many more contributions that may be easily overlooked, such as: providing a detailed analysis of types of systems; making a distinction between concrete and abstracted systems; discussion of physical space and time; placing emphasis on information processing; providing an analysis of entropy; recognition of totipotential systems, and partipotential (progressively higher-order) systems;[6] providing an innovative approach to the structure-process issue; and introducing the concept of *joint subsystem*—a subsystem that belongs to two systems simultaneously; of *dispersal*—lateral, outward, upward, and downward; of *inclusion*—inclusion of something from the environment that is not part of the system; of *artifact*—an animal-made or human-made inclusion; of *adjustment process*, which combats stress in a system; and of *critical subsystems*, which carry out processes that all living systems need to survive (pp. 292–296).

Bailey (1994) adds that LST's analysis of the 20 interacting subsystems, clearly distinguishing between matter/energy processing and information processing, as well as LST's analysis of the eight interrelated system levels, enables us to understand how social systems are linked to biological systems. Living systems theory also analyzes the irregularities or "organizational pathologies" of systems functioning (e.g., system stress and strain, feedback irregularities, information-input overload). It explicates the role of entropy in social research while it equates negentropy with information and order. It emphasizes structure and process, as well as their interrelations (pp. 209–210).

LST's Limitations

It omits the analysis of subjective phenomena, and it overemphasizes concrete Q-analysis (correlation of objects) to the virtual exclusion of R-analysis (correlation of variables). By asserting that societies (ranging from totipotential communities to nation-states and nonsupranational systems) have greater control over their subsystem components than supranational systems have, it dodges the issue of transnational power over the contemporary social systems. Miller's supranational system bears no resemblance to the modern world system that Wallerstein (1974) described, although both of them were looking at the same living (dissipative) structure (i.e., a dynamical self-organizing open system—as the world is presumed to be—that operates far from thermodynamic equilibrium in an environment with which it exchanges energy-matter and information).

Sawyer (2005) points out that although Miller occasionally uses the term *emergence*, "Miller does not argue that the levels are independent and autonomous, and Miller does not explain how one of his proposed levels might be later proven to be nonautonomous and thus mergeable with a nearby level" (p. 22).

Parallels in Buddhist/Daoist Philosophy

Western scholars have looked askance at the connections of modern systems approaches, including the LST, to Eastern philosophy, particularly the Buddhist dependent coarising (paticca samuppāda) paradigm and the Daoist Yijing paradigm (Gunaratne, 2008b).

Dependent Coarising Paradigm

This Buddhist approach illustrates network analysis of a high order that scholars in sociocybernetics have just begun to use. It presents the samsara (the cycle of rebecoming) as a nonlinear dynamic system comprising 12 coarising variables, none of which is independent or dependent. Its focus is on mutual causality—the impact of feedback loops of the 12 variables on one another—their interconnection and interdependence (Figure 2.2). It represents the rudiments of modern complexity science. The early texts (e.g., *Samyutta Nikaya* and *Majjhima Nikaya*) describe dependent coarising as a four-part formula expressed in four succinct lines:

> This being, that becomes;
> From the arising of this, that arises;
> This not being, that becomes not;
> From the ceasing of this, that ceases.

Buddhist texts also explain dependent coarising in terms of a chain of 12 conditional factors (*nidānas*) referred to as *this* and *that* in the four-part formula:

> *avijjā* (ignorance)
> *sankhārā* (volitional, or karmic formations)
> *viññāna* (consciousness or cognition)
> *nāmarūpa* (name and form, or the psycho-physical entity)
> *satāyatana* (the sixfold senses)
> *phassa* (contact)
> *vedanā* (feeling)
> *tanhā* or *trsna* (craving)
> *upādāna* (grasping)
> *bhava* (becoming)
> *jāti* (birth)
> *jarāmarana* (decay and death)

Many metaphors and analogies in the early scriptures clearly convey the interrelatedness of all causes. Textual evidence abounds that the

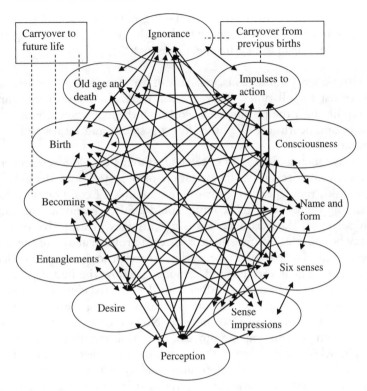

Figure 2.2 The dependent co-arising model. As explanation of the *Bhavacakra* (wheel of becoming).

relationship of the *nidānas* is one of mutual dependence. For example, *nāmarūpa* (name and form) arises conditioned by *viññāna* (consciousness) while *viññāna*, in turn, is conditioned by *nāmarūpa*. Thus the cybernetic feedback loops attached to the notion of mutual causality makes dependent coarising an "interdeterminative" process (Macy, 1991, p. 54).

The doctrine of impermanence (*anicca*) is integral to apprehend the meaning of dependent coarising. "No factor external to change, no absolute that is not definitive of process itself, secures our existence" (Macy, 1991, pp. 34–35). Existence is suffering becausee it is associated with the mutual causality of the 12 conditional factors, which represent attachment to desire. Furthermore, the appearance of continuity ("order") occurs within the reality of change ("chaos"). This contrasts with the linear view of causality that order requires permanence (equilibrium conditions). Trinh Xuan Thuan explains:

> The world is a vast flow of events that are linked together and participate in one another. There can be no First Cause, and no creation

> ex nihilo of the universe, as in the Big Bang theory. Since the universe has neither beginning nor end, the only universe compatible with Buddhism is a cyclic one. (Thuan, 2001, p. 206)

Matter-energy and consciousness have coexisted, coexist, and will coexist for all times. They are coarising. They rise from infinite potentiality into the phenomenal world, go through the cycle of birth, growth, and death just like other living systems, and return to infinite potentiality.

Just as much as LST's 20 critical subsystems enable a researcher to conduct a comprehensive investigation of a system and diagnose its faulty links, the dependent coarising paradigm's 12 conditional factors underlying the cycle of rebecoming could guide a researcher to inductively select all the pertinent *coarising* variables (irrespective of disciplinary boundaries) to investigate a selected problem at any of the seven system levels. The paradigm forces the researcher to discard the concept of the independent variable and demonstrate how the interdependence (coarising) and interaction (feedback) of the selected cluster/network of factors produced a given outcome. The universe is a giant network of *impermanent* networks of varying size. No two networks are identical. Because change is an ongoing process, no two situations are identical.

An IC scholar could deploy the DC paradigm alone or combined with LST's 20 subsystems to develop numerous hypotheses at the top two levels of the systems hierarchy. However, it is important to note that the DC emphasis is on the mental or psychological structure whereas the LST emphasis is on the physical structure. For simplicity, let us take up the DC paradigm's 12 *nidānas* to analyze the processes involved in the emergence of colonialism-imperialism-modernization-globalization complex.

Applying the DC paradigm, one could theorize that the c-i-m-g complex represents an endless cycle of a system of hierarchies resulting from the interplay of the selected *nidānas*. The researcher may see a cluster of the first four: *ignorance* (of the world circa end of 15th century) giving rise to *volitional action* (by European explorers funded by rulers) who had vague *cognitions* (visions) of *psychophysical entities* (strange countries and peoples across the oceans); coarising with the next five: their *six senses* discerned the possibilities of creating wealth through *contact* with these strange peoples whose *feelings* clashed with those of the explorers (and the nations who funded their actions) whose *craving* for the newly founded wealth grew to the extent of *grasping* (or colonizing and subjugating these strange people and their land); which gave rise to the last three: the mutual interaction of the foregoing factors engendered the *becoming* of colonialism, which paved the way for the *birth* of (European) imperialism, and its own *decay and death*.

The IC theorist could apply the same 12 *nidānas* (with revised meaning) to analyze how imperialism gives rise to the more complex system of modernization/ Westernization and to the most complex system of globalization. Such analysis will demonstrate the close links that exists between colonialism and globalization.

The combined DC+LST paradigm will generate much deeper insights. The template for theorizing could associate each of the 12 *nidānas* with the most appropriate 20 subsystems (e.g., birth with reproducer; cycle of becoming with boundary; decay and death with extruder and output transducer; ignorance with ingestor; input transducer and internal transducer; cognition with matter-energy storage and memory; volitional actions with converter and decoder; craving with producer and associator; six senses with decider; feeling with timer; and grasping with distributor and channel/net).

Yijing Paradigm

This is the expanded version of the Chinese *yin-yang* model explicated in the *Zhouyi* (*Book of Changes*).[7] This paradigm clearly illustrates Daoist founder Laozi's philosophy of emergence—a concept associated with modern systems theory, including Miller's LST—reflected in his classic *Daodejing*. Laozi held that every form of existence in the universe and the universe itself are the products of the interaction between *yin* and *yang*, two properties or two sets of properties, which, although differing from and even conflicting with each other, can connect and interact in various ways to generate one or more new forms (Gunaratne, 2005a).

As Laozi expressed it metaphorically, the *Dao* (Supreme Reality) produced the One (space-time?); the One produced the Two (*yin* and *yang*?); the Two produced the Three (energy, matter, and information?); and the Three gave birth to 10,000 beings (all things in the universe?). The *Yijing* model asserts that everything is made up of opposites or complements— *yin* and *yang*. Thus the universe is a unity of diversity—a result of several stages of bifurcation (twofold splitting) of each *yin* (--) and *yang* (—), which takes the form of an analog tree or a binary tree. Exponential bifurcation in the analog tree occurs at period 3 with eight trigrams. Each trigram forms a vertical *bagua* of three *yin-yang* lines. These eight trigrams mount each other to form 64 unique hexagrams representing numerous human situations. The *yin-yang* lines can be counted as binaries or fractals to derive meanings (Walter, 1994). The two trigrams comprising each hexagram become a strange attractor that forces it to self-organize into a more complex system (Gunaratne, 2006, 2008b).

The IC researcher can fit these complexity science principles into the LST framework to provide new insights. The bifurcation process in the *Yijing* paradigm is similar to the *emergence* /transformation process shown in LST's eight hierarchical system levels—the cell giving rise to the organ, which gives rise to the organism, which gives rise to the group, and so on through the supranational system. Each higher level represents greater complexity. The *Yijing* paradigm illustrates the successive progression of the *yin* and *yang* into bigrams, trigrams, and hexagrams. Applying the dependent coarising paradigm, one can conceptualize all components of the LST or of the *Yijing* as interconnected and interdependent, a presumption backed by the implications of Bell's theorem.

Equilibrium/Homeostasis to Entropy/Emergence

Systems approaches in social science research shifted their emphasis from *equilibrium* to *homeostasis*—a term coined in 1932 by W. B. Cannon to mean dynamic equilibrium adjustment within a stable range (as done by a thermostat), and then to *entropy* and *emergence*.[8] The concept of entropy, also used in information theory, became the focus of the new systems approaches that came to be bundled as complexity science (e.g., Prigogine's theory of dissipative structures). Thermodynamic equilibrium, associated with the new systems approaches (Gunaratne, 2003, 2007a), has a different meaning: a condition where the entropy of a system is greater than that of any other condition, given the same level of energy. Entropy means waste or used-up free energy. Prigogine and Stengers (1984) maintained that living-systems or dissipative structures are far from (thermodynamic) equilibrium.

Three "Waves"

The "first-wave" systems theory, viz., Parsons's (1951) structural–functionalist theory of society, was based on systems concepts borrowed from postwar cybernetics (prominently associated with Norbert Wiener and W. Ross Ashby). Parsons (1937) began as the inheritor of classical sociology—Max Weber's action theory, and the works of Vilfredo Pareto and Emile Durkheim—out of which he tried to derive a single action theory. Being a proponent of grand theory, he was naturally attracted to the cybernetic notion of effecting self-regulation through negative feedback. Parsons presumed social systems to be hierarchical and decomposable structures, and placed emphasis on the maintenance of equilibrium of the component units. Sawyer (2005) says that in the Parsonian system, "the behavior of any part is intrinsically determined" (p. 11)

First-order cybernetics became the model for interdisciplinary social science, including communication and mass communication, from the middle of the last century, when the Westley-MacLean model of the communication process hit the field (Westley & MacLean, 1957). A few American communication scholars—notably Fisher (1975), Krippendorf

(1975), and Monge (1977)—championed the older systems approaches. Notable among systems opponents was Berger (1977), who championed the Newtonian–Cartesian covering laws approach (Gunaratne, 2003). Thus, his subsequent advocacy of a *communication science* merely meant the unification of the postpositivist approaches at the four hierarchical levels of communication—individual, group, organization, and society. Communication scholars deemphasized systems approaches when the traditional Parsonsian systems model (homeostasis) lost ground in the 1970s and 1980s.

Sawyer (2005) identifies the general systems theory and chaos theory as the "second wave" of systems approaches. This wave of social systems theory, which drew on chaos theory, emerged in the 1960s and 1970s. Bertalanffy (1968) published his work on general systems theory and Miller (1978) published his work on living systems a decade later. These works also were inspired by cybernetics-related models, and their emphasis was on dynamics and change rather than on the first-wave's equilibrium/ homeostasis.

Although many people use the terms *chaos* and *complexity* interchangeably, Sawyer (2005) makes the following distinction:

> "Chaos" refers to turbulent behavior in a low-dimensional system (i.e., with low degrees of freedom) where the behavior is completely determined by nonlinear laws that may exaggerate minor changes to the initial conditions and thus make the system's behavior unpredictable in practice beyond a certain time period. "Complexity" refers to ordered phenomena in a high-dimensional system (i.e., with high degrees of freedom) that emerge from a large number of interactions among system components. (p. 15)

Sawyer (2005) says that the "third-wave" of system theory draws on complexity theory. The theorists in this wave are basically "concerned with emergence, computer interactions, and relations between levels of analysis" (p. 22). This category is better known as complex dynamical systems theory or complex adaptive systems theory. An outstanding example in this category is second-order cybernetics, which calls itself sociocybernetics.

Communication Scholarship

Scholars in communication science have been tardy in picking up the "new" systems approaches embedded in sociocybernetics (Geyer & van der Zouwen, 1986), such as social autopoiesis (Luhmann, 1995), living systems theory (Miller, 1978), complexity science or nonlinear dynamics (Prigogine & Stengers, 1984), social entropy theory (Bailey,

News Flow Example

To enable the system (e.g., Sri Lanka) to communicate with its surrounding systems (e.g., India, Pakistan, Bangladesh, the Maldives, etc.), the system (Sri Lanka) must be able to take in the available output of foreign news and extract what it deems necessary. This is realized by *the input transducer subsystem* (e.g., foreign news editors of all the news media in the country and the bureaucrats who control the inflow of foreign news received via direct TV or the Internet).

But not all news originates from outside Sri Lanka. When news is originated from within Sri Lanka and enters the news channels, it is done through the *internal transducer* subsystem (e.g., the reporting teams of all the media in Sri Lanka).

News not readily usable by the multiethnic news consumers in Sri Lanka is translated or decoded by the *decoder* subsystem (e.g., journalists assigned to translate news from English to vernacular languages or vice versa).

The *timer* subsystem (e.g., editors responsible for maintaining deadlines for different editions or newscasts in Sri Lanka media) functions as the time coordinator in the system. The timer transmits to the decider subsystem information about time-related states of other subsystems and components or processes within the system. The timer also time coordinates the decider of the system to deciders of subsystems (if they exist).

The *channel and net* subsystem (e.g., TV channels, newspapers, radio stations, and the Internet operators in Sri Lanka) functions as the distributor in the system. This subsystem distributes news to the various members or components of the system.

The *associator subsystem* (e.g., journalism educators and others involved in teaching news reporting and production in Sri Lanka) manages the first stage of the learning process, and helps trainees to sort out the enduring associations between items of information in a complex system.

The *memory subsystem* (e.g., libraries, databases, news-clipping services that are essential for every reporter in Sri Lanka to get the necessary background) stores information within the system. (The ability to remember past actions and past perceptions without actually interacting with the environment provides the ability to "think through" possible actions and possible consequences.)

The *decider subsystem* (e.g., executive editors of all news media at the higher echelon; and editors heading section desks at the lower echelon) controls and regulates the operation of the news flow in Sri Lanka. However, during the ongoing state of emergency, the news flow is also subject to the control and regulation of the government of Sri Lanka (via the Media Centre for National Security of the Ministry of Defense,

Public Security Law and Order). The decider is the keystone subsystem in the system.

The *encoder subsystem* (e.g., journalists and officials who select local news stories and translate them into English for news consumers in other countries) changes the information from the systems code to a public code that can be understood outside the system.

Once news is encoded (prepared for release) it is sent from the system by the *output transducer subsystem* (e.g., overseas broadcasting service, overseas telecommunication services, etc., in Sri Lanka). A variety of means is available for output transducing.

Challenge to IC Scholars

LST can provide the incentive to solidify the field of communication science by stimulating cross-level research of the eight hierarchies of systems. Miller (1978) has provided 173 examples of representative cross-level hypotheses, as well as outlines for cross-level research designs, to assist system researchers to apply the LST model (incorporating complexity science) to test relationships among subsystems or components. The following four hypotheses will give their flavor:

- Two-way channels which permit feedback improve performance by facilitating processes that reduce error. (An IC example: Online news sites that permit readers to provide prompt feedback are less likely to make errors than those which do not.)
- In a channel there is always a progressive degradation of information and decrease in negative entropy. The output information per unit time is always less than it was at the input. (An IC example: Cable TV news network channels repeat the same news per unit of time more often than other channels.)
- Channels in living systems have adjustment processes which enable them to maintain stable, within a range, the similarity of the information output from them to the information input to them. The magnitude of these adjustment processes rises as information input rates increase up to and somewhat beyond the channel capacity. These adjustments enable the output rate to remain at or near channel capacity and then to decline gradually, rather than to fall precipitously to zero immediately whenever the information input rate exceeds the channel capacity (Miller, 1978, p. 103). (An IC example: When the external (foreign) news input to the press system [in Sri Lanka] increases up to and somewhat beyond its channel capacity, the (domestic) news output [in Sri Lanka] will not precipitously fall but rather remain at or near channel capacity and then decline naturally.)

- Positive feedback may produce continuous increments of output which give rise to 'spiral effects' destroying one or more equilibria of a system (Miller, 1978, p. 106). (An IC example: If the demand for the Inter Press Service from advanced countries were to increase substantially, it is likely to engender a spiral of nonlinear effects that will diminish both the quality and the quantity of its development-oriented news output.)

Miller (1978) points out that "multilevel researches are not easy" because they require "the most careful and rigorous conceptualization and research design," and also the "skills of several disciplines" (p. 114). Bailey (2005) avers that an important reason for the decline of multilevel systems theory is "the extreme degree of specialization, or even hyper-specialization found in the world today" (p. 356). Systems analysts say that many of the hyperspecialized nonsystems models widely used today probably could not stand careful critical analysis. Therefore, the future of communication science will to a large extent depend on the multidis-ciplinary background of its research community.

Miller (1987) has provided a strategy to analyze systems at any hier-archical level, and has outlined the applications carried out using the LST framework (Appendix 2.2). The largest application of LST has been a study of the performance of 41 U.S. Army battalions (Ruscoe et al., 1985). This study indicated important relationships between characteristics of matter-energy and information processing and battal-ion effectiveness.

Using LST's most exhaustive integrative framework, communication researchers can investigate the communication dimensions of the global information flows (e.g., news/advertising/ entertainment, digitized infor-mation, the Internet, world money) in the context of matter-energy flows (e.g., imports and exports, travel and tourism, immigration and emigra-tion). They could improve on Miller's classic cross-level studies of infor-mation-input overload. The system can turn "dysfunctional" when it is unable to process or store input overloads of information (and matter-energy). If communication researchers venture into the study of negent-ropy inputs in relation to entropy outputs in living systems, it would not only break down disciplinary barriers but also enhance the qualitative status of communication research.

World-Systems Analysis Plus LST

Thus, communication researchers who use the world-systems framework could adapt Miller's 20 subsystems for more comprehensive analyses of the impact of matter-energy and information inputs on the world system as a single unit. World-systems analysis was in its incipient stage at the time Miller presented his general theory of living systems. Although positivist testing of the theory of living systems at the supranational level might be a formidable task, the idea of focusing on the components of the 20 subsystems constituting the structure of the supranational (or world) system would allow world-system analysts to widen their scope of analysis. Arrighi and Silver (1999) and their collaborators, who have used the world system as the unit of analysis to interpret the transition of hegemonic power in the modern world economy—from the Dutch to the British to the United States—using four perspectives at the supranational level, could have produced a more comprehensive history had they paid attention to all or most of the 20 subsystems however they chose to define them.

Researchers who aspire to write horizontally integrative macrohistories of mass communication could adopt Miller's comprehensive framework. Moreover, researchers engaged in studying organizational communication or group communication could refer to the 20 subsystems at the levels of organization and group to examine the impact of the interactions between information inputs and matter–energy inputs on organizational or group dynamics.

Cosmopolitan Communication?

Miller's living systems theory provides the guidelines for us to grasp the scope and limits of the putative field of "international" communication. Because the term *international* communication basically refers to interactions among nation-states (as exemplified by the communication processes associated with the United Nations and its agencies, international treaties, and international customs and tariffs regulations), that term no longer adequately describes the field. However, scholars have been prone to use *global, international, transnational, multinational,* and *regional* as coequal adjectives modifying the noun *communication*. Very careful distinctions are now being made between *international* or *multinational*—relationships between and among nation-states—and *transnational*—relationships between and among individuals and other entities, regardless of nation-state boundaries.

Applying the LST terminology, global communication relates to what transpires at the eighth hierarchical level (i.e., the supranational system, which, in Miller's view, still lacked several subsystem components, including a decider). The world as a single unit, in the sense of Wallerstein's (2004) world-systems analysis, could be a better way to conceptualize this level in the context of the emergence of a global information infrastructure. The term *global* connotes the inclusion of the entire globe. It involves much more than the limits connoted by "supranational." Organizations concerned with such entities as global climate change or ecological pollution are engaged in global communication.

International or multinational communication relates to communication between two or more societies (nations) at the seventh hierarchical level. The term *transnational* focuses on the heightened interconnectivity between people all around the world and the loosening of boundaries between countries. It also denotes communication that takes place at the intersociety level but is confined mainly to foreign owned organizations (e.g., the Microsoft network located in different countries). Regional communication at the intersociety level, refers to communication among a group of countries in a particular geographical region (e.g., the Middle East, Southeast Asia).

Miller's hierarchy of system levels also helps us to delineate the boundaries of the misnamed field of "international" communication. Clearly, the focus of the field must be communication among supranations, nations, organizations, and peoples at the seventh and eighth hierarchical levels. However, communication at the levels of organism (individual), group, organization, and community across two or more societies appears to fall outside the field of international communication. These belong to the field of intercultural communication.

In an age when the nation-states are ceding parts of their sovereignty to wider geographical unions or supranations (e.g., European Union), the customary emphasis of the suffix *national* (as in inter*national* or trans*national*) appears to be an anomaly. A more accurate term is necessary to describe the varieties of communication at the top two hierarchical levels.

Held (2000) has introduced the term *cosmopolitan democracy* to match the emerging global reality of a world where citizens enjoy multiple citizenships and where democracy needs to be thought of as a double-sided process—deepening of democracy within a national community combined with the extension of democratic forms and processes across territorial borders. Held's macroscopic view of cosmopolitan democracy has some commonalities with Eastern philosophy and the theory of living systems. The future of democracy will indeed be cosmopolitan—a concept which needs further refinement to accommodate Eastern thinking, which looks at the entire cosmos as interdependent and interconnected (Gunaratne, 2005).

On the basis of the foregoing reasoning, the term *cosmopolitan communication* might be a good substitute for the misnamed field of "international" communication.

Summary and Conclusions

In summary, this chapter has made a case for transforming the highly specialized IC field into a more general field under a new rubric called *cosmopolitan communication*. Miller's LST model allows us to compare what we do with what we should do. Miller's comprehensive delineation of the world into eight "nested" hierarchical systems, each with 20 critical subsystems, enables us to understand the interconnectivity of everything as attested by Buddhist philosophy. Because it is unreal to study communication as an isolated factor by holding other factors constant, scholars in communication science, of whose fraternity the IC scholars are a part, must move into conducting interdisciplinary research with colleagues in all sciences to capture how various phenomena reverberate across the hierarchies, paying particular attention to emergence at each higher level.

This suggestion should not be dismissed as a pipe dream, for we know the existence of advanced computer technology to conduct complex simulations with time-series data, and capable of computing nonlinear effects coarising with positive feedback loops. The new approach to research must adapt itself to studying wholes. It can discard the "independent variable" and the traditional "scientific method." It can follow the sociocybernetic approach and let the computer sort out any number of dependent coarising factors (comprising a multitude of webs) engendering a variety of impermanent and ongoing outcomes. (There are no permanent problems or solutions because everything is always evolving.)

Sociocybernetic theories avoid generating hypotheses about bivariate distributions. Researchers translate the theories involved into simulation models and do a computer run to ascertain the predictions they can derive from the theory. They compare the computer output of time-series, or trajectories, with the observed time-series to establish the degree of fit between the trajectories (van der Zouwen & van Dijkum, 2001). Sociocybernetic researchers claim that because they work with feedback models, they cannot use linear equations, which assume unidirectional causality, such as regression equations, linear structural models, differential equations, and survival analysis.

In conclusion, it is essential for scholars in communication science, of which IC is a component, to embrace "third-wave" systems thinking. Perhaps a good start to develop simulation models is to think in terms of Miller's eight nested hierarchical systems. This hierarchy of living systems can guide us on the limits and scope of our field. Although IC scholars' inclination would be to limit the scope of cosmopolitan communication to the two top hierarchical systems, a better strategy is to move successively into the other nested systems levels to seek connections with organizational communication, group communication, and intrapersonal communication.

Acknowledgments

A preliminary condensed version of this chapter appeared in *Global Media and Communication* (Gunaratne, 2007b). Some concepts mentioned in this chapter are explicated in several other publications by the author (e.g., Gunaratne, 2003, 2004, 2005a, 2005b, 2006, 2007a, 2007c, 2007d, 2008a, 2008b).

Appendix 2.1

Miller's General Descriptions of the 20 Critical Subsystems Common to All Living Systems at Each Hierarchical Level (with examples applicable to Level 7—Society)

- Processors of both *matter-energy* and *information*:
  1. *Reproducer*, the subsystem that gives rise to other systems similar to the one it is in (Miller, 1978, p. 55); for example, a structure, like the Constitutional Convention, that creates and implements the society's charter or constitution; the structure that creates and implements the society's information and communication policy.
  2. *Boundary*, the subsystem at the perimeter that holds together the components which make up the system, protects them from environmental stresses, and excludes or permits entry to various sorts of matter-energy and information (p. 56); for example, organization of border guards; customs service; information security agency.
- Processors of *matter-energy*:
  3. *Ingestor*, the subsystem which brings matter-energy across the system boundary from the environment (p. 57); for example, import company, immigration service.
  4. *Distributor*, the subsystem which carries inputs from outside the system or outputs from its subsystems around the system to each component (p. 57); for example, transportation services like railroad and truck operators.
  5. *Converter*, the subsystem which changes certain inputs to the system into forms more useful for the special processes of that particular system (p. 57), e.g., oil refinery, nuclear industry.
  6. *Producer*, the subsystem which forms stable associations that endure for significant periods among matter-energy inputs to the system or outputs from its converter, the materials synthesized being for growth, damage repair, or replacement of components of the system, or for providing energy for moving, or constituting the system's outputs of products or information markers to its suprasystem (p. 58); for example, all farmers and factory workers of a given society.
  7. *Matter-energy storage*, the subsystem which retains in the system, for different periods of time, deposits of various sorts of matter-energy (p. 58); for example, soldiers in Army barracks, warehouse company.

8. *Extruder,* the subsystem which transmits matter-energy out of the system in the form of products or wastes (p. 59); for example, export organizations of a given society.

9. *Motor,* the subsystem which moves the system or parts of it in relation to part or all of its environment or moves components of its environment in relation to each other (p. 59); for example, trucking company, aerospace industry that builds spacecraft.

10. *Supporter,* the subsystem which maintains the proper spatial relationships among components of the system so that they can interact without weighting each other down or crowding each other (p. 60); for example, officials who operate national public buildings and lands.

- Processors of *information*:

11. *Input transducer.* The sensory subsystem which brings markers that bear information into the system, changing them to other matter-energy forms suitable for transmission within it (p. 62); for example, foreign news services.

12. *Internal transducer,* the sensory subsystem which receives, from subsystems or components within the system, markers bearing information about significant alterations in those subsystems or components, changing them to other matter-energy forms of a sort which can be transmitted within it (p. 62); for example, public opinion polling organizations; voters.

13. *Channel and net,* the subsystem composed of a single route in physical space, or multiple interconnected routes, by which markers bearing information are transmitted to all parts of the system (p. 63); for example, telephone and communication organizations.

14. *Timer,* the subsystem which synchronizes internal processes of the system and coordinates the system with its environment (Miller & Miller, 1992); for example, legislators who decide on time and zone changes.

15. *Decoder,* the subsystem which alters the code of information input to it through the input transducer or the internal transducer into a "private" code that can be used internally by the system (p. 64); for example, cryptographers; language-translation unit.

16. *Associator,* the subsystem which carries out the first stage of the learning process, forming enduring associations among items of information in the system (p. 65); for example, all teaching institutions of a given society.

17. *Memory,* the subsystem which carries out the second stage of the learning process, storing various sorts of information in the system for different periods of time (p. 66); for example, library; keepers of national archives.

18. *Decider,* the executive subsystem which receives information inputs from all other subsystems and transmits to them information outputs that control the entire system (p. 67); for example, voters and officials of national government.
19. *Encoder,* the subsystem which alters the code of information input to it from other information processing subsystems from a "private" code used internally by the system into a "public" code which can be interpreted by other systems in the environment (pp. 68–69); for example, press secretary; drafters of treaties.
20. *Output transducer,* the subsystem which puts out markers bearing information from the system, changing markers within the system into other matter-energy forms which can be transmitted over channels in the system's environment (p. 69), e.g., national representatives to international meetings..

Miller explains that relationships among subsystems or components are based on *structure, process,* or *meaning.*

Structural relationships pertain to containment, number, order, position, direction, size, pattern, and density.

Process relationships are twofold: (1) *temporal*—containment, number, order, position, direction, duration, and pattern (all in time)—and (2) *spatiotemporal*—action, communication, direction of action, pattern of action, entering or leaving containment.

Meaning relationships (e.g., love, friendship, etc.) cannot be quantified.

Appendix 2.2

LST Research Strategy, Validation, and Applications

Researchers have applied LST to systems as different as psychiatric patients and organizations. Those interested in following Miller's (1987) research design will find detail at http://www.belmont.k12.ca.us/ralston/programs/itech/SpaceSettlement/spaceresvol4/applications.html

Miller suggests the following strategy to analyze systems at any level:

Research Strategy
1. Identify and make a two- or three-dimensional map of the structures that carry out the 20 critical subsystem processes in the system being studied.
2. Identify a set of variables in each subsystem that describe its basic processes. At levels of group and below, these represent aspects of the flows of matter, energy, and information. At levels of organization

and above it has proved useful to measure five instead of three flows: MATFLOW, materials; ENFLOW, energy; COMFLOW, person-to-person, person-to-machine, and machine-to-machine communications information; PERSFLOW, individual and group personnel (who are composed of matter and energy and also store and process information); and MONFLOW, money, money equivalents, account entries, prices, and costs—a special class of information.

3. Determine the normal values of relevant variables of every subsystem and of the system as a whole and measure them over time, using appropriate indicators. (Miller (1987) points out that the normal values of innumerable variables have been established for human organisms. A physician can make use of reliable tests and measurements and accepted therapeutic procedures to discover and correct pathology in a patient. Similar information is not available to the specialist who seeks to improve the cost-effectiveness of an organization. Studies that make it possible to generalize among organizations are few, with the result that the usual values of most variables are unknown at organization and higher levels. This lack makes it difficult to determine to what extent an organization's processes deviate from "normal" for systems of its type. Pathology in an organization may become apparent only when deviation is so great that acceptance of the organization's products or services declines or bankruptcy threatens.)

4. Take action to correct dysfunctional aspects of the system and make it healthier or more cost-effective, by, for example, removing a psychiatric patient from an unfavorable environment, altering the structure or process of a work group, or introducing nonliving artifacts (like computers or faster transport equipment) into an organization. Miller (1987) says that researchers applied the above strategy to evaluating the cost effectiveness of the operations of a crew of a space station, tracking the five categories of flows through its 20 subsystems, identifying its strengths and dysfunctions, and recommending ways to improve its operations.

Validation

Miller (1987) points out that LST arises from the integration of a large number of observations and experiments on systems of a variety of types that represent all eight levels. As with other scientific theories, however, its assertions cannot be accepted without validation.

Miller (1987) asserts that if LST is to have validity and usefulness, confirmation of hypotheses related to it is essential. The first test of an LST hypothesis was a cross-level study of information input overload at five levels of living systems, carried out in the 1950s. It confirmed the hypothesis that comparable information input-output curves and adjustment processes to an increase in rate of information input would occur in systems at the level of cell, organ, organism, group, and organization. Numerous other quantitative experiments have been done on systems at various levels to test and confirm cross-level hypotheses based on living systems theory (e.g., Rapoport & Horvath, 1961; Lewis, 1981). Such tests support the validity of living systems theory.

Applications

Miller (1987) says that LST has been applied to physical and mental diagnostic examinations of individual patients and groups (Bolman, 1970; Kluger, 1969; Kolouch, 1970) and to psychotherapy of individual patients and groups (Miller & Miller, 1983) An early application of LST at organism, group, and organization levels was a study in the social service field by Hearn (1958).

An application of living systems concepts to families described the structure, processes, and pathologies of each subsystem as well as feedbacks and other adjustment processes (Miller & Miller, 1980). Miller (1987) adds that a subsystem review of a real family was carried out in a videotaped interview that followed a schedule designed to discover what members were included in each of several subsystems, how the family decided who would carry out each process, how much time was spent in each, and what problems the family perceived in each process.

Research at the level of organizations includes a study of some large industrial corporations (Duncan, 1972); general analyses of organizations (Alderfer, 1976; Berrien, 1976; Lichtman & Hunt, 1971; Merker, 1985; Noell, 1974; Rogers & Rogers, 1976); an explanation of certain pathologies in organizations (Cummings & DeCotiis, 1973)); and studies of accounting (Swanson & Miller, 1989), management accounting (Weekes, 1983), and marketing (Reidenbach & Oliva, 1981). Other studies deal with assessment of the effectiveness of a hospital (Merker, 1987) and of a metropolitan transportation utility (Bryant, 1987).

Several researchers (Bolman 1967; Baker & O'Brien 1971; Newbrough 1972; Pierce 1972; Burgess, Nelson & Wallhaus 1974) have used LST as a framework for modeling, analysis, and evaluation of community mental health activities and health delivery systems. LST has also provided a theoretical basis for assessing program effectiveness in community life (Weiss & Rein 1970).

After a protest of comparable methods of evaluation, a study of public schools in the San Francisco area was carried out (Banathy & Mills 1985). The International Joint Commission of Canada and the United States has used LST as a conceptual framework for exploring the creation of a supranational electronic network to monitor the region surrounding the border separating those two countries (Miller 1986b).

Notes

1. The terms in square brackets are improvements suggested by Kenneth Bailey. *Institutions* are those related to science, religion, law, medicine, education, finance, etc.—very similar to the social systems in Niklas Luhmann's (1995) systems theory.
2. The original LST model (Miller, 1978) had seven hierarchical levels. Miller and Miller (1992) added another level, *community*, between the levels of *organization* and *society*; and they added the *timer* as another critical information-processing subsystem to the original total of 19.
3. Hays (2006) says that in complex systems various processes sometime "shred out" across multiple structures. Miller (1978) coined these terms to explicate how various structures in a complex system share different roles to complete a specific process.
4. Note how Niklas Luhmann (1995) adjusted this process to define his functional social systems as phenomena that filtered and processed *communicative events* (i.e., the outcomes of the *information-utterance-understanding* process) related to its concerns. Chaffee and Berger (1987) have proposed the term *communication science* to integrate all postpositivist quantitative empirical research (excluding critical and cultural studies) on communication done at intraindividual, interpersonal, network or organizational, and macroscopic societal levels.
5. Macy (1991) and Capra (1996) have documented that mutual interdependence/interaction and other main concepts of the general systems theory are found in Buddhist philosophy and Chinese ontocosmology. LST is a broad-scale application of general systems theory; also, see Gunaratne (2007b, 2008a).
6. At a generic level, Miller (1978) refers to the hierarchy of "totipotential," "partipotential," and "fully functional" systems to illustrate his thinking.
7. Because several scholars, such as Cheng (1988), Gunaratne (2005a, 2006, 2008b), and Walter (1994) have explained the merits of the *Yijing* paradigm, this chapter provides only a brief description.
8. Sawyer (2005) associates the focus on *emergence* with the "third wave" of systems theory (beginning with the developments in computer technology in the mid-1990s) that emphasized social systems rather than natural systems. Sawyer defines emergence as "the processes whereby the global behavior of a system results from the actions and interactions of agents" (p. 2). Sawyer points out that "contemporary uses of emergence in sociology and economics are contradictory and unstable...one consistent with methodological individualism and one inconsistent with it" (p. 11). Sawyer adds that multiagent systems simulation can help resolve and integrate these two conflicting perspectives.
9. Whether the studies on the topics listed by Mowlana meet the definitions (derived from complexity science and world-systems analysis) assigned in this chapter to his three models is questionable. However, this is not a criticism of the topics themselves.

References

Alderfer, C. P. (1976). Change processes in organizations. In M. D. Dunnette (Ed.), *Handbook of industrial and organizational psychology* (pp. 1592–1594). Chicago: Rand-McNally.

Arrighi, G., & Silver, B. J. (1999). *Chaos and governance in the modern world system*. Minneapolis: University of Minnesota Press.

Bailey, K. D. (1994). *Sociology and the new systems theory: Toward a theoretical synthesis*. Albany, NY: SUNY Press.

Bailey, K. D. (2005). Fifty years of systems science: Further reflections. *Systems Research and Behavioral Science, 22*, 355–361.

Bailey, K. D. (2006), Living systems theory and social entropy theory. *Systems Research and Behavioral Science, 23*, 291–300.

Baker, F., & O'Brien, G. (1971). Intersystem relations and coordination of human service organizations. *American Journal of Public Health 61*, 130–137.

Banathy, B. S., & Mills, S. R. (1985). The application of living systems process analysis in education. *ISI Monograph 85-7*. San Francisco: International Systems Institute.

Baran, S. J., & Davis, D. K. (2006). *Mass communication theory: Foundations, ferment, and future* (4th ed.). Belmont, CA: Thomson Wadsworth.

Berger, C. R. (1977). The covering law model in communication inquiry. *Communication Quarterly, 25*(1), 7–18.

Berrien, F. K. (1976). A general systems approach to organizations. In M. D. Dunnette (Ed.), *Handbook of industrial and organizational psychology* (pp. 42–43). Chicago: Rand-McNally.

Bertalanffy, L. von (1968). *General systems theory: Foundations, development, applications*. New York: Braziller.

Bolman, W. M. (1967). Theoretical and community bases of community mental health. *American Journal of Psychiatry 124*, 7–21.

Bolman, W. M. (1970). Systems theory, psychiatry, and school phobia. *American Journal of Psychiatry, 127*, 65–72.

Bryant, D. D. (1987). A living systems process analysis of a public transit system. *Behavioral Science, 32*, 293–303.

Burgess, J., Nelson, R. H., & Wallhaus, R. (1974). Network analysis as a method for the evaluation of service delivery systems. *Community Mental Health Journal, 10*(3), 337–345.

Capra, F. (1975). *The Tao of physics: An exploration of the parallels between modern physics and Eastern mysticism*. Boston: Shambala.

Capra, F. (1996), *The web of life: A new scientific understanding of living systems*. New York: Doubleday.

Chaffee, S. H., & Berger, C. R. (1987). What communication scientists do. In C. R. Berger & S. H. Chaffee (Eds.), *Handbook of communication science* (pp. 94–122). Newbury Park, CA: Sage.

Chaffee, S. H., & Metzger, M. J. (2001). The end of mass communication? *Mass Communications and Society, 4*, 365–379.

Cheng, C-Y. (1988). The *I Ching* [*Yijing*] as a symbolic system of integrated communication. In W. Dissanayake (Ed.), *Communication theory: The Asian perspective* (pp. 79–104). Singapore: Amic.

Cummings, L. L., & DeCotiis, T. A. (1973). Organizational correlates of perceived stress in a professional organization. *Public Personnel Management, 2*, 277.

Duncan, D. M. (1972). James G. Miller's living systems theory: Issues for management thought and practice. *Academic Management Journal, 15,* 513–523.

Fisher, B. A. (1975). Communication study in system perspective. In B. D. Ruben & J. Y. Kim (Eds.), *General systems theory and human communication* (pp. 191–206). Rochelle Park, NJ: Hayden.

Geyer, F., & van der Zouwen, J. (Eds.). (1986), *Sociocybernetic paradoxes: Observation, control, and evolution of self-steering systems.* London: Sage.

Gunaratne, S. A. (2003). Thank you Newton, welcome Prigogine: "Unthinking" old paradigms and embracing new directions. Part 1: Theoretical distinctions. *Communications: The European Journal of Communication Research, 28,* 35–455.

Gunaratne, S. A. (2004). Thank you Newton, welcome Prigogine: "Unthinking" old paradigms and embracing new directions. Part 2: The pragmatics. *Communications: The European Journal of Communication Research, 29,* 113–132.

Gunaratne, S.A. (2005a). *The Dao of the press: A humanocentric theory.* Cresskill, NJ: Hampton Press.

Gunaratne, S. A. (2005b). Public diplomacy, global communication and world order: An analysis based on theory of lining systems. *Current Sociology, 53,* 749–772.

Gunaratne, S. A. (2006). A *Yijing* view of world system and democracy. *Journal of Chinese Philosophy, 33,* 191–211.

Gunaratne, S. A. (2007a). Systems approaches and communication research: The age of entropy. *Communications: The European Journal of Communication Research, 32,* 79–96.

Gunaratne, S. A. (2007b). A systems view of "international" communication: Its scope and limits. *Global Media and Communication, 3,* 267–271.

Gunaratne, S. A. (2007c). World-system as a dissipative structure: A macro model to do communication research. *The Journal of International Communication, 13*(1), 11–38.

Gunaratne, S. A. (2007d). *A Buddhist view of journalism: Emphasis on mutual interdependence.* Unpublished paper, Minnesota State University Moorhead.

Gunaratne, S. A. (2008a). Understanding systems theory: Transition from equilibrium to entropy. *Asian Journal of Communication, 18*(3), 175–192.

Gunaratne, S. A. (2008b). Falsifying two Asian paradigms and de-Westernizing science. *Communication, Culture & Critique, 1*(1), 72–85.

Hayek, F. A. (1942). Scientism and the study of society. Part 1. *Economica, New Series, 9,* 267–291.

Hays, R. T. (2006). *The science of learning: A systems theory approach.* Boca Raton, FL: Brown Walker Press.

Hearn, G. (1958). *Theory building in social work.* Toronto: University of Toronto Press.

Held, D. (2000). Regulating globalization? The reinvention of politics. *International Sociology, 15,* 394–408.

Kluger, J. M. (1969). Childhood asthma and the social milieu. *Journal of the American Academy of Child Psychiatry, 8,* 353–366.

Swanson, G. A., & Miller, J. G. (1989). *Measurement and interpretation in accounting.* New York: Quorum Books.

Thuan, T. X. (2001). Cosmic design from a Buddhist perspective. In J. B. Miller (Ed.), *Cosmic questions* (pp. 206–214). New York: New York Academy of Sciences.

Wallerstein, I. (1974). *The modern world-system: Capitalist agriculture and the origins of the European world economy in the sixteenth century.* New York: Academic Press.

Wallerstein, I. (2004). *World-systems analysis: An introduction.* Durham, NC: Duke University Press.

Wallerstein, I. (2006). *European universalism: The rhetoric of power.* New York: New Press.

Walter, K. (1994). *Tao of chaos: Merging East and West.* Austin, TX: Kairos Center.

Weekes, W. H. (1983). *A general systems approach to management accounting.* Salinas, CA: Intersystems.

Weiss, R. S., & Rein, M. (1970). The evaluation of broad-aim programs: Experimental design, its difficulties, and an alternative. *Administrative Science Quarterly, 15*(1), 97–109.

Westley, B. H., & MacLean, M. (1957). A conceptual model for mass communication research. *Journalism Quarterly, 34,* 31–38.

Chapter 3

International News Determinants in U.S. News Media in the Post-Cold War Era

Kuang-Kuo Chang and Tien-Tsung Lee

Chang, Shoemaker, and Brendlinger published a landmark study in 1987 that summarizes previous major research in international news coverage and theoretically outlines the determinants of international news by the U.S. media. They investigated seven predictive variables that may influence how the U.S. news media selected international events to cover. Significant predictors, according to Chang and colleagues, included normative deviance of an event, relevance to the United States, potential for social changes, and geographic distance. Poor determinants were: language affinity, press freedom, and economic system.

The present study seeks to reexamine and expand Chang et al.'s theoretical framework and methodological scope. Since the publication of the original study, the world has become a different place, partly because of the fall of communism. Therefore, the world news determinants proposed by Chang and associates may have shifted significantly because the world has changed.

A few studies on the same subject have been conducted since 1987. However, they either have a narrower focus or take a significantly different approach from Chang et al.'s investigation. The present study attempts to fill a number of theoretical and methodological voids in the 1987 research, some of which were suggested by Chang et al. themselves. Thus, an examination of U.S. news media's selection criteria for international events, with newer data but similar and additional methods (e.g., examining newshole assignments), is the goal of the present study. Specifically, the 1987 Chang et al. article use data from 1984. For comparison, the present study purposely examines data collected a decade later in 1994.

It is important to point out that the present study, like the original, does not attempt to measure how editors in the U.S. news media decide which international events to cover. Such examinations should be approached with surveys of the gatekeepers, and it has been conducted by a number of scholars, including Chang and his colleagues (Chang, 1998; Chang & Lee, 1992). Content analysis remains an important tool to determine what is out there for the audience to consume. Therefore, this method of inquiry is still widely utilized by researchers of international communication (e.g., Golan, 2009; Johnson, 1997; Wu, 1998, 2000).

Literature Review

Since Ostgaard's (1965) and Rosengren's (1974) pledge to using extramedia materials to better gauge the impact of news determinants on international news reporting, scholars have explored many variables that can be put into three basic categories: organizational, context-oriented, and event-oriented.

The organizational approach (e.g., Lacy, Chang, & Lau, 1989) indicates that factors internal to news institutions would influence the nature of media coverage due to activities within and outside the newsroom, as well as the choices of available news reports for publication. For example, news organizations with correspondents stationed in foreign countries are more likely to cover events overseas.

The context-oriented approach (Ahern, 1984; Chang et al., 1987) examines the interactive relationship of the foreign nation where events occurred with such contextual elements as economic relations, political affiliation, geographic proximity, and press freedom. In other words, U.S. media are more likely to cover countries with stronger economic or political relations, more geographic proximity, or greater press freedom.

The event-oriented approach (Ahern 1984; Chang et al. 1987) suggests that regardless of those external contextual factors, some internal characteristics inherent in global events, such as the negative nature of the events, can determine whether such events are covered. While news organizations can have a great impact on the choices of international news, little research has adopted this approach to examine the nature of world news transmissions. Ostgaard (1965), for instance, argued that internal or external information controls by media organizational goals or governmental regulations could effectively undermine message flow across borders.

In a study of 114 American newspapers, Lacy and associates (1989) concluded that circulation size and level of reliance on wire services were the two strongest predictors for the percentage of news space assigned to world news. They also found dependence on wire service was positively associated with the amount of conflict or disaster news.

Their findings confirmed the evidence reported by Hart (1961, 1963, 1966) who argued that the vast majority of world news provided by wire services was about conflict, crime, and disaster and that the Associated Press and United Press International accounted for nearly two-thirds of international news in the newspaper examined. Comparable results were disclosed in Cho and Lacy's (2000) national studies of Japanese local press coverage of world affairs. They nevertheless found a negative correlation between the number of wire services and number of conflict and disaster news stories. They offered two possible reasons for the difference: the allocation of newsroom resources and the existence of only two news services in Japan. Editors either assigned fewer resources to a second agency, or they selected stories with fewer conflict or disaster elements from available stories provided by the two agencies, which further limits the purview of choice.

The impact of circulation size on the amount of international news reporting was also supported in Johnson's (1997) content analysis study of 515 articles from 34 U.S. newspapers' coverage of Mexico. Circulation size was not only the second most important predictor but also the predominant factor in deciding the length of the stories.

The context-oriented approach has created conflicting results, mostly because of different operational definitions of the concepts and methods. The key contributors to this orientation include Galtung and Ruge (1965), Hester (1971), Rosengren (1974), and Wu (2000). Galtung and Ruge investigated 12 factors in the reporting of international issues. They concluded that events are more likely to receive coverage if they are frequent, innovative, relevant, consonant (expected), scarce, or referent to elite nations. Regardless of their pioneering contribution, Galtung and Ruge were criticized for their methods. Some of their 12 factors were difficult to measure because most of them were psychological variables (Hur, 1984).

Hester (1971), who adopted an international relations approach, which belongs to the contextual category, defined the hierarchy of the nation as trade volume, economic association as economic development, and cultural association as shared language. Hester's national hierarchy notion defined in terms of trade volume was different from Chang's (1998) world system concept, which was expressed in terms of three echelons of world power—core, semiperiphery, and periphery. Chang's world system notion was borrowed from Wallerstein (1974). However, the operational definition of trade volume has been used mostly in the sense of a reported nation's trade exchange not with all trade partners but only with the United States instead (Chang et al. 1987; Hester, 1971; Wu, 2000). As a result, the likely predicting power of this factor was not present.

The significance of event-oriented variables on world news coverage was illustrated in Chang et al.'s work (1987). Chang and colleagues further theorized the determinants of world news coverage by examining the patterns in the mainstream U.S. newspapers and ABC, CBS, and NBC. Integrating previous theoretical notions and adopting extramedia information, they conceptualized seven independent variables as either context-oriented or event-oriented factors to examine whether certain events were covered or not in those American news outlets. Event-oriented factors, such as normative deviance of issues (the extent to which the event would have broken norms if it had occurred in the United States), and relevance to the United States, and potential for social change, were found to be strong determinants in their study. In comparison, contextual variables were mostly insignificant.

Additionally, they found some variations in the salience of those deciding factors between the *Times* and the Big Three networks. Relevance to the United States was the greatest discriminant for news choices in the flagship daily, followed by potential for social change and normative deviance. On the other hand, normative deviance accounted the most for news selections in the three television networks, preceding factors of relevance to the United States and geographic proximity. Given the outcomes, Chang and associates argued that the event-driving perspective with its implicit characteristics (simply the news criteria), was more prominent than its contextual counterpart in terms of determining why and how a particular international event was covered or not.

In another related study conducted years later, Chang and Lee (1992) unveiled the filtering process of international news events by directly surveying gatekeepers (news editors) of 279 newspapers of various sizes. The authors specifically examined how editors' perception of the importance of 12 news criteria may have influenced their selection international events. The 12 factors were: (1) threat of the event to the United States; (2) threat of events to the world; (3) readers' interest; (4) timeliness; (5) U.S. involvement; (6) loss of lives or property; (7) human interest; (8) cultural relevance to the United States; (9) U.S. trade relations; (10) physical distance from the United States; (11) military strength of country; and (12) economic development of country.

The first five factors were rated "very important" by their respondents in terms of news election criteria. Loss of lives or property, human interest, and cultural relevance were considered "important" by considerably fewer editors, who deemed trade relations, physical distance, economic development, and military strength as unimportant. Such findings were congruent with those of Chang's previous study: contextual factors were of less importance in the U.S. news media's selection of international events.

The interesting concept of deviance was generated by an earlier study by the same set of authors. Shoemaker, Chang, and Brendlinger (1986) defined deviance as a result of some act, the breaking of some norm. The normative definition of deviance therefore connoted negativity for an individual or society. They argued that this construct, which underpins the criteria of newsworthiness for both domestic and international news reporting, was positively correlated with the likelihood of being selected for coverage. In other words, deviant people, events or even deviance itself are often part of the newsworthiness definition. The more deviant an event is, according to Shoemaker et al. (1986), the more likely it would be covered by the news media.

Although the 1987 research by Chang and colleagues, as well as a few other studies (e.g., Riffe & Shaw, 1982), has offered an insight into why and how certain global affairs were selected for coverage in U.S. media, it did not include important information or analysis of the coverage of selected events: the newshole size and location of those stories. Thus, in addition to investigating whether there has been a change over time in terms of the nature of stories of international events that appear in the U.S. media, the present study also includes newshole assignments (the location or length of each story) in our analyses.

The 1987 content analysis study by Chang et al. is important because it encompassed the methods and expanded the scope of previous research. Specifically, it incorporated factors of both context- and event-oriented categories. Since then, besides the studies by Chang himself and a number of his associates, there have been few major developments in this line of research in terms of methodology.

Most studies in this line of research focus on coverage of international news. Barnett and colleagues used an organizational communication method called network analysis to analyze the flow of international news. For example, Barnett and Choi (1995) examined physical distance and language as determinants of the international telecommunication network. Later Kim and Barnett (1996) used the same approach to investigate international news flow in print media. They explained, "International news flow analysis deals mainly with the volume and direction of news flow, whereas international news coverage analysis focuses on the amount, nature, and type of foreign news disseminated across national boundaries" (p. 400).

The independent variables in Kim and Barnett's 1996 study include political freedom, GNP per capita, language, and physical distance. The dependent variable is international newspaper and periodicals trade data. They found that economic development is the most important factor behind news flow. Specifically, the Western industrialized countries dominate such flow. This approach is a clear departure from most research reviewed above. First, the number of potential determinants is much fewer. Second, while previous studies focus on which countries receive more coverage in the news, and what types of events receive more attention, Kim and Barnett's focus is not messages (news coverage) but media that carry such messages. There is no doubt that it is important to investigate the trading of print media around the world. However, most scholars interested in international news flow may still prefer to focus on what is covered in the news.

Major Differences between the Original and the Present Study

While the original study investigated only one dichotomous dependent variable (whether an event was covered by the U.S. news media or not), the present study examined the coverage and noncoverage of an event, as well as the location or length of a story. In other words, unlike the original study with only one dependent variable (whether an event was covered in the U.S. news media), this present study has two dependent variables: whether an event was covered or not, and the relevant importance of placement (location, length, or order of newscast).

Another difference between the original and present study is the coding and statistical treatment of independent variables. While using a dichotomous variable as the dependent variable in a discriminant analysis is correct, using independent variables that are dichotomous is less than ideal statistically and may not be satisfactory conceptually. Specifically, relevance to the United States was expanded into two variables, which are measured as interval rather than dichotomous variables: threat of event to the United States and nonthreatening events. Similarly, the variable of economic system in the original study was expanded into two variables: trade relations and economic development.

This present study also added one variable: loss of lives or property, and changed the name of "social change deviance" to "national change deviance" to represent a broader scope of events.

Conceptual and Operational Definitions of New Variables

Relevance to the United States   An event's relevance to the United States was one of the independent variables in Chang and associates' 1987 study. They determined whether an event was relevant to the United States or not as a dichotomous variable. The present authors argue that whether an event would threaten the national interest may influence how a news media outlet determines its newsworthiness. Thus, two new categories about relevance were generated.

Threatening Event Relevant to the United States   An event was defined as threatening to the United States if the occurrence of such event would negatively influence the national interest, welfare, or image of the United States economically, politically, or militarily. For instance, an Asian or European economic crisis could pose potential threats to the health of the U.S. economy. This variable was measured on a 4-point scale: (1) no threat (no action being in progress); (2) low threat (little discussion by political leaders on how to deal with it); (3) moderate threat (much discussion by political leaders on how to handle); and (4) high threat (retaliatory or protective laws or actions being initiated or taken).

Nonthreatening Event Relevant to the United States   This type of event is defined as relevant to the interest of the United States but in a positive or neutral manner (versus negative or threatening). It is also measured by a 4-point scale: (1) no involvement (if the United States is not mentioned in the story); (2) low involvement (if the United States appeared after the fifth paragraph in a newspaper story or after the fifth story in order in a newscast); (3) high involvement (if the United States appeared in the first two to five paragraphs or order of a newscast); and (4) very high involvement (if the United States appeared in the headline or news lead).

Economic System   A country's economic system may not have much to do with its trade relations with the United States. One may argue that the U.S. news media may pay more attention to a country whose trade connection with the United States is close, regardless of how rich this country is. Also, a rich country, which literally is influential in international politics, may not have a close trading tie to the United States. Therefore, the old category was expanded and alternated into two new ones as follows.

Trade Relations of the Foreign Country with the United States   This construct was determined by the ranking of trade partnerships with the United States, which is based on the trade records issued by the U.S. Department of Commerce from 1993 (Barton, 1993). This trade variable was measured on a 4-point scale: (4) very close, if the country ranked among the top 10 partners of the United States; (3) moderately close, if the country is ranked among 11 to 25; (2) close, if it is ranked 26 to 50; and (1) not close, if it is ranked below the top 50.

Economic Development of the Nation   Economic development, which often initiates political change in a country, serves as a key indicator for a country's development. The degree of economic development of a nation, based on the World Bank record in 1993, was measured on a 4-point scale: (4) high-income country; (3) upper-income country; (2) middle-income country; and (1) low-income country.

Loss of Lives and Property in a Human or Natural Disaster   Apparently such events were included in the "potential for social change" category in the original study because it may change the status quo of a particular society. However, one may argue that a political movement is very different in nature from a flood. Also, as stated earlier, natural disasters abroad are frequently covered by the U.S. news media. Therefore, such events deserve their own category. The old category was renamed as "National Change Deviance." The loss of lives and property variable was measured on a 5-point scale: (5) very severe, (4) severe, (3) moderate, (2) low, and (1) none.

Statistical Procedure

To test RQ1 (which variables determine coverage), a discriminant analysis was run, which followed the procedure of the original article. This same technique was used to test the hypothesis as well. To answer RQ2 and 3, correlations, chi-square tests, t-tests, and ANOVAs were conducted to compare differences between media content.

Findings

Tables 3.1 and 3.2 show the pooled within-group correlation matrix for the 10 independent variables used in the discriminant analysis. Most of the coefficients are small enough that interdependency is not a concern. Two moderate coefficients are seen between potential for national change deviance and normal deviance (.73 for newspapers and .74 for television networks), and between press freedom and economic development (.54 and .55). Chang and colleagues in their 1987 study reported a very similar pattern in terms of correlation. They also found greater

Table 3.1 Pooled Within-Groups Correlation Matrix for Newspapers (the *New York Times* and the *Washington Post*).

					Variables					
	1	*2*	*3*	*4*	*5*	*6*	*7*	*8*	*9*	*10*
1	–									
2	–.59	–								
3	.03	–.12	–							
4	.15	.06	.09	–						
5	–.03	–.18	.73	.12	–					
6	–.15	–.15	–.06	–.08	–.04	–				
7	.07	.19	.003	–.10	–.06	.40	–			
8	–.09	–.02	–.02	–.01	.03	.40	.23	–		
9	–.09	–.13	–.18	–.10	–.02	.54	.38	.30	–	
10	.04	–.13	.18	–.04	.20	.23	.07	.01	.07	–

Variables:
1. Threat of event to the U.S. 2. Non-threatening events
3. National change deviance 4. Loss of lives or property
5. Normative deviance 6. Press freedom 7. Geographic proximity
8. Trade relations 9. Economic development 10. Language affinity

Table 3.2 Pooled Within-Groups Correlation Matrix for Television Networks (ABC, CBS and NBC)

	Variables									
	1	2	3	4	5	6	7	8	9	10
1	–									
2	–.66	–								
3	.12	–.01	–							
4	.22	–.14	.12	–						
5	.05	–.08	.74	.13	–					
6	–.15	–.14	–.07	–.09	–.06	–				
7	.07	.18	.01	–.08	–.05	.41				
8	–.07	–.002	–.02	–.01	.02	.40	.24	–		
9	–.13	–.18	–.19	–.11	–.03	.55	.37	.31	–	
10	.04	–.12	.17	–.13	.20	.23	.07	.01	.07	–

Variables:
1. Threat of event to the U.S. 2. Non-threatening events
3. National change deviance 4. Loss of lives or property
5. Normative deviance 6. Press freedom
7. Geographic proximity 8. Trade relations
9. Economic development 10. Language affinity

coefficients between potential for social change deviance and normal deviance (.56 and .57), and between press freedom and economic system (.56 and .56).

Table 3.3 reveals the means for the explanatory variables for the world events that were and were not covered in the U.S. news media. This table shows that most means have a higher intensity for covered events than noncovered ones for both newspapers and television networks. Also, all means have a lower intensity for not covered events than covered ones in both types of media. Tables 3.4 and 3.5 report the findings of discriminant analyses for newspapers and TV.

The chi-square tests (not shown in a table) for the group means (group centroids) of newspapers and TV networks are statistically significant (chi-square = 123.19 and 115.59 for newspapers and TV, respectively, with $p< .001$.) This indicates the two groups of events (covered and not covered) do not have identical means and are highly differentiated from each other in the discriminant function. In other words, those factors found to be statistically significant are good predictors of news coverage of world events in U.S. news media.

Unexpectedly, normative deviance, which was the strongest determinant (.79) in the original study, turned out to be not significant in both Tables 3.4 and 3.5. Therefore, H1 is not supported.

Table 3.3 Group means for Newspapers and Television Networks

	Newspapers		TV Networks	
	Covered	Not covered	Covered	Not covered
1	2.02	1.04	2.21	1.34
2	2.26	1.09	2.79	1.20
3	3.31	2.66	2.92	2.76
4	1.36	1.13	1.21	1.16
5	2.64	2.18	2.00	2.27
6	1.56	1.76	1.38	1.74
7	2.67	2.45	2.92	2.46
8	1.22	1.24	1.13	1.25
9	1.36	1.50	1.50	1.47
10	2.89	3.22	3.33	3.15

Variables:
1. Threat of event to the U.S.: 4-point scale (1-4)
2. Non-threatening events: 4-point scale (1-4)
3. National change deviance: 4-point scale (1-4)
4. Loss of lives or property: 5-point scale (1-5)
5. Normative deviance: 4-point scale (1-4)
6. Press freedom: 3-point scale (1-3)
7. Geographic proximity: 4-point scale (1-4)
8. Trade relations: 4-point scale (1-4)
9. Economic development: 4-point scale (1-4)
10. Language affinity: 3-point scale (1-3)

As for RQ1, two independent variables are significant for both newspapers and television networks: threat of events to the United States and nonthreatening events. Two other variables that contribute to the discriminant function for newspapers are: potential for national change deviance and loss of lives or property. For television newscast, the additional significant variables are: press freedom and geographic proximity.

In the present study, the single most important explanatory variable for both newspaper and TV is events that are nonthreatening to the United States. Threat of event is the second most important determinant for both types of media.

Tables 3.4 and 3.5 show the discriminant function coefficients for explanatory variables in coverage in both types of news media. For RQ1, nonthreatening events relevant to the United States contributed the most to the discriminant function for newspapers, followed by threat of events, potential for national change, and loss of lives and property. In the original study, relevance to the United States was also the strongest predictor, followed by potential for social change and normative

Table 3.4 Determinants of International Events Selection for Newspapers

Variables	Standardized Coefficients	F-value	d.f.	p.-value
Non-threatening events involving the U.S.	.66	113.10	264	< .001
Threat of events to the U.S.	.40	101.35	264	< .001
National Change deviance	.29	9.06	264	< .01
Loss of lives or property	.09	7.30	364	< .01
Normative deviance	.05	3.39	364	> .05

deviance in *The New York Times* coverage. By comparison, in the present study nonthreatening events relevant to the United States is also the best determinant for network broadcast, followed by threat of event, press freedom, and geographic proximity. In the original study, the best determinant for TV news coverage was normative deviance, followed by relevance to the United States and geographic distance.

As for RQ2 and 3, chi-square tests show that there was no difference in page location assignment between the two newspapers (p > .05) or the three networks (p > .05). Specifically, the *Times* reported 44 (25%) out of the total 176 events, and assigned nine events to the front page, 31 to the international section, and four to the business section. In comparison, the *Post* covered 26 events, assigned 10 to the front page, 14 to the international section, and two to its business section. Among the TV networks, ABC selected 13 out of the 176 events and NBC covered only nine, while CBS chose 14.

In terms of the order of newscast, ABC assigned five events to be its lead stories, two to the second, zero to the third, one to the fifth, four to the eighth, and one to the tenth story of the day. NBC had three as its headline news, two to the second, one to the third, two to the fifth, one

Table 3.5 Determinants of International Events Selection for TV Networks

Variables	Standardized Coefficients	F-value	d.f.	p.-value
Non-threatening events involving the U.S.	.99	114.18	397	< .001
Threat of events to the U.S.	.04	60.01	397	< .001
Press freedom	−.30	5.52	397	< .05
Geographic proximity	−.01	4.43	397	< .05
Trade relations	−.08	1.12	397	> .05
Normative deviance	−.22	.68	397	> .05

to the eighth, and zero to the tenth. CBS used six as its first story, three to the second, one as the fifth, one as the 8th, and three as the tenth. No statistically significant difference was found.

However, there is a significant difference in the length of selected news events between the two newspapers (t = 2.57, p < .05). The *Post* is more likely than the *Times* to have a longer piece (1,016.50 vs. 656.55 words per story on average). The ANOVA test showed no difference in the length of time given to covered events among the three television networks (F = .23, p > .05).

Discussion and Conclusion

The present study has made a meaningful contribution to the understanding of international news flow in terms of methodology, by expanding conceptualizations as well as using more appropriate statistics. Present data also reveal new patterns of international news flow in this post-Cold War era.

The results in the present study as a whole differ much from those of the original study. First, the importance of normative deviance has changed over the years (1984 to 1994). One possible explanation is that what deviance is may have switched over time because the world has changed significantly. What used to be deviant may have become more acceptable or normal, and thus is no longer newsworthy. For instance, internationally, as more countries democratically choose their leaders, elections in those nations are a routine rather than novelty. Another possibility is that many countries have experienced social and political disorder between 1984 and 1994, and the large number of such events has made each event seem trivial to the U.S. media. One example is how often the Japanese have changed their prime ministers. Such changes have become routine and thus U.S. journalists may not find them interesting.

Another explanation for the difference between the two studies is a methodological one. The current study has made some changes in the level of measurement (such as not using a dichotomous variable as well as including more and new variables). Such differences may change the relative weight of each variable.

The findings of the present study are in fact a lot more similar to those of a later study by Chang and Lee (1992), a survey of U.S. news editors. That study listed 12 selection criteria. It is interesting, but not surprising, to see that U.S. involvement and threat of event to the United States were the top two factors considered "very important" by those editors surveyed. These are the same two most significant determinants for newspapers and TV networks in the present study. It is perfectly logical that when the United States is involved in any international event, threatening or nonthreatening, such events will become prominent and newsworthy in the eyes of the news media in this country (Shoemaker, Danielian, & Brendlinger, 1991).

Loss of lives or property, the next most important factor ranked by the surveyed editors, is also found significant in the present study between the two newspapers. Since the world went through a lot of political and social changes between 1984 and 1994, naturally many lives and properties were lost or damaged in the growing confrontations in various countries. Even though such losses may not seem very unique to U.S. news media, the frequency of such tragedies might have translated to more coverage. Also, conceptually, loss of lives or property is different from normative deviance.

An interesting finding appeared in the comparisons of Chang et al.'s 1987 study and the 1992 survey. Two key determinants (potential for social change and normative deviance) in the 1987 study were not included in Chang and Lee's survey. And while these editors' survey rejected the assumption made in the 1987 original study that U.S. editors would judge the foreign affairs newsworthiness based on a U.S. norm, it lends some support to our findings that normative deviance is not a significant determinant for international world coverage.

Press freedom is found to be a significant factor in the present study. It functions as the central brain that influences the government's control of information inflow and outflow. The degree of press freedom may not only affect how much access to information domestic and foreign reporters would have, but also influence how they would behave on their job. Lack of press freedom indicates that the U.S. media may become hesitant to dispatch their news crews to certain countries where these reporters' lives and freedom may be in danger (Moody, 2006; Parks, 2002).

As for geographic proximity, considering the fact that today news outlets care more about the bottom line, fewer news outlets are willing to maintain a news bureau in many countries. With a limited budget, news editors have to decide which countries or territories to place their correspondents permanently or to parachute them when needed (Riffe, Aust, Jones, Shoemake, & Sundar, 1994). As a result, geographically proximate countries are more feasibly to cover.

The present study found little difference on the placement of stories between news organizations. Previous research has reported that major news organizations tend to have similar views on what stories are important to report (Carpenter, Lacy, & Fico, 2006).

From the above analyses it is clear that international news determinants have changed and differed to a certain degree from those of the original study published in 1987. The once highly significant factor, normative deviance, was dropped from the discriminant function in the present study, while other variables carried more predictive power. Nevertheless, the present study revealed a similarity to the initial research: world events selected by the U.S. news media are more likely to be event driven (threatening or nonthreatening events) than context-oriented (e.g., language affinity). For example, all four significant determinants for newspapers are event-oriented: nonthreatening events, threat of events, potential for national change, and loss of lives or property.

It seems clear then that the impact of trade volume and economic development disappeared when event-oriented variables were included but resurfaced when they were excluded. However, these two context-oriented variables were gaining strength. Moreover, the predictability of these two economic variables could have been stronger if the real dollar terms, rather than scales of the economic activity, had been adopted. Future studies then should consider using the real dollar amounts for the measures.

In addition, the present study used 1994 data. Many major changes that could affect international news determinants have occurred in the world since 1994, such as the birth of the European Union, Euro currency, and the World Trade Organization. Future research should replicate this study with up-to-date data. Finally, because of the proliferation of news sources in recent years, future studies should include additional news outlets such as cable news channels.

References

Ahern, T. J. Jr. (1984). Determinants of foreign coverage in U.S. newspapers. In R. L. Stevenson & D. L. Shaw (Eds.), *Foreign news and the new world information order* (pp. 217–236). Ames, IA: Iowa State University Press.

Barnett, G. A., & Choi, Y. (1995). Physical distance and language as determinants of the international telecommunication network. *International Political Science Review, 16,* 249–265.

Barton, D. R. (Ed.). (1993). *U.S. foreign trade highlights.* Bethesda, MD: CIS/ Washington, DC: U.S. Department of Commerce.

Carpenter, S., Lacy, S., & Fico, F. (2006). Network news coverage of high-profile crimes during 2004: A study of source use and reporter context. *Journalism & Mass Communication Quarterly, 83,* 901–916.

Chang, T-K. (1998). All countries not created equal to be news: World system and international communication. *Communication Research, 25,* 528–563.

Chang, T-K., & Lee, J. (1992). Factors affecting gatekeepers' selection of foreign news: A national survey of newspaper editors. *Journalism Quarterly, 69,* 554–561.

Chang, T-K., Shoemaker, P. J., & Brendlinger, N. (1987). Determinants of international news coverage in the U.S. media. *Communication Research, 14,* 396–414.

Cho, H., & Lacy, S. (2000). International conflict coverage in Japanese local daily newspapers. *Journalism & Mass Communication Quarterly, 77,* 830–845.

Galtung, J., & Ruge, M. H. (1965). The structure of foreign news. *Journal of Peace Research, 2,* 64–91.

Hart, J. A. (1961). The flow of international news into Ohio. *Journalism Quarterly, 38,* 541–43.

Hart, J. A. (1963). The flow of news between the United States and Canada. *Journalism Quarterly, 40,* 70–74.

Hart, J. A. (1966). Foreign news in U.S. and English daily newspapers: A comparison. *Journalism Quarterly, 43,* 443–448.

Hester, A. (1971). An analysis of news flow from developed and developing nations. *Gazette, 17,* 29–43.

Hur, K. K. (1984). A critical analysis of international news flow research. *Critical Studies in Mass Communication, 1,* 365–378.

Johnson, M. A. (1997). Predicting news flow from Mexico. *Journalism & Mass Communication Quarterly, 74,* 315–330.

Keesing's Contemporary Archives. (1994). *Record of world events.* New York: Longman.

Kim, K., & Barnett, G. A. (1996). The determinants of international news flow: A network analysis. *Communication Research, 23,* 323–352.

Lacy, S., Chang, T., & Lau, T. (1989). Impact of allocation decisions and market factors on foreign news coverage. *Newspaper Research Journal, 10,* 23–32.

Moody, B. (2006, Summer). Teamwork replaces ego on the frontline of war. *Nieman Reports, 60,* 67–68.

Ostgaard, E. (1965). Factors influencing the flow of news. *Journal of Peace Research, 2,* 39–63.

Parks, M. (2002, May-June). Weighing risks. *Columbia Journalism Review, 41,* 19–23.

Riffe, D., Aust, C. F., Jones, T. C., Shoemake, B., & Sundar, S. (1994). The shrinking foreign newshole of the New York Times. *Newspaper Research Journal, 15*(3), 74–88.

Riffe, D., & Shaw, E. F. (1982). Conflict and consonance: Coverage of third world in two U.S. papers. *Journalism Quarterly, 59,* 617–619.

Rosengren, K. E. (1970). International news: Intra and extra media data. *Acta Sociologica, 13,* 96–109.

Rosengren, K. E. (1974). International news: Methods, data and theory. *Journal of Peace Research, 11,* 145–156.

Shoemaker, P. J., Chang, T., & Brendlinger, N. (1986). Deviance as a predictor of newsworthiness: Coverage of international events in the U.S. media. In M. L. McLaughlin (Ed.), *Communication yearbook* (Vol. 10, pp. 348–365). Newbury Park, CA: Sage.

Shoemaker, P. J., Danielian, L. H., & Brendlinger, N. (1991). Deviant acts, risky business, and U.S. interests: The newsworthiness of world events. *Journalism Quarterly, 68,* 781–795.

Wallerstein, I. M. (1974). *The modern world system.* New York: Academic Press. World Bank (1993). *World development indicators.* Washington, DC: Author.

focuses on the microlevel, such as journalists' perceptions, values, and social norms as influences on international news coverage (Chang & Lee, 1992, chapter 3 this volume; Shoemaker, Danielian, & Brendlinger, 1991). The context-oriented perspective focuses on macrolevel factors, such as international relations as the determinants of news coverage. The perspective suggests that international news coverage reflects the structural characteristics of world systems theory in terms of volume, direction, and selected content (Chang, 1998; Kim & Barnett, 1996; Pietiläinen, 2006; Wu, 2000, 2003). In addition, recent research suggests an organizational perspective considering media market factors, such as organizational resources and editorial policies associated with media management (Kim, 2003).

This study focuses on the structural determinants of international news coverage in the global system. Galtung and Ruge (1965) proposed a systematic approach that considered international characteristics, such as geographical distance, political stability, and economic development. However, although they considered the macrolevel factors that influence the amount and the content of news coverage, psychological elements determine the newsworthiness of international news. For this reason, their theory has had a limited influence on empirical research (Hur, 1984).

Previous studies have tried to clarify the determinants of international news coverage without a psychological perspective. Dupree (1971) empirically tested 11 macrofactors, such as trade, population, GNP, and geographical distance. He suggested that population and geographical distance are the major determinants of international news coverage. Rosengren (1974, 1977) also found that trade and population influence the amount of international news coverage. Hester (1974) categorized macrosocietal factors based on international relations: national hierarchy, cultural affinity, economic relationship, and news conflict. National hierarchy is related to geographical country size, population, and economic growth. Cultural affinity involves shared language, travel, migration, and colonial history. Economic relationships include trade, international aid, and business investment. These macrolevel determinants of international news were examined in other empirical studies. Golan (chapter 6 this volume) reviews the extensive literature on the determinants of international news coverage and indicates that several macrolevel factors, including instability, geographic proximity, investment, international aid, religious diversity, military expenditures, and population, are significantly associated with international news coverage on U.S. news media.

Wu (2000) emphasized more integrative and systematic approaches to examine the determinants of international news coverage and flows. Kim and Barnett (1996) examined the structure of international news flows and its determinants by using network analysis regarding the global system. They found that the structure of international news flows is influenced by economic development, language, geographical location, political freedom, and population. Specifically, economic development was the most important determinant of international news flows.

Wu (2000, 2003) examined the systemic determinants of international news coverage and flows in the global system. He suggested that population, the presence of news agencies, and geographic distance globally contribute to transnational news flows. Also, international trade was considered the dominant determinant of international news coverage. Pietiläinen (2006) found that trade and news flows are highly correlated in the majority of countries with geographic, political and cultural proximity, and historical associations.

Determinants of International Aid

The determinants of international aid have been explained from three perspectives: realism, idealism, and globalism (Degnbol-Martinussen & Engberg-Pedersen, 2003; Van Belle, Rioux, & Potter, 2004). These perspectives focus on a donor country's motives and foreign policy interests. The realist paradigm is related to the political and strategic interests of the donor; the idealist paradigm concentrates on humanitarian motives; and the globalist or world system paradigm is based on economic interests.

Each perspective provides specific determinants of international aid allocations. The realist paradigm regards international aid as an extension of national security policy. The strategic motives of the donor country are important in determining international aid. These motives include the recipient's alliances, military ties, and economic or political positions (Walt, 1990; Waltz, 1959).

The idealist perspective is based on the humanitarian or neoliberal paradigm and is more optimistic about cooperative relations between nations (Lumsdaine, 1993). It emphasizes the potential of international aid to promote the economic development of recipient countries and the benefits of improved international trade. The main variables are associated with the need of recipient countries, which is usually indicated by low Gross Domestic Product (GDP) per capita and high population (Alesina & Dollar, 2000; Zhang, 2004).

The globalist or world-systems perspective is closely connected to the neo-Marxist approach (Shannon, 1996; Wallerstein, 1976). It argues that international aid is an extension of the exploitative relationships based on the economic disparity between rich and poor countries. That is, the rich core nations in the global economic system use international aid to maintain the economic dependency of poor peripheral countries (Chase-Dunn & Grimes, 1995; Shannon, 1996; Wallerstein, 1976). Thus, international aid is usually related to the trade flows between recipients and donors (Meernik, Krueger, & Poe, 1998; Schraeder, Hook, & Taylor, 1998).

Historically, national security was a critical determinant of international aid. Its importance has decreased since the end of the Cold War (Degnbol-Martinussen & Engberg-Pedersen, 2003; Hjertholm & White, 2000). On the contrary, the considerations of economic motives have increased, even though these interests are not apparent because they generally hide behind the humanitarian motives. Recent studies on international aid allocations have considered the determinants of all three major perspectives (Alesina & Dollar, 2000; Hjertholm & White, 2000; Hopkins, 2000; Meernik et al., 1998; Rioux & Van Belle, 2005; Schraeder et al., 1998; Van Belle, 2003).

Several determinants, such as population, economic development (GNP or GDP per capita), and trade are commonly used for the analysis of international aid. These are the same as the major determinants of international news coverage. Recent research reported that the direct effect of trade volume is insignificant (Lim, Barnett, & Kim, 2006; Rioux & Van Belle, 2005; Van Belle, 2003). However, there is a possibility of the indirect effect on international aid. Thus, this study focuses on population, GDP per capita representing economic development, and trade as control variables for the effect of news coverage on international aid.

Global Bystander Intervention Model

In 1964, a young woman was cruelly killed in New York City. Although at least 38 people witnessed the murder, nobody helped the victim (Rosenthal, 1999). Latané and Darley tried to analyze the situation from the actor's perspective, and then argued that individuals are less likely to help others in an emergency when onlookers are present (Darley & Latané, 1968; Latané & Darley, 1968, 1969, 1970).

Latané and Darley (1970) proposed three processes that determine the bystander nonintervention effect: audience inhibition, social influence, and diffusion of responsibility. First, the audience inhibition process concerns others' evaluation. People may be reluctant to help others in emergencies due to the fear of making a bad impression on onlookers. Although a situation may seem to be urgent, in the presence of others, it may be hard to decide whether to help because it might not be serious. There is a possibility that helpers will look foolish to onlookers. Thus, the presence of an audience can inhibit people from helping.

Second, the social influence process is closely related to a social psychological term, pluralistic ignorance—"private thoughts, feelings, and behaviors are different from those of others even though one's public behavior is identical" (Miller & McFarland, 1987). The pluralistic ignorance is a tendency to follow the norm that is supported by every group member rather than show individual disagreement. In ambiguous events like most emergencies, people tend to observe others' reactions before making a decision about what actions to perform. Although people may think that a situation is an emergency, if nobody around them appears to regard the event as serious, their potential intervention may be inhibited.

Finally, the diffusion of responsibility may lessen the psychological burden connected to nonintervention (Darley & Latané, 1968). If only one person witnesses an emergency, all responsibility to help the other is focused on the bystander. In this situation, there is a greater likelihood that the bystander will help because of the psychological pressure to intervene. On the contrary, if there are several onlookers, the responsibility for helping the other is shared among all the bystanders. Thus, each individual's responsibility would be lessened, so it is possible that nobody will help.

Based on these processes, Latané and Darley (1970) proposed the model of bystander intervention. To help a victim, an individual should notice the situation; interpret it as an emergency; assume personal responsibility; feel capable of helping; and then help. Each step could be influenced by the situational factors like "the presence of other bystanders." If any one of the steps is not fulfilled, a bystander would fail to help a victim.

Pittinsky and Matic (2005) suggested that the bystander intervention model may be applied to international relations, such as international aid. They suggested that the model can explain "the circumstances in which, and the mechanisms by which, individuals in one nation do not help individuals in other nations who are clearly in need" (Pittinsky & Matic, 2005, pp. 5–6). The Darfur conflict in western Sudan is the worst humanitarian crisis among current international issues. It is an ongoing armed conflict between ethnic African tribes and the Arab-dominated government which has continued since 2003. The government supports armed Arab militias that suppress rebel groups. The Arab militias have destroyed hundreds of villages, killing the inhabitants, raping women, and blocking international assistance. At least 200,000 people have died because of disease and starvation. Approximately, 2.5 million refugees have fled from the region (Mortimer, 2006). However, the international community has ignored or overlooked the emergency situation as a regional conflict. As such, onlookers are present in the global system.

According to Pittinsky and Matic (2005), rich countries may be potential donors or bystanders in the global system, and can decide to help poor countries by following the bystander intervention model. That is, the global bystanders should notice the situation that the poor countries suffer from severe circumstances, such as poverty, disaster, and conflict; interpret the situations as an emergency; feel responsibility; have the capability to help; and then provide assistance. Thus, the extended bystander intervention model can reveal the processes of decision making that influence one nation's policy when it comes to assisting another.

Relationship between Global News Coverage and International Aid

The global bystander intervention model provides a mechanism to facilitate international aid. If severe situations of poor countries are known and the responsibility of the situations is clear, the responsibility can weigh heavily on the global bystanders, and the possibility of global intervention to help the victims would be high. This mechanism may be connected to the role of global news networks as agenda-setting agents in the global system. Agenda-setting theory is related to the formation of public awareness and appreciation of salient issues by the mass media (McCombs & Shaw, 1972). The global bystanders can recognize the situations of the global victims through global news networks. The news networks can make the bystanders feel strong responsibility for these situations as a result of high levels of news coverage. According to the mechanism of the bystander intervention model, the global news networks can increase the possibility of the bystander intervention to help victims in the global system.

Although Livingston (1997) indicated that most international humanitarian assistance is irrelevant with respect to news media effects as agenda-setting agents, the study narrowly examined the correspondence between news coverage and international assistance focusing on a specific event. Recent research has provided evidence that news coverage influences international aid allocations (Rioux & Van Belle, 2005; Van Belle, 2003). The recent studies indicate that news media coverage is a crucial determinant of international aid even though most of them focused on particular nation-states rather than the entire global system.

This study examines the influence of global news coverage on international aid in the global system. If the global news networks play their role as agenda-setting agents reflecting the mechanism of the global bystander intervention, then the level of news coverage that each recipient country receives from news networks would be positively associated with international aid allocations. Thus, the following hypotheses are suggested.

H1. The level of news coverage that each recipient country receives from global news networks is positively related to the level of international aid received.

H2. The level of news coverage that each recipient country receives from global news networks is positively related to the number of donor countries providing assistance.

Relationships among Control Variables

To develop a more specific research model, it is necessary to determine the relationships among a set of control variables. Population, trade, and GDP per capita are control variables. Generally, population and trade are major factors used to measure GDP per capita. Population negatively affects the level of GDP per capita because it is the denominator. Conversely, the total volume of trade that a country engages in might positively influence it because it is the numerator. Although the volume of net exports is considered in the equation of GDP per capita, a national strategy of international trade is mainly to increase the profits of trade by maintaining the balance between exports and imports. Thus, the volume of trade might positively affect GDP per capita.

Galor and Mountford (2003, 2006) explained the relationships between trade and population size. They suggested that international trade is a significant determinant of the distribution of world population. Specifically, they argued that increased trade in less developed countries leads to higher population growth. Also, this effect becomes a major cause of the "Great Divergence," the unequal growth in the global economic system. Judging from their arguments, the indirect effect of trade on the economic growth of a country would be negative even though the direct effect seems to be positive.

Figure 4.1 shows the hypothesized research model for the study, including the research hypotheses and the relationships among control variables.

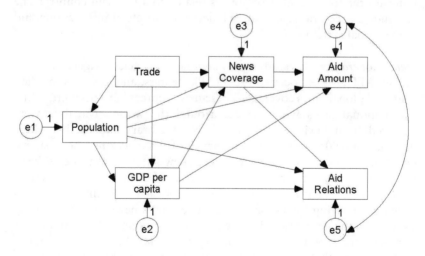

Figure 4.1 Hypothesized research model of news coverage impact on international aid.

Method

Data

International Aid The data were obtained from International Development Statistics (IDS), an online database constructed by the Organization for Economic Co-operation and Development (OECD). The database provides detailed information on official developmental aid (ODA) activities, such as volume, sectors, countries, IGOs, and descriptions, including humanitarian and development assistance for the time period 1993 to 2001. This study focused on two aspects of international aid: aid allocation and the number of relations for each recipient country. The two data sets were calculated by using the measure of degree centrality through network analysis. Degree centrality is defined as the number of links incident upon a node (nation) or the sum of the strength of links (Borgatti, Everett, & Freeman, 2002). Nodes that have more links to other nodes may be less dependent upon individual nations because they have alternative donors from whom to receive assistance. For directional data, it is necessary to discriminate between indegree centrality and outdegree centrality. Indegree centrality is based on the links received by a node. Alternatively, outdegree centrality is based on the links initiated by a node. Thus, the measure of indegree centrality was used for two aid variables. The indegree centrality of the valued aid network indicates the total aid allocation received from donor countries and IGOs. The indegree centrality of the binary aid network indicates the total number of donors related to a recipient country. The two indegree centrality measures reflect the aspects of international aid in the global system.

News Coverage This study used major news agencies—Agence France-Presse (AFP), the Associated Press (AP), Reuters, and CNN as the data source of global news coverage. These news sources have been providing transnational news wire services around the world. The data were acquired from LexisNexis Academic News Library and Factiva. These databases provide news stories and articles from magazines, newspapers, broadcast transcripts, and specialized newsletters. From LexisNexis, CNN transcripts were obtained. News stories of other news agencies were gathered from Factiva. The news coverage for each recipient country was coded by counting the number of each country's news stories including its name in the news title using the news search engine. The total number of news stories about a specific country represents the overall amount of news coverage that the country receives from the global news agencies. This measure of news coverage is commonly used in recent studies (Golan, chapter 6 this volume; Rioux & Van Belle, 2005; Van Belle, 2003). The time period for news coverage data was from 1990 to 2000. Note that the measure of news coverage precedes the measure of aid by 3 years. This lag allows time for the agenda-setting effect of global news coverage to occur (McCombs & Shaw, 1972).

International Trade   The data for 1990 to 2000 were compiled from the World Trade Organization Statistics Database. They include the value of merchandise exported and imported by trade partners and the use of commodity trade data as the sole measure of international trade transactions, excluding trade in commercial services. This study used the value of exports and imports of each recipient country with world partners.

GDP Per Capita   The data for 1990 to 2000 were collected from the United Nations (UN) Common Database. The GDP per capita of each recipient country was converted to US dollars in current prices, based on UN Statistics estimates.

Population   The data were gathered from the *CIA World Factbook* (2005). The population has been used as a control variable accounting for the country size of each nation-state (Rioux & Van Belle, 2005; Van Belle, 2003).

Analysis Strategy

This study used path analysis to examine the causal relationships among variables. This study employed a model-generating approach, the process of final model construction. The maximum likelihood (ML) estimation procedure in AMOS software was used to specify the path model. Model fit was judged by a combination of four indices: chi-square (χ^2) goodness-of-fit, comparative fit index (CFI), standardized root mean square residual (SRMR), and root mean square error of approximation (RMSEA). For a good model fit, chi-square values should be statistically insignificant. Also, CFI values should exceed .90, SRMR close to .09 and RMSEA close to .06 or less (Hu & Bentler, 1999).

Results

Data for 159 recipient countries were used to test the hypothesized model. Through the network analysis of international aid data, the valued indegree centrality indicates aid amount each recipient country received and the binary indegree centrality indicates the number of donors. This is shown in Table 4.1. The average value of indegree centrality was $2,617.40 million ($SD$ = 4,545.36) in valued aid network: 25.06 (SD = 12.42) donors in binary aid network.]

Table 4.1 International Aid Amount ($ Million) and the Number of Donors in 159 Recipients

Countries	Amount	Relations	Countries	Amount	Relations
China	22636.1	39	Mali	3724.7	36
Egypt	16132.3	36	Madagascar	3707.4	35
India	15709.8	39	Burkina Faso	3627.5	36
Indonesia	13914.8	38	Nepal	3599.6	38
Russia	13271.5	36	Serbia &	3530.0	34
Poland	13160.2	32	Montenegro		
Bangladesh	11827.0	37	Cambodia	3341.9	35
Pakistan	10262.3	39	Ukraine	3288.7	33
Israel	9715.3	26	Angola	3287.8	34
Viet Nam	9709.9	37	Haiti	3211.1	34
Tanzania	8942.6	37	Zimbabwe	3207.2	39
Mozambique	8942.4	39	Romania	2899.3	34
Philippines	7469.3	36	Guinea	2802.2	33
Ethiopia	7458.5	38	Papua New Guinea	2800.9	30
Zambia	7101.5	37	Yemen	2642.0	32
Cote d'Ivoire	7041.6	36	Brazil	2560.5	33
Uganda	6611.2	38	Niger	2521.1	34
Thailand	6286.6	36	Laos	2496.4	35
Bosnia-Herzegovina	6215.6	37	El Salvador	2401.3	36
Ghana	5816.6	37	Algeria	2398.3	31
Bolivia	5797.7	35	Albania	2338.0	37
Nicaragua	5686.7	37	Benin	2261.9	35
Kenya	5353.9	36	Mauritania	2247.2	35
Morocco	4959.4	35	Tunisia	2224.8	33
Senegal	4633.8	38	Sudan	2184.0	34
Cameroon	4482.2	37	Czech Rep.	2163.1	31
Sri Lanka	4453.0	38	Guatemala	2117.9	35
Jordan	4014.5	34	Mexico	2050.2	34
Malawi	3949.9	36	Hungary	2036.1	31
Honduras	3909.7	37	Georgia	1954.7	37
Peru	3904.4	35	Bulgaria	1945.6	32
Rwanda	3870.2	37	Kyrgyz Rep.	1941.9	38
South Africa	3766.0	32	Colombia	1919.8	35

Table 4.1 Continued

Countries	Amount	Relations	Countries	Amount	Relations
Afghanistan	1878.5	33	Paraguay	872.3	30
Nigeria	1842.7	35	Liberia	848.5	29
Chad	1815.0	35	Malaysia	846.3	29
Mongolia	1813.2	37	Djibouti	788.2	27
Turkey	1804.6	36	Lesotho	774.2	30
Armenia	1794.9	35	Belarus	763.5	32
Ecuador	1752.2	36	Gabon	742.6	25
Iraq	1750.4	32	Jamaica	736.7	30
Sierra Leone	1717.0	37	Botswana	727.7	31
Syria	1714.1	32	Latvia	690.4	32
Congo, Rep.	1631.4	32	Croatia	623.4	33
Congo, DR	1608.2	35	North Korea	622.2	26
Namibia	1452.5	35	Moldova	614.8	37
Burundi	1435.6	34	Bhutan	574.9	28
Iran	1412.5	33	Costa Rica	574.4	31
Lebanon	1377.4	34	Estonia	572.4	27
Eritrea	1301.5	34	Slovenia	568.2	27
Chile	1261.9	31	Suriname	553.3	19
Azerbaijan	1253.8	34	Cuba	510.0	31
Argentina	1230.9	35	Marshall Islands	500.8	10
Central African Rep.	1170.8	31	Gambia	465.8	33
Slovak Rep.	1146.1	30	Solomon Islands	442.7	19
Guyana	1109.6	29	Panama	437.0	28
Kazakhstan	1090.6	34	Uruguay	426.6	30
Togo	1037.0	31	Venezuela	388.2	36
Cape Verde	1005.4	30	Sao Tome & Principe	387.5	28
Dominican Rep.	996.0	30			
Uzbekistan	991.8	32	Cyprus	373.6	23
Lithuania	985.7	29	Fiji	373.5	26
Guinea-Bissau	965.7	35	South Korea	365.0	27
Myanmar	963.5	28	Swaziland	350.9	26
Tajikistan	911.4	35	Samoa	337.4	21
Micronesia	880.5	15	Vanuatu	336.1	19

(continued)

Table 4.1 Continued

Countries	Amount	Relations	Countries	Amount	Relations
Mauritius	318.5	30	Seychelles	132.4	29
Comoros	300.6	23	Singapore	111.2	19
Malta	284.9	19	Grenada	81.7	20
Maldives	273.0	28	Tuvalu	65.4	14
Equatorial Guinea	266.8	29	Bahamas	58.8	14
Tonga	254.4	18	Barbados	56.5	20
St. Lucia	227.8	22	Libya	52.8	17
Oman	223.6	18	St. Kitts-Nevis	50.4	17
Turkmenistan	223.2	27	Antigua & Barbuda	43.2	19
Belize	195.6	30			
Trinidad & Tobago	186.3	23	United Arab Emirates	34.6	14
Dominica	174.8	25	Kuwait	31.2	16
Saudi Arabia	150.5	15			
Kiribati	143.5	15	Bahrain	25.0	9
			Brunei	20.9	10
St. Vincent & Grenadines	142.6	21	Qatar	17.5	7

To determine the international news coverage variable, factor analysis was conducted. The correlations (see Table 4.2) among news sources were strong—greater than .50—and statistically significant ($p < .01$). Also, based on the results of Kaiser-Meyer-Olkin (.78) and Bartlett's test ($\chi^2 = .548.28$, $df = 6$, $p < .01$), factor analysis is appropriate. Through factor analysis, only one factor was derived accounting for 81.99% of the variance. The factor loadings were .94 in AFP; .93 in AP; .89 in Reuters; .86 in CNN. Regarding the factor score coefficients, AFP was .29, AP .28, Reuters .27, and CNN .26. All news coverage data were weighted on the basis of those coefficients. Then, the four types of news coverage data were combined as one variable. That is, the news coverage variable in each country is a weighted sum accounting for the four news sources. The average of 159 countries was 2,909.16 ($SD = 5,054.56$).

Table 4.3 shows the descriptive statistics of the variables. The observed data were far from the multivariate normality assumption for the ML estimation. However, recent research has investigated the robustness of structural equation modeling (SEM) to nonnormality. Fan and Wang (1998) suggested that a nonnormality condition in SEM does not affect the standards errors of parameter estimates regardless of estimation methods, such as ML and GLS. Also, Lei and Lomax (2005) argued

Table 4.2 Correlations among News Coverage Variables

	1	2	3	4
1. AFP	–	.82**	.75**	.84**
2. AP		–	.78**	.77**
3. CNN			–	.59**
4. Reuters				–

Note: n = 159, **p < .01.

that the interpretation of parameter estimates in SEM can be accepted even though nonnormality conditions of observed data are severe. Thus, although the data for this study violate the assumption of multivariate normality, they can be acceptable for ML estimation.

Table 4.4 presents the results of the correlations among positions in the international aid network, news coverage, and the control variables. The correlation between the two aid networks was .50 ($p < .01$). The correlations between aid amount and other variables were all significant. News coverage ($r = .64$, $p < .01$) and population ($r = .65$, $p < .01$) were closely related to the aid amount, and GDP per capita ($r = -.22$, $p < .01$) showed a negative relationship the lower the GDP, the greater the aid amount. The correlation between the number of aid relations and news coverage was .24 ($p < .01$), population .22 ($p < .01$), GDP -.62 ($p < .01$). International trade ($r = .04$, $p > .05$) was not significant. News coverage was closely related to population ($r = .79$, $p < .01$) and trade ($r = .69$, $p < .01$), but GDP per capita ($r = .10$, $p > .05$) was not significant.

The hypothesized research model resulted in a $\chi^2 = 2.78$, $df = 2$, $p = .25$, a CFI of .999, a SRMR of .01, and an RMSEA of .050. This indicates a reasonable model fit. However, the path from GDP per capita to news coverage was not significant ($\beta = .05$, $p > .05$). Since the

Table 4.3 Descriptive Statistics

Variables	M	SD	Skewness	Kurtosis	n
Aid Amount[a]	2640.74	3560.67	2.67	8.67	159
Aid Relations	30.30	7.27	−1.22	.78	159
News Coverage	2909.16	5054.56	3.75	18.31	159
Trade[b]	176679.00	425376.23	4.21	19.87	159
GDP per capita	2825.60	3971.16	2.75	8.25	159
Population[c]	34.70	136.61	8.08	68.92	159

Note: Aid Amount[a] and Trade[b] are expressed in terms of million dollars. Population[c] is million people.

Table 4.4 Correlations among Aid Amount, Aid Relations, News Coverage, and Control Variables

	1	*2*	*3*	*4*	*5*	*6*
1. Aid Amount	–	.50**	.64**	.35**	–.22**	.65**
2. Aid Relations		–	.24**	.04	–.62**	.22**
3. News Coverage			–	.69**	.10	.79**
4. Trade				–	.31**	.54**
5. GDP per capita					–	–.10
6. Population						–

Note: n = 159, **p < .01.

correlation between them was also not significant, the direct effect of GDP per capita on news coverage was removed from the final model.

The respecified model resulted in a χ^2 = 3.91, *df* = 3, *p* = .27, a CFI of .998, a SRMR of .02, and an RMSEA of .044. It reveals a good model fit. Also, the values of χ^2 and RMSEA were better than the previous model. Thus, this study considered it the final model.

Figure 4.2 shows the results of the final model for this study. This model accounts for more than 50% of the variance in aid amount and aid relations. All paths were statistically significant. The path coefficient of news coverage on aid amount was .45 (*p* < .01). It supports the first

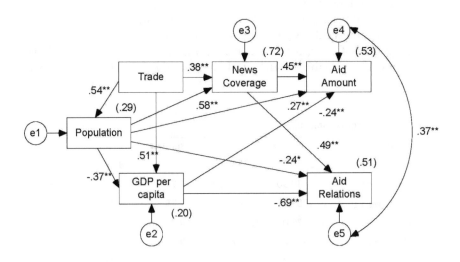

Figure 4.2. Final model, with standardized coefficients, of news coverage impact on international aid. Parentheses indicate variance explained. *p < .05. **p < .01.

hypothesis that news coverage positively affects aid amount. Also, the path coefficient between news coverage and aid relations was .49 ($p <$ .01). This supports the second hypothesis that news coverage positively affects the number of donors.

The effect of GDP per capita on aid amount was -.24 ($p < .01$), and the effect on aid relations was -.69 ($p < .01$). The standardized total effect of population on aid amount was .62 (standardized direct effect = .27, $p < .01$; standardized indirect effect = .36). The total effect of population on aid relations was .31 (standardized direct effect = -.24, $p < .05$; standardized indirect effect = .54). Trade has only indirect effects on aid amount (standardized indirect effect = .38) and aid relations (standardized indirect effect = -.00).

A total of 72% of the variance in news coverage is explained by trade and population. The standardized total effect of trade on news coverage was .69 (standardized direct effect = .38, $p < .01$; standardized indirect effect = .31). Population has only direct effect on news coverage (standardized direct effect = .58, $p < .01$). In addition, the total effect of trade on GDP per capita was .31 (standardized direct effect = .51, $p < .01$; standardized indirect effect = -.20).

Discussion

The results here show positive associations between the levels of global news coverage and international aid. That is, recipient countries with a high level of news coverage receive more aid and have more international aid relations than those with less coverage.

A contribution of this study is to provide empirical evidence that global news networks significantly affect international relations in the global system. This study suggests that global news networks enhance international communication and play an important role in the foreign policy decision-making process related to international aid commitment. Communication may be defined as a process by which information is exchanged among two or more systems existing within a larger supra-system with a goal of reducing uncertainty in the future behavior of the interacting systems. In this study, the communicating systems are nation-states and the suprasystem is the global community of nations. According to the global bystander intervention model (Pittinsky & Matic, 2005), to help victim countries, most of all, global bystanders must recognize the severe situations of the victims and feel strong responsibility. That is, the global bystander intervention model emphasizes the importance of com-munication among members in the global system. Consequently, this study indicates that global news networks practically embody the key mechanism of the global bystander intervention model by intensifying the international communication process.

Galor, O., & Mountford, A. (2006). *Trade and the great divergence: The family connection.* Retrieved October 15, 2006, from http://www.brown.edu/Departments/Economics/Papers/2006/2006-01_paper.pdf

Galtung, J., & Ruge, M. H. (1965). The structure of foreign news. *Journal of Peace Research, 2*(1), 64–91.

Giddens, A. (1990). *The consequences of modernity.* Stanford, CA: Stanford University Press.

Hester, A. (1974). The news from Latin America via a world news agency. *International Communication Gazette, 20*, 82–98.

Hjertholm, P., & White, H. (2000). Foreign aid in historical perspective: Background and trends. In F. Tarp (Ed.), *Foreign aid and development: Lessons learnt and directions for the future* (pp. 80–102). New York: Routledge.

Hopkins, R. F. (2000). Political economy of foreign aid. In F. Tarp (Ed.), *Foreign aid and development: Lessons learnt and directions for the future* (pp. 423–449). London: Routledge.

Hu, L., & Bentler, P. M. (1999). Cutoff criteria for fit indices in covariance structure analysis: Conventional criteria versus new alternatives. *Structural Equation Modeling, 6*, 1–55.

Hur, K. K. (1984). A critical analysis of international news flow research. *Critical Studies in Mass Communication, 1*, 365–378.

Kariel, H. G., & Rosenvall, L. A. (1984). Factors influencing international news flow. *Journalism Quarterly, 61*, 509–516.

Kim, K. (2003). Organizational determinants of international news coverage in Korean newspapers. *International Communication Gazette, 65*(1), 65–85.

Kim, K., & Barnett, G. A. (1996). The determinants of international news flow: A network analysis. *Communication Research, 23*, 323–352.

Latané, B., & Darley, J. M. (1968). Group inhibition of bystander intervention in emergencies. *Journal of Personality and Social Psychology, 10*(3), 215–221.

Latané, B., & Darley, J. M. (1969). Bystander "apathy." *American Scientist, 57*, 244–268.

Latané, B., & Darley, J. M. (1970). *The unresponsive bystander: Why doesn't he help?* New York: Appleton-Century-Crofts.

Lei, M., & Lomax, R. G. (2005). The effects of varying degrees of nonnormality in structural equation modeling. *Structural Equation Modeling, 12*(1), 1–27.

Lim, Y. S., Barnett, G. A., & Kim, J. H. (2008). The structure of international aid flows and global news media. *The Journal of International Communication, 14*(2), 117–142.

Livingston, S. (1997). *Clarifying the CNN effect: An examination of media effects according to type of military intervention.* Retrieved May15, 2008, from http://www.hks.harvard.edu/presspol/research_publications/papers/research_papers/R18.pdf.

Livingston, S., & Van Belle, D. A. (2005). The effects of satellite technology on newsgathering from remote locations. *Political Communication, 22*, 45–62.

Lumsdaine, D. (1993). *Moral vision in international politics: The foreign aid regime, 1949–1989.* Princeton, NJ: Princeton University Press.

McCombs, M., & Shaw, D. L. (1972). The agenda-setting function of mass media. *Public Opinion Quarterly, 36*, 176–187.

Meernik, J., Krueger, E. L., & Poe, S. C. (1998). Testing models of US foreign policy: Foreign aid during and after the Cold War. *Journal of Politics, 60*, 63–85.

Miller, D. T., & McFarland, C. (1987). Pluralistic ignorance: When similarity is interpreted as dissimilarity. *Journal of Personality and Social Psychology, 53*, 298–305.

Mortimer, J. (2006). Questions and answers about Darfur. *Associated Press.* Retrieved October 24, 2006, from http://news.yahoo.com/s/ap/20061024/ap_on_re_af/sudan_darfur_q_a_2

Pietiläinen, J. (2006). Foreign news and foreign trade: What kind of relationship? *International Communication Gazette, 68*(3), 217–228.

Pittinsky, T. L., & Matic, T. (2005). Global bystander non-intervention: Cross-level insights on cross-national helping. Retrieved April 25, 2005, from http://ksgnotes1.harvard.edu/research/wpaper.nsf/rwp/RWP05-006/$File/rwp_05_006_Pittinsky.pdf

Rioux, J.-S., & Van Belle, D. A. (2005). The impact of Le Monde coverage on French foreign aid allocations. *International Studies Quarterly, 49*(3), 481–502.

Rosengren, K. E. (1974). International news. Methods, data and theory. *Journal of Peace Research, 11*, 145–156.

Rosengren, K. E. (1977). Four types of tables. *Journal of Communication, 27*(1), 67–75.

Rosenthal, A. M. (1999). *Thirty-eight witnesses: The Kitty Genovese case.* Berkeley: University of California Press.

Schraeder, P. J., Hook, S. W., & Taylor, B. (1998). Clarifying the foreign aid puzzle: A comparison of American, Japanese, French, and Swedish aid flows. *World Politics, 50*(2), 294–323.

Shannon, T. R. (1996). *An introduction to the world-system perspective* (2nd ed.). Boulder, CO: Westview Press.

Shoemaker, P. J., Danielian, L. H., & Brendlinger, N. (1991). Deviant acts, risky business and US interests: The newsworthiness of world events. *Journalism Quarterly, 68*, 781–795.

Van Belle, D. A. (2003). Bureaucratic responsiveness to the news media: Comparing the influence of the New York Times and network television news coverage on US foreign aid allocations. *Political Communication, 20*, 263–285.

Van Belle, D. A., Rioux, J.-S., & Potter, D. M. (2004). *Media, bureaucracies, and foreign aid: A comparative analysis of the United States, the United Kingdom, Canada, France, and Japan.* New York: Palgrave-Macmillan.

Wallerstein, I. (1976). *The modern world system.* New York: Academic.

Walt, S. M. (1990). *Origins of alliances.* Ithaca, NY: Cornell University Press.

Waltz, K. N. (1959). *Man, the state, and war; a theoretical analysis.* New York: Columbia University Press.

Wu, H. D. (2000). Systemic determinants of international news coverage: a comparison of 38 countries. *Journal of Communication, 50*(2), 110–130.

Wu, H. D. (2003). Homogeneity around the world? Comparing the systemic determinants of international news flow between developed and developing countries. *International Communication Gazette, 65*(1), 9–24.

Zhang, G. (2004). The determinants of foreign aid allocation across China: The case of World Bank loans. *Asian Survey, 44*(5), 691–710.

Chapter 5

Coverage of Foreign Elections in the United States

A Model of International News Flow

Wayne Wanta and Guy J. Golan

Important events happen throughout the world every day. Because of time and space limitations, news media must sort through the endless stream of these international events and make value judgments regarding which are important enough to receive coverage. Thus, only a small portion of international events ever gets through the media gatekeepers.

Despite the fact that the flow of international news has received extensive attention from scholars—Hur (1982, p. 531), for example, believes that research in this area has reached "almost landslide proportions"— some critics have noted deficiencies in much of the research. Stevenson (1992, p. 552), for example, claims that many studies "document interesting facets of the field but offer no explanation." Chang (1998, p. 530) argues that scholars "need to take a more interconnected approach to creating synergies between theory and research."

The current study attempts to add to an emerging theory by proposing and testing a model of news flow involving non-U.S. elections in the U.S. news media. Through a content analysis of the newscasts of CNN and the three national networks, our study will investigate whether several factors can predict when an election held abroad is an important enough event to warrant media coverage.

The current study presents and tests a model that predicts coverage of international elections based on the nations' location in the world system. The study is based on research on the determinants of international news flow and coverage that integrated the world system perspective as a theoretical framework for predicting coverage (T. Chang, 1998; Gunaratne, 2001). We predict that core nations will be more likely to receive coverage from American television news networks than peripheral nations and that the likelihood of semiperipheral nations to receive coverage will largely depend on their relationship with core nations. Specifically the model predicts that amount of coverage depends on (1) location in the world system, with core nations receiving more coverage than semiperipheral or peripheral nations; (2) international interactions, with semiperipheral countries that have close ties with core nations through strong trade relations, cultural ties, or because they are receiving foreign aid from the core nations, which in turn receive more coverage from U.S. media than other countries not closely aligned with the elite nations; (3) positive attributes, with peripheral nations that have aa large gross domestic product, a large population, or high oil production receiving high levels of coverage; and (4) negative attributes are also considered newsworthy, for example, peripheral nations that may pose a threat to the United States because of military expenditures, drug production, or the possession of nuclear weapons.

Literature Review

International news has been an important part of evening newscasts. Larson (1982) found that 40% of the air time on ABC, CBS, and NBC news in the late 1970s was devoted to international affairs. It is no surprise, then, that the flow of international news has been one of the most highly researched areas in mass communication (e.g., Galtung & Ruge, 1965; Stevenson & Shaw, 1984).

While the quantity of international news coverage has been high, some scholars argue that the quality of this coverage has often been lacking. Larson (1982), for example, is critical of correspondents who lack linguistic, cultural, or political knowledge about the nations on which they report. Peterson (1979) noted that story selection tends to vary with the cultural background of the reporters rather than newsworthiness. Paik (1999) analyzed coverage of international news in the *Wall Street Journal*. The results of his analysis indicated that news from Europe and Asia received the majority of coverage while South America, the Caribbean, and Africa received limited coverage. This lack of balance in international coverage was further supported by Golan's (2006) analysis of international news coverage on three American television networks' news in the New York region. His study revealed a pattern that demonstrated less than 20 nations accounted for more than 85% of international news stories.

International News and World-Systems Theory

In their attempt to go beyond the mere identification of some of the key determinants of international news flow and coverage, scholars proposed several models for predicting international news coverage.

Chang and Lee (chapter 3 this volume) replicated a determinants' model originally proposed by Chang, Shoemaker, and Brendlinger (1987). The original study identified such variables as normative deviance of an event, relevance to the United States, potential for social changes, and geographic distance to be the key predictors of international news coverage. However, Chang and Lee's model suggested that threat to the

United States and U.S. involvement were the two leading determinants of coverage for both newspapers and television.

Golan (chapter 6 this volume) proposed and tested a model that incorporated 14 key variables drawn from determinants research that he argued could be used to predict international coverage. The results from a series of multivariate regression tests found reliable support for his model and for his assertion that international coverage may be predicted by country-based variables. Specifically instability, distance from the United States, U.S. investment, U.S. aid, religious diversity, military expenditures, and population all predicted coverage on CNN and the U.S. network news.

Chang (1998) has proposed a model of international news flow based on world-systems theory (Wallerstein, 1974, 1979, 1996). World-systems theory argues that the global system has two tiers, with Western developed countries forming the core and the rest of the world forming the periphery. This global system originated through an evolutionary process in which countries were subsumed under the capitalist world economy dominated by the United States through a complex network of interdependence. Based on their economic, political, and social and cultural relations, countries are located in three zones: core, semiperipheral, and peripheral. Consequently, the hierarchical position of nations could explain the disproportionate quantity and quality of news, where nations nearer or in the core receive more and better coverage than nations in the periphery.

Chang (1998), therefore, argues that the world-system theory fits in well with international communication. World-system theory merges an individual nation's goals, its global exchange of trade, and its flow of international relations, capital, and information. At the center of this news hierarchy are core nations, the elite nations that dominate world markets and world media outlets. Nations in the core, then, are naturally deemed newsworthy in international news. With strong ties to the world economic, political, and cultural infrastructure, core nations command attention from news media around the globe.

Indeed, several studies (e.g., Golan & Wanta, 2003; Kim & Barnett, 1996) have found that Western industrialized countries dominate news coverage. News from nations in Africa, Asia, and Latin America, meanwhile, are less likely to pass through the world's gatekeepers (Golan, 2008). Noncore nations have significantly less impact on the world's economy and thus command significantly less attention from news media around the globe. Nonetheless, events from noncore nations occasionally receive news coverage, pointing to the likelihood that other factors play roles in the news selection process. Two such variables form the basis for the model proposed here. They are international interactions and international attributes.

variables that could differentiate between semiperipheral and peripheral nations. Nations with strong ties with the United States culturally and economically should be deemed more newsworthy than nations with weak links to the United States. Thus, these nations with close U.S. ties will form the semiperipheral layer of our model and will be more likely to pass through the news gates than will nations outside this layer with weak U.S. ties.

Newsworthiness Factor 3: International Attributes   Core nations have newsworthiness because of their importance in the world's economic and political infrastructure. Semiperipheral nations have newsworthiness because of their interactions with core nations. Peripheral nations, however, need some additional element to reach the newsworthiness threshold that will allow stories dealing with their elections to pass through the U.S. gatekeepers. Thus, only peripheral nations that have certain international attributes—important characteristics linked to countries—will pass this third newsworthiness test and receive coverage in the U.S. media. Peripheral nations, then, need a large gross domestic product, a large population, or high oil production to make them newsworthy. In addition, negative factors that may make a nation appear to be a threat to the United States also would be important newsworthy criteria. Thus, military expenditures, drug production within a country, or the presence of nuclear weapons would increase a nation's newsworthiness. The more important attributes a nation has, the more likely it will be to receive media coverage.

Generally, factors related to a country's impact on the world and its relative reputation for deviance could be important attributes that would allow peripheral countries to pass through gatekeepers and appear on the evening news. Logically, if a country has a large population, the nation would be more newsworthy than a smaller nation. Likewise, if a country has a reputation as being radically deviant, its elections would hold high interest among U.S. news consumers. Previous research has found deviance to be perhaps the strongest predictor of international news coverage (Chang, Shoemaker, & Brendlinger, 1987; Shoemaker, Chang, & Brendlinger, 1986; Shoemaker, Danielian, & Brendlinger, 1991). Thus, the size of a country and its political climate should influence the amount of coverage that it would receive.

Previous studies consistently found that a nation's population serves as a strong predictor of coverage (Kim & Barnett, 1995). Ishii (1996) found that population was a significant predictor of the quantity of international news in a Japanese newspaper. Population, in fact, was the second most powerful predictor—after "eliteness" of nations—in an analysis conducted by Kariel and Rosenvall (1984). Wu (2000), however, found that population was a significant predictor of coverage in Cyrus, Gambia, and Senegal, but only a modest predictor in Germany, Kenya, Nigeria, Turkey, Ukraine, and the United Kingdom. Thus, population may be important in some countries only under certain circumstances.

Thus, international attributes form the third stage of our model. News of peripheral nations will not pass this third newsworthiness test unless the nations have important attributes that make the countries newsworthy.

Hypotheses

The overall model, then, proposes and tests the following hypotheses:

H1. Core nations will be more likely than noncore nations to receive media coverage.

If a nation is a Western industrialized nation or a member of the United Nations Security Council, it will be deemed newsworthy by U.S. gatekeepers. These elite nations do not need other factors to increase their newsworthiness and so should receive more news coverage than other nations.

H2. The stronger the ties to core nations that a noncore nation has, the more likely it will be to receive media coverage.

Noncore nations need additional factors to make them newsworthy. If a noncore nation has strong international interactions with a core country—specifically, the United States—the U.S. media should deem it newsworthy enough to merit coverage. Thus, international, cultural, and economic interactions will transform some peripheral nations into semiperipheral nations, making them more worthy of coverage than peripheral nations.

H3. The more important attributes that a peripheral nation possesses, the more likely it will be to receive media coverage.

Nations outside the core and outside the semiperiphery will need additional factors before they will be deemed newsworthy by the U.S. media. If a peripheral nation has important attributes, this would increase its newsworthiness and increase its chances of passing through the U.S. gatekeepers. These attributes can be in the form of negative characteristics that position a country as a threat to the United States—drug production or military expenditures, for example—or positive characteristics that improve a country's image—population size or gross domestic product, for instance.

Method

To examine the nature of the coverage of international elections by the U.S. broadcast media, we conducted a content analysis of four U.S. evening newscasts. The content analysis included CNN and the evening news programs of the three U.S. television networks: ABC, CBS, and NBC. The content analysis focused specifically on the main evening news shows. Programs were analyzed through the Vanderbilt News Abstracts Archive (2000).

The unit of analysis was the individual election. The study analyzed all elections that took place from January 1, 1998, through May 1, 2000. Of the 138 elections, only eight received coverage on all four newscasts, 10 received coverage on more than one newscast, 18 received coverage on one newscast, and 102 received no news coverage.

The dependent variable, then, was whether the election was covered by any of the newscasts. The variable could range from zero if the election received no coverage to 4 if it received coverage on all four networks.

Each election was coded for several independent variables. To maintain consistency across the items, the range was restricted for all of the variables except for stage 1—location in the world system. Thus, the international interaction and the international attributes variables all had ranges of 1 to 3. All of the interaction and attribute indexes were computed by summing three individual variables then dividing by the number of items in the indexes (3). Thus, the indexes had ranges from 1 to 3.

Factor 1: Location in World System

The first factor determining whether a country's election is newsworthy enough to warrant coverage is the nation's location in the world system. Core nations will pass through the first news gate while noncore nations will not. As Gunaratne (2001) explains, traditional world-system studies often base their classification of nations using a formula that weighs a nation's gross national product against its share of exports. Answering critics who believe that economic factors are not sufficient in the determination of a nation's location in the world system (e.g., Bergesen, 1990), the current study introduces Western industrialized nations and permanent membership in the UN Security Council as variables that impact the location of a nation in the world system. Chang (1998) argues that Western industrialized nations dominate the world's economic and political infrastructure and thus rank higher in the world system than other countries. In addition, permanent membership in the UN Security Council clearly positions nations as central in the shaping of international diplomacy. This is the same way in which Chang (1998) measured core nations.

Factor 2: International Interactions

International interactions deal with links between peripheral nations and core nations. Three items were summed to form an index. The variables were:

The Amount of Trade a Nation Had with the United States   This was determined here by the ranking of the nation on the U.S. list of trading partners. The categories were: Top 20 trading partner, top 50 trading partner, not in the top 50 trading partner ranking. Data were based on the Office of Trade and Economic Analysis, International Trade Administration, U.S. Department of Commerce (2000).

The Number of Immigrants in the United States from an Individual Nation   The categories were: more than 10 million, between 5 million and 1 million, less than 1 million. Data were based on the U.S. Census Bureau (1990).

The Amount of Foreign Aid a Country Receives   The categories were: Receives less than $1 billion, receives more than $1 billion, donor nation. Data come from the *CIA World Factbook (1999).*

The three variables, then, dealt with cultural and economic links to the core countries. After the three measures were summed and divided by the number of items in the index (3), the international interactions variable could range from 1 to 3. The larger the score, the closer a nation would be linked to a core country. The Cronbach's alpha for the index was .82.

Factor 3: International Attributes

Several attributes that could influence the newsworthiness of a nation's election were included in our analysis. The variables were combined to form two indexes, one of which dealt with positive attributes and one that dealt with negative attributes.

The positive attributes variables were factors that would increase a nation's impact in the world, and thus were a measure of a nation's importance. The positive variables were:

Population   This variable was based on the number of people living in a nation. Categories were: Less than 20 million, between 20 and

100 million, more than 100 million. Since the size of population is one indicator of a country's importance, we may find a positive relationship between population and media coverage. Coding was based on the official U.S. Census Bureau's 2000 International Database.

Gross Domestic Product   This was coded as under $50 billion total GDP, between $50 billion and $1 trillion, over $1 trillion. Data come from the CIA World Factbook 1999.

Role in Oil Production   This was coded as the nation does not export oil, it exports oil but is not a member of OPEC, it is a member of OPEC. Data come from the *CIA World Factbook 1999*.

The three measures all deal with positive aspects of a country's image. If a nation is perceived as having a strong economy or a powerful image, the U.S. media should provide more coverage of the nation than weaker countries. The more positive a nation's attributes, the higher it would score on this measure. The alpha was .80.

The negative attributes index involved three factors that would make a country appear to be a threat to U.S. security and thus was a measure of deviance. The variables were:

Narcotics Involvement   This was measured by whether a nation is a known producer or trafficker in narcotics. Categories were: Production and transport country, transport country, no drugs. Data were based on the *CIA World Factbook 1999*.

Nuclear Arms Capabilities   This was measured by a country's current ability to produce nuclear arms. Categories were: Nuclear arms capability, developing nuclear arms, and no nuclear capabilities. Variable coding was based on data from the Bureau of Nonproliferation, U.S. Department of State (2000). Since nuclear arms pose a threat to the United States, countries that have nuclear capabilities or are developing such capabilities may be more likely to receive coverage in the U.S. media than would other countries.

Military Expenditures   This was coded as under $1 billion in annual military expenditures, between $1 billion and $10 billion in annual military expenditures, over $10 billion. Data come from the *CIA World Factbook 1999*.

These three measures all deal with negative characteristics of countries that would pose a threat to other nations. Nations posing a threat to the United States should be deemed more newsworthy than nonthreatening nations. The more negative a nation's attributes, and thus the larger the threat to the United States, the higher they would score on this measure. The alpha was .74.

Data Analysis

A series of regression analyses tested the model in Figure 5.1. The regression analyses examined whether the three factors could predict whether a nation's election would receive media coverage on U.S. newscasts.

Factor 1 involved a nation's location in the world system. Here, core nation was examined as a dummy variable with the amount of coverage nations received as the dependent variable.

Factor 2 involved international interactions. Since core nations were involved in the first stage and the model was designed to differentiate only between semiperipheral and peripheral nations in this second stage, only noncore nations were included in this part of the analysis. This analysis essentially tested whether semiperipheral nations, those with close ties to core nations, would be more likely to receive media coverage than peripheral nations.

Factor 3 involved international attributes. Since core nations were involved in the first stage and semiperipheral nations were involved in the second stage, only noncore nations scoring below the median on the international interactions variable were included in this analysis, which essentially removed core nations and semiperipheral nations from this final analysis. The third stage, then, was designed to examine whether peripheral nations scoring high on international attributes, both positive and negative, would be more likely to receive media coverage than peripheral nations scoring low on international attributes.

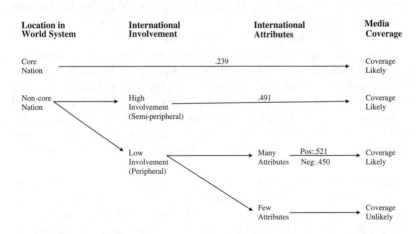

Figure 5.1 Model of international election news coverage in the U.S. media.

Note: Hypothesis 1 compares core nations vs. non-core nations.
Hypothesis 2 compares semi-peripheral nations (those with high international involvement) vs. peripheral nations.
Hypothesis 3 compares peripheral nations with many international attributes (positive and negative) vs. peripheral nations with few attributes.

The international interaction and international attributes variables were examined both through the indexes and through the individual variables that comprised the indexes.

Results

Figure 5.1 shows the results of the analysis. The data fit the model extremely well. Hypothesis 1 predicted that core nations would be more likely to receive news coverage in the U.S. media than nations on the periphery. The beta was .239 (p = .005). Thus, core nations were more likely to pass this newsworthiness test and receive media coverage than other nations.

Hypothesis 2 predicted that international interactions would allow semiperipheral nations—those countries with strong ties to core nations—to receive media coverage. In this test, the beta was .491 (p = .000). Thus, the stronger a peripheral nation's ties to the United States, the more likely it was to receive coverage in the U.S. media, which supported the hypothesis.

Hypothesis 3 predicted that international attributes would make some peripheral nations more newsworthy than others. Here, the beta for the negative attribute index, involving items that would make a country appear to be a threat to the United States, was .450 (p = .000). The positive attribute index, which included items that would increase a country's standing in the world, produced a beta of .521 (p = .000). Again, the results strongly support the hypothesis that the more international attributes a nation possessed, the more likely it would be to receive coverage in the U.S. media.

To further examine the international news model, the indexes were deconstructed and individual variables were analyzed. All but one of the individual variables produced statistically significant betas.

In Stage 2, both international trade with the United States (.492, p = .000) and ancestral ties to the United States (.277, p = .001) predicted media coverage. The beta for foreign aid, however, was not significant (-.103, p < .05). Thus, only two of the measures of international interaction were predictors of whether a noncore nation's elections were covered.

Stage 3, meanwhile, showed statistically significant betas for all the variables. Population (.456), gross domestic product (.519), oil production (.449), nuclear arms capability (.494) and military expenditures (.422) all were significant at the p = .000 level. Drug involvement (.239) was significant at the p <,05 level. Thus, all of these variables were strong predictors of whether peripheral nations' elections received media coverage.

Discussion

The present study proposed and tested a model of international news coverage that employed a series of three factors: location in the world system, international interactions, and international attributes. The data from our analysis of 138 elections from 1998 to 2000 fit the model extremely well.

As previous research has found, elite nations were more likely to receive media coverage than other nations. These elite nations form the core of the news flow model tested here. These Western industrialized nations or members of the UN Security Council were deemed newsworthy by themselves and did not need additional factors before warranting news coverage from U.S. media.

Noncore nations, however, did need additional factors before they could pass through the news gates. The first such set of factors formed the international interactions index. If nations had strong ties to core nations—notably, the United States—U.S. media were more likely to give them coverage. Thus, if a nation had strong trade relations with the United States or had a cultural link through ancestors who migrated to the United States, these nations passed this second newsworthiness test and received media coverage on the U.S. newscasts.

Notably here, though, was the lack of an impact of the aid variable. How much aid a nation received did not increase its newsworthiness. U.S. news media may not care about the amount of aid a country receives. Indeed, some countries that received relatively high amounts of aid, such as Guatemala, received little or no media coverage, while other countries that received low amounts of aid, such as Iran, received significant media coverage. Indeed, the fact that a country did not receive aid from a core nation may be an indication that the country is a threat to the United States—low aid means a nation is too deviant to warrant support from a core nation. Thus, these deviant nations deserve more media coverage, which is why the beta for this variable was negative (-.103). While this coefficient was not statistically significant, it does indicate the direction of the relationship between the two variables: countries receiving less aid from core nations tended to get more media coverage. The aid variable, then, may not have been an indication of ties to core nations so much as a measure of a country's deviance.

Regardless, other variables play a clearer role in the news decision process. Trade, for instance, has a direct influence on the U.S. economy. Thus, while both trade and aid involve economic links to a country, the trade variable has a greater direct impact on the average U.S. citizen and thus is more important in the news selection process.

In addition, the aid variable was the only interactions item used here that did not involve a direct link to the United States. The other two factors looked at trade with the United States and number of ancestors who migrated to the U.S. The aid variable looked broadly at the overall amount of aid a country received. Perhaps interactions variables need links to a specific core nation before the core nation's media will deem it newsworthy.

In the final stage of our model, nations outside the core and semiperiphery needed additional factors before they were deemed newsworthy. This third stage involved international attributes.

Both positive and negative attributes played a role in the news selection process for these peripheral nations. If countries were viewed as a threat to the United States because they possessed nuclear arms, were involved in drug trafficking, or had high military expenditures, they increased their chances of passing through the U.S. gatekeepers. In addition, if countries were viewed as important by having large populations, high oil production, or high gross domestic products, they too increased their chances of receiving coverage.

All of these variables produced strong betas. Only the drug involvement measure, in fact, produced a beta that was not significant at the $p < .001$ level. This measure, as with the aid variable, may have produced a stronger beta had we used a wider range. The 1 to 3 range used here may have restricted the variance of this measure, which lessened the ultimate impact of this variable in our model. Even with the compressed range, however, drug involvement produced a significant beta ($p = .018$).

While the present study demonstrates clear trends in international news coverage, international elections are just one segment of the international news agenda. Future research should continue to monitor media coverage patterns of other topics of international news.

In addition, future studies should examine the type of coverage devoted to international elections. While our study examined frequency of election coverage, it did not look at the framing of the coverage. Perhaps, newscasts were focusing on improprieties in elections, concentrating on negative aspects of international news. Future research also may utilize variables employing wider ranges. While we felt maintaining consistency across our measures was important, and most of the variables here were robust enough to produce statistically significant results, increasing the variance on some measures may have produced different results.

Overall, though, our model successfully linked world systems theory to international news flow. Clearly, all nations are not equal in the eyes of the U.S. news media gatekeepers. Chang's (1998) suggestion that world-system theory serves as an appropriate theoretical framework for the study of the determinants of international news coverage and flow is supported by the results of the current study, which like other studies (Chang et al. 2000; Golan, 2008; Gunaratne, 2001) tested and supported the world-system model.

News selection is a complex and often subjective process, as White's classic study showed (White, 1950). The model examined here is an attempt at grounding international news flow into the emerging theoretical framework that others, such as Chang (1998) and Wu (2000), have initiated.

References

Bergesen, A. (1990). Turning world system theory on its head. *Theory, Culture & Society, 7,* 67–81.

Bureau of Nonproliferation, U.S. Department of State. (n.d.). Retrieved February 11, 2003, from http://www.state.gov/www/global/arms/bureaunp.html

Burrowes, R. (1974). Mirror, mirror on the wall: A source comparison study of international event data. In J. N. Rosenau (Ed.), *Comparing foreign policies: Theories, findings, and methods* (pp. 383–405). Beverly Hills, CA: Sage.

Chang, T-K. (1998). All countries not created equal to be news: World system and international communication. *Communication Research, 25,* 528–566.

Chang, T-K., & Lee, J. (1992). Factors affecting gatekeepers' selection of foreign news: A national survey of newspaper editors. *Journalism Quarterly, 69,* 554–561.

Chang, T-K., Shoemaker, P., & Brendlinger, N. (1987). Determinants of international news coverage in the U.S. media. *Communication Research, 14,* 396–414.

CIA World Factbook 1999. (1999). Retrieved March 20, 2003, from http://www.odci.gov/ cia/publications/factbook/indexgeo.html

Gatlung, J., & Ruge, M. (1965). The structure of foreign news. *Journal of Peace Research, 2,* 64–91.

Golan, G. (2006). Inter-media agenda setting and global news coverage: Assessing the influence of the *New York Times* on three network television evening news programs. *Journalism Studies, 7*(2), 323–334.

Golan, G. J. (2008). Where in the world is Africa? Predicting coverage of Africa by U.S. television networks. *International Communication Gazette, 70*(1), 43–59.

Golan, G., & Wanta, W. (2003). International elections on the U.S. network news: An examination of factors affecting newsworthiness. *Gazette, 65*(1), 25–39.

Gunaratne, S. A. (2001). Prospects and limitations of world system theory for media analysis: The case of the Middle East and North Africa. *Gazette, 63*(2–3), 121–148.

Hester, A. (1971). An analysis of news from developed and developing nations. *Gazette, 7,* 30–40.

Hur, K. K. (1982). International mass communication research: A critical review of theory and methods. In M. Burgoon & N. E. Doran (Eds.), *Communication yearbook* (Vol. 6, pp. 531–554). Beverly Hills, CA: Sage.

Ishii, K. (1996). Is the U.S. over-reported in the Japanese press? *Gazette, 57,* 135–144.

Kariel, H. G., & Rosenvall, L. A. (1984). Factors influencing international news flow. *Journalism Quarterly, 60*, 434–436.

Kim, K., & Barnett, G. A. (1996). The determinants of international news flow: A network analysis. *Communication Research, 23*, 323–352.

Larson, J. F. (1982). International affairs coverage on U.S. evening news networks news. In W. C. Adams (Ed.), *Television coverage of international affairs* (pp. 15–39). Norwood, NJ: Ablex.

McCombs, M. E., Lopez-Escobar, E., & Llamas, J. P. (2000). Setting the agenda of attributes in the 1996 Spanish election. *Journal of Communication, 50*, 77–92.

Office of Trade and Economic Analysis, International Trade Administration, U.S. Department of Commerce. (2000). http://www.ita.doc.gov/td/ industry/ otea/

Ostgaard, E. (1965). Factors Influencing the flow of news. *Journal of Peace Research, 2*, 39–64.

Peterson, S. (1979). Foreign news gatekeepers and criteria of newsworthiness. *Journalism Quarterly, 56*(1), 116–125.

Shoemaker, P. J., Chang, T-K., & Brendlinger, N. (1986). Deviance as a predictor of newsworthiness: Coverage of international events in the U.S. media. In M. L. McLaughlin (Ed.), *Communication yearbook* (Vol. 10, pp. 348–365). Beverly Hills, CA: Sage.

Shoemaker, P. J., Danielian, L. H., & Brendlinger, N. (1991) Deviant acts, risky business and U.S. interests: The newsworthiness of world events. *Journalism Quarterly, 68*, 781–795

Stevenson, R. L. (1992). Defining international communication as a field. *Journalism Quarterly, 69*, 543–553.

Stevenson, R. L., & Shaw, D. L. (1984). *Foreign news and the New World Information Order*. Ames: Iowa State University Press.

U.S. Census Bureau, International Data Base. (2000). http://www.census.gove/ cgi/bin/ipc/idbrank.pl

Vanderbilt Television News Archive (2000). Collection at Vanderbilt University. http://tvnews.vanderbilt.edu/search.html

Wallerstein, I. (1974). *The modern world system*. New York: Academic Press.

Wallerstein, I. (1979). *The capitalist world-economy*. New York: Cambridge University Press.

Wallerstein, I. (1996). National development and the world system at the end of the Cold War. In A. Inkeles & M. Sasaki (Eds.), *Comparing nations and cultures: Readings in a cross-disciplinary perspective* (pp. 484–497). Englewood Cliffs, NJ: Prentice-Hall.

White, D. M. (1950, Fall). The gatekeeper: A case study in the selection of news. *Journalism Quarterly, 27*, 383–390.

Wu, H. D. (2000). Systemic determinants of international news coverage: A comparison of 38 countries, *Journal of Communication, 50*(2), 110–130.

Wu, H. D. (2007). A brave new world for international news?—Exploring the determinants of the coverage of foreign nations on U.S. web sites. *International Communication Gazette, 69*(5), 539–551.

Chapter 6

Determinants of International News Coverage

Guy J. Golan

Introduction

The world we live in is shaped daily by events that occur all around the globe. Such events might include terror attacks, natural disasters, armed conflict, political elections, and celebrity weddings. Due to limitations of time and space, news media gatekeepers must identify a few events as more newsworthy than others. As noted by Chang, Shoemaker, and Brendlinger (1987), research into international news coverage has yielded a rich body of empirical research describing the various aspects of how the news media cover the world. A more specific emphasis within research of international news coverage is research of the determinants of international news coverage.

Decades of research have studied many news factors that are associated with an international event's newsworthiness. As noted by Wu (1998), the determinants of international news have been widely investigated. Wu notes that 15 relevant studies were completed prior to 1980, 23 between 1981 and 1990, and 17 since 1991.

Research into the determinants of international news coverage has been traditionally divided along two theoretical approaches: the event-oriented approach and the contextual approach (Chang et al., 1987). Both approaches attempt to provide operational definitions of the newsworthiness concept. While the former focuses on the nature of the international news event, the latter focuses on the contextual characteristics of the countries involved. Research findings identify several different factors as determinants of international news coverage. These include such event-oriented variables as normative and potential for social change deviance (Chang et al., 1987; Shoemaker, Chang, & Brendlinger, 1986; Shoemaker, Danielian, & Brendlinger, 1991) and relevance to the United States (K. Chang & Lee, 1992; Chang et al., 1987) and such contextual variables as population (Dupree, 1971; Kim & Barnett, 1996), cultural affinity (Hester, 1973), location in the world system (Chang, 1998), geographic distance from the United States (Van Belle, 2000), and economic variables (Rosengren & Rickardsson, 1974).

Recently, scholars argued for the need to move beyond a mere taxonomy of news factors and toward a more systematic investigation of news factors. This includes the inclusion of multivariate techniques that allow scholars to synthesis and evaluate which determinants serve as the strongest predictors of coverage (Shoemaker et al., 1991; Wu, 2003).

The current study aims to contribute to the rich literature on the determinants of international news coverage through its examination of the country based factors that are associated with the amount of coverage that nations receive from U.S. television network news programs. The current study will make a contribution to knowledge in the field by providing one of the first multivariate measurements of country-based variables that are associated with international news coverage.

Review of Literature: The Determinants of International News Coverage

One of the first and most influential studies concerning newsworthiness and its definition is the Galtung and Ruge (1965) study. In the past few decades, scholars have continued to research the newsworthiness concept. For example, Harcup and O'Neil (2001) argued the need for a more "contemporary" taxonomy of news values than that of the original study by Galtung and Ruge. The authors offered an alternative operationalization of the newsworthiness concept that included the following news values: the power elite, celebrity, entertainment surprise, bad news, good news, magnitude, relevance, and follow-ups.

Moving beyond a mere taxonomy of news values, researchers of international news coverage have argued for a more theoretical approach to the study of the factors that determine the newsworthiness of international news. Shoemaker et al. (1986) argued that such variables as those identified by Galtung and Ruge (1965) lack a theoretical underpinning and instead hypothesized and supported deviance as the main predictor of coverage. Research into the determinants of international news coverage has been traditionally divided along two theoretical approaches: the event-oriented approach and the contextual approach (Chang et al., 1987; Wu, 1998). Both approaches attempt to provide operational definitions of the newsworthiness concept using different approaches.

Over the past two decades three main event-oriented variables emerged as the key determinants of international news coverage. These are: normative deviance, which was operationalized by Chang et al. (1987) as the extent to which an event would violate U.S. norms; potential for social change deviance, which was operationalized by Chang et al. (1987) as the extent to which an event violated the status quo in the country in which it occurred and relevance to the United States. The current study will argue that these operational definitions of deviance are likely to lead to measurement errors since they are both highly subjective and both require a high degree of expertise concerning international politics from the coders. The current study will argue for an alternative operational definition of deviance in its methodology section.

While event-oriented variables serve as powerful predictors of international news coverage, they fail to fully explain the international news selection process. A review of research into the determinants of international news coverage identifies several key contextual variables found to be associated with international news coverage. These include: geographic variables (Van Belle, 2000; Wang, 2009; Wu, 2003); cultural affinity variables (Hester, 1973; Shoemaker et al., 1991); and location in the world system/hierarchy of nations (Chang, 1998; Kim & Barnett, 1996).

Geographic Variables

One key variable that has consistently been found to be a strong determinant of international news coverage is geography, more specifically, geographic proximity between the nation in which an event occurs and the nation in which the event is covered. It would be logical that media consumers would be more interested in events that occur close to them than those that occur far away (K. Chang & Lee, 2009; Chang et al., 1987; Van Belle, 2000; Wu, 2000, 2003). Indeed, Wu's study has (2003) identified geographic proximity as one of the key determinants of international news coverage.

Cultural Affinity

Cultural affinity has been found to be a strong determinant of international news coverage in several key studies. Hester (1973) proposed a research design for studying the relationship between cultural affinity and coverage. However, Hester left the actual measurements for future research. Unfortunately, a review of the literature indicates that the majority of variables suggested by Hester have not been measured frequently against coverage. Rather, many studies identified different variables from those of Hester that are based on his cultural affinity hypothesis. For example, Shoemaker et al. (1991) introduced ethnic similarity as one variable under their cultural significance variable category.

The main assumption in Hester's proposal is that news media gatekeepers are more likely to view an international event as newsworthy if the event occurred in a nation that is culturally similar and familiar to the United States. One possible theoretical explanation for this phenomenon might be found in social identity theory. This theory posits that individuals conceptualize their self-concept based on their group membership (Tajfel, 1978). The theory further identifies how people

of the United Nations. In addition, the current study will also include the recently created Palestinian Authority. While this political entity does not represent a sovereign nation, it does govern more than 3 million people and therefore cannot be excluded from the current study.

The selection of 1999 as the sample year was based on the need to include the most recent year, while searching for a year that might be considered to be a typical year of coverage that is much like previous years. The year 2001 could not be selected because of the September 11 story which dominated all news coverage during the second half of that year. The year 2000 was also not included in the sample because of the fact that the year included the 2000 U.S. presidential election, which much like the September 11 megastory, dominated all coverage and therefore was not representative of most typical coverage periods.

Each news story was coded for the identity of the nations that were the main subjects of the story. When aggregated, this will produce for each country a frequency that will represent the overall amount of coverage the nation received during 1999. So for example, a story about a car bombing in Jerusalem will be coded with the number that is assigned to Israel. If a story focused on more than one nation, it was double coded. For example, a story about peace talks between India and Pakistan was coded for both India and Pakistan. It ought to be noted that a nation was not coded unless it was the main subject of the news story. For example, a story that mentioned U.S. Air Force strikes on Iraq might mention that the planes flew out of a base in Turkey. Since Iraq was the main news object in the story and the mention of Turkey was just incidental, only the prior country was coded.

Upon the completion of the content analysis, a frequency will be run to determine how many stories included each one of the nations of the world as their main subject. This total frequency count for each nation represents the dependent variable in the current study: coverage. Since previous research indicates that CNN coverage of world events is much more extensive than that of the three other networks (e.g., Golan & Wanta, 2003), a separate combined score will be presented for the aggregate country coverage on the three networks and a separate score will be presented for the nation's coverage on CNN. The aggregate frequency scores for each country are presented in the results section.

Subsequent to the completion of the content analysis, a second coder coded 10% of the stories in order to measure the reliability of the measurement. The following intercoder reliability scores were derived using the Holsti (1969) method: ABC .91, CBS .89, NBC .93, CNN .86.

Independent Variables

Upon the completion of the content analysis, each of the 190 UN member nations were coded the 14 different variables. The main criterion for the inclusion of a variable in this study was inclusion in at least two previous studies that related directly to international news coverage. The only exceptions to this rule are the religious affinity variables and the variables in the "deviance" and "relevance" categories.

Deviance

Several benchmark studies have identified normative deviance and potential for social change deviance as the two key predictor of international news coverage (Chang et al., 1987; Shoemaker, Chang et al., 1986; Shoemaker, Danielian et al., 1991).

The current study will argue that the operational definitions of both the normative and potential for social change deviance as offered by the previous studies are likely to result in errors. The nature of both definitions is highly subjective and both require the coder to hold a high degree of expertise regarding international politics.-

The current study operationalizes deviance as the level of instability in a nation. This coding was based on an international conflict report published by the National Defense Council Foundation (1999), a Virginia based think tank that specializes in research on national defense and foreign affairs. The overall instability score that is assigned to each nation in the world by the NDFC reflects that overall level of economic, political, military, and social instability in a nation during the year 1999.

Relevance to the United States

Previous studies of the determinants of international news coverage indicate that nations (or events) that are of relevance to the United States are more likely to receive coverage than those that are not (e.g., Shoemaker et al., 1991). The current study operationalizes relevance to the United States by using the following previously tested relevance variables: trade with the United States (K. Chang & Lee, 2001, chapter 3 this volume; Lim & Barnett, chapter 4 this volume; Shoemaker et al., 1991), geographic distance from the United States (Wu, 2003), foreign aid from the United States (Lim & Barnett, chapter 4 this volume; Shoemaker et al., 1991; Wanta & Golan, chapter 5 this volume) and U.S. private investment in a nation (Hester, 1973; Shoemaker et al., 1991). The trade variable will represent the sum of imports from and exports to the United States during 1999. The data are derived from the U.S. Census Bureau (1999) and represent the total amount of overall trade between the nation and the United States in millions of dollars. The current study will code geographic distance from the United States in the exact same manner as the Shoemaker et al. (1991) study. Coding of the aid from the United States variable will be on the total amount of U.S. military and economic aid that the nation received during 1999 in thousands of dollars. Data were obtained from the U.S. Census Bureau (1999). Finally, coding for the U.S. private investment in nation variable will be based on the total amount of dollars (in thousands) that U.S. residents invested in the nation based on data from the Bureau of Economic Analysis (1999).

Cultural Affinity

Hester (1973) proposed incorporating cultural affinity variables in research of international news flow and coverage. Several recent studies incorporated included several cultural affinities as possible determinants of international news coverage (Chang et al., 1987; Shoemaker et al. 1991) including such variables as language, religion, and press freedom.

Press Freedom   One of the cultural foundations of the United States is commitment to individual freedom and liberties. In the United States, basic freedoms such as the freedom of speech and freedom of press are not only a right but also a cultural value (Rokeach, 1974). Logically, nations that share a commitment to the freedom of its citizens (e.g., Britain) will be more culturally similar to the United States than those nations who deny their citizens basic freedoms (e.g., Iran).

The current study will base its coding of press freedom on data from the Freedom House survey (2000, which is used to measure press freedom around the world by the World Bank, the International Monetary Fund, and the U.S. Agency for International Development. Coding will be based on the 2000 press freedom survey and will reflect press freedom in the nation during 1999. Each nation will be coded with a score from 0 to 100, such that a score of 100 (e.g., Afghanistan) indicates complete absence of press freedom while a score of 5 (Norway) indicates large scale press freedom.

Religious Composition Previous studies (e.g., Shoemaker et al., 1991) have operationalized cultural affinity by measuring similarities in religious composition. The current study codes each country in the world for the percentage of Christians, the percentage of Muslims, and the overall level of religious diversity in a nation. Coding is based on religious data from the *CIA World Factbook* (2000).

Position in Hierarchy of Nations

As indicated by the findings of previous studies, a nation's position within the hierarchy of nations or within the world system influences the amount of coverage that nation receives from U.S. news media (Chang, 1998; Chang et al. 2000). Gatekeepers might consider events that occur in large powerful nations (such as Russia and France) to be more news-worthy than similar events that occur in small and impoverished nations (such as Bolivia and Chad). A nation's position in the hierarchy of nations/world system has traditionally been operationized using a nation's GNP, exports, military expenditures, population, and geographic size.

Gross National Product

Several studies have used a nation's gross national product as an indica-tor of its location within the hierarchy of nations (Dupree, 1971; Hester, 1973; Wang, chapter 13 this volume). Coding for the GNP variable was based on data from the World Bank (2000) and will reflect a nation's Gross National Product (in U.S. dollars) from 1999.

Exports

A nation's location within the hierarchy of nations can be measured in part by its level of trade. Several studies have found trade variables to be key determinants of international news coverage (Wu, 2000, 2003) Coding of the export variable was based on nations' overall export sta-tistics from the year 1999. Coding will be based on data from the *CIA World Factbook 2000* and will reflect the overall exports from a nation in U.S. dollars.

Military Expenditure

A nation's location within the hierarchy of nations is not limited to eco-nomic variables. A recent study by Golan and Wanta (2003) found an association between a nation's military capabilities and the amount of coverage it receives from U.S. television networks. Coding for the mili-tary expenditure variable was based on the data from the *CIA World Fact Book 2000*. Coding of the military expenditure variable was based on the total amount (in thousands) of dollars that a nation allocated toward military expenditures during the year 1999.

Population

Several studies provided evidence of the strong association between the population size of nations and the amount of news coverage and flow (Dupree, 1971; Kim & Barnett, 1996). It is likely that nations with large populations such as India and Nigeria will rank higher on the hierarchy of nations than nations with small populations such as Belize and Arme-nia. The coding of the population variable was based on data from the World Bank (2000).

Geographic Size

Previous research has indicated an association between the amount of coverage a nation receives and its geographic size (Kim & Barnett, 1996; Wu, 2003). Nations with large geographic areas (e.g., China and Russia) are more likely to be rated higher on the hierarchy of nations than nations with very small land size (Cyprus and Malta). Coding of the geographic size variable was based on data from the *CIA World Factbook 2000* that indicated the total amount of square kilometers (in thousands) in its domain.

Analysis

In the past two decades, scholars have incorporated regression analysis in an attempt to synthesize and analyze the large number of possible determinants of international news flow and coverage (Shoemaker et al., 1991; Wu, 2003). The current study hopes to contribute to research by providing one of the first regression models that is based solely on country based contextual variables.

Unlike most previous studies, the current study will argue for the use of a generalized linear model (GLM) rather than ordinary least squares (OLS) regression and the classic linear model. Ordinary least squares regression would not be appropriate in the case of the current study, based on the nature of the dependent variable in the study ,which is a count variable and which is not normally distributed; that is, it is a discrete, not a continuous, outcome variable.

The news coverage measure is a count variable—an indicator of the number of times a nation was covered in the four television networks during 1999. Coverage is thus always positive and always an integer. The OLS regression requires the dependent variable to range from negative infinity to positive infinity, and therefore is not appropriate for measurement of the current data. Based on the nature of the dependent variable (discrete) and its distribution (non-normal distribution), the current study uses a GLM with a Poisson as the most appropriate distribution to model the current data (Agresti, 1996).

The OLS regression requires that the dependent variable be distributed normally and therefore is not the appropriate statistical procedure for testing these data. The nature of the distribution of the dependent variable would likely violate the normality of the error term distribution and the constant variance of the error terms, the key assumptions of OLS regression. Such violations of the OLS assumptions are likely to result in serious errors in the estimation that might lead to mistakenly failing to reject a null hypothesis (Gill, 2001).

Upon completion of the content analysis, two dependent variables were identified: overall network coverage and overall CNN coverage. As argued in the methodology section and later highlighted by the content analysis results, the nature of news coverage differs significantly between the three networks and CNN and therefore requires a separate analysis.

Two separate Poisson models were created, based on the regression of the 14 independent variables with two dependent variables.

Results

As indicated by Table 6.1, both Poisson models provided strong evidence of the association between the news determinants and the CNN and network coverage variables. The majority of independent variables were found to be significant predictors of coverage when regressed with the overall country coverage on the networks: Instability, Trade with the United States, Distance from the United States, U.S. investment, U.S.

Table 6.1 Poisson Model: Network and CNN (Unstandardized b, P-value)

Variable	b networks	P value networks	B (CNN)	P value (CNN)
Intercept	−3.814e+00	< 2e-16 ***	−2.880e+00	< 2e-16 ***
Instability	1.008e-01	< 2e-16***	8.688e-02	< 2e-16***
Trade with US	8.003e-06	< 2e-16***	7.037e-06	< 5.28e-13***
Distance US	−1.762e-04	< 2e-16***	−1.203e-04	5.81e-10***
US Investment	5.818e-06	< 2e-16***	5.724e-06	3.76e-14 ***
US Aid	2.762e-06	< 2e-16***	2.662e-06	< 2e-16 ***
Press Freedom	2.146e-03	0.2594	−8.678e-04	0.66966
% Christians	1.651e-02	< 2e-16***	1.064e-02	7.03e-09 ***
% Muslims	2.072e-04	0.9012	5.341e-04	0.74622
Religious Diversity	−9.655e-03	3.09e-09***	−1.396e-02	1.12e-15 ***
GNP	2.161e-07	0.0160*	3.902e-08	0.67976
Exports	1.302e-06	0.0444*	4.985e-07	0.49544
Military Expend.	6.880e-05	< 2e-16***	7.545e-05	< 2e-16 ***
Population	1.439e-09	< 2e-16***	1.642e-09	< 2e-16 ***
Geographic Size	−5.509e-08	3.06e-05***	−4.249e-08	0.00214 **

Significance codes: *** 0.001; ** 0.01; * 0.05
For networks: Null deviance: 7916.9 on 167 degrees of freedom, Residual deviance: 3285.0 on 153 degrees of freedom, AIC: 3633.8
For CNN: Null deviance: 5835.0 on 167 degrees of freedom, Residual deviance: 2061.1 on 153 degrees of freedom, AIC: 2416

aid, percentage of Christians, religious diversity, Gross National Product, exports, military expenditures, population, and geographic size.

The Poisson model indicated significant associations between the following independent variables and overall coverage on CNN: instability, trade with the United States, distance from the United States, U.S. investment, U.S. aid, percentage of Christians, religious diversity, military expenditures, population, and geographic size.

Influential Case Analysis

Upon completion of the Poisson tests, an influential case analysis was conducted to identify those cases that might have a strong influence on the Poisson models. As indicated by the Cook's distance plot, France, Israel, and Yugoslavia were identified as influential cases. This does not necessarily indicate that these cases were outliers but rather that these cases had a strong impact on the model results. To correctly assess the impact of the influential cases on the two Poisson models, separate Poisson tests were conducted for both the networks and CNN, each omitting the influential cases one at a time. In addition to the three countries that were identified as influential cases, this study also ran the Poisson models excluding Russia. Russia ranked second after Yugoslavia because it served as a strong outlier in both dependent variables and is likely to have some influence on the Poisson models.

Tables 6.2 and 6.3 demonstrate the effect that dropping the individual influential cases had on the Poisson models. Unlike the initial models that found the majority of independent variables to be significant (12 for the networks and 10 for CNN), the Poisson models yielded different results when dropping the influential cases.

The overall network coverage Poisson model yielded different results when the different cases were included and removed. Only 7 out of 14 variables were found to be consistently significant, regardless of case inclusion or exclusion: instability, distance from the United States, U.S. investment, U.S. aid, religious diversity, military expenditures, and population. Consistent with these findings, the same seven variables were found to be consistently significant despite the exclusion or inclusion of the different influential cases. Trade with the United States was found significant three out of the four times in which influential cases were included or excluded for the networks model. Trade with the United States and the percentage of Christians were found significant three out of four times for the CNN model.

Based on the consistent significance and nature of the coefficient direction, the current study can assess the proposed hypotheses, as presented in the literature review.

Table 6.2 Poisson Model: Excluding Influential Cases: Networks (Unstandardized b, P-value)

Variable	Excluding Yugoslavia	Excluding France	Excluding Israel	Excluding Russia
Intercept	−5.341e-01 0.0395 *	−3.684e+00 < 2e-16 ***	−5.341e-01 0.0395 *	−3.799e+00 < 2e-16 ***
Instability	4.570e-02 2e-16 ***	1.110e-01 < 2e-16 ***	4.570e-02 < 2e-16 ***	9.947e-02 < 2e-16 ***
Trade with US	5.370e-06 9.22e-10 ***	−5.326e-08 0.9653	5.370e-06 9.22e-10 ***	8.304e-06 < 2e-16 ***
Distance US	−1.278e-04 1.61e-08 ***	−1.920e-04 < 2e-16 ***	−1.278e-04 1.61e-08 ***	−1.759e-04 < 2e-16 ***
US Investment	6.816e-06 < 2e-16 ***	2.948e-06 7.66e-05 ***	6.816e-06 < 2e-16 ***	6.007e-06 < 2e-16 ***
US Aid	2.320e-06 < 2e-16 ***	2.942e-06 < 2e-16 ***	2.320e-06 < 2e-16 ***	2.784e-06 < 2e-16 ***
Press Freedom	1.489e-03 0.4943	−1.864e-03 0.3539	1.489e-03 0.4943	2.779e-03 0.15219
% Christians	3.540e-03 0.08007	1.293e-02 3.79e-12 ***	3.540e-03 0.0696	1.678e-02 < 2e-16 ***
% Muslims	2.592e-03 0.1404	−3.996e-03 0.0221 *	2.592e-03 0.1404	6.494e-04 0.70126
Religious Diversity	−1.242e-02 2.22e-10 ***	−1.672e-02 < 2e-16 ***	−1.242e-02 2.22e-10 ***	−8.919e-03 1.36e-07 ***
GNP	−8.188e-08 0.3609	−1.099e-07 0.2480	−8.188e-08 0.3609	2.206e-07 0.01482 *
Exports	6.986e-07 0.2866	1.381e-05 < 2e-16 ***	6.986e-07 0.2866	1.529e-06 0.02010 *
Military Expend.	6.106e-05 < 2e-16 ***	1.725e-05 0.0341 *	6.106e-05 < 2e-16 ***	6.408e-05 < 2e-16 ***
Population	1.734e-09 < 2e-16 ***	7.790e-10 2.85e-07 ***	1.734e-09 < 2e-16 ***	1.654e-09 < 2e-16 ***
Geographic Size	2.514e-08 0.0563	3.359e-08 0.0357 *	2.514e-08 0.0563	−8.793e-08 0.00043 ***

Significance codes: *** 0.001; ** 0.01; * 0.05

Evaluating the Hypotheses

Hypothesis 1 predicted that a nation's level of deviance is positively associated with the amount of coverage it receives from U.S. television news programs. In the current study, deviance was operationalized in terms of instability and was based on NDFC data. Instability was found to have

Table 6.3 Poisson Model: Excluding Influential Cases: CNN (Unstandardized b, P-value)

Variable	Excluding Yugoslavia	Excluding France	Excluding Israel	Excluding Russia
Intercept	−1.172e+00 9.53e-06 ***	−2.693e+00 < 2e-16 ***	−3.677e+00 < 2e-16 ***	−2.871e+00 < 2e-16 ***
Instability	5.592e-02 < 2e-16 ***	9.603e-02 < 2e-16 ***	8.339e-02 < 2e-16 ***	8.478e-02 < 2e-16 ***
Trade with US	5.922e-06 3.16e-09 ***	−5.379e-07 0.694185	6.162e-06 1.41e-09 ***	7.632e-06 5.11e-14 ***
Distance US	−6.934e-05 0.00267 **	−1.401e-04 7.21e-13 ***	−1.103e-04 1.23e-08 ***	−1.197e-04 4.67e-10 ***
US Investment	6.461e-06 < 2e-16 ***	3.251e-06 4.41e-05 ***	6.751e-06 < 2e-16 ***	5.911e-06 1.69e-14 ***
US Aid	2.401e-06 < 2e-16 ***	2.807e-06 < 2e-16 ***	7.035e-07 0.034019 *	2.697e-06 < 2e-16 ***
Press Freedom	−3.085e-03 0.15819	−4.842e-03 0.023071 *	1.072e-03 0.611692	2.408e-04 0.908139
% Christians	3.371e-03 0.08007	7.289e-03 8.78e-05 ***	2.071e-02 < 2e-16 ***	1.108e-02 1.87e-09 ***
% Muslims	3.039e-03 0.07487	−3.157e-03 0.061802	1.032e-02 1.14e-05 ***	1.236e-03 0.461423
Religious Diversity	−1.497e-02 1.74e-14 ***	−2.114e-02 < 2e-16 ***	−1.290e-02 3.65e-12 ***	−1.280e-02 1.96e-12 ***
GNP	−1.599e-07 0.09067	−2.345e-07 0.017632 *	4.017e-07 0.227991	3.493e-08 0.714577
Exports	3.899e-07 0.59172	1.158e-05 2.30e-13 ***	-9.809e-07 0.227991	8.237e-07 0.261092
Military Expend.	7.037e-05 < 2e-16 ***	2.931e-05 0.000446 ***	7.057e-05 < 2e-16 ***	6.944e-05 < 2e-16 ***
Population	1.755e-09 < 2e-16 ***	1.164e-09 6.59e-16 ***	2.387e-09 < 2e-16 ***	1.949e-09 < 2e-16 ***
Geographic Size	1.036e-08 0.45909	3.694e-08 0.024652 *	−3.742e-08 0.007100 **	−9.277e-08 0.000919 ***

Significance codes: `***' 0.001 `**' 0.01 `*' 0.05 `

a positive direction and found to be significant in all 10 Poisson models that were generated by the current study. The results of the Poisson models strongly support hypothesis 1.

Hypothesis 2 predicted that a nation's relevance to the United States is positively associated with the amount of coverage it will receive from

U.S. television news programs. In the current study, relevance to the United States was operationalized by trade with the United States, proximity to the United States, U.S. investment in the nation, and U.S. aid. Distance from the United States, U.S. investment, and U.S. aid were significant in all 10 Poisson models that were generated. The negative coefficient in front of the distance from the U.S. coefficients in all 10 models suggest the lower the distance from the United States, the higher the coverage. This finding is consistent with Hypothesis 2 since the I argue that nations that are close to the United States are more likely to be considered relevant to the United States than nations that are far away.

The positive direction of the U.S. investment and U.S. aid coefficients suggest a positive association between U.S. economic involvement in a country (relevance) and the amount of coverage the nation received from US television networks (including CNN). Based on the significant p values and direction of coefficients for distance from the United States, U.S. investment, and U.S. aid variables, the data provide support for hypothesis 2.

Hypothesis 3 predicted a positive association between cultural affinity of nations with the United States and coverage. In the original design, cultural affinity was operationalized through the press freedom, migration and travel from the U.S. variables.

Due to inability to gather data for the majority of cases, both migration and the travel variables were not included in the Poisson. Therefore, press freedom was the sole variable used to measure press freedom. In all 10 Poisson models, press freedom did not produce significant p values. Furthermore, the direction of the coefficients suggests mixed results as to the association between press freedom and coverage.

In the original Poisson models, press freedom produced a positive coefficient (2.146e-02) for the networks and a negative coefficient (-8.678e-04) for CNN. Therefore, the original Poisson models suggest that networks are more likely to cover nations with lower degrees of press freedom, and CNN is more likely to cover nations with higher degrees of press freedom.

The Poisson models that excluded influential cases also produced mixed results concerning press freedom. None of the eight models produced significant p values for the press freedom variable. The coefficients of the variable were consistently positive with the exception of the models that excluded France (networks) and France and Yugoslavia for CNN. Based on the nonsignificant p-scores and contradictory direction of the coefficients of the press freedom variable, Hypothesis 3 can be rejected.

Hypothesis 4 predicted a positive association between religious affinity with the United States and coverage. Three variables were used to operationalize religious affinity: the percentage of Christians, religious

The second contribution of the current study is the presentation of one of the first comprehensive determinants models that also includes world-system variables in its analysis.

The results of the Poisson models identify 7 variables that were found to be significant for both the networks and CNN in all 10 Poisson models. These variables include: instability, distance from the United States, U.S. investment, U.S. aid, religious diversity, military expenditures, and population. The consistency of coefficient direction and significant p values across all 10 models suggest that these 10 variables are strong predictors of international news coverage.

One specific new value identified by the study was relevance. The results indicate that nations that are relevant to the home nation (in this case the United States) were likely to receive coverage. This is supported by the significance of the geographic proximity, trade with the United States and the U.S. investment variables. These findings support previous research that identified relevance as a key predictor of coverage (Chang et al., 1987; K. Chang & Lee, 1992). The importance of relevance as a news value should be further examined by future research as shifts in the global political paradigm as represented by the U.S. war on terror may in itself impact the very notion of what makes a nation relevant.

Another important contribution of the current study had to do with the introduction of the religious diversity variable as a possible determinant of international news coverage. This variable's significance in all 10 models justifies its inclusion in future studies on determinants of international news coverage. Again, the new global paradigm that entails tensions between the Muslim world and the West may make this variable even more relevant to understanding what makes nations and world events newsworthy than in previous years.

Finally, the results of the study indicate that deviance and hierarchy of nations are consistent predictors of coverage. These findings are consistent with the seminal studies by Shoemaker et al. (1986) for deviance and by Chang (1998) for hierarchy of nations that set these two variables as key theoretical frameworks for understanding the determinants of international news coverage.

Future studies should further test the proposed model and further apply general linear models for the analysis of the contextual approach to research on the determinants of international news coverage. In addition, scholars ought to examine the influence of the U.S. led war on terror on American gatekeepers' news selection process and test previous models in order to see if they are still useful in predicting coverage.

References

Agresti, A. (1996). *An introduction to categorical data analysis*. New York: Wiley-Interscience.

Bureau of Economic Analysis, U.S. Department of Commerce. (1999). http://www.bea.gov/

CIA World Factbook 2000. (2000). http://www.odci.gov/cia/publications /factbook/country.html

Chang, K., & Lee, T. (2001, August). *Revising the determinants of international news coverage in the U.S. media: A replication and expansion of the 1987 research on how the U.S. news media cover world events*. Paper presented at the AEJMC Conference, Washington, DC.

Chang, T.-K. (1998). All countries not created equal to be news: World system and international communication. *Communication Research, 25*, 528–566.

Chang, T.-K., Lau, T. Y., & Hao, X. (2000). From the United States with news and more: International flow, television coverage and the world system. *Gazette, 62*, 505–522.

Chang, T-K., & Lee, J. (1992). Factors affecting gatekeepers' selection of foreign news: A national survey of newspaper editors. *Journalism Quarterly, 69*, 554–561.

Chang, T-K., Shoemaker, P., & Brendlinger, N. (1987). Determinants of international news coverage in the U.S. media. *Communication Research, 14*, 396–414.

Dupree, J. D. (1971). International communication: View from a window on the world. *Gazette, 17*, 224–235

Flournoy, D. M., & Stewart, R. K. (1997) *CNN making news in the global market*. Eastleigh, England: Libbey. (University of Luton Press)

Freedom House. (2000). Election freedom rating: Annual survey of free country rating. http://www.freedomhouse.org/ratings/

Galtung, J. (1971). A structural theory of imperialism. *Journal of Peace Research, 8*, 81–118.

Galtung, J., & Ruge, M. (1965). The structure of foreign news. *Journal of Peace Research, 2*, 64–91.

Gill, J. (2001). *Generalized linear models: A unified approach*. Thousand Oaks, CA: Sage.

Golan, G., & Wanta, W. (2003) International elections on the U.S. network news: An examination of factors affecting newsworthiness. *Gazette, 65*(1), 25–39

Gunaratne, S. (2001). Prospects and limitations of world system theory for media analysis: The case of Middle East and North Africa. *Gazette, 63*, 2–3, 121–148.

Harcup, T., & O'Neill, D. (2001). What is news? Gauteng and Ruge revisited. *Journalism Studies, 2*, 261–280.

Hester, A. (1973). Theoretical consideration in predicting volume and direction of international information flow. *Gazette, 19*, 238–247.

Hicks, R. G., & Gordon, A. (1974) Foreign news content in Israel and US newspapers. *Journalism Quarterly, 51*, 639–644.

Holsti, O. (1969). *Content analysis for the social sciences and humanities.* Reading, MA: Addison-Wesley

Kim, K., & Barnett, G. (1996). The determinants of international news flow: A network analysis. *Communication Research, 23,* 323.

National Defense Council Foundation. (1999). http://www.ndcf.org/Conflict_List/World99.html

Rokeach, M. (1974). Change and stability in American value systems: 1968–1971. *Public Opinion Quarterly, 38,* 222–239.

Rosengren, K. E., Rickardsson, G. (1974). Middle East news in Sweden. *Gazette, 20,* 99–116.

Shoemaker, P., Chang, T. K., & Brendlinger, N. (1986). Deviance as a predictor of newsworthiness: Coverage of international events in the U.S. media. In M. L. McLaughlin (Ed.), *Communication yearbook* (Vol.10, pp. 348–365). Beverly Hills, CA: Sage.

Shoemaker, P. J., & Cohen, A. (2006). *News around the world: Content, practitioners, and the public.* New York: Routledge.

Shoemaker, P., Danielian, H. L., & Brendlinger, N. (1991). Deviant acts, risky business and U.S. interests: The newsworthiness of world events. *Journalism Quarterly, 68,* 781–795.

Shoemaker, P. J., & Reese, S. D. (1996). *Mediating the message.* New York: Longman.

Tajfel, H. (1978). Inter-individual behavior and intergroup behavior. In H. Tajfel (Ed.), *Differentiation between groups: Studies in the social psychology of intergroup* (pp. 27–60). London: Academic Press,

U.S. Census Bureau. (1999). *Statistical abstract of the United States.* http://www.census.gov

Van Belle, D. A. (2000). New York Times and network TV news coverage of foreign disasters: The significance of insignificant variables. *Journalism and Mass Communication Quarterly, 77*(1), 50–70.

Wallerstein, I. (1974). *The modern world system.* New York: Academic Press.

World Bank. (2000). http://www.worldbank.org/ data/databytopic/databytopic.html

Wu, H. D (1998). Investigating the determinants of international news flow: A meta-analysis. *Gazette: The International Journal for Communication Studies, 60*(6), 493–512.

Wu, H. D. (2000). Systemic determinants of international news coverage: A comparison of 38 Countries. *Journal of Communication, 50*(2), 110–130.

Wu, H. D. (2003). Homogeneity around the world? Comparing the systematic-determinants of international news flow between developed and developing countries. *Gazette, 65*(1), 9–24.

Part II

The Language of International News

How Could So Much Produce So Little?

Foreign Affairs Reporting in the Wake of 9/11

Shahira Fahmy

Just as a great cook cannot work miracles with poor ingredients, foreign news cannot be any better than the quality of news stories upon which it is based. In other words, the quantity of international news does not necessarily equal comprehensive and useful coverage of international news events. High-quality international reporting attempts to convey the economic, historical, political, and social dimensions of international issues and makes an effort to convey the importance of events as they affect international relations and international cooperation.

Scholars have repeatedly criticized the American news media for reporting foreign news in a less complex manner and for oversimplifying and decontextualizing international news events. For example, in a visual content analysis of the Tiananmen Square coverage, Perlmutter (1988) found that the U.S. media focused on the image of the man blocking the tanks, making it the super-icon of the entire revolution. Perlmutter thus concluded that the U.S. media presented an oversimplified and decontextualized view of the large student demonstrations.

Although it has been shown that the volume of foreign news increased after 9/11, many suggest the breadth of the news was reduced (Lichter, Butterworth, & Amundson, 2004). Scholars believe the oversimplified nature of U.S. foreign coverage has provided Americans with little understanding of international problems and diplomacy. For instance, after the fall of the Taliban regime, the U.S. media avoided delving into the ethnic, political, and social problems that overwhelmed Afghanistan (Lichter et al., 2004). Overall then, scholars agree that the U.S. media do not cover much international news, and when they do, they fail to meaningfully translate foreign news for the American people.

In the face of perceived public disinterest, however, news professionals may feel oversimplification of international news events is a legitimate public service. The viewers, who are assumed to know nothing of foreign lands and in general to perceive foreign news as having little influence on their everyday lives, are also assumed to care little about having their news world translated into symbols, ideas, and slogans that make sense to them. In the long term, however, this superficial style of international reporting may be less of a service to the audience and the industry overall.

Few scholars have explored quantity versus quality of international reporting. The debate over whether an increase in the volume of foreign coverage is always beneficial, suggests that more attention needs to be paid to the issue. In other words, does more foreign news necessarily lead to better informed citizens?

While several scholars have criticized the decrease in both quantity and quality of foreign news, this essay suggests that quantity of foreign news does not necessarily equal comprehensive and useful coverage of foreign news events. Specifically, this work examines how news selection and gatekeeping differs from culture to culture, often representing the individual governments' views on international issues. In addition, it explores the current challenges to good reporting of international events. Finally, the author examines solutions on how to supply the public with international coverage that is as comprehensive as possible.

A Self-Reinforcing Prophesy

If news professionals widely perceive that the quality of international news is not very important to the audience, this in turn may lead the audience to receive superficial forms of reporting. And the results may be cyclical. In other words, when the media continue to oversimplify foreign news on the assumption that the American audience is not interested, the news industry will continue to suffer a self-inflicted wound more grievous than any adversary is likely to inflict.

In the first phase of the news-making process, the presumption that the audience is disinterested in foreign news leads the media to oversimplify international news events. The understanding is that news consumers have increasing demands on their time, so they must prioritize information, and local news is generally held to be more important than foreign news. The audience seems only interested in simple explanations of foreign news events—especially news of distant nations, such as in the case of many African nations where news may not seem relevant to them. In order to gain audience appeal, the foreign correspondent reports the news in a one-dimensional frame and in a less complex manner. For example, research shows that 99% of AP photographs depicted Afghan women wearing the burqa after the fall of the Taliban regime (Fahmy, 2004). The editors back home, however, elected to publish photographs of women in Afghanistan removing their burqas as a sign of liberation. The U.S. media, thus, oversimplified and decontextualized the Afghan issue for the American public by finding symbols that matched with Western ideals about appropriate social policies while ignoring native symbolism. The media failed to communicate that the burqa is a cultural phenomenon that could not have been thrown away overnight. Many women in Afghanistan still rely on it for a false sense of security under oppressive and unsafe conditions. Afghanistan, like many of the surrounding Muslim nations, remains an uncompromising and patriarchal society that would like to keep its women covered.

In the second phase of the news-making process, then, the audience, which already has limited understanding of foreign cultures, is forced to rely on episodic or skewed reports for information, which may have a direct impact on their perceptions of reality. For example, while the U.S. media have focused primarily on Iraq in recent years, they have ignored many other regions of conflict around the world. In the case of the African continent, for example, more than 3.9 million people have died as a result of the war in the Democratic Republic of Congo (DRC) (Coghlan et al., 2006). And while the humanitarian crisis in Congo was rated one of the worst in recent history, results of a content analysis show the critical situation in Congo was featured in only 0.04% of U.S. foreign news coverage. Consider that television remains the primary news source for most Americans. In a 15-month period of analysis, ABC, NBC, and CBS ran 4,997 reports on Iraq and broadcast only four reports on Congo (Media Tenor, 2005). As such, the framework the networks create for understanding foreign events is troubling. Similarly, the media paid little attention to Sudan where the longest civil war in recent history has been ongoing. Despite the massive humanitarian crisis in African countries and while the fighting in Congo claimed 10 times as many lives as the December 2004 tsunami, the majority (57%) of Americans perceived the earthquake and tsunami in Southeast Asia to have claimed more lives than the war in Congo (Harris Poll, 2005).

The media, therefore, by selecting some stories while ignoring others, frames news events and directly influences public perception of these events. Gamson (1989) defines a frame as "a central organizing idea for making sense of relevant events and suggesting what is at issue." Entman (1989) explains the process of framing as involving selection and salience, in which some aspects of a perceived reality are selected and made more salient in a communicating text, in such a way as to promote a particular problem definition, causal interpretation, moral evaluation, and treatment recommendation from the vast pool of daily occurrences. For instance, an examination of press coverage in an American newspaper and an Arabic newspaper revealed the coverage of the Iraq War as being framed differently in each outlet (Ghanem, chapter 10 this volume). These differences, thus, lend credence to the idea that the war issue was framed differently in different parts of the world. What is more, these constructed news frames in turn conventionalize the way future foreign correspondents and editors perceive foreigners and foreign places and the way they look at foreign news events in general. So, in a sense, reductionism and superficial reports over time reproduce consistent and distorted news frames. And these news frames create preconceived views about the world that become inherently part of the newsroom culture. In this regard, Eric Louw (2004) writes:

> These existing images determine the questions they ask and the images they seek. Hence, the partiality of news frames tends to be recycled and reproduced, so that discourses about foreigners and foreign places are resistant to change. (pp. 153–154)

When Bad Things Happen to Strange Countries

The U.S. media have traditionally only paid attention to foreign countries in the case of war or natural disaster. They have eliminated most events and issues that are not directly related to the United States, deepening divisions among peoples and nations. Thus, the world outside of the United States was only worth reporting when it was engulfed by natural disaster or engaged in war (Kalyango, chapter 11, this volume; Lichter et al., 2004; Martin-Kratzer & Thorson, chapter 8 this volume).

Further, when journalists and news editors have reported *bad things* in foreign contexts, news professionals engaged in the news-making process already have mental images of the events. In other words, these news professionals *construct* the way we see other countries in the news. What is more, these constructions have often represented the government's views on international issues.

For example, in analyzing the visual coverage of war and terrorism in English- and Arabic-language newspapers, a recent study found differences in the overall theme of photographs, topics, and level of *graphicness* (Fahmy, 2007a). The English-language newspaper, the *International Herald Tribune*, published proportionally more images depicting the 9/11 attack, and its Arabic counterpart, *Al-Hayat,* published proportionally more images depicting the Afghan War. In terms of level of *graphicness*, the Arabic-language newspaper consistently published more graphic images of both events.

What is interesting is that when elite editors of the newspapers were contacted in order to ask them to discuss the photo selection process of the events in question, they claimed their selection was solely based on how newsworthy the photographs were and how well they illustrated the accompanying news story. A high-ranking editor of the U.S. newspaper said there was no conscious effort to differentiate between the coverage of 9/11 and the Afghan War. The editor explained that the editing staff tried to choose the visuals that told the story in the most objective manner and added that if the outcome portrayed only one side of the story, it was never intentional.

While the less cynical may believe any skewing or oversimplification in international reporting is not intentional, the news-making process is clearly subjective. The editors' personal prejudices and values inevitably affect news judgment and media content.

It comes as no surprise, then, that the news industry currently faces a *Catch* 22 in being pressured to act and then repeatedly criticized for whatever it does. Even if it is argued that the U.S. media have tried to increase the quantity of foreign reporting in the wake of 9/11, scholars have continued to criticize the quality of U.S. international reporting as inept. As discussed earlier, this has not been a predicament unique to the U.S. media.

Scholars suggest news selection and gatekeeping vary from culture to culture. Scholars have established models of selective gatekeeping, arguing that the process is often determined by numerous factors, among them the intensity of the issue based on national interest, cultural proximity, and continuity. For example, a newspaper with a large ethnic group in its area of coverage will likely pay more attention to issues involving that group. Further, if an event or news story passes through the media gate once, it is likely that it will pass through the gate again. And while journalists are often faced with the issue of rendering complex foreign contexts comprehensive for audiences back home, the process whereby journalists make sense of distant places have had real consequences for American lives.

The 9/11 terrorists attack confirmed the importance of assessing the state of international reporting in the United States. Not only did 9/11 change the way Americans look at international news events, it also suggested the media failed to inform the American people about foreign affairs (Lichter et al., 2004). The 9/11 attack influenced how we assess the quality of international journalism that brings us news and opinions about peoples from faraway countries. For example, the terrorist attacks in New York, London, and most recently in Sharm Al-Sheikh (Egypt) and the emergence of the al-Qaida terrorist organization in countries such as Afghanistan and Sudan, demonstrated the need for a more global perspective in the coverage of international issues.

At its heart, the problem lies in increasingly overestimating public disinterest in foreign news. As mentioned earlier, the strong presumption that the audience is disinterested in international issues has deterred the media from increasing costly foreign news coverage, which has influenced the quality of the news reports. For example, a great deal of evidence suggests there have been significant declines in resources allocated to foreign news (Riffe & Budianto, 2001). More specifically, there

access to the Internet or other research sources that would have provided them with a more comprehensive picture (Fahmy & Johnson, 2005).

Thus, the ability of news organizations to send embedded journalists may have provided a limited perspective of the conflict. True, there was more coverage of the Iraq War than of previous wars, but it was fragmented war coverage, and as a result some Americans were less informed about the war in Iraq.

This phenomenon of partial or total misinterpretation of news events is not, however, limited to one national medium over another. A great deal of evidence suggests news is reported according to an interpretation of the events in a politically and culturally advantageous manner that reflects the societies that journalists cover.

As noted earlier, English- and Arabic-language newspapers published different images of 9/11 and the Afghan War (Fahmy, 2007a). Research shows the news coverage of the English-language newspaper emphasized the emotion of guilt in the 9/11 attack by running photographs that humanized the victims. It deemphasized the bombing of Afghanistan by running photographs that focused less on the victims and more on aid, patriotism, and weaponry, thus placing the Afghan War in a technical rather than an emotional frame. In the same way, the news coverage in the Arabic-language newspaper emphasized the emotion of guilt in the Afghan War by running photographs that humanized the victims. It deemphasized 9/11 by running photographs that focused less on the victims and more on material destruction and planes crashing into the buildings, thus also placing the terrorist attack in a more technical frame.

What is noteworthy, however, is that more than nine in 10 of the photographs analyzed were from the main Western news agencies: Associated Press (AP), Agence France-Presse (AFP), and Reuters (Fahmy, 2005a). In other words, the Arabic- and English-language newspapers had access to similar pools of photographs and yet chose to run different images of the events under study. Interestingly, along the lines of cultural and political relativism, the editors of the newspapers were not surprised by the findings because of the differences between the target audiences their newspapers serve. What is more, the editors did not express concern for the lack of all-inclusive coverage or the overall challenges involved in international reporting.

Why This Difficulty, Anyway?

Good reporting of any international event is difficult and requires knowledge of the culture if a more complex perspective on the situation is to be presented. Successful communication depends on the source and the receiver having sufficient language and cultural background in common. Media scholar Wilbur Schramm explains that when these vital commonalities are not shared, reporting is negatively affected. The literature suggests it is not only audiences who misunderstand distant places; journalists regularly misinterpret the foreign contexts to which they are sent (Louw, 2004). They may reinforce stereotypes, which can have severe consequences. When journalists cover international issues, they often do not have the time or the space to address issues in a comprehensive, in-depth fashion. News events are fast moving, and thus journalists are often rushed in with no experience of the area in question, and are under pressure to produce stories. For example Edward Said wrote that journalists who visited the Orient quickly developed an ill-informed opinion of the Arabs and Islam (Said, 1978).

Journalists arriving in a foreign land often lack necessary historical background knowledge or knowledge of the contemporary society they are to cover. Most journalists are not equipped to understand the full complexity of foreign events. Difficulties could be based on unfamiliar geography, culture, or religion. During the coverage of the Israeli pullout from the Gaza strip in August 2005, for example, a CNN correspondent referred to the Mediterranean Sea as the ocean.

The literature also suggests many foreign correspondents do not speak the language of the country they are covering. While, Wu and Hamilton (2004) found more than eight in 10 U.S. foreign correspondents surveyed speak at least one foreign language, they also noted that Spanish, French, and German are the primary non-English languages these foreign correspondents can speak. Foreign correspondents, therefore, should learn to communicate in a variety of different languages and navigate in a variety of cultures and not be limited to only a few. In other words, they should try to move beyond communicating in Spanish, French, and German.

Further, it is important to note that there are about 200 languages that have a million or more native speakers, with Mandarin Chinese being the most common—spoken by around 874 million people as a native language (Ethnologue, 2000). Further, some parts of the world have unusually high concentrations of different languages. For example, there are around 900 native languages spoken by the 5 to 10 million people of New Guinea and its neighboring islands (Ethnologue, 2000). Put in context, then, foreign correspondents sent to cover news events in non-European nations most likely face a language barrier when they are not able to converse in the native tongue of the region, in particular in nations where more than one tribal/official language exists. Moreover, while journalists often arrive at the news location without much background knowledge, when they do come with more expertise, the editors back home may not be much help, such as when they ran images of Afghan women without their burqas immediately after the fall of the Taliban regime to imply liberation from a strictly Western cultural perspective.

News skewing and oversimplification of distant news events could be due to both the cultural biases in reporting foreign contexts and a response to the pressures of the target audience back home. A survey of photojournalists and photo-editors in U.S. dailies suggested political sensitivity ranked higher for selecting graphic images of the Afghan War than for selecting graphic images of 9/11 (Fahmy, 2005b). For instance, the photograph below depicts a man crying over the body of his son and neighbors who died in U.S. raids in Kabul in October 2001. The photograph refers to the human cost of the U.S. attack on al-Qaeda, the Taliban, and the population of Afghanistan. But when this image of an Afghan father crying over the body of his baby ran on the front page of the *Harford Courant* newspaper, the newspaper reported 550 complaints concerning the picture selection and placement (Elliot & Lester, 2001). The complaints focused upon the display as representing unpatriotic sympathies for Afghan civilians and described it as the newspaper taking sides against U.S. war efforts.

Undeniably, the literature strongly suggests that the media are often expected to frame international news in a patriotic framework in an effort to meet the people's and the U.S. government's expectations—especially when the lives of citizens are at stake. Carragee (2003) for example, explains that past studies of U.S. press coverage of international affairs suggest that media reports were frequently consistent with the objectives and interests of the U.S. government. A Gallup Poll survey conducted in February 2003 showed the majority of Americans (57%) were in favor of invading Iraq with American ground troops in an attempt to remove Saddam Hussein from power (Curtin, 2003). According to a *Foreign Policy in Focus* article, the "U.S. media outlets seem to be competing for a place among the most patriotic news sources" (Siegel, 2003).

Researchers who examined the coverage of the Iraq War noted the U.S. media reinforced versions of events that have already been established in public discourse and entrenched in media institutions by powerful social interests. For example, a visual content analysis examined the tone of coverage of the toppling of the Saddam statue in 43 newspapers of 30 countries (Fahmy, 2007b). The study revealed that U.S. newspapers portrayed the event favorably, representing a victory/liberation frame. The data showed that by and large U.S. newspapers—with the exception of the *Christian Science Monitor*—shied away from images that showed a more critical view of the toppling of the statue. The U.S. newspapers overall ran images that implied a large number of Iraqis had participated in the toppling event and close-up shots of Iraqi people destroying the head of the Saddam's statue. Major and Perlmutter (2005) explain that such favorable portrayals were to be expected. They represented predictable war imagery, such as showing U.S. troops being welcomed by Iraqi citizens, as promised by administration officials in the months leading up to the war (Aday, Cluverius, & Livingston, 2005).

While news professionals understand the value of putting a patriotic spin on foreign news events to meet audience expectations, the U.S. media are now facing new challenges as a result of globalization and inexpensive digital technology. The U.S. media are being faced with diverse representations of news events by international media organizations, news professionals, and citizens around the world over the World Wide Web. The fact that many countries may have shared different perceptions of the recent Iraq War is a good reason why the U.S. media need to improve foreign affairs coverage to increase news credibility at home and abroad.

In conclusion, the U.S. media need to explain the complex range of economic, national, and global issues that confront our world today. First, news professionals need to show how foreign events can have a direct impact on American lives. Many agree that for people to care about foreign news, the media need to acquire relevant information and put it into context. Second, the media need to humanize news events from abroad. Perhaps Americans fail to identify with raw numbers, but if foreign news includes humanizing frames, viewers can empathize. For example, photographs of war and famine, such as the powerful photographs of children dying painfully from starvation that appeared in U.S. media and eventually helped mobilize U.S. public opinion leading to the intervention in Somalia in December 1992 (Perlmutter, 1998). Third, editors may consider increasing the use of local correspondents, which may increase news consumers' perceived involvement with foreign news. One way is to rely on foreign nationals as a less expensive and better way to get complex and humanized news reports from abroad. This simple device may be important in the current news environment, and may well be one that news consumers will respond to and one which may also help them process foreign news. Fourth, editors may want to carefully consider their use of visuals of foreign events. Past literature suggests news consumers respond more positively to larger graphics and more photographs (Wanta & Gao, 1995). Visuals provide readers with important information in a concise manner and thus make it easier to process information. Fifth, allocation of space to foreign news also should be reexamined. Editors have the ability and the responsibility to devote more space to high quality foreign news, with the use of more graphics and photographs. Foreign news needs to move up the ladder of concern for the news industry. Foreign affairs coverage cannot remain far down the news scale in U.S. media, with local and domestic news on the top. It is essential for the news industry to try to make foreign news relevant to the American audience. With the development of transnational mass

media, satellite technology, and the diffusion of information via the
Internet, along with political and military propaganda, a more complex
and comprehensive quality of international reporting must be developed
and maintained.

References

Aday, S., Cluverius, J., & Livingston, S. (2005). As goes the statue, so goes the
war: The emergence of the victory frame in television coverage of the Iraq
War. *Journal of Broadcasting and Electronic Media, 49*(3), 314–331.

Carragee, K. M. (2003). Evaluating polysemy: An analysis of the New York
Times coverage of the end of the Cold War. *Political Communication, 20*,
287–308.

Coghlan, B., Brennan, R. J., Ngoy, P., Dofara, D., Otto, B., Clements, M. et
al. (2006). Mortality in the Democratic Republic of Congo: A nationwide
survey. *The Lancet, 367*(9504), 44–51. Retrieved February 6, 2006, from
http://www.thelancet.com/journals/lancet/article/PIIS0140673606679233/
fulltext

Curtin, J. S. (2003). *Japanese anti-war sentiment on Iraq in accord with global
opinion. Glocom Platform: Japanese Institute of Global Communications.*
Retrieved February 6, 2007, from http://www.glocom.org/ special_topics/
social_trends/20030224_trends_s28/

Elliot, D., & Lester, P. (2001). Ethics of patriotism: When is it OK to break the
law? *News Photographer, 56*(11), 10–12.

Entman, R. M. (1993). Framing: Toward clarification of a fractured paradigm.
Journal of Communication, 43, 51–58.

Ethnologue. (2000). *Languages of the world* (Vol. 1, 14th ed.). Retrieved February
6, 2007, from http://www.ethnologue.com

Fahmy, S. (2004). Picturing Afghan women: A content analysis of AP wire photographs
during the Taliban regime and after the fall of the Taliban regime.
Gazette, 66(2), 91–112.

Fahmy, S. (2005a). Emerging alternatives or traditional news gates: Which news
sources were used to picture the 9/11 attack & the Afghan War. *Gazette
67*(5), 383–400.

Fahmy, S. (2005b). Photojournalists' and photo-editors' attitudes and perceptions:
The visual coverage of 9/11 and the Afghan War. *Visual Communication
Quarterly, 12*(3–4), 146–163.

Fahmy, S. (2007a). *Filling out the frame: Transnational visual coverage and
news practitioners' attitudes towards the reporting of war and terrorism.*
Saarbrücken, Germany: VDM.

Fahmy, S. (2007b). "They took it down": Exploring determinants of visual
reporting in the toppling of the Saddam Hussein statue in national and international
newspapers. *Mass Communication & Society, 10*(2), 143–170.

Fahmy, S., & Johnson, T. J. (2005). How we performed: Embedded journalists'
attitudes & perceptions towards covering the Iraq War. *Journalism & Mass
Communication Quarterly 82*(2), 301–317.

Fox News Spins 9/11 Commission Report. (2004, June 22). Retrieved February 1, 2007, from http://www.fair.org/index.php?page=1577

Gamson, W. A. (1989). News as framing: Comments on Graber. *American Behavioral Science, 33*(2), 157–161.

Harris Poll. (2005). *Most U.S. adults feel good about nation's response to the recent tsunami.* Retrieved March 10, 2007, from http://www.harrisinteractive.com/harris_poll/printerfriend/ index.asp?PID=538

Hess, S. (1996). Media mavens. *Society, 33*(3), 70–78.

Kull, S., Ramsay, C., Subias, S., Lewis, E., & Warf, P. (2003). *Misperceptions, The media and the Iraq War, The PIPA/knowledge networks poll.* Retrieved February 1, 2007, from http://64.233.167.104/search?q=cache:y3mBJCObArYJ www.pipa.org/OnlineReports/Iraq/Media_10_02_03_Report.pdf+Misperceptions,+The+Media+and+the+Iraq+War&hl=en&client=safari

Lichter, R. S., Butterworth, T., & Daniel A. Daniel (2004). A world apart. Global news media in the U.S. media pre-and post-9/11. *Media Tenor Quarterly Journal, 2,* 20–22.

Louw, P. E. (2004). Journalists reporting from foreign places. In A. S. de Beer & J. C. Merrill (Ed.), *Global journalism: Topical issues and media* (pp. 151–162). Boston: Allyn & Bacon.

Major, L., & Perlmutter, D. (2005). The fall of a pseudo-icon: The toppling of Saddam Hussein's statue as image management. *Visual Communication Quarterly, 12*(1–2), 38–45.

Media Tenor (2005). *Media neglects conflicts in Africa.* Retrieved February 1, 2006, from http://www.mediatenor.com/

Perlmutter, D. (1998). *Photojournalism and foreign policy: Framing icons of outrage in international crisis.* Westport, CT: Greenwood.

Perry, D. K. (1990). News reading, knowledge about, and attitudes toward foreign countries. *Journalism Quarterly, 67*(2), 353–358;

Pew Research Center. (2004). *News audiences increasingly politicized: Media credibility declines.* Retrieved February 1, 2006, from http://people-press.org/reports/display.php3? ReportID=215

Riffe, D., & Budianto, A. (2001). The shrinking world of network news. *International Communication Bulletin, 36*(1–2), 18–35.

Said, E. (1978). *Orientalism.* New York: Pantheon.

Salwan, M. B., & Frances R. M., Frances R. (1992). Public salience of foreign nations. *Journalism Quarterly, 69*(3), 623–632.

Siegel, P. C. (2003). Changing rules of U.S. journalism, *Foreign Policy in Focus* Retrieved February 1, 2006, from http://www.fpif.org/index.htm

Wanta, W., Golan, G., & Lee, C. (2004). Agenda setting and international news: Media influence on public perceptions of foreign nations. *Journalism and Mass Communication Quarterly, 81*(2), 364–377.

Wanta. W., & Gao, D. (1995). Young readers and the newspaper: Information recall and perceived enjoyment, readability, and attractiveness. *Journalism Quarterly, 71*(4), 926–936.

Wu, H. D., & John M. H. (2004). U.S. foreign correspondents: Changes and continuity at the turn of the century. *Gazette, 66*(6), 517–532.

Chapter 8

Patterns of News Quality

International Stories Reported in American Media

Renee Martin-Kratzer and Esther Thorson

The amount and type of information provided to Americans about other countries has been a focus of social science researchers in mass communication for many years. One rationale for the importance of international news is that it reduces Americans' ignorance about their world. An example of that ignorance comes from the answer the 2007 Miss Teen USA candidate from South Carolina made to the question "Recent polls have shown that a fifth of Americans can't locate the United States on a world map. Why do you think this is?" Although Miss South Carolina's answer[1] suggests that information is not always effectively processed, it also hints at the extent of the ignorance problem. Fortunately, however, research indicates that international news consumption has a positive impact on world knowledge, and that it influences people's perceptions about what is important in the world, and perhaps even makes them less negative about "foreign others."

The present study makes use of a significant national-level content analysis of American media provided by the Project for Excellence in Journalism (2005). That study looked at newspapers, both elite and local, network and cable news programs, and Internet news sites created by newspapers, television, and Internet aggregators like Google and Yahoo. The present study involves a secondary analysis of the data to determine the frequency and characteristics of international news across media. The findings suggest that news about other countries is more likely to be included if there is a link to U.S. interests. Also, the medium matters when it comes to the frequency of international news and the types of topics that are covered.

Why International News Coverage is Important

There is a significant literature that demonstrates that exposure to international news increases knowledge and changes images of "foreign others" (e.g., Perry, 1987, 1990). Korzenny, del Toro, and Gaudino (1987) found that newspaper readership of international news was a predictor of international knowledge and that it was associated with less negative attitudes about the Third World. Brewer, Graf, and Willnat (2003) showed in an experiment that framing stories about nations in specific ways influenced how people evaluated those countries. Similarly, Beaudoin (2004) found greater knowledge levels in those who reported higher consumption of international news in print, broadcast, and on the Internet. Wanta and Hu (1993) showed that four areas of international news coverage had the greatest influence on what people thought were important issues; that is, had agenda-setting effects: international conflicts that the U.S. was involved in, terrorism related to the United States, crime/drugs, and military information. In general, then, we need to have a sense of what international news looks like because it affects Americans in important ways.

Citizen Interest in International News

Consistent with U.S. involvement in Iraq and the more general challenge of terrorism, the latest figures on American interest in international news are high. In 2004, more than half of Americans (52%) reported following international news closely most of the time, which is up from 37% in 2002 (Pew Research Center for People and the Press, 2004). The percent of females who follow international news closely most of the time has grown from 32% in 2002 to 51% in 2004. This is similar to the percent of male readers (52%).

Nevertheless, the gender gap remains among the group that expresses the strongest interest in international news; males with college educations continue to make up this audience. The Pew study found that overall, more people express a strong interest in international news (24% in 2004 compared to 14% in 2000), but most of these are men (28% male to 19% female).

Hargrove and Stempel (2002) used a national survey to gauge reader interest in international news. They showed that readers preferred good news to bad, and news about ordinary people to news about politics and government, economics or disasters. It is ironic that the most preferred topics are, as we will see in the next section, those least provided by international news in U.S. media.

Foreign News Coverage in American News Media: The Last 40 Years

One of the earliest empirical studies of the content of news (Galtung & Ruge, 1965) was concerned with the presence of inaccuracies and bias in news about other countries. Weaver and Wilhoit (1983) demonstrated that international news on American news wires was inaccurate and incomplete. Shoemaker, Danielian, and Brendlinger (1991) showed that the *New York Times* covered only about 25% of reported world events, and that the three American network news programs covered only about 10% of those stories. There has been continued demonstration of U.S. media shortcomings in regard to international news (e.g., Golan & Wanta, 2003; Wanta & Golan, chapter 5 this volume; Wu, 2003).

Weaver and Wilhoit (1981) showed that the content of international stories increased its emphasis on crisis and conflict (from 14% in 1979 to 27% in 1981), but Kirat and Weaver (1984) discovered a decline that was most pronounced in developing nations (47% in 1979 and 10% in 1983). Giffard's study (1984) found that media portrayal of developing nations showed them to be "relatively more prone to internal conflicts and crises; more likely to be the setting of armed conflict; more frequently the recipients of disaster relief, or economic and military aid; and proportionately more often the location of criminal activities" (p. 19).

Another important topic has been the relative representation of different countries in U.S. foreign news. Schramm (1964) argued that there was little flow of news among countries, and that the developed countries played a far greater role than undeveloped countries. Indeed, during the 1970s there was growing interest in the direction of news flow (e.g., Hester, 1974). By 1980, the "New World Information and Communication Order" was articulated by the MacBride Commission of UNESCO (1980). The pattern of international news across the world was one of many issues in this debate. It was argued that news about the developing world was dominated by disasters and governmental breakdown, while the coverage of the developed world was much broader.

The comparative role of countries in the overall pattern of news remains an issue. For example, Kang and Choi (1999) looked at international news online, suggesting that Southeast Asia and China, plus Middle East hotspot countries like Israel and Iraq, play central roles, along with the United States, the United Kingdom, and Japan. Others have found that Western nations and powerful countries have the greatest amount of media coverage (Mowlana, 1986; Wu, 2000). Thus, the uneven-handed nature of foreign news in the United States continues to be observed.

From the 1980s onwards, the research conversation about international news in the United States became focused on whether its incidence was decreasing. In one of the earliest examples, Emery (1989) showed that international news, as a percent of total newshole, fell from 10% in 1971 to just under 3% in 1988. In contrast, Davis (1999) reported that in the *New York Times*, probably the nation's most elite newspaper, the international newshole was 14% of the total. Beaudoin and Thorson

(2001) reported that in the *Los Angeles Times*, another elite newspaper, international news was fully 19% of the total newshole.

As mentioned earlier, public interest in international news has grown following the terrorist attacks of September 11, 2001, and continuing throughout the second Iraq war (see Project for Excellence in Journalism studies of 2004–2007 news content; http://www.journalism.org/). Shoemaker and Cohen (2006) used a smaller sample and a narrowed definition of international news but found that the frequency of "international politics" in U.S. newspapers was 6.3% and on U.S. television was .7%. Other countries in that study showed much higher coverage of international politics. For example, newspaper coverage of international politics was 12% in China and 18% in Jordan. Television percentages were 13% for India, 39% for Jordan, and 18% for Russia. Thus, the previous literature indicates that some countries receive more media attention than others, and that overall, news coverage of international news in U.S. media is scarce compared to other topics.

Investing in International News Coverage

Maintaining foreign newspaper news bureaus costs about $200,000 to $300,000 yearly (Carroll, 2007), and the costs rise for television because of the additional people involved in each report. Wu and Hamilton (2004) argue that investment in specialists in other countries is crucial for quality international news, but that profit pressures on newspapers and what they claim are editors' assumptions that Americans are not interested in foreign news have led to dwindling numbers of correspondents.

Wu and Hamilton (2004) found far more foreign nationals (69%) were serving as correspondents for U.S. media, with only 31% of them American. Twenty-six percent of the correspondents were women (identical to Kliesch's finding from 1991), and 83% were White/European.

Among newspapers, the elite publications such as the *New York Times* and the *Washington Post* are more likely to invest in international news coverage than smaller circulation newspapers that serve local audiences. "But, in a sense, they are outstanding in the coverage of foreign news because they have to be to maintain their reputations and their readership" (Stacks, 2003–2004, p. 15). In 1996, Hess reported that the number of correspondents representing elite media continued to decrease. More recently, the *Baltimore Sun* and the *Boston Globe* announced bureau closings (Gavin, 2007). "Between 2002 and 2006, the number of foreign-based newspaper correspondents shrank from 188 to 141 (excluding the *Wall Street Journal*, which publishes Asian and European editions)" (Constable, 2007, para. 5).

This decline is also reflected in network news in which the number of foreign bureaus for each network has dwindled from about 15 to six or fewer. "Aside from a one-person ABC bureau in Nairobi, there are no network bureaus left at all in Africa, India or South America—regions that are home to more than 2 billion people" (Constable, 2007, para. 11).

Among the cable news networks, CNN maintains numerous foreign bureaus and offers an international edition viewed overseas. Its competitors, MSNBC and Fox News Channel, were created with a focus on domestic news and did not invest as heavily in international news. However, MSNBC can use correspondents from NBC news while Fox has access to owner Rupert Murdoch's broadcasting stations in other countries (Fleeson, 2003). Indeed, the different media can offer international news by establishing partnerships with other networks, hiring freelancers, or relying on wire services. However, Parisa Khosravi, CNN's senior vice president and managing editor of international news-gathering, cautions against this practice. "As a news organization, what do you have but your credibility? If you're going on anonymous wire reports by people you don't know, then what is it? It's rip and read" (quoted in Fleeson, 2003).

Audiences are turning to Web sites for news about the world, and they are going beyond U.S. media sites. One study found that nearly a quarter of its sample of Internet users visited foreign Web sites to read international news (Best, Chmielewski, & Krueger, 2005). Research on the content of Internet sites shows that frequently, the information that is posted is similar to the information that appeared in the source (Thalhimer, 1994). Because of the prevalence of this "shovelware," the content of the Internet sites is expected to be a reflection of the medium that posts the online stories. In other words, the amount of international news on a newspaper's Web site will be similar to the amount of international news in the same newspaper's printed edition.

Why International News Looks As It Does

To understand the incidence and pattern of foreign news in American media, there are a number of theoretical areas that provide insight. Shoemaker and her colleagues (1991; Shoemaker & Cohen, 2006) provide rich theory of news coverage as determined by "deviance" and "social significance" of events. Differences in the news media have been theorized about in terms of media economics and the sociology of newsrooms (Lowrey, Becker, & Punathambekar, 2003). It is also clear that the structure of world systems, organizations, and governments makes a difference. Aggregation of these approaches leads to seven important hypotheses and one research question that are then tested with the Project for Excellence In Journalism data.

Hypotheses about the Current State of International News

The present study takes an in-depth look at the content analysis that the Project for Excellence in Journalism executed in 2004. Based on the literature reviewed above, we generated six hypotheses and one research question.

H1. There will be more domestic than international news in U.S. media.

H2. International stories that relate to the United States will appear more frequently in each of the media.

H3. Elite newspapers will have the highest level of international news compared to other media and will publish more international news than local newspapers.

H4. Cable news will show high levels of coverage of international news, higher than network news and higher than local newspapers.

H5. International coverage on Internet sites will be consistent with the medium that produces those sites.

H6. There will be significant distributions of topics between domestic and international news.

H7. Newspapers will have more staff-generated content than other media and Web sites will have less staff-generated content.

There was one area where the previous research was not clear enough to justify hypotheses; thus, we posed a research question.

Research question 1. Will there be significant patterns of difference in international news topics across the media? Will the topics that are covered in international news vary across the media?

These expectations and questions were asked and answered in a secondary analysis of the larger content analysis data provided by the Project for Excellence in Journalism in their 2005 annual study of American journalism.

Method

This study examined stories that were published in newspapers and on Internet sites, as well as stories that aired on network and cable news programs.

Newspaper Sample

Sixteen newspapers were chosen based on circulation size and geographic location. The daily circulation categories were more than 750,000;

300,001 to 750,000; 100,001 to 300,000; and 100,000 and below. There are five U.S. newspapers with circulations 750,000 or higher. The Wall Street Journal was one of these, but it was excluded because it is a specialty publication. Thus, the four elite newspapers included were *USA Today*, the *Los Angeles Times*, *The New York Times*, and *The Washington Post*.

The following process was used to select 12 more newspapers.[2] First, *Editor and Publisher's Yearbook* was used to make a list of daily U.S. newspapers. The newspapers were assigned a random number and then the list was re-sorted. Newspapers were chosen by going down the list and finding the publications that were not tabloids, that had a Sunday section, and whose stories were indexed in a database so coders could access them. Geographical diversity was achieved by making sure the four newspapers in each category were from different regions of the country as defined by the U.S. Census Bureau.

Randomly constructed weeks were used in order to have a better representation of the news from different days. The 28 days chosen included four days that represented each day of the week. This was done to avoid bias in coverage related to a particular news day. Riffe, Aust, and Lacy (1993) have shown that two randomly constructed weeks is a good representation for a year of a daily newspaper; therefore, the 4 weeks used here is more than sufficient.

Stories were selected from those published from January 1 to October 13, 2004. Stories were accessed through a combination of electronic databases and hard copies. To be chosen, the stories had to have distinct bylines and appear on the newspaper's front page or the local/metro section's front page.

Internet Sample

The selected sites were taken from the Nielsen/NetRatings list of the top 20 news sites. The list had four categories of news sites: newspapers, network news, cable news, and news aggregators, which are sites that post stories but do not create them. Two sites from each category were selected. The network sites were ABC and MSNBC, which is the site for both NBC news and MSNBC news. The cable sites were Fox and CNN, and the aggregator sites were AOL and Yahoo. Newspapers that had active daily sites were randomly selected. One was selected from newspapers in the largest circulation group (*The Washington Post*), and the other was selected from newspapers falling in the other three circulation categories (*Bloomington Pantagraph*). One site, CBS 11 TV, was chosen to represent the local television market.

On the same dates as in the newspaper sample, the stories were downloaded once a day, rotating from among four different times (9 a.m., 1 p.m., 5 p.m., and 9 p.m.). Featured stories that were tied to graphic elements at the top of the page were selected as well as the next three most prominent stories without graphics.

Network Sample

The weekday sample dates that were used for the newspapers were also used for the network sample. Saturdays and Sundays were excluded because the weekend newscasts do not always appear in all the markets. In some cases, special programming preempted the evening newscasts, so an alternative date for the same day of the week was randomly chosen. Both morning and evening programs were studied.[3] The broadcasts were videotaped live from the New York market. PBS supplied the tapes for NewsHour. The analysis relied on the broadcasts and not transcripts.

Cable Sample

The same weekday sample dates that were used for the other media were also used for the cable sample. Saturdays and Sundays were excluded. In some cases, special programming preempted newscasts, so an alternative date for the same day of the week was randomly chosen. The cable news stations studied were CNN, Fox, and MSNBC. Three different types of programming were studied: daytime programming (11 a.m. to noon); news digest programs and prime-time talk shows.[4] The broadcasts were obtained through videotapes and transcripts. Ten percent of the programming was recoded for intercoder agreement scores. These scores were 88% and above for the variables.

Coding Procedures for Newspaper and Internet Stories

Four people were trained as a group to code the newspaper stories. One publication from each circulation group was chosen as a control. A single person who worked separately from the others coded the control publications. Another person coded 20% of these control publications to determine intercoder reliability scores. The coders referred to a standardized codebook and coding rules when making decisions. Intercoder reliability tests were done on 5% of the inventory variables (publication date, story length, placement, and story origination) and resulted in agreement rates of 98% and higher. For the more difficult content variables, 20% of the publications were recoded. The intercoder reliability scores for these variables were 87% and above.

Coding Procedures for Network and Cable Stories

A team of three trained coders analyzed the television stories. All coders analyzed at least 20% of each of type of network programming. The network broadcasts were viewed twice. A random sample of dates was used to determine content that would be selected for recoding to determine intercoder reliability scores. Seven percent of the stories were used, and intercoder agreement scores were above 90% for all variables except story topic, which scored 83% for collapsed categories. For cable stories, 10% of the stories were randomly chosen to assess reliability. Intercoder agreements were above 88%.

Variables of Interest

This study involves a comprehensive content analysis of newspapers, network, cable, and Internet stories from 2004. The unit of analysis is a single news story. The variables are as follows:

Domestic news: The stories originally coded as local, regional, or national U.S. news were combined in this study to create this broader variable.

International news: These stories included those about other nations that involved a relationship with the United States (such as a trade story about Mexico and the United States) and stories of other nations that did not include direct involvement with the United States.

The main topic: Each story was identified as one of the following: government, election, domestic affairs, crime, terrorism, foreign affairs, accidents, disasters, unusual weather, science/technology, celebrity/entertainment, lifestyle, and other.

Story origin: Staff-produced content was written or produced by staff members; externally produced content was written by wire services or produced by outside employees.

Results

Hypothesis 1 suggested that there would be more domestic than international news in U.S. media. There were a total of 10,429 stories included in the analysis, with 8,268 U.S. stories (79%) and 2,161 international stories (21%) Clearly, the first hypothesis was supported.

Hypothesis 2 suggested that international stories that relate to the United States would appear more frequently in U.S. media. The international stories included 1,490 with U.S. involvement (69%) and 671 (31%) non-U.S. international stories. It is evident, then, that even when stories are about the rest of the world, there is an effort to link them with the United States. Thus, hypothesis 2 is supported. An additional analysis looked at the distribution of stories with and without U.S. involvement, but showed no difference among the media, χ^2 (3, N = 2161) = 7.25, p = .064.

The next two hypotheses examined the frequency of international news. Hypothesis 3 suggested that elite newspapers would show the highest level of international news among all media, and specifically, a much higher level than local newspapers. Hypothesis 4 suggested that cable news would show high levels of coverage of international news, higher than network news and higher than nonelite newspapers. Table 8.1 shows the distribution of domestic and international stories across the news media. Network and cable television had more international news than print. Internet news showed the highest percent of international stories. Thus, hypothesis 4 was not supported. However, there was a significant difference in the amount of coverage based on newspaper type, χ^2 (1, N = 4252) = 83.13, p < .001. Elite newspapers were more likely to include international stories than local newspapers, offering partial support to hypothesis 3.

Hypothesis 5 suggested that international coverage on Internet sites would be consistent with the medium that sources those sites. For example, sites of cable and network news would show high levels of international news. Sites of local newspapers would show much less coverage. Table 8.2 shows news types broken out by the type of Internet news site. Online only (AOL and Yahoo) showed about a 50-50 split between

Table 8.1 Frequency of International and Domestic News Across Mediums

	Medium					
	Elite Newspaper	Other Newspaper	Network	Cable	Internet	Total
Type of News						
Domestic	82.7%	92.5%	73.8%	76.1%	61.9%	79.3%
International	17.3%	7.5%	26.3%	23.9%	38.1%	20.7%

$\chi^2(4, N = 10429) = 693.33$, p <.001

Table 8.2 Percentage of International and Domestic News on Internet News Sites

	Type of Internet Site					
	Aggregate	Network	Cable	Newspaper	Local TV	Total
Type of News						
Domestic	49.5%	57.4%	54.8%	79.2%	76.3%	61.9%
International	50.5%	42.6%	45.2%	20.8%	23.7%	23.7%

$\chi^2(4, N = 1620) = 87.97$, p <.001

domestic and international news as did the two cable sites (Fox News and CNN). The two network sites (ABC and MSNBC) showed slightly fewer international stories (43%). The newspaper sites (*Washington Post* and *Bloomington Pantagraph*) and the local TV site showed many fewer international stories (around 22%). Thus, hypothesis 5 is supported.

Hypothesis 6 predicted that the distribution of topics within domestic and international news would vary. Table 8.3 shows the distribution of news topics in the two categories. As can been seen, there were fewer stories about campaigns/elections, domestic affairs, entertainment, and lifestyles in the international news. International stories showed higher coverage of foreign affairs and 15 times as much coverage of terrorism than domestic news, offering support for hypothesis 6.

Hypothesis 7 suggested that sourcing of international news would show the highest in-newsroom creation for newspapers and the lowest for the Internet. Hypothesis 7 looked at story origin to determine if staff members or external employees generated the most international news content. The results show a significant difference across media, $\chi^2(3, N = 1711) = 783.31, p < .001$. Network news features exclusively staff-produced content. This is similar to cable news, in which staff produce 97% of stories. In contrast, newspapers and the Internet rely more heavily on wire stories, with the Internet featuring the lowest percentage (23%) of staff-produced content (see Table 8.4). The low percentage of staff-produced content in newspapers is due to the sample. Small, medium, and large circulation newspapers were included, but the smaller newspapers

Table 8.3 Percentage of News Topics in International and U.S. News Stories

		Type of News	
		U.S.	International
Topics	Government	34.1%	35.4%
	Terrorism	2.7	32.6
	Foreign Affairs	.2	13.3
	Domestic Affairs	12.8	7.3
	Crime	5.3	2.1
	Election	11.6	1.9
	Lifestyle	9.6	1.9
	Entertainment	7.2	1.2
	Science/ technology	2.1	1.1
	Other	14.4	3.3

$\chi^2(9, N = 10429) = 3408.21, p < .001$.

Table 8.4 Origination of International News

	Medium				
	Newspaper	Network	Cable	Internet	Total
Story Origin					
Staff	57.7%	100.0%	97.6%	22.6%	61.1%
External	42.3%	0%	2.4%	77.4%	38.9%

$\chi^2(3, N = 1711) = 783.32, p < .001$

are less likely to have the resources to devote to international report-ing. An analysis of only the newspapers with circulations above 350,000 reveals drastically different results. The findings show that 80% of inter-national news stories at these newspapers are produced by staff, $\chi^2(1, N = 5313) = 88.57, p < .001$.

Research Question 1 focused on the distribution of international news topics across the news media. Table 8.5 shows the distribution. Cable news had more government stories than the other media. Newspaper and networks did more stories on domestic affairs than did cable and the Internet. Newspapers did far more stories on foreign affairs/diplo-macy, with cable coming in second. The Internet did far more stories on terrorism, with networks coming in second, and newspaper and cable a distant third. Clearly, there were differences in coverage, although the patterns were complex. More will be said about this in the discussion.

Table 8.5 Percentage of News Topics in International News Stories Across Mediums

	Mediums				
	Newspapers	Network	Cable	Internet	Total
Topics					
Government	24.3%	36.4%	45.6%	30.1%	35.4%
Terrorism	28.3%	34.9%	25.1%	42.8%	32.6%
Foreign Affairs	26.4%	2.5%	13.6%	11.0%	13.3%
Domestic Affairs	11.0%	14.6%	2.6%	5.7%	7.3%
Crime	1.9%	4.5%	1.1%	1.8%	2.1%
Election	1.0%	.5%	1.9%	3.6%	1.9%
Lifestyle	3.6%	.8%	2.8%	.3%	1.9%
Entertainment	0%	.5%	3.2%	.2%	1.2%
Science/technology	1.4%	1.3%	.4%	1.5%	1.1%
Other	2.1%	4.0%	3.7%	3.1%	3.3%

$\chi^2(27, N = 2161) = 321.13, p < .001.$

Discussion

This study focused on the prevalence of international news in a variety of media. The purpose was to discover how these media differ in the amount of international coverage as well as examining the types of international story topics that are included. The findings indicate that overall, the American media do not extensively cover international news. However, U.S. involvement in international topics makes it more likely for stories to appear.

News consumers who seek international coverage will find more at online news sites than on network, cable, or in newspapers. In fact, less than 10% of newspaper stories in this study were devoted to international coverage compared to 38% on cable. The findings suggest that the medium you choose heavily influences your chances of encountering international news. Moreover, the specific type of newspapers or Internet sites that you consume will also determine how much international news you receive, with elite newspapers, Internet aggregators, and cable Web sites offering the most.

The findings show that international news topics lack diversity. A majority of stories focus on government and terrorism, and few feature topics such as lifestyle, entertainment, and science/technology. This lack of diverse coverage across American media fails to provide news consumers with a broader view of the world. The exclusion of stories about everyday life in distant countries denies readers and viewers the opportunity to understand the lives and interests of regular citizens. Instead, the knowledge that is gained will mainly be constricted to the government as well as stories about terrorists.

The topics that are covered vary in frequency across the media. For example, cable has more government stories; the Internet has more terrorism stories; newspapers have more foreign affairs stories; and networks have the most domestic affairs stories. The gatekeepers at each of these mediums make different editorial decisions when it comes to selecting international news stories. So not only does the medium you choose play an important role in your likelihood of encountering international news, but it also influences the type of content that you will find. This is significant because studies have shown that news stories, including those on international topics, can set the agenda for what we think about (Wanta, Golan, Lee, 2004; Wanta & Hu, 1993). If the different media place emphasis on various topics, then news consumers may form quite different views of foreign nations depending on the medium that they turn to.

Network, cable, and elite newspapers share a commitment to devoting resources to international news reporting. Financing foreign news bureaus or correspondents is costly, but in this study, these three types of media include a high amount of staff-produced content. However, since this study's data were gathered, there has been continued pressure upon news organizations to produce greater profits and streamline budgets, leading to the closure to some foreign news bureaus and a potential decrease in the amount of original reporting. For example, the *Boston Globe* closed its three remaining offices in Jerusalem, Berlin, and Bogota, and the South Florida *Sun-Sentinel* eliminated its foreign desk (Ricchiardi, 2008). These cutbacks come at a time when Americans are fighting overseas. However, the Associated Press has made efforts to expand internationally (Ricchiardi, 2008), and this increased coverage from wire services can be helpful for smaller newspapers that lack the resources to have their own staff go abroad to cover stories. But having access to the international stories doesn't mean that gatekeepers will include them. The editor of a 22,000 circulation newspaper in Wisconsin said, "You have to focus on what you can do better than anyone else. What we can do best is cover Janesville, Wisconsin" (Ricchiardi, 2008). However, foreign correspondent Pamela Constable argues that the need to understand what is going on outside our borders has become increasingly important.

> We have been victimized by foreign terrorists, yet we still cannot imagine why anyone would hate us. Our economy is intimately linked to global markets, our population is nearly 20 percent foreign-born, and our lives are directly affected by borderless scourges such as global warming and AIDS. Knowing about the world is not a luxury; it is an urgent necessity. (2007, para. 3)

Despite these compelling reasons to understand the world beyond our borders, the American media coverage as demonstrated in this study falls short. The small amount of international news stories that are published or aired cover a limited range of topics. Thus, American news consumers are left with an incomplete picture of foreign nations at a time when the need for world understanding has never been more vital.

This study is significant because it offers a look at the prevalence of international news from a large sample taken from various media. The study offers insight into the story topics that dominate international news and includes an analysis of who is creating the content—staff or wire services. This examination of international news characteristics contributes to the literature because it offers a fuller description of the type and amount of international news that audiences will encounter in each medium.

This study involved secondary analysis of data, so the questions were limited to the data that was gathered. Also, the conclusions are limited to the chosen time period. Another study using more recent material could determine if recent cutbacks in newspaper staffs have led to a shrinking newshole for international news as well as domestic news. Also, the variables could be expanded to include the specific countries that receive coverage. This would provide greater insight into the news that is deemed worthy by gatekeepers and reveal if there is a difference in coverage among the various media. Such a study could build upon the previous literature on the determinants of foreign news coverage that are discussed elsewhere in this book (e.g., K-K. Chang & Lee, chapter 3 this volume; Golan, chapter 6 this volume; Wanta & Golan, chapter 5 this volume;). Interviews with news editors could provide insight into the news selection process. Because the need to be informed about global events will continue, the focus on the frequency and characteristics of this news in U.S. media will remain important.

Notes

1. "I personally believe that U.S. Americans are unable to do so because, uhm, some people out there in our nation don't have maps and uh, I believe that our, I, education like such as, uh, South Africa, and uh, the Iraq, everywhere like such as, and I believe that they should, uh, our education over here in the U.S. should help the U.S., uh, should help South Africa, it should help the Iraq and the Asian countries so we will be able to build up our future, for us."

2. Besides the four elite newspapers, the others chosen were the *Cleveland Plain Dealer, Dallas Morning News, Philadelphia Inquirer, Sacramento Bee, Albuquerque Journal, Asbury Park Press, Kansas City Star, San Antonio Express-News, Bloomington (Illinois) Pantagraph, Hanover (Pennsylvania) Evening Sun, McAllen (Texas) Monitor,* and *Vacaville (California) Reporter.*

4. The network morning programs were ABC's *Good Morning America,* CBS's *The Early Show,* and NBC's *The Today Show.* The network evening news programs were ABC's *World News Tonight,* CBS's *Evening News,* NBC's *Nightly News,* and PBS's *NewsHour.*

5. The cable programs included CNN's *NewsNight with Aaron Brown* and *Larry King Live;* Fox's *Special Report with Brit Hume* and *O'Reilly Factor;* MSNBC's *Countdown with Keith Olbermann* and *Hardball with Chris Matthews;* and each cable station's programming between 11 to noon.

References

Beaudoin, C. E. (2004). The independent and interactive antecedents of international knowledge. *Gazette, 66*(5), 459–473.

Beaudoin, C. E., & Thorson, E. (2001). Value representations in foreign news. *Gazette, 63*(6), 481–503.

Best, S., Chmielewski, B., & Krueger, B. (2005). Selective exposure to online foreign news during the conflict with Iraq. *Harvard International Journal of Press Politics, 10*(4), 52–70.

Brewer, P. R., Graf, J., & Willnat, L. (2003) Priming or framing: Media influence on attitudes toward foreign countries. *Gazette, 65*(6), 493–508.

Carroll, J. (2007). Foreign news coverage: The U.S. media's undervalued asset. Report from the Joan Shorenstein Center for Press and Politics, Harvard University. Retrieved January 22, 2008, from http://www.ksg.harvard.edu/press...papers/2007_10_carroll.pdf

Constable, P. (2007, February 18). Demise of the foreign correspondent. *Washington Post,* p. B01.

Emery, M. (1989). An endangered species. The international newshole. *Gannett Center Journal, 3,* 151–164.

Fleeson, L. (2003, October/November). Bureau of missing bureaus. *American Journalism Review, 25.* http:www.ajr.org/article_printable.asp?id=3409

Galtunge, J., & Ruge, M. (1965). The structure of foreign news: The presentation of the Congo, Cuba, and Cyprus crises in four Norwegian newspapers. *Journal of Peace Research, 2,* 64–91.

Gavin, R. (2007). Globe to close last three foreign bureaus. *The Boston Globe.* Retrieved August 1, 2007, from http://www.boston.com

Giffard, C. A. (1984). Developed and developing nation news in U.S. wire service files to Asia. *Journalism Quarterly, 61*(1), 14–19.

Golan, G., & Wanta, W. (2003). International elections in U.S, network news: An examination of factors affecting newsworthiness. *Gazette, 65*(10), 25–39.

Hargrove, T., & Stempel, G. H. III (2002). Exploring reader interest in international news. *Newspaper Research Journal, 23*(4), 46–51.

Hess, S. (1996). Media mavens. *Society, 33*(3), 70–78.

Hester, A. (1974). The news from Latin America via a world news agency. *Gazette, 20*(2), 83–98.

Kang, N., & Choi, J. (1999). Structural implications of the crossposting network of international news in cyberspace. *Communication Research, 26*(4), 454–481.

Kirat, M., & Weaver, D. (1984, August). *Foreign news coverage in three wire services: A study of AP, UPI, and the nonaligned news agency pool.* Paper presented at the annual meeting of the Association for Education in Journalism and Mass Communication, Gainesville, FL.

Kliesch, R. E. (1991). The U.S. press corps abroad rebounds. A 7th world survey of foreign correspondents. *Newspaper Research Journal, 12*(10), 24–33.

Korzenny, F. del Toro, W., & Gaudino, J. (1987). International news media exposure, knowledge, and attitudes. *Journal of Broadcasting and Electronic Media, 31*(1), 73–87.

Kwak, N., Poor, N., & Skoric, M. (2006). Honey, I shrunk the world! The relation between internet use and international engagement. *Mass Communication & Society, 9*(2), 189–213.

Lowrey, W., Becker, L. B., & Punathambekar, A. (2003). Determinants of newsroom use of staff expertise: The case of international news. *Gazette, 65,* 41–63.

Mowlana, H. (1986). *Global information and world communication: New frontiers in international relations.* New York: Longman.

Perry, D. K. (1987). The image gap: How international news affects perceptions of nations. *Journalism Quarterly, 64,* 416–421.

Perry, D. K. (1990). News reading, knowledge about, and attitudes toward foreign countries. *Journalism Quarterly, 67*(2), 353–358.

Pew Research Center for People and the Press. (2004, June 8). *News audiences increasingly politicized.* Retrieved June 24, 2007, from http://people-press. org/reports/display.php3?ReportID=215

Project for Excellence in Journalism. (2005). *The state of the news media.* Retrieved December 12, 2006, from http://www.stateofthenewsmedia. com/2005/

Ricchiardi, S. (2008–2009, December/January). Covering the world. *American Journalism Review,* Retrieved September 5, 2008, from http://www.ajr.org/ Article.asp?id=4429

Riffe, D., Aust, C., & Lacy, S. (1993). The effectiveness of random, consecutive day and constructed week samples in newspaper content analysis. *Journalism Quarterly, 70,* 133–139.

Schramm, W. (1964) *Mass media and national development: The role of information in the developing countries.* Stanford, CA: Stanford University Press.

Shoemaker, P. J., & Cohen, A. A. (2006). *News around the world.* New York: Routledge.

Shoemaker, P. J., Danielian, L. H., & Brendlinger, N. (1991). Deviant acts, risky business and U.S. interests: The newsworthiness of world events. *Journalism Quarterly, 68,* 781–795.

Stacks, J. (2003/04). Hard times for hard news: A clinical look at U.S. foreign news coverage. *World Policy Journal, 20*(4), 12–21.

Thalhimer, M. (1994). High-tech news or just "shovelware"? *Media Studies Journal, 8*(1), 41–51.

Wanta, W., Golan, G., & Lee, C. (2004). Agenda setting and international news: Media influence on public perceptions of foreign nations. *Journalism and Mass Communication Quarterly, 81*(2), 364–377.

Wanta, W., & Hu, Y. W. (1993).The agenda-setting effects of international news coverage: An examination of differing news frames. *International Journal of Public Opinion Research, 5,* 250–264.

Weaver, D., & Wilhoit, C. (1981). Foreign news coverage in two U.S. wire services. *Journal of Communication, 31*(2), 55–63.

Weaver, D., & Wilhoit, C. (1983). Foreign news coverage in two U.S. wire services: An update. *Journal of Communication, 33*(2), 132–148.

Wu, H. D. (2000). Systemic determinants of international news coverage: A comparison of 38 countries. *Journal of Communications, 50*(2), 110–130.

Wu, H. C., & Hamilton, J. M. (2004). US foreign correspondents: Changes and continuity at the turn of the century. *Gazette, 66*(6), 517–532.

Chapter 9

The Influence of Contextual Factors on the Selection of News Frames

A Cross-National Approach to the News Coverage of Severe Acute Respiratory Syndrome (SARS)

Kuang-Kuo Chang, Charles T. Salmon, Byoungkwan Lee, Jounghwa Choi, and Geri Alumit Zeldes

Traditional research on framing has focused primarily on clarifying and redefining its conceptualization (Entman, 1993; Gamson, 1989; Pan & Kosicki, 1993; Scheufele, 1999) and on rigorous empirical tests of media frames as independent variables that elicit subsequent effects on cognition and affect (Akhavan-Majid & Ramaprasad, 1998; Iyengar & Simon, 1993). However, research on media framing as a dependent variable is relatively rare and indeed has been singled out as an area of study that merits further empirical investigation (Scheufele, 1999). Scheufele (1999) argues that although "many researchers have examined extrinsic and intrinsic factors influencing the production and selection of news" (p. 109), no empirical evidence has been collected about specific factors that lead to corresponding media frames. In particular, contextual (extrinsic) factors—such as political or economic conditions and press freedom—have been shown to influence news content, but not news frames.

Much of the research examining the influence of contextual factors on news coverage has been done through cross-national studies by international communication researchers and has been limited to providing explanations of the selection of international news. Although many researchers (e.g., Akhavan-Majid & Ramaprasad, 1998; Iyengar, 1991; Massey, 2000) have recognized the need for cross-national studies of framing that will lead to theory-building, very few scholars (e.g., Y. L. Chang & Chang, 2003; Massey, 2000; Wanta & Chang, 2001) have tried to link contextual factors and news frames and to scrutinize the potential roles of those factors in the selection of news frames. Furthermore, such examinations are hard to conduct due, in part, to the lack of comparable issues that may have a potential geopolitical or economic impact across a region or the globe.

One issue that lends itself to cross-national research is Severe Acute Respiratory Syndrome (SARS), a mysterious contagious disease that dramatically stirred up an "epidemic of fear" for the American populace, which was afraid of getting infected and dying from the disease (Siegel, 2005). Siegel (2005) was critical of the media-generated fearful environment and resultant uncertainties that blew the seriousness of the disease out of proportion and left American society and other infected nations in limbo for a period of time. A contagious disease initiated in China that subsequently spread to Asia and North America, SARS claimed more than 800 lives worldwide in 2003. Back then, the SARS disease not only worsened the already deteriorating tourism industry and economies of infected nations but it also caused racial and political tensions between and within them. The growing global economic interdependence also forced those infected nations, along with other noninfected ones, to forge collaborative strategies to battle the disease and at the same time try to minimize their human and financial losses. Accordingly, the issue presents the opportunity for a good case study that compares media frames across nations and an investigation of factors that may have led to differences in those frames.

The present project thus proposes to conduct a cross-national study examining what and how news frames were adopted in mainstream newspapers in SARS-infected nations (Singapore, China, Hong Kong, Taiwan, and Canada, along with the United States, whose air and tourism industries were hurt badly by the combined impact of fear of the disease and the Iraq War). More specifically, the current research analyzes and compares news frames (e.g., economic threats) within each country, and examines contextual factors that may influence the selection of news frames regarding this issue of international consequence.

Media Frames and Context/Event-Related Approaches

Media frames provide structures for the working routines of journalists and news organizations in their efforts to organize, interpret, and present information efficiently to their audiences (e.g., Entman, 1993; Gamson, 1989; Gitlin, 1980; Pan & Kosicki, 1993). Defined as "a central organizing idea or story line that provides meaning to an unfolding strip of events..." a frame first of all offers an organizational structure and reportorial essence to an event that has no inherent meaning (Gamson & Modigliani, 1987, p. 143). In effect, as Entman notes (1993), media frames "promote a particular problem definition, causal interpretation, moral evaluation, and/or treatment recommendation" (p. 52) through their emphasis of certain facets of an event to the exclusion of others.

In terms of news production, Gitlin (1980) defined frames as the "persistent selection, emphasis, and exclusion" of news and argued that frames "enable journalists to process large amounts of information quickly and routinely package the information for efficient relay to their audiences" (p. 7). Tuchman (1978) argued that news organizations are complicated institutions subject to certain processes. Journalists are driven not only by their professionalism but also by newsroom sociology and constraints. In other words, Tuchman linked Goffman's (1974) study to the ideological and structural processes of journalism, news organizations, and above all, news sources which help structure "social reality." Berkowitz and Gavrilos (2001) suggested that news was shaped by three levels of influences; those of the journalism profession, the news organization, and of society at large.

In an effort to bridge the respective literature on framing and predictors of news coverage, Scheufele (1999), who adopts Shoemaker and Reese's (1996) hierarchy of influence hypotheses, suggests five factors that can influence media framing: social norms and values, organizational pressures and constraints, pressures of interest groups, journalistic routines, and the individual journalist's ideological or political orientations. Shoemaker and Reese (1996) hypothesize the five levels of hierarchy as: individual background, media routines, organizational restraints, extramedia influences, and ideological influences. Similarly, Hilgartner and Bosk (1988) have outlined a dynamic system of selection principles and factors that contribute to the rise and fall of social problems and their corresponding news frames. These factors include organizational characteristics of media, economies, and cultural myths. The aforesaid theorizations on framing and predictive factors apply equally and increasingly to international conflicts (e.g., Barnett & Kim, 2005; Entman, 1991; Leslie, 2006) and risk communication (Bowen, Heath, Lee, & Li, 2005; Qiu & Cameron, 2005), notably public health crises, and a combination of the two, in that international public health crises have become more local and threatening due to the expanding global village (Y. L. Lee, 2005).

It is particularly noteworthy that cultural and societal considerations influence a country's news media in terms of how information is processed on a given health epidemic, because such information flow or control will affect both domestic and international politics and images. In terms of international conflicts, Huntington (1993a, 1993b, 1996) and Ting-Toomey and Oetzel (2001), among other scholars, argue forcefully that cultural differences that often produce confrontations or emotional frustrations between political entities can lead to international conflicts between them. Such international or intercultural conflicts can further intensify and turn into wars if their news media lose neutrality in covering them (Gilboa, 2006; Wolfsfeld, 1997, 2004). However, those conflicts can be avoided or averted strategically if the nations involved and their news media are wary of the risk and its potential consequences

(Leslie, 2006). At issue are the divergent world images of China and Singapore that were associated with their contrasting risk management strategies over the SARS crisis, which were similar in terms of both having authoritarian political systems and political control (Chong, 2006).

The linkages among international conflicts, risk communication, and media framing have led us, at least indirectly, to two major genres of factors that explain international news coverage: intrinsic (or event-related) factors and extrinsic (or context-related) factors. The event-driven approach examines news values intrinsic to the news itself. In this context, for instance, McQuail (2000) has examined such factors as the location of a news event, its predictability, the size of the issue, and its timeliness, as well as the relationship of those factors to news coverage. More significantly, such factors as prominence/impact, conflict/controversy, novelty, timeliness, proximity, deviance, and human interest have been found to be predictive of whether an international event gets covered (e.g., T-K. Chang, Shoemaker, & Brendlinger, 1987; Wanta & Chang, 2001).

Directly tied to the present research is the concept of impact, which is usually measured by the magnitude of casualty and financial loss. T-K. Chang et al. (1987) and Van Belle (2000) argued that the number of people killed or the amount of property damaged are significant determinants of international news coverage. In the present study, the potential, and varied impacts of SARS in terms of human casualties and economic activities in infected countries, as well as countries that have close political and economic connections with the infected countries, would help determine coverage. Clearly, casualties resulting from the epidemic are expected to have an impact on addressing the threat to public health as a major news frame.

On the other hand, the context-oriented approach investigates how extrinsic predictors, such as economic, political, cultural, and social factors influence news coverage (T-K. Chang et al., 1987; Entman, 1991; Gamson & Modigliani, 1987; Shoemaker & Reese, 1996; Tuchman, 1978). In the context of international conflicts and associated news, specific factors such as trade relations, economic relations, political affiliation, and press freedom have been shown to affect news coverage between or among countries (Ahern, 1984; Dupree, 1971; Ishii, 1996; Kim & Barnett, 1996; Nnaemeka & Richstad, 1980; Robinson & Sparkes, 1976; Wu, 2000).

The Potential Impact of Economic and Political Factors on News Frames

Several economic factors are commonly examined as contextual variables whose predictability has been found to be inconsistent in terms of their impact on world affairs coverage. Wu (2000), for example, examined nine contextual factors—without any event-oriented factors—that might have affected world news coverage in 38 countries and found "trade volume" and "presence of world news agencies" to be the two primary predictors of whether a country gets covered in another country's news media. He disclosed a significant, positive relation between the two determinants and the quantity of a nation's news coverage. Similar findings about the influence of trade appeared in studies by Ahern (1984), Dupree (1971), Ishii (1996), Kim and Barnett (1996), Lim and Barnett (chapter 4 this volume), and Nnaemeka and Richstad (1980). Nonetheless, a comparable number of studies (e.g., T-K. Chang et al., 1987; T-K. Chang & Lee, chapter 3 this volume; Golan & Wanta, 2003; Robinson & Sparkes, 1976; Wang, chapter 13 this volume) found that trade had no effect on world news coverage.

In addition, how news frames are adopted also depends on the interplay of the various competing forces in the same issue. For instance, arguing that national interests affect international news discourse and that issues are framed accordingly, Lee and Yang (1995) showed how news coverage of a Chinese student movement was framed with respect to each country's national interest, such as economic impact (Japan) or ideological concern (U.S.). Since Japan had a closer economic relationship with China, the media in Japan adopted an "economic impact" frame in its coverage of the student movement. Therefore, it is inferred that economic conditions and economic relations may affect the media's news frame. It is logical to expect that the economic factor would link with the discussion of threat on economy as a major news frame.

Likewise, the political system, political freedom, and press freedom have been found to be strong forecasters of world news coverage. For example, Kim and Barnett (1996) found that political freedom positively affected the structure of world news flow. Nnaemeka and Richstad (1980) suggested that political control influenced the patterns of international news coverage in the Pacific region. They argue that authoritarian regimes aim to achieve a political consensus under which individual voices are suppressed in order to maintain social order. According to Edelman (1993), government authorities use news media to frame beliefs related to issues, which builds a frame of reference. Press freedom also has been a strong predictor in world news reporting (K-K. Chang, 2006; K-K. Chang & Freedman, 2008; Mishra, 1979) and can affect the fairness and balance of the coverage (K-K. Chang & Freedman, 2008; Bouzid & Stoll, 2003).

In short, in any political environments characterized by expansive government control and limited political and press freedom, media frames typically reflect authorities' agendas. This political control can be executed in a number of ways, including laws, licenses, regulations, and self-censorship that are imposed on the press (Shoemaker & Reese, 1996). Wolfsfeld (1997) further points out that when government authorities are in full control of the political environment, they also are in complete command of press access and, thereby, press coverage. As such, the press is fully manipulated by the authority that decides the frame of reference of the reporting. At this level, the government can force the press to become either wide open or tightlipped, depending on its situational evaluations of the issue. That means a government, particularly an authoritarian one with a high degree of political control, can conduct a risk analysis to decide its ad hoc press policy and risk management strategy, if any. As a result, it is expected that this political-control factor can lead news media to promote a consensus sought for by the authority and, therefore, frame news issues in a certain way.

Several contextual factors, alongside reported number of SARS cases as an event-driven impact variable, served as independent variables in this study. The factors under examination in the study include economic development, trade among the nations, foreign direct investment in another country, the nation's political and press freedom, and the number of SARS cases.

Research Questions and Hypotheses

We have come up with nine news frames based on and revised from past research (de Vreese, Peter, & Semetko, 2001; Luther & Zhou, 2005; Semetko & Valkenburg, 2000; Valkenburg, Semetko, & de Vreese, 1999), with additional ones to fit the nature and need of our study. Semetko and colleagues developed four news frames to examine news coverage of international affairs: economic consequences, responsibility, human interest, and conflict. Closely related to our investigation is Luther and Zhou's study (2005). They adopted the four news frames to compare press coverage of the SARS crisis between the U.S. and Chinese elite press. Luther and Zhou refer to economic consequences as the economic impact of the disease; responsibility as blame/credit claim; human interest as personalized or heroic behavior; and conflict as clashes between political entities. In an effort to outline a more holistic media framing of the crisis, our nine news frames that are defined in the methods section are: threat to economy (from economic consequences); threat to government credibility (from responsibility); individual survival or heroic acts (from human interest); threat to national or racial relations (from conflict); threat to public health (SARS being a legitimate threat); along with international aid; joint efforts on controlling SARS; medical investigation of the disease (all of which seem crucial in today's global society and therefore are logically included), and others.

Based on the literature and the eight news frames derived, the following research questions and hypotheses are proposed in this comparison of press coverage of the SARS epidemic in Canada, China, Hong Kong, Singapore, Taiwan, and the United States.

RQ1. Which nation has dedicated more news space to the SARS issue?
RQ2. What is the dominant news frame of SARS coverage in the six
  countries?

As discussed above, we assumed that economic factors could affect news frames and that economic development would be one of them. In this study, three factors were considered as economic contextual factors that can affect media news framing: economic development, total foreign trade, and total foreign direct investment (FDI). First, a country's gross domestic product (GDP) per capita has been widely used as a prime indicator of a country's economic strength. In the case of SARS, it is reasoned that the more economically developed the nation, the greater the potential economic impact of SARS, and, therefore, the more likely that economic frames would appear in the news.

Total foreign trade and total foreign direct investment (FDI) are also considered important economic factors for media framing. "Total foreign trade" is defined as a country's total trade volume—imports and exports—with the rest of the world measured in real-dollar terms in millions. "Total foreign direct investment" is defined as a country's total amount of FDI in the rest of the world and measured in real-dollar terms, in the unit of million of dollars. Since SARS, a contagious disease, motivated people to avoid crowds and international travel, we posited that newspapers in nations with higher economic development, greater total foreign trade and FDI would adopt the "threat to economy" news frame more frequently. Therefore, we suggest the first hypothesis:

H1. The greater the economy (economic development, trade, and foreign direct investment) of the nation, the more likely the "threat to economy" news frame would be used in its newspapers.

As documented, the degree of the impact of a news event or an issue is a major predictor of its news coverage. The number of SARS cases is considered an impact factor. This sole event-oriented variable is operationalized as the total number of probable cases and deaths on a weekly basis. This aggregate number was calculated by dividing the total number of cases during the period of November 1, 2002 to July 31, 2003 by 39 weeks (World Health Organization, n.d.). On the basis of the disparity among the countries, the following hypothesis is developed:

H2.   The more SARS cases the nation reported, the more likely the "threat to public health" news frame would be used in its newspapers.

The concept of political control covers the constructs of political freedom and press freedom. Political freedom typically refers to a country's political rights and civil liberties and is usually indexed according to the *Freedom House* rankings. Taking the time gap into account, data were obtained from the 2002–2003 edition of *Freedom in the World: The Annual Survey of Political Rights and Civil Liberties* (Gastil, 2003). Countries whose ratings average 1 to 2.5 are considered "free"; 3 to 5 "partly free"; and 5.5 to 7 "not free." In other words, the lower the score, the less political control is exerted in a country, and the higher the score, the more political control is exerted in a country. Press freedom is the level of government information control, which is operationally assessed in the annual *Freedom Review* by Sussman and Guida (2002). Similarly, the higher the score is, the less the press freedom and the more the political control. Taken together, political control is defined by adding the rating scores of the two constructs, and the higher the combined score, the greater the political control of a country, and vice versa.

We expect that political control of a country will significantly influence the orientation of news coverage and its associated news frames (Wolfsfeld, 1997). However, news orientation is also affected by a government's risk management strategy, which aims to minimize the risk, if not also to maximize the benefit (Bowen et al., 2005; Qiu & Cameron, 2005). The ultimate question for any government to make then would be: will this action do more good or bring more harm to the government politically and economically? How should the government act with regard to its press policy, for instance? As an example, the polarizing political decisions about political and news transparency made by China and Singapore, two authoritarian nations with a virtually total political control, generated contrasting political and economic outcomes and international images for them (Chong, 2006; Leslie, 2006; Qiu & Cameron, 2005).

While it is reasonable to reckon that a more authoritarian nation would seek a social consensus that coerces or encourages its press and populace to behave a certain way, this social model or its intended outcomes may not be always achievable due to its government's miscalculation of a crisis or adoption of a wrong strategy dealing with the ongoing crisis. In this light, it becomes more difficult to predict how an authoritarian government would exercise its political control and risk management in terms of steering press coverage of any crises. In the present research, we are also interested in the relationship between political control and two forms of social consensus, keeping in mind that two authoritarian nations being included for investigation approached and handled the issue in different ways. The following two research questions are then proposed.

RQ3. How would political control be associated with use of the "threat to government credibility" news frame?

RQ4. How would political control be associated with use of the "individual survival or heroic action" news frames?

Methods

Sampling

Six elite dailies from six nations or political entities were selected. They are: *Toronto Star* (Canada), *People's Daily* (China), *South China Morning Post* (Hong Kong), *The Straits Times* (Singapore), *United Daily News* (Taiwan), and *The New York Times* (the United States).

Rationales for selecting these newspapers include: (1) each newspaper is the elite daily of its country or political entity and has a large circulation there; (2) the four Asian nations were listed by the WHO as SARS-infected nations; (3) for Canada and the United States, each newspaper also is headquartered in the city with large Chinese immigrant populations and, therefore, faced the greatest threats from the SARS disease and concerns for international cultural confrontations.

The time frame of the study covered 4 months of news coverage on this issue, from March 1 to June 30, 2003. While news reports suggested that the disease seemed to originate in Southern China in November 2002, the news media did not to pick up the issue until early March 2003, and therefore, it is appropriate to include news stories from the selected time frame. As a result, a total of 1,464 issues, with 122 for each newspaper, were used in the analysis, and thus, the unit of analysis for this study is an issue.

An intercoder reliability test was conducted by three groups, each group with two coders, to overcome the geographic and language barriers. Each group of newspapers was treated as a subset of the whole data set, and each subset yielded its own intercoder reliability testing result. One group coded the U.S. and Canadian newspapers (*The New York Times* and *Toronto Star*), and the second group coded two Chinese-language Asian newspapers (*People's Daily* and *United Daily News*), and the last group coded the English-language Asian newspapers (*South China Morning News* and *The Straits Times*). For each coding group, intercoder reliability was assessed by randomly selecting and coding 80 issues of newspapers (Riffe, Lacy, & Fico, 2005) and yielded an acceptable agreement of .90 or higher; using Krippendorff's (2004) Alpha for all coding.

Measurement

The eight types of news frames were designated and defined as follows:

1. *Threat to the economy* is defined as referring to a threat to or disruption of economic or business activities, such as airline industry, travel, tourism, entertainment (e.g., movie-going), sports events, restaurants, regional or world trade (e.g., shipping), stock markets, employment, among others. This would include any postponement or cancellation of activities as a result of fear of getting infected from or spreading of the disease, or individuals, groups, or organizations being prevented from carrying out their plans or schedules, with corresponding implications for economics and business. An example might be a news story about problems in the airline or tourism industries attributable to people avoiding travel to infected areas/nations.

2. *Threat to public health* is operationally defined as a discussion of any actions or reports about new infection(s), death(s), updated death tolls, quarantine of individual(s), communities, or institution(s), or government's precautionary measures, such as temperature checking, airport screening, mask wearing, school closing, and cleaning/disinfecting.

3. *Threat to government credibility* is defined as discussions about credibility of a government being undermined as a result of its intentional cover-up of the occurrence or seriousness of the disease. For example, the Chinese government's well-documented cover-up of SARS invited criticism and damaged its world credibility/image.

4. *Threat to national or racial relations* is defined as discussions on actions that show dislike, condemnation, resent, hatred, or other offensive acts toward a different nation or toward a different racial or ethnic group within the nation. For instance, Toronto residents condemned Chinese immigrants were blamed for importing the SARS disease to Toronto; the contagious disease killed scores of people and severely disturbed the city's normal life.

5. *International aid* is defined as discussions about monetary, materialistic, or manpower assistance, such as donation of masks or screening equipment, from one nation to another to help fight the disease. For example, Singapore donated screening equipment to China, an occurrence which subsequently was reported in news coverage of the issue.

6. *Joint efforts on controlling the disease* refers to governmental decisions or actions in a nonresearch lab or hospital setting, such as discussions about any bilateral (e.g., Singapore/Malaysia), regional (e.g., ASEAN), or world (e.g., WHO) efforts announced or conducted in an attempt to fight or control the spread of the disease by exchanging knowledge about it.

7. *Medical investigation of the disease* refers to an examination involving a research lab or hospital setting, but not a conference meeting

or the like. Typical references pertain to medical studies of the disease's potential origins—such as from a civet cat, pig, or even outer space—and medical efforts in developing a vaccine.

8. Individual survival or heroic action/stories are defined as discussions or personal profiles about medical staff at risk or about individuals who have sacrificed their own lives trying to save the infected, or about any of the infected patients who survive the disease.

9. *Others* are defined as other dominant news frames not listed above.

Results

To examine which country and its newspaper dedicated more news coverage to SARS, the number and size of news coverage of SARS were compared among the dailies. In terms of the number of stories on the front pages, the analysis showed significant differences among the newspapers, F (5, 687) = 32.894, p< .001. Specifically, Hong Kong's *South China Morning Post* published the largest average number of front-page news stories per issue with a 1.42 pieces, followed by Singapore's *The Straits Times* (mean = .79) and Canada's *Toronto Star* (mean= .69), while the U.S. *New York Times* (mean = .29) published the least. However, when the whole first section was measured, Taiwan's *United Daily News*'s coverage had the greatest news space devoted to the disease with an average of 21.97 square-inches per issue, followed by *The Post* (mean = 3.92) and *The Straits Times* (mean = 3.92). Table 9.1 summarizes the result.

Using newshole percentage (on the front page) as the unit of measurement offers an additional interpretation and insight into how the issue was treated by these dailies. Table 9.2 shows that the amount of SARS news coverage in terms of percentage of news size on the front page differed significantly among the six newspapers, F (5, 685) = 18.215, p< .001. In this case, Canada's *Toronto Star* dedicated nearly half of its front page, or 47.73%, to SARS coverage compared to *The Straits Times*, which dedicated 32.68% of its front page to SARS, and the *South China Morning Post,* which dedicated 31.96%. China's *People's Daily* allotted the least amount of space of its front page to SARS coverage, only 6.2%. This additional finding could suggest, for one, that while China did cover the issue, it seemed to downplay its importance.

On the other hand, the analysis of stand-alone photos on the front page and the whole first section showed consistent results. Taiwan's *United Daily News* provided the largest average number of stand-alone SARS-related photos with .22 on the front page and 1.98 in the whole first section. Singapore's *The Straits Times* and Hong Kong's *The Post* placed second and third in both cases.

Table 9.1 Difference in the Number of the SARS News Coverage between the Newspapers

Country of the newspaper	N	Mean	SD	F(5, 687)
News Coverage in the Front Page				
Singapore (The Straits Times)	100	.79	.76	
China (People's Daily)	122	.45	.80	
Hong Kong (South China Morning Post)	119	1.42	1.13	32.894***
Taiwan (United Daily News)	111	.48	.60	
Canada (Toronto Star)	119	.69	.61	
United States (The New York Times)	122	.29	.52	
News Coverage in the Front Page and Section One				
Singapore	100	3.92	4.56	
China	122	2.03	2.69	
Hong Kong	119	7.37	5.41	85.253***
Taiwan	111	21.97	20.89	
Canada	119	2.74	2.32	
United States	122	1.65	1.52	
Stand Alone Photo in the Front Page				
Singapore	100	.12	.38	
China	122	.00	.00	
Hong Kong	119	.05	.22	14.239***
Taiwan	115	.22	.41	
Canada	119	.02	.13	
United States	122	.00	.00	
Stand Alone Photo in the Front Page and Section One				
Singapore	100	.62	1.27	
China	122	.00	.00	
Hong Kong	119	.17	.26	44.558***
Taiwan	115	1.98	2.74	
Canada	119	.08	.33	
United States	122	.02	.15	

# $p < .10$, * $p < .05$, ** $p < .01$, and $p < .001$.

Table 9.3 reports the results for research question 2: What is the dominant news frame of the main SARS story on the front page for each country? Apparently, the "threat to public health" was the dominant news frame in all countries, accounting for 62.7% for Taiwan and about 50% for Singapore and Canada. Hong Kong and China ranked the bottom two in using this frame. The salience of this public-health frame suggests the need to include it in any future research on public health-driven issues, particularly those with a great international significance and implication. "Threat to economy" was the second most important frame adopted by all six countries, and China placed an emphasis on this frame relatively more than other nations. Also notable is the high frequency of the frame of "threat to government credibility" in the news-

Table 9.2 Difference in the Percentages of the Size of the SARS News Coverage in the Front Page[a]

Country of the newspaper	N	Mean (%)	SD	F(5, 685)
Singapore	100	31.96	32.59	
China	122	6.2	11.28	
Hong Kong	119	32.68	27.81	18.215***
Taiwan	109	22.9	30.3	
Canada	119	47.73	63.98	
United States	122	16.56	34.58	

Note: To calculate the size of the SARS news coverage, the size of news story and stand-alone photo were combined for each newspaper.
# $p < .10$, * $p < .05$, ** $p < .01$, and $p < .001$.

papers of China and Hong Kong, compared to other countries. This particular outcome is quite surprising, considering the normally tight political control of the Chinese government over the *People's Daily*. Since the publication acts as the Chinese government's mouthpiece, we would expect that it would have toiled to cover up the SARS crisis, instead of attacking it. These two outstanding outcomes contradict those of Luther and Zhou (2005), who documented that the Chinese elite press (the *People's Daily* and *China Daily*) was less likely than its American counterparts to focus on the economic impact and responsibility perspectives of the issue. On the other hand, the *Straits Times*, being mum on the perspective of (attacking) government credibility is within the expectation in that this elite daily has long been regarded as the Singapore government's mouthpiece, given the country's friendly foreign policy toward its trade partners (Massey, 2000). As shown in Table 9.3, the difference in dominant news frames of the main SARS story on the front page among the six dailies was significant, $\chi^2 (40) = 73.84$, $p < .001$. It is also interesting to note that the "threat to national or racial relations" and the "international aid" frames are the two least used news frames across the six newspapers on their front pages. The former, in particular, appears once only in the *Star* and the *Times*, and does not appear at all in those four Asian elite dailies.

The Influence of Contextual Factors on News Framing

Hypothesis 1 focuses on the influence of economic factors on news frames. We hypothesized that the greater the economic factors of the nation (e.g., GDP per capita, trade and foreign direct investment), the more likely the "threat to economy" news frame would be used in its newspaper. Table 9.4 reveals the outcomes of bivariate correlation

Table 9.3 Dominant News Frame of the Main SARS Story in the Front Page by Country of the Newspaper

	Singapore	China	Hong Kong	Taiwan	Canada	United States	df	χ^2
Threat to economy	10 (16.7%)	23 (20.5%)	12 (13.3%)	6 (5.1%)	9 (11.1%)	5 (16.7%)	40	73.84***
Threat to public health	30 (50.0%)	44 (39.3%)	30 (33.3%)	74 (62.7%)	40 (49.4%)	12 (40.0%)		
Threat to government credibility	0 (0.0%)	4 (3.6%)	6 (6.7%)	2 (1.7%)	3 (3.7%)	2 (6.7%)		
Threat to racial relations	0 (0.0%)	0 (0.0%)	0 (0.0%)	0 (0.0%)	1 (1.2%)	1 (3.3%)		
International aids	1 (1.7%)	1 (0.9%)	0 (0.0%)	1 (0.8%)	1 (1.2%)	0 (0.0%)		
Joint efforts on controlling the disease	1 (1.7%)	4 (3.6%)	9 (10.0%)	7 (5.9%)	1 (1.2%)	4 (13.3%)		
Medical investigation of the disease	3 (5.0%)	5 (4.5%)	3 (3.3%)	2 (1.7%)	8 (9.9%)	3 (10.0%)		
Individual survival or heroic action/stories	1 (1.7%)	3 (2.7%)	4 (4.4%)	1 (0.8%)	3 (3.7%)	2 (6.7%)		
Others	14 (23.3%)	28 (25.0%)	26 (28.9%)	25 (21.2%)	15 (18.5%)	1 (3.3%)		
Total	60 (100.0%)	112 (100.0%)	90 (100.0%)	118 (100.0%)	81 (100.0%)	30 (100.0%)		

*** $p < .001$.

analyses. According to the results, all of the three economic variables were significantly negatively correlated to the "threat to economy" news frame ($r = -.40, p < .001$ for GDP per capita; $r = -.34, p < .001$ for trade; $r = -.37, p < .001$ for foreign direct investment). This opposite direction seems to be caused by the data from the United States and Canada. Thus, it seems that although the economic status of these two countries is higher than that of other countries, they made infrequent use of the "threat to economy" news frame, compared to other countries, particularly China. This may be due to the hysteria of American people which led to overreaction to the disease and therefore focused their attention on the public health perspective (Siegel, 2005). To assess this argument, correlation analysis was rerun after excluding these two countries. The results produced somewhat different relationships between economic factors and the "threat to economy" news frame. While a significant negative correlation between GDP per capita and the frame remains ($r = -.20, p < .01$), a significant positive correlation between trade and the frame was found ($r = .22, p < .01$). This paradoxical finding from the rerun analysis was probably due to the mixed role of China. While now being considered one of the twin engines of the world economy, China remains a poor country in terms of GDP per head. Therefore, while China as a trade giant is positively correlated with the corresponding use of the "threat to economy" frame, China as a poor GDP-per-capita country is negatively associated with the use of the same news frame. As to the relationship between foreign direct investment and the frame, no significance was found from the reanalysis.

In terms of the number of SARS cases as an event-oriented factor, we hypothesized that the more SARS cases the nation reported, the more likely the "threat to public health" news frame would be used in its newspapers. Once again, the opposite result was found. As shown in Table 9.4, the number of SARS cases was negatively related with the "threat to public health" frame ($r = -.21, p < .001$). Hypothesis 2 was not

Table 9.4 Pearson Correlations among Independent and Dependent Variables

	Threat to Economy	Threat to Public Health	Threat to Government Credibility	Individual Survival or Heroic Action
GDP per Capita	−.40***	.20***	.10*	.07
Trade	−.34***	.16**	.11*	−.08
Foreign Direct Investment	−.37***	.18**	.12*	−.05
Number of SARS cases	.38***	−.21***	−.06	−.12*
Political Control	.42***	−.18**	−.11*	−.17**

N = 372
* $p < .05$, ** $p < .01$, and $p < .001$

supported. America appears to account for these results even though it suffered few human losses from the disease, but the *Times* devoted much space to this perspective.

RQ3 and RQ4 examine the potential influences of political control on news framing. It turns out that significant negative correlations occur between political control and the "threat to government credibility" frame (RQ3, $r = -.11$, $p < .05$) and political control and the "individual survival or heroic action" frame (RQ4, $r = -.17$, $p < .01$). For RQ3, the outcome is most likely due to the unexpected, relatively high frequency of China's *People's Daily* use of "threat to government credibility" frame. This unanticipated result may have led to a sign reversal, from positive to negative. As pointed out earlier, while Singapore's *Straits Times* seemed to behave in accordance with its government control, the Chinese daily seemingly failed to follow suit and, instead, churned out quite a few news items that addressed the frame of "threat to government credibility." We would reason that *People's Daily*, the official mouthpiece, would have helped cover up the disease and remained mum about its government's wrongdoings.

As to RQ4, the outcome could be due to the simple consideration of human interest as a news criterion. After all, newspapers would simply eulogize any heroic behavior that drives up human spirits and collective social well-being. The human-interest consideration seems supported by the data in which the *New York Times* used the heroic frame only once as the dominant news frame on the front page when its home country indeed barely suffered from, though scared by, the epidemic. This particular outcome, however, is in conflict with that of Luther and Zhou (2005), who rejected their hypothesis that the human-interest news value would lead the Chinese elite press to have more coverage of individual heroic behavior, compared to the U.S. elite dailies; they found instead that the latter devoted slightly more than the former to that perspective even though the difference is far from being statistically significant.

However, it is important to note that the insignificant relations associated with the two news frames may in part be due to their very low frequency, which caused the corresponding correlations tests to become less robust and their outcomes much weaker.

Discussion and Conclusions

The SARS epidemic was a tragedy for individuals and families, and it illustrated the vulnerability of global health systems and economies. The ease and efficiency of transcontinental travel have created conditions for future epidemics of this sort, and medical science will be severely tested with each new such outbreak. Moreover, the epidemic had profound implications for businesses and governments not just in afflicted nations but also in countries with close political and trade ties with them. Reports of empty hotels and planes served as the barometers of conditions in the industries of tourism and travel and of the lack of confidence travelers had in government responses to the disease. This negative influence on the travel industry hit countries at both ends.

News organizations face special challenges in these situations. On the one hand, they have a professional responsibility to accurately report sources of danger to citizens and to critique governmental responses that are inadequate. On the other, a substantial body of literature shows news organizations often reflect national priorities, values, and agendas, even in political systems characterized by high degrees of press freedom and autonomy (e.g., Bennett, 1990; Entman, 1991; Herman & Chomsky, 1988). Legitimate threats to a nation, whether in the form of military invasion, terrorism, or disease, pose a threat to the political and economic viability of the system, and thus to the ability of the press to balance its dual roles of reporting information and reflecting national interests.

In the current study, we found key differences and similarities in news coverage of SARS in six nations affected by the disease. Far more people died of SARS in China and Hong Kong than other countries, and yet businesses suffered in nations at least to some extent because news reports led to diminished economic activities notably in the form of tourism and travel. First, SARS was far more likely to be framed as a "threat to public health" in Taiwan, Singapore, and Canada, than other countries. However, contrary to the hypothesis, the result showed that this disparity cannot be attributed to the number of SARS cases. Although the number of SARS cases in China and Hong Kong was far greater than in other countries, the "threat to public health" frame was adopted relatively less in those two places in terms of percentage, even though the public health frame remained dominant for the two political entities. Moreover, the United States as a noninfected country saw considerable coverage of the issue from this particular angle. Conceptually, research on risk management and international conflicts might help explain the potential shift in frames in the Chinese daily, and at least two possible explanations exist. First, the Chinese government tried to cover up the outbreak of the disease (Bowen et al., 2005; Wang, 2007) in an effort to sustain its economic growth via undisrupted foreign trade, foreign direct investment, tourism, and other types of economic activities, and therefore the news coverage was focused more on the epidemic's threat to the economy. But, when international conflicts occurred, in the form of cultural confrontations overseas, and continued to intensify, Chinese rulers were forced by the WHO and other world powers to uncover the black box that allowed world governments and health experts to scrutinize the reality of the epidemic, accordingly forcing the Chinese government and its news reportage to engage in discussing the public health perspective. As is widely known, racial tension in North America was heightened to the level of an international political confrontation, which resulted in Chinese immigrants in Toronto and other world cities being accused of importing the terrifying disease into those cities, and thereby posing a severe threat to other residents and economies (Bowen et al, 2005; Leslie, 2006). This public relations strategy, which aimed to avert the damaging international image of the Chinese government likely propelled its rulers to permit more and easier information flow (Qiu & Cameron, 2005). As a result, Wang (2007) criticizes the Chinese government for caring more about its political gains than about its populace's public health. Also, under the ultimate oversight of the Chinese government, Hong Kong, while controlling its own economic leverage, could have been forced to act in line with the Chinese central government in reporting the disease.

It turned out that newspaper coverage in China and Hong Kong was far more likely to emphasize SARS as constituting a "threat to the economy" than in other countries, in terms of frequency. Nevertheless, the level of adoption of the "threat to economy" frame did not show significant correlations with economic indicators—GDP, trade, and the FDI. This finding perhaps derives from China's rapid economic growth and its interest in economic development. Thus, maybe China as a trade giant but a poor GDP-per-head country exerted opposite impacts via it's press coverage.

Furthermore, U.S. news coverage placed much less emphasis on the "threat to the economy" frame than on the "threat to public health" frame, even though this epidemic appeared to have a greater impact on its economy than on its public health. It could be that American news media overemphasized the seriousness of the disease and thus concentrated on the public health-related perspectives. It was very likely to be the case, as Siegel (2005) argues, that Americans suffering from an "epidemic of fear" were inclined to become terrified by unknown contagious diseases given that the United States suffered few human losses from this disease compared with the casualty level in other places, such as China. This unspeakable fear, Siegel further claims, was also shown in the "crises" of anthrax and avian flu, which led its populace to unreasonable panic. In short, according to Siegel, Americans were infected more by the fear of the disease than by the disease itself. In addition, rather than SARS, the war in Iraq was the most urgent issue facing the United States, and U.S. newspapers at that time dedicated much of their space to the war in Iraq. It is possible that reporting of the war in Iraq would have affected coverage of SARS in a different way in America compared to other countries. The long-lasting preoccupation with the Iraq war as a front-page headline news story probably crowded out the SARS issue as being more newsworthy. As the data showed, the *New York Times* had devoted the least effort—in terms of average number of news items on front pages and of news spaces in the first sections—to this health crisis. As a result, this variation might help explain the rejection of the two hypotheses. Thus, adopting the public arena model in a future study is recommended in order to analyze news frames in conjunction with contextual factors. The model (Hilgartner & Bosk, 1988) suggests that issues gain public attention and salience from a very competitive and limited capacity of public arenas such as news media, if its persuasiveness, refreshment, importance, and interest to the arena and the public are sustained. In short, claim-makers' PR efforts along with the characteristics of the media and the audience should be taken into account.

Finally, it is well to remember that the potential influence of political control on the "threat to government credibility" and the "individual survival" frames might have been lost due in part to the low frequency of the two frames. Moreover, use of the "individual survival" frame could be a simple reflection of human interest as a commonplace news value. As to the "threat to government credibility" frame, the Chinese daily's unexpectedly heavy reportage of the perspective due to its shifting risk management strategy—from purposeful cover-up to unwilling open-up—may have also erased the impact of political control on selecting the frame.

Although empirical implications are limited, this study shows some differences and similarities in the news coverage among the countries and allows us to reconsider possible contextual factors that influence news frames. Clearly, further research is needed to delve into possible explanations for these content analytic findings, and to further study coverage of issues in other countries both within and outside the Asian and the North American region. As the results suggest, it is necessary to elaborate the study by controlling potential confounding cultural, economic, and journalistic variables, whenever possible, in examining the impact of contextual factors on news frames. This type of research will eventually lead to a greater understanding of the relationship between culture and news, and will shed particular light on the role of various contextual factors in shaping the frames that reporters use in their daily routines.

References

Ahern, T. J. (1984). Determinants of foreign coverage in U.S. newspapers. In R. L. Stevenson & D. L. Shaw (Eds.), *Foreign News and the New World Information Order* (pp. 217–236). Ames: Iowa State University Press.

Akhavan-Majid, R., & Ramaprasad, J. (1998). Framing and ideology: A comparative analysis of U.S. and Chinese newspaper coverage of the fourth United Nations Conference on Women and the NGO forum. *Mass Communication & Society, 1*(3–4), 134–152.

Barnett, G., & Kim, J. H. (2005). *A structural analysis of international conflict from a communication perspective.* Paper presented to the International Communication Association, New York City.

Bennett, W. L. (1990). Toward a theory of press–state relations in the United States. *Journal of Communication,40,*103–25.

Berkowitz, D., & Gavrilos, D. (2001). *News of terrorism in Israel through an American lens.* Paper presented to the Association for Education in Journalism and Mass Communication, Washington, DC.

Bouzid, A., & Stoll, I (2003, May/June). The other war: A debate. Questions of balance in the Middle East. *Columbia Journalism Review, 54–57.*

Bowen, S., Heath, R., Lee, J., & Li, F. (2005). *Narratives of the SARS epidemic and ethnical implications for public health crises.* Paper presented to the International communication Association, New York City.

Chang, K. K. (2006). *Constructing a theoretical framework for sourcing pattern: A case study on selection of news sources in Israeli-Palestinian conflict.* Paper presented to the Political Communication Division, ICA, Dresden, Germany.

Chang, K. K., & Freedman, E. (2008). *Political contest, news bias and the Israeli–Palestinian conflict: How and why rival official sources were unevenly treated in four major U.S. newspapers?* Paper presented to the International Communication Division, AEJMC, Chicago.

Chang, T. K., & Lee, J. W. (1992). Factors affecting gatekeepers' selection of foreign news: A national survey of newspaper editors. *Journalism Quarterly,* 69(3), 554–561.

Chang, T. K., Shoemaker, P. J., & Brendlinger, N. (1987). Determinants of international news coverage in the U.S. media. *Communication Research,* 14, 396–414.

Chang, Y. L., & Chang, K. K. (2003). World editorials on the Sept. 11 terrorist attacks: Integrating news flow analysis in international communication and framing analysis *International Communication Bulletin, 38,* 42–60.

Chong, M. (2006). A crisis of epidemic proportions: What communication lesions can practitioners learn from the Singapore SARS crisis? *Public Relations Quarterly, 51,* 6–11

Dupree, J. D. (1971). International communication: View from "A window on the world." *Gazette, 17,* 224–235.

Edelman, M. (1993). Contestable categories and public opinion. *Political Communication, 10,* 231–242.

Entman, R. M. (1991). Framing US coverage of international news: Contrasts in narratives of the KAL and Iran Air incidents. *Journal of Communication,* 41(4), 6–27.

Entman, R. M. (1993). Framing: Toward clarification of a fractured paradigm. *Journal of Communication, 43,* 51–58.

Freedom House. (n.d.). Press freedom rankings 1994–2002 in Excel format. Retrieved October 24, 2003, from http://www.freedomhouse.org/research/ratings.XLS

Gamson, W. A. (1989). News as framing. *American Behavioral Scientists, 33,* 157–161.

Gamson, W. A. & Modigliani, A. (1987). The changing culture of affirmative action. In G. B. Braungart & M. M. Braungart (Eds.), *Research in Political Sociology* (pp. 137–177). Greenwich, CT: JAI Press.

Gastil, R. D. (2003). *Freedom in the world: The annual survey of political rights and civil liberties 2002–2003.* New York: Freedom House.

Gilboa, E. (2006). Media and international conflict. In J. G. Oetzel & S. Ting-Toomey (Eds), *The Sage handbook of conflict communication* (pp. 596–626). Thousand Oaks, CA: Sage.

Gitlin, T. (1980). *The whole world is watching: Mass media in the making and unmaking of the new left.* Berkeley, CA: University of California Press.

Goffman, E. (1974), *Frame analysis: An essay on the organization of experience.* Berkeley: University of California Press.

Golan, G., & Wanta, W. (2003) International elections on US network news: An examination of factors affecting newsworthiness. *Gazette. 65*(1), 25–39.

Herman, E. S., & Chomsky, N. (1988). *Manufacturing consent: The political economy of the mass media.* New York: Pantheon Books.

Hilgartner, S., & Bosk, C. (1988). The rise and fall of social problems: A public arenas model. *American Journal of Sociology, 94,* 53–78.

Huntington, S. P. (1993a). The clash of civilizations? *Foreign Affairs, 72,* 22–49.

Huntington, S. P. (1993b). If not civilizations, what? *Foreign Affairs, 72,* 186–194.

Huntington, S. P. (1996). *The clash of civilizations and the remaking of world order.* New York: Simon & Shuster.

Ishii, K. (1996). Is the U.S. over-reported in the Japanese press? Factors accounting for international news in the Asahi. *Gazette, 57,* 135–144.

Iyengar, S. (1991). *Is anyone responsible? How television frames political issues.* Chicago: University of Chicago Press.

Iyengar, S., & Simon, A. F. (1993). News coverage of the Gulf War and public opinion: a study of agenda-setting, priming and framing. *Communication Research, 20,* 365–383.

Kim, K., & Barnett, G. A. (1996). The determinants of international news flow: A network analysis. *Communication Research, 23*(3), 323–352.

Krippendorff, K. (2004). *Content analysis: An introduction to its methodology.* Thousand Oaks, CA: Sage.

Lee, C. C., & Yang, J. (1995). National interest and foreign news: Comparing U.S. and Japanese coverage of a Chinese student movement. *Gazette, 56,* 1–18

Lee, Y. L. (2005). Between global and local: The globalization of online coverage on the trans-regional crisis of SARS. Asian *Journal of Communication, 15,* 255–273.

Leslie, M. (2006). Fear and coughing in Toronto: SARS and the uses of risk. *Canadian Journal of Communication, 31,* 367–389.

Luther, C., & Zhou, X. (2005). Within the boundaries of politics: News framing of SARS in China and the United States. *Journalism & Mass Communication Quarterly, 82,* 857–872.

Massey, B. L. (2000). How three Southeast-Asian newspapers framed "the haze" of 1997–98. *Asian Journal of communication, 10,* 72–94.

McQuail, D. (2000). *Mass communication theory* (4th ed.). Thousand Oaks, CA: Sage.

Mishra, V. M. (1979). News from Middle East in five U.S. media. *Journalism Quarterly, 56,* 374–378.

Nnaemeka, T., & Richstad, J. (1980). Structured relations and foreign news flow in the Pacific region. *Gazette, 26,* 235–257.

Pan, Z., & Kosicki, G. M. (1993). Framing analysis: An approach to news discourse. *Political Communication, 10,* 55–75.

Qiu, Q., & Cameron, G. T. (2005). *A public relations perspective to manage conflict in a public health crisis.* Paper presented to the International Communication Association, New York City.

Riffe, D., Lacy, S., & Fico, F. (2005). *Analyzing media messages: Using quantitative content analysis in research.* Mahwah, NJ: Erlbaum.

Robinson, G. J., & Sparkes, V. M. (1976). International news in the Canadian and American Press: A comparative news Flow study. *Gazette, 22,* 203–218.

Scheufele, D. (1999). Framing as a theory of media effects. *Journal of Communication, 49,* 103–122.

Semetko, H. A., & Valkenburg, P. M. (2000). Framing European politics: A content analysis of press and television news. *Journal of Communication, 50,* 93–109

Shoemaker, P. J. & Reese, S. D. (1996). *Mediating the message: Theories of influences on mass media content* (2nd ed.). White Plains, NY: Longman.

Siegel, M. (2005). *False alarm: The truth about the epidemic of fear.* Hoboken, NJ: Wiley.

Ting-Toomey, S., & Oetzel, J. (2001). *Managing intercultural conflict effectively.* Thousand Oaks, CA: Sage.

Tuchman, G. (1978). *Making news: A Study in the construction of reality.* New York: Free Press.

United Nations Conference on Trade and Development's Foreign Direct Investment Database. (n.d.). Retrieved October 24, 2003, from http://www.unctad.org/Templates/Page.asp?intItemID=1923&lang=1

Valkenburg, P. M., Semetko, H. A., & de Vreese, C. H. (1999). The effects of news frames on readers' thoughts and recall. *Communication Research, 26,* 550–569.

Van Belle, D. (2000). New York Times and network TV news coverage of foreign disaster: The significance of the insignificant variables. *Journalism & Mass Communication Quarterly, 77,* 50–70.

Wang, X. (2007). For the good of public health or for political propaganda: *People's Daily* coverage of the Severe Acute Respiratory Syndrome epidemic. *China Media Research, 3,* 25–32.

Wanta, W., & Chang, K. K. (2001). Visual depiction of President Clinton in the international press after the release of Starr Report. *Visual Communication Quarterly, 8*(9–11), 14.

World Health Organization. (n.d.). Summary of probable SARS cases. Retrieved October 24, 2003, from http://www.who.int/csr/sars/country/table2003_09_23/en/

Wolfsfeld, G. (1997). *Media and political conflict: News from the Middle East.* Cambridge, England: Cambridge University Press.

Wolfsfeld, G. (2004). *Media and the path to peace.* Cambridge, England: Cambridge University Press.

Wu, H. D. (2000). Systematic determinants of international news coverage: A comparison of 38 countries. *Journal of Communication, 50*(2), 110–130.

Chapter 10

News as Culture

A Comparative Study of Newspaper Coverage of the War in Iraq

Salma I. Ghanem

Since the war in Iraq began in 2003, the performance of the media in terms of war coverage has been the target of much condemnation. Criticism of media coverage is not new, but it became even more scathing after the events of September 11 and the second invasion of Iraq. Massing (2003) came down hard on American reporters and claimed that they didn't ask any of the tough questions for fear of reprisal from the Coalition Media Center and that the reporters were submissive to the Pentagon and the White House. He indicated that the British press did a much better job in terms of war analysis. Others criticized the media for serving as propaganda tools and as mouthpieces for the administration. According to Hackett (2001), the dominant frame in U.S. media coverage since the 9/11 attacks has been that of total support of government rhetoric and action.

Many scholars ripped the media's claim of objectivity by providing evidence of the American media's tendency to rally behind the government. According to Seib (2004), "...objectivity in war reporting is skewed from the start, distorted by boosterism that is dressed up as 'patriotism'" (p. 31). Fahmy (chapter 7 this volume) also reiterates that the media often frame international news in a patriotic framework. MSNBC in particular was criticized because of its focus on tales of American bravery (Massing, 2003), while CNN was repudiated for helping perpetuate official viewpoints and for functioning as a source of propaganda and disinformation (Vincent, 1992). Interestingly, some claim that CNN International offered more serious accounts than the American version (Massing, 2003). Coe, Domke, Graham, John, and Pickard (2003) also assert that the news media frequently align closely with national themes emanating from political leaders and reminded their readers that the networks incorporated the colors of red, white, and blue in their promotions. Jensen (2004) pointed out that every time the phrase "Operation Iraqi Freedom" appeared in the corner of the television screen, the news media were endorsing the administration's claims about the motives for war.

Some critics went so far as to state that: "The world is watching two entirely different wars" (Seib, 2004 quoting Saad, 2004). Others claimed that Europeans and Americans have different views partly because they see different news. And that U.S. cable news, in particular, seems to be reporting about a different world than the one covered by foreign media (Krugman, 2003). Others claim that U.S. coverage of the Middle East is distorted because reporters lack an understanding of the region and thus coverage of the first Persian Gulf War presented the triumph of image over reality (Mowlana, 1995).

The purpose of this study is to investigate the claims presented by the media critics by examining the coverage of the war in the U.S., British, French, and Arab media. This content analysis compares the coverage using framing as the theoretical underpinning. By comparing home-team coverage, this study illustrates the various cultural and ideological prisms through which news is reported.

News and Ideology

In 1959, Wilbur Schramm published a book titled *One Day in the World's Press*. The book consisted mainly of articles in 14 newspapers published on Friday, November 2, 1956. On that day, two international crises were taking place. Soviet units were threatening Hungary, and the British, French, and Israelis were about to engage in a full-scale war with Egypt because of its president's policy on the Suez Canal. No two newspapers in the collection were alike in their coverage for each one carried "many of the qualities of their nations" (p. 5). Schramm points out that each paper provided a different picture and slant for events. He also points out that each paper used a different prism to filter events and that some aspects of an event might be left out entirely. Schramm's thesis indicates that news is a rhetorical artifact. It is the message about an event and not the actual event. All rhetorical artifacts, and the news is no exception, serve as evidence of ideology which provides the values, beliefs, and interpretations of the world for a particular group or culture (Foss, 1996). Snow and Benford (1988) propose that societies have their cultural heritage in the form of cultural narrations, stories, myths, and folk tales which function to inform events and experience. The news as a cultural narrative is "produced by people who operate, often unwittingly, within a cultural system, a reservoir of stored cultural meanings and patterns of discourse" (Schudson, 1995, p. 14). Journalists tend to reflect broad cultural assumptions about reality (Haque, 1995). Reese (2001a) considers ideology as the ultimate level in the hierarchy of influences on media content.

Ideology provides the framework through which events are represented. This representation is not necessarily a conscious process on the part of journalists but rather an assumption about the social world in which news must be embedded. Thus, news reports are generated out of a limited ideological matrix (Hackett, 1984). Durham (1998) indicates that journalists bring an ideological perspective to the framing table in their attempts to determine the dominant frames of news stories, thus reifying the legitimacy of certain interpretations over others. Journalism like any other narrative form is essentially ideological and the news does not just transmit facts but also the attitudes, beliefs, and values of its makers (Johnston-Cartee, 2005).

From a critical perspective, some see the news as favoring those in power and reflecting the needs of certain groups over others (Molotoch & Lester, 1974). Steuter (1990) examined the coverage of terrorism in *Time* magazine in 1986 and found that ideology is manifested in terrorism news through semantics, language, headlines, social and historical context, treatment of objectives, trivialization, and amplification of violence. He concluded that the coverage of terrorism is not a neutral representation and by relying on authority sources, the coverage mirrors conservative ideologies and an "Us versus Them" mentality.

Framing and Ideology

Hyun (2004) classifies frames into deep frames, working frames, news frames, and individual (audience) frames. Deep frames represent deep-rooted belief systems or culture. Gamson (1988) argues that cultural themes "transcend the particular issue in question and suggests [a] broader world view" (p. 167), and that media frames reproduce the dominant political culture. The link between ideology and frames ties into McCombs and Ghanem's (2001) discussion of micro- and macroattributes, with frames serving as efficient bundling devices of microattributes, which, in turn, can be thought of as macroattributes. A frame possesses gestalt qualities derived from cultural and ideological assumptions. Culture can be defined as the stock of commonly invoked frames (Entman, 1993).

This comparative study of the coverage of the war in Iraq in Arab, British, French, and U.S. media provides evidence of the ideological differences in media coverage. According to Entman (1991),

> comparing media narratives of events that could have been reported similarly helps to reveal the critical textual choices that framed the story but would otherwise remain submerged in an undifferentiated text. Unless narratives are compared, frames are difficult to detect fully and reliably, because many of the framing devices can appear as "natural," unremarkable choices of words or images. (p. 6)

For example, a study comparing *The New York Times* and *The Guardian* found that British reporters used as sources Al-Jazeera affiliated personnel and Muslim nonofficials much more than their American counterparts. The British newspaper also gave more positive coverage of Al-Jazeera than did *The New York Times* (Kim & Jang, 2004).

The News and the Construction of Reality

This macroprism through which news is transmitted shapes the reality provided to the reader or the viewer. Communication thus creates reality and there is no single reality or objective truth (Johnston-Cartee, 2005). "Every narrative account of reality necessarily presents some things and not others; consciously or unconsciously, every narrative makes assumptions about how the world works, what is important, what makes sense, and what should be" (Schudson, 2003, pp. 35–36). In addition, "Frames are the focus, a parameter or boundary, for discussing a particular event. Frames focus on what will be discussed, how it will be discussed and, above all, how it will not be discussed" (Altheide, 2002, p. 45).

The frames used by journalists "assign meaning to and interpret relevant events and conditions" (Snow & Benford, 1988, p. 198). The media do not reflect reality but frame reality through their selection and rejection of what is covered and how it is covered (Hackett & Zhao, 1994). Frames organize social events and structure the social world (Goffman, 1974; Reese, 2001b; Tuchman, 1978). The media frame issues through the way they select and organize information (Altheide, 2002; Gamson & Modigliani, 1989). Similarly, Tankard, Hendrickson, Silberman, Bliss, and Ghanem (1991) view framing as "a central organizing idea for news that supplies a context and suggests what the issue is through the use of selection, emphasis, exclusion, and elaboration" (p. 5). Frames make it possible for news reporters to package information to their readers while ultimately supporting society's ideology. Framing, according to Iyengar (1991), alters the presentation of issues and thus promotes a particular definition of the issue, its causes, and possible solutions (Entman, 1993; Pan & Kosicki, 1993).

Consequences of Frames

The public relies predominantly on the media for its information, and, in foreign affairs, the media have been its sole source of information (Cohen, 1963; Hafez, 2000). Most politicians also make it a point to keep abreast of media coverage (Paletz & Entman, 1981). The media are very effective in shaping social definitions that govern social action (Altheide, 2002). Studies have shown that the media do set the public agenda, particularly in foreign affairs. More importantly the presentation of reality through the media could lead audiences to have different reactions in how they evaluate a problem (Entman, 1993). The way journalists present and frame issues impacts public understanding and policy formation (Pan & Kosicki, 1993). Even subtle differences in coverage can alter the way people understand problems and thus their level of support for public policy (Gandy, Koop, Hands, Frazer, & Phillips, 1997). Experimental studies have also demonstrated how the emphasis given to competing frames is reflected in subjects' interpretations of the issue manipulated (Nelson, Clawson, &Oxley, 1997; Price, Tewksbury, & Powers, 1997).

If minor alterations in the frames presented can affect the way people react to issues, it would be logical to conclude that the world looks different to people because of what they read and see in the media. Framing of the news, influenced by ethnocentricity and cultural conditions, often results in diametrically opposed coverage in different countries (Hafez, 2000).

Coverage of the Iraq War

Researchers have examined the coverage of the war in different countries and have found that the media frame the war differently in each country, reflecting its interests.

Lee (2004) compared the coverage of the Iraq War in *The New York Times, The Arab News,* and *The Middle East Times* and indicated that the various newspapers reflected their national interests in their coverage of the war. The U.S. paper emphasized U.S. war efforts and cited primarily U.S. officials, while the Arab newspapers cited Arab sources primarily and devoted more space to antiwar voices. Lee also concluded that *The Arab News* and *The Middle East Times* were not as critical of U.S. interests in the Gulf region and the U.S–Israel relationship as expected.

The differences in media coverage should be even more apparent in this study because Lee's study examines newspapers published in English in the Arab world whose audience is not really the Arabs. Lee himself indicates that the papers he examined serve a predominantly expatriate community. According to Lee, *The Arab News'* audience is 85% non-Arab.

Dimitrova and Connolly-Ahern (2007) compared the Web sites of prestige news media in the United States, United Kingdom, Egypt, and Qatar and the results of the content analysis revealed that the Arab media used the military conflict and violence of war frame more than the other sources. The Coalition media, on the other hand, emphasized the rebuilding of Iraq frame.

Aday, Cluverius, and Livingston (2005) and Aday, Livingston, and Hebert (2005) also examined the coverage of the war in U.S. broadcast news and on Al-Jazeera and noted that the U.S. media tended to focus on the victory frame and provided very little coverage of the dissent against the war which took place both in the United States and elsewhere. The Arab channel, on the other hand, mentioned the dissent against the war in 6.7% of its articles. In addition the U.S. media hardly covered international diplomacy or the role of the United Nations, while Al-Jazeera included them in 13% of its stories. In addition, the researchers concluded that the majority of all reports in the media examined were considered objective.

Other researchers also conducted comparative studies but focused on embedded and nonembedded American reporters. Their study revealed that news stories reported by embedded reporters tended to be more episodic in nature and contain more positive messages (Pfau, Haigh et al. 2004; Pfau, Wittenberg et al., 2005).

Schudson's (2003) suggestion of examining the "what," "who," and "why" of an event can be used to summarize the literature on the war coverage and help categorize the frames used in the different media in this study. Researchers have found differences in what was covered, with the American media focusing more on the military frame (Lee, 2004) and the Arab media focusing more on international diplomacy or the political frame (Aday Cluverius, & Livingston, 2005). In terms of the who, both U.S. and Arab reporters relied on sources from their own countries (Lee, 2004). The different media also focused on different players, with the Arab media giving more coverage to antiwar protestors than the American media (Aday, Cluverius, & Livingston, 2005; Lee, 2004). The researchers also indicate that the mention of casualties was minimal in U.S. media.

The purpose of this paper is to compare coverage of the war in Arab, British, French, and U.S. media in both tone and frames used. In terms of tone, if media coverage indeed reflects the dominant ideology, then the American newspaper's coverage, for example, will reflect the Bush administration's position and would be more in favor of the war than that of Arab media. Most Arab governments opposed the war and called for a political solution even after the battles began. The French held a similar position. The British media would be more difficult to characterize because even though the British government was part of the coalition forces, public opinion was for the most part against the war. In terms of frames, the study will examine the coverage in the four newspapers in terms of what was covered, who was covered, and an additional category dealing with "why" or the reasons given for the invasion.

In addition to comparing coverage and identifying the different frames and thus ideology, this study helps fill a void in media studies pertaining to the examination of Arab media (Lee, 2004). Recently, scholars have started developing an interest in the Arab media, especially the Qatar-based Al-Jazeera channel (Fahmy & Johnson, 2007; Seib 2008).

Methods

This study examined the coverage for a 17-day period immediately before and after the second invasion of Iraq in 2003 in four newspapers of record: *The New York Times, Le Monde, The Guardian*, and *Al-Ahram* (the leading Egyptian newspaper). The Egyptian newspaper was selected because it is considered an important source for understanding what is happening in the Middle East from the Arab point of view (Nasser, 1990). The study examined the coverage from March 11 through March 27. The bombing of Iraq started on March 19 and was covered in the newspapers on March 20.

The examination of the coverage focused on the amount and placement of the coverage. It also examined whether the coverage was positive, neutral, or negative. According to the critics, the media tend to reflect the dominant political ideology. Although the critics tend to focus on the American media, this research will attempt to discover whether the government positions in the United States, United Kingdom, France, and the Middle East are apparent in news coverage. The assumption is that the U.S. coverage will be positive while that of the Egyptian and French newspapers will be negative because these two countries opposed the invasion. The British paper, on the other hand, will be more neutral in coverage to reflect the contradictory positions of the government and British public opinion.

H1a. There will be more positive coverage of the war in the U.S. newspaper, followed by the British, the French, and the Egyptian paper.

The reverse should also be apparent:

H1b. Negative coverage of the war will be higher in the Egyptian and French papers, followed by the British newspaper and the American paper.

The media tend to reflect the official viewpoint through the sources they use (Aday Cluverius, & Livingston, 2005; Vincent, 1992). This study will also examine the country of origin of the sources used to determine the reliance of each newspaper on American, Arabic, French, and British sources.

H2. Each newspaper will quote more sources from its country/region of origin than other papers.

Schudson (2003) suggests that "to understand news as culture, how-ever, requires asking what categories of person count as a 'who,' what kinds of things pass for facts or 'what,' what geography and sense of time is inscribed as 'where' and 'when,' and what counts as an explanation of 'why'" (p. 160). Using Schudson's suggestions, this paper examined a variety of frames using the "who," "what," and "why" as an organiz-ing principle. The "who" was examined by focusing on the portrayal of Saddam Hussein, who was presented in the press during the 1991 Per-sian Gulf War as a criminal and a beast. Corcoran (1992) indicated that Hussein was demonized in the press and Lang and Lang (1994) indicate that Hussein was linked to Hitler. This paper will compare the negative portrayal of Hussein in the four newspapers with the assumption that he was portrayed more negatively in the American and the British media. After all, Hussein was an Arab leader and the Egyptian newspaper will not be as critical of him as its American or British counterparts.

H3. The negative coverage of Hussein in the American and British news-papers will exceed that of the Egyptian newspaper.

The "who" in this war goes beyond the leaders and extends to the casualties in military and civilian personnel. Critics claim that the American media did not do an adequate job of covering Iraqi casualties in either Gulf war (Aday, Livingston, & Herbert, 2005; Youssef, 2004). Because Egypt and France opposed the war, this study predicts that the Egyptian and the French newspapers will devote more coverage to Iraqi casualties while the American newspaper will focus more on American and coalition forces casualties. The British newspaper's coverage of casu-alties will be more equally divided between Iraqi and coalition forces.

H4a. The Egyptian and French newspaper will focus more on Iraqi casualties while the American newspaper and British newspapers will focus more on coalition forces casualties.

In addition, the American and the British media will focus more on the bravery of the coalition forces than Egyptian and the French papers.

H4b. The American and the British media will give more coverage to the bravery of the coalition military forces than the French and Egyptian newspapers.

In addition, the study focused on other players in the conflict by examining the amount of coverage given to antiwar demonstrations, positions of other countries, the role of the United Nations. The men-tion of Israel in conjunction with the war will also be examined. The assumption is that the American and British media will focus less on antiwar demonstrations and more on other countries' support for the war than the Egyptian and French media to boost their administrations' prowar stance. Similarly, the Egyptian and French media will focus more on the other countries' opposition to the war than the American and British media to show that the coalition forces are acting in isolation.

H5. The American and the British media will focus less on antiwar demonstrations, less on other countries' opposition to the war, and more on other countries' support for the war than the Egyptian and French media.

Following the same rationale, the French and the Egyptian media will devote more space to the role of the United Nations. In addition, the American media and the British media will focus less on the United Nations because of their administrations' disregard to its resolutions. It is also hypothesized that the Egyptian media will mention Israel and the Palestinian conflict more often than the other three because for Arabs, every conflict in the Middle East involves the Israeli–Palestinian conflict.

H6. The American and British media will focus less on the United Nations than the Egyptian and French media.

H7. The Egyptian media will focus more on the Israeli-Palestinian conflict than the British, French, and American media.

The "what" will be investigated by examining the overall context used for the coverage. The military frame seems to be the frame of choice for the U.S. media in times of war (Aday, Livingston, & Herbert, 2005). Security was paramount in the rationale that the administration provided for the war. In addition, many opposing the war worried about the costs and the economic implications. Previous studies have also showed that in the American media international diplomacy or the political frame was almost entirely absent while the Arab media devoted a substantial portion to the political frame (Aday, Livingston, & Herbert, 2005). This study will examine whether the war was framed in political, economic, military, or security frames.

RQ 1. What is the context used to cover the war in each newspaper?

The "why" will be examined by focusing on the reasons given for the war in the four newspapers. The Arabs and the French see the war as an imperialist, colonialist move to ensure the interests of the United States in the region (Sachs, 2003) while the United States and Britain touted the war as a vehicle to democratize Iraq and free the Iraqi people.

RQ 2. What are the main reasons for the war as indicated in the four newspapers?

Results

All articles printed in the 17-day period were examined for the four newspapers from online sources and the total number of articles for that period amounted to 1,874. Intercoder reliability was established at .86. Because only the researcher could code in Arabic, the intercoder reliability was determined on 15% of the English-language papers. *The New York Times* published 23% of those articles, *The Guardian* published 24%, *Al-Ahram* newspaper published 24%, and *Le Monde* published 25.1% of the articles. Because total coverage for the newspapers varied, comparisons will be provided using percentages of total articles published by each newspaper. Out of all the articles published in *The New York Times*, 20.6% were located on the front page, while 31.4% of war articles were published on the front page of *Al-Ahram*, and only 8.2% of war articles were published on the front page of *The Guardian*. The researchers could not determine the number of articles located on the front page of *Le Monde* because the online articles did not include page numbers. Table 10.1 lists whether the article overall was supportive of the war, neutral, or against the war.

Hypothesis 1a stated that there will be more positive coverage of the war in the U.S. newspaper, followed by the British, the French, and the Egyptian paper. Hypothesis 1a was supported. The American paper provided more positive coverage of the war, followed by the British, the French, and the Egyptian newspaper. As for the negative coverage of the war, the British, French, and Egyptian newspapers were around 31% while the *New York Times* was only at 14.4% and thus hypothesis 1b, negative coverage of the war will be higher in the Egyptian and French

Table 10.1 Percentage of Articles per Paper that were Supportive, Neutral or Against the War

	For the War	Neutral	Against the War	Total
The New York Times	7%	78.7%	14.4%	100% (N=431)
The Guardian	3.3%	65.6%	31%	100% (N=449)
Al-Ahram	.8%	68.1%	31.2%	100% (N=523)
Le Monde	2.6%	65.7%	31.7%	100% (N=470)

$X^2 = 71.02$ p < .001

papers, followed by the British newspaper, was partially supported. The overwhelming tone of coverage for all papers was neutral, ranging from the *Guardian* at 65.6% to *The New York Times* at 78.7%. This finding supports Aday, Livingston, and Herbert's (2005) finding that both the U.S. and the Arab media were neutral in coverage.

Hypothesis 2 stated that each newspaper will quote more sources from its country/region of origin than other papers. Hypothesis 2 was partially supported. Each newspaper, with the exception of the French paper, relied on sources from its own country more than sources from other countries. The *New York Times* relied on American sources 70% of the time, *The Guardian* relied on British sources approximately 52% of the time, and the Egyptian newspaper relied on Arabic sources 36.1% of the time. *Le Monde*, on the other hand, relied on American sources more than it did on French sources. Because most articles include more than one source and possibly sources from different countries, articles were coded for each country in the study.

Table 10.3 examines frames by focusing on the coverage of the "who" in the war as suggested earlier by Schudson (2003). The table displays the amount of negative coverage of Hussein, the amount of coverage devoted to Iraqi and U.S. casualties, Iraqi infrastructure, and American military heroics. Specifically, hypothesis 3 asserted that negative coverage of Hussein in the American and British newspapers will exceed that of the Egyptian newspaper. Hypothesis 4a claimed that the Egyptian and French newspaper will focus more on Iraqi casualties while the American newspaper and British newspapers will focus more on coalition casualties. Finally, hypothesis 4b stated that the American and the British media will give more coverage to the bravery of the coalition military forces than the French and Egyptian newspapers.

Hypothesis 3 was supported. The *New York Times* and *The Guardian* devoted over eight times as much coverage to negative portrayals of Hussein as *Al-Ahram*. In terms of casualties, hypothesis 4a was partly supported where the Egyptian newspaper reported Iraqi casualties twice as much as the American newspaper. *The Guardian*, on the other hand,

Table 10.2 Sources

	American	British	Arabic	French	Other
NY Times	70.1%	8.4%	15.8%	3.2%	17.4%
The Guardian	30.1%	52.3%	14.3%	3.8%	14.9%
Al-Ahram	28.9%	10.9%	36.1%	4.8%	20.1%
Le Monde	29.7%	8.9%	15.5%	17.4%	24.2%
	$X^2 = 229.84$ $p < .001$	$X^2 = 397$ $p < .001$	$X^2 = 100.15$ $p < .001$	$X^2 = 93.93$ $p < .001$	

Table 10.3 Portrayal of Hussein, mention of Iraqi/coalition casualties, Iraqi, and American heroics

	Demonizing Hussein	Iraqi Casualties	Coalition Forces Casualties	Coalition Heroics
NY Times	6.5%	7%	18.6%	6.5%
The Guardian	6.9%	17%	12.1%	3.4%
Al-Ahram	.8%	12.6%	4.0%	0
Le Monde	5.9%	9.3%	5.3%	.4%
	$X^2 = 26.7$ $p < .001$	$X^2 = 25,44$ $p < .001$	$X^2 = 71.91$ $p < .001$	$X^2 = 80.95$ $p < .001$

reported more on the Iraqi casualties than the Egyptian, the American, or the French newspapers. The American and the British newspapers reported substantially more on the casualties of the coalition forces than did the Egyptian and the French papers.

Once the war started, the *New York Times* included stories of coalition forces military heroics in over 6% of its articles, the British in 3.4%, the French in only 4% of articles, while the Egyptian newspaper never mentioned them at all. Thus, hypothesis 4b is also supported. Even though there are differences in coverage, the amount of coverage given to coalition military heroics did not exceed 6% in the American media. One has to keep in mind that this study examined the coverage before and after the war for a total of 17 days and thus the incidence of heroism could be rather few in number.

Table 10.4 continues with "who" was covered and provides the percentages of articles that mentioned antiwar demonstrations, the pro- and antipositions of international governments, the United Nations, the Iraqi position, and the Israeli–Palestinian conflict. Specifically, hypothesis 5 posited that the American and the British media will focus less on

Table 10.4 Coverage of anti-war demonstrations, governments that are pro-war, governments that are anti-war, the United Nations and the Israeli-Palestinian conflict

	Anti-War Demon-strations	Governments Pro-War	Governments Anti-War	United Nations	Israeli-Palest. Conflict
NY Times	11.8%	4.6%	15.3%	19.5%	5.8%
The Guardian	11.6%	4.2%	15.4%	31.9%	7.6%
Al-Ahram	14.1%	2.3%	24.1%	26.8%	13.8%
Le Monde	17.6%	10%	15.3%	38.6%	8.3%
	$X^2 = 9.045$ $p < .05$	$X^2 = 31.73$ $p < .001$	$X^2 = 19.85$ $p < .001$	$X^2 = 42.89$ $p < .001$	$X^2 = 21.15$ $p < .001$

antiwar demonstrations, less on other countries' opposition to the war, and more on other countries' support for the war than the Egyptian and French media. Hypothesis 6 contends that the American and British media will focus less on the United Nations than the Egyptian and French media.

Finally, hypothesis 7 states that the Egyptian media will focus more on the Israeli–Palestinian conflict than the British, French, and American media.

There was a three to six percentage difference in coverage of antiwar demonstrations between the Egyptian and French papers and the American and British papers. In terms of coverage of other countries' prowar stance, the British and American newspapers published double the amount of such coverage as the Egyptian paper. Interestingly, the French newspaper had the highest percentage of articles on other governments' prowar stance. As for articles mentioning other governments' antiwar stance, the Egyptian paper took the lead at 24% while the three Western papers were around 15%. Thus hypothesis 5 was partially supported.

In terms of coverage of the United Nations, hypothesis 6 was partially supported with the United States focusing the least on the role of the United Nations. Hypothesis 7 dealing with the Egyptian media focusing the most on the Israeli–Palestinian conflict was supported.

Table 10.5 examines the context for the war. It examines whether the article focused on the political, economic, military, or security frame. Research Question 1 asked what is the context used to cover the war in each newspaper?

The French newspaper used the political frame the most with almost 45% of articles taking a political twist. The American paper used the political frame the least with only 26.2% of articles using the political frame. Once again this result confirms the results by Aday, Livingston, and Herbert (2005) that an international diplomacy frame was minimal in the American media. The military frame and the security frames were used the most by the American paper. Once again these findings support other studies on the military frame being the frame of choice

Table 10.5 Context Used for Coverage of the War

	Political	Economic	Military	Security
NY Times	26.2%	13.5%	40.4%	8.6%
The Guardian	37.4%	18.2%	35.9%	1.1%
Al-Ahram	38.2%	13.8%	36.5%	2.5%
Le Monde	44.8%	18%	31.4%	.2%
	$X^2 = 34.19$ $p < .001$	n.s.	$X^2 = 7.93$ $p < .05$	$X^2 = 64.98$ $p < .001$

Table 10.6 Reasons for the Invasion

	US Interests	Iraqi Interests	Get Rid of Weapons	To Help Israel
NY Times	20.8%	33.3%	45.8%	0%
The Guardian	21%	43.5%	35.5%	0%
Al-Ahram	71.2%	13.6%	10.2%	5.1%
Le Monde	58.8%	14.7%	26.5%	0%

$X^2 = 58.71, p < .001$

for the American media (Lee, 2004). In addition to supporting previous research, these findings indicate that the war was seen differently in different parts of the world. In many places, people called for a political resolution to the war while the United States emphasized the need for military action as a way to guarantee its security.

Table 10.6 examines the frames in terms of the "why" or the reasons for the invasion. Research Question 2 asked: what are the main reasons for the war as indicated in the four newspapers?

The reasons for the invasion varied greatly by newspaper with the Arabic and French newspapers portraying the war as serving American interests while the American and British papers indicated that the war was waged to serve Iraqi interests. Getting rid of weapons of mass destruction was given more prominence by the American paper, followed by the British, French, and Arabic papers. The Egyptian newspaper alone provided the rationale for the war as somehow helping Israel, and it only focused a little attention on that possible reason.

Discussion

This content analysis lends quite a bit of support to the notion that the war is different depending on which country's media you follow, and also lends empirical evidence to the criticisms waged against the U.S. media. Obviously all four newspapers devoted quite a bit of their newshole to war coverage. Most articles in the newspapers were neutral and thus followed the rules of objectivity. Although few articles supported the war, we do note a difference between the amount of support provided by each newspaper. For the countries involved in the war, the support for the war was higher than for those countries opposed to the war. *The New York Times* was supportive of the war in 7% of its articles, *The Guardian* in 3.3%, while *Le Monde* and *Al-Ahram* were only at .8 and 2.6% respectively. Even though the number of articles for all four papers that objected to the war was greater than those in support of the war, the objection was more evident in countries that opposed the war, such as Egypt and France. In the British paper, coverage seemed to echo the public's opposition to the war. The Egyptian, French, and British papers included approximately 31% of articles classified as antiwar, while only 14.4% of articles in the American paper were opposed to the war. The low percentage of antiwar articles in the American newspaper is further evidence that the media support the position of the government (Jensen, 2004; Massing, 2003).

This content analysis also revealed that newspapers rely on official sources and thus tend to reflect their government positions (Steuter, 1990). The American newspaper relied the most on ethnocentric sources with 70% of sources in the *Times* coming from American sources, namely officials. The *Guardian* relied on British sources over 50% of the time. Even though the Egyptian newspaper relied heavily on official sources, those sources were distributed much more evenly among American, Arab, British, French, and other sources.

Even though the majority of articles examined appeared to be neutral, frames and subsequently ideology should not be equated with objectivity. Frames and ideology can be revealed in terms of what is selected and emphasized, but also what is excluded (Entman, 1993; Tankard et al, 1991). The focus on coalition casualties was much more evident in the countries supporting the war. In addition, the *Times* downplayed the casualties inflicted on Iraqis, lending support to the critics that claim that Iraqi suffering was underemphasized in the American media (Aday Livingston, & Herbert, 2005; Fahmy & Johnson, 2007; Seib, 2004). Too much focus on the harm inflicted by the war could lead to public opinion turning against the government. The British paper, on the other hand, covered the Iraqi casualties even more than the Egyptian paper. The Egyptian paper never mentioned the heroics of the coalition forces, and the American paper's coverage of heroics was almost double that of the British newspaper. Hussein was portrayed much more negatively in the *Times* and in *The Guardian*, lending support to media critics that the media demonized Hussein to bolster their governments' position. By focusing more on certain players, the media tend to reflect the ideology of their country.

In addition, the Egyptian and French newspapers focused more on the antiwar stance by international governments, thus selecting information that provides support for their governments' positions, while the American and British newspapers focused more on those countries with a pro-war stance for the same reason. The role of the United Nations was more apparent in the French newspaper, reflecting the government's position that the United States should not invade Iraq without the UN permission (Sciolino, 2003). The mention of Israel and the Israeli–Palestinian conflict was much higher in the Egyptian press, supporting the claim made earlier that in the minds of the Arab world, all conflicts in the area involve Israel (Jacobs, 2007).

In terms of the context provided for the coverage, some differences do emerge. *The New York Times* used the security frame more extensively, thereby reflecting the administration's "War on Terror." This frame lends some credence to Kellner's statement that the mainstream media served as a mouthpiece for U.S. foreign policy (1993). Also, *The New York Times* provided less emphasis on the political context of the invasion as compared to the French and Egyptian papers whose governments pleaded for a political solution for the conflict.

The major difference that the content analysis revealed was in terms of the "why" or reasons given for the invasion of Iraq. *The New York Times* and *The Guardian* emphasized Iraqi interests as the main reason for the invasion. Such interests included democratizing and liberating Iraq and helping the Iraqi citizens get rid of Saddam Hussein. The second reason provided by the American and British papers was to get rid of weapons of mass destruction. The Egyptian and the French newspapers, on the other hand, focused on U.S. interests as the rationale for the war. In addition the Egyptian newspaper cited Israel's security as another reason for the war. Israel was never mentioned as a rationale for the war in the American, British or in the French newspaper.

Conclusion

This preliminary study provides quite a bit of evidence that indeed the "World was watching two different wars." The difference was revealed by the "who," "what," and "why" each newspaper decided to emphasize. Major differences were found in the rationale for the war and thus problem definition and causes for the invasion were revealed by comparing the narratives produced by different countries reflecting the ideological makeup of the country of origin. The British and the American papers provided similar rationales for the war as compared to the Egyptian paper. Based on the sources used, all four countries can be accused of boosterism and propaganda reflecting nationalistic perspectives. The role of Israel in any Middle East conflict is much more paramount in the minds of Arabs, as evidenced in the rationale for the war.

This study focused only on four newspapers from four different countries and yet significant differences in coverage emerged that reflected the different perspectives on the conflict and perhaps explain why it is so difficult for different political entities to reach resolutions. Each entity is dealing with a different frame of reference, and the conflicts will continue unless more overlap in perspectives is reached.

References

Aday, S., Cluverius, J., & Livingston, S. (2005). As goes the statue, so goes the war: The emergence of the victory frame in television coverage of the Iraq war. *Journal of Broadcasting & Electronic Media, 49*, 314–331.

Aday, S., Livingston, S., & Herbert, M. (2005). Embedding the truth: A cross-cultural analysis of objectivity and television coverage of the Iraq war. *The Harvard International Journal of Press/Politics, 10*, 3–21.

Altheide, D. L. (2002). *Creating fear: News and the construction of crisis.* New York: Aldine de Gruyter.

Coe, K., Domke, D., Graham, E., John, S., & Pickard, V. (2003, August). *Beyond good and evil: The binary discourse of George W. Bush and an echoing press.* Paper presented at the meeting of the Association for Education in Journalism and Mass Communication, Kansas City, MO.

Cohen, B. (1963). *The press and foreign policy.* Princeton, NJ: Princeton University Press.

Corcoran, F. (1992). War reporting: Collateral damage in the European theater. In H. Mowlana, G. Gerbner, & H. I. Schiller (Eds.), *Triumph of the image: The media's war in the Persian Gulf—A global perspective* (pp. 106–117). San Francisco: Westview Press.

Dimitrova, D., & Connolly-Ahern (2007). A tale of two wars: Framing analysis of online news sites in coalition countries and the Arab world during the Iraq war. *The Howard Journal of Communications, 18*, 153–168.

Durham, F. D. (1998). News frames as social narratives: TWA flight 800. *Journal of Communication, 48*, 100–117.

Entman, R. M. (1991). Framing U.S. coverage of international news: Contrasts in narratives of the KAL and Iran air incidents. *Journal of Communication, 41*, 6–27.

Entman, R. M. (1993). Framing: Toward clarification of a fractured paradigm. *Journal of Communication, 43*, 51–58.

Fahmy, S., & Johnson, T. J. (2007). Show the truth and let the audience decide: A web-based survey showing support for use of graphic imagery among viewers of Al-Jazeera. *Journal of Broadcasting & Electronic Media, 51*(2), 245–252.

Foss, S. (1996). *Rhetorical criticism: Exploration and practice.* Prospect Heights, IL: Waveland Press.

Gamson, W. (1988). The 1987 distinguished lecture: A constructionist approach to mass media and public opinion. *Symbolic Interaction, 11*(2), 161–174.

Gamson, W. A., & Modigliani, A. (1989). Media discourse and public opinion on nuclear power: A constructionist approach. *American Journal of Sociology, 95*, 1–37.

Gandy, O., Jr., Koop, K., Hands, T., Frazer, K., & Phillips, D. (1997). Race and risk: factors affecting the framing of stories about inequality, discrimination and just plain bad luck. *Public Opinion Quarterly, 61*, 158–182.

Goffman, E. (1974). *Frame analysis.* New York: Free Press.

Hackett, R. A. (1984). Decline of a paradigm? Bias and objectivity in news media studies. *Critical Studies in Mass Communication, 3*, 229–259.

Hackett, R. (2001). Covering up the "war on terrorism." The master frame and the media chill. *Canadian Business and Current Affairs, 8*(3), 8–11.

Hackett, R. A., & Zhao, Y. (1994). Challenging a master narrative: Peace protest and opinion/editorial discourse in the U.S. press during the Gulf War. *Discourse and Society, 5*, 509–541.

Hafez, K. (2000). International news coverage and the problems of media globalization: In search of a "New Global-Local Nexus." In K. Hafez (Ed.), *Islam and the west in the mass media: Fragmented images in a globalizing world* (pp. 3–24). Cresskill, NJ: Hampton Press.

Haque, M. (1995). Elements of cross-cultural communication and the Middle East. In Y. R. Kamalipour (Ed.), *The U.S. Media and the Middle East* (pp. 16–24). Westport, CT: Praeger.

Hyun, K. (2004, August). *Framing frames: Locations of frames and their connections in signifying processes.* Paper presented at the meeting of the Association for Education in Journalism and Mass Communication, Toronto, Canada.

Iyengar, S. (1991). *Is anyone responsible? How television frames political issues.* Chicago: University of Chicago Press.

Jacobs, M. (2007, July 17). Mideast madness: Region lacks a culture of conflict resolution and compromise. *Toronto Sun,* p. 18.

Jensen, R. (2004). The military's media. In R. W. McChesney & B. Scott (Eds.), *Our unfree press: 100 years of radical media criticism* (pp. 430–435). New York: New Press.

Johnston-Cartee, K. S. (2005). *News narratives and news framing: Constructing political reality.* New York: Rowman & Littlefield.

Kellner, D. (1993). The crisis in the Gulf and the lack of critical media discourse. In B. Greenberg & W. Gantz, (Eds.), *Desert Storm and the mass media* (pp. 37–47). Cresskill, NJ: Hampton Press.

Kim, N., & Jang, S. (2004, August). *Reporting Al-Jazeera's close encounter with U.S. militarism: A comparative content analysis.* Paper presented to the meeting of the Association for Journalism and Mass Communication Education, Toronto, Canada.

Krugman, P. (2003, February 18). Behind the great divide. *New York Times,* p. A23. http://www.nytimes.com

Lang, G. & Lang, K. (1994). The press as prologue: Media coverage of Saddam's Iraq, 1979–1990. In L. Bennett & D. Paletz (Eds.), *Taken by storm: The media, public opinion, and U.S. foreign policy in the Gulf War* (pp. 3–7). Chicago: University of Chicago Press.

Lee, C. (2004, August). *News coverage of U.S. war in Iraq: A comparison of The New York Times, The Arab News, and the* Middle East Times. Paper presented at the meeting of the Association for Education in Journalism and Mass Communication, Toronto, Canada.

Massing, M. (2003, May 29). The unseen war. *The New York Review of Books,* pp. 16–19.

McCombs, M., & Ghanem, S. (2001). The convergence of agenda setting and framing. In S. Reese, O. Gandy, & A. Grand (Eds.), *Framing in the new media landscape* (pp. 67–82). Mahwah, NJ: Erlbaum.

Molotoch, H., & Lester, M. (1974). News as purposive behavior: On the strategic use of routine events, accidents and scandals. *American Sociological Review, 39,* 101–12,

Nasser, M. K. (1990, December). Egyptian mass media under Nasser and Sadat: Two models of press management and control. *Journalism Monographs, 124,* 1–26.

Paletz, D. L., & Entman, R. (1981). *Media, power, politics.* New York: Free Press.

Pan, Z., & Kosicki, G. M (1993). Framing analysis: An approach to news discourse. *Political Communication, 10,* 55–76.

Pfau, M. Haigh, M. Gettle, M., Donnelly, M. Scott, G., Warr, D., & Wittenberg, E. (2004). Embedding journalists in military combat units: Impact on newspaper story frames and tone. *Journalism & Mass Communication Quarterly, 81,* 74–88.

Pfau, M., Wittenberg, E., Jackson, C., Mehringer, P., Lanier, R., Hatfield, M. et al. (2005). Embedding journalists in military combat units: How embedding alters television news stories. *Mass Communication & Society, 8,* 179–195.

Price, V., Tewksbury, D., & Powers, E. (1997). Switching trains of thought: The impact of news frames on readers' cognitive responses. *Communication Research, 24,* 481–506.

Reese, S. (2001a). Framing public life: A bridging model of media research. The convergence of agenda setting and framing. In S. Reese, O. Gandy, & A. Grant (Eds.), *Framing in the new media landscape* (pp. 7–31). Mahwah, NJ: Erlbaum.

Reese, S. (2001b). Understanding the global journalist: A hierarchy-of-influence approach. *Journalism Studies, 2,* 173–187.

Sachs, J, (2003, August 13). The real target of the war in Iraq was Saudi Arabia. *Financial Times,* p. 17.

Schramm, W. (1959). *One day in the world's press: Fourteen great newspapers on a day of crisis.* Stanford, CA: Stanford University Press.

Schudson, M. (1995). *The power of the news.* Boston, MA: Harvard University Press.

Schudson, M. (2003). *The sociology of news.* New York: W. W. Norton.

Sciolino, E. (2003, March 11). Threats and responses: Discord; France to veto resolution on Iraq war, Chirac says. *The New York Times,* p. 10.

Seib, P. (2004). *Beyond the front lines: How the news media cover a world shaped by war.* New York: Palgrave Macmillan.

Seib. P. (2008). *The Al Jazeera effect: How the new global media are reshaping world politics* Dulles, VA: Potomac Books.

Snow, D., & Benford, R. (1988). Ideology, frame resonance, and participation mobilization. *International Social Movement Research, 1,* 197–217. Dulles, VA: Potomac Books.

Steuter, E. (1990). Understanding the media/terrorism relationship: An analysis of ideology and the news in *Time* magazine. *Political Communication and Persuasion, 7,* 257–278.

Tankard, J. W., Jr., Hendrickson, L., Silberman, J., Bliss, K., & Ghanem, S. (1991, August). *Media frames: Approaches to conceptualization and mea-*

surement. Paper presented at the meeting of the Association for Education in Journalism and Mass Communication, Boston, MA.

Tuchman, G. (1978). *Making news: A study in the construction of reality.* New York: Macmillan.

Vincent, R. C. (1992). CNN: Elites talking to elites. In H. Mowlana, G. Gerbner, & H. Schiller (Eds.), *Triumph of the image: The media's war in the Persian Gulf—A global perspective* (pp. 181–201). San Francisco: Westview Press.

Youssef, M. (2004, August). *Their word against ours: News discourse of the 2003 Gulf War civilian casualties in CNN and Al-Jazeera.* Paper presented at the meeting of the Association for Education in Journalism and Mass Communication, Toronto, Canada.

Chapter 11

Frame Building and Media Framing of the Joint Counterterrorism

Comparing United States–Uganda Efforts

Yusuf Kalyango Jr.

Global terrorism has become a daunting challenge for nations around the world, and scholars from the social and behavioral fields have invested considerable time in trying to understand this challenge.

This chapter examines how state actors propagate counterterrorism efforts and how the press frames such efforts, taking as examples *The New York Times* of the United States and *The Daily Monitor* of Uganda.[1] Before the August 1998 attacks on U.S. embassies in Nairobi, Kenya and Dar Es Salaam, Tanzania, the U.S.-sponsored joint counterterrorism efforts were concentrated on the countries of the Arabian Peninsula, South Asia, and the Middle East. The U.S. embassy bombings in East Africa were proof that terrorism could target U.S. assets and citizens anywhere, particularly in countries that were lax in their counterterrorism preparedness (Cronin, 2002). Since then, the United States has fostered joint counterterrorism efforts with some African states to empower them to combat international terrorism.[2] Thus, since 9/11, the United States has offered financial and technical support to East African countries to fight terrorism;, for instance $100 million was donated by America to the East African Counterterrorism Initiative (EACTI) in 2003 to cultivate cooperation among the Ugandan, Kenyan, and Tanzanian governments to fight international terrorism. Millions of dollars are disbursed annually to African governments through the Terrorist Finance Working Group (TFWG) to curb the flow of money from terrorist organizations to individuals (Silke, 2004). More monetary assistance in millions of dollars is channeled through the Anti-Terrorism Assistance (ATA) program to the East African governments to support their National Counterterrorism Centers (Copson, 2005). The U.S. sponsors counterterrorism missions to ensure that African nations such as Uganda do not become a haven for terrorists and international criminal activity.

The U.S. government's counterterrorism financing of African states such as Uganda is made on the reasonable assumption that those states also have terrorism problems that are similar to those faced by the United

States (Copson, 2005). However, this chapter is based on the idea that newspapers from unique political cultures, on different continents, face different terrorist threats, and report their domestic and international terrorism problems in different ways. It is important to study how joint counterterrorism goals across political cultures could be allied since such bilateral efforts involve monetary support and military technical assistance. The theoretical propositions, frame building, and media framing of terrorism attempt to address the idea that frame sponsors propagate their preferred interpretation of events by means of powerful, persuasive messages and actions of conflict aggravation through the press. The analysis focuses on how power persuasion and conflict aggravation differed in frames propagated from both countries by state actors and other interest groups. Drawing from Wanta and Kalyango (2007), terrorism is defined in this chapter as the unlawful use or threat of violence by disgruntled factions, which have an ethnic, religious, or political agenda against a state/states or a group of citizens, with intentions to impair, intimidate, frustrate, or coerce a government, individuals, or any sector thereof.

Terrorism

A comprehensive definition of terrorism is nonexistent and all scholarship contributes to its understanding through theory building and conceptualization (Sorel, 2003). Policy makers have propagated a definition of terrorism through a power persuasion schema that describes it as the use of fear, anxiety, destruction, and loss of life against random targets designed to cause aggravation to and challenge the authority of the state (Crenshaw, 1972, 1981). The term *terrorism* was coined to describe the systematic inducement of fear and the escalation of conflict by using acts or threats of violence to control and influence a civilian population (Crenshaw, 1981). Terrorists also have power persuasion attributes such as attracting media attention to their cause, appealing for sympathy, impressing an audience, or promoting the adherence of the faithful (Dershowitz, 2002; Wilkinson, 1997).

Differences in definitions and conceptualizations of terrorism in unique political cultures make the global war on terrorism a daunting task for state actors and the press (Sorel, 2003). With the enormous U.S. financing of antiterrorism missions in Uganda and other East African nations, one would expect some conventional policies in their joint counterterrorism efforts. Corsi's (1981) key work on terrorism as a desperate game showed how regimes that deny other able leaders access to power and persecute dissenters create dissatisfaction and motivate terrorism. International terrorism has been a bigger threat for democratic societies like the United States than for Third World nations because the developing nations are neither perceived as transnational cultural imperialists, unwanted external influences on the political economy of weaker states, nor as globalization exploiters (Corsi, 1981; Enders & Todd, 2000).

Terrorism in the United States

Terrorists who have targeted the United States, its property, and its citizens are portrayed by U.S. state actors through the media as irrational agitators, religion-inspired (Islamic) fundamentalists such as the Al-Qaeda and Taliban networks, fascists bent on undermining Western influence, and left-wing terrorists.[3] The left-wing terrorism factor refers to international movements such as communist movements during the Cold War, Marxist political philosophers, and others.

Terrorist acts that target U.S. citizens and their property occur as a result of anti-Westernism and Islamic fundamentalism (Cronin, 2002; Enders & Todd, 1999; Rapoport, 2001), which emanate from anti-Americanism, and are closely related to antiglobalization (Elliot, 2004; Enders & Todd, 2000). Anti-Americanism is also a result of dashed expectations and a heightened resentment of the perceived U.S.-led Western hegemonic system vis-à-vis other regions such as Africa. This kind of terrorist activity targets symbolic American targets to get public attention and to provoke a public outcry in the hope of upending U.S. foreign policy (Cronin, 2002). Fantu (2002) explained that this is due to a general belief that the United States is the primary driver of the powerful forces that result in globalization and Western influence.

Comparative political literature shows that international terrorists do not seek political power in the United States (Ballard, 2005). The threats and attacks are designed to win political leverage and express a desire to change U.S. foreign policy toward regions with disenfranchised groups such as the Middle East, the Arab world, Asia, and parts of Africa (Enders & Todd, 1999; Jenkins, 1986). In addition, Cronin (2002) concluded that the international terrorists' goal is to destabilize the strategic U.S. global leadership in the world by influencing and enlisting the weak and the disenfranchised to move against the United States.

Terrorism in Uganda

Since 2001, the Uganda government has condemned and prosecuted individuals suspected of committing acts of terrorism, using the Antiterrorist Act of 2002. Some of the clauses in the Act include violence characterized by spontaneity, instigation of mass participation in uprisings, a primary intent of physical destruction of state property, libel or defamation of the name of the president by the press, and treason. A notable example of how the Uganda government enforced the laws under this Act occurred in late 2005 when presidential candidate Dr. Kizza Besigye was arrested on charges of terrorism. During the 2006 presidential elections, Ugandan president Yoweri Museveni employed an extreme act of presidential coercion by bringing charges of terrorism against Dr. Besigye. He accused Besigye of leading an armed insurgency called the People's Redemption Army (PRA) against the state (president). The state also linked him to the Lord's Resistance Army (LRA) that had politically destabilized northern Uganda for the last 24 years and the Allied Democratic Forces (ADF) in Southwest of the country for the last 12 years (Rubongoya, 2007). The government registered the LRA and ADF with the U.S. Department of State in 2002 as terrorist organizations.

Upon his return from exile in October 2005, Besigye announced his intention to defeat Museveni in the presidential elections. Two weeks after his return, Besigye was incarcerated on charges of terrorism and concealment of treason (*The Daily Monitor*, November 15, 2005). Museveni ordered the same charges of terrorism and illegal possession of firearms to be brought against Besigye before the military General Court Martial (GCM). Museveni addressed the nation on state-owned television and reiterated that the state had received reliable information that Besigye planned a terrorist attack. He said Besigye's arrest prevented a coup and maintained peace (*The New Vision*, November 20, 2005).

Other opposition politicians were also arrested on the same terrorism charges in late 2005 during the presidential campaigns. Besigye spent the better part of his campaign in jail while Museveni vigorously campaigned for reelection. The terrorism case was dismissed by the Supreme Court and all other charges against Besigye were dropped by the state after the March 2006 General Elections. According to press reports, Besigye and his FDC party were considered by the government as a serious political and foreign relations threat to Museveni's political fortunes. That's why they declared him an international terrorist. Some opposition politicians told *The Daily Monitor* that the State House (official presidential palace) locked up Besigye to wreck his presidential ambitions (*The Daily Monitor*, December 14, 2005).

Apparently, Besigye was facing identical charges before both the High Court and a military tribunal—a duplication of charges. According to Besigye's lawyers, it meant that if their client was released by the High Court, he would be legally detained by the Court Martial and imprisoned in a military barracks. It turned out that the Court Martial did not have jurisdiction to try terrorism charges. Besigye's legal team challenged the twin trials in the Constitutional Court, calling the military hearing "a kangaroo court." The Anti-Terrorism Act 2002 says that charges of terrorism can only be tried by the High Court (*The Daily Monitor*, January 6, 2006).

The U.S. Department of State expressed deep concern about Besigye's arrest and illegal detention. In his statements to the press in Washington, DC, on November 17, the U.S. Department of State Deputy Spokesman, Adam Ereli, expressed disapproval of the Uganda government's behavior toward Besigye. He called on the government to carefully examine the basis for the charges against these opposition politicians and to honor Uganda's commitments to the International Covenant for Civil and Political Rights.

The Constitutional Court that ultimately handled the case ruled that the GCM was subordinate to the High Court. The court ruled that the trial of Besigye at the GCM on charges of terrorism and unlawful possession of firearms, with the ultimate penalty being death, contravened articles 22(1), 128(1), and 210 of the Uganda Constitution. Shortly after this ruling, President Museveni secured his reelection in March 2006. In April 2006, High Court Judge John Bosco Katutsi said in his ruling that the prosecution had "dismally failed" to prove its case against the opposition leader. "He is accordingly acquitted and set free forthwith."

The Uganda Antiterrorist Act of 2002 describes terrorism as a criminal, libelous act which aims, or is directed against, a state to instigate terror;[4] and "any act or threat of violence and unlawful opposition to state policy, which causes emotional anxiety to the person of the president and produces social defiance, is punishable under that law" (p. 11c). This law provides for a possible death sentence for anyone reporting and publishing news that is likely to promote terrorism (Rubongoya, 2007); three well-known journalists were prosecuted under this archaic law between 2006 and 2007. In August 2008, three other cases were under way in the High Court of Uganda, charging three politicians and a talk-show host (journalist) of terrorism for openly opposing the proposed government-sponsored Land Bill on national radio.

Frame Building and Media Framing

Framing refers to the typical manner in which news reporters and their editors shape content by selecting particular statements from state actors and other communication sponsors, based on some underlying structure of meaning. Reese (2007) noted that terrorism is a very important framing case of our time. The construction of terrorism is carried out by state actors who build the frames with a specific manifest message (Rachilin, 1998; Reese, 2007). Frame building takes place through specific ideology based on targeted persuasion of political or national security interests (Cooper, 2002). The process of building counterterrorism messages for the public sphere is largely done through an interaction between journalists and elites (Norris, Kern, & Just, 2003). It is the press that provides interpretations and meaning to such frames.

Frame building is used here as a communication process from state leaders and other message sponsors to structure meaning of the term *terrorist* and *terror* when combating international terrorism. Media framing deals with how journalists choose certain viewpoints of a political order from news sources such as state actors and other interest groups to provide meaning, in this case to terrorism and terrorist acts. It entails selecting and highlighting some facets of events in order to promote a particular interpretation, evaluation, or solution (Entman, 1993, 2003). The outcome of the frame building of terrorism is the frames manifest in the media through power persuasion.

In a recent study on the framing of terrorism, Norris et al. (2003) concluded that perceptions and evaluations of terrorism in the United States differ sharply between the political elite and the public. Entman (2003), for instance, found that the media portrayal of terrorism significantly contributes to what people think they know about it, which comes from the journalistic rationalization of terror that is built from elite influence and political persuasion. State actors build frames that influence how the press interprets and depicts terrorism (Norris et al., 2003). The routine begins with a consensual interpretation of events from political actors which is then passed on to the media (Nelson, Oxley, & Clawson, 1997).

Meanwhile, frame building and media framing relate to the persistent political culture of states and their regime types, which stress specific values, facts, and other considerations to shape content. In this case, frames are tied in with culture as a macrosocietal structure moderated by political actors, press systems, and interest groups (Van Gorp, 2007). Media framing also deals with how journalists choose certain interpretations of elite dissatisfaction and mass protests against the state to provide meaning to conflict aggravation in order to rationalize actions of disgruntled interest groups or "terrorists" (Cronin, 2002; Norris et al., 2003). Framing is thus an important approach for this comparison of two newspapers in two unique political cultures. State actors are political leaders in the executive and legislative arms of government, and interest groups refer to other frame sponsors such as terrorist organizations or individual terrorists.

Conceptualizing Frame Building

The two concepts of power persuasion and conflict aggravation are used to explain frame building of terrorism. Decades of research show that terrorists employ diverse strategies of ideological power persuasions and conflict provocations designed to influence change by inducement of threat, fear, or extreme violence (Crenshaw, 1981; Rapoport, 1984, 2001). In this case, state actors pursue their political–ideological persuasions about terrorism to frame the content for the media to shape public opinion (Jablonski & Sullivan, 1996). Other frame sponsors or interest groups (terrorists) expect the press to frame their messages as conflict aggravations to bring about a political advantage.

Political actors use their position of power to portray terrorists, at a macrolevel, as agitators for irrational beliefs such as socioeconomic opportunism, a power struggle for a particular political ideology, and radicalism against the status quo. Yet at a microlevel, the activities of terrorists may also elicit power persuasion through intense media coverage that sometimes frames their actions as struggles for power against the state as a result of elite dissatisfaction (Elliot, 2004; Rapoport, 1984). Figure 11.1 is a typology that illustrates an abstract concept of power persuasion in media framing of terrorism.

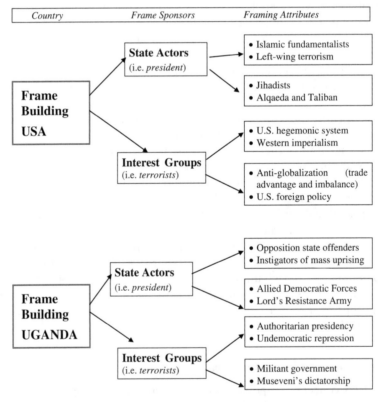

Figure 11.1 Power persuasion as applied to frame building of terrorism

*Figure 1 is a schematic representation of message construction derived from frame building. Both political actors and terrorists try to influence the framing of media messages. To test inter-coder reliability, two cases/codes in frame building were set up for the variable 'power persuasion': state actors = 1 and terrorists = 2, which were distributed in fixed cells/columns to thematically code (based on structural relationships of themes/concepts emerging from the frames) all the attributes.

The concept of power as an act of persuasion in Figure 11.1 illustrates how (in the Interest Groups column) terrorists commit or commission acts such as a political protest designed to cause political change. Terrorists single out the executive government or state institutions to blame for popular suffering as part of their campaign of political power persuasion. This political ideology is also propagated by state actors as a mobilization strategy in order to garner mass support against terrorists (Cronin, 2002). The executive branches of both governments, supported by the U.S. Congress or the Ugandan parliament (in the State Actors column) portray terrorists as agitators, religious fundamentalists, and nonconformists who use acts of violence to achieve their objectives (Okumu, 2007).

Terrorists draw on conflict aggravation because they can achieve certain instantaneous ends, such as general insecurity, disorientation of the public and the government, which attract media publicity. This concept has been tested by several students of terrorism such as Jenkins (1986) and Fantu (2002). Conflict aggravation relates to international terrorist actions such as kidnappings, bombings (mortars and suicide blasts), assassinations, barricades, hostage taking, armed attacks, and skyjackings directed toward the United States and her allies (Enders & Todd, 1999, 2000; Fantu, 2002).

On the contrary, some studies have shown that the media exaggerate the real risks of terrorism when framing conflict aggravation. Bassiouni (1981) argued that terrorists tailor their acts and choice of target to ensure media framing of the threats and underlying message to achieve terror-inspiring effects from political conflicts. Bassiouni analyzed the role of the media in handling terror–violence coverage. That study echoed the attributes of conflict aggression used by terrorists and their networks to spark mass dissatisfaction and elite discontent of the regime. He identified terrorism as including the use of the media to impress an audience, to promote the adherence of the faithful, and to dramatize a particular claim or grievance. Bassiouni stated that the overt fear inspired in the public by terrorist acts may be attributed to the media framing of conflict escalation.

Other studies on media coverage of terrorism tend to support the relationship between media coverage of terrorism and propagation of domestic political ideologies. For instance, Entman (2003) introduced the cascading activation concept that focused on the White House framing and promotion of the war against terrorism after 9/11 through the media. Entman analyzed stories in major U.S. newspapers and on network television and determined that the media guard the boundaries of culture and maintain domestic dissent within conventional bounds when covering crises like international terrorism. He found that during its campaign to attack Iraq in 2002, the White House deployed its power

Table 11.1 Conflict Aggravation from Frame Sponsors of Terror Incidents

Country	Conflict aggravation ->	Target of aggression
United States	• Airline hijacking →→→ • Hostage taking →→→→ • Suicide bombing →→→ • Kidnapping →→→→ • Car bombing →→→→ • Assassination →→→→	• Passenger commercial planes • U.S. journalists/ workers/troops • Civilians, U.S. citizens/troops • U.S. Citizens/tourists/polit. elites • State property/monuments/etc... • Diplomats /pol. elites/aid workers
Uganda	• Mutilation →→→→ • Arson →→→→ • Abduction/Rape →→→ • Barricades →→→→ • Protests/Demos →→→ • Hostages →→→→ • Libel /Treason→→→→	• Children and women • On homes in villages • Coercing boys and girls • On state & civilian vehicles • Against state autocracy/injustice • Women and children • Journalists/opposition/activists

* Frames for United States were drawn from terrorism literature as types of aggression and modes of conflict (Jenkins, 1986; Enders et al., 2000; Fantu, 2002).
* The frames for Uganda are anecdotal evidence from the Ugandan press (*The New Vision* & *The Daily Monitor*) which refer to aggression and modes of terror.
* In the Ugandan case, some conflict aggravations are state-inspired acts of aggression.

over the media to reassert frame building that would promote support for its proposed attack. Table 11.1 presents a typology that illustrates the concept of conflict aggravation from earlier literature on the antiterrorism challenges avowed by U.S. and Ugandan newspapers.

The Media, Politics, and Terrorism

The Western press, such as *The New York Times,* has covered state-sponsored and organizational terrorism in Africa. However, few studies have been conducted by Western scholars of terrorism and the media about the new terrorist breeding grounds in sub-Saharan Africa. The focus of antiterrorism research has been on Egypt, Libya, and more recently Somalia because most of the known terrorist activities in sub-Saharan Africa had not directly targeted Western governments and their property before the 1998 bombings in East Africa (Cilliers, 2003; Wanta & Kalyango, 2007). Seminal works on terrorism and the media examined the acts of terror, terrorists, and how governments use the media in their campaign to fight terrorism, fight freedom of the press, and promote censorship (Paletz & Schmid, 1992).

Recent contributions on media and terrorism addressed political aggression and the ways that sponsors of a particular terrorism frame shape messages for the media (Ballard, 2005). Hess and Kalb (2003) looked at freedom of information and how leaders build news frames that support international military action against terrorism. When terrorists attacked the United States on September 11, television coverage was heavy and continuous, with the victims, newsmakers, and emergency workers displaying emotionally charged reactions (Cho et al., 2003). According to Cho and colleagues (2003), television cameras were able to reveal the emotional reactions of television journalists and other contributors who shared a collective sense of shock, grief, and anger. The authors opined that by producing such intense coverage, people become emotionally aroused, using verbal and visual imagery of the unfolding terror events to provoke positive and negative factors such as aggression, blame, praise, satisfaction, and tenacity, among other factors. Hence, terrorists achieve their intended goals of winning media coverage and attention to their grievances or cause (Carey, 2002; Schudson, 2002) by means of conflict aggravation.

This chapter examines two central questions: Do state actors frame international terrorism and build the case for joint counterterrorism efforts differently in the United States and Uganda? How do *The New York Times* and *The Daily Monitor* frame the joint counterterrorism efforts in the two countries?

Methods

Data, Sampling, and Coding

A comparative content analysis was conducted to determine how terrorism was framed in *The Daily Monitor* and *The New York Times*. The data used were generated from LexisNexis academic search for *The Daily Monitor* and *The New York Times* index. The unit of analysis was a paragraph. News and feature stories published in both papers between December 31, 2002 and December 31, 2004 that contained the words *terror, terrorism, terrorists*, and *terrorist acts* were collected. The rationale for choosing these 2 years was that they were considered salient for the Bush administration's start of the global war against terrorism, as the U.S. troops deployed on the frontlines in Afghanistan and Iraq, and other U.S.-led foreign counterterrorism engagements. Second, several notable incidents framed as terrorism related in Uganda appeared in the Ugandan press during the same period after the enactment of the antiterrorism bill.

By using instruments of categorization (Stempel, 1989; Wimmer & Dominick, 2003), the study assessed the relevance of stories collected from both newspapers to the research question. A total of 179 stories were published by *The Daily Monitor* during that period on terrorism, and 674 stories were published by *The New York Times* on terrorism that occurred in the United States or against U.S. interests abroad and in Uganda. A sampling using the constructed week approach (Riffe, Aust,

& Lacy, 1993) ensured that all days of the week had equal chances of being represented, to arrive at the total of 200 stories from both newspapers in the sample.

One hundred stories were identified from *The Daily Monitor* and 100 stories from *The New York Times* during that period. To arrive at 100 stories for each newspaper, stories were eliminated from the sampling data due to lack of relevance to the theoretical concepts or because they were repetitive, were opinion pieces rather than news stories (Stempel, 1989), or lacked general suitability (Cresswell, 2003; Wimmer & Dominick, 2003). Data were coded by evaluating and dividing them into appropriate variable categories.

Frames were identified from hard news stories, feature stories, and staff writers' columns from each paragraph. Hard news stories included terrorist attacks that had just taken place and had been reported in the press as well as breaking news on terrorism; feature stories included reports from press briefings by state actors and follow-up stories on terrorist incidents; and the columns included stories from regular columnists who are staff writers of these papers or special contributors who wrote about conflicts or terrorism. Conflict aggravation variables, namely suicide bombings, airline hijackings, kidnappings, car bombings, assassinations, mutilations, arsons, abductions, raping/defiling, barricades, and others were coded to determine the correlation between *The Daily Monitor* and *The New York Times*. The frames examining power persuasion which were measured in units of terrorism attributes (e.g., radical jihadist, Islamic extremist, and others) were also coded to determine frame building from state actors and other frame sponsors.

Once the initial coding of 100 stories from *The Daily Monitor* and 100 from *The New York Times* was completed, two independent coders, both graduate students, were recruited to establish reliability. Coders were trained to acquaint them with Uganda's polity as well as style of news reporting and writing, and to ensure a common frame of reference. The intercoder reliability over a systematic subsample of 10% of the stories was calculated with Scott's *pi* formula (1955). The observed agreement of the overall intercoder reliability calculated was 86%.

Construct validity was obtained with chi square to determine the significant differences in frequencies of the categorical frames between *The Daily Monitor* and *The New York Times* when framing terrorism. Content construct validity refers to the degree to which inferences can justifiably be made from the operationalizations on which the initial assumptions were based (Angoff, 1988). The purpose of this statistical analysis was to determine which frames contributed to the differences in frame building and the media framing of international terrorism from both newspapers.

Results

Overall results in frame building of terrorism in terms of power persuasion and conflict aggregation showed significant differences between *The Daily Monitor* and *The New York Times*. Both conflict aggravation $\chi^2 = (1, N = 8) = 58.469, p < .000)$ and power persuasion $(\chi^2 = (1, N = 9) = 43.394, p < .000)$ frames were significantly different. As expected, actions and violent incidents framed as terrorism by *The Daily Monitor* that occurred in Uganda were significantly different from those in *The New York Times*.

Of the articles on suicide bombings and other bombings that were framed as terrorist attacks, 93% appeared in *The New York Times* and only 6.7% of the same frames appeared in *The Daily Monitor*. On the contrary, 95.5% of the frames that described raping and defilement of women as acts of terrorism appeared in *The Daily Monitor* while only 0.5% of similar frames were characterized as acts of terrorism in *The New York Times*. Results show that internal (civil domestic) mutilations (87.5%) and domestic arson (78.6%), which occurred in East Africa were among types of actions and violent incidents considered as acts of terrorism in *The Daily Monitor*. The same incidents received less attention: (12.5%) for internal (civil domestic) mutilations and (21.4%) for domes-

Table 11.2 Conflict Aggravation Frames and Frequencies – Uganda and USA

Conflict Aggravation Frames	Between newspapers		Within newspapers	
	NYT	DM	NYT	DM
Bombings	93.3	6.7	20.0	1.3
Airline hijacking	87.5	12.5	10.7	1.3
Arson	21.4	78.6	4.3	14.1
Assassinations	50.0	50.0	17.1	15.4
Barricades	66.7	33.3	8.6	3.8
Suicide Bombings	93.3	6.7	20.0	1.3
Kidnappings	40.7	59.3	15.7	20.5
Mutilations	12.5	87.5	2.9	17.9
Raping/Defilement	4.5	95.5	1.4	24.4
	Total: 100		Total: 100	

$$\chi^2(1, N=8)=58.469, p < .000$$

Total # of variable-freq.:	N = 70	→	N = 78	→	N = 148
Stories	N = 10	→	N = 10	→	N= 20
Paragraphs	N = 107	→	N = 131	→	N = 238

- Frequencies between newspapers are shown in percentages.
- NYT stands for *The New York Times* and DM stands for *The Daily Monitor*.

tic arson in *The New York Times*. One exception in conflict aggravation was on assassination (no matter where it occurred), which was similarly framed as an act of international terrorism in both newspapers.

Results show that Al-Qaeda terror cells dominated the content of international terrorism in *The New York Times*, appearing 37.2% of the time between December 31, 2002, and December 31, 2004. In contrast, Al-Qaeda terror cells in *The Daily Monitor* constituted 4.9% of all content characterized as international terrorism in the same period. Data show that incidents characterized as international terrorism that occurred in East Africa appeared 5.4% in *The New York Times* with the rest of 94.6% incidents that occurred in other regions. In *The Daily Monitor*, 16.5% of articles referred to the U.S.-led international counterterrorism efforts.

The Daily Monitor featured U.S. counterterrorism efforts more often than *The New York Times* featured counterterrorism efforts in Uganda. Ugandan state actors characterized the guerrilla rebellion in Northern Uganda [internal civil-political threat] as countering international terrorism. Such frames appeared in *The Daily Monitor* 88.9% of the time as counterterrorism efforts. In contrast, these incidents appeared 11.1% of the time in *The New York Times* but were framed as East Africa's domestic terrorism threats. As Table 11.3 shows, the frames frequently propagated and used in *The New York Times* as countering international terrorism were Islamic militants, radical jihadists, Al-Qaeda fighters, Islamic extremists, and Islamic terrorists and Islamic fundamentalists in global counterterrorism efforts. They were significantly different from those propagated by Ugandan state actors as international [external] terrorism threats in *The Daily Monitor*. Counterterrorism efforts reported in *The Daily Monitor* included responses to acts perpetrated by rebel leaders, bandits, irate (libelous) journalists, and other typical[5] criminals.

Discussion

The comparative examination of these two counterterrorism bedfellows has produced valuable results in understanding the challenges involved in combating international terrorism. The analysis compared the power persuasion and conflict aggravation frames in *The Daily Monitor* of Uganda and *The New York Times*. First, it was noted earlier in the introduction that the United States is leading transnational efforts, specifically investing financial and technical resources in East Africa to combat international terrorism.

The data reveal that the power persuasion of counterterrorism in Uganda is shaped differently by Ugandan state actors from the way it is shaped by the U.S. government. Hence the two newspapers framed

Table 11.3 Power Persuasion Frequencies and Frames – Uganda and USA

Power Persuasion Frames	Within newspapers		Between newspapers	
	NYT	DM	NYT	DM
Radical jihadism	9.3	1.6	80.0	20.0
Religious fundamentalism	7.0	1.6	75.0	25.0
Nonconformist	2.3	6.6	20.0	80.0
Fascism	2.3	8.2	16.7	83.3
Left-wing terrorism	7.0	6.6	42.1	57.9
Political agitation	7.0	18.0	21.4	78.6
Al-Qaeda terror cells	37.2	4.9	84.2	15.8
Guerrilla rebellion	7.0	39.3	11.1	88.9
Islamic extremism	20.9	4.9	75.0	25.0
Libelous journalism	00	8.2	0	100
	Total: 100		Total: 100	
	$(\chi 2(1, N=9)=43.394, p<.000)$			

Total # of variable-freq.:	N = 70	→	N = 78	→	N = 148
Stories	N = 10	→	N = 10	→	N= 20
Paragraphs	N = 107	→	N = 131	→	N = 238

- Frequencies between newspapers are shown in%ages.
- NYT stands for *The New York Times* and DM stands for *The Daily Monitor*.

both the internal and external threats of terrorism in different ways. For instance, *The Daily Monitor* reported that terrorists had committed atrocious and psychologically shocking acts of terrorism such as physical mutilation of Ugandan victims, cutting off ears and noses by rebels fighting a guerrilla war. Although this was an internal political rebellion, Ugandan state actors built the frames as fighting international terrorism and as part of global counterterrorism efforts.

The imprisonment of the Ugandan presidential candidate, Dr. Kizza Besigye, by the state as a terrorist during elections and the media framing of this political leader who heads a major opposition political party as a state terrorist is another example. Terrorism frames in *The Daily Monitor* included, but were not limited to: rebel insurgents killing civilians; acts of treason by opposition politicians; armed bandits robbing and occasionally murdering residents; carjacking "for economic gains"; and publication of "harmful" news that was said to promote rebel/civil conflicts against the government.

The provocations and violent incidents framed as terrorism in *The Daily Monitor* that occurred in East Africa were significantly different from those framed in *The New York Times*, such as kidnappings, abduction of diplomats, and rebel attacks. Most of these incidents were not framed as terrorism in *The New York Times*. This inconsistency in frame building of terrorism by state actors and in their respective newspapers shows that the U.S.-led joint counterterrorism efforts with Uganda were not executed in unison by the two cultures, by targeting international terrorists with similar traits. These significant differences in frame building of terrorism and media framing may bring into question the efficiency of the joint counterterrorism efforts.

The findings support arguments by Norris and colleagues (2003) and Entman (2003) that the news media guard the boundaries of culture and maintain a remarkably parochial stance even when covering international terrorism. There were several other instances where frames in *The Daily Monitor* indicated unique conflict aggravations unlike those in *The New York Times*. In Uganda for example, school children had been abducted by terrorists;[6] the boys were forced to join the rebellion against the government as freedom fighters and the girls were forced to serve as the rebel commanders' concubines. Rebel attacks on military barracks and exchange of fire in the jungles between the Uganda army and rebel fighters were also framed as terrorism in *The Daily Monitor*. The newspaper reported common patterns of Uganda's use of excessive force to quell protest or squash dissent, in some cases arresting journalists and also charging activists as terrorists in its counterterrorism efforts. These incidents do not appear on the long list of the U.S. Department of State's terrorism incidents in Uganda. However, Ugandan leaders framed these incidents and they were reported in *The Daily Monitor* as global counterterrorism efforts, a position which does not reflect the reality of the U.S.-led counterterrorism effort, the United States defining international terrorism in quite different terms from the way it was defined by the Ugandan government and media.

Coverage of internal threats, which are promoted by Ugandan leaders as global counterterrorism efforts, indicates inconsistent and contradictory frame building from state actors of both countries. It is therefore determined that the joint counterterrorism efforts between the United States and Uganda as well as their media do not reflect consistent efforts of to create a common front against international terrorism. In support of Schmid and Jongman (1988), literature and statutes on terrorism in these two countries and other counterterrorism allies reveal variations in statutes and policy implementation of counterterrorism efforts. Consistent with previous findings from Corsi (1981), Entman (2003), and Elliot (2004), the United States and her citizens are victims of a different conflict aggravation from many of the Third World countries allied with it in the global effort to jointly counter terrorism, since countries like Uganda also indict and prosecute actions of their political opponents and civil activists as terrorism.

"Terrorists" also build power persuasion frames such as fighting an autocratic state, a tyrant, political imbalance, military dictatorship, and so forth, and succeed in exploiting the frustrations of the ordinary people. The Uganda government, for example, declared the ADF an international terrorist group which destabilizes Uganda by kidnapping and murdering civilians in northern and western towns resulting in hundreds of deaths. When the government built its case against ADF, it eventually linked the rebel forces to powerful opposition politicians who are Members of Parliament representing major opposition political parties. The opposition politicians then used the press to provoke and shape media frames that captured the image of the ADF as liberators and revolutionary heroes whose major crime was to liberate citizens from President Museveni's "oppressive government."

Some disgruntled and deprived citizens end up believing in the "liberation cause" of violent activists and "terrorists" if their frame-sponsors succeed in getting constant coverage in the press. This happened when crowds protested the arrest and continued remand in custody of presidential candidate Dr. Besigye as a terrorist suspect. Government property was destroyed in the second wave of riots and this prompted police to unleash more tear gas and pepper spray at onlookers (*Daily Monitor*, November 23, 2005). Placards described Besigye as a liberator at a time when government was building its case to charge him as a terrorist (*Daily Monitor*, November 26, 2005). Both state and private businesses came to a standstill for one week following Besigye's continued incarceration.

Once political leverage or state power is attained, some present-day liberators and statesmen have been known to have once been former terrorists (Ahmad, 2001; Nathanson, 2004). These maladies of presidential supremacy and prosecution of politicians and activists as "international terrorists" as displayed by President Museveni of Uganda further weaken the legitimacy of a cohesive global fight against terrorism. Sometimes *The New York Times* framed as absolute truth the crackdown on political activists who were framed as terrorists in Uganda. The ADF is still listed as a terrorist organization but no known leader has ever been convicted by the Ugandan government, yet some prominent opposition politicians who were named ADF terrorists by the state in 2005 still loom large in the city and still served as opposition Members of Parliament in 2008.

Stories in *The Daily Monitor* on violations of human rights as a result of Uganda's Anti-Terrorism Act 2002 reflect arguments similar to findings from earlier studies by Enders and Sandler (2000) as well as Cronin (2002). The authors argued that circumstances also provide terrorists with compelling reasons to commit criminal acts while seeking political change. These latter assessments are proffered with a caution that they are precipitating assumptions not empirically supported by these data, and other causations are plausible.

Implications and Conclusion

The question of why there are these cross-political cultural differences despite joint counterterrorism efforts is salient and will continue to be debated beyond this assessment. It is apparent from these data that Uganda's power persuasion ideology on terrorism goes beyond fighting conventional international terrorism. Nonetheless, the United States continues its counterterrorism funding programs despite these differences that include significant disregard of human rights on the Ugandan part. Moreover, *The Daily Monitor* reported that Uganda's state actors have their own unique frame building of terrorism, which is used to fight domestic political contestation and civil conflicts. Thus, the implication could be that the U.S. counterterrorism program funds Uganda, which stifles domestic political competition and dissent using the Anti-terrorist Act 2002 to guarantee presidential supremacy.

Data collected in *The New York Times* during the period examined in this chapter had no editorial investigation as to why the U.S.-sponsored allies such as Uganda pursue different forms of antiterrorism not conventionally consistent with U.S. counterterrorism policies. Uganda should be seen as an example of a political culture marred by a history of presidential supremacy, which still hampers its democratic institutional building, this along with a defective joint counterterrorism effort. It is also important for the U.S. press to be cautious of stereotyping an international terrorist based solely on propaganda by other governments, due to the bifurcated antiterrorist laws and political efforts of some foreign leaders. The dislodging of the rule of law in Uganda during the 2005–2006 presidential elections on flawed international terrorism charges is an example of how leaders can easily manipulate antiterrorism laws for their own political benefit. As Okumu (2007) argued, these bifurcated antiterrorism laws are so broadly legislated that they have been used in Uganda to prosecute members of the civil society, such as trade unionists and independent journalists on terrorism charges without guarantees of a fair trial.

With this evaluation, it can be argued that these inconsistent power persuasion strategies in Uganda could lead to other social negatives, such as human rights violations, which may also engender mass protests, elite dissatisfaction, and terror from interest groups. It also appears that the joint counterterrorism efforts may sometimes increase anti-American sentiments in Third World nations where the rights of citizens are violated by leaders who use the U.S.-sponsored antiterrorism missions for their own political ends. According to editorials and commentaries from a variety of independent newspapers across Africa,[7] some governments on the continent, including Uganda, have allegedly used the enormous financial backing and technical support of the United States to thwart their political opponents. They have also prosecuted civil activists, protesters, and ethnoconflict dissidents under the disguise of the joint counterterrorism efforts.

This study has explored how state actors from two independent nations on separate continents build frames and how the press frame counterterrorism efforts. Power persuasion and conflict aggravation have also been introduced as testable framing concepts for understanding the political game of joint counterterrorism. This is by no means preordained as a comprehensive comparative analysis of frame building and media framing of the joint counterterrorism efforts, since several questions remain unanswered. Global joint counterterrorism efforts are a recent development, and the press should rise to the occasion to address this phenomenon. Future research should examine how the press can independently address these inconsistent counterterrorism efforts without a clear universal definition of terrorism. Why these differences exist despite joint counterterrorism efforts should be explored beyond this content analysis.

Because most governments that are engaged in joint counterterrorism efforts seek cooperation, understanding, and loyalty from the press in their efforts to curb terrorism (Perl, 1997; Wilkinson, 1997), a solution to this crisis is thus proposed: first, to create a universal intergovernmental news media pool on counterterrorism for the international press. Second, define the dynamics of joint counterterrorism efforts and develop policies that are recognized by and serve all nations, the international news media, and global interests. What Corsi (1981) predicted 25 years ago still stands the test of time. If the current trends of the global joint counterterrorism efforts continue unchanged, in a dyad of unique political cultures and coverage from distinctive systems, these findings potentially illustrate how the war on international terrorism may last for generations unabated.

Notes

1. The *Daily Monitor* is an independent, privately owned commercial newspaper. It steers away from government influence and propaganda in its coverage of national affairs. *The Daily Monitor* and the *New York Times* are widely respected and to a large extent influence public opinion in their respective countries.
2. This is contained in a (2004) memorandum presented to the U.S. House of Representatives by the U.S Department of State.
3. These portrayals are contained in memoranda from the U.S. State Department (August, 2004) and testimonies from the Department of Homeland Security (April, 2006) before the House International Relations and House Security Committees.
4. This clause is also reprinted in the *Ugandan Law Society Review* booklet (2004), 2(4).

5. These are people who commit misdemeanors like disobeying common law, habitual banditry, possession of unlicensed arms, and so forth.
6. Terrorists in that paragraph referred to the Lord's Resistance Army (LRA) rebel group, led by Joseph Kony, which operates from northern Uganda. The Ugandan government says that this terrorist group commits all of these atrocities as it tries to topple government using guerilla warfare and terrorism tactics.
7. The independent newspaper commentaries in Africa referred to here include the *Monitor* newspaper (Uganda), *The Daily Nation* (Kenya), *The Accra Mail* (Ghana), *The Star* (South Africa), *The Post* (Zambia), *The Guardian* (Nigeria), and *The Addis Tribune* (Ethiopia).

References

Ahmad, E. (2001). *Terrorism: Theirs and ours.* New York: Seven Stories Press.

Angoff, W. H. (1988). Validity: An evolving concept. In H. Wainer & H. I. Braun (Eds.), *Test validity* (pp. 19–32). Hillsdale, NJ: Erlbaum.

Ballard, J. D. (2005). *Terrorism, media, and public policy: The Oklahoma City bombing.* Cresskill, NJ: Hampton Press.

Bassiouni, C. M. (1981). Terrorism, law enforcement, and the mass media: Perspectives, problems, proposals. *The Journal of Criminal Law and Criminology, 72*(1), 1–51.

Carey, J. W. (2002). American journalism on, before, and after September. In B. Zelizer & S. Allan (Eds.), *Journalism after September 11* (pp. 71–90). London: Routledge.

Cho, J., Boyle, M., Keum, H., Shevy, M., McLeod, D., Shah, D. et al. (2003). Media, terrorism, and emotionality: Emotional differences in media content and public reactions to the September 11th terrorist attacks. *Journal of Broadcasting & Electronic Media, 47*(3), 309–327.

Cilliers, J. (2003). Terrorism and Africa. *Africa Securities Review, 12*(4), 91–103.

Cooper, A. H. (2002). Media framing and social movement mobilization: German peace protest against INF missiles, the Gulf War and NATO peace enforcement in Bosnia. *European Journal of Political Research, 41*, 37–80.

Copson, R. W. (2005). Africa: U.S. foreign assistance issues. *Congressional Research Service* (order code IB95052). Washington, DC: Library of Congress.

Corsi, J. R. (1981). Terrorism as a desperate game: Fear, bargaining, and communication in the terrorist event. *Journal of Conflict Resolution, 25*(1), 47–85.

Crenshaw, M. (1972). The concept of revolutionary terrorism. *Journal of Conflict Resolution, 16*(3), 383–396.

Crenshaw, M. (1981). The causes of terrorism. *Comparative Politics, 13*(4), 379–399.

Creswell, J. W. (2003). *Research design: Qualitative, quantitative, and mixed methods approaches.* Thousand Oaks, CA: Sage.

Cronin, A. K. (2002). Behind the curve: Globalization and international terrorism. *International Security, 27*(3), 30–58.

Dershowitz, A. (2002). *Why terrorism works*. New Haven, CT: Yale University Press.

Elliot, D. (2004). Terrorism, global journalism, and the myth of the nation state. *Journal of Mass Media Ethics, 19*(1), 29–45.

Enders, W., & Todd, S. (1999). Transnational terrorism in the post-cold war era. *International Studies Quarterly, 43*(1), 145–167.

Enders, W., & Todd, S. (2000). Is transnational terrorism becoming more threatening? A time-series investigation. *Journal of Conflict Resolution, 44*(3), 307–332.

Entman, R. M. (1993). Framing: Toward clarification of a fractured paradigm. *Journal of Communication, 43*(4), 51–58.

Entman, R. M. (2003). Cascading activation: Contesting the White House's frame after 9/11. *Political Communication, 20*, 415–432.

Fantu, C. (2002). *African renaissance: Roadmaps to the challenge of globalization*. London: Zed Books.

Gamson, W. A. (1989). News as framing, comment of Graber. *The American Behavioral Scientist, 33*(2), 157–162.

Hess, S., & Kalb, M. L. (2003). *The media and the war on terrorism*. Washington, DC: Shorenstein Center on the Press/Brookings Institution Press.

Jablonski, P. M., & Sullivan, C. (1996). Building the terrorism agenda, 1981–1994: The media, the president, and real world cues. *World Communication, 25*(4), 191–201.

Jenkins, B. M. (1986). Defense against terrorism. *Political Science Quarterly, 101*(5), 773–786.

Nathanson, S. (2004). Prerequisites for morally credible condemnations of terrorism. In W. Crotty (Ed.), *The politics of terror* (pp. 3–34). Boston: Northeastern University Press.

Nelson, T. E., Oxley, Z., & Clawson, R. A. (1997). Toward a psychology of framing effects. *Political Behavior, 19*(3), 221–246.

Norris, P., Kern, M., & Just, M. (2003). *Framing terrorism: The news media, the government and the public*. New York: Routledge.

Okumu, W. (2007). Gaps and challenges in preventing and combating terrorism in East Africa. In W. Okumu & A. Botha (Eds.), *Understanding terrorism in Africa: Building bridges and overcoming gaps* (pp. 60–70). Tshwane, Pretoria, South Africa: Institute for Security Studies.

Paletz, D. L., & Schmid, A. (1992). *Terrorism and the media*. Newbury Park, CA: Sage.

Perl, R. F. (1997). Terrorism, the media, and the government: Perspectives, trends, and options for policymakers. *Congressional Research Service* (order code 97-960F), 10–22. National Defense Division.

Rachilin, A. (1998). *News as hegemonic reality: American political culture and the framing of news accounts*. New York: Praeger.

Rapoport, D. C. (1984). Fear and trembling: Terrorism in three religious traditions. *American Political Science Review, 78*(3), 658–677.

Rapoport, D. C. (Ed.). (2001). *Inside terrorist organizations*. Thousand Oaks, CA: Sage.

Reese, S. D. (2007). The framing project: A bridging model for media research revisited. *Journal of Communication, 57*(1), 148–154.

from the celebrity to the product and from the product to the consumer (McCracken, 1989).

Several researchers have documented that Al-Jazeera is increasingly emerging as a credible source of news in the Arab world (Arab Advisors Group, 2004; Auter, Arafa, & Al-Jaber, 2005; Johnson & Fahmy, 2005) but little attention has been paid to a Western audience's perception of its credibility.

This study will explore the meaning transfer model in a news setting by examining the degree to which those who have viewed the English-language Al-Jazeera Web site judge the Arabic-language Al-Jazeera television channel as credible, even if they have not personally viewed the network. Specifically, this study will examine how credible viewers of the English-language Al-Jazeera Web site rate the television version of the network and whether Al-Jazeera Web site users who have never actually seen Al-Jazeera television view it as more or less credible than regular viewers' perceptions of it. This study will also examine the degree to which ever watching the Al-Jazeera television network as well as reliance on it as a news source, predict credibility of Al-Jazeera television after controlling for demographic, political, and cultural factors.

Source Credibility

Source credibility has long been of interest to communication scholars who have studied how speakers' characteristics can affect the persuasive influence of a communication message. Studies have consistently supported what Hovland and associates (Hovland, Janis, & Kelley, 1953; Hovland, Lumsdaine, & Sheffield, 1949) discovered more than 50 years ago: The credibility of a source is primarily influenced by a source's perceived expertise (the degree to which audience members consider someone is qualified to know the truth) and truthfulness (the degree to which the audience perceives that a person is motivated to tell the truth) (Metzger, Flanagin, Eyal, Lemus, & McCann, 2003). Highly credible sources typically have more influence on a receiver's attitudes and behaviors than less credible ones (Sternthal, Dholakia, & Leavitt, 1978).

Johnson and Fahmy (2008) found that when users of the Arabic-language Al-Jazeera Web site were judging credibility of various news sources, trustworthiness impacted credibility more than expertise. Respondents did not question that the BBC and CNN were news authorities. However, respondents distrusted the message that the BBC and CNN provided, perceiving it as distorted through the lens of Western values. Consequently, viewers of Al-Jazeera rated Western news sources low on other measures, such as accuracy, believability, and fairness. But Johnson and Fahmy (2008) and others who have explored the credibility of Al-Jazeera (i.e., Auter et al., 2004a, 2005) have surveyed Arabic-language audiences who are loyal viewers of Al-Jazeera and are therefore in a strong position to judge its expertise and trustworthiness. However, Westerners who have never watched Al-Jazeera TV, both because of lack of access and lack of understanding of the Arabic language, may also pass judgment on the network even though they have never seen it.

Researchers suggest credibility is not inherent in a source but results from audience perceptions (Berlo, Lemert, & Mertz 1969). Therefore, perceived expertise may not reflect actual knowledge. We may take financial advice from a trusted friend even if she or he has no real expertise in the area (Ohanian, 1991). Similarly, many advertising studies have suggested that we will trust a source, such as a celebrity, even though that individual may possess little or no actual knowledge about the product he or she endorses (Atkin & Block, 1983).

Some advertising researchers have advanced a meaning transference model to explain why celebrities—who often have little actual expertise—are nonetheless perceived as credible sources. Advertisers first identify the cultural meanings intended for a certain product, such as the gender, status, age and lifestyle it is designed for. They then choose celebrities who they feel embody the characteristics of the product that they intend to promote. The characteristics of the celebrity, through the endorsement, are transferred to a product. Thus, if an actress is perceived as attractive, intelligent, and classy, consumers will consider the cell phone she endorses as possessing those same characteristics (McCracken, 1989).

Similarly, some researchers have advanced a match-up hypothesis in which the effectiveness of a celebrity endorsement is determined by the level of congruence between the image of the celebrity and the product advertised (Ohanian, 1991).

Researchers examining Web credibility have also suggested a transference credibility model where those who judge a traditional source as credible transfer that judgment onto its Web counterpart (Finberg, Stone, & Lynch, 2002). For instance, Flanagin and Metzger (2000) indicated that people trusted media organizations the most for news and information, while sites created by individuals were judged the least credible.

Studies that have compared credibility ratings between online and traditional sources typically find that differences are greater between individual media than between the online and traditional form of the same medium (Johnson & Kaye, 2000, 2002). Johnson and Kaye indicate that Internet users recognize that content is often similar between a source and its online counterpart: the difference lies in how it is delivered.

While studies suggest that people transfer their judgments to the online counterpart, the opposite may also be true: People who have visited the English-language Al-Jazeera Web site and judge its credibility, may pass on those judgments to the television network.

Credibility of Al-Jazeera Television Network

Scholars agree that the coming of satellite television and the Internet in the 1990s has transformed Arab broadcasting so that it has come to resemble Western-style broadcast journalism (Ayish, 2004, 2006; Lynch, 2006; Mellor, 2005; Miles, 2005). But they disagree on the extent to which Arab journalists enjoy more freedom (Miles, 2005).

Because credibility is not inherent in a source, but rather is a perception held by audience members (Berlo et al., 1969), sources have debated how much credence to put in news from Al-Jazeera. Indeed, while U.S. officials and Arab governments brand Al-Jazeera as unreliable and propagandistic at best, and charge it with being irresponsible and dangerous at worst (el-Nawawy & Iskandar, 2002; Zayani & Ayish, 2006), Al-Jazeera has emerged as perhaps the most watched and credible source of news for Arab audiences. Ironically, it has built its credibility by adopting many characteristics of Western news organizations, and has thereby earned the title "The CNN of the Arab World" (Auter et al., 2005; el-Nawawy, 2003; Mellor, 2005).

Most of the reporters initially recruited by Al-Jazeera were from the BBC's Arabic TV service, and reporters who have been hired more recently have often been trained in Western journalism techniques (el-Nawawy, 2003). Al-Jazeera has employed the BBC and CNN as models in developing news gathering techniques, such as seeking out multiple perspectives on the news, tackling controversial issues, and featuring Western-style talk shows such as *The Opposite Direction*, *More than One Opinion*, *No Limits,* and *Open Dialogue* where viewers can call and freely express their views (el-Nawawy, 2003; Lynch, 2005, 2006). Al-Jazeera doesn't deny that it focuses on news of interest to an Arab audience and presents it from an Arab perspective. However, the network argues that it embodies its motto *The opinion and the other opinion* because its television shows present the audience with all viewpoints with objectivity, integrity, and balance to allow the audience to form its own views (el-Nawawy, 2003). The network's supporters claim Al-Jazeera is transforming Arab political culture by expanding what is considered news and by giving Arab citizens a voice through its talk shows (Lynch, 2006).

Not surprisingly, because Al-Jazeera has not simply parroted the Arab governments' perspectives nor been afraid to criticize the West, it has emerged as a highly credible source among Arab audiences (Powers & Gilboa, 2007; Seib, 2007) and is increasingly finding an audience in the West.

In a survey of users of the Arabic-language Al-Jazeera Web site, Johnson and Fahmy (2008), found viewers of the television network gave it high ratings for believability, accuracy, depth of information, trustworthiness, and expertise. Only scores for fairness dipped below 4 on a 5-point scale, although the network was praised for presenting the Arab perspective on the news (Johnson & Fahmy, 2008) and for presenting a more honest portrayal of the Iraq War by not shying away from graphic images (Fahmy & Johnson, 2007a).

No studies have been found that have examined Western audiences on Al-Jazeera credibility or have compared credibility of Al-Jazeera Web sites with the actual television network. However, Al-Emad (2005) examined how the Arabic-language vs. the English-language Web sites framed the news of the U.S./Iraq and U.S./al-Qaeda conflicts. He found significant differences between how the two Web sites covered the news. Because of differences between the network's two Web sites, this suggests that while people might transfer opinions of Al-Jazeera Web sites onto the television network, even if they haven't actually viewed it, that transference may not be valid because the English-language Web site offers more negative content than the Arabic-language one.

Credibility and Reliance on Al-Jazeera Network

Studies have consistently shown that how credible one views a medium to be is strongly related to how often one relies on it (Wanta & Hu, 1994), although this finding is not universal. For instance, studies have found that traditional media use can be a stronger predictor of online credibility than Internet use (Johnson & Kaye, 2000, 2002).

Studies by Johnson and Fahmy (2008) and Auter, Arafa, and Al-Jaber (2004b, 2005) found that Al-Jazeera viewers are extremely loyal. Auter and associates (2004b) found that a third of those surveyed watched Al-Jazeera for 5 hours or more a day. Not surprisingly, then, these studies found that heavy viewing of Al-Jazeera was linked with higher levels of credibility. Reliance may make more of a difference with Al-Jazeera than Western media because Al-Jazeera does not adhere to Western values of taste. For instance, Al-Jazeera has tried to put a human face on the Iraq War, presenting bloody and wounded civilians, including women and children. To an irregular viewer of Al-Jazeera, particularly from the West, Al-Jazeera's presentation of graphic images may be perceived as shocking and sensationalistic (Fahmy & Johnson, 2007a).

Cultural Factors and Media Credibility

Only a handful of studies have explored credibility outside of the United States and fewer still have examined cultural factors that explain differences in credibility.

The World Internet project at UCLA (Lebo & Wolpert, 2004) compared 10 nations on the degree to which they perceive the Internet as accurate and credible. Scores tended to be higher in countries with fewer press freedoms (Korea, Hungary, China, and Singapore) than in predominantly Western countries with a freer press (Japan, Germany, Sweden, and Spain). Internet scores were higher for more repressive regimes, indicating that people in those countries do not trust their national media and use the Internet to seek out more reliable sources outside their country.

Studies of media credibility in the Arab world suggest until recently that the Internet was considered more credible than the heavily censored Arab state-run news channels (Al-Makaty, Boyd, & Van Tubergen, 1994). However, the development of independent satellite news services, such as Al-Jazeera, has shifted perceptions of Arab media from state-run channels to Western media and more recently transnational Arab satellite television. Results from the Arab world and elsewhere suggest, not surprisingly, that the more the state controls the information it allows people to access, the less they will trust the media.

Few studies have explored specific cultural factors and their potential influence on credibility. Yoon, Chung, and Kim (1998) examined whether collectivist nature of Korean culture influenced attitudes toward credibility, but they found few differences. Similarly, Johnson and Fahmy (2008) found that one's nationality failed to influence credibility judgments regarding Al-Jazeera.

No studies could be found that have explored how other cultural variables, such as whether one has visited one's country of origin (if applicable), fluency in a language, and whether one has ever traveled abroad, influence credibility ratings. However, studies do suggest that the degree of familiarity with a source influences how much one trusts it (Wanta & Hu, 1994). Therefore, those who are more familiar with the Arabic language or have visited Arab nations are more likely to be more familiar with, and interested in, Arab news. They may be more likely to seek out news from Al-Jazeera and therefore judge it as more credible.

Based on the review of the literature and the meaning transfer model theory, the following is hypothesized:

H1. Those who have visited the English-language Al-Jazeera Web site will judge the Arabic-language Al-Jazeera television network as credible even if they have not personally viewed the television channel.
H2. Those who have visited the English-language Al-Jazeera Web site will judge the Arabic-language Al-Jazeera television network high on (a) expertise and (b) trustworthiness.
H3. Those who have visited the English-language Al-Jazeera Web site will judge the Al-Jazeera television network as more credible than (a) the BBC, (b), CNN, and (c) local Arab media.

H4. Reliance on the Al-Jazeera English-language Web site will predict credibility of the television network after controlling for demographic (income, age, gender, and education), political (activity, interest, and ideology), and cultural variables (religion, Arab nations visited, Arabic-language proficiency, and country of origin—if applicable).

H5. Those who have watched the Al-Jazeera television network will be more likely than those who have never watched it to rate the TV channel as credible after controlling for demographic (income, age, gender, and education), political (activity, interest, and ideology) and cultural variables (religion, visited Arab nations, Arabic-language proficiency, and country of origin—if applicable).

Method

An English-language survey that examined viewers' beliefs about the credibility of Al-Jazeera was posted on the Al-Jazeera English-language Web site (http://english.aljazeera.net). The hyperlink was posted for 3 weeks, from November 23, 2004 to December 14, 2004, on the Arab World news page and the Global news page of the Al-Jazeera news Web site.

The English-language questionnaire was pretested to ensure that valid and reliable data were collected. The online questionnaire was completed by 913 respondents. The survey's respondents were users of Al-Jazeera who seek information from the Al-Jazeera English-language Web site. Using an online questionnaire proved to be the preferred method for this study as it allowed us to directly survey users of Al-Jazeera English-language Web site, who are not necessarily proficient in the Arabic language. This study's respondents therefore, can be classified as a purposive sample of Al-Jazeera users who have not necessarily watched the Arabic television network but seek information from its English-language news Web site.

The Dependent Measure

Al-Jazeera Credibility To address hypotheses testing predictors of Al-Jazeera credibility, a summated index measuring media credibility was made up of the following six items: believability; fairness; accuracy; depth of information; trustworthiness; and expertise. The response options for each item was a 5-point scale that ranged from "not at all" to "very." The reliability of the credibility index is .95.

The Independent Measures

Al-Jazeera Reliance   Respondents first were asked whether they watch the network. Next, a reliance index was computed. The index was composed of two measures. Respondents were asked to assess their level of attention paid to Al-Jazeera television in the past 3 days and assess their level of reliance on Al-Jazeera television for information. Response categories ranged from "a lot"; "considerable"; "some"; "little"; and "not at all." The Cronbach alpha testing the reliability of the reliance scale was .77.

Political Variables   Measures of political activity and political interest were also employed. Respondents were asked to rate their level of political activity and their level of political interest on a scale that ranged from 0 to 10. Respondents were also asked to report whether they viewed themselves as politically "very liberal"; "liberal"; "independent"; "conservative"; or "very conservative."

Demographic Variables   A set of background questions used for descriptive and comparison purposes were used. This study specifically examined associations between perceptions of Al-Jazeera credibility and gender, age, education, and income.

Cultural Variables   Respondents were asked whether they had ever visited an Arab country and about their proficiency in the Arabic language, their country of original nationality, their country of residency, and their religion.

Results

A total of 913 usable responses were analyzed for this study. Respondents who completed the survey listed 76 different countries as their country of origin, with almost half of the respondents (47%) listing the United States, 20% listing Canada, Australia, and the United Kingdom, and only 14.4% of the respondents indicating backgrounds from 20 Arab countries and five Muslim countries (Afghanistan, Pakistan, Bangladesh, Azerbaijan, and Iran).

Overall, the respondents represented an international and highly educated elite group. Almost two thirds (61%) reported they have lived outside their native country, with an average of 11 years spent abroad. Almost half (44.1%) reported that they had visited an Arab country, and nearly two thirds (65.3%) reported they were not at all proficient with the Arabic language, with 11% reporting they were "proficient" or "very proficient." Almost three fourths (73.6%) indicated at least a university degree and almost one third (31.2%) reported they had graduate degrees.

Respondents ranged in age from 15 to 96 years old, with a mean of 44. Males greatly outnumbered females (85.3 to 14.7%). About one third (30.1%) reported they were Christians, about one fourth (23.7%) reported they were Muslims, less than 3% (2.3%) reported they were Jewish, and 43% listed "other." In terms of income, one quarter (25.7%) reported an annual income that ranged between $1,001 and $25,000 and one quarter (25.4%) reported an annual income between $75,001 and more than $100,000. More than 40% (43.1%) indicated an annual income between $25,001 and $75,000. Few of the respondents (5.9%) indicated an annual income of less than $1,000. Almost 7 out of 10 respondents reported they have never watched the Al-Jazeera network. Only one third of the respondents (32.5%) reported watching the network channel. These respondents who watched Al-Jazeera were attentive to and relied on the network for news (mean = 3.92 and 3.65 respectively). The mean scores were between the "considerable" and the "some" response categories. Regarding political ideology, almost 40% (38.1%) reported they were "very liberal" or "liberal," 45.6% considered themselves "independents," and 16.3% reported they were "very conservative" or "conservative."

Media Credibility

Hypothesis 1 predicted that those who have visited the English-language Al-Jazeera Web site would judge Al-Jazeera television network has having high credibility. Table 12.1 shows responses concerning credibility measures of Al-Jazeera. The majority of the respondents reported they perceived the network as "considerable" and "very" credible on the six measures examined, with scores ranging from 54.3% for fairness to 66.7% for expertise. Table 12.2 compares means of responses to credibility measures among those who have and have not watched Al-Jazeera TV. These results suggested those who had watched Al-Jazeera TV scored consistently higher on all Al-Jazeera credibility measures than those who had never watched the television news channel. Our findings, thus, showed support for hypothesis 1.

Our data analysis also showed support for hypothesis 2—those who have visited the English-language Al-Jazeera Web site would judge Al-Jazeera television network high on (1) expertise and (2) trustworthiness. The hypothesis was partially supported. Our results show the mean scores for both expertise and trustworthiness, neared "considerable." The mean score was higher for level of expertise (mean = 3.77) than trustworthiness (mean = 3.54) (Table 12.2). However, respondents judged the Al-Jazeera English-language Web site higher on believability and depth than on trustworthiness.

Hypothesis 3 predicted those who have visited the English-language

Table 12.1 Percentage Ages of Respondents Regarding Credibility Measures of Al-Jazeera TV Network (N=913).

	Percent reporting "Very much" & "Considerable"	Percent reporting "Not at all" & "Little"
Believability	66.3%	14.8%
Fairness	54.3%	24.7%
Accuracy	64.7%	16.3%
Depth of Information	60.6%	16.4%
Trustworthiness	59.0%	21.6%
Expertise	66.7%	15.4%

Note: 1=Not at all; 2=little; 3= Somewhat; 4= Considerable; 5=Very much.
The 'Don't know' response category was coded as missing.

Al-Jazeera Web site would judge Al-Jazeera television network as more credible than the (1) BBC, (2) CNN, and (3) local Arab media. By and large, our data analysis indicated support for hypothesis 3. Overall, respondents rated the credibility of Al-Jazeera higher than the credibility of the BBC, CNN, and local Arab media. The mean scores for all credibility measures were between the "somewhat" and the "considerable" response categories. As shown in Table 12.3, the mean score for the credibility index of Al-Jazeera scored the highest with a mean of 3.69, followed by the BBC, then CNN, and local Arab media. The data showed the mean scores for believability, fairness, accuracy, depth of information, and trustworthiness of the Al-Jazeera network scored the highest when compared to mean scores of all other networks examined.

Table 12.2 Comparing Means of Responses of Those Who Have Watched and Who Have Not Watched Al Jazeera to Statements Assessing Credibility Measures of Al-Jazeera TV Nnetwork (N=913).

	Mean "Do Watch Al-Jazeera"	Mean "Do NOT Watch Al-Jazeera"	T-Score
Believability	3.97	3.63	-59.77***
Fairness	3.62	3.25	-48.09***
Accuracy	3.82	3.58	-57.69*
Depth of Information	3.87	3.54	-56.92**
Trustworthiness	3.81	3.62	-50.05***
Expertise	3.91	3.68	-59.24*
Credibility Index	3.88	3.56	-58.78**

Note: 1=Not at all; 2=little; 3= Somewhat; 4= Considerable; 5=Very much.
The 'Don't know' response category was coded as missing
*p < .05, **p < .01, ***p < .001

Table 12.3 Respondents' Mean Responses to Questions Regarding Credibility Measures of Al-Jazeera, the BBC, CNN and Local Arab Media (N=913).

	Believ-ability	Fairness	Accuracy	Depth of Information	Trust-worthiness	Expertise	Credibility Index
Al-Jazeera	3.76	3.39	3.67	3.67	3.54	3.77	3.69
BBC	3.41	3.10	3.35	3.43	3.24	3.86	3.43
CNN	2.55	2.10	2.51	2.30	2.20	3.13	2.47
Local Arab Media	2.25	2.03	2.26	2.12	2.03	2.42	2.21

Note: 1=Not at all; 2=little; 3= Somewhat; 4= Considerable; 5=Very much.
The 'Don't know' response category was coded as missing.

Thus, overall, in six of the seven credibility measures, the hypothesis was fully supported. Only the score for expertise for Al-Jazeera (mean = 3.77) was lower than the score of expertise for the BBC (mean = 3.86). And although the mean score for the expertise of CNN was the highest (mean = 3.13) among all of the other credibility measures, it was still lower than the mean score for the expertise measure of both Al-Jazeera and the BBC.

Predictors of Al-Jazeera Credibility

Hypothesis 4 predicted reliance on the Al-Jazeera English-language Web site will predict credibility of the television network after controlling for demographic (income, age, gender, and education), political (activity, interest, and ideology) and cultural (religion, visited Arab nations, Arabic-language proficiency, and country of origin) variables. As shown in Table 12.4, results of a hierarchical regression indicated support for hypothesis 4. The credibility of Al-Jazeera can be predicted by income (beta = –.171, p < .031) and media reliance (beta = .526, p < .000). Reliance on Al-Jazeera is a strong and positive predictor of credibility. Indeed, reliance predicted more than 20% of the variance in credibility. The more the respondents rely on Al-Jazeera, the more likely they are to judge it as credible. Results also showed lower income respondents are more likely to view the television network as more credible than higher income respondents.

Hypothesis 5 predicted those who have watched the Al-Jazeera television network will be more likely than those who have never watched it to rate the TV channel as credible after controlling for demographic (income, age, gender, and education), political (activity, interest, and ideology) and cultural (religion, visited Arab nations, Arabic-language proficiency, and country of origin) variables. However, hierarchical

Table 12.4 Hierarchical Regression Analysis of Reliance on the English Language *Al-Jazeera* Web Site as a Predictor of the Network's Credibility (N=913).

Demographics	Standardized Beta	T- Score	Sign.
Income	-.171*	-2.496	.031
Age	-.111	-1.775	.078
Gender	-.034	-.529	.597
Education	.033	.487	.627
R-square = .084*			
Political Variables			
Politically	.004	.055	.956
Political Interest	.102	1.443	.151
Political Ideology	-.090	-1.408	.161
R-square = .122			
R-square change = .038			
Cultural Variables			
Religion	-.011	-.148	.882
Visited an Arab country	-.019	-.254	.800
Arabic-language proficiency	.059	.727	.468
Country of origin	.075	1.177	.241
R-square = .166			
R-square change = .044			
Reliance index	.526***	7.939	.000
R-square = .374			
R-square change = .208***			

F value= 8.61***
*p < .05, **p < .01, ***p < .001

regression results show that after controlling for demographic, political, and cultural variables, hypothesis 5 was not supported (Table 12.5). In this model watching Al-Jazeera TV was not linked to perceptions of the network's credibility. Our results showed the credibility of Al-Jazeera can be predicted by income (beta = −.257, p < .019), political interest (beta = .122, p < .015), political ideology (beta = −.232, p < .000), and whether a respondent had visited an Arab country (beta = .257, p < .000). Again, results showed higher income respondents are less likely to view the television network as credible. Our findings suggested conservatives are less likely than liberals to view the channel as credible. The more politically interested respondents are, the more likely they are to

Table 12.5 Hierarchical Regression Analysis of Viewing *Al-Jazeera* Television as a Predictor of the Network's Credibility (N=913).

Demographics	Standardized Beta	T-Score	Sign
Income	−.257***	−5.34	.000
Age	−.058	−1.33	.184
Gender	−.004	−.08	.936
Education	.006	.12	.905
R-square = .095*			
Political Variables			
Politically activity	.011	.230	.818
Political Interest	.122*	2.445	.015
Political Ideology	−.232***	− 5.248	.000
R-square = .157			
R-square change = .062*			
Cultural Variables			
Religion	.020	.465	.642
Visited an Arab country	.257***	− 4.554	.000
Arabic-language proficiency	.068	1.299	.195
Country of origin	.016	258	.797
R-square = .218			
R-square change = .061*			
Do you watch *Al-Jazeera TV?*	−.067	−1.322	.187
R-square = .221			
R-square change = .0003			

F=9.964***
*p < .05, ***p < .001

view the network as credible. Results also suggest respondents who had visited an Arab country are more likely to view Al-Jazeera TV as more credible than respondents who had never been to the region.

Discussion

This study tested the meaning transfer model in a news setting by examining the degree to which those who have viewed the English-language Al-Jazeera Web site judge the Arabic-language Al-Jazeera television network as credible even if they have not personally viewed the satellite television station. This study is based on a survey of those who had visited the English-language version of Al-Jazeera Web site for the purpose of examining how credible these users view its network counterpart to be; whether Al-Jazeera Web site users who have never actually seen Al-Jazeera television view it as more or less credible than regular viewers, as well as the degree to which ever watching Al-Jazeera television as well as reliance on it as a news source predict its credibility, after controlling for demographic, political, and cultural factors.

Al-Jazeera has been subjected to withering criticism from U.S. officials as being anti-American and a propaganda tool for terrorists (el-Nawawy & Iskandar; 2002; Lynch, 2005; Mekay, 2004). However, as noted above, such criticisms are not always based on actually viewing the Arabic-language Al-Jazeera network, but are based on what the critics heard from sources they trust (Lynch, 2005).

Previous credibility research (Finberg et al., 2002; Johnson & Kaye, 2000, 2002) as well as advertising studies (McCracken, 1989) have suggested a transference credibility model in which media users will assess credibility of an unfamiliar source based on their knowledge of a familiar source.

In two important ways those who had visited the English-language and Arabic-language Al-Jazeera Web sites are quite similar. Both audiences said they spent considerably time with Al-Jazeera. More importantly, both considered it as a credible source, although scores for those who viewed the English-language site were lower than the Arabic-language site, where scores for all measures were above 4 on a 5-point scale (Johnson & Fahmy, 2008).

Like the Arabic-language survey (4.55), scores were highest for level of expertise (3.77). Ironically, as noted above, the network gained its expertise by emulating Western news styles and practices, such as presenting multiple perspectives on the news, featuring slick, polished graphics and reports, and creating Western-style news magazine shows (Auter et al., 2005; el-Nawawy, 2003).

Also, like the Arabic-language Web site (Johnson & Fahmy, 2008) viewers rated Al-Jazeera lowest on fairness (3.77 vs. 3.39). Objectivity is held up as the standard for American media and Al-Jazeera executives also strive to present the news from many perspectives. Indeed, the network has been praised for its willingness to tackle controversial views, seeking out a balance of Western and Middle Eastern views, and for its talk shows that allow average citizens a platform from which to present their views (el-Nawawy, 2003; el-Nawawy & Iskander, 2002; Lynch, 2005, 2006). However, executives concede they put out an Arab perspective on the news to correct the anti-Arab distortion they perceive is presented by Western media, particularly on issues such as the Iraq War and the Israeli–Palestinian conflict (el-Nawawy, 2003).

Those who have visited the English-language Web site value the network for its willingness to support Arab perspectives in the face of Western media that they perceive parrot the U.S. government line. For instance, more than two thirds of those surveyed (66.9%) said the station promotes the belief that the Iraq War is unjust and an almost equal percentage (65.1%) said it promotes the Palestinian cause. Almost half (47.5%) agree that it promotes press freedom. As one respondent wrote:

> CNN and Western media are as biased as Al-Jazeera is in its own way. CNN and Western media are serving a certain kind of public, Westerners, and giving them what they expected. Those who use the English-language Al-Jazeera Web site are ready to accept Al-Jazeera does the same for its own Arab public.

Studies have identified expertise and trustworthiness as the major factors that impact source credibility (Metzger et. al., 2003). Johnson and Fahmy (2008) found that viewers of the Arabic-language Al-Jazeera Web site considered truthfulness more important than expertise in assessing credibility. This study generally supports those findings. Like the study of Arabic-language Web site users, those surveyed did not question that the BBC was a news authority; indeed, the BBC rated higher than Al-Jazeera on expertise (3.86 vs. 3.77). However, while trustworthiness scores for Al-Jazeera approached those for expertise (3.54 vs. 3.77), trustworthiness scored lower for both the BBC (3.24) and CNN (2.20) than on the expertise measures. Audience members did not trust Western media because they perceive them as filtering the news through the distorting lens of Western values (Auter et al., 2005; Fahmy & Johnson, 2007b; Johnson & Fahmy, 2008). Consequently, CNN and the BBC also scored lower on measures such as believability, fairness, accuracy, and depth. Therefore, this study supports the earlier work of Johnson and Fahmy (2008) that while the audience may not question the expertise of an established news organization, they may not always believe the message the source presents.

But while Johnson and Fahmy (2008) found that those who viewed the Arabic-language Al-Jazeera Web site judged the BBC as more credible than CNN, differences were even more pronounced for those who use the English-language Al-Jazeera site. While overall credibility was somewhat higher for Al-Jazeera than the BBC (3.69 to 3.43), it was almost a point higher than CNN (2.47).

Several of those surveyed lumped CNN together with Fox in presenting the news with a pro-U.S. bias. As one respondent humorously noted:

> CNN and Fox News are leaders in feeding the American public the snippets of "news" designed to placate and mislead its viewers

concerning the major issues of the day. It would be productive and informative if the American news networks would wire into the White House each evening and let the President's press secretary give the daily news for NBC, CBS, CNN, and Fox. At least the public could see the source of the "nightly news program." Condolezza Rice could give the weather and Colin Powell broadcast the sports.

While nearly half of the respondents of this survey were from the United States, that does not mean they support the way the U.S. media present the news. Westerners answering this survey were less likely than Arab audiences to view U.S. media as free (5.35 to 5.03) and more likely to see the Arab media as free (3.76 vs. 2.82). Many respondents said they distrusted President Bush's policies, particularly his stand on the Iraq War. They sought out views from Al-Jazeera because they believed Western, particularly U.S. media, censored the news while Al-Jazeera presented news and images that U.S. media were unwilling to show (Fahmy & Johnson, 2007b). As one respondent claimed:

America sanitizes the war for their people back in America. This gives the impression that the war in Iraq is just a video game and not all that bloody. I appreciate Al-Jazeera's journalism for showing what war is REALLY like.

This study sought to explore whether those who have watched Al-Jazeera television are more or less likely to judge the network as credible. More importantly, this study attempted to test the transference credibility model found in advertising research in which media users will assess credibility of a source they don't know, based on their knowledge of a similar source they have familiarity with (McCracken, 1989). Credibility of a medium is typically tied to reliance, with people judging those sources they rely on most as more credible (Johnson & Kaye, 2000, 2002; Wanta & Hu, 1994). But because credibility is based on audience perceptions, not necessarily experience with a medium, sources that the audience members have never seen can still be viewed as credible.

This study does suggest audience members were transferring credibility judgments of the Al-Jazeera television network based on their views of the English-language Web site. More than two thirds (67.5%) of those surveyed said they have never watched Al-Jazeera television. Yet, only a handful would not pass judgment on Al-Jazeera's credibility. For instance only 3.7% said they did not know whether or not Al-Jazeera TV was believable. Past studies have found that those who judge a traditional source as credible sometimes transfer those ratings to its online counterpart (Finberg et al., 2002; Johnson & Kaye, 2000, 2002). This may be the first study that has found the reverse: People judge a Web site as credible and transfer those beliefs to the traditional form—in this case the Arabic news television channel.

While those who had not watched Al-Jazeera TV were still likely to pass judgments on its credibility, it is not clear the degree to which having viewed the network influences how credible English-language viewers judge its credibility. Those who have watched Al-Jazeera TV scored consistently higher on all Al-Jazeera credibility measures than those who have never watched it (Table 12.2). However, relationships proved insignificant after controlling for other factors (Table 12.5), suggesting that political, cultural, and demographic differences between users and nonusers of the English-language Web site accounted for differences in attitudes.

Few studies have examined how well cultural variables explain credibility. This research discovered that those who had visited Arab nations are more likely to judge the English-language Al-Jazeera Web site as more credible. Past studies suggest that degree of familiarity with a source influences how much one trusts it (Wanta & Hu, 1994). Therefore, those from the West who have visited the Arab world may be more familiar with the language and are more likely to be familiar with and interested in Arab news. They may seek out information from Al-Jazeera because they are aware that most other Arab media remain under the control of their governments and Al-Jazeera has been freer to present alternative perspectives. As one respondent noted:

> My experience is that Al-Jazeera is doing real reporting, unvarnished, unadulterated reporting in a way that other state sponsored news agencies, and in the case of the U.S., corporate sponsored news agencies are editorially not interested in doing. One measure of the quality of Al-Jazeera's reporting is how often they are bad mouthed by governments and other media sources. That is a sure sign the truth is coming out.

While this study found that the majority of those who have never viewed Al-Jazeera were still willing to pass judgment on its credibility, this does not mean that reliance had no influence on credibility. Indeed, among those who have watched Al-Jazeera TV, reliance was clearly the strongest predictor of credibility. Most studies find that reliance is a strong predictor of credibility (i.e., Johnson & Kaye, 2000, 2002). Reliance may be a stronger predictor of credibility for Al-Jazeera than for Western media because Al-Jazeera does not follow Western values of taste. While Western media have been accused of sanitizing the war by avoiding graphic images because of their perception that their audience does not want to view disturbing material, Al-Jazeera coverage has emphasized the suffering brought upon Iraqi civilians, by showing images of dead or wounded Iraqis, particularly women and children. Al-Jazeera editors claim that its audiences expect to see bloody images during a war (Fahmy & Johnson, 2007b). Indeed, when Fahmy and Johnson (2007a) surveyed those who had visited the Arabic-language Al-Jazeera Web site about their views on graphic images, more than 80% supported the network's use of graphic images saying that Al-Jazeera did a better job than Western media of presenting the realities and consequences of the war. Al-Jazeera's presentation of graphic images, then, may be perceived as shocking and sensationalistic (Fahmy & Johnson, 2007a) among Western viewers with little experience with the Arab network.

Limitations

This study assessed how those who have visited Al-Jazeera's English-language Web site judge the credibility of the network. Because this study relied on a self-selected sample of those viewers who visit Al-Jazeera's English-language Web site, results may not be representative of all Al-Jazeera users and certainly are not representative of American and Western audiences as a whole. However, a random sample would have likely found that few people had even heard of Al-Jazeera. This study was interested in the views of a specifically targeted group: Westerners familiar with and interested enough in Al-Jazeera to have visited the Web site. Such a sample was ideal to study transference credibility, the degree to which those who have not actually viewed Al-Jazeera television network are still willing to pass judgment on it. Babbie (2001) suggests that careful use of purposive sampling generates results that may be representative of a specific subset of Internet users, but may not be representative of the larger population.

This study used a host of variables to explore what predicts perceptions of Al-Jazeera's credibility among a Western, primarily U.S. audience. However, the variables relating to demographics, political culture, and Al-Jazeera use explained only 33% of the variance on attitudes regarding credibility. Future studies could include other variables, such as political trust and support for press freedom, which might provide additional insight into what can predict audience perceptions of credibility regarding an alternative media site such as Al-Jazeera.

References

Al-Emad, M. (2005). *Al-Jazeera news framing online: A comparative study of the Arabic version and the English version of its news Web sites.* Unpublished master's thesis, University of Oklahoma.

Atkin, C., & Block, M. (1983). Effectiveness of celebrity endorsers. *Journal of Advertising Research, 23*(1), 57–61.

Auter, P., Arafa, M. M., & Al-Jaber, K. (2004a). *News credibility in the Arab world: An analysis of Arabic people's usage patterns of Al-Jazeera after September 11, 2001 and before the Iraq War.* Paper presented at the Global Fusion annual conference, St. Louis, MO.

Auter, P., Arafa, M. M., & Al-Jaber, K. (2004b). Who is Al-Jazeera's audience? Deconstructing the demographics and psychographics of an Arab satellite news network. *Transnational Broadcasting Studies.* Retrieved July 22, 2006, from http://www.tbsjournal.com/html12.auter.htm

Auter, P., Arafa, M. M., & Al-Jaber, K. (2005). Identifying with Arabic journalists: How Al-Jazeera tapped parasocial interaction gratifications in the Arab world. *Gazette, 67*(2), 189–204.

Ayish, M. I. (2004). News credibility during the 2003 Iraq war: A survey of UAE students. In R. D. Berenger (Ed.), *Global media go to war: The role of news and entertainment media during the 2003 Iraq war* (pp. 321–332). Spokane, WA: Marquette Books.

Ayish, M. I. (2006). Heroes and villains in the land of two rivers: How aljazeera. net told the story of the Anglo-American invasion of Iraq. In R. D. Berenger (Ed.), *Cybermedia go to war: Role of converging media during and after the 2003 Iraq War* (pp. 126–148). Spokane, WA: Marquette Books.

Babbie, E. R. (2001). *Survey research methods.* Belmont, CA: Wadsworth.

Berlo, D. K., Lemert, J., & Mertz, R. (1969). Dimensions for evaluation the acceptability of message sources. *Public Opinion Quarterly, 33*(4), 563–576.

El-Nawawy, M. (2003). Why Al-Jazeera is the most popular network in the Arab world. *Television Quarterly, 34*(1), 10–15.

El-Nawawy, M., & Iskandar, A. (2002). *Al-Jazeera: How the free Arab news network scooped the world and changed the Middle East.* Cambridge, MA: Westview Press.

Fahmy, S., & Johnson, T. J. (2007a). Show the truth and let Al-Jazeera audience decide: Support for use of graphic imagery among Al-Jazeera viewers. *Journal of Broadcasting & Electronic Media, 51*(2), 245–264.

Fahmy, S., & Johnson, T. J. (2007b). The caged bird sings: How reliance on Al-Jazeera affects views regarding press freedom in the Arab World. In P. Seib (Ed.), *New media and the new Middle East* (pp. 81—100). New York: Palgrave Macmillan.

Finberg, H. I., Stone, M. L., & Lynch, D. (2002). Digital journalism credibility study. OnlineNews Association. Retrieved July 22, 2006, from http://www.onlinenewsassociation.org

Flanagin, A. J., & Metzger, M. J. (2000). Perceptions of Internet information credibility. *Journalism and Mass Communication Quarterly, 77*(3), 515–540.

Hovland, C. I., Janis, I. L., & Kelley, H. H. (1953). *Communication and persuasion.* New Haven, CT: Yale University Press.

Hovland, C. I., Lumsdaine, A. A., & Sheffield, F. D. (1949). *Experiments on mass communication: Studies in social psychology in World War II.* Princeton, NJ: Princeton University Press.

Johnson, T. J., & Fahmy, S. (2008). The CNN of the Arab world or a shill for terrorists?: How support for press freedom and political ideology predict credibility of Al-Jazeera among its audience. *International Communication Gazette, 70*(5), 338–360.

Johnson, T. J., & Kaye, B. K. (2000). Using is believing: The influence of reliance on the credibility of online political information among politically interested Internet users. *Journalism & Mass Communication Quarterly, 77*, 865–879.

Johnson, T. J., & Kaye, B. K. (2002). Webelievability: A path model examining how convenience and reliance predict online credibility. *Journalism & Mass Communication Quarterly, 79*, 619–642.

Lebo, H., & Wolpert, S. (2004). The UCLA World Internet Project. Retrieved July 27, 2006, from http://www.digitalcenter.org/downloads/World_Internet_Project.doc

Lynch, M. (2005). Watching Al-Jazeera. *Wilson Quarterly, 29*(3), 36–45.

Lynch, M. (2006). *Voices of the new Arab public: Iraq, Al-Jazeera and Middle East politics today.* New York: Columbia University Press.

McCracken, G. (1989). Who is the celebrity endorser? Cultural foundations of the endorsement process. *The Journal of Consumer Research, 16*(12), 310–321.

Mekay, E. (2004, May 26). Washington urges media freedom—But not for Al-Jazeera. InterPress Service. Retrieved July 22, 2006, from http://www.commondreams.org/headlines04/0526-06.htm

Mellor, N. (2005). *The making of Arab news.* Lanham, MD: Rowman & Littlefield.

Metzger, M. J., Flanagin, A., Eyal, K., Lemus, D. R., & McCann, R. M. (2003). Credibility for the 21st century: Integrating perspectives on source, message, and media credibility in the contemporize environment. *Communication Yearbook, 27*, 293–335.

Miles, H. (2005). *Al-Jazeera: The inside story of the Arab news channel that is challenging the West.* New York: Grove Press.

Ohanian, R. (1991). The impact of celebrity spokespersons' perceived image on consumers' intention to purchase. *Journal of Advertising Research, 31*(1), 46–54.

Powers, S., & E. Gilboa, E. (2007). The public diplomacy of Al-Jazeera. In P. Seib (Ed.), *New media and the new Middle East* (pp. 53–80). New York: Palgrave Macmillan.

Seib, P. (2007). New media and prospects for democratization. In P. Seib (Ed.), *New media and the new Middle East* (pp. 1–17). New York: Palgrave Macmillan.

Sternthal, B., Dholakia, R., & Leavitt, C. (1978). The persuasive effect of source credibility: Tests of cognitive response. *Journal of Consumer Research, 4*(4), 252–260.

Wanta, W., & Hu, Y. H. (1994). The effects of credibility, reliance, and exposure on media agenda-setting: A path analysis model. *Journalism Quarterly, 71*(1), 90–98.

Yoon, K., Chung, K-H., & Kim, M. S. (1998). A cross-cultural comparison of the effects of source credibility on attitude and behavioral intentions. *Mass Communication and Society, 1*(3–4), 153–173.

Zayani, M., & Ayish, M. I. (2006). Arab satellite television and crisis reporting: Covering the fall of Baghdad. *The International Communication Gazette, 68*(5–6), 473–497.

Chapter 13

An Exploration of the Determinants of International News Coverage in Australia's Online Media

Xiaopeng Wang

As one of the major approaches in international media studies, international news flow research has received continuing attention from scholars in past decades (Wu, 1998). A wealth of research indicates that gatekeeper factors, organizational constraints, sociocultural structures, and logistical concerns have a significant impact on the ways in which the media of one country cover events in other countries (Hur, 1984). However, Sreberny-Mohammadi (1995) pointed out that previous studies were largely framed within the Cold War context. The rapidly changing political and economic environments of the world since the end of the Cold War might have altered the determinants of international news coverage. In particular, after the tragedy of 9/11, global terrorism is considered to greatly influence media's coverage.

In terms of communication channels, through which international news spreads, there is a gap in our knowledge about the role of the Internet in covering the world. The majority of the international news flow research focuses on newspaper and television news, while only a few studies have attempted to map the world reflected on the Internet (Gasher & Gabriele, 2004; Wu, 1998). Given the advanced new technologies, the Internet has dramatically reduced the logistical constraints in global communication. Thus, the assumption that geographic relations between nations influence media's coverage (Galtung & Ruge, 1965) may need a reexamination in the context of the online media environment.

Besides, geographical areas in prior international news flow research are unevenly studied. The most frequently studied region is North America, followed by Western Europe, Asia, Latin America, Eastern Europe, and Africa (Wu, 1998). Little effort has been devoted to investigating Australia's media coverage of the world.

Australia is a member of the Commonwealth of Nations, with the world's sixth largest land area and the largest in the southern hemisphere (*CIA World Factbook*, n.d.). In 2007, it had a population of approximately 20.7 million, 90% of whom were of European descent (The Commonwealth, n.d.). In a democratic political system, Australia has established a free media system (Freedom House, 2006). It has two public broadcasters, the Australian Broadcasting Corporation (ABC) and the Special Broadcasting Service (SBS), as well as multiple commercial television networks. Newspapers have a high circulation rate throughout the country. *The Australian* and *Australian Financial Review* are the two major national dailies (The Commonwealth, n.d.). The Internet is popular in Australia. There are approximately 15.3 million Internet users in 2007, about 74% of its total population (*CIA World Factbook*, n.d.). Over the past 50 years, Australian politics, economy, media, and culture have been strongly influenced by both American and British popular culture (Craig, 2004).

Australia's democratic politics, prosperous economy, and Western culture make it natural to compare it with North America and Western Europe in terms of international news flow. The purpose of this study is to explore the determinants of online international news coverage in the post-9/11 era through a content analysis of Australia's media.

Literature Review

Studies on News Flow Determinants

Studies on determinants of international news are built on Galtung and Ruge's (1965) theoretical framework, which suggests that world news coverage is not only influenced by news events themselves, but also determined by economic, social, political, and geographic relationships between countries. In other words, whether a foreign event will be covered is reliant on its internal news values, such as deviance, unexpectedness, and meaningfulness, as well as its external factors, such as cultural similarity, social distance, and geographical proximity.

For instance, Ostgaard (1965) pointed out that in addition to the factors inherent in the news process, political and economic forces had an impact on the news flow among countries as well. Hester (1973) proposed that a set of external factors (the hierarchy of nations, cultural affinities, and economic association between nations) and internal factors (news and information conflicts) could define the flow of news information. He specified that the variables of physical size, population, economic development, and the period of time the country has existed as a sovereign nation contributed to the hierarchy of nations; cultural affinities included variables like language, immigrants, tourists, and historical and colonial relationships; and international trade, foreign aid, and investment variables involved in the economic association between nations (Hester, 1973).

Similarly, Chang, Shoemaker, and Brendlinger (1987) described the studies of news flow determinants as taking two approaches: the event-oriented or the context-oriented approach. They stressed the theoretical and operational differences between these two approaches. The event-oriented approach looked at the internal nature of events, whereas the context-oriented approach assumed that foreign news coverage was determined by the context where events occurred. The context-oriented approach emphasized the origin of foreign news, and its relationships with the external environments.

Among the few news flow studies about Australia and online media, the event-oriented approach was mostly employed to illustrate the news values represented in the international coverage. For example, Hanusch (2003) examined newspapers in Australia and Fiji, and identified negative events as a predominant determinant in covering foreign countries. Gasher and Gabriele (2004) compared online and off-line versions of the *Montreal Gazette* and discovered that the online coverage of foreign countries was more geographically diverse and favored international sports news.

This study, instead, will look at online news coverage of the world from the contextual perspective. On the one hand, the Internet has become an increasingly important channel for people to seek news information. It is valuable to assess the validity of those external context-oriented determinants identified by traditional media research on new media outlets (Sosale, 2003). On the other hand, new technologies, including the Internet, not only change the way in which people receive information, but also change the way journalists gather and disseminate news information (Hachten & Scotton, 2002). The advance of the Internet, along with the shifting political environment, can become a critical variable that determines the flow of international news information.

Context-Oriented Determinants

Studies inspired by earlier research of Galtung and Ruge (1965), Hester (1973), and Ostgaard (1965), show that a number of contextual determinants have influenced international news flow, such as the geographic distance between host and foreign nations (Chang et al., 1987; Kim & Barnett, 1996; Van Belle, 2000; Wu, 2003); languages (Hester, 1973; Kim & Barnett, 1996); populations (Hester, 1973; Kim & Barnett, 1996; Wu, 2003); economic development (Kim & Barnett, 1996); international trade volume (Hester, 1973; Wu, 2003); and political freedom (Kim & Barnett, 1996; Ostgaard, 1965). However, this list of external determinants is not comprehensive or consistently significant. Findings vary depending on different media, events, and other conditions. The international news flow is usually determined by a combination of those factors (Chang et al., 1987). As a result, the analysis of external determinants becomes rather complex.

Given the exploratory nature of this study and the prior findings in the news flow research tradition, this study includes 11 variables to examine Australia's news coverage of the world: geographic distance, land area, population, tourism, trade, gross domestic product (GDP), press freedom, active troops, defense expenditures, colonial relations, and Internet users.

Geographic Distance   The physical distance from the host nation of the location where events have occurred can impact the news editorial decisions for at least two reasons. First, a news event that takes place in a distant country may not be able to attract the interest of a local audience. Chang et al.'s (1987) study has supported such a proximity rule. The second reason is logistic concerns. Despite the international news information available through news wire services, many news media, especially elite newspapers and networks, tend to use their own sources (Gasher & Gabriele, 2004). Accordingly, the travel cost and time will offset the newsworthiness of some events that occur in foreign countries (Tuchman, 1997).

However, new technologies and advanced transportation are reducing the distance and time constraints, so geographic distance should become a less important factor in shaping the news flow. Besides, the comparison between online and off-line newspapers has indicated that online media use more information from wire services than their off-line counterparts (Gasher & Gabriele, 2004). Therefore, whether the variable of geographic distance significantly affects the international news flow is indefinite for the online new media.

Land Area   Land area refers to the physical size of a country. Many studies have found that the variable of land area is positively related to news coverage (Kim & Barnett, 1996). Nations with large land areas are more likely to be rated higher on the hierarchy of nations in news coverage than those with small land areas (Wu, 2003). However, this hypothesis is not supported by all studies. Rather than proposing hypotheses in relation to the variables of geographic distance and land area, this study raises the following research questions for academic consideration:

RQ1. Will the geographic distance between the host country and the country to be covered affect the amount of news coverage on an online news site?

RQ2. Is a country's land area associated with the online news coverage of that country in the host country?

Population   Previous studies suggest population is a factor in explaining the media's world coverage (Kim & Barnett, 1996; Wu, 2003). It is assumed that the larger a nation's population, the greater will be its personal contact and information exchange with other nations. Thus, this study proposes that:

H1. The larger the population of a nation, the more news this nation will receive online in the host nation.

Tourism   Related to the variable of population, the number of tourists is also introduced to predict international news flow (Hester, 1973). To some extent, as a variable to measure the contact between two nations, tourism is more accurate than population because it also implies cultural and social proximity (Adams, 1986). One will expect that the flow of tourists should influence the flow of news. Tourists crossing national borders will advance economic, cultural, and news information exchanges among nations.

H2. The more tourists there are traveling from and to a nation, the more news coverage that nation will receive in the host nation.

Trade   The variable of international trade is one of the most important factors in shaping the flow of news (Chang et al., 1987). Economic interactions between nations encourage people in each country to learn more about the other nation or nations. Indeed, people may have little interest in nations that are unrelated economically to the country in which they live. Beyond the trade relationship, dependency theory further reveals the historic and cultural influences that developed countries have on developing countries: developed countries produce and market their industrial products as well as news information to developing countries, and developing countries consume and depend on information from developed countries (Kim & Barnett, 1996). Trade is conceptually and practically correlated to the variables of tourism and population. Therefore, the trade volume between two countries alters their mutual news coverage of each other's events.

H3. The greater the trade volume between a host and a foreign country, the more the foreign country will be covered online in the host country.

Gross Domestic Product (GDP)   Unlike the variable of trade, GDP indicates the wealth of a country in general. Actually, the advance of international news flow research has roots in the debate about the new world information and communication order (NWICO) (Wu, 2003).

The developing countries complain that there is an imbalance of news flow across national borders, and that developed countries' wire services have not sufficiently covered developing countries. Since GDP is one of the most frequently used measurements of economic development level, it can serve as a predictor of the direction of international news flow.

Moreover, the development level can also indicate the communication infrastructure of a country. With a better communication infrastructure, the information transmission will be faster and more frequent. In particular, the Internet will have a greater impact on a nation's economic and social changes. Studies discover that GDP is a valid predictor of foreign news coverage (Wu, 2003).

H4. The larger a nation's GDP is, the more that nation will be covered online in the host country.

Press Freedom   The variable of press freedom is commonly used in the news flow literature to assess the influence of government on world news coverage (Chang et al., 1987; Golan, chapter 6 this volume). One can assume that freedom of speech should make it easier to gather and transmit news information. Since the end of the Cold War, the right to freedom of the press has become expected all over the world. Although countries are located in different positions on a continuum of press freedom, new technologies are believed to offer people more opportunities to express and receive diverse opinions.

H5. The more freedom the press system has in a foreign country, the more that country will be covered online in the host country.

Active Troops   In addition to press freedom, military power is one of the crucial political influences especially on intercountry relationships (Oneal & Russett, 1997). After the 9/11 attacks, national security and the war on terrorism began to have a worldwide impact, which makes the power of the military an important variable to study. Van Belle (2000) suggests using the number of active troops and defense expenditures to measure the power of the military.

H6. The greater the number of active troops a foreign country has, the more that country will be covered online in the host country.

Defense Expenditures   As mentioned before, the variable of defense expenditures measures the power of the military from an economic angle (Oneal & Russett, 1997). The assumption is that expenditures on weapon development, military training, and defense construction will enhance the comprehensive power of the armed forces. Besides, the defense expenditures are expected to correlate to a country's economic and technologic development, as well as its population and land area.

H7. The more defense expenditures a country has, the more that country will be covered online in the host country.

Colonial Relations   To speculate about the cultural links among nations, some researchers have integrated colonial ties into their studies (Meyer, 1984). The investigation on this variable is rational because Australia is a member of the Commonwealth of Nations, among which common values are shared and closer relations are expected. United by a common allegiance to the British Crown, the Commonwealth consists of 53 sovereign nations.[1] If colonial ties can predict the foreign news coverage, then,

H8. The members of the Commonwealth of Nations will receive more news coverage than other countries in Australia's online media.

Internet Users   The variable of Internet users is employed to evaluate Internet development and uses in a country. The Internet has been perceived to be a more important information source than all other traditional media (Annenberg News, Annual Internet Survey, 2008). A Pew Internet study has found that there is an increase in the number of people who regard the Internet as a primary medium of rapidly spreading news information (Horrigan, 2006). Research shows that news Web sites present more international news than network, cable, or newspapers (Martin-Kratzer & Thorson, chapter 8 this volume). It is expected that growth in the number of Internet users will accelerate the distribution of online information. Also, the number of Internet users should be a credible indicator of the development of the communication infrastructure, which is positively correlated to the news coverage of this country (Wu, 2003). Furthermore, the diffusion of the Internet will improve the freedom of the traditional media within a country. As a result, the number of Internet users in a particular country is assumed to positively correlate to its news coverage in the host country.

H9. The more Internet users a country has, the more coverage this country will receive online in the host country.

Method

The study to identify the major determinants of online international news flow consisted of three steps. First, a content analysis was conducted to discover how often each nation is covered in the Australian online media, which was used as the dependent variable in regression analyses. Then, data for the 11 variables were collected in response to the nations covered in the online media, which were used as the independent variables in regression analyses. Finally, regression analyses were performed to discover the determinants of online international news flow.

Content Analysis

Media   Australia was chosen for this study because not many news flow studies have focused on that country (Hanusch, 2003). Australia's media are independent of the government and have a tradition of free expression (Craig, 2004; Deuze, 2002), and Australia has a diverse media market with a condensed population, favorable Internet accessibility, and nationally circulated newspapers (Department of Foreign Affairs and Trade of Australia, n.d.). Yahoo!7, a partnership between the largest television network, Seven Network, and Yahoo! Australia & New Zealand (Yahoo!7 Redefines, 2006), was analyzed because it was one of the most influential online media identified by native Australians (Widing, personal communication, March 3, 2006). In contrast to online media, this study also examined the international news coverage in *The Australian*, one of the two major national dailies in Australia.

Sampling   This study randomly selected March 3, 2006, as a starting point from which to study news stories for one consecutive week. All news stories listed under the "world news" category on Yahoo!7 beginning March 3 through March 9, 2006, were sampled in the analysis. In the meantime, the researcher located seven days of international news in *The Australian* through the LexisNexis database. A total of 469 online international stories and 57 offline international stories were sampled.

Coding   This study coded only the primary nations mentioned in each story. To define the primary nations in stories, the researcher decided to code those identified in the headline or lead. Multiple nations were coded if more than one country was identified in the headline or lead. If no country was specified in the headline or lead, the researcher read the rest of the story until one could be identified. If the researcher could only identify a region, such as the Middle East, the story was coded as "others."

One graduate student and the researcher coded 100 online international stories, approximately 20% of the overall sample, to test intercoder reliability. Using the simple agreement between the two coders, the intercoder reliability of this study was 94.7%. The researcher completed the rest of coding and found 71 countries were covered in online news, and 15 countries were covered in off-line news, which echoed Martin-

Table 13.1 The Numbers of Stories about 10 Most Frequently
Covered Nations at Yahoo!7 and the Australian, March 3 to 9, 2006

Nation	Yahoo!7	The Australian
U.S.A	67	11
Iraq	43	13
Israel	30	0
India	29	7
China	27	10
Afghanistan	27	2
U.K.	22	2
Iran	22	0
Pakistan	18	0
The Philippines	12	1

Kratzer and Thorson's (chapter 8 this volume) finding that news Web sites cover broader issues and more nations than traditional media. Table 13.1 shows the 10 most frequently covered nations.

Independent Variables

The researcher used varying methods and resources to collect data regarding the independent variables.

The *geographic distance* between Australia and a foreign country was defined as the distance between the two capital cities. For instance, the distance between Australia and America was computed as the distance from Canberra to Washington, DC, which was 9,908 miles. The researcher used an online database, *Bali & Indonesia on the Net*,[2] to calculate the distance from Canberra, Australia, to 71 capital cities. The most distant city from Canberra, Australia, was Madrid, Spain (10,924 miles); and the closest city was Noumea, New Caledonia (1,393 miles).

The raw figures for the variables of land area, population, GDP, active troops, and defense expenditures were directly collected from the *World Almanac and Book of Facts* (2006). The Internet user statistics from 71 countries were also collected from the *World Almanac and Book of Facts* (2006), which, however, missed a few nations' figures. The researcher then searched the Central Intelligence Agency's (*CIA World Factbook*, n.d.) Web site and obtained the raw figures for Iraq, Afghanistan, Somalia, and New Caledonia.

The raw figures of tourists from 71 countries traveling to Australia and those of Australians traveling to those 71 countries were obtained from *Annuaire des Statistiques du Tourisme* (*Yearbook of Tourism*

Statistics; World Tourism Organization, 2005) published in Madrid. However, the tourism statistics seemed rather fragmented and unsystematic. This study combined four types of statistics as the number of tourists, including arrivals of nonresident tourists at national borders, arrivals of nonresident visitors at national borders, arrivals of nonresident tourists in hotels and similar places of accommodation, and arrivals of nonresident tourists in all types of places of accommodation. Yet, not all four statistics were available for each nation. And a few nations, such as Iraq and Iran, did not have tourism records for the most recent 5 years. Therefore, the quality of this variable was not highly consistent.

Mutual trade was calculated as the sum of the import and export volumes between the foreign nation and Australia, which were available at *Direction of Trade Statistics Yearbook, 2004* (International Monetary Fund, 2004)—the data were for 2003. For the colonial ties, a list of the Commonwealth countries was downloaded from the Web site of the Commonwealth Secretariat (The Commonwealth, n.d.). This was coded as a dummy variable used in regression analyses as nations of the Commonwealth and coded "1"; other nations were coded "0."

Freedom House's *Freedom in the World* offers an interval scale to measure the variable of press freedom, which was superior to an ordinal scale that Chang et al. (1987) used. This study adopted Freedom House's 2006 survey that analyzed 194 countries and territories on a basis of universal criteria concerning a society's press freedom. Each nation is assigned a score from 0 to 100, where a score of 0 indicates a large degree of press freedom while a score of 100 indicates a complete lack of press freedom. For instance, the press in Australia is considered free with a score of 19, and the press in North Korea, rated 97, is not considered free, (Freedom House, 2006).

Regression Analyses

All dependent and independent variables were input into SPSS for statistical analyses. Q-Q plots and standardized residual plots were used to examine the assumptions of linearity, normality, and homogeneity of variances. With the help of residual diagnostics, specifically examining the studentized deleted residual, Cook's distance, and centered leverage values, the researchers identified the coverage frequencies of the United States, Iraq, Israel, India, China, Afghanistan, United Kingdom, Iran, and Pakistan as nine influential outliers. Conceptually, the coverage of these nations is the essence of international news flow. Simply dropping these cases from the regression analyses would potentially damage the validity of the determinant study. Therefore, the researcher removed those outliers to conduct a regression analysis first; then reassigned the outliers three standard deviations to the mean and included them into a second regression analysis. With outliers removed and reassigned, these two regression analyses reached the same result.

Results

The 11 determinants of online news flow were regressed on amount of online coverage by Australian media. Only two variables, Internet users and GDP were significant determinants of online international news flow.

Thus, the researcher entered the amount of online coverage as the dependent variable, and Internet users and GDP as independent variables to establish full regression models. Table 13.2 shows the regression model when the outliers were removed and the model when the outliers were reassigned. When the outliers were removed, the full regression model was significant $(R^2 = .361, F (2, 48) = 15.111, p < .001)$. The full regression model was significant, too, when the outliers were reassigned $(R^2 = .358, F (2, 67) = 20.236, p < .001)$. In other words, only the number of Internet users and GDP were significant predictors of the amount of news coverage of that nation in Australia's online media. And the combined two predictors could explain about 36% of the variations of online international news coverage.

Accordingly, a country's geographic distance (RQ1) to Australia, land area (RQ2), population (H1), mutual tourists (H2), bilateral trade (H3), level of freedom of press (H5), number of active troops (H6), defense expenditures (H7), and colonial ties did not significantly correlate with

Table 13.2 Predictions of International News Covered on Australia's Online Media, Outliers Removed and Reassigned Models, March 3 to 9, 2006.

Independent Variables	B	β	t	sig.
Outlier removed model				
Constant	2.072			
GDP	.010	1.899	4.281	.000
Internet users	.00000056	1.447	3.261	.002
Adjusted R^2 = .361, F = 15.111, d.f. = (2, 48), p < .001.				
Outlier reassigned model				
Constant	4.335			
GDP	.008	1.524	3.435	.001
Internet users	.00000039	.971	2.189	.032
Adjusted R^2 = .358, F = 20.236, d.f. = (2, 67), p < .001.				

the news coverage of that country in Australia's online media. Instead, a country's GDP (H4) and Internet users (H9) were found to be significant predictors of the news coverage in the regression model, and therefore hypotheses 4 and 9 were supported. In particular, H9 suggested that the greater number of Internet users a foreign country has, the more news that country would receive online in Australia. This result indicates that nations with more Internet users and better high technological infrastructures might receive more attention in Australian online news. On the one hand, the development of the Internet is associated with another predictor, GDP, because they both can suggest the nature of a nation's economic development. On the other hand, one can assume that the use of the Internet will accelerate the worldwide information diffusion. The Internet and new technologies enable media workers to gather and transmit foreign news information efficiently.

Intriguingly, even though the international news coverage on Australia's off-line and online media is rather similar ($r = .818$, $p < .001$), there were 56 countries that were ignored by off-line news, but were covered by online news. This gap between the numbers of nations covered in online news and offline news supported previous studies that online news covered broader issues and more nations than its counterparts (Martin-Kratzer & Thorson, chapter 8 this volume). Part of the reason is that online media have almost unlimited newsholes, which allows journalists to include more international news provided by a variety of sources including wire services.

However, the interesting question became what contextual factors had altered online news editors' decisions. The researcher separated the 56 nations only covered in online media from those 15 nations also covered in off-line media. Another stepwise regression was executed to investigate the determinants that extended online editors' vision of the world.

After reassigning the outliers inspected by the residual diagnostics, the hierarchy regression identified the variable of active troops as the only significant predictor for the online-only coverage. The researcher reentered the number of online stories as the dependent variable, and active troops as an independent variable to create a full regression model (see Table 13.3.). With the adjusted $R^2 = .173$, $F (1, 52) = 12.050$, $p < .001$, the online-only regression model was significant, too.

In the online media, when editors expanded their views to survey those nations that were "traditionally" not covered, the nations' active troops became the predominate determinant, which could explain 17.3% of the variations of the online-only international news. In this circumstance, however, hypothesis 6 was supported. This result could predict that after the 9/11 attacks and other global terrorism events, the war on terrorism was at the top of media's agenda. Online news media are

Table 13.3 Prediction of International News Exclusively Covered on Australia's Online Media, March 3 to 9, 2006

Independent Variables	B	β	t	sig.
Constant	2.426			
Active troops	.0000096 I	.434	3.47 I	.00 I

Adjusted R^2 = .173, F = 12.050, $d.f.$ = (1, 52), p < .001.

playing a keen role in surveillance, watching other nations with active militaries. Australia was also part of the coalition operations in Iraq until June 2008 (The War in Iraq, n.d.), and had a contingent of troops there at the time of the study. The issues of national security and military conflicts diverted the flow of international news online.

Conclusion and Discussion

This study examined the contextual determinants of online international news flow by analyzing Australia's media. The researcher discovered that GDP and the number of Internet users of a nation were major determinants of the online international news flow. If a nation has a strong economy and larger numbers of Internet users, it will receive more coverage in Australia's online media. The findings support the previous studies that discovered GDP to be a valid predictor of news coverage (Wanta & Golan, chapter 5, this volume; Wu, 2003).

With the increased interest in national security following the 9/11 attacks, foreign countries that are not generally covered by traditional newspapers could attract more attention from online media if they have a powerful, active military. Previous research consistently identified military power as an important factor in international news coverage (Golan, chapter 6 this volume; Oneal & Russett, 1997).

Some expected predictors were found to be insignificant. Australia's media seemingly did not pay much attention to the culturally, historically, and economically related Commonwealth nations. The colonial tie was not a profound determinant in the flow of international news in this study. This result echoes the studies by Herr (2006) and Yeomans (1999) that suggested Australia was not closely connected to other Commonwealth nations in improving regional security, cultural, economic, and environmental well-being. Although it was often identified as a crucial predictor (Chang & Lee, chapter 3 this volume; Chang et al., 1987; Golan, chapter 6 this volume), geographic proximity did not lead Australians to look at their neighboring nations in this study. New Zealand, for instance, was not one of the frequently covered countries in Australia's media. Given Australia's geographical isolation, distance between nations turned out to be an insignificant factor in changing the shape of the world presented in the news.

In dealing with influential cases, this study employed the method of reassigning outliers to three standard deviations to the mean. However, Myers and Well (2003) recommended another approach to detect the influence of outliers, suggesting researchers add outliers one at a time to the regression model without outliers present. To further evaluate the possible determinants owing to those outliers, the researcher added the nine nations, namely the United States, Iraq, Israel, India, China, Afghanistan, United Kingdom, Iran, and Pakistan, one at a time to the "outlier removed model" in Table 13.2. The results showed that GDP became the only predictor of international news flow when including U.S. into the model. When China was involved, the Internet users and GDP remained the dominant determinants. Active troops and defense expenditures, which imply military activities, were strong predictors when Iraq, Israel, Iran, and Afghanistan joined the regression model.

The variable of population was a significant predictor when India and Pakistan were added to the analyses. By contrast, the involvement of Britain made tourism and mutual trade the significant determinants of international news coverage. These two variables could denote the ties between Commonwealth nations. Even though this is considered an alternative approach to examine outliers, the researcher found it troublesome to interpret the results. Nevertheless, the results obtained through this approach were expected to attract the attention of researchers for future investigations on these variables. In the meantime, a refined method to assess influential cases in regression studies is needed for future research.

Other future research may investigate more online news sites and traditional news outlets for a better understanding of the international news flow presented in online media. Expanding the international news flow research to more countries may help find some common and unique criteria that gatekeepers of different countries have been using to cover foreign countries.

Finally, missing data and incomparable raw figures, such as tourism statistics, have caused problems for news determinants studies. It will be valuable if future studies can refine the methods used to collect more reliable statistics.

Notes

1. The 53 Commonwealth nations are Antigua and Barbuda, Australia, The Bahamas, Bangladesh, Barbados, Belize, Botswana, Brunei Darussalam, Cameroon, Canada, Cyprus, Dominica, Fiji Islands, The Gambia, Ghana, Grenada, Guyana, India, Jamaica, Kenya, Kiribati, Lesotho, Malawi,

Malaysia, Maldives, Malta, Mauritius, Mozambique, Namibia, Nauru, New Zealand, Nigeria, Pakistan, Papua New Guinea, St Kitts and Nevis, St Lucia, St Vincent and the Grenadines, Samoa, Seychelles, Sierra Leone, Singapore, Solomon Islands, South Africa, Sri Lanka, Swaziland, Tonga, Trinidad and Tobago, Tuvalu, Uganda, United Kingdom, United Republic of Tanzania, Vanuatu, and Zambia (The Commonwealth, n.d.).

2. Bali & Indonesia on the Net: http://www.indo.com/distance/

References

Adams, W. C. (1986). Whose lives count? TV coverage of natural disasters. *Journal of Communication, 36*(Spring), 113–122.

Annual Internet survey by USC Annenberg's Center for the Digital future finds shifting trends among adults about the benefits and consequences of children going online. *University of Southern California Annenberg News.* (2008, January 17). Retrieved July 12, 2008, from http://annenberg.usc.edu/AboutUs/PublicAffairs/AbergNews/080117CDFsurvey.aspx

Chang, T. K., Shoemaker, P. J., & Brendlinger, N. (1987, August). Determinants of international news converge in the U.S. media. *Communication Research, 14,* 396–414.

CIA world factbook. (n.d.). Retrieved March 21, 2006, from http://www.cia.gov/cia/publications/factbook/rankorder/2153rank.html

The Commonwealth. (n.d.). *Commonwealth secretariat.* Retrieved July 10, 2008 from http://www.thecommonwealth.org/Internal/180380/

Craig, G. (2004). *The media politics and public life.* Crows Nest, NSW, Australia: Allen & Unwin.

Department of Foreign Affairs and Trade of Australia. (n.d.). *The media in Australia.* Retrieved March 6, 2006, from http://www.dfat.gov.au/facts/media.html

Deuze, M. (2002). National news cultures: A comparison of Dutch, German, British, Australian, and U.S. journalists. *Journalism & Mass Communication Quarterly, 79,* 134–149.

Freedom House. (2006). *Freedom of the press 2006: A global survey of media independence.* Lanham, MD: Rowman & Littlefield.

Galtung, J., & Ruge, M. H. (1965). The structure of foreign news. *Journal of Peace Research, 2,* 64–91.

Gasher, M., & Gabriele, S. (2004). Increasing circulation? A comparative news-flow study of the *Montreal Gazette*'s hard-copy and on-line editions. *Journalism Studies, 5*(3), 311–323.

Hanusch, F. (2003). Coverage of international and Pacific news in the *Fiji Times* and *The Australian. Pacific Journalism Review, 9,* 59–78.

Hachten, W. A., & Scotton, J. F. (2002). *The world news prism: Global media in an era of terrorism* (6th ed.). Ames, IA: Iowa State University Press.

Herr, R. (2006). Australia, security and the Pacific Islands: From empire to Commonwealth. *The Round Table, 95,* 705–716.

Hester, A. (1973). Theoretical considerations in predicting volume and direction of international information flow. *Gazette, 19,* 239–247.

Horrigan, J. B. (2006). For many home broadband users, the Internet is a primary news source. *Pew Internet & American Life Project*. Retrieved July 12, 2008, from http://www.pewinternet.org/PPF/r/131/report_display.asp

Hur, K. K. (1984). A critical analysis of international news flow research. *Critical Studies in Mass Communication, 1,* 365–378.

International Monetary Fund. (2004). *Direction of trade statistics yearbook.* Washington, DC: Author.

Kim, K., & Barnett, G. A. (1996). The determinants of international news flow: A network analysis. *Communication Research, 23,* 323–352.

Meyer, W. H. (1984). Global news flows: Dependency and neoimperialism. *Comparative Political Studies, 22*(3), 243–264.

Myers, J. L., & Well, A. D. (2003). *Research design and statistical analysis* (2nd ed.). Mahwah, NJ: Erlbaum.

Oneal, J., & Russett, B. (1997, June). The classical liberals were right: Democracy, interdependence, and conflicts, 1950–1989. *International Studies Quarterly, 41,* 267–294.

Ostgaard, E. (1965). Factors influencing the flow of news. *Journal of Peace Research, 2*(1), 39–63.

Sosale, S. (2003). Envisioning a new world order through journalism. *Journalism: Theory, practice and criticism, 4*(3), 377–392.

Sreberny-Mohammadi, A. (1995). Global news media cover the world. In J. Downing, A. Mohammadi, & A. Sreberny-Mohammadi (Eds.), *Questioning the media: A critical introduction* (pp. 428–433). Thousand Oaks, CA: Sage.

Tuchman, G. (1997). Making news by doing work: Routinizing the unexpected. In D. Berkowitz (Ed.), *Social meanings of news: A text-reader* (pp. 173–192). Thousand Oaks, CA: Sage.

Van Belle, D. A. (2000). *New York Times* and network TV news coverage of foreign disasters: The significance of the insignificant variables. *Journalism & Mass Communication Quarterly, 77,* 50–70.

The war in Iraq: ADF operations in the Middle East in 2003. (n.d.). *Australian Government, Department of Defense.* Retrieved July 12, 2008 from http://www.defence.gov.au/publications/lessons.pdf

The World Almanac and Book of Facts, 2006. (2006). New York: World Almanac Books.

World Tourism Organization. (2005). *Annuaire des Statistiques du Tourisme* [Yearbook of Tourism Statistics] (56th ed.). Madrid: Organisation Mondiale du Tourisme.

Wu, H. D. (1998). Investigating the determinants of international news flow: A meta-analysis. *Gazette: International Journal of Communication Studies, 60*(6), 493–512.

Wu, H. D. (2003). Homogeneity around the world? Comparing the systemic determinants of international news flow between developed and developing countries. *Gazette, 65*(1), 9–24.

Yahoo!7 redefines Australian media landscape: Partnership announces new corporate identity & chairman. (n.d.).*Yahoo! Media Relations.* Retrieved January 30, 2006, from http://au.docs.yahoo.com/info/pr/pr.html?id=57

Yeomans, K. (1999). Commonwealth island states in the global information society: A narrow window of opportunity. *The Round Table, 351,* 423–431.

Chapter 14

Blogs as Stealth Dissent?

"Eighteen Touch Dog Newspaper" and the Tactics, Ambiguity, and Limits of Internet Resistance in China

Wei Zha and David D. Perlmutter

The Problem: The People's Media?

Here we consider two paradoxes of modern global media. First, in an age when all online communication is accessible to international audiences even if produced for local consumption, how do we "read" across borders, cultures, and symbol systems? Second, how can a local communicator produce oppositional communication within a restrictive society that, in theory and legal fact, controls the information its citizens can gather, disseminate, and exhibit? The polity at issue is the People's Republic of China, a nation that is accelerating its development of the infrastructure of the Internet and other modern telecommunications technology. At the same time, the Middle Kingdom has, within the last decade, widely expanded the types and degrees of its restrictions on the political content of new media, especially on the booming native online blog community.

In the West, the weblog is often portrayed as the ultimate expression of "people's media," allowing individuals to create idiosyncratic, interactive online journals of news and commentary that bypass the normal channels of the elite media. In China, the situation is different: Outright public affairs argumentation is either banned or discouraged, and the use of legal sanctions and technological blocks and filters are on the increase. At the same time, worldwide, China leads the blog population in terms of growth (Perlmutter, 2008; Perlmutter & Hamilton, 2007; Sifry, 2005, 2006). Can blogs operate in their ascribed democratizing tendency in such a controlled environment? In this study we examine a famous and extremely popular Chinese blog and discuss how it can be a vehicle of dissent *without* incurring the wrath of the state. We further speculate whether this blog might serve as a model for others wishing to express unapproved messages via personal Web sites in societies that limit freedom of expression.

Three Kinds of Dissent in Controlled Societies

Dissent in a controlled society, where open physical, written, or verbal protest against the ruling regime is dangerous, can operate in several forms. Each is in tension with the state not only because it is in opposition but because it can erupt into outright rebellion. The first and most common variety of indirect dissent is nonmediated interpersonal or small-group communication: gossip, rumor, and conversation. Anthropologist James Scott has argued that among all subordinate groups there is a rich history of the "'hidden transcript'...[that] represents the critique of power spoken behind the back of the dominant" (Scott, 1990, p. xii). In Chinese tradition these "common voices" of the streets, marketplace, fields, and now the office water cooler is "small way" or "folk talk" and *xiaodao xiaoxi* (rumors or gossip) (Chang, 1990; Dittmer, 1994; Hamrin, 1994).

A second form of indirect opposition is samizdat (literally, to "do the publishing oneself"), protest literature not printed by formal means. The term arose from dissenters against Communist regimes in the Soviet Union and Middle and Eastern Europe, whose clandestine mimeographs and newsletters laid the groundwork for popular upheavals against many governments (Johnston, 1999; Telesin, 1973). China has a tradition of such literature through its most famous incarnation, the *dazibao* ("big-character posters"), pasted on the "democracy wall" near Tiananmen Square both in the late 1980s and in earlier times (Hamrin, 1994; Liu, 1996; Zhao, 1998).

A third traditional way in which people can express dissent in a controlled society is via visual or verbal allusions (from irony to allegories, metaphors, and symbols): Creating media content that seems to be about one thing (an innocuous subject or even praise of the regime) but is understood (that is, decoded) by oppositional audiences to be actually criticism of the regime. *The key for such media to survive is their very ambiguity and indeterminacy of meaning.* China's most famous modern case of protest of this kind in the pre-Tiananmen era was probably *He Shang*, translated variously as "River Dirge," "River Elegy," or "early death on the river," a six-part documentary film shown on Beijing's Central Television starting June 12, 1988. By one estimate, it drew 600 million viewers in its various showings. A version of the series script became a bestseller and was renowned for its symbolic and inferred criticism of the ruling regime (Cheng, 1990, pp. 89–90).

The Prospects and Perils of International e-Dissent

Chinese dissidents have always been entrepreneurial in exploiting technology to get their messages out to the world. During the Tiananmen movement, while the "whole world was watching" via television, other media such as faxes constituted significant venues for internal dissidents to get out their message and receive information from abroad (Evan, 1981; Forsythe, 1991; Johnson-Eilola, 1997; Sproull & Keisler, 1991; Vaney, Gance, & Mar, 2000). And then, on the surface, the Internet offered an opportunity to revert from indirection, circuitousness, and subtlety and proceed to open opposition in word and image in the PRC. By 2001, China comprised the second largest population of Internet users in the world (Bowman, 2002) and by 2007 the numbers of Chinese Web users was greater than the adult population of the United States (Internet Coaching Library, 2007; *Wall Street Journal*, 2007). From the 1990s through today, thousands of Internet newspapers and other kinds of Web sites that directly criticized the Chinese government sprang up on servers outside China and were available to the careful Chinese Internet user. Among the major players in oppositional information are Big Reference [*Da Cankao*], Small Reference [*Xiao Cankao*], and the "*Huaxia* Digest" (http://www.cnd.org), which are forwarded by e-mail or available to Chinese who can access their sites (China's Internet Information Skirmish, 2000). By January 2005, China also boasted an estimated 700,000 bloggers (Gillmor, 2005). By late 2007 that number had reached an estimated 47 million, with the number of blog spaces jumping to 72.82 million in China (The Survey Report, 2007). Hundreds of thousands of blogs about China are posted by Chinese and foreigners and members of the ethnic Chinese Diaspora abroad.

The Chinese government, however, has worked actively to control Internet-derived content through the Ministry of Information Industry, which regulates access to the Internet, and the Ministry of Public and State Security, which monitors use of the Internet (Cox, 2003). These agencies now have Internet administrative offices in more than 700 cities and provinces and search the Web as well as personal and commercial e-mails for "heretical teachings or feudal superstitions" and any postings "harmful to the dignity or interests of the state"—commonly referred to in state literature as "poisonous weeds" (*New Scientist*, 2004).

Techniques for censorship include blocking certain Web sites from Chinese servers and filtering e-mails with search engines that seek out trigger words, ranging from the names of Chinese leaders to suspicious terms such as *freedom* and *democracy* (Zittrain & Edelman, 2003). Other methods include changing IP addresses on forbidden Web sites and redirecting them to a single server for deletion (Dong, 2002; IDG News Service, 2002). Government officials log onto foreign Internet chat rooms to argue in favor of PRC policies; the Ministries also issued a decree warning "Web administrators at popular online services...that they will be held responsible for politically offensive communications, thereby enlisting them in the policing efforts" (French, 2005).

The "great firewall of China" is variable and spotty, however. Sometimes officials block Web sites because proscribed groups are associated with them. For example, the Web site of Stanford University is blocked because of a Falungong (the banned Chinese spiritual society) club on campus (China's Internet Information Skirmish, 2000). On the other hand, Web content may be blocked via one portal but not another. *Foreign Affairs* magazine published an article on the Tiananmen protests in its first issue of 2001; its site was consequently blocked by the PRC censors but the article was still available to Chinese Internet users via the Web site of the Council on Foreign Relations (Chase & Mulvenon, 2002). In other instances, a foreign site will find itself unblocked, only to be blocked again a few weeks later. In a major case in October 2004, the PRC government tried to ban "links to foreign Chinese language newspapers from PRC news Web sites" but apparently stopped the policy a few months later (China's Internet Information Skirmish, 2000; see also BBC, 2005; Boxun.com, 2005; Shen, 2005; Zittrain & Edelman, 2003).

More recently, in the run-up to the Olympics, restrictions on censorship of the Internet in China have grown. Among the new targets are Web sites that transmit video content. Most recently, foreign Web sites outside China, including YouTube.com, have been blocked due to their video presentation of contentious issues like protests in Tibet (China Ties U.S., 2008). This is not an isolated event, since January 31, 2008, the State Administration of Radio, Film and Television has stipulated that those Chinese sites will be punished if they distribute online videos that concern national secrets, hurt the reputation of the country, destabilize the society, or promote pornography. One of the victims is Totou.com, one of the well-known Chinese Web sites that carry videos (China to Shut or Punish, 2008). In May 2008, China's technology minister, Wan Gang, promised that China would guarantee Internet access but defended the country's censorship, which he said aims at illegal and offensive content (Serrie, 2008).

Self-censorship has also accelerated. The supervisory bodies of the government have established different kinds of communication channels to monitor the leading commercial Web sites through phone, e-mail, SMS text messages, MSN, QQ, and RTX (Real Time eXchange) instant messaging, Web platforms, and a weekly meeting. The most preferred is RTX, an instant messaging service offered by Chinese company Tengxun (China Journey to the Heart, 2007). In order to have ideological control over its employees and to conduct better censorship and self-censorship practices, relevant government institutions have sponsored training courses, and only executives and editors who get a certificate of compliance can work at Internet companies (China Journey to the Heart, 2007).

Ironically, and to the surprise of Westerners, a new study (Surveying Internet Usage, 2007) founded by the Markle Foundation found that the majority of Chinese approve of the government's control over the Internet, perhaps because "Internet addiction" is a large social concern in China (Fallows, 2008). Even though there are many Chinese Internet users writing blogs, and many participate in online discussions, most of them are actually using blogs as a record of their daily lives. The most popular topics on Chinese blogs are hobbies, pets, pop culture, and rumors about entertainers. The Internet has brought an unprecedented chance for ordinary people to be heard or to communicate with each other (Fallows, 2008).

The future, of course, is unwritten (and as yet unblogged). Certainly, as has been claimed, "you can't stop the flow of information by tanks" (Berkowitz & Quittner, 1991). But obviously the challenges to dissident blogs in the PRC are numerous. High-level filterware, tough laws, and dedicated "Internet police" can restrict information and intimidate those who seek to disseminate or consume it. Of some controversy is the fact that Microsoft, Cisco Systems, Nortel Networks, Sun Microsystems, and Websense have assisted the Chinese government in creating detection, filtering, and blocking software (International Freedom of Expression eXchange, 2005). As a result, as one major report noted:

> China's Internet filtering regime is the most sophisticated effort of its kind in the world. Compared to similar efforts in other states, China's filtering regime is pervasive, sophisticated, and effective. It comprises multiple levels of legal regulation and technical control. It involves numerous state agencies and thousands of public and private personnel. (Open Initiative, 2005)

Some observers, however, believe that the sheer numbers of Chinese Internet users, and the great weight of complaints about the government on issues ranging from corruption to lack of civil liberties and freedoms, will eventually break through the web of censorship. The *Guardian's* John Gittings wrote:

> The government is engaged in a losing battle against a news-hungry and increasingly sophisticated people who are finding creative ways to get past the high-tech word-based filters. Chairman Mao was right when he said that the course of battle was determined not by machines but people. (*Yaleglobal*, 2003, p. 2)

Taking more of a middle ground, a 2002 Rand Corporation study on strategies of Internet dissent and censorship in China suggested:

> While Beijing has done a remarkable job of finding effective coun-
> terstrategies to the potential negative effects of the information revo-
> lution, the scale of China's information-technology modernization
> would suggest that time is eventually on the side of the regime's
> opponents. (cited in Chase & Mulvenon, 2002, p. 89)

Nevertheless, two of the normal channels for dissent in China are
no longer available to online dissidents. They cannot "small talk" other
Web sites and they cannot engage in open "postering" on their own
blogs or foreign blogs via e-mail. For those who violate the laws, the
outcome is potentially grim. Amnesty International lists a number of
Chinese bloggers and Web posters who have been jailed for their activities (Amnesty International, 2004).

It follows that the third option, stealth dissent by allusion, is the only
one available that provides any modicum of safety. This paper examines
a major Chinese blog—indeed, the most famous PRC-based blog in the
world—that, to the outside eye, may be an example of indirect opposition. We seek to understand how the content, style, and language of
this blog can create ambiguities that allow it to be seen by some audiences as shrewd political allegory, irony, and satire, and others (presumably the PRC government) as innocuous or inconsequential. We use the
results of the analysis to speculate on the future of blogging in China
and the role of the Internet as a medium of opposition in controlled
societies. Our intention is not to render a final verdict, nor to propel the
bloggers into jail; we will argue, rather, that the very indeterminacy of
the Chinese blog allows it to survive as a meaningful tool of political
communication.

And the Winner Is…Eighteen Touch Dog Newspaper

In 2004, the Best Weblog Award of Deutsche Welle's 2004 International
Weblog Awards was conferred on blogger Aggressive Little Snake's
(Meng Xiaoshe) Eighteen Touch Dog Newspaper, a blog that, as its
title suggests, focused on the canine. According to Guido Baumhauer,
one of the jury members of the Awards, the blog was "a good example
of Weblogs bringing up an issue that is not tackled by the traditional
media"; furthermore, the blog constituted a successful metaphor for the
situation of people living in China and other nations by presenting the
unfair conditions suffered by dogs in China and Asia compared to the
treatment of animals in the Western world (DW-WORLD DE, 2004). In
short, the judges clearly assumed that Eighteen Touch Dog Newspaper
was, like George Orwell's Animal Farm, concerned with the political
affairs of humans, not the life of our four-legged friends. But how could
they, or anyone, be sure? When examined closely, the content of the blog

does not lend itself to one-to-one allegorical explication and extrapolation; this fact in itself suggests some of the parameters of quasi-oppositional media in modern China.

Metaphors and Allusions: Dogs and Fondling

Eighteen Touch Dog Newspaper made its debut on December 9, 2003. The blog's title, pronounced as "ShiBaMo GouRiBao," was posted in Chinese characters at the left side of the blog banner. Its layout consisted of four major columns, respectively titled "Dog," "Coquette," "Causality," and "Amorism." The "Dog" column is ostensibly devoted primarily to dogs and dog-related events. Most stories deal with relations between dogs and human beings and sometimes dogs and other animals. Some of the stories focus not so much on dogs as they do on entertainment news, partly in connection with dogs, such as films, cartoons, Christmas postcards, and high-tech products with images of dogs. For example, on January 28, 2005, a posted message in the "Dog" column introduced a new intelligent dog toy, developed by a well-known Japanese company, possessing (virtual) "emotions" and an ability to "communicate" with its master.

The column "Coquette" is attributed to a woman named XiaoMo Zhang (who, presumably, is a pseudonym of Aggressive Little Snake). The name translates to "someone named Zhang who would like to be (sexually) fondled." Zhang presents herself as a concubine of Aggressive Little Snake. The tone of her writing suggests that this is meant in jest. In her column, she describes her personal life, her work, and her relations with colleagues and friends. She often uses puns and intentionally misconstructs Chinese characters as well as using exaggerated language to describe events occurring around her. For instance, in April 2004, she wrote,

> Sister Yang wants to co-rent a house with me. Applying a well-known line of the leading actor Wei Xiaobao in a well-known martial arts film, *Fighting for the Almighty Power*, "I only know that I am lovely, but don't know how lovely I am." Now, working in a company and getting along with those decent persons, I really know the degree of my loveliness. Oh, Sister Yang, don't be so Delphic as to eat and live together with me; I will get married someday, and living together with somebody else will smudge my reputation. (Zhang, 2004)

The "Causality" column is used by Aggressive Little Snake and several other pseudonymous authors to address general subjects unrelated to the canine. For example, Snake posted a thank-you letter for a friend who found him a beautiful knife. Another message showed that

he was once invited to write a one-sentence commentary on the film
Cell Phone (*Shou Ji*), a 2004 black comedy portraying the psychological
distance between people, especially spouses, enabled by the use of cell
phones for all conversations. In his review, Snake used his trademark
"sexing up" of formerly august and somber Communist Party dictums
and platitudes. In 1976, after the death of Mao, there was a leadership
struggle in China; as a result, the so-called Gang of Four—the ultra-
leftists, including Mao's wife—were purged. The rallying cry of the coup
was, "Practice is the only criterion of testing truth." Snake, in his movie
review, quipped, "Cell Phone is the only criterion of testing fornication"
(Aggressive Little Snake, 2003a).

The final column, "Amorism," highlights the daily life of one "Alice
Kelp" (AiLiSi Haidai), which reads like a conventional personal Web
page with no attempts to make fun of anything, For example, in February 2004, Alice Kelp wrote, "Due to vanity or love, I really care about
what my boyfriend will do on Valentine's Day. There is no need for him
to spend a lot of money to buy flowers or other expensive gifts; I do want
him to show his love [with a] postcard, a phone call, or a message" (Alice
Kelp, 2004).

Although entitled *Eighteen Touch Dog Newspaper*, the weblog content seemed to be distributed equally among its four major columns,
with a slight emphasis toward "Coquette," until it highlighted its dog
theme on June 17, 2004. After that time, almost all the news stories
ostensibly focused on dogs.

What does this all signify? The complexities of the meanings of elements of the blog defy easy translation (and transliteration) into English
and Western culture. Puns, in particular, do not cross borders well. Take
the original title of the blog itself: *Eighteen Touch Dog Newspaper* (Shi-
BaMo GouRiBao). The Chinese character *Mo*, in the context of *Eighteen
Touch*, could only be interpreted as "touch or grope for an object." The
title *Eighteen Touch* is the same as a well-known song of the "Kejia,"
that is, Han (the majority ethnicity of China) people who migrated from
the north of China to the south after the end of the reign of the Xijin
Dynasty (A.D. 265–316) (Qiao, 2005). The lively tune is composed of
18 lines of Chinese characters and describes—in the vocative tense—the
process of a male fondling his female lover. An approximation of the
song in English is as follows (Qiao, 2005):

> the head smells wonderful like [incense];
> the hair is really dark,
> the hair in the front looks attractive,
> the hair on the back
> of the head curls beautifully,
> the hair at the sides holds upward,

the forehead shines with light,
both sides of the eyebrow raise upward,
the eyes glance attractively upward,
the breath is sweet,
the lip is red,
the chin is lovely,
the ear listens keenly,
the neck is white and clean,
the shoulder curves upward,
the hands are white and delicate,
and the back could be
touched and scratched.

In each line, the first three Chinese characters detail the places on the woman's body to be fondled, with the following five characters depicting the feeling of touching or viewing or smelling the body parts. The second through 6th lines refer to the sensation of stroking the lover's hair, with the 7th to 13th focusing elsewhere on her head, and the next 4 parsing out the touch of, respectively, her neck, shoulders, hands, and back. But the implied concluding two sentences are missing. Generations have mentally filled in the body parts to be fondled next accompanied by the Chinese versions of a smirk and wink (Gu, 2005).[1] *Eighteen Touch* falls into the genre of the ribald folk song, sung by peasants in the field, soldiers in the bivouac, or workers trudging home from the factory, but it is also a famous tune of the bordello, sung and pantomimed by prostitutes, or even in prerevolutionary China a "gorging song," to be sung for patrons at high-end restaurants while they feasted on large meals.

The rest of the blog's title, *Dog Newspaper*, in Chinese characters, could be interpreted as even more directly obscene, figuratively "*dog [fornicating] paper.*" In Chinese, "daily newspaper" is composed of two characters, with the first sounding the same as "fornicate" and the second meaning "paper." *Gouri* is a malicious cursing term, equivalent to "son of a bitch" in English. When asked once in person why the weblog was named *Dog Newspaper*, Aggressive Little Snake replied, holding up a copy of *People's Daily*, the official newspaper of the Chinese government, "Human beings fornicate, so do dogs; if someday human beings stop fornicating, dogs will never stop" (Aggressive Little Snake, 2003b).

Snake has repeatedly stated within the blog that it is about dogs and other common subjects and has *no* political content (Aggressive Little Snake, 2003b). However, on another occasion, when Sina.com interviewed Snake after he received the blog award, he admitted that he introduced some social factors into his dog news (Interview Dog Newspaper Webmaster, 2004).

Dogs by the Numbers

The story behind *Eighteen Touch Dog Newspaper*'s startling victory in the weblog contest establishes a method by which to measure its level of political dissent. According to the introduction of Aggressive Little Snake, after he submitted his Web content for the competition, the single Chinese judge Muzimei briefed other judges (who did not understand Chinese) about the substance of the weblog. She implied, and they concluded, that the blog presented the unfair conditions suffered by dogs in China and other Asian countries *by comparing and contrasting them to the happy lives of animals in the Western world* (Interview Dog Newspaper Webmaster, 2004). The judges apparently reasoned then that the blog delivered brilliant political satire, cunning in its subtlety, and bold in its allegory.

When we examined the content of *Dog* from December 2003 (the first day this blog made its debut) to March 2005, we found that there were altogether 228 entries referring to dogs and anecdotes occurring around dogs. Among them, 146 entries referred to dogs in China and Asian countries, while 78 were about dogs in the West, with four not discernible as being in either category (see Table 14.1). Our inferential measure of the political implications of the blog's theme was to contrast its portrayal of Chinese and non-Chinese dogs.

Among all the entries about dogs in China and other Asian countries, 23 (15.8%) showed dogs being badly treated by human beings. Here, abuse is defined as when dogs were killed, captured, or used for brutal entertainment by human beings or neglected without care while ill. For example, there was a news item about dog fights in Handan, China that left the dogs severely injured (Deng, 2004). "Good" stories refer to those situations when human beings attended to dogs' welfare, as, for example, by building various facilities to make them comfortable or rescuing them from danger, and stories of dogs that rescued or helped their masters. The majority of the message entries referring to dogs in China or Asian countries (74, nearly 51%) constituted news stories indicating that dogs were well treated or that dogs had good relations with their masters. "Neutral" stories (49, or around 34%) were defined as those that did not

Table 14.1 Frequency and Percentage of Dog News

	Bad	Neutral	Good	Others	Total
China or Asian Countries	23 (15.8%)	49 (33.6%)	74 (50.6%)		146
Western Countries	17 (21.8)	37 (47.4%)	24 (30.8%)	4 (missing)	78

$X^2 = 8.197, p = .017$

touch relations between human beings and dogs and focused only on dogs. For example, a post on February 19, 2005 described a dog show in which a dog called Cali won the championship.

As for the stories concerning dogs of Western countries, 17 entries belong to the "bad" category, while those in the "good" category numbered 24 (30.8% of the total stories concerning dogs—20 percentage points less than the same category for Chinese and Asian dogs).

Although there are 74 dog news stories that depict good relations between dogs and human beings in China and other Asian countries (50 stories more than those about Western dogs), the Western judges viewed the blog content as a whole as alluding to Chinese people's "terrible" lives by discussing dogs having been killed or eaten. This leap could be attributed to Muzimei's subjective introduction of the content of the blog as mentioned earlier. Another reason might be that Western judges saw the *Dog* blog through native values and practices (cf. Gans, 1979). Perhaps, for example, the judges had heard about dogs being killed and eaten in Asia, and these photos further confirmed their expectation about dogs' fate. But economics also may have played a role. In Western Europe, the dog no longer has a work life, except for security or in a service capacity for the blind. Most dogs are family pets; their role is that of pampered companion and entertainer. In folk legend in China, for many years, the Western dog has been conceived of as a creature living a better life than most poor people in the rest of the world.

In China, in contrast, a dog might be found in a small village pulling a cart for its owner. Yet, we can understand the willingness of the European judges to read in metaphor. After all, and perhaps significantly, Aggressive Little Snake did not add any commentary to the photos he posted; what he wanted was to let the photos or stories speak for themselves (Zhou, 2004), thus creating a situation in which anyone could interpret what he or she was inclined or wanted to interpret from the blog according to his or her own expectations and values.

Other hints that *Dog* is satire come from its humor. In fact, here political metaphor seems downright transparent. Aggressive Little Snake graduated from the Chinese department of Nankai University in Tianjin around 1994. After graduation, he worked as both a magazine and newspaper editor for several years. Then he became an Internet commentary writer and often appeared on the IT bulletin board service of Sina.com. cn. His style was metaphorical: He used wrongly written Chinese characters to express his daily work routine, his contacts with friends, and sometimes his feelings about life. For example, he used the word *laozi* as satire. In China, if you have children, you can tell them that you are their laozi (dad). The word when used to others, however, stands somewhere between cynicism and hooliganism, mostly meaning you are afraid of nothing with nothing to lose, or even with the implication that you have fathered children illegitimately. When discussing J. R. R. Tolkien, author of *The Lord of the Rings* (who died in 1973), Aggressive Little Snake said, "Laozi was born in 1973 when a foreigner died. Even though he was a dead person, he earned $22 million in 2002, which make me envious and angry" (Aggressive Little Snake, 2003c). Snake estimated that all the authors together in China could not have made so much money that year and would himself have been satisfied to earn one thousandth of the money.

It was typical of Aggressive Little Snake, or the blogger Zhang Xiaomo, to deprecate others' personal lives with such salty language. Occasionally, the result has been conflict with *Dog*'s audience. Some wrote to him in anger about his 2004 annual review's cornucopia of expletives and obscenities. But Snake fought back, saying that "these groups of doggerels surpass illusionary realism and could be called 'mind-wanton realism.' You should raise your literature common sense. Otherwise, I will have others and dogs fornicate you one hundred times" (Aggressive Little Snake, 2005). In short, from the Chinese perspective, such self-critical humor is political. It reminds the reader of the practice during the Cultural Revolution of subjecting suspected and real dissidents to "self-criticism" sessions (Macfarquhar, 1974; Schoenhals, 1996; Wen, 2005).

But Snake satirizes a broad range of targets besides his own situation. According to a legend, Chinese (Han) people were created by a goddess from the rich earth of the banks of the Yellow River. In one post, Aggressive Little Snake referred to this story and delved into the origin of this goddess. He said that because of the yellow soil, Chinese are yellow. But he expressed in a somewhat sarcastic way that Chinese seemed to demand more of their complexion, willing to be black through tanning or white by using various cosmetics (Aggressive Little Snake, 2003d). When talking about Majiang (mah-jongg in the West), a popular game in China, he said Sichuan province was renowned for its skilled players. But he added that the people across the Taiwan Straits were experts at playing Majiang. His suggestion: Reunite China and Taiwan via the board game (Aggressive Little Snake, 2004)—an allusion to the "Ping-Pong" diplomacy that helped bring Nixon to China? It is hard not to read in these statements explicit sociopolitical commentary.

Snake also makes reference to Mao Zedong. For example, Chairman Mao once wrote a poem that reads, "Dating back to ancient history, we try to find real heroes, but eventually we can only find them in the current era." With this verse, Chairman Mao referred to himself as one of China's heroes. But Aggressive Little Snake changed the poem to, "Dating back to ancient history, the heroes are doing eighteen touch and fornicating," apparently suggesting that today's "hero" leaders were overpaid, overbearing, and oversexed—a perspective that would not have pleased the Chairman or his heirs (Aggressive Little Snake, 2003e). In another poem, Mao urged people to be physically fit, to study well, and to work diligently. Snake morphed those high-minded exhortations into the following satire of modern China's mores and social issues: "to be physically well, with energy to fornicate; to study well, with skill to spread rumor; and to work well, with supporting skill to migrate" (Aggressive Little Snake, 2003f).

Another technique used by Snake is to expose a phenomenon without mentioning the factors precipitating it. One may complain about poor inner city transit service, for example, but not speculate on those government polices that led to the problem. Symptoms are usually allowable as the objects of critique; causes are dangerous to ruminate upon. One may, within limits, attack a corrupt individual or government section— again, while not implying that the government itself is the problem. For example, one of Snake's copied posts concerned a prevalent situation in China of private or public building contractors delaying or skipping out altogether on paying construction workers for jobs completed (Aggressive Little Snake, 2003g). One CCTV program, "News 30 Minutes," revealed that a Hebei province labor department delayed handling complaints from a group of laborers of nonpayment by their employer (a contractor) for months, but quickly solved the problem when the news crew's camera appeared on the scene. Snake attributed the original outrage to the social tendency of "admiring richness." He stated, "Admiring richness directly leads to local officials' greed for economic achievements, the most obvious representative of which was real estate development" (Aggressive Little Snake, 2003f). In another article, Snake sneered at the newly issued "Lowest Salary Regulation" for its complicated and unreasonable calculation method. Nevertheless, he said the exploitation of Chinese workers was a phenomenon occurring not only in China but also in other countries.

Conclusions

This paper has been an exercise in ambiguity—intentionally so, in light of the case studies—a blog that survives by slippery allusions and puns but also ambiguity in the context of understanding other cultures via new media or any media. The West has had a long history of looking at China and seeing, for good and ill, what it wanted to see. General views of China paralleled this structure of enthusiasm followed by disdain. Indeed, the weight of scholarship on this issue argues that American and Western views of China followed cyclical patterns. As Harold Isaacs described it, the 18th century constituted the "Age of Respect" while the 19th century through World War I was the "Age of Contempt" (Isaacs, 1958; Perlmutter, 2007). Writing before the 1989 Tiananmen events,

Warren Cohen argues that American views of China followed eras in which one cultural filter tended to dominate (Cohen, 1978). As shifts occurred, the same Chinese character types, holding the same social positions, espousing the same values, making the same actions, could be viewed with opposite attitudes:

> The Chinese are seen as a superior people and an inferior people; devilishly exasperating heathens and wonderfully attractive humanists; wise sages and sadistic executioners; thrifty and honorable men and sly and devious villains; comic opera soldiers and dangerous fighters. (Isaacs, 1958, p. 4)

Today's China represents a similar paradox. Polling in America and Europe shows a favorable view of China's people (which probably has been heightened by the politeness and respect to all athletes shown by the Chinese Olympic audiences) and a negative view of its government. China is ubiquitous in American and European life: toys, clothes, and other merchandise made in China and exported. Its energy consumption is surpassing our own, with a consequential effect on global climate change. It is one of the leading holders of American debt. There are many worries about China's military build-up and threats of forced unification with Taiwan. In looking at China via its blogs, we naturally assume that dissent must be there, indeed should be there, since of course, for most Westerners, Western democracy is the gold standard of all other polities.

But Aggressive Little Snake's *Eighteen Touch Dog Newspaper* is perhaps a new way of looking at Chinese through Western eyes and seeing what we want to see. On the one hand, the case for its winning an award for political satire because of its main subject, canines, is thin: We found that there was no pattern of Chinese and Asian dogs appearing worse off than Western dogs. So it was probably the case that Western European judges were grasping at the metaphorical wind, assuming that a few examples of canine contrasts were examples of deep political satire. Nevertheless, they may not have been wholly off the mark. After all, in the China of the Mao era *any* showing of negativity in society was forbidden: All dogs and all people (save traitors and dissidents) were happy. To show dog fights and malnourished dogs in China in 2004 was, by the standards of 1964, a revolutionary act, although an even more subtle one than the award judges noticed. But parceling out "bad" dog images to East and West allows Snake, if confronted by the Ministry police, to say, "Look, I'm even-handed." Perhaps that is a sign that the climate of political tolerance in the Middle Kingdom is appreciably greater than in many periods in China's past.

In short, we argue that Snake overturned the typical linear convention of China watching. He presented the awards committee with interesting, arresting pictures that seemed to hint at metaphorical and allegorical dissent. But those same pictures could be shown to prove to the China censor that the site had no political content. Meanwhile, Snake, the jester, is using words to make clever political satire about China's situation.

Only one of the judges in the competition was Chinese, and she did not translate the written parts of the blog that did not pertain to dogs. In fact, according to Aggressive Little Snake's introduction, what the Chinese judge Muzimei passed on to other judges were visual portions of the blog, without mentioning any written parts. The Western judges did not know about the rich puns, wordplays, allusions, and text of Snake's and his partners' posts that were politically oriented. Those items stopped short of actually blaming the government of China for any of the problems he lamented and lampooned. Snake's political satire is both brilliant and skirting the bounds of a prison offense. To "sex up" the injunctions and aphorisms of Mao, to complain of the corruptions and thieveries of Chinese society—again, these would have been offenses that would have merited prison sentences in 1954, 1964, 1974, and 1994.

Here, too, is confusion. Why is this critical mass communicator not in prison? In discussion with Chinese students and academics abroad, this is a topic of extensive "small talk" debate. Some suggest that the government cannot pay attention to all blogs, so Snake is under the radar. But certainly the award brought him front and center into the scan zone of the Internet police. Alternatively, it is possible that his international status makes it politically unwise to persecute him. The problem with that conjecture is that notoriety has never stopped the Chinese government from curtailing the activities of opponents, although human rights protests from abroad have resulted in some political prisoners being released *after* imprisonment.

Another possibility is that the government realizes that China has so many problems that a safety valve of complaint is needed, that no one can ban all political satire because the alternative, keeping a lid on a boiling pot, would be worse. Is Snake, then, a jester of the Web, tolerated as long as he seems to restrict himself to veiled humor, not outright protest? In any case, Dog blog is a premier example of the complexity of the Internet as a tool of political argumentation in a society trying to control political dissent while spurring economic development. It is not just about dogs, or sex, or the trivia of everyday life.[2] And that is perhaps as it should be: If Dog blog were simple and clear and direct enough to fit into preconceptions of either the government of China or that of liberal Europeans eager to see signs of dissent in China, then ironically *Eighteen Touch Dog Newspaper* would not have survived and prospered long enough to gain world attention. Aggressive Little Snake endures, at least as of this writing, because he is not what anyone wants or expects him to be.

Notes

1. Another *Eighteen Touch* folk song prevails in Taiwan, but the places touched or viewed are somewhat different, but with 10 of them identical to the former song.
2. One Chinese acquaintance who has lived in America called it "China's Seinfeld."

References

Aggressive Little Snake. (2003a). Mobile phone is the only criterion of testing fornication. Retrieved June 19, 2005, from http://www.18mo.com/index.asp?vt=default&page=33

Aggressive Little Snake. (2003b). Reply to a newspaper reporter. Retrieved June 20, 2005, from http:www.18mo.com/indes.asp?vt=bycat&cat_id=39

Aggressive Little Snake. (2003c). Superb Foreign Writer. Retrieved June 19, 2005, from http://www.18mo.com/index.asp?vt=default&page=32

Aggressive Little Snake. (2003d). Yellow complexion. Retrieved June 19, 2005, from http://www.18mo.com/index.asp?vt=default&page=32

Aggressive Little Snake. (2003e). Long live Chairman Mao. Retrieved June 19, 2005, from http://www.18mo.com/index.asp?vt=default&page=32

Aggressive Little Snake. (2003f). Chairman Mao guides us. Retrieved June 19, 2005, from http://www.18mo.com/index.asp?vt=default&page=32

Aggressive Little Snake. (2003g). 100 billion Yuan owed to construction workers. Retrieved June 19, 2005, from http://18mo.com/index.asp?vt=default&page=31

Aggressive Little Snake. (2004). Majiang with Red China. Retrieved June 19, 2005, from http://www.18mo.com/index.asp?vt=default&page=30

Aggressive Little Snake. (2005). Don't drive Laozi crazy, otherwise I will loose my dog to bite you. Retrieved June 20, 2005, from http://www.18mo.com/showlog.asp?cat_id=26&log_id=657

Alice Kelp. (2004). I am really afraid of having Valentine Day. Retrieved June 18, 2005, from http://www.18mo.com/index.asp?vt=default&page=21

Amnesty International. (2004, January 28). People's Republic of China: Controls tighten as Internet activism grows. Retrieved June 19, 2005, from http://web.amnesty.org/library/Index/ ENGASA170012004

BBC News World Edition. (2005, June 7). Chinese blogs face restrictions. http://news.bbc.co.uk/2/hi/technology/4617657.stm.

Bell, D. A. (1999). Democracy with Chinese characteristics: A political proposal for the post-Communist era. *Philosophy East & West, 49*, 451–493.

Berkowitz, H., & Quittner, J. (1991, August 22). Media and message. *Newsday*, pp. 14, 16.

Bowman, L. M. (2002, July 31). China No. 2 in web population. *CNET News.com*. Retrieved June 20, 2005,from http://news.com.com/China+No.+2+in+Web+population/2110-1023_3-947458.html?tag=nl

Boxun.com. (2005, June 7). China: Authorities declare war on unregistered web sites and blogs. Retrieved June 25, 2005, from http://www.peacehall.com/news/gb/english/2005/06/200506070644.shtml

Chang, S. H. (1990). *History and legend, ideas and images in the Ming historical novels*. Ann Arbor: University of Michigan Press.

Chase, M. S., & Mulvenon, J. C. (2002). You've got dissent! Chinese dissident use of the Internet and Beijing's counter-strategies. Washington, DC: Rand Publishing.

Cheng, C. Y. (1990). *Behind the Tiananmen massacre: Social, political, and economic ferment in China* (pp. 89–90). Boulder, CO: Westview Press.

China journey to the heart of internet censorship: Investigative report. (2007). http://crd-net.org/Article/ShowClass.asp?ClassID=9

China ties US in total number of users. (2008, April 24,). Associated Press. http://www.foxnews.com/story/0,2933,352412,00.html. China to shut or punish video-sharing sites over security, threats, porn, violence. (2008, March 21,). Associated Press. http://www.foxnews.com/story/0,2933,340410,00.html

China's Internet information skirmish (2000). A January 2000 report from U.S. Embassy, Beijing. Available at: http://www.usembassy-china.org.cn/sandt/webwar.htm

Cohen, W. I. (1978). American perceptions of China. In M. Oksenberg & R. B. Oxnam (Eds.), *Dragon and eagle: United States-China relations, past and future* (pp. 54-86).New York: Basic Books.

Cox, C. (2003). Establishing global internet freedom. In C. W. Crews Jr. & A. Thierer (Eds.), *Who rules the net? Internet governance and jurisdiction* (pp. 3–12). Washington, DC: Cato Institute.

Deng, Y. (2004). Handan bloody dog-fighting place. Retrieved June 26, 2005, from http://www.18mo.com/index.asp?vt=default&page=25

Dittmer, L. (1994). The politics of publicity in reform China. In C. C. Lee (Ed.), *China's media, media's China* (pp. 89–112). Boulder, CO: Westview Press.

Dog Newspaper Webmaster, Aggressive Little Snake, Interview. (2004). Retrieved June 21, 2005, from http://life.sina.com.cn/art/2004-12-21/59962.shtml

Dong, B. (2002). How China censors the Net by domain name hijacking. Retrieved June 20, 2005, from http:// www.rense.com/general30/sase.htm

DW-WORLD DE. (2004, June 12). Chinese blog wins "Best Blog Awards." http://www.dw-world.de/dw/article/0,1564,1418080,00.html

Evan, W. M. (1981). *Knowledge and power in a global society*. Beverly Hills, CA: Sage.

Fallows, D. (2008, March 27,). Few in China complain about internet controls. Pew Research. http://pewresearch.org/pubs/776/china-internet

Forsythe, D. P. (1991). *The internationalization of human rights*. Lexington, MA: Lexington Books.

French, H. W. (2005, June 8). China tightens restrictions on bloggers and web sites. *The New York Times*, p. 6.

Gans, H. J. (1979). *Deciding What's News — a Study of CBS Evening News, NBC nightly News, Newsweek, and Time*. New York: Random House.

Gillmor, D. (2005, Jan. 6). Chinese blogs slowly give voice to the masses. *Knight Ridder*, p. F4.

Gu, G. (2005). Eighteen touch. *Kejia Magazine, 50*. Retrieved June 18, 2003, from http://chineseculture.about.com/library/literature/classics/other/nsgd 126.htm

Hamrin, C. (1994). China's legitimacy crisis: The central role of information. In C. C. Lee (Ed.), *China's media, media's China* (pp. 59–74). Boulder, CO: Westview Press.

IDG News Service. (2002, September 10). China hacks Google's domain name. Retrieved June 18, 2005, from http://www.idg.net/ic 946304 4394 1 1681. html

International Freedom of Expression eXchange. (2004). Is Microsoft aiding Internet censorship in China? *International Freedom of Expression eXchange.* Retrieved June 24, 2005, from http://canada.ifex.org/en/content/view/full/56592/

Internet Coaching Library. (2007). Asia marketing research, internet usage, population statistics and information. http://www.internetworldstats.com/asia.htm.

Isaacs, H. R. (1958). *Scratches on our minds: American images of China and India*. New York: J. Day.

Johnson-Eilola, J. (1997). *Nostalgic angels: Rearticulating hypertext writing*. Norwood, NJ: Ablex.

Johnston, G. (1999). What is the history of samizdat? *Social History, 24*(2), 115–133.

Liu, A. P. L. (1996). *Mass politics in the people's republic: State and society in contemporary China* (pp. 162–166). Boulder, CO: Westview Press.

Macfarquhar, R. (1974). *The origins of the cultural revolution* (Vol. 2). New York: Columbia University Press.

New Scientist. (2004, November 27). Chinese whispers: Human rights campaigner Xiao Qiang meets the bloggers who are keeping one step ahead of the censors. http://www.newscientist.com/channel/info-tech/mg18424755. 500

Open Initiative. (2005). Internet filtering in China in 2004-2005: A country study. Retrieved June 20, 2005, from http://www.opennetinitiative.net/studies/china/ONI_China_Country_Study.pdf

Perlmutter, David D. (2007). *Picturing China in the American press: The visual portrayal of Sino-American relations in* Time *magazine, 1949–1973*. Lanham, MD: Lexington Books.

Perlmutter, D. D. (2008). *Blogwars: The new political battleground*. New York: Oxford University Press.

Perlmutter, D. D., & Hamilton, J. M. (Eds.). (2007). *From pigeons to news portals: Foreign reporting and the challenge of new technology*. Baton Rouge, LA: Louisiana State University Press.

Qiao, H. (2005). Kejia residents and kejia culture. *People's Forum, 1*. Retrieved June 18, 2005, from http://culture.people.com.cn/GB/40483/40488/3159094. html

Schoenhals, M. (1996). *China's cultural revolution, 1966–1969*. Armonk, NY: Sharpe.

Scott, J. C. (1990). *Domination and the arts of resistance: Hidden transcripts.* New Haven, CT: Yale University Press.

Serrie, J. (June 20, 2008), Breaking down the Great Firewall of China. Fox News. http://www.foxnews.com/story/0,2933,368985,00.html

Shen, H. (2005, June 7). Zhong guo jia jin kong zhi shang ye wang zhan. [China strengthens control of commercial Web sites]. *VOANews.Com.* Retrieved June 18, 2005, from http://www.voanews.com/chinese/w2005-06-07-voa71.cfm

Silfry, D. (2005, October 17,). Technorati: State of the blogosphere. http://www.sifry.com/alerts/archives/000343.html

Silfry, D. (2006, May 1). State of the blogosphere, April 2006. Part 2: On language and tagging. http://technorati.com/weblog/2006/05/100.html

Sproull, L., & Keisler, S. (1991). *Connections: New ways of working in networked organizations.* Cambridge, MA: MIT Press.

Survey Report on Blogs in China 2007. (2007, December 26). http://www.cnnic.cn/html/Dir/2007/12/27/4954.htm

Surveying Internet Usage and Its Impact in Seven Chinese Cities. (2007). Center for Social Development, Chinese Academy of Social Sciences. Available at http://www.markle.org/downloadable_assets/china_internet_survey_11.2007.pdf

Telesin, J. (1973). Inside samizdat. *Encounter, 40(2),* 25–33.

Vaney, A. D., Gance, S., & Ma, Y. (2000). *Technology and resistance: Digital communications and new coalitions around the world.* New York: Lang.

Wall Street Journal. (2007, December 8). China closes in on U.S. as largest web market. http://online.wsj.com/article/SB120062064572399407.html?mod=rss_whats_news_technology&apl=y&r=110846

Wen, Z. (2005). A Chinese-American woman's plight during the Cultural Revolution. *Chinese America: History and perspectives.* http://goliath.ecnext.com/coms2/gi_0199-3580527/A-sense-of-home.html

Yaleglobal Online. (2003, July 21). Beijing is losing the people's war in cyberspace. Retrieved June 25, 2005, from http://yaleglobal.yale.edu/display.article?id=2133&page=2

Zhang, X. M. (2004, April 9). One month memory. Retrieved June 20, 2005, from http://18mo.com/index.asp?vt=default&page=31

Zhao, D. (1998). Ecologies of social movement: Student mobilization during the 1989 prodemocracy movement in Beijing, *The American Journal of Sociology, 103*(6), 1493–529.

Zhou, X. (2004). Aggressive Little Snake's "dogitarianism" care. *Chinese Youth.* http://tech.sina.com.cn/i/2004-12-22/1806481908.shtml

Zittrain, J., & Edelman, B. (2003). Empirical analysis of internet filtering in China. http://cyber.law.harvard.edu/filtering/china/

Part III

Strategic Global Communication

Chapter 15

Global Integration or Local Responsiveness?

Multinational Corporations' Public Relations Strategies and Cases

Joon Soo Lim

Multinational corporations (MNCs) are increasingly dominating the world economy. U.S. companies have expanded their markets by opening foreign subsidiaries in ever-increasing numbers. European and East Asian companies have also extended their reach since the late 1980s by opening subsidiaries across the globe (Shuter & Wiseman, 1994). According to Bartlett and Ghoshal (2000), MNCs account for more than 40% of the world's manufacturing output and almost a quarter of world trade. About 85% of the world's automobiles, 70% of computers, 35% of toothpaste, and 65% of soft drinks are produced and marketed by MNCs.

With the internationalization of business and world communication systems, it has become almost a truism to say that public relations has also become "international" or "global" (Verčič, Grunig, & Grunig, 1996, p. 32). The advances in information technology in particular have made it possible for an international business operation to achieve greater integration through a constant flow of communication within geographically dispersed organizations (Molleda, 2000a; Molleda & Laskin, chapter 16 this volume).

To many public relations scholars, however, understanding international public relations has been confined to the "public relations programs conducted on the other side of the ocean" (Anderson, 1989). As a result, most scholarly attempts at international public relations have disproportionately dealt with country-specific anecdotal stories. However, as Wakefield (1999) pointed out, rapid changes and complex forces are shaping an uncertain international environment in which effective public relations is essential. Therefore, what is needed is a foundation of principles and assumptions that come from scholarly research on what comprises effective practices in international public relations (Wakefield, 1996).

In accordance with the global firms' expansion around the world, much of the scholarship in international public relations has also focused on global management theories for explaining global public relations effectiveness (e.g., Falconi, 1989; Molleda, 2000a; Molleda & Laskin, chapter 16 this volume; Ovaitt, 1988; Wakefield, 2001). Wakefield (1996) aptly states this trend: "Just as organizational theory has guided domestic public relations research, comparative management theory can assist with international public relations research" (p. 24).

Drawing from the comparative international business management theory, considerable scholarship has debated the MNCs' communication effectiveness in terms of the global integration and local responsiveness paradigm. The field of public relations has also had a debate extending over several decades, and still not settled, regarding standardization versus adaptation of the international public relations approach (Ovaitt, 1988).

This chapter delineates an optimizing framework for effective international public relations management strategy by applying the integration–responsiveness grid (I-R grid) proposed by Prahald and Doz (1987) to the MNCs' international public relations setting. According to Prahald and Doz's (1988) seminal framework, integration and local responsiveness strategies each brings different benefits to MNCs. Briefly, the integration strategy brings a cost reduction benefit while local responsiveness has much to do with external effectiveness. Public relations scholars have long argued that the debate that MNCs face when practicing international PR should be viewed on a continuum rather than as an either–or situation (Bardhan & Patwardhan, 2004; Burk, 1994).

How can MNCs employ integration or local responsiveness strategy to international public relations to optimize their organizational effectiveness? In answering this question, this chapter introduces the key strategies and cases of multinational corporations' public relations.

Global Integration of Public Relations Strategy and Cases

Globalization is causing multinationals to sell the same brands globally and adopt global standards as a way to present a clear corporate identity (Ogrizek, 2002). Several international business scholars have provided a rationale for global integration strategy (Bartlett & Ghoshal, 1989; Doz, Prahalad, & Hamel, 1990; Ghoshal, 1987; Lorange & Probst, 1990; Prahalad, & Doz, 1987). They argue that an effective global strategy requires strategic control (Doz, et al., 1990; Lorange & Probst, 1990) and coordination mechanisms (Bartlett & Ghoshal, 1989; Prahalad & Doz, 1987) between an MNC's headquarters and subsidiaries as well as among subsidiaries.

Due to institutional pressure from global and local stakeholders, to gain legitimacy and build trust, parent MNCs need to control strategic communication (Hunter & Bansal, 2007). One area that deserves attention in terms of integrated public relations practices is MNCs' global corporate social responsibility communication. For instance, in facing institutional pressures from stakeholders to present environmental communications, multinational corporations usually standardize their messages across countries to make them more credible (Hunter & Bansal, 2007).

Ongoing pressure from NGO sectors also makes global companies undertake standardized public relations practices across countries. For instance, global coffee MNCs such as Kraft, Nestlé, and SLDE established The Common Code for the Coffee Community (4C) to enable social, environmental, and economic sustainability in coffee production (Kolk, 2005).

Today's worldwide competitive environment and the emerging new communication technologies also demand collaborative information sharing and problem solving, cooperative resource sharing, and collective implementation—in short, a relationship built on interdependence (Bartlett & Ghoshal, 1989). Global information systems help facilitate exchange of information and sharing of best practices among managers in different locations throughout the globe. Organizational learning (knowledge) is transferred across borders and provides a richer base of knowledge and skills to enhance the firm's competitiveness in global markets. Skills, experience, and capabilities developed in response to a specific market environment or market conditions can be transferred to other similar market conditions. Equally, skills and capabilities that are culturally embedded or location specific (e.g., public relations creativity) can be used to broaden the range of skills and capabilities supporting the firm's operations in another market (Craig & Douglas, 2000).

Worldwide companies have traditionally attempted to use so-called pooled interdependence to make unit managers responsive to global rather than local interests (Bartlett & Ghoshal, 1989). By definition, tighter integration between a subsidiary and the rest of the global network increases the degree of mutual interdependence between the subsidiary and the network. In this context of high interdependence, it becomes crucial for the subsidiary and the network to pursue shared goals; and for the firm to be able to reshape the subsidiary puts major constraints on the firm's ability to achieve such congruence in goals and have the requisite freedom to reshape subsidiary operations as needed (Gupta & Govindarajan, 2000). Hulbert and Brandt (1984) state, "integration relies heavily on communication flow between subunits, and in the multinational company, flows between headquarters and the foreign subsidiary are critical" (p. 89).

Effective global public relations strategy also can be achieved by establishing a strong coordination system between an MNC's headquarters and its subsidiaries (Mangee, 1989; Molleda, 2000b; Molleda &

Laskin, chapter 16 this volume; Wakefield, 1997, 2001). According to Newbury and Yakova (2006), PR activities in global PR MNCs must be coordinated based on reciprocal work interdependencies that involve at least three dimensions: (1) Coordination between offices is needed to ensure that PR campaigns maintain a degree of consistency from market to market. (2) Employees need to communicate across offices to perform specific activities in servicing both clients and general operations. (3) Because clients are more international, employees have to focus on interconnectedness because their clients operate in multiple locations (p. 50).

Newbury and Yakova (2006) conducted survey research for a global PR firm headquartered in the United Kingdom to examine what factors contributed to employee preference in terms of standardization. Their results indicate that shared clients, interoffice communication, and client multinationality were positively related to employee preference for integration strategy; however, this tendency appeared quite uneven in different cultures. For instance, activity communication and local service were the strongest factors in Europe to lead to standardization, whereas shared clients seemed to have the strongest effect in Asia.

This integrative public relations strategy of MNCs is directly related to a global public relations goal—worldwide development of best public relations practices. That is, a global corporation can try to bring people together to talk about what they have in common, to share best public relations practices, to learn what others are doing, and to discover common issues and problems (Lucenko, 1999). For example, globally integrated public relations makes practitioners among the subsidiaries share information about activism and helps them manage a global scale crisis in an efficient manner. Familiarity with the failure as well as the success gives modern public relations professionals basic information on which to build a case for their own company's entry into another country. Some firms have in fact established "educational institutions"; for example, Matsushita has an overseas training center in Osaka, Japan. Managers and supervisors from around the world come to this center to learn specific skills, but more importantly they are exposed to the theory and in practice of Matsushita philosophy (White & Poynter, 1990).

Wouters (1991) contends, "As corporations become more global, coordination of their information dissemination becomes more critical" (p. 73). Thus, integration of public relations programs becomes more urgent, both in terms of cost-efficiency and impact.

A case study by O'Neil (2008) compared the communication output and outcome of a major international firm before and after its new integrated communication programs were launched to enhance employee comprehension of business strategy and goals and to increase employee action in support of the body of knowledge. The multinational firm that

O'Neil (2008) examined had no strong global, corporate-wide employee communication strategy in 2003 and faced an internal communication challenge. The company upgraded its Intranet system to improve global integration between the headquarters in North America and its regional offices across countries. With the global integration strategy of internal communication, the multinational firm observed a significant increase in employee comprehension of company strategy and employee confidence that they could access all the information they needed to do an effective job.

By their use of the integrative communication strategy, global companies can enjoy enormous cost advantages over competitors. This is possible because modern communications facilities have created a worldwide commonality of interests that has surpassed national interests (Wouters, 1991). That is, in today's world of intense competition, the benefits from economies of scale are necessary. Therefore, the integrative (or federal) and intensive communication forms are an important characteristic of newly emerging organizational models (Rockart, 1998).

Molleda (2000a) found that integrative public relations is accomplished by the use of "integrative communication devices." These devices include corporate Web sites, Intranet, conferences, seminars, teleconferencing, newsletters, corporate publications, and codes of ethics/conduct. Cesaria (2000) also contends that the influence of the Intranet, phone, fax, e-mail, and Web integration has required researchers to rethink processes of organizational communication needed to support all business activities. Thus, Ruigrok, Achtenhagen, Rüegg-Stürm, and Wagner (2000) call attention to the integrative communication programs in any company that has the majority of its employees working in countries other than the country where the company headquarters is situated.

In summary, as Wakefield (2001) states, effective public relations tends to combine the best domestic and international programs in one unified worldwide function. In other words, public relations practitioners must create global strategies to preserve the entity's reputation, to retain consistent messages and identity, and to anticipate and handle problems that might cross borders.

Yet the idea that a company can operate as if the entire world were a single entity is something more aptly discussed under the heading of reality versus fantasy. By definition, management from the home office on a global basis means overlooking cultural details in various overseas markets. International public relations guru David Drobis notes:

> borderless credibility requires a seamless network of communications professionals who share a company's vision, who understand a company's core messages, and who know how to work cooperatively

to deliver those messages consistently across different cultures, races and religions. (Drobis, 1998, p. 34)

In Wakefield's (1997) Delphi study, the majority of respondents acknowledged that in theory integration of public relations programs around the world would be valuable. However, when it came to practical implementation of an integrated program, there was a widespread debate among the respondents who agreed with the theoretical proposition. That is, when actual practice was examined, most panelists expressed discomfort with the role of local general managers or other local officers in public relations due to their limited understanding of its purpose.

The implication is, of course, that formulating and communicating a vision is not enough, no matter how clear, durable, and consistent it may be. Central to the effectiveness of a shared vision is the ability of individual organization members to collaboratively use goals, professional knowledge, methods, experience, and values with others in the organization (Cesaria, 2000).

Therefore, this integration of public relations programs is often not a problem of communication, but of receptivity (Bartlett & Ghoshal, 1989). Tobias (1996) stresses that integration does not just mean integrated communication but means "shared values" and "shared behaviors" (p. 22). The best example of integration of shared value and practice is often found in a widespread concern among MNCs about global environmental regulation. Most firms with proactive environmental management systems require all of their operating units both to share their green policy and audit their facilities for compliance with global and local environmental regulations and company policies (Rondinelli & Berry, 2000).

Local Responsiveness of Global Public Relations Practice

Beyond global integration strategy coordinated by MNCs parent company or headquarters, flexibility is often required. Global companies should anticipate that whatever local market they enter, they will not know as much about the workings of the place as do local citizens. Therefore, while business issues are often global and should be addressed on a global basis, they are also interpreted locally. For example, if a company claims to be environmentally responsible, that message may carry more weight in some places than others. Germany takes seriously the notion of cradle-to-grave product responsibility, and so being "green" may be a tremendous asset. In other countries, however, environmentalism is not such a hot subject and so a company that markets itself as green might not succeed. Therefore, the issue may be global, but how a company communicates its position can be very local (Lucenko, 1999).

Local responsiveness refers to resource commitment decisions taken autonomously by a subsidiary in response to primarily local competitive or customer demands (Prahalad & Doz, 1987, p. 15). Lee (2000) defines this term as a firm's ability to respond to various demands in dynamic competitive environments. The need for flexibility is often increased by the varying extent of external pressures such as government influences, and differing government policies, from country to country in the same industry (Doz, 1986).

For instance, MNCs in China acknowledge the existence of a universal set of corporate social responsibility strategies but they also emphasize the strategic adaptation of these strategies so as to reflect local culture and politics (Shen, 2007). In interviews with public relations practitioners in the Chinese branches of Japanese MNCs, Shen (2006) found that they were entitled to make some of their own decisions insofar as corporate social responsibility (CSR) was concerned. For instance, a PR manager in the Japanese MNC could propose local-specific CSR programs with permissible budgets, and her American counterpart only needed to inform the global headquarters of his CSR initiatives to confirm if those initiatives were in line with the company's global guidelines for CSR.

In contrast with the integrated strategy, locally responsive public relations strategy aims at customizing its practices to the local environment, local organizational culture, and needs/interests of local stakeholders. Especially, under environmentally uncertain conditions, the local responsiveness strategy is often regarded as a major competitive priority (Lee, 2000). Environmental uncertainty describes an organizational decision makers' perceived inability to make an accurate prediction about the organizational environment, which is generated by inadequate information about the forces outside organizational boundaries and the forces important to decision-making processes (Lawrence & Lorsch, 1967). Lawrence and Lorsch (1967) demonstrated that organizations facing a high degree of environmental uncertainty tended to cope by using less formal coordination and control mechanisms in structuring their operations. Grunig (1992) also argues that one effective way to reduce the environmental uncertainty is to design an organizational structure that is flexible enough to adapt to rapidly changing external conditions.

As an environment becomes more complex and turbulent, companies will use whatever means they have at their disposal to deal with conditions, which in turn will result in the increase of all types of boundary-spanning activities (Meznar & Nigh, 1995). Lorange and Probst (1990) assert that managing in turbulent times calls for flexibility in the design, control, and development of strategies. Wakefield (1997) states, "because the organization faces a turbulent, dynamic environment internationally, the public relations program is structured to be flexible and adaptable to that environment, worldwide" (p. 246). For instance, when allegations of pesticide contamination resulted in partial bans on Coke and Pepsi products in India, some public relations experts wondered if the local employees' sensitivities to local priorities came into conflict with corporate hierarchies and the need to get approval from headquarters in the United States (Gentleman, 2006).

Shen's (2007) in-depth analysis of four Asian MNCs' CSR programs shows how a turbulent political or diplomatic environment could influence global companies' public relations strategies. Shen examined whether historically hostile Sino-Japan relations and surging anti-Japan sentiments, due to Japan's new history textbook that played down Japan's wartime atrocities, have changed the ways in which Japanese MNCs in China implemented their CSR programs. Shen found that they all recognized universal CSR codes, especially in terms of environmental protection and education, but also adapted themselves to satisfy local needs from China. For instance, emphasizing similarities in culture between Koreans and Chinese, Samsung China aimed to reflect the Chinese cultural value of respecting the elders and caring for children. However, the Japanese MNCs organized their CSR strategies mainly around their business or Sino-Japanese relations, paying little attention to traditional Chinese cultural values, presumably because the Japanese MNCs felt a greater need to ease the Sino-Japanese tension caused by historical relations.

Another force that requires locally flexible public relations strategy is the different cultural setting. Grunig, Grunig, Sriramesh, Huang, and Lyra (1995) contend that cultural interpreters would play an essential role in the two-way symmetrical model in a multi-(cultural) organization by helping to facilitate dialogue and understanding between organizations and publics from different cultures. They observed that international public relations firms or MNCs typically hire local citizens for their public relations departments and this trend would seem to fit into the cultural interpreter model.

While many global companies have recognized the importance of global public relations integration, however, not many Western firms put enough emphasis on adaptation to the local culture (Leichsering, 1998; Wang, 2005). They used Western values in managing the companies they ran in those countries. However, the MNCs' desire to prosper in the developing countries often faces challenges and threats that derive from a local desire to retain national and cultural identity and traditions (Friedman, 1999). The most effective way to solve this dilemma is to localize public relations programs as well as business practices (Gadiesh & Pean, 2003; Wang, 2005). Not only does it address local communications directly to the local audience, but it also requires tailoring the message to mirror the cultural perspective of the local audience. In other words, it is imperative for PR practitioners in host countries to become aware of how their message would be understood by the host culture (George, 2003).

During crisis time, misunderstanding local culture often fosters public anger and aggravates the situation. In 2006, when the Indian news media accused Coca-Cola and PepsiCo of pesticide contamination in India, executives in the companies were confident that they could handle the crisis (Gentleman, 2006). Initially, they hoped that the crisis would blow over and thus adopted a policy of virtual silence, which eventually turned out to be a public relations disaster. Suhel Seth, an adviser to Coca-Cola India, was quoted in the *International Herald Tribune* as saying that, "In the U.S. and the West there is a certain dignity to silence. But here people interpret silence as guilt. You have to roll up your sleeves and get into a street fight. Coke and Pepsi didn't understand that" (Gentleman, 2006).

However, Lee (2004) found that a company's no-comment response during the crisis situation received more positive evaluation among participants from Hong Kong than the minimization response, presumably because silence is often considered as an act of wisdom, as taught in Confucius' maxim to "think three times before you act."

Many of the same mistakes of Western MNCs are also made by many Asian global firms in the West. For example, when Mitsubishi, the Japanese car giant, was involved in a sexual harassment case in the United States, it was ignorant of U.S. regulation on the issue. The company resisted the U.S. regulation system rather than adapting its system to U.S. public relations practice, and as a result it made a bad situation worse (Paul, 1999).

The local responsiveness strategy of public relations can be further discussed in terms of the stakeholders' perspective, because doing business means personalizing the business relationship in an obsessively intimate fashion (Levitt, 1983). Botan (1992) warns that failure to recognize underlying (national) differences reduces the potential for using public relations as a lens for better understanding how organizations in other cultures use communication to adapt their relationships with relevant publics (p. 152).

Because MNCs are not able to manage diverse stakeholders around the nations, Cesaria (2000) states that it is impossible for management of global organizations to successfully control all communication processes. A company's stakeholders may vary from one product and country market to another. Those stakeholders' expectations will also vary concerning the company's behavior and outcomes. Therefore, Mühlbacher, Dahringer, and Leihs (1999) argue that effective public relations activities may be mostly local in nature.

Mackiewicz (1993) added that global companies should prepare for environmental challenges from two fronts: government regulatory policy and public activism (p. 85). Taylor and Kent (1999) argue that it is government officials rather than the general public who are of great importance to effective public relations in many developing countries. Yi-Ru Regina Chen (2007) interviewed 25 MNCs' public relations managers in China and examined how they interacted with Chinese government. Multinationals whose business is significantly affected by the government will often provide their public relations department with a managerial role whereby they either lead or work closely with other business departments such as marketing and sales. For instance, a PR manager of an aerospace MNC set up the firm's lobbying priority based on "the understanding of China's publics, sensitive to the Chinese political environment, and accurate judgment of the government's agenda priority" (Chen, 2007, p. 291).

The potential for activism makes the international environment particularly turbulent. Domination or exploitation in developing countries, pollution of the environment, industrial accidents, or occupational diseases such as asbestosis among asbestos miners all have the potential to mobilize social opposition against the offending organization (Grunig, 1987). Thus, Wakefield (1997) maintains that excellent international public relations contain a component in each country that can scan the environment, identify potential activist groups, and build programs to deal with them (p. 279). Then, it is imperative that MNCs should broaden their definition of the terms *environmental regulators* and *constituencies*.

Child and Tsai (2005) who studied two U.S.-based chemical MNCs and a British chemical MNC's public relations strategies in China and Taiwan, demonstrated that informal local constituencies often pose a real challenge for MNCs. Indeed, adhering to local standards and environmental regulations in emerging economies has become a sine qua non for the legitimacy of MNC operations, because of their global scope. However, they observed, the real challenge comes from informal local constituencies such as local politicians, NGOs, and a concerned public, and they played a more prominent role than the formal regulators. Even the slightest improper conduct in an obscure corner could have wide ramifications, thanks to the Internet and new communication technologies. In Child and Tsai's (2005) case study, a British chemical MNC in Taiwan disposed of acid waste through a contractor who used ships that failed to discharge it at the specified locations, which was detected by local fishermen, and followed by a large-scale protest that brought in politicians and NGOs. As a result, the MNC was forced to shut down its production for a while.

This was particularly the case when six Indian states imposed whole or partial bans in 2006 on Coke and Pepsi after a research group reported that the soft drinks contained harmful levels of pesticides (Rai, 2006). Amelia Gentleman of the *International Herald Tribune* states the lesson clearly:

> Coke and Pepsi stumbled badly in their response to the pesticide allegations: they underestimated how quickly this would spiral into a nationwide scandal, misjudged the speed with which local politicians would seize on an Indian environmental group's report to attack a powerful global brand and failed to respond swiftly to quell the anxieties of their customers. (Gentleman, 2006)

Experience from the Coke and Pepsi crisis in India has proved that the news media in host cultures are intrinsically not favorable to multinational corporations. When the negative event develops into a "focusing event" that captures millions of consumers' attention and generates intense controversy, it becomes a threat to the survival of international businesses operating in foreign countries (Birkland, 1997).

Thus, Wakefield (1997) contends that an effective local component of an excellent international public relations program will build relationships with local media and with publics who may have received unrealistic pictures about the multinational organization. Media relations are particularly vital for companies operating overseas, and public relations managers should cultivate relationships with local media (Gonring, 1997). With MNCs' growth and expansion in emerging Asian countries, the unique characteristics of those countries' media relations have been introduced (Huang, 2000). In essence, the most notable characteristic of the journalist–PR practitioner's relationship in the East Asian countries can be explained by the collectivist cultures and social relationships, which are a stark difference from the media relations practices in Western culture, which is grounded on the social exchange theory. For instance, the relationship between journalists and PR practitioners in China, Taiwan, and South Korea is culturally different from that of Western countries: *quanxi* (Huang, 2000) in Chinese does not merely indicate *relationship* in English. Both PR practitioners and journalists often seek some commonalities via numerous social ties or networks. Rooted in collectivist culture as well as Confucianism, *quanxi* is sustained by the motivation to help in-group members (favor) and to keep favorable social perceptions about one's prestige (face).

Balancing Global Integration and Local Responsiveness

The integration–responsiveness paradigm has proven to be a robust framework for describing and analyzing the strategies of international firms at the corporate and subsidiary levels (Taggart, 1997). Bartlett and Ghoshal (2000) assert that global efficiency must develop the infrastructure and capabilities for simultaneously managing both costs and revenues. In terms of public relations, the cost side can be linked to internal efficiency of public relations that results from the integrated public relations programs for research, publicity, Web site development, annual reports, and publications. Estimating such an economic value of public relations can be an important public relations evaluation, because the logic underlying the economic issues of public relations focuses on the relationship between benefits and costs associated with the implementation of a public relations program (Ehling, 1992). Internal efficiency is achieved by sharing an MNC's mission, public relations goals, business philosophy, and policies.

The local responsiveness strategy is conceptualized as "decentralization" in terms of external effectiveness. Given the difficulty of community-based standards of responsibility and the integration of different community values to direct a sense of global responsibility (Deetz, 1999), MNCs are finding it necessary to move toward more decentralized forms of management (Mackiewicz, 1993). The heads of sectors, branches, divisions, or subsidiaries are generally encouraged to think of themselves as the heads of independent or autonomous businesses. For instance, firms have increasingly decentralized their philanthropic programs so that subsidiaries around the world can design their own community relations philanthropy programs, while ensuring that they are linked to the MNC's overall business strategies (Shen, 2006; Wright, 1996).

Coombs, Holladay, Hasenauer, and Signitzer (1994) contend that international public relations often confronts the choices between globalization (integration) and localization (local responsiveness). In practice, however, polarization can be harmful (Wakefield, 1997). Several scholars proposed a normative idea that integration and local responsiveness must be viewed as complementary options rather than as either–or choices (Coombs et al., 1994; Lucenko, 1999) and for selection to be made for the best global communications strategy (Falconi, 1989).

Coordinating between integration and responsiveness can be achieved by giving tactical autonomy to local subsidiaries within the boundary in which the MNC's mission, goals, and specific program's themes are kept. For instance, IBM's regional and local offices exercise their own judgment about what to fund, while they follow the firm's two global themes— education and the environment (Mackiewicz, 1993).

MNCs' Public Relations Effectiveness in the I-R Grid

The change in international operating environments has forced MNCs to simultaneously optimize global efficiency and local responsiveness.

However, it has been the dilemma of MNCs to reconcile the benefits of local tailoring with those of global integration in every business function such as R&D, manufacturing, marketing, and communications. System theory holds that efficiency and adaptiveness (flexibility) are trade-offs, but Phillips and Tuladhar (2000) argue that it is not appropriate to define flexibility simply as the inverse of economic efficiency.

Prahalad and Doz (1987) came up with the integration-responsiveness (IR) grid. They explain that "the purpose of the IR framework is to assess the *relative importance* of the two sets of conflicting demands on a business and to determine which of the two provides strategic leverage at a given point in time" (p. 22).

The I-R grid is a suitable frame for identifying the characteristics of a business in a global setting. The unit of analysis is a discrete business. However, functions within a business may respond differently to each strategic pressure (Prahalad & Doz, 1987). For example, in an industry, integrated R&D may be common while manufacturing may be somewhat decentralized, and marketing fairly locally responsive.

Unlike other business departments or functions in an MNC, the global public relations strategies should ensure that internal efficiency and external effectiveness could be achieved simultaneously. On the one hand, organizational mission, public relations goals, and public relations training programs need to be strategically coordinated by the parent company or MNC's headquarters and shared through the local entities. On the other hand, adapting or responding to the local business environment in terms of public relations practices should be implemented tactically to build effective relationships with diverse stakeholders in a local setting.

Observing two successful cases of MNC entrants in India, Bardhan and Patwardhan (2004) concluded that two MNCs' success resulted from their cultivating healthy relationships with local stakeholders while they were following headquarters' norms and conducting frequent in-house training and professional development programs for employees. This optimization is often achieved by global training of managers of subsidiaries to serve as cross-cultural boundary spanners.

Figure 15.1 shows the I-R grid for developing a normative theoretical framework for optimizing global public relations strategies according to the business environment and organizational culture. While the basic framework is adopted from Prahalad and Doz (1987), the conditions or pressures on each strategy have been modified in terms of an international public relations perspective. The I-R grid for MNCs' public relations is drawn in the two-dimension grid instead of a continuous line. Strategic redirections of integration and responsiveness of public relations should be contingent on different business competitions and issue settings. That is, in structuring relationships between headquarters and

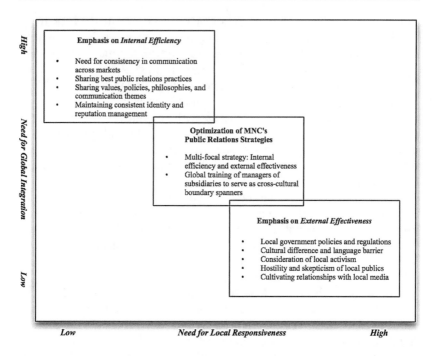

Figure 15.1 *Optimization model for international public relations of MNCs.*

affiliates, managers must be sensitive not only to the present responsiveness and integration needs, but also to possible changes in the underlying competitive and economic conditions of a business (Doz et al., 1990).

Depending on the relative intensity of pressures for integration or responsiveness, when a national issue emerges onto the global stage

> the headquarters–subsidiary relationship can be altered strategically to achieve the best fit of the time responding to shifting needs for integration and responsiveness (Doz & Prahalad, 1987). For instance, even though senior managers in each country are responsible for activities in that country, it is the headquarters of MNCs that [are] ultimately responsible. (Wakefield, 1997, p. 218)

A rapidly changing global business setting often forces multinational organizations to change their global public relations strategies in accordance with the restructuring organizational system. Especially, when a multinational corporation experiences a fundamental change in its organization structure because of mergers and acquisitions, public relations needs to consider many constituent groups with diverse cultural and societal backgrounds (Golitsinski, 2000). Of course, corporate communications during the merger must be consistent and inclusive, reaching all audiences, both external and internal, especially placing much emphasis on employees (Drobis, 1998). However, communicating complex mergers across borders and cultural divides requires a lot more than consistency.

Conclusion

As multinational corporations evolve into global networks, the capability to coordinate their operating units' public relations programs becomes important. The goal of integrative public relations strategy is to have a closely coordinated, and strategically controlled international public relations programs that builds an integrative communication network between headquarters and subsidiaries or among subsidiaries in a multinational corporation. By taking this global integration strategy, not only can an MNC share organizational mission, goals, values, and publications among global units but it also implements PR programs with an integrated voice to project consistent corporate identity and values.

An MNC can achieve this goal by integrating its communication devices such as corporate Web sites, Intranet, newsletters, blogs, and publications, and by establishing an institutionalized training program to share the success and failure of global public relations programs from different regions. This integrative public relations strategy helps organization achieve internal efficiency that benefits organizations by reducing operating costs.

As globalization increases, so do the challenges from the external business environment that require multinational companies to implement locally adaptable public relations programs. Local responsiveness of public relations strategy for MNCs can be defined as designing and customizing public relations programs to be adaptable to local environmental uncertainty and national regulatory barriers. Its goal is to decentralize public relations programs and give autonomy to local business units to build effective relationship with diverse publics. The needs for being locally responsive increase during the crisis situations. Faced with the uncertain local business environment, an MNC may try to avoid that uncertainty by designing organizational structures to be flexible to local conditions. Public relations managers of an MNC must be aware that global public relations programs are often constrained by the national variation and the external environment on which organizational survival depends.

With the increasing globalization of world economy, it is necessary that the role and expectations of public relations also be increased. Public relations practitioners working for an MNC are required to interact with diverse stakeholders and to represent their firm's interests (Burk, 1994). In doing so, practitioners working in multinational corporations should keep it in mind that many factors—such as market conditions, legal or regulative restrictions, competition, cultural diversity, and communication differences—are to be considered in the decision-making process when developing public relations strategies.

References

Anderson, G. (1989). A global look at public relations. In B. Cantor (Ed.), *Experts in action* (2nd ed., pp. 412–422). White Plains, NY: Longman.

Bardhan, N., & Patwardhan, P. (2004). Multinational corporations and public relations in a historically resistant host culture. *Journal of Communication Management, 8*, 246–263

Bartlett, C. A., & Ghoshal, S. (1989). *Managing across borders: The transnational solution.* Boston: Harvard Business School Press.

Bartlett, C. A., & Ghoshal, S. (2000). *Transnational management: Text, cases, and readings in cross-border management* (3rd ed.). Boston: Irwin McGraw-Hill.

Berenbeim, R. E. (1983). *Operating foreign subsidiaries: How independent can they be?* New York: Conference Board.

Birkland, T. A. (1997). *After disaster: Agenda setting, public policy, and focusing events.* Washington, DC: Georgetown University Press.

Botan, C. (1992). International public relations: Critique and reformation. *Public Relations Review, 18*, 149–159.

Burk, J. (1994). Training MNC employees as culturally sensitive boundary spanners. *Public Relations Quarterly, 39*, 40–44.

Cesaria, R. (2000). Organizational communication issues in Italian multinational corporations. *Management Communication Quarterly, 14*, 161–172.

Chen, Y-R. R. (2007). The strategic management of government affairs in China: How multinational corporations in China interact with the Chinese government. *Journal of Public Relations Research, 19*, 283–306.

Child, J., & Tsai, T. (2005). The dynamic between firms' environmental strategies and institutional constraints in emerging economies: Evidence from China and Taiwan. *Journal of Management Studies, 42*, 95–125.

Coombs, W. T., Holladay, S., Hasenauer, G., & Signitzer, B. (1994). A comparative analysis of international public relations: Identification and interpretation of similarities and differences between professionalism in Austria, Norway, and the United States. *Journal of Public Relations Research, 6*, 23–39.

Craig, C. S., & Douglas, S. (2000). Configural advantage in global markets. *Journal of International Marketing, 8*, 6–26.

Deetz, S. (1999). Multiple stakeholders and social responsibility in the international business context: A critical perspective. In P. Salem (Ed.), *Organizational communication and change* (pp. 289–319). Cresskill, NJ: Hampton Press.

Doz, Y. (1986). Government policies and global industries. In M. E. Porter

(Ed.), *Competition in global industries* (pp. 96–118). Boston: Harvard Business Press.

Doz, Y., & Prahalad, C. K. (1987). A process model of strategic redirection in large complex firms: The case of multinational corporations. In A. Pettigrew (Ed.), *The management of strategic change* (pp. 63–83). Oxford: Basil Blackwell.

Doz, Y., Prahalad, C. K., & Hamel, G. (1990). Control, change, and flexibility: The dilemma of transnational collaboration. In C. A. Bartlett, Y. Doz, & G. Hedlund (Eds.), *Managing the global firm* (pp. 117–143). London: Routledge.

Drobis, D. (1998, December). Global mergers at the flood. *International Public Relations Review*, 33–35.

Dunning, J. (1989). Multinational enterprises and the growth of services. *The Service Industries Journal*, 9, 5–39.

Ehling, W. P. (1992). Estimating the value of public relations and communication to an organization. In J. Grunig (Ed.), *Excellence in public relations and communication management* (pp. 617–638). Hillsdale, NJ: Erlbaum.

Falconi, T. M. (1989). Management of international public relations. In B. Cantor (Ed.), *Experts in action* (2nd ed., pp. 444–449). White Plains, NY: Longman.

Friedman, T. (1999). *The Lexus and the olive tree*. New York: Farrar, Straus & Giroux.

Gadiesh, O., & Pean, J-M. (2003, September 9). Think globally, market locally. *The Wall Street Journal*, p, B2.

Gentleman, A, (2006, August 23). Coke and Pepsi stumble in India. *The International Herald Tribune*. Retrieved July 18, 2008, from http://www.iht.com/articles/2006/08/22/business/coke.php

George, A. M. (2003). Teaching culture: the challenges and opportunities of international public relations. *Business Communication Quarterly*, 66, 97–113.

Ghoshal, S. (1987). Global strategy: An organizing framework. *Strategic Management Journal*, 8, 425–440.

Golitsinski, S. (2000). *A study of the Daimler–Chrysler merger portrayal in U.S. and European media*. Project report in Communication Studies. Retrieved July 8, 2008, from http://www.lordofthewebs.com/communication/

Gonring, M. P. (1997). Global and local media relations. In C. L. Caywood (Ed.), *The handbook of strategic public relations and integrated communication* (pp. 63–76). New York: McGraw-Hill.

Grunig, J. E., Grunig, L. A., Sriramesh, K., Huang, Y-H., & Lyra, A. (1995). Models of public relations in an international setting. *Journal of Public Relations Research*, 7, 163–186.

Grunig, L. A. (1987). Variation in relations with environmental publics. *Public Relations Review*, 13, 46–58.

Grunig, L. A. (1992). How public relations/communication departments should adapt to the structure and environment of an organization...and what they actually do. In J. Grunig (Ed.), *Excellence in public relations and communication management* (pp. 467–481). Hillsdale, NJ: Erlbaum.

Gupta, A. K., & Govindarajan, V. (2000). Managing global expansion: A conceptual framework. *Business Horizon, 43*, 45–54.

Guth, D. W. (1998). Public relations in the new Russia. *The Public Relations Strategist, 4*, 51–54.

Huang, Y.-H. (2000). The personal influence model and the Gao Guanxi in Taiwan Chinese public relations. *Public Relations Review, 26*, 219–236.

Hulbert, J. M., & Brandt, W. K. (1984). *Managing the multinational subsidiary*. New York: Holt Rinehart & Winston.

Hunter, T., & Bansal, P. (2007). How standard is standardized MNC global environmental communication? *Journal of Business Ethics, 71*, 135–147.

Kolk, A. (2005). Corporate responsibility in the coffee sector: The dynamics of MNC responses and code development. *European Management Journal, 23*, 228–236.

Lawrence, P., & Lorsch, J. (1967). *Organization and environment: Managing differentiation and integration*. Cambridge, MA: Harvard Business Press.

Lee, B. K. (2004). Audience-oriented approach to crisis communication: A study of Hong Kong consumers' evaluation of an organizational crisis. *Communication Research, 31*, 600–618.

Lee, S-H. (2000). Creating organizational flexibility by reengineering HR activities: Implications for economic uncertainties. *Global Focus, 12*, 89–97.

Leichsering, V (1998). Tradition vs. transition: The changing role of public relations. *International Public Relations Review, 21*, 33–35.

Levitt, T. (1983). The globalization of markets. *Harvard Business Review, 61*, 92–103.

Levitt, T. (1985). Global companies to replace dying multinational. *Marketing News, 19*, 15.

Lorange, P., & Probst, G. (1990). Effective strategic planning processes in the multinational corporation. In C. A. Bartlett, Y. Doz, & G. Hedlund (Eds.), *Managing the global firm* (pp. 144–163). London: Routledge.

Lucenko, K. (1999). *Communicating the future*. New York: Conference Board.

Mackiewicz, A. (1993). *The economist intelligence unit guide to building a global image*. New York: McGraw-Hill.

Mangee, C. (1989). Building an international public relations network. In B. Cantor (Ed.), *Experts in action* (2nd ed., pp. 434–443). White Plains, NY: Longman.

Meznar, M. B., & Nigh, D. (1995). Buffer or bridge? Environmental and organizational determinants of public affairs activities in American firms. *Academy of Management Journal, 38*, 975–996.

Molleda, J. C. (2000a). *Integrative public relations in international business: The impact of administrative models and subsidiary roles*. Unpublished doctoral dissertation, University of South Carolina, Columbia.

Molleda, J. C. (2000b). *An exploration of integration of the public relations function in international business operations*. Paper presented to the AEJMC annual convention, Phoenix, AZ.

Mühlbacher, H., Dahringer, L., & Leihs, H. (1999). *International marketing: A global perspective* (2nd ed.). London: International Thomson Business Press.

Newbury, W., & Yakova, N. (2006). Standardization preferences: A function of national culture, work interdependence and local embeddedness. *Journal of International Business Studies, 37*, 44–60.

Newsom, D., Scott, A., & Turk, J. V. (1992). *This is PR: The realities of public relations* (5th ed.). Belmont, CA: Wadsworth.

Ogrizek, M. (2002). The effect of corporate social responsibility on the branding of financial services. *Journal of Financial Services Marketing, 6*, 215–229.

O'Neil, J. (2008). Measuring the impact of employeee communication on employee comprehension and action: A case study of a major international firm. *Public Relations Journal, 2*, 1–17.

Ovaitt, F. Jr. (1988). Pr without boundaries: Is globalization an option? *Public Relations Quarterly, 33*, 5–9.

Paul, E. F. (1999). *Business ethics in the global market*. Stanford, CA: Stanford University Press.

Phillips, F., & Tuladhar, S. D. (2000). Measuring organizational flexibility: An exploration and general model. *Technological Forecasting and Social Change, 64*, 23–38.

Prahalad, C. K., & Doz, Y. (1987). *The multinational mission*. New York: Free Press.

Rai, S. (2006, August 15). Move in India to ban Coke and Pepsi worries industry. *The New York Times*, p. C1.

Rockart, J. F. (1998). Towards survivability of communication-intensive new organization forms. *Journal of Management Studies, 35*, 417–420.

Rondinelli, D. & Berry, M. (2000). Corporate environmental management and public policy. *American Behavioral Scientist, 44*, 168–187.

Ruigrok, W. Achtenhagen, L., Rüegg-Stürm, J., & Wagner, M. (2000). Hilti AG: Shared leadership and the rise of the communicating organization. In A. M. Pettigrew & E. M. Fenton (Eds.), *The innovating organization* (pp. 178–207). Thousand Oaks, CA: Sage.

Shen, H. (2006). *Public relations and MNCs' corporate social responsibility: From developing country's perspective*. Unpublished master's thesis, University of Maryland, College Park, MA.

Shen, H. (2007, March 8-11). Cultural and historical variances of multinational corporations' social responsibility. In M. W. DiStaso (Ed.), *Proceedings of the Tenth Annual International Public Relations Conference* (pp. 477–492), Gainesville FL: Institute for Public Relations.

Shuter, R., & Wiseman, R. L. (1994). Communication in multinational organizations. In R. Wiseman & R. Shuter (Eds.), *Communicating in multinational organizations* (pp. 3–11). Thousands Oaks, CA: Sage.

Taggart, J. H. (1997). An evaluation of the integration-responsiveness framework: MNC manufacturing subsidiaries in the UK. *Management International Review, 37*, 295–318.

Taylor, M. (2000). Cultural variance as a challenge to global public relations: A case study of the Coca-Cola scare in Europe. *Public Relations Review, 26*, 277–293.

Tobias, R. L. (1996). Communicating core values. *The Public Relations Strategist, 2*(1), 19–22.

Verčič, D., Grunig, L. A., & Grunig, J. E. (1996). Global and specific principles of public relations: Evidence from Slovenia. In H. M. Culbertson & N. Chen (Eds.), *International public relations: A comparative analysis* (pp. 31–65). Mahwah: NJ: Erlbaum.

Wakefield, R. I. (1996). Interdisciplinary theoretical foundations for international public relations. In H. M. Culbertson & N. Chen (Eds.), *International public relations: A comparative analysis* (pp. 17–30). Mahwah, NJ: Erlbaum.

Wakefield, R. I. (1997). *International public relations: A theoretical approach to excellence based on a worldwide Delphi study.* Unpublished doctoral dissertation, University of Maryland, College Park.

Wakefield, R. I. (1999). Preliminary Delphi research on international public relations programming. In D.Moss, D. Verčič, & G. Warnaby (Eds.), *Perspectives on public relations research* (pp. 179–208). London: Routledge.

Wakefield, R. I. (2001). Effective public relations in the multinational organization. In R. L. Heath (Ed.), *Handbook of public relations* (pp. 639–647). Thousand Oaks, CA: Sage.

Wang, J. (2005). Consumer nationalism and corporate reputation management in the global era. *Corporate Communication, 10,* 223–239.

White, R. E., & Poynter, T. A. (1990). Organizing for world-wide advantage. In C. A. Bartlett, Y. Doz, & G. Hedlund (Eds.), *Managing the global firm* (pp. 95–111). London: Routledge.

Wouters, J. (1991). *International public relations: How to establish your company's product, service, and images in foreign markets.* New York: AMACOM.

Wright, P. D. (1996). Making the corporate giving programs strategic. In S. J. Garone (Ed.), *Strategic opportunities in corporate community activity* (pp. 19–21). New York: Conference Board.

Zaidman, N. (2001). Cultural codes and language strategies in business communication: Interactions between Israeli and Indian business people. *Management Communication Quarterly, 14,* 408–441.

Chapter 16

Coordination and Control of Global Public Relations to Manage Cross-National Conflict Shifts

A Multidisciplinary Theoretical Perspective for Research and Practice

Juan-Carlos Molleda and Alexander Laskin

Public relations, public affairs, and communication professionals working for nonprofit, for-profit, and governmental transnational organizations (TNOs) are challenged by a world in which the need for interdependence is increasing all the time. International markets are flattened by technologies that allow us to move faster and farther and communicate more widely in real time (Friedman, 2005). Social interdependence joins forces with the spread of democracy and alternative political systems that empower public opinion nationally and internationally (Sharpe & Pritchard, 2004). Morley (2002) explains that significant changes

> have reshaped the world in which we live and the techniques we use to communicate: the Internet, religious fundamentalism, global terrorism, increasingly strident NGOs seeking to de-rail globalization, the concentration of power into new communications conglomerates, the boom and bust of the "new economy" along with the rapid deployment of the Internet in a 24/7 mobile and continuously connected society. (p. vii)

The local and global impact of communication, the empowerment of public opinion, and democracy each presents practitioners and TNOs with an opportunity to balance those forces. The achievement of local and global impact is possible with the mechanisms of coordination and control for efficient and effective management of the public relations or public affairs function (Molleda, 2000a, 2000b). The efficiency is necessary to master internal operations and effectiveness is necessary in order to achieve public relations goals and objectives with a variety of stakeholders. Internal efficiency and external effectiveness is a day-to-day preoccupation of large domestic organizations with branches or subsidiaries in several locations within a country, such as national banks and social-driven foundations (see Lim, chapter 15 this volume).

The complexity of coordinating and controlling the public relations or public affairs function in TNOs increases because of distance, a diversity of contexts (i.e., country differences in terms of market size, competition, nature of product/service, and labor), uncontrollables (i.e., foreign stockholders and host government regulations), degree of certainty (i.e., stability versus change), and multiple layers of authority and decision making (Daniels, Radebaugh, & Sullivan, 2004). Complexity intensifies when TNOs face crises or difficult situations that have a potential to cross borders and thus exert great pressure on the organization's headquarters or in their home markets. "Business practices, even those conducted a very long way from their home markets, can be subject to intense scrutiny and comment by customers, employees, suppliers, shareholders, and governments, as well as other groups upon whose support the business relies," Knox and Maklan state (2004, p. 509).Taylor (2000) also explains:

> Today, successful organizations must operate in a global market-place. American companies now have subsidiaries all over the world. Likewise, companies from Europe and Asia have operations in the United States. Globalization means that what happens to an organization in one part of the world will affect the organization in other parts of the world. (p. 278)

The purpose of this chapter is to review pertinent literature from public relations and international business concerning transnational crises and coordination and control mechanisms. The intersections between the two bodies of literature are summarized and analyzed. Finally, after this multidisciplinary literature review, a set of presuppositions are introduced to guide future research and point out lessons learned for teaching and practicing global public relations.

Literature Review

Coordination and Control Mechanisms

According to Daniels et al. (2004), these are the questions facing all TNOs: "Where should decision-making power reside? How should foreign operations report to headquarters? How can the company ensure that it meets its global objectives?" (p. 442). Managers' toughest challenge is to balance a TNO's global needs with its needs to adapt to country-level differences. In general, these questions and a need for maintaining balance have guided research on coordination and control mechanisms in the field of international business studies. "The new paradigm ought to account for a more comprehensive approach that creates thinking and acting at both the local and global levels of the organization," says

Wakefield (2001) in reference to the role of global public relations practitioners in TNOs (p. 641).

Martinez and Jarillo (1989) define a mechanism of coordination as "any administrative tool for achieving integration among different units within an organization" (p. 490). After reviewing the work of more than 80 scholars from 1953 to 1988, Martinez and Jarillo conclude that research has focused on the more formal tools to the detriment of the subtler forms of coordination, such as acculturation and the creation of networks of informal communication. Some examples of coordination mechanism are: global, cross-functional, virtual teams (members from various functional areas who work from a variety of geographical locations and are connected by communication technology, such as Web sites and intranets); advisory personnel; management rotation; keeping international and domestic personnel in closer proximity; establishing liaisons among subsidiaries; placing foreign personnel on the board of directors and top-level committees; basing reward systems partially on global results; and giving divisions and subsidiaries credit for their accomplishments and contributions.

Control mechanisms keep a TNO's direction and strategy on track. "Control is the management's planning, implementation, evaluation, and correction of performance to ensure that the organization meets its objectives," Daniels et al. write (2004, pp. 442–443). Examples of control mechanism are: visits to subsidiaries, management performance evaluation, cost and accounting comparability through standardized procedures and methods, evaluative measurement with similar indicators for all subsidiaries, and information systems.

The benefits of exploiting global economies of scale and scope give integration and coordination of activities a prominent role in strategic management (Bartlett & Ghoshal, 1987a). The multiple interactions among subsidiaries and between subsidiaries and headquarters is a management process in which control was made less dominant by the increased importance of interunit integration and collaboration (Bartlett & Ghoshal, 1987b). "[T]oday's game of global strategy seems increasingly to be a game of coordination—getting more and more dispersed production facilities, R&D laboratories, and marketing activities to truly work together," Porter writes (1986, p. 36).

Control and coordination are two of the main elements of the integration process of TNOs (Cray, 1984). Cray identifies size and location in the organizational structure, technology, foreign commitment, financial performance, and nationality as variables that affect the extent of control and coordination used by a foreign subsidiary to manage its operations and the interaction with the parent company and other subsidiaries. Cray (1984) elaborates:

A subsidiary which is large, technologically complex, located in a product division, and highly profitable will very likely be integrated through extensive coordination with other parts of the organization while retaining a good deal of control over its own affairs. A small subsidiary, located at a long administrative distance from the center of the organization, and sharing a simple technology with its parent, will be subject to higher levels of control and lower levels of coordination. (p. 96)

Martinez and Jarillo (1989) explain that simple strategies demand simple coordination so that they are implemented with the use of formal structural mechanisms. In contrast, complex strategies—such as interrelated, multiple plants, or multiple markets policies—demand a great amount of coordinating effort, and therefore are implemented by using both structural/formal and informal/subtle mechanisms.

According to Martinez and Jarillo (1989), studies of the coordination mechanisms in an international context can be divided into three main streams of research: (1) studies on organizational structure; (2) studies of centralization of decision making and bureaucratic control; and (3) studies of the informal, subtler mechanisms, such as cultural control or control by socialization. They state that from 1953 to 1975 international business scholars focused their attention on structural and formal coordination mechanisms (e.g., Child, 1972a, 1972b, 1973; Pugh, Hickson, & Hinings, 1968; Pugh, Hickson, Hinings, & Turner, 1968). Since 1976, according to the authors, while researchers continued their interest in structural and formal mechanisms of coordination, they began to concentrate more on informal and sophisticated administrative tools (e.g., Baliga & Jaeger, 1984; Bartlett & Ghoshal, 1987a, 1987b; Edström & Galbraith, 1977; Ghoshal & Bartlett, 1988; Mascarenhas, 1984; Van Maanen, 1978). Thus, a more multidimensional perspective in the study of coordination mechanisms appears to have taken hold since the mid-1970s.

Martinez and Jarillo (1991) investigated managers' perception of the relationship between integration and mechanisms of coordination and concluded:

The more managers expect their subsidiaries to be integrated with the group, the more they plan to use all mechanisms of coordination.... [A]n increase in the firm's integration level must be accompanied by an increase in coordination, and that the mechanisms to be introduced or reinforced will probably be the more subtle ones. (pp. 440–441)

Coordination mechanisms seem to be an essential part of international strategic management. The flexibility achieved by more coordination and less control appears to facilitate the adoption of a global corporate vision without leaving out domestic concerns.

Ricart, Enright, Ghemawat, Hart, and Khannaet (2004), reporting on the results of the First Annual Conference on Emerging Research Frontiers in International Business Studies, conclude that modern international business research in the area of international coordination and control uses a simple antagonistic framework of globalization versus localization: "Technological change was bringing convergence in tastes, customs, and products. However, implementation required some degree of localization to respond to local needs and cultures, as well as to benefit from local advantages" (p. 177). Such an approach, however, focuses the research "on *how* multinationals do what they do, rather than *what* they do, or *why* they do it in the first place" (Ricart et al., 2004, p. 176). The literature review that the authors conduct allows them to suggest a different "ecological" approach, where the focus of the research is the understanding of the underlying reasons for coordination and control choices TNOs make. Such choices generally depend on four key areas:

- Differences between countries (Ghemawat, 2001) such as cultural sensitivity, administrative sensitivity, geographic sensitivity, and economic sensitivity. In other words, to understand why business strategies differ across countries, one should answer the question why countries themselves differ from each other. Different geographic locations, climates, cultures, or economies create these varieties between countries and they lead to different business strategies. Even more, these differences create complex dimensions as their interactions also influence corporate strategies. Thus, multidimensional and cross-country analysis is required to evaluate this complexity.
- Configurations of local institutions such as paucity of the specialized intermediaries needed to consummate transactions. Khanna (2002) explains that absence of intermediaries in a foreign location, which a company relies on at home, requires such a company to change its competitive strategy and implement local modifications to take into account these localized voids.
- Integration of home and foreign locations into a corporate strategy. It can be a part or even a key element of a company's business strategy—achieving the international level creates internal efficiency and external effectiveness. Thus, the third area of analysis looks at firm-specific and location-specific advantages—"collocating firms

and places" (Ricart et al., 2004, p. 178). Internationalization of a company's business becomes a competitive advantage in itself.

- Place as an ingredient for competitive advantage (Hart & Milstein, 1999) such as targeting not only one billion or so people currently targeted by multinationals but the other 5 billion people, the bottom of the pyramid, "living *in* poverty who have been largely bypassed, or even damaged, by globalizations" (Ricart et al., 2004, p. 193).

- Another area of research that analyzes the differences between host and home countries' cultures as a factor in shaping the coordination and control mechanism uses the *National Trade Bank and American Wholesalers and Distributors Directory* to identify U.S. manufacturers and their international distributors to investigate the relations between them (Griffith, Hu, & Ryans, 2000). The article relies primarily on Hofstede's cultural dimensions (i.e., individualism, power distance, and uncertainty avoidance) in order to understand the possibility of businesses to have a globally standardized strategy. The research, then, compares so-called intra- and intercultural relationships. "International business relationships...can consist of two partners from the same cultural type (intra-cultural) or two different cultural types (inter-cultural)" (Griffith et al., 2000, p. 305). Standardization may be appropriate "when both partners emanate from the same cultural type" (p. 306). When, however, partners are "members of different culture types...the differences...could create unexpected consequences in the relationships" (p. 306).

- The authors suggest four relational constructs: trust, commitment, conflict, and satisfaction.

The results show interdependence of the relational variables: trust is positively related to commitment in intercultural and in intracultural relationships. Commitment is inversely related to conflict in both intra- and intercultural relationships. Commitment is positively related to satisfaction and a relationship is significantly stronger in intercultural relationship over the intracultural. Conflict is negatively related to satisfaction in intracultural relationships but no relationship is determined in intercultural relationships. In other words, the study results show that when both parties are from the same culture they perceive conflict similarly as something negative and detrimental to their relationships with each other; however, it is not necessarily the case in communications between members of different cultures.

The authors summarize their findings by concluding that "businesses should carefully weigh the potential disadvantages of employing a globally standardized process approach in developing international relationships, particularly those consisting of partners from different cultural types" (Griffith et al., 2000, p. 317). A coordination and control mechanism successfully working in the United States can probably be extended to Canada, a culturally similar country, but may prove disastrous if extended into a culturally different country such as Mexico.

Luo (2003) similarly investigates parent–subsidiary links but focuses on one country, China. The sample of 196 subsidiaries of TNOs is drawn from the *Directory of Foreign-Invested Industrial Enterprises* and the parent–subsidiary relations are assessed. The key concept of the study is the interconnectedness of parent–subsidiary relationships with resource dependence and dynamic capability. Resource-dependency is being defined broadly as "a foreign market environment is a source of scarce resources" meaning not only natural resources, but also, for example, informational, capital, or workforce; thus, as a local environment becomes more volatile, TNOs depending on this environment are subject to increasing uncertainty and exposure. The author suggests, "The reduction of external dependency requires improvements in parent–subsidiary relations on a number of fronts, notably resource support and intra-network information flow" (Luo, 2003, p. 292). At the same time, subsidiaries have not only to respond to the needs of the organization, but also to the realities of the local environment, and thus headquarters must "encourage local adaptation and responsiveness from their subsidiaries" (p. 292). As a result, these two complimentary and yet contradictory tendencies play in each subsidiary–headquarters interaction because "resource dependence explains the importance of intra-corporate links in reducing external dependence and thus alleviating emerging market threats, while the dynamic capability perspective explains the importance of such links in bolstering a subsidiary's strategic adaptation to the host country environment, which may in turn help reap benefits from emerging opportunities" (Luo, 2003, p. 291).

Based on the research findings, the author concludes that in emerging markets subsidiaries "tend to perform better in terms of sales and profitability when they receive more resources from parent firms, are supported by parental adaptation to host country operations, and are less rigidly controlled by headquarters" (Luo, 2003, p. 303). The findings validate key propositions:

> parent support reduces a subunit's dependency on external resources that are either governmentally controlled or involve enormous economic exposure, and this reduction in turn stimulates firm performance in this environment.... MNEs [also] need to depend on their subsidiaries in order to secure emerging market opportunities or acquire country-specific knowledge. This in turn requires a parent's local responsiveness and control flexibility so that subsidiaries can move quickly to seize opportunities or reap the gains. (Luo, 2003, p. 305)

Another similar study comes from Korea. Choi and Beamish (2004) conducted research on joint ventures in Korea to analyze coordination and control arrangements between TNOs and local Korean partners. The research yielded four possible types of coordination and control arrangements: split control management, shared management, TNOs-partner dominant management, and local-partner dominant management. These types are developed based on two dimensions: first, control over TNO's partners' "firm-specific advantages" and, second, control over "local emerging market partners' firm-specific advantages" (Choi & Beamish, 2004, p. 213). Thus, the study suggests another dimension to research: not just degree of control exercised by different parties, but also what specific areas they have control over. The study suggests that "the parent's choice of the activities over which control is exercised is much more important to the JV performance than the parent's choice in the extent of overall control" (pp. 213–214).

Choi and Beamish (2004) conclude that split control is the most effective for multinational operations. In a split-control structure, each partner controls certain functions of the corporate operations; for example, the local partner would control production and suppliers, while the international partner would control public relations, advertising, and sales. Such division of labor allows each party to "exercise dominant control" (p. 205) over the area in which they respectively have a specific advantage. Consequently, "the expertise or know-how needed to control or manage MNE [TNO] partners' firm specific advantages is different from that needed to control local Korean partners' firm-specific advantages" (p. 213). Split control allows the TNO and local partner to increase control over their own firm-specific advantages and thus allows the joint venture to "exhibit superior performance" (p. 213).

Coordination by Socialization

Edström and Galbraith (1977) argue that socialization is a third type of coordination that complements the personal or direct type of control (i.e., centralization/autonomy in decision making) and bureaucratic control (i.e., formalization of structure and processes). According to the authors, coordination by socialization is characterized by a significant proportion of expatriates in upper and middle management positions, frequent information exchange between headquarters and subsidiaries, and a deemphasizing formalization. Similarly, Bartlett and Ghoshal (1987b) point out various socialization processes, such as the transfer of people, the encouragement of informal communication channels that foster information exchange, and the creation of forums that facilitate interunit learning.

Socialization is the most flexible method for rapid responses in competitive world environments Bartlett and Ghoshal write: "The reality of today's worldwide competitive environment demands collaborative information sharing and problem solving, cooperative support and resource sharing, and collective action and implementation" (1987b, p. 47).

Martinez and Jarillo (1989) explain that the development of an organization's culture occurs through socialization of individuals within the corporation. Organizational members communicate with each other the preferred way of doing things, the decision-making style, and the company objectives and values. Thus, the new coordination mechanisms are informal and subtle; they rely on three key components, according to Martinez and Jarillo: (1) They establish cross-cultural teams and international committees that do not necessarily follow the lines of the formal international departmental structure, but develop interpersonal links and facilitate lateral relations. (2) They supplement the formal reporting channels with informal information exchange between managers and employees across departments and countries. (3) They inject a strong dose of corporate culture into employees all over the world, as a result of which employees are not simply familiar with the company's values but accept these values as their own.

Roth and Nigh (1992) investigated the relationship between coordination, control, and conflict on the effectiveness of the headquarters–subsidiary relationship. They reported that more effective headquarters–subsidiary relationships are associated with greater levels of coordination, lower levels of conflict, and greater use of personal integrating mechanisms. The increasing use of personal integrating mechanisms reinforces the understanding of the headquarters–subsidiary relationship and fosters the commitment of subsidiary managers to the TNO as a whole. "Apparently, the development of a shared culture with its more flexible channels of communication leads to more effective headquarters–subsidiary relationships," Roth and Nigh conclude (1992, p. 295).

Ghoshal, Korine, and Szulanski (1994) explored the influence of formal organization structure and informal relationships between managers on the frequency of communication between the subsidiaries and headquarters as well as among the subsidiaries. They measured informal relationships and socialization among managers through their participation on teams, task forces, and conferences. Formal organizational structure was measured by the autonomy of the subsidiary managers in making a set of key decisions. "While subsidiary autonomy has almost no effect on either subsidiary–headquarters or intersubsidiary communication, interpersonal networking has significant positive effects on the ongoing communication of subsidiary managers, both with their counterpart in the headquarters and with managers in other subsidiaries," Ghoshal et al. report (1994, p. 106).

Deemphasizing centralization and formalization to increase the use of socialization as the main coordination mechanism is a key characteristic of the transnational mentality (i.e., worldwide learning, national responsiveness, and global efficiency). It is important to note that deemphasizing those formal coordination mechanisms does not mean they are eliminated. The fact is that the need for adapting and coming up with rapid organizational responses to ever-changing organizational, social, and political/legal environments gives socialization a leading role in fostering interunit collaboration. It appears that socialization encourages personal and functional interdependence, which, at the same time, fosters the exchange of ideas and information, collective action, and implementation of common strategies.

Coordination and Control in Public Relations, Public Affairs, or Communication Activities

Although there is a dearth of research on how TNOs manage relationships with noneconomic stakeholders, international business scholars offer a considerable number of studies that explore the relationships among units in TNOs. Notable exceptions to the lack of research that exclusively explores the public relations or public affairs function are Blumentritt (1999); Dunn, Cahill, and Boddewyn (1979); Mahini and Wells (1986); and Meznar (1993). Other researchers have studied coordination and control function as it pertains to marketing activities (Hewett, Roth, & Roth, 2003) and advertising (Laroche, Kirkpalani, Pons, & Zhou, 2001). Since the 1980s, there has been significant growth in international business scholars' interest in noneconomic issues that affect business operations in different markets. The rationale behind the focus on the social and political environments is the assumption that TNOs are "open systems" that interact, to different extents, with foreign governments and communities.

Transnational organizations' use of coordination and control mechanisms to cope with the complexity of global public affairs management was explored by Meznar (1993); they relate to the social and political and legal environments either by complying with them or attempting to alter the social contract with those sectors. "The social contract perspective holds that a firm must obtain legitimacy from society in order to survive," Meznar states (1993, p. 27). He explores the relationships between two public affairs strategies, buffering and bridging,1 using the boundary spanning literature, and the coordination and control systems used to manage the public affairs function in TNOs. Meznar reported a strong positive association between the control mechanisms—goal internalization and performance evaluation—and the use of bridging and buffering strategies. He also finds a strong positive relationship between the control mechanisms and the centralization of the public affairs function. Similarly, he finds strong positive correlations between coordination mechanisms—impersonal and personal—and the use of buffering, bridging, and public affairs centralization. Other sets of associations are reported by Meznar, such as public affairs effectiveness and goal internalization, impersonal coordination, and increase of both buffering and bridging activities.

Blumentritt (1999) studies the organizational characteristics of foreign subsidiaries and their effects on the subsidiaries' government affairs activities, such as lobbying and relationship building with influential local and national officials and their agencies. He finds that the more a subsidiary's top management believes in government affairs as a strategic function, the more the subsidiary will formalize these types of public affairs activities. "[T]he top management beliefs variable was suggested to be a predictor of formalization, as subsidiaries with management teams inclined toward government affairs activities would tend more to create organizational structures dedicated to government affairs activities," Blumentritt writes (1999, p. 111). Similarly, he reports a positive association between the extent of economic integration with affiliates and the subsidiary's degree of intersubsidiary coordination of government affairs activities.

Laroche et al. (2001) developed a model of advertising standardization in TNOs and suggest that advertising standardization depends on the degree of control exercised by the TNO over a subsidiary. They follow the Tai and Wong's (1998) assumption that the degree of control is the major driving force behind the choice between standardized or localization. Laroche et al. (2001) conduct a survey of advertising executives from all over the world (i.e., North America, Asia, Europe, and South America) to confirm the assumption that degree of control plays a "central and mediating role...in influencing the level of advertising standardization" (p. 262). The authors also suggest that standardization can go beyond advertising and affect standardization of approach in other communication activities as well.

Hewett et al. (2003) make an attempt to integrate the external and internal pressures that subsidiaries experience. From the industrial organization theory standpoint, firms try "to become aligned with or fit its external market and industry conditions" (p. 568). On the other hand, institutional theory suggests that firms try "to conform to pressures within the firm's environment" (p. 568). So, a subsidiary of a TNO has a dual role and dual pressures, "Within the MNC [TNO], foreign subsidiaries operate in a host country environment and, at the same time, they are part of an MNC [TNO] environment" (p. 569). A subsidiary thus has to find an ideal balance between these two competing pressures. The authors ask, "Under what conditions should specific activities and capabilities be the responsibility of subsidiaries rather than headquarters?" (p. 567). The researchers claim that an answer to this question is a source of competitive advantage for TNOs and "deviation from an ideal profile for either a greater headquarters or a greater subsidiary role in marketing activities will result in lower product performance in individual markets" (p. 573).

Similar results are introduced in Lim's chapter 15 (this volume) specific to the public relations function of TNOs. He observes that on the one hand, "global integration of public relations" that is defined as "a closely coordinated, and strategically controlled international public relations strategy" will allow TNOs to speak in one unified, integrated voice across national borders and to share "organizational mission, goals, values, communication themes and best public relations practices." On the other hand, however, different countries will present TNOs with different settings and with different challenges and to a certain degree require TNOs to digress from the unified global strategy and lead to TNOs "designing and customizing public relations programs to be adaptable to local environmental uncertainty and national regulatory barriers."

Lim (chapter 15 this volume) recommends looking for a balance between global integration of public relations and local responsiveness, by applying the "Integration-Responsiveness Grid" initially proposed by Prahalad and Doz (1987). This framework allows TNOs to evaluate which strategy, integration, or responsiveness will be the most beneficial for each specific place and time. Lim (chapter 15 this volume) suggests that public relations may be a "multi-focal strategic area where internal efficiency and external effectiveness could be achieved simultaneously." The mission and strategy of TNOs public relations is upheld on the global level, while specific tactics are adapted to local environments and locally implemented.

Molleda (2000a) examines the relationships between the public relations function of subsidiaries and their parent companies as well as other subsidiaries or sister companies. In particular, his research looks at coordination mechanisms (i.e., socialization, formalization, and centralization) used to manage the public relations function. Positive associations were found between integrative communication devices (e.g., Web site, intranet, and annual reports), communication quality (e.g., relevance/importance, amount, and timeliness), parent company–subsidiary relationship quality, and integration. Positive associations also are found between corporate socialization and both global efficiency (i.e., the use of common public relations resources by both headquarters and subsidiaries) and worldwide learning (i.e., sharing successes and failures of public relations practices in various world locations); between integration and communication quality and overall transnational mentality (i.e., the presence of global efficiency, worldwide learning, and multinational flexibility or national responsiveness in managing the global public relations function).

More specifically, Molleda's (2000a) study finds that more than 60% of the TNOs reported a medium level of centralization; that is, half of the coordination and control was in the hands of headquarters and the rest was the responsibility of the subsidiaries. The highest level of centralization is found in the shareholder or investor relations function and the lowest level in the community relations function. Media relations, government relations, and consumer relations show a medium level of centralization, and internal communication or employee relations a low level of centralization.

More than half of the public relations executives at a subsidiary report having a mentor at the TNO's headquarters. This is where the socialization process works as a coordination mechanism. More than 40% of public relations managers have worked at headquarters and more than 30% at a sister subsidiary or company; both groups reported the length of stay as being less than one year. The public relations personnel also reported that they kept in touch with the parent company via trade shows and special events, committees and meetings, annual assembly of shareholders, teamwork and taskforces, and training programs. The most important integrative communication devices to keep up with the relationship between public relations units at both the home- and host-country levels are: annual reports, Web sites, newsletters, intranets, teleconferences, videoconferences, conferences, and codes of conducts and ethics.

Another study that directly addressed the issue of integration in the public relations literature is reported by Wakefield (1997). He conducted a Delphi study with practitioners and academicians in various countries. The outcome of Wakefield's research was the statement of 14 research propositions. The fourth of those propositions deals with normative integration:

> Excellent international public relations is integrated, meaning that worldwide, practitioners report to the public relations department at headquarters and work under a single umbrella (as opposed to, for example, public relations in one country under marketing, in another country under human resources, etc.). It is recognized that senior managers in each country are responsible for activities in that country and that the senior practitioner must work closely with that senior manager. But if something negative happens anywhere, headquarters is ultimately responsible. Public relations must

be connected worldwide to build consistent programs and respond quickly to problems that arise. A senior practitioner at headquarters must supervise all communication programs, and local practitioners must be trained to carry out the same organizational philosophies, themes and goals. This requires close cooperation and communication between offices and headquarters. (p. 218)

This normative proposition explains how international corporate public relations ought to be managed to be excellent. Nevertheless, according to the literature review for this chapter and Molleda's (2000a, 2000b) findings, there are certain elements of Wakefield's proposition that do not appear to work as stated. Some previous research indicates that directly reporting to the parent company (formal control mechanism) is not a condition for achieving integration, nor is placement of the public relations unit under a single umbrella.

According to the transnational mentality (i.e., the combination of global efficiency, worldwide learning, and national responsiveness), responsibilities are shared. Both the parent company and its subsidiaries are interested in major events that affect local and global markets simultaneously or independently. A domestic event can become a global trend or a global issue can affect domestic operations in the future. Definitely, local issues should be the main concern of the subsidiary, but they are a great source of public relations knowledge and, therefore, local issues are of interest for the transnational operation as a whole. This seems to be the case whether those issues have domestic or transnational implications. According to Roth and Morrison (1990), "Competitive forces are not constrained within a single market location, but rather a strategic action in one country will concurrently impact other locations" (p. 542).

Of course, those issues that have transnational implications will be monitored closely by the parent company, which is particularly the case for what has been defined as "cross-national conflict shifting" (Molleda, Connolly-Ahern, & Quinn, 2005; Molleda & Quinn, 2004; Welge & Holtbrügge, 1998), where publics in one country condemn a TNO for what they are doing in other countries. Similarly, many sociopolitical issues are not limited to individual countries but are globally important, such as human rights, individual freedoms, and governmental accountability. For this reason, TNOs must develop organizational strategies to coordinate their worldwide public relations strategies.

Wakefield (2001) introduces five key aspects necessary for effective public relations management in TNOs: balancing the global and the local, one unit or single coordinated department, horizontal and team-oriented structure, being a team leader instead of a manager, and whether to hire agencies or external resources on a global, regional, or local basis. One autonomous public relations unit at a TNO is ideal because "[t]hey will create global strategies to preserve the entity's reputation, to retain consistent messages and identity, and to participate and handle problems that might cross borders" (Wakefield, 2001, p. 644). Crises that might cross borders are explained by the evolving theory of cross-national conflict shifting.

Cross-National Conflict Shifting

According to German international business scholars Welge and Holtbrügge (2001, p. 323), today TNOs are confronted with "globally active groups" that closely watch their behaviors in different world locations where they operate. Berg and Holtbrügge (2001) acknowledge that "interest groups in one country condemn multinational corporations for what they are doing in other countries" (p. 112). Conflicts, therefore, are no longer isolated in a single country where they originated, but may be fought in other countries where interest groups can "best push through their position" (Welge & Holtbrügge, 2001, p. 324).

Molleda and Connolly-Ahern (2002) borrowed this concept of cross-national conflict shifting (CNCS) from the discipline of international management and introduced it to public relations scholars. They illustrate and expand the concept to a systematic conceptualization of CNCS theory as it relates to the global public relations field.

With today's unprecedented power of Internet communications, a local issue could easily shift across national borders and impact stakeholders internationally. Such cross-national conflict shifts involve a variety of publics at various geographical levels, namely, host, home, and transnational publics (e.g., NGOs and activist groups, global media outlets, international news agencies, pan-regional media, shareholders) (Molleda & Connolly-Ahern, 2002).

To illustrate the CNCS conceptualization, Molleda and Connolly-Ahern (2002) provide a case study where a legal incident involving America Online Latin America (AOLA) in Brazil caused repercussions in the U.S. and European financial markets. Molleda and Connolly-Ahern (2002) further elaborate the conceptualization of CNCS as:

> There are organizational decisions, actions and operations that affect publics in one country and have an impact internationally. This impact seems to be greater at the home country of the organization or organizations involved, which could be explained by the relevance and proximity of organization for the home publics. Domestic conflicts are increasingly shifting worldwide because of the growth of international transactions, transportation and communication, especially information technology. (p. 4)

Molleda and Quinn (2004) expand the dynamic of CNCS theory and use four additional cases to illustrate its various components, including: (1) the characteristics of the issue; (2) the ways a national conflict reaches transnational audiences; and (3) the parties involved or affected (p. 3). Molleda and Quinn propose 10 propositions for further testing:

P1. Cross-national conflict shifting is mainly related to corporate social performance issues and negative economic consequences of globalization.

P2. The magnitude of a cross-national conflict shifting will increase when it starts in an emergent or developing economy because of the greater pressure the transnational corporation will face in the host country and from the international activist community. For instance, weaker labor and environmental regulatory frameworks and legal enforcement may allow for business operations, practices, and actions that may not be allowed in developed economies. This may produce greater irregularities that will be denounced and penalized at the home country of the TNO or where NGOs or activist groups exert their major influence and presence.

P3. Conflicts that occur in developed nations usually have a shorter life and do not cross borders as often as conflicts that start in developing nations or emergent economies.

P4. A greater number of involved parties will characterize a cross-national conflict shift in which a developed nation's transnational corporation is the principal participant of the crisis.

P5. A lower number of involved parties will characterize a cross-national conflict shift in which a developing nation or emergent economy corporation is the principal participant of the conflict.

P6. Transnational corporations that produce or commercialize tangible, boycottable products are more likely to receive attention than those who produce and commercialize intangible services.

P7. Transnational corporations headquartered in developed nations that produce or are part of a national conflict outside their home country will attract significant attention from global NGOs, international regulatory bodies, national governments, organized citizen groups, and international news agencies and global media outlets.

P8. The direct involvement of a transnational corporation in a cross-national conflict shift will produce greater consequences and demand a more comprehensive set of responses than a transnational corporation that is indirectly related to the issue.

P9. National conflicts shift to the international arena when (primarily) global NGOs or media report on the situation to audiences or publics in different parts of the world. However, there will be occasions in which the transnational corporation itself alerts authorities in its home country about improper actions or behaviors it is involved in overseas.

P10. National conflicts with a great human-interest focus are likely to be shifted to the international arena. Human interest is an important news value. Putting a face and using testimonials to develop an international news story seems to increase audiences' and active publics' attention and interest in the situation reported. For example, many TNOs' operations and actions in the border town of Ciudad Juarez, Mexico have been questioned because of the lack of safety measures to protect female workers. There have been a series of murders focusing on female workers of transnational maquiladoras or manufacturing plants who have to walk or take precarious public transportation to get from their poor housing arrangements to their workplace. International news agencies and global media have presented emotional and well-documented portrayals of some women killed in Juarez. (pp. 5–7)

To test these propositions, Molleda, Connolly-Ahern, and Quinn (2005) conducted a content analysis of news coverage of a Lesotho (a Southern African nation) bribery scandal which shifted to the international scene, which indicated the intricacy and magnitude of interactions amongst different players involved. Three hypotheses were tested and supported: (1) news media outlets will publish stories about international conflicts in greater length when the story focuses on corporate players from the news media's country of origin; (2) the news coverage of the Lesotho case will be characterized by the use of more sources and quotes in the North American (Canada-United States) news coverage than in the European and African coverage; and (3) the news coverage of the Lesotho case will be more extensive (i.e., number of sources and number of quotes) in Europe than Africa, yet less intensive than in North America (Canada-United States).

Kim and Molleda (2005) analyzed the bribery probe by the Nigerian government against Halliburton. In particular, this study analyzed

impossible (Griffith et al., 2000). Even more, we can suggest that lack of understanding of local peculiarities (or improper adaptation to them) could be one of the contributing factors to the appearance of a conflict in the first place and then to its spreading internationally. Localization and independence of public relations or public affairs functions at the subsidiary level could become a factor in preventing the development and spread of a conflict. Luo (2003) explains that TNOs depend on their subsidiaries for providing country-specific information and taking advantage of country-specific events. This is virtually impossible without flexibility in coordination and control mechanisms. As a result, both bodies of literature merge to inform the inquiry into the area of managing cross-national conflict shifts.

Discussion and Presuppositions

Global public relations can be managed with this integration/localization principle in mind to become an efficient function that coordinates its activities with other functions within the local operation and with public relations functions in diverse locations as well. Most importantly, with the use of integrative communication devices such as corporate publications, public relations may contribute to the diffusion of organizational values, norms, and perspectives that work to hold together the overall transnational operation.

Global public relations practitioners must collaborate with each other to pull together resources, ideas, and strategies that are dispersed in different operational facilities around the world. Collaboration implies working together toward the fulfillment of a common organizational goal. Martinez and Jarillo (1989) traced a tendency to employ more informal/subtle coordination mechanisms, although an expensive and time consuming process seems to be the formula with which normative integration is achieved. Thus, it is expected that public relations functions that have the added responsibility of achieving normative integration would make use of both formal and informal types of coordination, but with an emphasis on cultural coordination or coordination by socialization. This particularly should be the case where the public relations function is managed using a model approaching the transnational mentality (i.e., worldwide learning, global efficiency, and national responsiveness). Following are a set of presuppositions or guiding points for further analysis and research to capture the complexity of coordination and control of the global public relations function, especially in times of transnational crises.

PS1. Public relations and public affairs executives working at large-size or strategic subsidiaries of TNOs will have greater power than small-size and ordinary branches to influence policy decision making and obtain relevant levels of autonomy for the planning, implementation, and evaluation of public relations actions and operations within their regional or local market. Laroche et al. (2001) find that capabilities of a subsidiary will influence the level of its independence from the headquarters.

PS2. Different areas of public relations or public affairs activities will have different levels of integration. For example, Molleda (2000a) discovered the differences across functions with investor relations being among the most integrated functions and community relations being among the most autonomous functions.

PS3. Standardization of a public relations function as a strategy is more appropriate among countries with similar cultural, economic, or political environments and less appropriate among countries in which environments vary greatly from each other. Griffith et al. (2000) argue that standardization may be appropriate when both partners are from a similar cultural type; otherwise, the differences may create unexpected consequences in the relationships in terms of trust, commitment, conflict, and satisfaction.

PS4. Overcentralization of most of the public relations or public affairs functions in the TNO's headquarters may limit regional or local managers because they cannot react timely and appropriately to incidents, delicate issues, rapid changes, and crises emerging in their domestic market. Lascu (2006) observes that "high flexibility is essential to react to changes quickly" (p. 275). Overcentralization can deprive local managers of such flexibility.

PS5. The more confidence in host public relations or public affairs executives, the more delegation occurs to take charge of their domestic relationship building efforts. Laroche et al. (2001) found that professionalism of the subsidiary managers and their perceived decision-making capabilities display a positive correlation with the amount of independence that these subsidiaries have.

PS6. Large TNOs will tend to have specialized staff at their home offices with global public relations expertise. Similarly, large operations in a given country are likely to have specialized public relations or public affairs staff to perform the function instead of staff from other operational areas, such as legal, human resources, or engineering departments. Cray (1984) explains that "a subsidiary which is large, technologically complex, located in a product division, and highly profitable will very likely be integrated through extensive coordination with other parts of the organization while retaining a good deal of control over its own affairs" (p. 96).

PS7. Native public relations or public affairs executives trained at the TNO's headquarters are more likely to think and act in ways that are similar to home office personnel. Molleda (2000) reports that public relations executives intern at or frequently visit the TNO's headquarters and sister companies. This is defined by international business scholars as coordination via socialization, and it is a key element (i.e., worldwide learning) of the transnational mentality.

PS8. A global public relations system of a TNO that relies on a combination of common planning, and measurement and evaluation devices or mechanisms is more reliable than one that does not. Control mechanisms include evaluation performance and reporting procedures, which implies a comprehensive and consolidated view of global operations of a TNO (Martinez & Jarillo, 1989).

PS9. Coordination and control of the public relations function in TNOs—during day-to-day operations and, most importantly, during a transnational crisis or cross-national conflict shift—demand talented professionals who enjoy the respect of their organizational peers and management. The influence and leadership of talented and respected global public relations professionals will be felt, impacting the coordination and control efforts. This will happen despite their geographic location and the level of importance of the subsidiary or sister company from which they work.

Each of these nine presuppositions must be supported or rejected with research evidence. In addition, further research is needed to assess how normative integration is achieved by the public relations function in TNOs and how organizational and contextual variables affect the management arrangements needed for such integration. Future studies are needed to determine the levels of centralization, standardization, coordination, and control for specific practices (i.e., media relations, investor relations, community relations) and how these functions are managed during cross-national conflict shifts, such as operation of crisis plans and work of crisis teams, spokespeople intervention and availability, media inquiries domestically and transitionally, and internal communication.

An additional area of research is coordination and control in global public relations agencies. Global public relations agencies work with global, regional, subregional, and domestic clients. The orchestration of crisis responses and actions for each of this type of clients may indicate diverse degrees of coordination and control complexity.

Note

1. Buffering is a defense strategy with which an organization seeks to alter or influence social contract terms. An example of buffering activities is lobbying of governments to block new laws, which would require changes in the production process. In contrast, bridging is an adaptive and collaborative posture an organization holds to assimilate and accommodate itself to the changes in both the political/legal and social environments. That is, organizations that approach the bridging role promote organizational compliance to social contract terms. These two strategies are similar to the concepts of two-way asymmetrical and two-way symmetrical communication defined by public relations scholars.

References

Baliga, B. R., & Jaeger, A. M. (1984). Multinational corporations: Control systems and delegation issues. *Journal of International Business Studies, 15,* 25–40.

Bartlett, C. A., & Ghoshal, S. (1987a, Summer). Managing across borders: New strategic requirements. *Sloan Management Review, 7–17.*

Bartlett, C. A., & Ghoshal, S. (1987b, Fall). Managing across borders: New organizational responses. *Sloan Management Review,, 43–53.*

Berg, N., & Holtbrügge, D. (2001). Public affairs management activities of German multinational corporations in India. *Journal of Business Ethics, 30,* 105–119.

Blumentritt, T. (1999). *An examination of foreign subsidiary government affairs activities: Effects of subsidiary and host-country characteristics.* Unpublished doctoral dissertation, University of South Carolina, Columbia.

Child, J. (1972a). Organization structure and strategies of control: A replication of the Aston study. *Administrative Science Quarterly, 17,* 163–177.

Child, J. (1972b). Organizational structure environment and performance: The role of strategic choice. *Sociology, 6,* 2–22.

Child, J. (1973). Strategies of control and organizational behavior. *Administrative Science Quarterly, 18,* 1–17.

Choi, C., & Beamish, P.W. (2004). Split management control and international joint venture performance. *Journal of International Business Studies, 35*(3), 201–215.

Coombs, W. T. (1998). An analytic framework for crisis situations: Better responses from better understanding of the situation. *Journal of Public Relations Research, 10*(3), 117–191.

Coombs, W. T. (1999). *Ongoing crisis communication: Planning, managing, and responding.* Thousand Oaks, CA: Sage.

Cray, D. (1984, Fall). Control and coordination in multinational corporations. *Journal of International Business Studies, 85–98.*

Daniels, J. D., Radebaugh, L. H., & Sullivan, D. P. (2004). *International business: Environments and operations.* Upper Saddle River, NJ: Pearson Prentice Hall.

Dunn, S. W., Cahill, M. F., & Boddewyn, J. J. (1979). *How fifteen transnational corporations manage public affairs.* Chicago: Crain Books.

Edström, A., & Galbraith, J. R. (1977). Transfer of managers as a coordination and control strategy in multinational organizations. *Administrative Science Quarterly, 22,* 248–263.

Friedman, T. L. (2005). *The world is flat: A brief history if the twenty-first century.* New York: Farrar, Straus & Giroux.

Ghemawat, P. (2001). Distance still matters: The hard reality of global expansion. *Harvard Business Review, 79*(8), 137–147.

Ghoshal, S., & Bartlett, C.A. (1988, Fall). Creation, adoption, and diffusion of innovations by subsidiaries of multinational corporations. *Journal of International Business Studies,* 365–388.

Ghoshal, S., Korine, H., & Szulanski, G. (1994). Interunit communication in multinational corporations. *Management Science, 40,* 96–110.

Griffith, D. A., Hu, M. Y., & Ryans, J. K. (2000). Process standardization across intra- and inter-cultural relationships. *Journal of International Business Studies, 31*(2), 303–324.

Hart, S., & Milstein, M. (1999). Global sustainability and the creative destruction of industries. *Sloan Management Review, 41*(1), 23–33.

Hewett, K., Roth, M. S., & Roth, K. (2003). Conditions influencing headquarters and foreign subsidiary roles in marketing activities and their effects on performance. *Journal of International Business Studies, 34*(6), 567–585.

Khanna, T. (2002). *Local institutions and global strategy.* Boston: Harvard Business School Press.

Kim, J. R., & Molleda, J.C. (2005, March). *Cross-national conflict shifting and crisis management: An analysis of Halliburton's bribery probe case in Nigeria.* Paper presented at the 8th Annual International Public Relations Research Conference, Miami, FL.

Knox, S., & Maklan, S. (2004). Corporate social responsibility: Moving beyond investment towards measuring outcomes. *European Management Journal, 22*(5), 508–516.

Laroche, M., Kirpalani, V. H., Pons, F., & Zhou, L. (2001). A model of advertising standardization in multinational corporations. *Journal of International Business Studies 32*(2), 249–266.

Lascu, D-N. (2006). *International marketing* (2nd ed.). Cincinnati, OH: Atomic Dog.

Luo, Y. (2003). Market-seeking MNEs in an emerging market: How parent–subsidiary links shape overseas success. *Journal of International Business Studies, 34*(3), 290–309.

Mahini, A., & Wells, L.T. (1986). Government relations in the global firm. In M. E. Porter (Ed.), *Competition in global industries* (pp. 291–312). Boston: Harvard Business School Press.

Martinez, J. I., & Jarillo, J. C. (1989). The evolution of research on coordination mechanisms in multinational corporations. *Journal of International Business Studies, 20,* 489–514.

Martinez, J. I., & Jarillo, J. C. (1991). Coordination demands on international strategies. *Journal of International Business Studies, 22,* 429–444.

Mascarenhas, B. (1984). The coordination of manufacturing interdependence in multinational companies. *Journal of International Business Studies, 15,* 91–106.

Meznar, M. B. (1993). *Public affairs management in multinational corporations: an empirical examination.* Unpublished doctoral dissertation, University of South Carolina, Columbia.

Molleda, J. C. (2000a). *Integrative public relations in international business: The impact of administrative models and subsidiary roles.* Unpublished doctoral dissertation, University of South Carolina, Columbia.

Molleda, J. C. (2000b, August). *An exploration of integration of the public relations function in international business operations.* Paper presented at the convention of the Association for Education in Journalism and Mass Communication, Phoenix, AZ.

Molleda, J. C., & Connolly-Ahern, C. (2002, August). *Cross-national conflict shifting: conceptualization and expansion in an international public relations context.* Paper presented at the convention of the Association for Education in Journalism and Communication, Miami, FL.

Molleda, J. C., Connolly-Ahern, C., & Quinn, C. (2005). Cross-national conflict shifting: expanding a theory of global public relations management through quantitative content analysis. *Journalism Studies, 6*(1), 87–102.

Molleda, J. C., & Quinn, C. (2004). Cross-national conflict shifting: A global public relations dynamic. *Public Relations Review, 30*(1), 1–9.

Molleda, J. C., Solaun, L., & Parmelee, K. (2008, October). *Advancing the theory of cross-national conflict shifting: An analysis of international news agencies' coverage of lead-tainted toys from China.* Paper presented at the Americas Congress II, Mexico City, Mexico.

Morley, M. (2002). *How to manage your corporate reputation; a guide to the dynamics of international public relations* (2nd ed.). New York: New York University Press.

Porter, M. E. (1986). Changing patterns of international competition. *California Management Review, 27,* 29–40.

Prahalad, C. K., & Doz, Y. L. (1987). *The multinational mission: Balancing local demands and global vision.* New York: Free Press.

Pugh, D. S., Hickson, D. J., & Hinings, C. R. (1968). An empirical taxonomy of structures of work organizations. *Administrative Science Quarterly, 13,* 115–126.

Pugh, D. S., Hickson, D. J., Hinings, C. R., & Turner, C. (1968). Dimensions of organization structure. *Administrative Science Quarterly, 13,* 65–105.

Ricart, J. E., Enright, M. J., Ghemawat, P., Hart, S. L., & Khannaet, T. (2004). New frontiers in international strategy. *Journal of International Business Studies, 35*(3), 175–200.

Roth, K., & Morrison, A. J. (1990). An empirical analysis of the integration-responsiveness framework in global industries. *Journal of International Business Studies, 21,* 541–564.

Roth, K., & Nigh, D. (1992). The effectiveness of headquarters-subsidiary relationships: The role of coordination, control, and conflict. *Journal of Business Research, 25,* 277–301.

Sharpe, M. L., & Pritchard, B. J. (2004). The historical empowerment of public opinion and its relationship to the emergence of public relations as a profession. In D. J. Tilson & E. C. Alozie (Eds.), *Toward the common good: Perspectives in international public relations* (pp. 14–36). Boston, MA: Allyn & Bacon.

Tai, S. H., & Wong, Y. H. (1998). Advertising decision making in Asia: Glocal versus regcal approach. *Journal of Managerial Issues, 10*(3), 318–339.

Taylor, M. (2000). Cultural variance as a challenge to global public relations: A case study of the Coca-Cola scare in Europe. *Public Relations Review, 26*(3), 277–293.

Van Maanen, J. (1978). People processing: Strategies of organizational socialization. *Organizational Dynamics, 7,* 19–36.

Wakefield, R. I. (1997). *International public relations: A theoretical approach to excellence based on a worldwide Delphi study.* Unpublished doctoral dissertation, University of Maryland, College Park.

Wakefield, R. I. (2001). Effective public relations in the multinational organization. In R. L. Heath & G. Vasquez (Eds.), *Handbook of public relations* (pp. 639–647). Thousand Oaks, CA: Sage.

Wang, Y. (2005). Cross-national conflict shifting: a case study of the DuPont Teflon crisis. Unpublished master's thesis, University of Florida, Gainesville.

Welge, M. K., & Holtbrügge, D. (1998). *Internationales management* [International management]. Germany: Verlag Moderne Industrie.

Welge, M. K., & Holtbrügge, D. (2001). *Internationales management* (2nd ed.) [International management]. Germany: Verlag Moderne Industrie.

Chapter 17

Netizens Unite!

Strategic Escalation of Conflict to Manage a Cultural Crisis

Sooyoung Cho and Glen T. Cameron

On February 12, 2004, a press conference that would drive heated discussions among Koreans was taking place in Seoul, South Korea. Netian Entertainment Corporation held the press conference to announce the release of a nude photo project, the first section of which had just been finished. Seemingly, it was just another celebrity nude collection, a popular genre in Korea. What was unusual about this project was that the model who posed nude in these photographs was the well-known actress, Lee Seung-yeon. The company and the actress announced that they would release the photos through a mobile phone service and the Internet. The idea of making celebrity nude photos available on cell phones so that people can look at them during a subway commute is a daring marketing method that has recently become popular in South Korea.

However, as a few of the photographs were shown at the press conference, everyone in the room was stunned because the photos were based on the theme of Korean comfort women who were abducted, raped, and ruthlessly used by the Japanese army as sex slaves during World War II. The term *comfort women* refer to the young women of various ethnic and national backgrounds who were forced into sexual slavery by Japanese troops during World War II. Numerous women labored as comfort women in the military brothels and it is believed that about 80% of them were Korean (Soh, 2000). Comfort women are a living symbol of sorrow and tragedy in Korea's history, remaining a very sensitive issue to this day because of the country's historical relationship with Japan (Korea was declared a protectorate of Japan in 1905 and annexed in 1910. It only regained its independence at the end of World War II). Immediately after the news conference, many human rights groups and angry citizens expressed disgust at the photos, expressing their feelings through protests and Internet discussions, vehemently insisting that the project be stopped. The company and the actress faced savage criticism from the public for the next several days.

Based on Cameron's contingency theory of conflict management in public relations (Cameron, Cropp, & Reber, 2001; Cancel, Cameron, Sallot, & Mitrook, 1997; Cancel, Mitrook, & Cameron, 1999) and Coombs's crisis management typology (1999), the present study aims to describe how the company managed its publics, how two parties involved in the conflict changed their stance over the conflict period, and what strategies the corporation and its publics used in this crisis situation. The majority of tests of contingency principles and factors have taken place in the United States. Although contingency theory has helped our understanding of effective conflict management, it is important to test the rigor of the theory through further applications in international settings. A number of U.S. studies have identified several important potential contingent factors that make an organization's strategy change in conflict situations. Societal and cultural factors may have a powerful impact on public relations practices in different cultures (Botan, 1992; Kim & Hon, 1998; Sriramesh, Kim, & Takasaki, 1999). There might be potentially important contingent factors that have not emerged in U.S settings but have significant impact on practices in other cultures.

During the crisis period, the company had to deal not only with activists and former comfort women directly engaged in the situation, but also huge numbers of the Korean population who remain sensitive about this terrible period in Korean history, and who still have nightmares about the past. We hope that this study can offer a unique chance to contemplate how one organization managed a severe conflict situation that involved an emotionally and historically sensitive issue accompanied by massive public attention and news coverage, all in a very short period of time. We also hope that we can identify some unique, but generalizable, contingent factors that previous quantitative studies conducted within a U.S. setting have not detected to help with the elaboration of contingency theory. This dramatic incident serves as a case study to track the changing stances of the corporation in response to contingent factors. And we set out to integrate contingency theory in crisis situations with crisis management strategies that become the tools for enactment of a contingent approach to public relations.

Theoretical Background

Contingency Theory of Conflict Management

The basic idea of contingency theory (Cameron et al., 2001; Cancel, Cameron, et al., 1997; Cancel, Mitrook, & Cameron, 1999) is that there is no one proper way to practice public relations that will be optimal for all situations. Contingency theory posits that true excellence in public relations requires the strategic management of conflict, which is achieved by picking the right point along the continuum ranging from pure advocacy to pure accommodation that best fits the current need of the organization and its publics (Cancel et al., 1997). In other words, different strategies corresponding to different points on the continuum should be adopted as the dynamic situation unfolds. The theory examines how the stance an organization takes toward publics changes over the course of interaction and why an organization moves toward or away from accommodation when confronted with publics in a conflict situation.

According to contingency theory, the stance of the organization can change depending on the circumstances and is affected by a variety of factors. Cameron and his associates offered 87 factors that influence the stance and practice, then organized them into 11 groups: (1) threats; (2) industry environment; (3) general political/social/cultural environment; (4) the external public; (5) issue under question; (6) organization's characteristics; (7) PR department characteristics; (8) top management characteristics; (9) internal threats; (10) individual characteristics; and (11) relationship characteristics. Scholars agree that certain factors among the 87 are more influential than others. Cameron et al. (2001) have argued that an organization would not change its stance if the situational variables were not compelling enough to affect the position or if the opportunity costs of the situational variables do not bring any benefits. The situational variables that have received support are: (1) the urgency of the situation; (2) characteristics of the external public; (3) potential or obvious threats; and (4) potential costs or benefit for the organization from choosing the various stances (Cameron et al., 2001; Cancel et al., 1999; Yarbrough, Cameron, Sallot, & McWilliams, 1998).

Importance of Understanding Cultural Environments in International Public Relations

Using surveys and quantitative content analysis methods, previous studies on contingency theory have identified some prominent variables that influence an organization to change its stance. However, many of the studies have tested the theory within the United States; thus there has been a lack of an international perspective, which has limited the scope of the theory. For instance, Cancel et al. (1999) reported that external cultural, social, political, and regulatory environments were not supported as potential contingent factors in their studies. However, scholars of international public relations argue that cultural and society-specific factors are important in examining public relations practices in international settings. Hofstede's (1984) five cultural dimensions (power distance, collectivism versus individualism, femininity versus masculinity, uncertainty avoidance, and Confucian dynamism) have been employed by many scholars to understand how culture shapes public relations practices in international settings.

Choi and Cameron (2005) noted that even though Hofstede's five dimensions of culture made contributions to building knowledge of international public relations practice, it is important to explore indigenous, perceptual cultural dimensions that may have been overlooked and that may have a significant impact on public relations practices in conflict situations in cultures other than the United States. Interviewing leaders of public relations agencies in South Korea whose major clients are multinational corporations, Choi and Cameron (2005) found that fear of the media, local culture, especially nationalism, and patriotism seem to make multinational corporations move toward accommodations in conflict situations. Researchers found the concept of "We-ness," a discourse of collectivism, within Korean culture. That is, Korean people often separate "we" from "others" and foreign businesses or multinational corporations are considered as "others." Also, one of their interviewees also pointed out the enormous collective power of Korean Netizens in building public opinion, especially issues related to nationalism. Unlike Cancel et al.'s (1999) study, in which external culture and social environment were not supported as contingent variables, Choi and Cameron concluded that local cultural factors (collectivism and nationalism) are crucial elements, which influence public relations practices in Korea. They suggested that public relations practitioners should develop their public relations programs based on clear understanding of local cultures (e.g., nationalism) in order to practice effective communication.

Employing qualitative case study analysis, the present study tries to find and expand the horizon of the contingent variables that are applicable to international settings, in this instance South Korea.

Conflict Management Strategies for Crises Resulting from Pitched Conflict

Generally, conflict occurs when two groups come into conflict because of incompatible goals, resources, and values, and where, often, two parties have unequal power (Rubin, Pruitt, & Kim, 1994). In the course of creating a crisis management literature, scholars have developed crisis life-cycle models. For example, in a model proposed by Coombs (1999), a crisis has three stages: the precrisis, crisis, and postcrisis. In the first stage, precrisis, an organization should prevent and prepare for a crisis before it takes place (p. 15). In the second crisis stage, an organization should communicate with its publics (p. 16). The postcrisis stage is equally important, Coombs argues, because organizations must think about and prepare a better way of handling the next crisis and make sure that stakeholders have a positive impression about the organization's crisis management endeavor.

Further, Coombs notes the strategies that organizations employ during the stages of a crisis. According to Coombs (1999), an organization's reaction to conflict may vary from defensive to accommodation: Defensive strategies include attacking the accuser, denial and excuses, and accommodating strategies that include ingratiation, corrective action, and full apology. He notes, "Accommodative strategies emphasize image repair, which is what is needed as image damage worsens. Defensive strategies, such as denial or minimizing, locally become less effective as organizations are viewed as more responsible for the crisis" (p. 187).

In their content analysis of the Chinese government's management of the SARS crisis, Pang, Jin, and Cameron (2004) adapt and add to Coombs's crisis communication strategies and propose eight strategies: (1) attack—confrontation and active advocacy; (2) denial—statement that the the party in question is not culpable or denial that the crisis is of any consequence; (3) excuse—minimizing the party's responsibility for the crisis, or shifting responsibility for the crisis to an external factor; (4) justification—explaining why the party has taken a certain course of action; (5) corrective action—the party actively addresses the problems; (6) ingratiation—the party acts to ensure that the other party will approve of its actions, with the aim of making a favorable impression; (7) cooperation—the party makes overtures to the other party with the goal of resolving the problem; and (8) full apology—the party takes full responsibility for the crisis and asks for forgiveness, with the promise of some form of compensation.

Using eight strategies suggested by Pang et al. (2004), this study examined what strategies were employed to resolve the conflict over the time of crisis as shown in the nude photo news coverage.

Method

Employing a case study method, this research examined 98 news stories and TV news transcripts about the incident, twenty-two columns, and seven readers' letters from 10 Korean national newspapers (*Kyunghyung Shinmun, Kookmin Ilbo, DongA Ilbo, Munhwa Ilbo, Seoul Shinmun, Saegye Ilbo, Chosun Ilbo, Hangyerye Shinmun, Hankook Ilbo*, and *Naeil Shinmun*), three major networks (MBC, SBS, and KBS), and two English-language dailies (*Korea Times* and *Korea Herald*) over a period of 8 days—from when the conflict began until it was resolved. These newspapers and networks were selected due to their influence and prominence.

Yin (1994) defines a case study as "an empirical inquiry that investigates a contemporary phenomenon within its real-life context, especially when the boundaries between phenomenon and context are not clearly evident" (p. 13). The strength of case studies lies in their use in understanding complex social phenomena. Yin notes that case studies are particularly effective when the researcher has little control over events, and when the focus is on explaining a current phenomenon within a real-life context. Both the nature of the incident and the study inquiries suggest that a case study method is a reasonable way to attain the goal of the study. The stories, columns, and letters regarding the incident were researched and downloaded from a news database Korean Integrated News Database System (KINDS) with the key terms of *Wee-an-bu* (comfort woman) *nude, Lee Seung-yeon nude*, and *Netian Entertainment* from February 12 to February 25, 2004.

Findings

The conflict took place and was resolved during a very short time period. It was a very intense, pitched battle and received extensive media coverage as well as tremendous public attention. We examined the event in chronological order.

Day 1: The Development of the Crisis

The Netian Entertainment Corporation held a press conference on February 12, 2004, to introduce nude photographs recently taken on Palau, an island where Japanese bases were located during World War II. The company announced that these were part of its upcoming nude photo collection, "Woman" and they were going to take more pictures in Japan and Nepal later that month ("Actress Lee Seung-yeon's Nude," 2004; "Nude Photos Featuring Lee Seung-Yeon as a Comfort Woman Repel Civic Groups," 2004).

Celebrity nude collections had been a trend in South Korea prior to this incident and they made huge profits by selling pictures through the Internet and mobile phone services ("Lee Seung-Yeon's Nude Photos Insult Comfort Women " 2004). In this case, because Lee Seung-yeon, the former Miss Korea who went on to become an actress, posed nude, public attention was higher even before the pictures were revealed. However, the photos presented in the conference were quite shocking because, in the photos, Lee poses in the role of a comfort woman forcibly drafted into sexual slavery by the Japanese Army during World War II with breasts exposed and wearing transparent clothes.

The Japanese government has denied governmental involvement in the forced draft of Korean women as comfort women and has refused to offer an official apology (Soh, 2000). The comfort women issue has been a very sensitive one in Korea because of the historical relationship between the two nations and survivors are the living symbol of national sorrow, tragedy, and anger. Some women's organizations and former comfort women are still protesting every Wednesday in front of the Japanese Embassy, requesting a formal apology.

The company claimed that they planned the nude project based on the comfort women theme "to express the sacrifices, revenge, and overcoming of anger that comfort women must have experienced" ("Actress Lee Seung-yeon's Nude," 2004) and "was intended to shed new light on the historic Korea–Japan relationship" ("Actress Lee's Nude Project Angers," 2004). Also, Lee asserted that "the collection will include topless photographs. However, I don't believe that the degree of nudity is what is important but rather the motive" ("Actress Lee Seung-yeon's Nude," 2004; "Can the Nude Photos Soothe Comfort Women?" 2004). The company and actress argued that their project differs from those of other celebrities because it focuses on the pain of comfort women and contains the message of social consciousness ("Outrageous Business," 2004). The company said a considerable proportion of the profits would be donated to help former comfort women ("Actress Lee Seung-yeon's Nude," 2004; "Nude Photos Featuring Lee Seung-Yeon as a Comfort Woman Repel Civic Groups," 2004).

This case instantly triggered a clamor from women's rights activists and Netizens in Korea: A few hours after the conference, 132 former comfort women and several civic groups including the Korea Council for Women Drafted for Military Sexual Slavery by Japan (hereafter the Korea Council) and Korea Women's Associations United expressed outrage at the nude photos and issued a joint statement insisting that the project be ended. In the statement, they denounced the photos as commercializing female sex and degrading the comfort women ("Outrageous Business," 2004), saying that, "They [Netian Entertainment and actress Lee] really hurt victims who have suffered and fought against the Japanese government for the past 14 years" ("Lee Commented that She Intended to Express the Sorrow of Comfort Women," 2004). These organizations also accused Netian and the actress of being phony, saying that their sole purpose was to make money by utilizing a very painful episode in history. In addition, "Internet bulletin boards are already filling up with messages criticizing Lee [and the company] casting doubt on her intentions" ("Actress Lee Seung-yeon's Nude," 2004). Newspapers and networks also harshly criticized them through news stories and editorial comments.

Despite intense criticism from the civic groups and angry Netizens, however, the company insisted that they had no intention of exploiting comfort women for commercial purposes. They said that they would take more photos and complete the project and would provide the photos and videos via the Internet and mobile services as originally scheduled ("Lee Seung-Yeon's Nude Photo Project Stirred Criticism,2004).

> **Interpretation and Commentary:** Although faced with sharp criticism from the start, the company defended its position, refused to budge from its original plan, and tried to justify its stance. Its initial statement, made during the press conference, seemed to indicate that the company had expected some degree of controversy surrounding the pictures. To advocate its stance, the company used strategies such as denial that it was making commercial use of comfort women and justification of its business. Three types of publics were identified in the very early stage of the crisis—former comfort women, who could be named as direct victims; activists such as the Korea Council; and citizens who are confronted with the company's behavior through cyberspace (Netizens). Those publics also actively advocated their stance and attacked the company.

Day 2: Maturation of the Crisis

On the second day of the conflict, civic groups and former comfort women filed for an injunction with the Seoul District Court to prevent the pictures from being distributed ("Actress Lee's Nude Project Angers," 2004). The groups demanded an official apology, and said that if the company didn't stop the project, they would visit company headquarters to protest. The media echoed the feelings of the groups through their editorial columns ("Commercialized Nude Photos Insulting Comfort Women Are Not Allowed," 2004; "Destroy the Nude Photos Insulting Comfort Women," 2004; "Don't Insult Comfort Women with the Nude Photos," 2004; "Regret Choice of Comfort Women for Nude Photo Project," 2004; "Crazy Nude Photo Trend Even Utilized Comfort Women," 2004a; "Mean Moneymakers Disgrace the History," 2004b; "Stop the Nude Photo Project Insulting Comfort Women," 2004; "Mean Nude Photo Project Insults Comfort Women," 2004). In cyberspace, anger mushroomed rapidly: Angry citizens set up an electronic bulletin board at Daum, a popular domestic site, and criticized Lee and the company as traitors who sold the nation's soul for money ("Nude Photo Injunction Application Was Filed," 2004a; "Crazy Publisher Should Leave for Japan," 2004). Daum conducted an opinion poll at its site, asking, "How do you feel about Lee's nude project?" Within one day, "more than 140,000 people responded to the poll and 84.1% of them opposed Lee's nude project" ("Crazy Publisher Should Leave for Japan," 2004). At Naver's poll, another site, "approximately 90% of Netizens claimed that the project should be stopped because it hurts comfort women" ("Nude Photo Injunction Application Was Filed,"

2004b). Responding to the negative public mood, broadcasters fired Lee from their TV programs, worrying that her appearance would further infuriate the audience.

Even in the face of public criticism and protest, Netian Entertainment announced that they would stick to the original plan "because we want to show that our intentions are innocent," ("Nude Photo Injunction Application Was Filed," 2004). The company also wanted to meet the comfort women and show all the photographs taken in Palau to persuade them to cancel their legal action ("Lee Seung-Yeon's Nude Photo Project Stirred Criticism," 2004). However, civic groups and comfort women refused to talk with the company ("Netizens Anger at Lee Seung-Yeon's Nude Photo Project," 2004). Three wireless carriers that initially planned to provide Lee's nude images via mobile service canceled the plan ("Mobile Service Providers Decided Not to Offer Lee's Nude Photos," 2004). In addition, stocks of companies engaged in the project plummeted on this day ("Lee's Nude Photos Depreciated Stock of the Lototo," 2004).

Interpretation and Commentary: The crisis intensified as the civic groups sought litigation and increasing numbers of citizens became intensely interested in the incident. The civic groups and comfort women strengthened their position by taking legal action and their claim was legitimized by numerous citizen supporters (mostly in cyberspace). As news stories indicate, enormous numbers of Netizens expressed their opposition to the company and the actress. As a result, the company and the actress began to suffer financial damage and lost a conduit for the photographs because wireless carriers refused to carry the photos. Despite the critical public mood due to the sensitive issue (both the issue itself and the cultural factor) and threats of litigation and economic loss, the company still advocated its initial position. Meanwhile, it tried to engage comfort women and civic groups in a dialogue to make them cancel the litigation by employing strategies such as excuses and corrective action. It seemed that the company had not fully realized the seriousness of the public mood but thought that the problem would be solved if they could persuade the activists to cancel the litigation.

Day 3

Through a press release, Netian still argued that they "were not trying to make money out of the pictures, rather, we were trying to raise the social consciousness and to protest against Japan which would not make an apology after committing a historical crime" ("Broadcasters Withdraw Lee," 2004). The company's spokesperson and CEO disappeared following the press release, so news organizations could not contact them for follow-up questions. The Korean Council announced that if the company would not officially cancel the project in 2 days, they would lead a huge protest with other women's organizations as well as sue the company for defamation of character ("Broadcasters Withdraw Lee," 2004). As with the off-line movement to stop the project, countless online messages opposing the project filled cyberspace in the third day of the incident.

> Interpretation and Commentary: Seemingly, the company realized that the public mood was getting serious and, startled by the negative public mood (from the Netizens), extensive media criticism, and legal action, retreated somewhat from its strong advocacy. However, the company did not change its initial stance but just attempted to justify its intention via news releases.

Day 4

More than 40,000 people participated in the Daum Internet chat room to express their opposition to the nude project and some participants even met together in person to discuss the next step they would take ("Citizen Groups Urged Netian to Suspend the Nude Photo Project and to Apologize," 2004). The Netizens had sent money to the Korean Council to express their support ("Actress Lee May Be Withdrawn from the Entertainment Industry," 2004). In addition, Netizens posted messages on the Web page of the Korean Attorneys' Association, requesting, "Please don't defend the company and actress so they can pay for their own misconduct" ("Lee's Nude Photo Project Comes to Litigation," 2004).

> Interpretation and Commentary: The public's actions were becoming concrete: Some Netizens were no longer remaining in cyberspace but communicating with each other off-line. News coverage did not report anything about the company's reaction and the company seemed to continue avoiding media contact.

Day 5: Changing the Stance

On the 5th day, Netian Entertainment held a news conference and announced that the company would immediately suspend any further production of the nude project. Park, a director of the company pleaded for forgiveness for the company's indiscreet conduct saying, "We never intended to upset the comfort women who are still tormented by their past memories. But if the photos are insulting to them, then we will stop all photography from now on" ("Lee Seung-yeon Nude Photo Project Canceled," 2004); "I have total responsibility for this project. All the staff, including Lee, were innocent participants in the project" ("Netian Announced a Stop to the Nude Photo Project...," 2004). However, he still argued that, "The project had no commercial purpose but was designed for distribution in Japan and the United States to get international attention for comfort women" ("Netian Stopped the Nude Photo Service...," 2004). Park also avoided giving a clear answer as to whether the company was still going to release photographs that had already been taken, but just responded that he wished to find a positive way after discussing the situation with the comfort women.

Despite the company's apology, comfort women and the Korean Council organized a demonstration in front of Netian's office and demanded that the company promise to destroy all the existing pictures ("Netian Announced End of Nude Photo Project...," 2004). Through columns and readers' letters, newspapers and networks continued to express severe criticism of the company, Lee, and their ignorance of history as well as the commercial nature of the project which they tried to conceal ("Japanese Would Sneer At the Comfort Women Nude Photos," 2004; "Shameless Nude Business Rips Off History," 2004; "Popular Nude Photos," 2004; "Nude Photos, Is It Art or Obscenity?" 2004; "Is It a Phony Apology?" 2004). In the stock market, the stocks of companies related to the project plummeted again. These companies also made apologies and promised that all future production would be suspended ("Stocks Involved in Lee's Nude Project Slump, 2004).

Interpretation and Commentary: After 2 days of silence, Netian Entertainment suddenly changed its stance from advocacy of its position to accommodation to the public's demand and actively managed the crisis by holding a press conference and making an apology (Ingratiation). According to a *Korea Times* article, "Until last week, Netian had stuck to its plan to go ahead with the project even in the face of public criticism. But the company was forced to change its mind after public sentiment turned decidedly against it" ("Nude Photo Project Suspended," 2004). The company still tried to justify its position by saying that its intention was a good one (Justification). Moreover, the company seemed to try to avoid taking responsibility at a company level; an individual employee (Park) took full responsibility for the crisis to minimize the damage done to the company's reputation. As with Netian, the related companies also apologized, presumably to offset further financial damage. Nonetheless, the publics refused to accept the apology and took a stronger advocacy stance, demanding that Netian stop circulating all existing videos and photos.

Day 6

In addition to the apology given by the company, actress Lee visited a shelter for comfort women and kneeled before them to seek their forgiveness. But the comfort women did not accept Lee's apology, saying, "Unless you get rid of them [existing photos], your apology is just a sham," ("Lee Apologizes to Comfort Women," 2004). They also demanded the president of Netian Entertainment should make an apology ("Actress Lee Apologized, But Anger Still Remains," 2004). Meanwhile, on the 6th day, more than 45,000 citizens had participated in the Daum Internet chat room (http://www.café.daum.net/antilee) and some of them contributed to set up a memorial building for comfort women ("Former Comfort Women Refuse Actress Lee's Apology...," 2004).

> **Interpretation and Commentary:** The actress made her public apology without giving any excuses (Full Apology). Kim (2002) noted that, in crisis situations, it is more effective for companies to show Korean citizens a human face and to deliver compassion (emotional approach) rather than to announce that the crisis is under control (logical approach). Actress Lee also utilized this emotional approach, visiting comfort women. However, the comfort women and civic groups had not changed their stance, and they refused to accept the apology and demanded that the pictures be destroyed. The Netizens' were still angry and they continued to take action for the comfort women.

Day 7: Reverse Turn

The controversy took a new twist on the 7th day of conflict: Netian Entertainment proposed a press screening of all the photographs they took in Palau and asked for an unbiased judgment from the media, civic groups, and citizens. The company spokespeople asserted that the company had been mistreated and said, "If our original intention is not clear after the open press screening, we will destroy all of the original images. However, if attendees understand our purpose after the screening, then we will donate all the profits from the photos to help the comfort women" ("Netian's Nude Photo Preview Proposal Brought Public Rage," 2004; "Netian Proposed the Nude Photo Preview," 2004). Civic groups argued that the apologies the company and actress made were phony, calling them "liars." ("Nude Photo Preview Proposal Caused Outrage," 2004b). All news media and Netizens also harshly criticized the company's indiscreet proposal ("Preview Proposal Caused Anger," 2004; "Preview Proposal of Lee's Nude Photo Arouse Criticism," 2004;

"Lee's Nude Photo Project Stirred Criticism," 2004; "Phony Apology? Netian's Preview Proposal Angers Public," 2004; "Fake Apology?" 2004; "Netian Evaded Its Responsibility," 2004). Regarding the open screening, the newspaper *Chosun Ilbo* conducted a poll on its Web site asking, "What do you think about the open screening? Do you think that we should judge the photos after seeing them through screening? Or, do you think that the company should not hold the open screening of photos?" Among 3,390 people participating in the poll, 2,641 participants (77.91%) responded that there was no need to look at the photographs (Readers' forum poll data, 2004).

> **Interpretation and Commentary:** Netian suddenly changed its stance from accommodation to advocacy and expressed discontent at what it regarded as mistreatment by the public. It could be seen as an indirect form of attack on the public as well as a way of excusing its behavior. Right after making an apologetic gesture, the company's sudden change of stance was somewhat puzzling. The company might have felt that it needed to take some action to restore its image for the sake of future business while giving up the immediate economic profits that would have derived from the sale of the nude photos. Internal threat (economic loss, stockholder perception of the company) seemed to be an important contingent factor in changing its stance. Nevertheless, the publics did not permit the company to make over its image in this way.

Day 8: The End of the Crisis

Finally, on the 8th day of the conflict, the controversy began to die down as the company totally changed its stance from the previous day and decided to destroy all materials. "Yielding to the simmering public outcry, Park, director of Netian Entertainment, burned all photographs and images of Lee before reporters" ("Publisher Destroys Nude Photos," 2004). Park claimed that nothing remained, adding that further photo shoots had all been canceled. Civic groups welcomed the destruction of the photographs, accepting it as a form of apology. But they said they would continue their court battle against the Lee photos if they were circulated on the Web ("Netian Destroyed All Original Photos," 2004; "Nude Photos Were Finally Destroyed," 2004).

> **Commentary and Interpretation:** At last, the company totally surrendered to the public and fully accommodated to their demands by destroying the photos (Full Apology). The company might have felt that this was a battle they had no chance of winning because of

the enormous power of the public (the External Public), threats of litigation, negative media coverage (threats), and the fact that it was a sensitive and important issue for several different Korean publics (issue under question and cultural factor).

Aftermath

On February 25, 2004, 6 days after the incident ended, civic groups withdrew an application for a court injunction, signaling an end to the controversy ("Nude Photo Injunction," 2004).

Discussion

Based on contingency theory, the present study tried to analyze (1) the change in the company position and its publics during the crisis; (2) the contingent factors associated with stances as well as possible new factors that are applicable to an international setting; (3) the crisis management strategies the company and its publics utilized and how the strategies were associated with the stances.

First, the study found that the company's stance toward the publics changed over time, associated with contingent factors. Contingency theory has argued repeatedly that accommodation is not necessarily ethical, particularly when the organization accommodates what may be viewed as a morally repugnant public. In a variation of that argument, accommodative behavior that is forced through circumstances, through contingent factors, may not be ethical so much as expedient. *Expediency* is probably the operative term in this case.

Even though the organization may already have been predisposed to take an advocacy stance, Cameron and his colleagues argued (Cancel et al., 1999) that the collective demands of the public may be powerful enough to impel the organization to take an accommodating position as a means to resolving the conflict situation. So it is with Netian. Initially, the company took a headstrong advocacy stance until the crisis reached the point where the company had no choice but to give up its original stance and accommodate the collective demands of the powerful public.

Second, the important contingent factors associated with the company's accommodation level were threats (litigation and scarring of the organization's reputation due to negative news coverage), the external publics (powerful activists and Netizens), issue under question, cultural factors (sensitive historical issue and nationalism), and internal threat (economic loss and marring of stockholders' perception of the company). Among others, threats appear to be the predominant factor that moved the company's stance from advocacy to accommodation.

Previous studies analyzing the conflict situation also found that threat was the predominant factor (Pang et al., 2004; Shin, Jin, Cheng, & Cameron, 2003). All public relations practitioners whom Cancel et al. (1999) interviewed agreed that their organization's actions in potentially negative situations have been influenced by a threat to the organization. The greater the threat, the faster the organization will take action, and the more accommodating it will be to its public. The most frequently mentioned threat by their interviewers was the threat of negative media coverage because it seriously damages the organization's reputation (Cancel et al., 1999). In addition, interview participants in Choi and Cameron's study (2005) also pointed out that multinational corporations' stances move toward accommodation during crisis situations once the media cover the story or when an issue is related to national sentiment. In our case, news media ardently covered the issue and expressed outrage toward the Netian, emphasizing historical wounds and encouraging nationalism among local publics. The media played an important role in legitimating the public outcry. By publishing news stories and editorials that denounced the company's indiscreet behavior, the news media became a real threat to the company. If the news media had approved the nude project as an expression of freedom of speech, the conflict resolution process would have been much different.

Powerful activists and huge numbers of supporters (external public) were also an important contingent variable that forced the company to quickly change its stance. Public relations practitioners in the Cancel et al. (1999) study said that an external public's power, its size, level of organization, ability to get media coverage, clout, or support from influential people or groups, and reputation are closely related to an organization's change in stance during a crisis (Cancel et al., 1999). The central publics in our case were the former comfort women and various civic groups. They actively sought legal action and protested against the company. Meanwhile, the level of power attained by these activists and the extensive amount of news coverage they received during the crisis would not have been possible without support from the Korean Netizens. In other words, the enormous support from the Netizens significantly helped activists and comfort women force the company to yield to their demands.

During the past several years in South Korea, the Internet has served as the most important public opinion forum: Whenever huge controversial issues have broken out, citizens set up chat rooms or bulletin boards in cyberspace and hotly debated the issues in question. One of the interviewees of the Choi and Cameron (2005) study also pointed out the importance of understanding the collective power of Korean Netizens in building public opinion, which can often lead to boycotts. Usually, these chat rooms on popular Web sites provide space for the public to debate the issues but also actively conduct polls regarding the issues. The traditional news media often report the poll results through their stories as we witnessed in the present case. In this light, Netizens are no longer invisible entities but become a very important public with whom corporate crisis management experts must interact. Furthermore, people actively participating in the online public forum often made an effort to make their presence even more visible by protesting in the street or setting up off-line meetings. Discovering the importance of the Internet and Netizens in current crisis management is one of the significant findings in this study. The powerful Internet community should be added to the contingent variables in the matrix. The life-cycle of the crisis was brief because of the powerful public. Considering the company's initially strong advocacy stance, this case could have dragged on if the power of the public had been weak and without determined support from the Netizens for civic groups. This case happened in South Korea where the Internet is highly developed and has penetrated into the general population ("Top 35 countries with the Highest Internet Penetration Rate," 2007). Because the Internet is becoming important in every country, practitioners throughout the world could learn a lesson from this case.

Third, the issue itself and cultural forces were important factors that influenced the company's change in position. Cancel et al. (1999) found that if a particular issue is seen by the general public as an important one, the organization is more likely to accommodate and is more willing to deal with the concerns of its public (Cancel, Mitrook, & Cameron, 1999). The nature of the issue in our study was sensational enough to grab public and news media attention. It has all sorts of eye-catching elements in it, such as nudity, a beautiful actress, and, most of all, a painful historical wound, which reminds Koreans of the past relationship with Japan. As Choi and Cameron (2005) suggested, Korean culture often makes a distinction between "we" and "others." Koreans see the Japanese as clearly "others," a country that caused permanent psychic wounds; and the company appeared to be making use of a particularly painful part of Korean national history for commercial purposes. In a culture where national identity is very powerful, there was a good chance that local publics would collectively respond to the issue. As with findings of Cancel et al. (1999) and Choi and Cameron (2005), because the issue of our case was important to the local publics, the company needed to quickly deal with the issue. As a result, the period of the crisis was brief. Again, if the general public, particularly Netizens, did not express their interest and intense anger regarding the issue, the period of the incident would have been longer (see Figure 17.1).

Lastly, the study examined strategies the company employed during

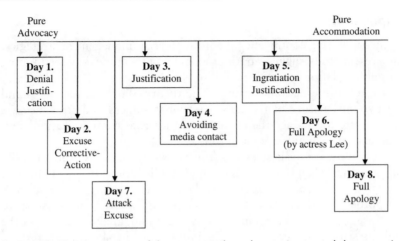

Figure 17.1 Changing stances of the company along the continuum and the strategies employed during the conflict period.

the crisis. We found that the company's position was associated with the strategies it used. For example, in our case, denial, justification, and excuse were used when the company advocated for its stance. Corrective action was associated with a relatively neutral stance. And ingratiation and full apology were the two main strategies for accommodating the public. Generally, the company employed more than one strategy to advocate its stance or accommodate to its public. For example, on the first day, when advocating its stance, the company used denial and justification, and on the second day, it utilized excuse and corrective action to advocate its stance as well as to show a somewhat accommodating position. Overall, an organization's stance and the strategies were associated with each other (see Figure 17.2).

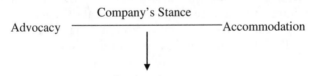

1. Powerful Activists
2. Litigation Threats
3. Negative News Coverage
4. A sensitive Cultural Issue that public regards as important
5. Extensive Internet Community Activity by Netizens (important new variable)

Figure 17.2 Main forces that move company's stance from advocacy to accommodation.

Implication

By incorporating contingency theory with crisis management strategies, the present study suggests both practical and theoretical understanding for public relations practitioners about how they can and must deal with crises in an international setting. The theory allows us to understand the dynamic nature of the crisis and what stances and strategies are appropriate to manage the external and internal communication environments at each given point in time.

We could learn the best lessons from the worst case. The overall finding suggests that when the issue under question is serious to the public, if it is related to nationalism or culture like our case, the organization needs to approach the issue in a more accommodating way from the start. In our case, although the company fully accommodated its publics in the end, its strong advocacy at the beginning and the shirking attitude in the middle of the crisis left a negative impression among the publics and its stakeholders. In addition, if a company wants to use bold and edgy marketing-PR tactics to get the public's attention and news coverage, as in our case, the company may be putting itself in a more risky position in terms of crisis management. Therefore, the company must have a well-prepared crisis management tactic or plan before it launches this sort of promotional event. However, rapid response is still difficult, particularly when company professionals may have truly believed that what they were proposing was acceptable. They might have sought the buzz in the marketplace and the extensive mobile service charges that would follow, but they allowed a quest for some notoriety and revenue to cloud their judgment as well as their crisis management planning.

The findings also suggest that it is very important for PR practitioners and crisis management experts of today to understand and be aware of the power of Netizens and the Internet community in current crisis management. And this should be included in the matrix as a new variable. Our international case study shows that Netizens are an important force to make a company move from its original stance over the period of conflict. The power and capacity of the Internet as a public opinion forum has been increasing. Public relations practitioners must understand Netizens' characteristics and the importance of them as a significant public to successfully manage the crisis. Also, practitioners and PR scholars need to develop ways to monitor and measure this important public's activity.

Acknowledgments

An earlier version of this chapter appeared in the *Public Relations Review* as a Research in Brief.

References

Actress Lee apologized, but anger still remains. (2004, February 17). *SBS News*.

Actress Lee may be withdrawn from the entertainment industry. (2004, February 16). *Hankook Ilbo*, p. 9.

Actress Lee Seung-yeon's nude photographs spark controversy. (2004, February 12). *Korea Times*.

Actress Lee's nude project angers comfort women. (2004, February 14). *Korea Herald*, p. 16.

Botan, C. (1992). International public relations: Critique and reformation. *Public Relations Review, 18*, 149–159.

Broadcasters withdraw Lee. (2004, February 14). *MBC News*.

Cameron, G. T., Cropp, F., & Reber, B. H. (2001). Getting past platitudes: Factors limiting accommodation in public relations. *Journal of Communication Management, 5*(3), 242–261.

Cancel, A. E., Cameron, G. T., Sallot, L. M., & Mitrook, M. A. (1997). It depends: A contingency theory of accommodation in public relations. *Journal of Public Relations Research, 9*(1), 31–63.

Cancel, A. E., Mitrook, M. A., & Cameron, G. T. (1999). Testing the contingency theory of accommodation in public relations. *Public Relations Review 25*(2), 171–197.

Can the nude photos soothe comfort women? Chongdaehyop urges a stop. (2004, February 13). *Hangyerye Shinmun*, p. 9.

Choi, Y., & Cameron, G. T. (2005). Overcoming ethnocentrism: The role of identity in contingent practice of international public relations. *Journal of Public Relations Research, 17*(2), 171–189.

Citizen groups urged Netian to suspend the nude photo project and to apologize. (2004, February 16). *Chosun Ilbo*, p. 11.

Commercialized nude photos insulting comfort women are not allowed. (2004, February 14). *Kyunghyung Shinmun*, p. 4.

Coombs, W. T. (1999). *Ongoing crisis communication*. Thousand Oaks, CA: Sage.

Crazy nude photo trend even utilized comfort women. (2004a, February 14). *Chosun Ilbo*, p. 22.

Crazy publisher should leave for Japan. (2004, February 13). *Naeil Shinmun*, p. 22.

Destroy the nude photos insulting comfort women. (2004, February 14). *Kookmin Ilbo*, p. 19.

Don't insult comfort women with the nude photos. (2004, February 14). *Seoul Shinmun*, p. 12.

Fake apology? (2004, February 18). *Seoul Shinmun*, p. 9.

Former comfort women refused actress Lee's apology and claim to destroy all photos. (2004, February 18). *Kyunghyung Shinmun*, p. 7.

Hofstede, G. (1984). *Culture's consequences: International differences in work-related values*. Beverly Hills, CA: Sage.

Is it a phony apology? (2004 a, February 17). *Saegye Ilbo*, p. 26.

Japanese would sneer at the comfort women nude photos. (2004, February 17). *DongA Ilbo*, p. 7.

Kim, Y. (2002). 위기관리의 이해 [*Understanding crisis management*]. Seoul, Korea: Book & Road.

Kim, Y., & Hon, L. (1998). Craft and professional models of public relations and their relation to job satisfaction among Korean public relations practitioners. *Journal of Public Relations Research, 10*, 155–175.

Lee apologizes to comfort women. (2004, February 18). *Korea Herald*, p. 20.

Lee commented that she intended to express the sorrow of comfort women. (2004, February 13). *Hankook Ilbo*, p. 9.

Lee Seung-yeon nude photo project canceled. (2004, February 17). *Korea Herald*, p. 13.

Lee Seung-Yeon's nude photo project stirred criticism. (2004, February 13). *SBS News*.

Lee Seung-Yeon's nude photos insult comfort women—Rude commercialization disgraces the history. (2004, February 13). *Munhwa Ilbo*, p. 3.

Lee's nude photo project comes to litigation. (2004, February 16). *Naeil Shinmun*, p. 23.

Lee's nude photo project stirred criticism. (2004, February 18). *SBS News*.

Lee's nude photos depreciated stock of the Lototo. (2004, February 14). *Hankook Ilbo*, p. 12.

Mean moneymakers disgrace history. (2004b, February 14). *Chosun Ilbo*, p. 31.

Mean nude photo project insults comfort women. (2004, February 14). *Hankook Ilbo*, p. 23.

Mobile service providers decide not to offer Lee's nude photos. (2004, February 14). *DongA Ilbo*, p. 30.

Netian announces the end of the nude photo project but still is uncertain whether to destroy the photos. (2004, February 17). *Chosun Ilbo*, p. 10.

Netian destroyed all original photos. (2004, February 19). *MBC News*.

Netian evaded its responsibility. (2004, February 19). *Naeil Shinmun*, p. 23.

Netian proposed the nude photo preview. (2004, February 18). *Kookmin Ilbo*.

Netian stopped the nude photo service...Chongdaehyop protested. (2004, February 17). *Kyunghyung Shinmun*, p. 7.

Netian's nude photo preview proposal brought the public rage. (2004, February 19). *Kyunghyung Shinmun*, p. 7.

Netizens anger at Lee Seung-Yeon's nude photo project. (2004, February 14). *Chosun Ilbo*, p. 10.

Nude photo injunction application was filed. (2004a, February 13). *KBS News*.

Nude photo injunction application was filed. (2004b, February 14). *Hangyerye Shinmun*, p. 7.

Nude photo injunction application retracted. (2004, February 25). *Korea Times*.

Nude photo preview proposal caused outrage. (2004, February 18). *Kookmin Ilbo*.

Nude photo project suspended. (2004, February 16). *Korea Times*.

Nude photos featuring Lee Seung-Yeon as a comfort woman repel civic groups. (2004, February 13). *Kookmin Ilbo*, p. 8.

Nude photos, is it art or obscenity? (2004, February 17). *Munhwa Ilbo*, p. 6.

Nude photos were finally destroyed. (2004, February 20). *Seoul Shinmun*, p. 9.

Outrageous business: Lee Seung-Yeon's nude photo project. (2004, February 13). *Kyunghyung Shinmun*, p. 7.

Pang, A., Jin, Y., & Cameron, G. T. (2004). *"If we can learn some lessons in the process": A contingency approach to analyzing the Chinese government's management of the perception and emotion of its multiple publics during the severe acute respiratory syndrome (SARS) crisis.* Paper presented at the annual meeting of the International Public Relations Research Conference, Miami, FL.

Phony apology? Netian's preview proposal angers public. (2004, February 19). *Chosun Ilbo*, p. 23.

Popular nude photos. (2004, February 17). *Kookmin Ilbo*.

Preview proposal caused anger. (2004, February 18). *KBS News*.

Preview proposal of Lee's nude photo arouse the criticism. (2004, February 18). *MBC News*.

Publisher destroys nude photos. (2004, February 19). *Korea Times*.

Readers' forum poll data. (2004, February 19). Chosun Ilbo. Retrieved February 23, 2004, from http://www.chosun.com/w21data/html/news/200402/200402190098.html

Regret choice of comfort women for nude photo project. (2004, February 14). *Saegye Ilbo*, p. 27.

Rubin, J. Z., Pruitt, D. G., & Kim, S. H. (1994). *Social conflict: Escalation, stalemate and settlement* (2nd ed.), New York: McGraw-Hill.

Shameless nude business rips off the history. (2004, February 17). *Kyunghyung Shinmun*, p. M2.

Shin, J., Jin, Y., Cheng, I., & Cameron, G. T. (2003). *Tracking messy organization public conflicts: Exploring the natural history of conflict management through the news coverage of unfolding cases.* Paper presented at the annual meeting of the International Communication Association, San Diego, CA.

Soh, C. S. (2000). *The comfort women project.* Retrieved February 25, 2004, from http://online.sfsu.edu/~soh/comfortwomen.html

Sriramesh, K., Kim, Y., & Takasaki, M. (1999). Public relations in three Asian cultures: An analysis. *Journal of Public Relations Research, 11*, 271–292.

Stocks involved in Lee's nude project slump. (2004, February 17). *Saegye Ilbo*, p. 19.

Stop the nude photo project insulting comfort women. (2004, February 14). *Hangyerye Shinmun*, p. 23.

Top 35 countries with the highest Internet penetration rate. (2007, January 11). *Internet world stats: Usage and population statistics* Retrieved February 10, 2007, from http://www.internetworldstats.com/top25.htm

Yarbrough, C. R., Cameron, G. T., Sallot, L. M., & McWilliams, A. (1998). Tough calls to make: Contingency theory and the Centennial Olympic Games. *Journal of Communication Management, 3*(1), 39–56

Yin, R. K. (1994). *Case study research: Design and methods* (2nd ed.). Thousand Oaks, CA: Sage.

Chapter 18

Communicating with Global Publics

Building a Theoretical Framework for International Public Relations

Paul S. Lieber and Colin Higgins

Public relations is experiencing arguably its most dramatic paradigm shift to date. Mainstream Internet acceptance has ushered in Marshall McLuhan's (1965) vision of a global village and with it new communication challenges and increased scrutiny of large (often global) business organizations (Wheeler & Silanpää, 1997). Not only has this generated unprecedented expectations of public relations practitioners to service a new, worldwide audience (Fitzgerald & Spagnolia, 1999), but it has also increased the complexity of the ethical issues these practitioners face on a daily basis (Hickson, 2004).

In addition to protecting client reputations, today's public relations practitioners must also ensure message consistency (Wakefield, 2001) and discharge accountability (Zadek, 1998) across multiple, often diverse, contexts. In this age of heightened demands for corporate accountability, public relations practitioners are also increasingly finding themselves in the role of "ethical guardians" of their organizations (L'Etang, 2003).

Public relations practitioners thus now require global strategies that reflect the complex reality of global communications practice. As trade barriers continue to fall and nations unite economically, globalization becomes more of a reality. Even a cursory glance at some statistics reveals the significance of emerging trends: the combined gross product produced by multinational corporations is an impressive $2,535.6 billion, with these organizations employing 31.6 million people worldwide (Mataloni, 2003). Moreover, nearly one-third of all U.S. corporate profits are generated internationally (Wilcox, Cameron, Ault, & Agee, 2006). The implications for public relations practitioners are clear: within seconds a press release originating in Shanghai about corporate operations in New Delhi is read by shareholders in New York City. Further, corporate Web sites and blogs communicate messages instantaneously to an international conglomerate of stakeholders, many of which are also active (and strategic) communicators in the electronic age (Rutherford, 2000).

Within such a global marketplace the stakes have never been higher for strategic communicators, as the sources of ethical mishaps multiply and the aftershocks resonate both worldwide and synchronously. For many public relations practitioners, nearly every communications decision (both in terms of advice provided internally to senior managers and those representing the organization's position to organizational constituents) potentially carries enormous global consequences (Hatcher, 2002). Such consequences require ethical approaches capable of maintaining global public relationships (Gower, 2003).

This chapter presents a theoretical analysis of the strengths or weaknesses of existing theoretical approaches to these global relationships and the strategic communication ethics which define them. To accomplish this analysis, we highlighted two of the world's largest public relations systems, those in Australia and New Zealand. Moreover, this chapter simultaneously addresses the challenges of conducting cross-cultural research for a now globally connected and diverse field.

Global Ethical Standards

Much is written about cross-cultural communication and the ethical issues that arise in a global business environment (Adler, 1983; Christie, Kwon, Stoeberl, & Baumhart, 2003). For the most part, significant culture-related differences (Alderson & Kakabadse, 1994; Becker & Fritzsche, 1987; Dubinsky & Jolson, 1991; Moore & Radloff, 1996) have been found in how managers identify (Vitell, Nwachukwu, & Barnes, 1993) and address (Husted, Dozier, McMahon, & Kattan, 1996) ethical issues.[1]

In terms of public relations practice, while there has been considerable academic and practitioner interest in ethical matters (e.g., Bivins, 1980; Bowen, 2002; Fitzpatrick & Bronstein, 2006), reflection about how these issues play out in a global context remains underdeveloped (although see Hickson, 2004).

One noteworthy exception is the attempt to develop a set of global ethical standards for those in the media and in public relations. The Media Transparency Charter, an ethical code recognized by the International Public Relations Association, the Institute for Public Relations, the International Communications Consultancy Organisation, and the Global Alliance for Public Relations and Communication Management attempts to compensate for the nuances of an individual country's public relations and journalistic systems. No document, however, can truly be a one-size-fits-all, ethical mandate considering the vast spectrum of ethical norms across the globe (Curtin, 2006).

Moreover, cultural disparities of what is "ethical" further obfuscate this attempt. Collectivist cultures, for example, shun codes that require individual practitioners to report each other for violations (Weaver, 2001). The same situation pertains for European-based systems, where in Germany ethics are considered private versus public realm issues (Palazzo, 2002). In authoritarian countries ethical codes might be perceived as something to work around versus adhere to (Husted, 2002).

Even in the United States, which has the world's oldest and most advanced public relations system, ethical expectations for its industry and practitioners continue to shift, even after 300 years. What began as a field intended to protect private interests at the expense of public ones soon merged the two in an attempt to advance railroad and utility company holdings (Olasky, 1987). Industry icons Ivy Lee and Edward Bernays introduced more scientific methods of persuasion to public relations, and likewise a new role as guardians of the public opinion formation process.

While issues such as ethical relativism, the possibility and desirability of some kind of universal ethics code, and reflections about cultural imperialism (Beauchamp & Bowie, 2004; De George, 2006) continue to occupy philosophers and academics (and rightly so) these debates provide little in the way of accessible guidance for public relations practitioners caught in the current mire of global communications practice.

In one attempt to understand global advocacy issues, Day (2005) grouped modern-day, U.S. practitioners into two distinct roles. The first categorizes the practitioner, while paid, as a person simply advocating a principle that he or she already believes in (akin to expression of an opinion under the First Amendment freedom of speech protections). The second philosophy sees the public relations representative only as a hired conduit for a particular point of view; personal opinion on the issue is irrelevant. In this latter definition, the practitioner's role is to ensure voices are heard within the marketplace of public opinion. This second definition is arguably the field's standard worldwide, echoing both Grunig's (1992) two-way symmetrical model of public relations and Barney and Black's (1994) attorney–adversary explanation for practitioner role.

Still, global ethical conundrums persist. Neither of these positions provides a satisfactory remedy for issues that arise when the two imperatives collide; those situations where the practitioner's values clash with what may be in the organization's best interests. Take a few recent situations as examples of the potentially dire consequences. In August of 2000, the U.S.-based Ford Motor Company and the Japanese tire manufacturer Firestone/Bridgestone made front-page headlines when treads on certain Ford vehicles—most notably its very popular Ford Explorer—began to inexplicably peel. Nearly 90 Ford owners in the United States died from exploding tires before Firestone/Bridgestone initiated a formal recall. More troubling is that both companies had known of the defects for 7 years, initiating a similar recall overseas back in 1993 (Verschoor, 2001).

An ugly public relations, finger-pointing battle emerged between both companies. Two months later, public relations agency powerhouse Fleishman-Hillard dismissed themselves from service to Firestone/Bridgestone only 8 months after securing the high-paying account (Grodsky, 2000). Serious questions soon emerged both about an agency abandoning a client during a crisis plus the client's deliberate omission of tire safety information which had resulted in dozens of deaths.

In Australia and New Zealand—countries whose public relations systems rank as two of the most active and advanced in the Western hemisphere (Wilcox et al., 2006)—ethical questions likewise reside. In a study on New Zealand business managers' attitudes toward unethical behavior, Brennan, Ennis, and Esslemont (1992) uncovered individuals who viewed themselves as more ethical than the "average" executive but would simultaneously consider acting in unethical ways. Likewise, Story (1996) discovered New Zealand managers' tolerance of unethical behavior as higher than of their American counterparts across lower, middle, and senior management levels of the organization.

One such example was the recent Timberlands logging scandal (Hager & Burton, 1999). Timberlands is a New Zealand government-owned logging company. It hired British public relations firm Shandwick New Zealand to represent the company (Rowell, 1999). Shandwick spied on Timberlands critics, infiltrated opposition factions, and threatened to sue anyone who was counter to their interests. False declarations of public support for logging exacerbated Shandwick's wrongdoing, with New Zealand's then Prime Minister Jenny Shipley accused of leaking information to assist existing public relations efforts.

Increases in global trade and associated controversies,[2] the rise in visibility of the Australian indigenous population, and increased awareness about the need to address past injustices; government communication; intercultural communication and the increased prominence of the non-profit sector all have contributed to an Australian focus on ethics that mirrors the practice of its New Zealand public relations neighbors (Singh & Smyth, 2000). For Australia's public relations practitioners, trade-offs are often required between presenting the clients in the best possible light (including protecting their privacy) and telling the full truth (Motion & Leitch, 2000). This challenge, according to Motion and Leitch, often relegates discussion about truth and honesty to a question of "strategic choice rather than a moral imperative."

National Australia Bank (NAB) turned this choice into front-page news. In 2004, four of NAB's financial traders were cited for covering up $455 million in losses stemming from a foreign exchange trading scam (BBC, 2004a). The Australian Prudential Regulatory Authority condemned NAB for its lack of internal controls to prevent this scandal from occurring (BBC, 2004c). Internal fallout for National Australia Bank was substantial: three top managers and five traders were fired. Frank Cicutto, the bank's chairman and CEO, stepped down shortly after the allegations came to light (BBC, 2004b).

Corporate Accountability

Challenges for public relations practitioners multiply when growing demands for greater corporate accountability are factored into the equation. Technological developments, trends toward globalization, concerns for ethical and ecological issues, and the changing role of governments over the past 30 years (Post & Berman, 2001) have ushered in a new era of stakeholder scrutiny of global business operations (Logsdon & Wood, 2005). Not only are more groups able to communicate with the public about important issues, Internet technology enables these groups to communicate much faster and more directly than has previously been the case.

Increasing in number, and increasingly well organized, NGOs and other social/environmental pressure groups have successfully positioned a diverse and complex range of social and environmental issues as a core part of corporate image and reputation. The work of Amnesty International in Nigeria, for example, placed issues of indigenous rights, human rights, and cultural imperialism on the agenda for Shell. As Elkington (1998) reports, the accusations that Shell was complicit in the execution of Ogoni activists campaigning for a greater share of oil revenues had significant implications for its reputation in Europe.

Similarly, exposure of labor practices in sportswear factories in South East Asia has led to significant reactive activity on the part of Nike and others (den Hond & de Bakker, 2007). People for the Ethical Treatment of Animals (PETA) have had a similar effect on global fast-food giant McDonalds. Greater exposure of internal organizational practices have caught these companies by surprise and raised new communicative challenges.

Increasingly sophisticated in their own communication practices, den Hond and de Bakker (2007) point out that it is NGOs and other independent organizations' ability to inflict symbolic (rather than exclusively material) damage on an organization that has public relations and corporate affairs practitioners sitting up and taking notice.

Findings from the *Millennium Poll on Corporate Social Responsibility* (Environics & PWBLF, 1999)[3] that citizens across all six continents are prepared to reward or punish companies based on their *perceived* social performance, suggests that demands for greater accountability (Zadek, Pruzan, & Evans, 1999) and more detailed information about corporate impacts (Lodgson & Wood, 2005) have entered into the mainstream—trends further reinforced by a growing number of best sellers critical of the emerging world order and the role of business within it.

Naomi Klein's (2001) *No Logo* for example, challenged the positive *image* of globalization: "tribespeople in remotest rain forests tapp[ing] away on laptop computers, Sicilian grandmothers conduct[ing] E-business and 'global teens'...sharing a world-wide style culture" (p. xvii). She contends that the reality is a world of multinationals "mining the planet's poorest back country for unimaginable profits...where Bill Gates [amasses] a fortune of $55 billion while a third of his workforce is classified as temporary workers" (p. xvii). John Pilger's (2002) *The New Rulers of the World* added to David Korten's (1995) *When Corporations Rule the World* and Noreena Heertz's (2001) *Silent Takeover: Global Capitalism and the Death of Democracy* in firmly positioning business as a key contributor to many of the world's current social and environmental problems in a global context.

Arguments that global information flows, and thus democracy, is under threat from the activities of large business organizations (Heertz, 2001; Pilger, 2002) coupled with notions that reputation, image, and corporate identity are becoming more important than product price and quality for business survival (Post & Berman, 2001; Wheeler & Silanpää, 1997) have substantially increased the complexity of the public relations practitioner's job. Not only does public relations involve representing the organization's interests to the outside world, but if Zadek, Pruzan, and Evans' (1999) notion that two-way dialogue with stakeholders is necessary to build and maintain corporate reputation, L'Etang's (2003) observation must be taken seriously that "the public relations practitioner as an ethical guardian is gathering force to become a key occupational myth" (p. 53).

International Industry Codes

While arguably extreme instances of global communications practice, the examples cited above nevertheless highlight at a minimum some need for formal conduct guidance or enforcement within public relations' new global sphere. This sphere, however, lacks formalized educational, certification, and barrier-of-entry requirements for any individual country let alone collective. The solution to date is largely the conscription of industry-wide ethical codes ideally meant to guide both inter- and intranation ethical decision making, and a smattering of ethics checklists and models for practitioners to draw on in addressing ethical dilemmas. Tilley (2005) proposes an "ethics pyramid" in which "multistage, objective-based modeling" is applied to professional ethics. Practitioners consider ethical intent, ethical means, and ethical ends at various stages of a communication project. Bowen (2004) suggests that broader consideration needs to be given to management education. Baker's (1997) ethical decision check-list for media ethics is representative (see also Kidder, 1995):

1. Identify the relevant facts
2. Recognize and identify the relevant moral issue(s)
3. Determine the moral actor(s)
4. Investigate whether there's another way, the middle ground
5. Test for right vs. wrong issues (is it legal, does it feel right, what if it became public, would someone of high moral standing do this?)
6. Test for right vs. wrong dilemma paradigms (truth vs. loyalty, individual vs. community, short-term vs. long-term, justice vs. mercy)
7. Identify other role-specific values and duties (e.g., organizational policies)
8. Apply resolution principles (e.g., Kant's categorical imperative, Mill's principle of utility)
9. Make the decision
10. Justify the decision.

In addition to the Media Transparency Charter alluded to above (Curtin, 2006), several industry-related organizations feature ethical bylines for members aimed at curtailing transgressions. Arguably the most widely cited is the Public Relations Society of America (PRSA)'s Code of Ethics. The Code's first iteration appeared in December 1950, and its contents have been continuously revised over the next half-century in line with the changing roles of the field's practitioners. The PRSA Code "emphasiz[es] serving the public interest; avoiding misrepresentations to clients, employers and others; and the continuing development of public relations practitioners" (Fitzpatrick, 2002).

Codes akin to PRSA's, Huang (2001) suggested, are crucial for public relations to be granted status as a bona fide profession. The PRSA Code, however, contains no formal means of enforcement. Without punitive measures, code enforcement falls upon the shoulders of individual practitioners guided by subjective, ethical self-standards (Wright, 1993).

The Media Transparency Charter is not alone: similar international codes fare no better. The International Association of Business Communicators (IABC) Code of Ethics—adopted in 1976 and modified in 1985—does possess enforcement and sanction methods. These methods, however, are likewise nondisciplinary. Enforcement is intended only to serve informational and educational purposes (Briggs & Bernal, 1992).

In Australia and New Zealand, the two biggest public relations organizations—the Public Relations Institute of Australia (PRIA) and the Public Relations Institute of New Zealand (PRINZ, 2003)—likewise lack formal enforcement procedures for ethical violations.

The PRIA, founded in 1949, last updated its Code of Ethics in November 2001. While the PRIA requires its members to "adhere to the highest standards of ethical practice and professional competence" (PRIA, 2004) in a number of industry studies performed in Australia between 1983 and 1999, ethical issues were not specifically addressed (Singh & Smyth, 2000).

In New Zealand, Simpson (1999) challenged the notion of objectivity and impartiality of PRINZ ethics committees considering the small size of the country's public relations industry. As of May 2002, there were fewer than 700 PRINZ members nationwide (PRINZ, 2003).

Toward a Theoric Approach

As could be expected, current research on global public relations ethics struggles with the same challenges as its industry codes. In a field where self-enforcement, subjective standards, and cultural norms determine ethical practice, its scholars are often limited to proposing loose qualitative, operational guidelines to match (Lieber, 2005). Such an approach is logical for a trio of reasons: (1) the relative newness of the field (in comparison to other mass communication disciplines); (2) its constant evolution—for example, its recent global push; and (3) because of this relative newness, most public relations practitioners are veterans of related, mass communication disciplines, most notably, journalism (U.S. Department of Labor, 2003). Thus, gauging the attitudes of individuals from these sister disciplines provided ethical data arguably transferable to public relations.

Such data, however, do little to explain and remedy the scandals at Ford/Firestone, Timberlands, and National Australia Bank. Moreover, and as evidenced above, today's public relations environments are worldwide in every sense of the word. Not only do the ethics of sister disciplines fail to address a dynamic public relations discipline environment domestically, applying these ethics across countries would be an ethical disaster. In short, existing models are not adequate for the modern, global public relations landscape and its multitude of cultures and systems. It is therefore imperative for the public relations vocation and its scholars to adopt a cross-cultural approach for their industry, one that can more accurately assess the industry's realities.

There are two primary benefits of a cross-cultural research approach to public relations (Ho & Wu, 2001). First, it can uncover systematic relationships between behavioral and ethnic–cultural variables across public relations environments. Second, it allows for generalizations to be made about psychological principles governing the field's practitioners across the globe.

Cross-cultural researchers typically use three analytic concepts to help describe their work: emics, etics, and theorics. Emics are culture specific concepts, applicable in one particular culture alone; no research claim is made about their applicability elsewhere. In contrast, an etic approach looks for culture universals applicable to multiple cultures. Etics that are assumed but not yet demonstrated are known as imposed etics (Berry, 1969) or pseudoetics (Triandis, Malpass, & Davidson, 1972). Theorics, the highest level of cross-cultural analysis, are theoretical concepts that interpret and account for both emic variation and etic constants (Berry, 1980).

To elaborate, a theoric approach is a holistic one, where a researcher simultaneously looks for disparities and similarities within and among groups. With emic and etic data already in hand, this approach enables a researcher to form higher level data assumptions, or "big picture" type perspectives.

For a field still struggling with definitional norms, it is imperative for public relations to move toward theoric-level constructs if research and professional progress are to be made. Technological advances will not stagnate in hopes of the public relations vocation catching up; the worldview Kruckeberg (1993) argued for nearly a decade and a half ago remains sorely needed.

Data for this worldview should possess common variables that explain similarities and differences both within and across individual public relations systems. For example, multinational public relations agencies share two or three cultures: the culture of the host country and the culture of the parent company or nation. Research and theory should attempt to explain both where these cultures meet and likewise where they diverge.

Such an approach would not only combine emic and etic approaches, it would simultaneously provide new life for theory attached to a particular strategic communication problem, region, or paradigm. A related point is that ethical codes that arguably explain membership norms versus practice ones would discover newfound purpose.

Alluded to above, future research should ideally isolate variables that explain public relations from a theoric context, one that transcends individual cultural nuances and microscopic analysis levels. For example, research should analyze information disclosure patterns and justifications for such practices contingent on role, not geographic location. In addition, research should test predictive modeling, emphasizing client type in overall equation, and likewise technological infrastructure impact on word selection or announcement timing.

Conclusions

There remains an active dialogue about creating valid ethical and operational templates for this now-worldwide field. Dozens of industry organizations left these dialogues with a stated purpose of creating such templates (AFX News Limited, 2004; Associated Press, 2003; Cordasco,

2003). The reality, however, is that more often than not these conversations are simply just that: dialogues. There is little tangible proof that any such conversation is having an actual impact in shaping public relations activities. Shouting from the rooftops that quantifiable reform is needed does not equate to it actually taking place.

There is arguably no better time than the present to remedy these deficiencies. Current events in business and national security continue to spotlight strategic communication ethics, making the timing ripe to both research and quantify this topic. Funding should be sufficient to support studies possessing a global focus, with public relations agencies eager to regain lost budgets, practitioners aching for a return of credibility post the dot com crash.

The benefits of quantifying both public relations and its ethics are enormous. Similar to the aforementioned reforms by Lee and Bernays (making strategic communication a more scientific process) (Olasky, 1987), quantification of the field provides tangible, numerical data for an industry known more for spin-doctor rhetoric than ethical practice (Lovel, 2001; Penchansky, 2001). A theoric approach provides the global scope sorely needed to power such efforts.

Data obtained can bolster codes, standards, and general industry understanding. More importantly, it can shape the field, its practitioners, educators, and clients toward its global present and future.

Notes

1. Some, however, have found similar moral attitudes amongst those from different cultural backgrounds (see Abratt, Nel, & Higgis,1992; Lysonski & Gaddis, 1991; Tsalikis & Nwachukwu, 1988). The morality of managers is found to be influenced by education, gender, and position in the organizational hierarchy, rather than culture per se. McDonald and Pak (1996) argue that the inconclusive nature of these results tends to be related to a lack of consistency in samples and research instruments used.
2. Specifically related to the movement of manufacturing to cheaper, developing countries and consumer concern about the conditions under which goods are manufactured in these countries.
3. The Millennium Poll on Corporate Social Responsibility interviewed a total of 25,000 people in 25 countries across six continents in May 1999.

References

Abratt, R., Nel, D., & Higgs, N. S. (1992). An examination of ethical beliefs of managers using selected scenarios in a cross-cultural environment. *Journal of Business Ethics, 11*(1), 29–35.

Adler, N. J. (1983). Cross-cultural management: Issues to be faced. *International Studies of Management and Organization, 13*(1–2), 7–45.

AFX News. (2004). CEOs fund academic institute to teach ethics. (2004, January 14). http://www. AFX.com

Alderson, S., & Kakabadse, A. (1994). Business ethics and Irish management: A cross-cultural study. *European Management Journal, 12*(4), 353–487.

Associated Press. (2003, November 7). Tyco signs workers on for ethics lesson. *Associated Press.*

Baker, S. (1997). Applying Kidder's ethical decision-making checklist to media ethics. *Journal of Mass Media Ethics, 12*(4), 197–210.

Barney, R., & Black, J. (1994). Ethics and professional persuasive communications. *Public Relations Review, 20*(3), 233–248.

Beauchamp, T. L., & Bowie, N. E. (2004). *Ethical theory and business* (7th ed.). Upper Saddle River, NJ: Pearson Prentice Hall.

Becker, H., & Fritzsche, D. J. (1987). A comparison of the ethical behavior of American, French and German managers. *Columbia Journal of World Business, 22*(4), 87–95.

BBC News. (2004a January 29). NAB warns of rogue trading loss. *BBC News.* http://news.bbc.co.uk/1/hi/business/3408597.stm

BBC News. (2004b February 2). Bank boss quits over rogue trades. *BBC News.* http://news.bbc.co.uk/1/hi/business/3450357.stm

BBC News. (2004c March 24). Australian watchdog condemns NAB. *BBC News.* http://news.bbc.co.uk/1/hi/business/3563439.stm

Berry, J. W. (1969). On cross-cultural comparability. *International Journal of Psychology, 4*, 119–128.

Berry, J. W. (1980). Introduction to methodology. In H. C. Triandis & R. Brislin (Eds.), *Handbook of cross-cultural psychology*: Vol. 2, *Methodology* (pp. 1–28). Boston: Allyn & Bacon,.

Bivins, T. H. (1980). Ethical implications of the relationship of purpose to role and function in public relations. *Journal of Business Ethics, 1*, 65–73.

Bowen, S. A. (2002). Elite executives in issues management: The role of ethical paradigms in decision making. *Journal of Public Affairs, 2*(4), 270–283.

Bowen, S. A. (2004). Expansion of ethics as the tenth generic principle of public relations excellence: A Kantian theory and model for managing ethical issues. *Journal of Public Relations Research, 16*(1), 65–92.

Brennan, M., Ennis, M., & Esslemont, D. (1992). The ethical standards of New Zealand business managers. *New Zealand Journal of Business, 14*(2), 100–124.

Briggs, W., & Bernal, T. (1992). Validating the code of ethics. *Communication World, 9*(6), 40–44.

Campbell, J. (2007). Why would corporations behave in socially responsible ways: An institutional theory of corporate social responsibility. *Academy of Management Review, 32*(3), 946–967.

Christie, P. M. J., Kwon, I.-W. G., Stoeberl, P. A., & Baumhart, R. (2003). A cross-cultural comparison of ethical attitudes of business managers: India, Korea and the United States. *Journal of Business Ethics, 46*(3), 263–287.

Cordasco, P. (2003, October 6). PR coalition releases white paper on recovering trust [Electronic version]. *PR Week,*

Curtin, P. (2006). *International public relations ethics: A cross-disciplinary approachto the challenges of globalization, identity, and power.* Paper presented at the International Communication Association Conference, Dresden, Germany.

Day, L. A. (2005). *Ethics in media communication*. Belmont, CA: Thompson Wadsworth.

De George, R. T. (2006). *Business ethics* (6th ed.). Upper Saddle River, NJ: Prentice-Hall.

den Hond, F., & de Bakker, F. (2007). Ideologically motivated activism: How activist groups influence corporate social change activities. *Academy of Management Review, 32*(3), 901–924.

Dubinsky, A. J., & Jolson, M. A. (1991). A cross-national investigation of industrial salespeople's ethical perceptions. *Journal of International Business Studies, 22*(4), 651–670.

Elkington, J. (1998). *Cannibals with folks: The triple bottom line of 21st Century business*. Gabriola Island, Canada: New Society.

Environics International & PWBLF. (2000). *The millennium poll on corporate social responsibility*. London: Author.

Fitzgerald, S., & Spagnolia, N. (1999). Four predictions for PR practitioners in the new millennium. *Public Relations Quarterly, 44*(3), 12.

Fitzpatrick, K. (2002). Evolving standards in public relations: A historical examination of PRSA's codes of ethics. *Journal of Mass Media Ethics, 17*(2), 89–110.

Fitzpatrick, K., & Bronstein, C. (2006). *Ethics in public relations: Responsible advocacy*. Thousand Oaks, CA: Sage.

Gower, K. (2003). *Legal and ethical restraints on public relations*. Long Grove, IL: Waveland.

Grodsky, D. (2000). Even Fleishman-Hillard couldn't help Firestone. *St. Louis Journalism Review, 30*(230), 26.

Grunig, J. E. (1992). *Excellence in public relations and communication management*. Hillsdale, NJ: Erlbaum.

Hager, N., & Burton, B. (1999). *Secrets and lies: The anatomy of an anti-environmental PR campaign*. Arrowtown, New Zealand: Craig Potton.

Hatcher, M. (2002). New corporate agendas. *Journal of Public Affairs, 3*(1), 32–38.

Heertz, N. (2001). *The silent takeover: Global capitalism and the death of democracy*. London: Heinemann.

Hickson, K. (2004). Ethical issues in practicing public relations in Asia. Journal of Commercial Management, 8(4), 345–353.

Ho, D. Y-F., & Wu, M (2001). Introduction to cross-cultural psychology. In L. L. Adler & U. P. Gielen (Eds.), *Cross-cultural topics in psychology* (pp. 3–13). Westport, CT: Greenwood.

Huang, Y-H. (2001). Should a public relations code of ethics be enforced? *Journal of Business Ethics, 31*(3), 259–270.

Husted, B. W. (2002). Culture and international anti-corruption agreements in Latin America. *Journal of Business Ethics, 37*, 413–422.

Husted, B. W., Dozier, J. B., McMahon, J. T., & Kattan, M. W. (1996). The impact of cross-national carriers of business ethics on attitudes about questionalbe practices and form of moral reasoning. *Journal of International Business Studies, 27*(2), 391–411.

Kidder, R. (1995). *How good people make tough choices*. New York: Simon & Schuster.

Klein, N. (2001). *No logo*. London: Flamingo.

Korten, D. (1995). *When corporations rule the world*. London: Earthscan.

Kruckeberg, D. (1993). Universal ethics code: Both possible and feasible. *Public Relations Review, 19*(1), 21–31.

L'Etang, J. (2003). The myth of the "ethical guardian": An examination of its origins, potency and illusions. *Journal of Communication Management, 8*(1), 53–67.

Lieber, P. S. (2005). Ethical considerations of public relations practitioners: An empirical analysis of the TARES test, *Journal of Mass Media Ethics, 20*(4), 288–304.

Logsdon, J., & Wood, D. (2005). Global business citizenship and voluntary codes of conduct. *Journal of Business Ethics, 59*, 55–67.

Lovel, J. (2001, September 3). PR exec: Agencies share blame for crash. *Atlanta Business Chronicle*, p. 7.

Lysonski, S., & Gaidis, W. (1991). A cross-cultural comparison of ethics of business students. *Journal of Business Ethics, 10*(2), 141–150.

Mataloni, R. (2003). U.S. multinational companies: Operations in 2001. U.S. Department of Commerce, Bureau of Economic Analysis. http://www.bea.gov/bea/ARTICLES/2003/11November/1103multinational.pdf

McDonald, G., & Pak, P. (1996). It's all fair in love, war and business: Cognitive philosophies in ethical decision-making. *Journal of Business Ethics, 15*(9), 49–62.

McLuhan, M. (1965). *Understanding media: The extensions of man*. New York: McGraw-Hill.

Moore, R. S., & Radloff, S. E. (1996). Attitudes towards business ethics held by South African students. *Journal of Business Ethics, 15*(8), 863–869.

Motion, J., & Leitch, S. (2000). The truth games of public relations politics. *Australian Journal of Communication, 27*(2), 65–80.

Olasky, M. N. (1987). *Corporate public relations: A new historical perspective*. Hillsdale, NJ: Erlbaum.

Penchansky, A. (2001). New PR rules for tech firms in a new area. *B to B, 86*, 11.

Pilger, J. (2002). *The new rulers of the world*. London: Verso.

Palazzo, B. (2002). U.S.-American and German business ethics: An intercultural comparison. *Journal of Business Ethics, 41*, 195–216.

Post, J. E., & Berman, S. L. (2001). Global corporate citizenship in a dot.com world: The role of organizational identity. In J. Andriof & M. McIntosh *Perspectives on corporate citizenship: Rights, responsibility, accountability* (pp. 66–82). London: Greenleaf,.

Public Relations Institute of Australia (PRIA). (2004). *Code of ethics*. http://www.pria.com.au/page.asp?category_id=2&page_id=94

Public Relations Institute of New Zealand (PRINZ). (2003). *What is PRINZ?* http://www.prinz.org.nz/Prinz/prinzopen.nsf/htmlmedia/what_is_prinz.html

Rowell, A. (1999, September 29). Cutting edge. *The Guardian*. http://www.guardian.co.uk/guardiansociety/story/0,3605,258917,00.html

Rutherford, K. (2000). Internet activism: NGOs and the Mine Ban Treaty. *International Journal on Grey Literature, 1*(3), 99–106.

Simpson, M. (1999, September 3). PR industry braces for Timberlands ethics test. *The National Business Review*, p. 19.

Singh, R., & Smyth, R. (2000). Australian public relations: Status at the turn of the 21st century. *Public Relations Review, 26*(4), 387–401

Story, M. (1996, March). Are you ethically fit? *NZ Business*, p. 21.

Tilley, E. (2005). The ethics pyramid: Making ethics unavoidable in the public relations process. *Journal of Mass Media Ethics, 20*(4), 305–320.

Tobin, N. (2004). Can the professionalisation of the UK public relations industry make it more trustworthy? *Journal of Communication Management, 9*(1), 56–64.

Tsalikis, J., & Nwachukwu, O. (1988). Cross-cultural business ethics: Ethical beliefs difference between Blacks and Whites. *Journal of Business Ethics, 7,* 745–754.

Triandis, H. C., Malpass, R. S., & Davidson, A. (1972). Cross-cultural psychology. *Biennial Review of Anthropology*, 1–84.

Verschoor, C. C. (2001). Are companies paying more attention to ethics? *Strategic Finance, 82*(8), 22–24.

Vitell, S. J., Nwachukwu, S. L., & Barnes, J. H. (1993). The effects of culture on ethical decision-making: An application of Hofstede's typology. *Journal of Business Ethics, 12*(10), 753–760.

U.S. Department of Labor, Bureau of Labor Statistics (2003). *Outlook Occupational Handbook 2002–2003*. Washington, DC: Author, http://www.bls.gov/oco/ocos086.htm

Wakefield, R. I. (2001). Effective public relations in the multinational organization. In R.L. Heath & G. Vasquez (Eds.), *Handbook of public relations* (p. 639–647). Thousand Oaks, CA: Sage.

Weaver, G. R. (2001). Ethics programs in global businesses: Culture's role in managing ethics. *Journal of Business Ethics, 30*, 3–15.

Wheeler, D., & Silanpää, M. (1997) *The stakeholder corporation: The body shop blueprint for maximizing stakeholder value*. London: Pitman.

Wilcox, D., Cameron, G., Ault, P., & Agee. (2006) *Public relations: Strategies and tactics*. New York: Allyn & Bacon.

Wright, D. K. (1993) Enforcement Dilemma: Voluntary nature of public relations codes. *Public Relations Review, 19*(1), 13–20.

Zadek, S. (1998). Balancing performance, ethics and accountability. *Journal of Business Ethics, 17*(4), 1421–1441.

Zadek, S., Pruzan, P., & Evans, R. (1997). *Building corporate accountability: Emerging practices in social and ethical accounting, auditing and reporting*. London: Earthscan.

Chapter 19

Colombia's Juan Valdez Campaign

Brand Revitalization through "Authenticity" and "Glocal" Strategic Communications

Juan-Carlos Molleda and Marilyn S. Roberts

"Of all the challenges facing corporations in the emerging era of the authentic enterprise, perhaps the most fundamental are those surrounding the issue of trust," states the Arthur W. Page Society in the report summary of *The Authentic Enterprise* (n.d., p. 3). According to Kunczik (2003), "The main objective of international public relations is [to] establish (or maintain existing) positive images of one's own nation or to appear trustworthy to other actors in the world system. Trust is no abstract concept" (p. 413). Sometimes a spokesperson or character is chosen to assist in building a positive national identity. When a spokesperson is involved, she or he is usually integrated into multiple components of a nation's campaign strategic promotions. Taylor and Kent (2006) write that a public relations approach to nation building uses an "elaborate model of communication that focuses on how meanings such as national identity, national unity, and the nation state are socially constructed" (p. 342). Thus, strategic communication campaigns play an important role in building national trust.

Nation building also implies institution building. Taylor and Kent state: "the creation of institutions such as political parties, nonpartisan professional organizations, and nongovernmental organizations (NGOs) supportive of the government is an important part of the nation-building process" (p. 342). In June 1927, a private trade association with not-for-profit status was created in Colombia to support an important commodity: coffee. The creation of the National Federation of Coffee Growers of Colombia (the Federation) integrated the various regions of the country's coffee growers into one association (Molleda & Suárez, 2006).

Some 30 years after the Federation's creation, the organization created a character, Juan Valdez, to "represent the proud traditions of Colombia's rural coffee growers" ("The New Face," 2006a, 2006b). The success of Juan Valdez as an "Ambassador" of the Federation's strategic communication efforts to publicize 100% handpicked quality coffee from the Andes became one of the world's most successful icons. Global audiences identify Colombian coffee's country of origin with a man in a poncho, wearing a straw hat, carrying a leather bag, and standing along-side his mule Conchita, depicting a typical rural coffee grower.

Entering the 21st century, environmental conditions loomed as threats to the nation's coffee industry: internally in Colombia and externally in the global *marketspace*. Because of increased global competition, nation-states are facing domestic reactions from their citizens, as well as external pressures from competing global regions.

Molleda and Suárez (2005) state that, "[t]oday's volatile political and economic environments in Colombia demand public relations practitioners to focus on the need for developing campaigns to regain trust in organizations, encourage peace and promote organizational changes as well as nation-building efforts both internally and externally" (p. 28). The authors underscore that the social gap and increasingly critical environment full of difficulties, contradictions, resistance, displacement of rural populations, and bursts of violence necessitated an increased emphasis on community engagement.

The Federation also faced a major strategic communication decision regarding the replacement of the aging actor who had played the role of "Juan Valdez" for many years and whose retirement was imminent. How should the Federation go about replacing the world-recognized symbol of Colombian coffee, Juan Valdez? Nations attempt to differentiate themselves and leverage the assets of their unique country of origin through their commodities and products. Not only did Juan Valdez represent Colombian coffee as a "coffee brand," but he also had become the positive image of the "country brand" Colombia.

Streaming video can be accessed on one of the Federation's Web sites (http://www.juanvaldez.com), which introduces the process of selecting the new Juan Valdez. It begins with a view of Colombia's snow-covered Andes and the narrator's voice saying, "[t]he time has come to entrust a successor with the continuity of this meaningful character. This circumstance led the Federation towards the end of 2004, together with the aid of David Altschul, head of the specialized and well-known international firm, Character, leaders in the handling of advertising icons ("The Rich Heritage," 2006). Immediately, Altschul appears on screen saying, "[t]he most interesting part of the Juan Valdez story is clearly the authenticity of it. In North America, companies spend millions, tens of millions, to hire celebrities to stand in front of their brand. Celebrities have nothing to do [with the product]. Here you have the opposite. You have a modest 'cafetero' [coffee grower] who is a world celebrity" ("The Rich Heritage," 2006.).

The purpose of the present study is to underscore the dual-prong strategic communication campaign used to boost morale among the coffee growers of Colombia and solidify the coffee culture domestically, while simultaneously revitalizing Colombia's leading national brand externally in the global coffee market. A case study approach is used. Theoretically, a multidisciplinary perspective is required to fully examine this unique phenomenon, which consists of integrating concepts from public relations, advertising, and marketing.

Literature Review

This section presents four major theoretical perspectives. These include discussions on public relations and nation building, the country of origin effect, the concept of brand authenticity, and global branding, in addition to a historical overview of the Juan Valdez campaign and character creation.

Brief Political, Social, and Economic Background

It can be said that the Colombian history of major political conflicts was institutionalized in 1965 with the formation of the leftist National Liberation Army (ELN) and the Maoist People's Liberation Army (EPL) (Sánchez, Silva, Noreña, Asencio, & Blanco, 1997). In 1966, the Revolutionary Armed Forces of Colombia (FARC) was set up, which currently is considered the largest guerrilla group in the country. In addition, the National People's Alliance formed as a left-wing counterweight to the National Front and the left-wing M-19 guerrilla group emerged. Before the creation of these reactionary groups, there had only been two major political parties since 1849: Conservative and Liberal.

A series of unfortunate events led to the proliferation of left-wing guerrilla groups (Sánchez et al., 1997). The assassination of the leftist mayor of Bogotá ignited riots. Between 1948 and 1957 an estimated of 250,000 to 300,000 people were killed in a civil war. Conservatives and Liberals formed the National Front with the intention of ending the civil war.

Insurgency was not the only long-lasting issue affecting Colombia in political, social, and economic terms. President Julio Turbay (a Liberal who was in office between 1978 and 1982) began an intensive fight against drug traffickers (Sánchez et al., 1997). Following the assassination of a justice minister, the campaign against drug dealers and traffickers intensified in the early 1980s. The guerrillas added to an increased climate of violence. Eleven judges and 90 other citizens were killed after M-19 guerrillas forced their way into the Palace of Justice (Colombia, "Timeline," 2008). In 1989, the M-19 became a legal political party after reaching a peace agreement with the government. In the same year, Andrés Pastrana secured U.S. aid but failed to decrease the violence. Colombia is the third-largest recipient of U.S. foreign aid to combat drug trafficking, left-wing guerrillas, and right-wing militias ("Colombia's

Struggle," 2003; "Narcotics and Economics," 2008), joining other aid recipients such as Afghanistan, Egypt, Israel, and Iraq. Specifically, in 2000 the U.S. Congress approved "Plan Colombia;" an aid package, mainly military, of almost $1 billion to fight drug trafficking and the rebels who profit from and protect the drug trade ("Colombia, Timeline," 2008).

The headline of a 1996 public diplomatic advertising campaign states: "In Colombia, the soil and climate allow you to grow just about anything. We consider that a blessing and a curse" (cited in "Narcotics and Economics," 2008, ¶ 54). The ad was sponsored by the National Federation of Coffee Growers of Colombia and published in The National Peace Association's *Worldview*. Regardless of the curses of the drug trade and the guerrillas, Colombia remains one of South America's most stable and growing economies. Despite the presence of serious armed conflict, Colombia's economy experienced positive growth between 2002 and 2007, backed by exports such as petroleum, coffee, coal, nickel, emeralds, apparel, bananas, and cut flowers ("Colombia, Economy," 2008). While this is good economic news, some 49% of the population still lives below the poverty line ("Colombia, Economy," 2008). This socioeconomic situation may not have a significant turnaround any time soon. Since 2007 the Colombian peso has gained significant value against the U.S. dollar making exports to the United States more expensive ("Series estadísticas," 2008). This has caused higher rates of inflation and an increase in unemployment.

Coffee is not only one of Colombia's major export commodities, but also an important component of the country's overall culture (Sánchez et al., 1997). The war against drug trafficking, guerrillas, and paramilitary groups has had a negative impact on coffee production. The violence has resulted in the displacement of farm owners and workers away from the rural areas, where the commodity is cultivated, to urban centers ("Narcotics and Economics," 2008). The Colombian government and the Federation sought solutions that would increase security and develop better trading practices to benefit coffee growers and the industry.

In 2002, an independent politician, Alvaro Uribe Velez, was sworn in as president and declared a state of emergency because of a FARC-attributed explosion in Bogotá that killed at least 20 people ("Colombia, Timeline," 2008). Uribe's second term began in 2006, which was achieved after passing an amendment to the Constitution to allow the reelection of the president. Uribe is recognized as a leader in the fight against the curses that afflict the country. In July 2007, citizens numbering in the hundreds of thousands in various locations in Colombia and around the world protested against kidnappings and the conflict that have afflicted the country for more than five decades ("Colombia: Timeline," 2008). In 2008, a debate started about the possibility of allowing the reelection of the president for a third term. In the same year, the major guerrilla group, FARC lost two of its main leaders and 15 valuable hostages were freed by the Colombian army. Analysts are now predicting a rapid decline in the armed conflict and violence and perhaps the fragmentation of this insurgent group.

Nation Building

Scott (1966) suggested that the foundation of the nation building process is the creation of a national identity, which is defined as a conscious identification of a group of people with shared national goals. People identify with numerous identities to define who they are and what values they hold. Taylor and Kent (2006) state that "Communication is a central part of nation building because communication channels act as relationship-building tools that bring citizens together and, in times of crisis or threats, can help to unify them" (p. 343). The coffee industry crisis, resulting from drug war violence and worker displacement in rural areas and increasing competition worldwide, challenged Colombia to develop a nation building and global branding campaign centered on Juan Valdez.

Another important component of nation building is the role of national unity, which refers to the cultural orientation of events and institutions that bring people together. Through national unity and cooperation, national goals can be achieved. In addition to the strongly held cultural values of family, faith, and language, Colombians identify culturally with coffee growing, an industry that is made up of more than 560,000 *cafeteros*.

Molleda and Suárez (2005) argued that failures of previous Colombian governmental administrations to curb violence and corruption and to improve the lives of the country's poorest citizens had a negative influence on the level of trust in the institution of government. Institutional mistrust in the government also affects the business sector. As a consequence of mistrust, "Colombian people are apathetic, resisting engagement in civil society" (p. 25). While the current state of the political science literature is split on the nature of the relationship between nation building and communication, Molleda and Suárez conclude that a "reorientation of the public relations function" from external to internal communication may be the consequence of internal political and social instability. The current coffee situation created the need to increase the motivation internally to deal with the stress and frustration caused by the external environment.

Taylor and Kent (2006) suggest that, "Mediated channels alone cannot, and never will, be the sole communicative element of national unity and nation building. Interpersonal communication and inter-organizational relationships are also needed" (p. 345). The authors stress that "...the importance of communication in nation building is found not so much in the technological advances or the amount of information disseminated but in the relationships that communication creates, maintains, and alters" (p. 346). Communication campaigns are particularly useful in helping citizens during difficult times of social, economic, and identity transformations. Top-down communication efforts are not recommended during times of stress, instead applications using relational and coorientation theoretical perspectives and a dialogic approach to nation building assist in creating a unified national vision. Citizens' engagement and commitment in nation building allow them to adopt the process as their own; that is, with a strong sense of identification and purpose because of their voice and influence.

Country-of-Origin Effect

National unity can also be a by-product of the common pride that citizens have in a specific commodity or product produced in their own country. Coffee is Colombia's third largest export behind petroleum and coal. The country-of-origin effect is defined as the "close interconnections between the image of a nation and its economy" (Kunczik, 2002, p. 68). Papadopoulos and Heslop (1993) claimed that country of origin as "typically operationalized or communicated through the phrase 'made in___,' is an extrinsic product cue—an intangible product attribute—that is distinct from a physical product characteristic or intrinsic attribute" (cited by Peterson & Jolibert, 1995, p. 884).

The country-of-origin effect can take either a positive or negative valence. The less information that a consumer has about a product and the more crowded the product category of similar choices, the more important and influential a positive country-of-origin effect may become. Kunczik states that, "[i]n such cases the 'made in' designation often is a decisive factor whether or not to buy" (p. 73). Global consumers do not always perceive products or commodities from a particular country in the same way. Kunczik points out that persons in various global regions may use different criteria for product evaluation and decision making.

Brand Authenticity

In addition to the influence of the country-of-origin effect, the concept of authenticity is becoming increasingly important in strategic communication campaign planning. Cook (2007), writing in *The Public Relations Strategist*, examines future trends with a view to reaching a better understand of the issues facing professionals and their clients. Cook states:

> We're at the start of an era where people want authentic stories about authentic people. PR [public relations] professionals are the storytellers. It's our job to help find the authenticity at the core of our companies and clients, and to tell those stories to the world in words that will truly be heard. (p. 33)

According to Peñaloza (2000), marketers are increasingly turning to brand histories and historical associations as sources of market value. Brown, Kozinets, and Sherry (2003) argue that "the search for authenticity is one of the cornerstones of contemporary marketing" (p. 21). However, according to Beverland (2005), little is known about how firms "create and maintain" images of authenticity. Peterson (2005) asserts that authenticity is socially constructed, takes effort to maintain, and the saliency of authenticity changes over time. He further states, "[i]ssues of authenticity most often come into play when authenticity has been put in doubt" (p. 1083).

In an interpretive study, Holt (1998) argues that consumers with different levels of cultural capital search for different cues that signal authenticity. According to Holt, "cultural capital resources are accumulated in three primary sites of acculturation: family upbringing, formal education and occupational culture" (p. 7). Beverland writes that, "[t]he literature posits that authenticity can be inherent in an object, come from a relation between an object and/or historical period, an organization form, or nature, or be given to an object by marketers and consumers. Authenticity can also be true and/or contrived" (p. 1006). Meyer and Rowan (1991) note that the more an organization is derived from institutionalized myths, the more organizations use elaborate ceremonies to display confidence to both their internal and external publics to further underscore either "real" and "perceived" authenticity.

Beverland (2005) uses the case study method to examine the strategies used by 26 luxury wine firms when they decided to create brand authenticity. Beverland concludes, "[t]hese images of authenticity represent a mixture of the real and the imagined, in that product distinctiveness, although somewhat a result of local climatic and topographical conditions is also a creation by winemakers, marketers, governments, consumers, critics, and other relevant stakeholders" (p. 1027). The author remarks that brand management is an interactive process of meaning construction and reconstruction, whereas brand authenticity is infused in the product by marketers.

Scholars have begun to identify and examine various types of authenticity. Gilmore and Pine (2007) identified five genres of perceived authenticity corresponding to five economic entities. These are: commodities (natural authenticity), goods (original authenticity), services (exceptional authenticity), experiences (referential authenticity), and transformations (influential authenticity). The researchers acknowledge what they refer to as "the authenticity paradox." Noting that consumers long for authenticity, but businesses are challenged to provide it, Gilmore and Pine recommend that marketers follow a set of axioms to avoid consumer backlash and criticisms of being "inauthentic."

Beverland, Lindgreen, and Vink (2008) suggest that the term *authenticity* has recently taken on new meaning. Their findings support the notion that advertising plays a role in reinforcing images of authenticity. They also argue that "previous forms of authenticity—indexical and iconic—can be transferred from historic sites to marketing communications" (p. 13).

Global Brand Building

The concept of branding is a central tenet of marketing. Definitions vary as to exactly what constitutes "a brand." Kotler (1988) defines a brand as "a name, term, sign, symbol or design or combination of them, which is intended to identify the goods of one seller or group of sellers and to differentiate them from those of competitors" (p. 463). Aaker and Joachimsthaler (1999) wrote in the *Harvard Business Review* that "companies whose brands have become more global reap some clear benefits" (p. 137).

Aaker and Joachimsthaler also argue that "developing global brands should not be the priority. Companies should work on creating strong brands in all markets through global brand leadership" (p. 138). The authors state that, "[g]lobal brand leadership means using organizational structures, processes, and cultures to allocate brand-building resources globally, to create global synergies, and to develop a global brand strategy that coordinates and leverages country brand strategies" (p. 138).

Kyriacou and Cromwell (n.d.) state that "the branding process strengthens democracy and helps both internal development and successful integration into the world community, on all levels" (¶ 13). The authors underscore the importance of a "truthful" brand for products and services, as well as nation branding. They caution that "[a]ny attempt to brand a nation untruthfully will backfire, as people and organizations discover the brand to be dishonest.... For a nation, this can have far-reaching consequences" (¶ 22).

Holt (2002) cautions that today's brands are vulnerable to attack from an emerging countercultural movement, sparked by such works as Naomi Klein's *No Logo: Taking Aim at the Brand Bullies* (1999). Ironically, in marketing courses such megaglobal brands as Nike, Coca-Cola, McDonald's, Microsoft, and Starbucks are heralded for their success. These same brands are being attacked in reality by the antibranding movement whose concerns are focused on environmental issues, human

Cafés (interviewed by Ludden, 2004, radio broadcast). The icon Juan Valdez obtained a spot on Madison Avenue's Walk of Fame in 2005 ("The Iconic Juan," 2005).

Two research questions guided this study:

RQ1. How did the new Juan Valdez campaign develop and deal with the issue of authenticity?

RQ2. How were the nation building and global branding dimensions of the campaign communicated?

Method

This research uses a case study methodology, including in-depth interview and text analysis. A review of internal documents was conducted, as well as online and print communication materials produced by the Federation and its affiliated organizations. As Wimmer and Dominick (2006) explain: "a case study uses as many data sources as possible to systematically investigate individuals, groups, organizations, or events" (p. 136). This study takes Yin's (1994) approach for data analysis, named explanation building, which consists of the construction of a description and illustration of the phenomenon under investigation including causes, processes, and outcomes, based on the theoretical framework chosen to inform the situation or place it in context. The research questions are answered by using findings from the various methods of data gathering.

A 2-hour interview with Marcela Jaramillo Asmar, director of the General Office of Intellectual Property of the Federation (Dirección General de Propiedad Intelectual), was conducted in Bogotá, Colombia, on October 24, 2006. Analysis consisted of two streamed videos, three Web sites (Juan Valdez, Juan Valdez Café, and the Federation), and domestic and international news coverage of the strategic communication campaign and launching media event of the new Juan Valdez that took place in Bogotá on June 29, 2006.

Findings

The Campaign for a New Juan Valdez

In May 2006, the Federation announced the retirement of Carlos Sánchez, an actor hired to play the role of Juan Valdez for almost 4 decades, and the search for his successor (personal communication, 2006; Ryssdal, 2006). Sánchez inherited the role from Cuban-American actor José Duval. The actions that led to the announcement of Sánchez's retirement and the unveiling of a new Juan Valdez on June 29, 2006 included the following. In preparation for the new era of Juan Valdez and Colombia's coffee worldwide promotion, the Federation announced that Juan Valdez Cafés would offer Rainforest Alliance Certified coffee, which is grown according to rigorous social and environmental standards. Sabrina Vigilante, Rainforest Alliance Senior Manager of Marketing and Business Development, pointed out at the NGO's annual gala in New York City: "Together, Juan Valdez and the Rainforest Alliance are building a global marketplace for sustainably-certified (sic) Colombian coffee. That is a very powerful equation" ("What's New," 2006, ¶ 7).

In 2004, the six-person marketing company Character, based in Portland, Oregon, was hired by the Federation to select Juan Valdez's replacement and infuse the character with a distinct personality and authenticity (personal communication, 2006). In an interview given to *Fortune Small Business*, Character's creative director, Jim Hardison, explained that "creating characters is not about making stuff up but discovering the story inherent in the brand" (cited in Adler, 2006, p. 38). The search for a new Colombian coffee ambassador to the world started in 2004 and involved 318,000 candidates nationwide out of an estimated more than 560,000 coffee growers (personal communication, 2006). "In searching for a replacement, the federation sent teams across the streets, farms and—of course—cafes in the country's western coffee region," MSNBC reported ("Juan Valdez Takes," 2006, ¶ 9).

The ideal candidate's profile was a man with a young face between 30 and 45 years of age ("Learn More About," 2006). Humble and wealthy *cafeteros*, extension agents, and employees of the Federation were included in the pool of candidates. A preselection process resulted in 406 candidates from 14 different regions and 87 coffee growing districts. Ten finalists participated in the last stage of the selection process from which the new coffee ambassador of Colombia was chosen.

The 2-year selection process was used to rally support for the Colombian coffee industry, which faced fierce global competition and the internal obstacles imposed by the negative impact of the war against drug trafficking, guerrillas, and paramilitary groups in the coffee growing regions and the displacement of the rural growers and workers (personal communication, 2006). The entire country was informed by impressive media coverage and special events staged in various regions of Colombia. For instance, a reality show was created about the search (Tharp, 2006). According to Character's cofounder, David Altschul, "the federation is actually looking for a backstory rather than inventing one" (interviewed by Ryssdal, 2006, radio broadcast).

Visibly emotional, the new Juan Valdez was unveiled in a ceremony in the capital city of Bogotá on Thursday, June 29, 2006 ("Colombia Growers Choose," 2006). The new Juan Valdez is 39-year-old farmer Carlos Castañeda, the oldest of 10 children born on a coffee farm and a third-generation coffee grower himself. Until the selection, Castañeda lived a modest life with his wife of 17 years and three children on a 10-acre plot, the legacy of his parents and grandparents ("Colombia Growers Choose," 2006). Castañeda picked his first coffee bean at the age of 6. He had never boarded a plane before he flew to the capital as a finalist in May 2006.

The Nation-Building Dimension

The Colombian coffee sector has experienced a significant decline since 2000 because of plummeting international prices and security concerns due to the war against drug trafficking, guerrillas, and paramilitary groups, whose activities take place in the areas where coffee is cultivated and produced (personal communication, 2006). "When planning the retirement of Mr. Sánchez, we analyzed the internal and external threats facing our industry and decided to develop a program to invigorate the coffee growers' identification with their lands and the sector, and solidify the 100% Colombian Coffee[1] and Juan Valdez brands in the international market" (personal communication, 2006). Altschul says: "I think what they've done is take the opportunity to deepen the story and they've looked deliberately within the ranks of the 'cafeteros,' the small coffee farmers, and they have to have a personal story that connects them authentically with the coffee culture" (interviewed by Ryssdal, 2006, radio broadcast).

One of the missions of the new Juan Valdez is to reenergize the failing Colombian coffee industry, the country's third largest legal export(personal communication, 2006). "Coffee is the national product of this South American nation and was crucial in the country's early economic development," MSNBC.com reports ("Juan Valdez Takes," 2006, ¶ 7). "It's rare to find a Colombian who does not start his or her day with a shot of 'tinto,' heavily sweetened black coffee" ("Juan Valdez Takes," 2006, ¶ 7). At the media event when the new Juan Valdez was introduced, Gabriel Silva, General Manager of the Federation, said:

> ...this character reflects the nature, values, vision, honesty, and democratic vocation of the Colombian coffee growers. Juan Valdez transcends the commercial impact, transcends its contribution to the presence of the coffee of Colombia in the entire world. No one will be able to doubt that Carlos Castañeda and his family...have been the most loyal interpreters and representatives...of the essence of the coffee soul of Colombia. ("The New Face," 2006b)

The launch of the new Juan Valdez was webcast live. The master of ceremonies was the general manager of the Federation. Carlos Castañeda, after being invested by Carlos Sánchez with a poncho, a leather bag, and straw hat typical of rural Colombia where the world-famous Arabica coffee is grown, thanked the community of coffee growers and the Federation for his selection. The new Juan Valdez said "[w]e all feel like we're Juan Valdez." As he completed his statement, all the competition finalists joined Castañeda on stage to underscore the unity of Colombian rural coffee growers' sense of being Juan Valdez.

"The goal was to find the person who embodied the fictional, yet real Juan Valdez who would capture the essence and value of the people who inhabit Colombia's various coffee growing regions," says the narrator of the launching webcast ("Learn More About," 2006). The webcast includes the key messages and strategy behind the strategic communication campaign (personal communication, 2006). It continues, "…a member who will be representative of a huge group of hard-working cheerful and prosperous men who work in the Colombian Andes day after day to assure, through their efforts, the well-being of future generations since it is they who will be in charge of carrying on the transition of the time-honored occupation of cultivating the land" ("Learn More About," 2006). Finally the narrator says, "[h]is mission will consist of always keeping open a window of opportunity and following the path to conquer new markets, reinforcing at every step, the prestige obtained by the brands which have been associated with Colombian coffee for almost half a century" ("Learn More About," 2006).

The Global Branding Dimension

Colombia faced a 35-year low in the price of coffee, on top of decades of violence and displacement of rural populations including coffee growing families, which demanded the renewal of Colombian coffee as the finest with the highest quality globally (personal communication, 2006). Juan Valdez became the natural communication channel and tool to revamp Colombia's coffee identity globally, as Sanchez (2003) writes:

> For a war-torn country mostly known abroad for its rebel groups, death-squad warlords and cocaine traffickers, Valdez has arguably been Colombia's best diplomat. He has posed for pictures with former U.S. president Bill Clinton and was awarded Colombia's National Order of Merit in the Grade of the Silver Cross. With Juan, Colombia's mild, aromatic coffee became something more than a simple commodity. (¶¶ 9–10)

The main purpose of the global branding campaign was to remind the consumer that "our coffee is special and authentic because it is picked and washed by hand, as well as the best beans [being] selected for export.

In addition, if they go to the coffee regions, they will see hundreds of Juan Valdezes and Conchitas because this is the way we transport coffee out of the mountains to the consumers" (personal communication, 2006). Marketing consultant, David Altschul, explains: "And here we have a product that started out as a commodity and the coffee federation itself, beginning with the Juan Valdez campaign, developed a story that elevated it above the commodity status" (interviewed by Ryssdal, 2006, radio broadcast).

Another key message the Federation wanted to convey internationally was that the benefit of the coffee trade goes directly to the coffee growers via social investment. The Federation uses its profits to provide roads, schools, and hospitals in Colombian coffee regions and soon coffee growers will be also stockholders of the Juan Valdez chain of coffee shops (Ludden, 2004; personal communication, 2006).

The extensive international media coverage of the new Juan Valdez focused on the retirement of the actor who had portrayed Juan Valdez for 37 years (May 31, 2006) and the introduction of a "real" and "authentic" Coffee Ambassador to the world (June 29, 2006). According to the records of the Federation and a LexisNexis database search, media coverage included news sources from North and South America, Europe, Asia, and Africa. The Associated Press reported the story about the launch as: "Colombia's new Juan Valdez is an authentic coffee grower" (Goodman, 2006). AP included the message of "authenticity" in the news headline. *The New York Post* captures another key message: "New 'Juan' aims to perk up coffee exports"; and the story's lead paragraph read: "Colombia's new coffee ambassador to the world—an icon of advertising for nearly half century—is no longer an actor for hire but a real coffee grower working the lush slopes of Colombia's coffee country" (Tharp, 2006, p. 50).

One of the main strategies to keep up with the presence and "front and center" identification of the character and icon Juan Valdez is for Carlos Castañeda to be physically present at major events and trade shows all over the world. As Gabriel Silva, General Manager of the Federation, stated that "[h]e'll spend half the year traveling, sitting in a plane and far away from his family, in order to stand for hours at events posing for photos and signing autographs" (cited in Goodman, 2006).

Discussion and Conclusions

The case study of the selection and introduction of the new Juan Valdez documents a two-prong strategic communication campaign of nation building and global branding as a novel strategic communication model. It illustrates the interplay between local and global in an integrative and coordinated fashion. Moreover, the "glocal" needs of both domestic environmental factors and global challenges must be addressed simultaneously in developing a "dual-pronged" or "glocal" strategic communication campaign. This case study and its theoretical framework provide evidence of the interdependence of domestic and global *marketspace*. It provides national and international strategic communication scholars and professionals with a progressive vision to capitalize on issues of national priority, while dealing with the implications of "a flattening" communication world.

Actor Carlos Sánchez's retirement and the selection process and introduction of a new, younger, and more authentic Juan Valdez provided an opportunity for brand revitalization. The revitalization efforts provided a catalyst for international expansion of stand-alone Juan Valdez Cafés and the formative partnership with the Rainforest Alliance. These activities, which were cumulatively and strategically capitalized by the Federation and its affiliated company PROCAFECOL, brought new opportunities, both in domestic and international terms. As a coordinated team, the old and new Juan Valdezes, as well as the president and the general manager of the Federation, consistently expressed the national and international campaign's unified key messages during the 2-year search process.

Concerning the nation building dimension, the 2-year campaign provided an opportunity for the Federation to address current internal challenges of the coffee regions. The campaign provided a mechanism by which to reinstate pride, identity, and unity internally with the Colombian coffee culture and industry. The strategic communication campaign unified and served as a formula to inoculate the rural coffee growers from internal threats of violence and displacement. A shared goal became the selection of a replacement for Juan Valdez from among the ranks of more than 560,000 authentic coffee growers, providing a sense of "ownership" in Juan Valdez's role as their ambassador to the world.

A revitalized country-of-origin icon of the "coffee brand" commodity also served to revitalize "brand Colombia." The country-of-origin effect of Colombian coffee was reintroduced and reenergized through the massive level of global media attention given to the "unveiling" of the new Juan Valdez and the retelling of his story. The Federation's strategy of sharing the media's attention from the external global media coverage of the new Juan Valdez and the country-of-origin effect reinforced the importance of this humble *cafetero* and his faithful "Conchita" to the rest of the world and resonated back to the coffee regions of Colombia.

The "genuine" portrayal of the new Juan Valdez provided opportunities for the Federation to work with their communication partners to develop a story that created a newer, more powerful, more emotional bond with coffee consumers. Global consumers raised the bar. Their expectations are for "real" people, "real" stories, and "real" cultural by-products and meaning construction. In creating more "authenticity," the Federation inoculated itself against future attacks that Juan Valdez is only an actor, not a true representation of Colombian *cafeteros*. If such an attack materialized from the emerging antibranding countercultural movement, the Federation would have no defensible response. According to Holt (2002), the antibranding opposition is becoming "a full-fledged social movement" concerned about the environment, human rights, and unchecked globalization. Likewise, the strategic decision to form a partnership with the Rainforest Alliance was key to a holistic approach to serving the needs of *cafeteros* and the environmental concerns of the region. Thus, extending the purpose and the role of Juan Valdez further became a symbol of corporate social responsibility and global citizenship. The expanded role of the new Juan Valdez provides a unique selling opportunity and a key point by which to differentiate between Colombian coffee and coffee grown in other regions of the world. Never before have the profits of stand-alone coffee shops gone back so directly to the rural coffee growers. One of the major criticisms made by the antibranding or counterculture critics of multinational brands, such as Naomi Klein (n.d.) or Kalle Lasn's magazine *Adbusters* (n.d.) in North America to name a few, has been the lack of direct benefit from the sales of goods and commodities to those who labor to produce them.

When conceptual approaches such as nation building, country of origin, brand authenticity, and global brand building are combined to an original framework is developed so that strategic communication can be studied and practiced at the national and international levels. The concept of authenticity seems to permeate both domestic and international strategic communication environments. More than ever, strategic communication professionals need to continue to identify and tell true stories with a heavy component of realism, openness, and transparency. The complexity of the global marketspace demands duality—domestic and international—of campaign planning and execution that simultaneously creates a more dynamic and synergic strategy and, therefore, outcomes among key home, host, and transnational publics (Molleda & Quinn, 2004). "Glocal" strategies are vibrant, authentic, and effective and resonate in domestic, regional, and global terms.

When the Federation planned and executed the introduction of the new Juan Valdez, global brand leadership was achieved. Aaker and Joachimsthaler (1999) described global brand leadership as "using organizational structures, processes, and cultures" (p. 138). Holt's (2002) recommendation was that to be authentic, "brands must be disinterested; they must be perceived as invented and disseminated by parties without an instrumental economic agenda, by people who are intrinsically motivated by their inherent value" (p. 83). This viewpoint can be found in the remarks of Gabriel Silva, general manager of the Federation, on the day that the new Juan Valdez was presented. Silva stated, "Juan Valdez transcends the commercial impact, transcends its contribution to the presence of the coffee of Colombia in the entire world. No one will be able to doubt that Carlos Castañeda and his family...have been the most loyal interpreters and representatives...of the essence of the coffee soul of Colombia" ("The New Face," 2006). What began as a mythic advertising character created in 1959 has evolved into a global icon with an authentic story of much greater cultural value both in both domestic and international terms.

Limitations and Future Research

The case documented in this study pertains to a specific industry and country, which could not predict the dimensions of the same phenomenon among other top coffee producers and exporters, such as Brazil, Ethiopia, India, Indonesia, Hawaii, and Vietnam. These regions also are trying to establish a country-of-origin and brand authenticity for their coffee industry. To understand the broader implications of the concept of authenticity for a dual domestic and global strategic communication campaign, it is necessary to document future cases, including an array of economic sectors and national environments from diverse regions of the world.

This multidisciplinary theoretical framework could be developed as a model for future research. Measurements of authenticity are needed to determine its use and impact in brand revitalization efforts in developing future communication strategies that respond to the complexity and hostility of skeptical publics. It has been said that authenticity is part reality and myth, and by operationalizing the construct, researchers and practitioners can identify and use the power of authenticity to create more compelling and sustainable stories and identities.

Note

1. Coffee considered 100% Colombian needs to be labeled with the Juan Valdez icon or the statement "100% Colombian Coffee" or "Pure Colombian Coffee" ("Programa 100% café," 2004).

References

Aaker, D. A., & Joachimsthaler, E. (1999, November/December). The lure of global branding. *Harvard Business Review, 77(6)*, 137–144.

Adbusters. (n.d.).http://www.adbusters.org/

Adler, C. (2006, October). Mascot makeover: How the Pillsbury Doughboy explains consumer behavior. *Fortune Small Business*, 30–42.

Authentic enterprise report summary, The. (n.d.) Arthur W. Page Society. Retrieved August 2, 2008, from http://www.awpagesociety.com/images/uploads/AE_Summary_4.pdf

Beverland, M. B. (2005, July). Crafting brand authenticity: The case of luxury wines. *Journal of Management Studies, 42*(5), 1003–1012.

Beverland, M. B., Lindgreen, A., & Vink, M. W. (2008). Projecting authenticity through advertising: consumer judgments of advertisers' claims. *Journal of Advertising, 37*(1), 5–15.

Brown, S., Kozinets, R. V., & Sherry, J. F. Jr. (2003). Teaching old brands new tricks: Retro branding and the revival of brand meaning. *Journal of Marketing, 67*(3), 19–33.

Colombia, economy. (2008). *CIA world factbook.* Retrieved June 10, 2008, from https://www.cia.gov/library/publications/the-world-factbook/geos/co.html#Econ

Colombia growers choose a new Juan Valdez. (2006, June 29). Associated Press cited in MSNBC website. Retrieved September 1, 2008, from, http://www.msnbc.msn.com/id/13617899/

Colombia's struggle. (2003, May 14). [Editorial] *The New York Times,* p. A24.

Colombia, timeline. (2008). BBC News. Retrieved June 10, 2008, from http://news.bbc.co.uk/2/hi/americas/country_profiles/1212827.stm

Cook, F. (2007, Winter). It's a small world after all: Multiculturalism, authenticity, connectedness among trends to match in next 50 years. *The Public Relations Strategist, 13*(1), 30–33.

El proyecto de tiendas Juan Valdez. (2005). Juan Valdez Café. Retrieved March 24, 2007, from http://www.juanvaldezcafe.com/index.php?id=1215

Forero, J. (2001, November 24). A coffee icon rides his mule off into the sunset. The New York Times, A4. Retrieved September 1, 2008, from http://www.nytimes.com/2001/11/24/world/medellin-journal-a-coffee-icon-rides-his-mule-off-into-the-sunset.html?scp=1&sq=A%20Coffee%20Icon%20Rides%20His%20Mule%20off%20into%20the%20Sunset&st=cse

Futuro de las tiendas Juan Valdez. (2005). Juan Valdez Café. Retrieved March 24, 2007, from http://www.juanvaldezcafe.com/index.php?id=1455

Gilmore, J. H., & Pine, B. J., Jr. (2007). *Authenticity: What consumers really want.* Boston: Harvard Business School Press.

Goodman, J. (2006, June 29). Colombia's new Juan Valdez is an authentic coffee grower. *The Associated Press.*

Holt, D. B. (1998). Does cultural capital structure American consumption? *Journal of Consumer Research, 25,* 1–25.

Holt, D. B. (2002, June). Why do brands cause trouble? A dialectical theory of consumer culture and branding. *Journal of Consumer Research, 29,* 70–90.

Iconic Juan Valdez , The. (2005, November). Hispanic magazine. Retrieved April 1, 2007, from http://www.hispaniconline.com/magazine/2005/november/Panorama/latinos.html

Juan Valdez takes permanent coffee break; star of Colombia advertisements retiring, new one to be named soon. (2006). MSNBC. Retrieved March 30, 2007, from http://www.msnbc.msn.com/id/13068453/

Klein, N. (1999). *No logo: Taking aim at the brand bullies.* New York: Picador.

Klein, N. (n.d.). http://www.naomiklein.org/main/

Kolter, P. (1988). *Marketing management: Analysis, planning and control.* Englewood Cliifs, NJ: Prentice-Hall.

Kunczik, M. (2003). Transnational public relations by foreign governments. In K. Sriramesh & D. Verčič (Eds.), *The global public relations handbook: Theory, research, and practice* (pp. 399–424).Mahwah, NJ: Erlbaum.

Kyriacou, S., & Cromwell, T. (n.d.). The concept and benefits of nation building. Retrieved from March 26, 2007, from http://eastwestcoms.com/Concepts-and-benefits-of-nation-building.htm.

Learn more about. (2006). Juan Valdez. Retrieved March 24, 2007, from http://www.juanvaldez.com/jvcomnew/welcome.htm

Ludden, J. (2004, October 10). *Juan Valdez, now serving hot coffee* [Radio broadcast]. Washington, DC: All Things Considered, National Public Radio.

Marcas registradas, historias de las marcas. (2004). Federación Nacional de Cafeteros de Colombia. Retrieved March 24, 2007, from http://www.cafedecolombia.com/comercializacion/marcasregistradas/historia.html

Meyer, J. W., & Rowan, B. (1991). Institutionalised organizations: Formal structure as myth and ceremony. In W. W. Powell & P. J. DiMaggio (Eds.), *The new institutionalism in organizational analysis* (pp. 41–62). Chicago: University of Chicago Press.

Molleda, J. C., & Quinn, C. (2004). Cross-national conflict shifting: a global public relations dynamic. *Public Relations Review, 30*(1), 1–9.

Molleda, J. C., & Suárez, A. M. (2005). Challenges in Colombia for public relations professionals: a qualitative assessment of the economic and political environments. *Public Relations Review, 31,* 21–29.

Molleda, J. C. & Suárez, A. M. (2006). Engaging Colombian coffee growers in dialogue: social reports campaign of the departmental committee of Antioquia. In M. G. Parkinson & D. Ekachai (Eds.), *International and intercultural public relations: A campaign case approach* (pp. 306–319). Boston: Pearson Education.

Narcotics and Economics Drive U.S. Policy in Latin America. (2008). The Center for Public Integrity. Retrieved June 10, 2008, from http://www.publicintegrity.org/report.aspx?aid=254#

New face of Juan Valdez, The. (2006a). Retrieved March 24, 2007 from http://www.juanvaldez.com/jvcomnew/newjuan.htm

New face of Juan Valdez, The. (2006b). Retrieved March 24, 2007, from http://www.juanvaldez.com/jvcomnew/welcome.htm

Papadopoulos, N. G., & Heslop, L. A. (1993). *Product-country images: Impact and role in international marketing.* New York: International Business Press.

Peñaloza, L. (2000, October). The commodifaction of the American West: Marketers' production of cultural meanings at the trade show. *Journal of Marketing, 64,* 82–102.

Peterson, R. A. (2005). In search of authenticity. *Journal of Management Studies, 42*(5), 1083–1098.

Peterson, R. A., & Jolibert, A. P. (1995). A meta-analysis of country-of-origin effects. *Journal of International Business Studies, 26*, 883–900.

Quienes somos. (2005). Retrieved March 24, 2007, from http://www.juanvaldezcafe.com/index.php?id=1202

Responsabilidad social. (2005). Retrieved March 24, 2007, from http://www.juanvaldezcafe.com/index.php?id=1454

Rich heritage of Juan Valdez, The. (2006). Retrieved March 24, 2007 from http://www.juanvaldez.com/jvcomnew/welcome.htm

Ryssdal, K. (2006, May 31). *David Altschul of Character describes the search for a new Juan Valdez* [Radio broadcast]. Saint Paul, MN: Marketplace, Minnesota Public Radio.

Sánchez, C., Silva, F., Noreña, M. I., Asencio, R., & Blanco, J. (1997). Breviario de Colombia: una guía para todos (Compendium of Colombia: A guide for all). Bogotá, Colombia: Panamericana Editorial.

Sanchez, M. (2003). Colombia's Juan Valdez back with new ad campaign. *Forbes.* Retrieved March 30, 2007, from http://www.forbes.com/markets/commodities/newswire/2003/07/08/rtr1020686.html

Scott, R. E. (1966). Nation building in Latin America. In K. W. Deutsch & W. J. Foltz (Eds.), *Nation building* (pp. 73–83). Chicago: Atherton.

Series estadísticas, tasas de cambio. (2008). Banco de la República. Retrieved June 10, 2008, from http://www.banrep.gov.co/series-estadisticas/see_ts_cam_dia.htm

Taylor, M., & Kent, M. L. (2006). Public relations theory and practice in nation building. In C. Botan & V. Hazelton (Eds.), *Public relations theory* (Vol. 2, pp. 341–359). Mahwah, NJ: Erlbaum.

Tharp, P. (2006, June 29). New "Juan" aims to perk up coffee exports. *The New York Post,* p. 50.

What's new: Juan Valdez embraces sustainable coffee. (2003). Rainforest Alliance. Retrieved March 30, 2007, from http://www.rainforest-alliance.org/news.cfm?id=juan_valdez

Wimmer, R. D., & Dominick, J. R. (2006). *Mass media research: an introduction* (8th ed.). Belmont, CA: Thomson Wardsworth.

Yin, R. (1994). *Case study research* (3rd ed.). Newbury Park, CA: Sage.

Chapter 20

The Influence of Mobile Phone Advertising on Dependency

A Cross-Cultural Study of Mobile Phone Use between American and Chinese Youth

Ran Wei

Critics of advertising (Williams, 1980) have argued that advertising sells a product as well as a lifestyle. As Bandura (1969) put it, advertising disseminates product information from which people learn how to attach social meaning to material goods. According to Pollay (1986), advertising not only attempts to influence how people shop and actually use products, it also has an impact on the larger domain of consumers' social roles, goals, values, and meaning, among other things. Hence, the persuasive power of advertising lies in cultivating consumers and creating a consumerist culture. Ewen (2001) characterized this power of advertising as "captains of consciousness." Nevertheless, the influence of advertising as an "awareness institution" (Tussman, 1977) on the emergence of new media technology-centered consumer cultures is rarely studied; little is known about the social psychological process in which advertising cultivates relationships with target audiences and motivates consumption of high-tech products.

This study is set in the context of the explosive growth of mobile phone use among young people worldwide and the prominence of mobile phone advertising in the media. For example, among the top 10 product categories of ad spending in the United States, wireless telephone services ranked seventh with a total of $692 million in January–March 2005 (Nielsen, 2005). In addition, mobile phones are used as a popular marketing tool in South Korea (see Cho & Cameron, chapter 17 this volume). This study aims to explore the role of advertising in developing a mobile phone-driven way of life among youth. Specifically, this study analyzes the similarities and differences between American and Chinese young people's dependence on the mobile phone to attain such communication goals as understanding, orientation, and entertainment. Moreover, the study investigates how mobile phone advertising contributes to the dependency. The focus on the high-tech mobile phone to explore the relationships among advertising, new media technologies, and a mobile lifestyle in a cross-cultural context is based on these theoretical considerations:

First, the ubiquity of the mobile phone is a striking global phenomenon. There were 2.7 billion mobile handsets in use worldwide in 2007 (International Telecommunications Union [ITU], 2008), which is three times the number of computers in use. More important, an industry study (Mobile Marketing Association [MMA], 2007) found that 79% of surveyed mobile phone users indicated they were moderately or highly dependent on the cell phone. The mobile phone seems to have inspired young people as a new gateway to adult life (Charlton & Bates, 2000). In Europe, teenagers lead the rest of the population in adopting the mobile phone—for example, in Finland, use is as high as 90%—and Japan with a rate of 70% (see Yu, Loudoen, & Sacher, 2002), integrating it into their day-to-day life. Further, young users have created a culture around the mobile phone (for example, the use of text messaging, see Oksman & Turtiainen, 2004).

More important, youths take pleasure in putting a personal touch to a phone's functions, shapes, and looks to articulate their personality (Lee, 2002). In fact, the mobile phone has evolved from a talking device into a fashion accessory and "an icon for adolescents" (Ling, 2001). Oksman and Turtiainen (2004) suggested that mobile communication provides a social stage for young people to articulate personal space; the mobile phone is an enabling technology to present the self. Research on mobile phone use among youth (Leung & Wei, 2000) confirmed that the mobile phone was considered a marker of social identity and a status symbol. A consequence of mobile phone popularity among youth is their increasing dependence on the mobile phone to fulfill their needs for communication, symbolic interaction, and having fun. In the rise of a mobile phone driven way of life among youth, advertising may have a great deal of influence. As Kilbourne and Pipher (2000) argued, insecure adolescents tend to be most vulnerable to the persuasive power of advertising.

Second, culture is a key variable in the consumption of products. Past cross-cultural studies show that people who are members of collectivist cultures tended to rely on the in-group for information and feedback concerning their behaviors as compared to individualists (Markus & Kitayama, 1991). Chinese students were more likely than American students to define themselves with reference to others (Briley & Wyer, 2001). In theoretical terms (Hofstede, 1980), people in Western industrial cultures are "I" conscious, self-actualization is viewed as important, and individuals are autonomous and independent (Triandis, 1995). People are "we" conscious in collectivistic cultures (mostly Asian and Latin American countries). Their identity is more related to the social system, especially the in-group such as family, peers, and coworkers to which they belong, than it is to the big "I."

Given the cultural difference between the United States and Taiwan along the individualist–collectivist dimension, the varying degrees in mobile phone dependency will likely mirror the differences in their societal cultures. The way in which adolescents use their mobile phone may well be a consequence of their home culture. For example, Chinese youth may be more dependent on the mobile phone to meet social-oriented goals of surveillance, interaction with others, and social play, whereas American youth may be more dependent on the wireless technology to achieve self-oriented goals of communication in terms of self understanding, daily planning, and solitaire play. To put it differently, culture leads to differentiation. If not, the alternative explanation is that the role of communication technologies in fastening the pace of globalization (Levitt, 1983) and prevailing cultural influences (Hofstede, 1980). This explanation touches upon the broad issues regarding the influence of globalization and culture.

With regard to the diffusion of communication technology, globalization refers to the process of spreading various objects and experiences universally to people across the world (Scholte, 2000). The impact of globalization on culture might be aided greatly by communication technologies, which move across borders freely. Thus the trend of globalization is to bring nations together and minimize culture-based differences. This explanation rings a technological determinist tone, which views technological developments in general and communication technologies in particular as the antecedent cause of social changes and principal determinants of institutions and social relationships (McLuhan, 1964).

Hence, findings of the study will shed light on the debate on how culture vs. technology impacts globalization.

Literature Review and Research Questions

Individual Media Dependency

Examining the tripartite relationship between media, social systems, and the audience, media dependency theory (Ball-Rokeach & DeFleur, 1976) proposes that the three parties mutually influence one another. Thus, the theory deals with the relationship between media and society at a macro level and individuals and media at a micro level (DeFleur & Ball-Rokeach, 1989). At the micro level, the theory states that individuals in society rely on the media to meet their needs and achieve certain goals. The more alternatives that individuals have for meeting their needs, the less dependent they will be on a given medium. Conversely, the fewer alternatives they have, the more dependent they will be. Specifically, proceeding from the assumption that goal-attaining motives drive media consumption, the individual media dependency theory (Ball-Rokeach, 1985; DeFleur & Ball-Rokeach, 1989) holds that an audience actively chooses media content based on a preexisting psychological need—dependency (Ball-Rokeach, 1998; Ball-Rokeach, Rokeach, & Grube, 1984).

The concept of dependency refers to "a relationship in which the satisfaction of needs or attainment of goals by one party is contingent upon the information resources of another party" (Ball-Rokeach et al., 1984, p. 3). Media dependency theory (Ball-Rokeach, 1998; Grant, 1996) identifies three main goals or three types of dependency: understanding (i.e., an audience's need to understand the world and themselves), orientation (i.e., an audience's need to act and interact with others effectively), and play (i.e., an audience's need for entertainment). For each goal, there are two dimensions: social and self. Thus, there are six goals: social understanding, self-understanding, interaction orientation, action orientation, social play, and solitary play.

Previous empirical research on individual media dependency focused on use of traditional mass media such as radio, television, and newspapers for fulfilling an individual's goals of understanding, orientation, and play. Recent research expands the model to the Internet (Patwardhan & Ramaprasad, 2004; Patwardhan & Yang, 2003). Findings reported overall high dependency on the Internet, and higher dependency for social understanding, action orientation, and solitary play among surveyed college faculty and students.

Originally an interpersonal communication device, the high-tech mobile phone has evolved into a hybrid medium with characteristics of both person-to-person (such as voice calls and text messaging) and mediated communication (such as SMS—short message services; Wei, 2008). Nonvoice uses include information seeking like news and weather, playing interactive games, surfing the Internet, and e-mailing anywhere, anytime. The individual media dependency theory is thus highly applicable in examining use of the converged mobile phone. In addition, sleek and trendy mobile phones became a status symbol (Leung & Wei, 2000).

Moreover, the symbolic use of the mobile phone is rising. Adolescents are the most active in reinventing wireless technology as a personal medium and a social prop for self-presentation (Oksman & Turtiainen, 2004). Mobile phones are smart skins for young users (Lee, 2002). That is, mobile phones were designed as wearable fashion accessories. Fashion attentiveness, which refers to the extent to which mobile phones are considered as fashion (or fashion worthiness) was found by Katz and Sugiyama (2006) to affect the purchase, use, and replacement of mobile phones among American and Japanese college students. The mobile phone served as a fashion lens to present self. Similarly, Chinese yuppies tended to integrate mobile phones into their conspicuous, Westernized, and socially active lifestyle. Having a mobile phone became a means to achieve social differentiation and identity among peer yuppies (Wei, 2006).

In the context of this cross-cultural study, two research questions were raised to address concerns of whether there are differences in mobile phone dependency between American and Chinese youth.

RQ1. In overall terms, which group is more dependent on the mobile phone: American or Chinese youth?

RQ2. Do American youth differ from their Chinese counterparts in being dependent on the mobile phone to attain social vs. self-goals of understanding, orientation, and play? If so, how?

Predictors of Individual Media Dependency

Previous research on media dependency at the individual level has identified a number of factors that affect the degree of the dependency relationship one develops with the media. First, demographic variables influence individual media dependency. Significant linkages were found between age, education, and media dependency in the use of traditional media (Loges & Ball-Rokeach, 1993) as well as Internet use (Patwardhan & Yang, 2003). Specifically, age was found to be a significant predictor of dependency on newspapers and the Internet. Young Internet users are more dependent on the Internet than older users. In addition, educated people were found to be less dependent on TV shopping than less educated people (Ball-Rokeach, 1985), but were more dependent on the Internet (Loges & Jung, 2001).

Second, media use was identified as a significant predictor of individual media dependency. With regard to use of traditional media such as newspapers and television, de Boer and Velthuijse (2001) investigated linkages among individual dependency relations with the news, news exposure, and knowledge gain. They reported a significant and positive relationship between dependency relations with the news and actual news exposure. Respondents with varying degrees of media dependency were found to differ in the extent to which they used television to learn about current affairs. The amount of time spent reading newspapers was related to the intensity of media dependency, particularly the goals of social and self-understanding. Morton and Duck (2000) focused on the relationship between media dependency relations and media use, employing a sample of 76 gay men. The results were consistent. Frequency of use of media devoted to gay subjects was significantly related to media dependency relations. In the Internet use, experience and length of time using the Internet were identified as significant correlates of individual media dependency (Patwardhan & Ramaprasad, 2004).

Third, factors that showed significant linkages with individual media dependency included audience attitudes toward a medium. Their attitudinal evaluation affected the media they chose to use (Morton & Duck, 2000). In addition, the role of advertising in influencing the varying degrees of dependency on the mobile phone was examined in this study. Past research shows that exposure to advertising has a socializing effect on consumers (Bush, Smith, & Martin, 1999; Wackman, Wartella, & Ward, 1977). At the societal level, Schudson (1986) suggested that the influence of advertising is derived from its ubiquitous presence. Advertising served as a constant reminder of consumption, legitimizing a consumption-oriented way of life. Myers and Biocca (1992) articulated the mechanisms in which advertising influences the mind or consciousness of consumers: advertising influences consumers as hidden motives or a form of social cues. Young people tend to be particularly sensitive to social cues coming from advertising and turn to advertising for guidance (Myers & Biocca, 1992).

In the context of mobile phones, fashionable phones have been reinvented by young users as a medium for self-expression. As Osgerby (2004, p. 210) argued, the mobile phone represents "an avenue for the creation of their individuality and self-image." Hence, it is important to explore the influence of symbolic use of the mobile phone as self on mobile phone dependency.

With all the above-mentioned factors being considered, the present study sought to explore whether predictors of mobile phone dependency would differ given the cultural differences between the United States and Taiwan. These two research questions were raised:

RQ3. What are the predictors of overall mobile phone dependency between American and Chinese youth? Are they different or similar? What is the impact of advertising?

RQ4. What are the predictors of mobile phone dependency for attaining social vs. self-related goals between American and Chinese youth? Are they different or similar? What is the impact of advertising?

Method

Sample

The present study relied on two parallel surveys conducted in the United States and Taiwan to answer the four research questions. The U.S. survey involved a convenience sample of high school students from eight Southeastern states. Prior consent was obtained from faculty before the questionnaires were distributed to the students attending a regional scholastic journalism convention in a Southeast state in March 2004. The survey was self-administered under the supervision of trained graduate assistants. The number of completed questionnaires totaled 334.

The Taiwan survey used a probability sample of five high schools. Both public and private schools were included to ensure students represented a wide range of socioeconomic backgrounds. With the approval of the schools' officials, three classes were selected in each school. The self-administered questionnaires were distributed to selected classes in May 2004. Respondents were assured of anonymity, and participation was voluntary. The sample included 620 respondents, among which 525 were mobile phone users and 75 were nonusers. Only the 525 mobile phone users were used for subsequent data analyses.

The two samples were comparable with the exception of gender ratio. The U.S. sample consisted of 32.4% male students and 67.6% female students. The average age of the respondents was 17.21 (SD = 1.12), slightly older than that of the Taiwan sample. The youngest was 15 and the oldest was 21. In terms of grades (the United States has a 4-year system for high schools), 36.5% were in the 11th grade, followed by the 12th grade (21.1%), the 10th grade (21.4%), and the 9th grade (11.0%). In addition, 75.7% of the respondents were White, and 17.4% were African American. Asians and Hispanics accounted for 3.8% and 3.2% of the sample respectively. Of the Taiwan sample, 51.8% were male and 48.2% were female. The mean age was 16.68 (SD = .94) with the youngest being 15 and the oldest being 20. In a system that features a 3-year program for high-school education, nearly half of the respondents were first-year high school students (49.4%); second-year students were more than one-fourth (28%); and the rest were third-year students (22.6%).

Measures of Key Variables

To ensure comparability, the questions used in the two surveys were identical. In addition, the same scales were used. The dependent variable of this cross-cultural analysis was mobile phone dependency (overall dependency and dependency for attaining social and self goals). The independent variables that were used to predict mobile phone dependency included control variables (e.g., age, gender, and cultural values), mobile phone use (e.g., general use, extended use, and symbolic use), consciousness of mobile phone advertising, and attitudinal variables (e.g., attitudes toward the mobile phone and viewing the mobile phone as projected self).

Mobile Phone Dependency The concept of individual media dependency refers to an individual's reliance upon the information resources of the media system to understand the society and self, to get information to coordinate daily routines and interaction with others, and to relax and entertain oneself (Grant, 1996; Grant, Kendall, & Ball-Rokeach, 1991; Loges & Ball-Rokeach, 1993). The 18-item individual media dependency scale thus has two distinctive dimensions: social and self. Operationally, respondents were asked to rate how helpful the mobile phone was to achieve goals of understanding, orientation, and play. The scale was 1 to 5, where "1" meant "not helpful at all" and "5" meant "extremely helpful." Responses to the 18 items were used to build an overall scale of mobile phone dependency. Specifically, for the U.S. data, the 18 items were summed and divided to construct an overall mobile phone dependency scale ($M = 2.64$, $SD = .84$, $a = .91$). Then, two separate subscales were built by averaging the nine items tapping social ($M = 2.67$, $SD = .82$, $a = .82$) and self goals ($M = 2.57$, $SD = .95$, $a = .87$). Similarly, the overall mobile phone dependency for the Taiwan data was summed and then divided to yield the composite scale ($M = 2.81$, $SD = .96$, $a = .94$). Two separate subscales were constructed by averaging the nine items tapping social ($M = 2.66$, $SD = .96$, $a = .87$) vs. self-oriented goals ($M = 2.95$, $SD = 1.02$, $a = .89$). Higher scores indicated more dependency on the mobile phone to attain the goals of understanding, orientation, and play.

General Mobile Phone Use   General use of the mobile phone refers to use of the mobile phone for voice calls and text messages. Respondents were asked to estimate the number of calls they made and received separately in a day. The two items were highly correlated in both samples ($r = .91$ for the U.S.; $r = .71$ for Taiwan). A composite scale of calling was created by combining the two ($M = 15.81$, $SD = 28.96$ in the U.S.; $M = 10.95$, $SD = 23.38$ in Taiwan). Similarly, respondents were requested to report the number of text messages received and sent in a day ($r = .76$ for the U.S. data; $r = .96$ for the Taiwan data). A scale was generated by combining the two questions on number of text messages received and sent ($M = 11.74$, $SD = 18.21$ for the U.S. sample; $M = 8.46$, $SD = 12.36$ for the Taiwan sample). Finally, respondents were asked to report the average minutes per call ($M = 11.80$, $SD = 12.97$ in the U.S.; $M = 5.70$, $SD = 11.97$ in Taiwan).

Extended Use of the Mobile Phone   Extended mobile phone use refers to using the mobile phone beyond voice calls to take advantage of the built-in functions and add-on mobile data services of mobile communication. On a 1 to 3 point scale, where "1" meant "never," "2" "sometimes," and "3" meant "often," respondents were requested to indicate how often they played video games on the mobile phone ($M = 1.97$, $SD = .66$ for the U.S. sample; $M = 2.12$, $SD = .53$ for the Taiwan sample), e-mailed ($M = 1.20$, $SD = .48$ for the U.S.; $M = 1.38$, $SD = .61$ for Taiwan), voice mailed ($M = 2.36$, $SD = .74$ for the U.S.; $M = 1.61$, $SD = .55$ for Taiwan), and used the mobile phone as a PDA (personal assistant) such as scheduling and alerts (M = 1.63, SD = .77 for the U.S.; M = 1.99, SD = .75 for Taiwan).

Symbolic Use of the Mobile Phone   Symbolic use of the mobile phone refers to self presentation through customization and personalization of one's mobile phone by adding ring tones, changing faceplates or functions to match the user's taste and interests (Osgerby, 2004). Operationally, respondents were asked to report the extent to which they had personalized their mobile phone. The personalization included changing the phone's appearance, functions, and accessories. To be specific, using "1" (yes) and "0" (no), they were asked to indicate if they had personalized the faceplate, the number pad, ring tones, the screen, banner, hologram sticker, voice mail, and the like. Responses to the 15 questions were summed to build an index of symbolic use of the mobile phone (M = 6.55, SD = 3.55, a = .81 for the U.S. sample; M = 6.39, SD = 3.78, a = .93 for the Taiwan sample). The index ranged from "0" (meaning personalized nothing) to "15" (meaning personalized everything). Higher numbers meant that more aspects of the mobile phone were personalized.

Consciousness of Mobile Phone Advertising   Consciousness refers to a mental construction of the world, particularly how people perceive the world around them (Berger, Berger, & Kellner, 1974). Three items were used to measure this variable. Respondents were asked to indicate the level of attention paid by them to mobile phone ads in newspapers, on TV, and on billboards. The scale ranged from 1 (not at all) to 4 (a great deal). Results of an exploratory factor analysis showed a single-factor salutation for the U.S. data and Taiwan data (Eigenvalue = 2.10, explaining 70.17% of variance in U.S.; Eigenvalue = 2.47, explaining 82.16% of variance in Taiwan). A composite scale was created based on these items (M = 1.92, SD = .76, a = .79 for the U.S. sample; M = 2.66, SD = .90, a = .89 for the Taiwan sample).

Attitudes toward the Mobile Phone   To measure this variable, respondents were given eight items on a 1 to 5 point semantic differential scale to rate mobile phone attributes and benefits. The items included pairs of opposing adjectives such as useless-useful; unimportant-important; invaluable-valuable; negative-positive; boring-exciting; difficult-easy; bad-good; disagreeable-agreeable. Exploratory factor analysis using varimax rotation resulted in a single-factor solution with an eigenvalue of 4.65 and explained 58.16% of the variance in the U.S. data; an eigenvalue of 4.78 and explained 59.74% of the variance in the Taiwan data. Item loadings were all greater than .60, indicating the measured

Table 20.1 Between-Country Comparison of Factor Loadings of Attitudes toward the Mobile Phone

The mobile phone is …	U.S. (N=334)	Taiwan (N=525)
not valuable—valuable	.78	.86
unimportant—important	.85	.84
negative—positive	.80	.82
not useful—useful	.79	.82
boring—exciting	.66	.76
bad—good	.81	.74
disagreeable—agreeable	.68	.68
difficult—easy	.71	.64
Eigenvalue	4.65	4.78
Total variance explained	58.16%	59.74%

Notes: The scale is 1 to 5. Reverse items were recoded in subsequent analysis.

underlying concept was unidimensional (Table 20.1). A composite scale of mobile phone attitudes was created by adding the eight items and then dividing by eight after achieving sufficient reliability ($M = 3.95$, $SD = .90$, $a = .90$ for the U.S.; $M = 3.71$, $SD = .77$, $a = .90$ for Taiwan). The higher the score, the more positive attitudes there were toward the mobile phone.

Viewing the Mobile Phone as Projected Self The apparatgeist (spirit of the machine) perspective of information technology (Katz & Aakhus, 2002) suggests that IT users tend to develop a relationship with the technology, viewing information technologies in an emotional and self-extensive way. In the context of the mobile phone, this study included another affective measure: viewing of the mobile phone as projected self. Operationally, respondents were asked to rate the nine items such as "having a mobile phone makes me look smart, cool, trendy" (see Table 20.2 for details). The scale ranged from 1 to 5 where "1" meant "completely disagree" and "5" meant "completely agree." Exploratory factor analysis using varimax rotation of the nine items yielded a single-factor solution. The factor structure held for the U.S. and Taiwan data, making it comparable for subsequent analyses. With sufficient reliability, the nine items were built into a composite scale after adding and then dividing by nine ($M = 2.62$, $SD = 1.23$, $a = .96$ in the U.S.; $M = 2.71$, $SD = .85$, $a = .94$ in Taiwan). The higher the rating, the more the mobile phone was viewed as a reflection of oneself.

Finally, control variables included age, gender, years of study, and race (U.S. survey only). Cultural values were also measured as a control variable. Culture refers to "the collective programming of the mind

Table 20.2 Between-Country Comparison of Factor Loadings of Viewing the Mobile Phone as One's Extended Personality

Having a mobile phone makes me ...	U.S. (N=334)	Taiwan (N=525)
look more attractive	.86	.92
feel confident	.90	.91
look sophisticated	.89	.88
look high-tech savvy	.87	.86
look cool	.88	.83
look socially dependable	.88	.80
look smart	.90	.80
look trendy	.85	.80
look good	.87	.70
Eigenvalue	6.97	6.27
Total variance explained	77.48%	69.64%

Notes: The scale is 1 to 5, where 1 means "completely disagree," 2 means "disagree," 3 means "partially agree, partially disagree," 4 means "agree," and 5 means "completely agree."

which distinguishes the members of one group or category of people from another" (Hofstede, 1991, p. 260). This study focused on individualism as a key aspect of culture. Conceptually, individualism is defined as "a tendency to think of oneself as a unique individual and to define oneself independently of others." On the other hand, collectivism refers to "a disposition to think of oneself as part of a group and to define one's own attributes and behavior in relation to those of other group members" (Briley & Wyer, 2001, p. 201). The individualism-collectivism scale (Triandis, 1995) was adopted. The scale contains 18 items, using a 1 to 5 point Likert scale. Responses in the U.S. and Taiwan surveys were summed up and divided by 18 to generate a composite scale ($M = 3.45$, $SD = .46$, $a = .69$ for the U.S.; $M = 3.36$, $SD = .43$, $a = .47$ for Taiwan). Higher scores indicated stronger individualist tendencies.

Findings

In terms of length of having a mobile phone, the Chinese high school students in Taiwan adopted the mobile phone earlier than their American counterparts ($M = 29.37$ months in Taiwan vs. $M = 25.60$ months in the United States). But American high school students outspent the Chinese high school students on the mobile phone. More than half (52.8%) of American youth reported spending $21 to $50 per month. On the other hand, 38.6% of Taiwan respondents spent $299 TWD (US$8.83) per month, and 33% reported $300–$599 (US$8.86–17.59). Further,

12.8% reported monthly spending of between $600 (US$17.72) and $899 (US$26.54). The rest spent $900 (US$26.57) or more per month.

Between-Country Differences in Mobile Phone Dependency

RQ1 explored whether there was any difference in mobile phone dependency between American and Chinese youth. Results of t-tests in Table 20.3 show that the two samples differed significantly in overall mobile phone dependency. The Chinese respondents were more dependent on the mobile phone for understanding, orientation, and play than their American counterparts.

RQ2 explored whether American youth would differ from Chinese youth in their dependency on the mobile phone to attain social vs. self-related goals of understanding, orientation, and play. As t-test results in Table 20.3 further show, the dependency on the mobile phone for the three social goals was about the same between the U.S and Taiwan samples. However, the Chinese high school students had a higher dependency for attaining the goals of self-understanding, orientation, and solitary play than the Americans. The between-country difference was statistically significant (Table 20.3).

In addition, it is interesting to note that American high school students were less conscious of mobile phone ads appearing in newspapers, on TV, and on billboards than their Chinese counterparts. The mean of the former was 1.92 with a standard deviation of .76, whereas the mean of the latter was 2.66 with a standard deviation of .90. The difference was statistically significant ($t = -12.61$, $df = 754$, $p < .001$), indicating the Chinese respondents tended to pay more attention to and became more aware of mobile phone advertising than the American respondents.

Table 20.3 Mean Comparisons between the U.S. and Taiwan on Mobile Phone Dependency

Mobile Phone Dependency	U.S.*	Taiwan**	t-test
Overall mobile phone dependency	2.64 (.84)	2.81 (.96)	$t = 2.56$, $df = 580$, $p < .05$
Dependency on the mobile phone for attaining social-oriented goals	2.67 (.82)	2.66 (.96)	$t = .36$, $df = 837$, non-significant
Dependency on the mobile phone for attaining self-oriented goals	2.57 (.95)	2.95 (1.02)	$t = -5.36$, $df = 832$, $p < .001$

Notes: *The U.S. scores 91 on the same index. **Taiwan has a score of 17 on Hofstede's individualism index. The scale is 1 to 5, where 1 means "not helpful at all", and 5 means "extremely helpful."

Predictors of Overall Mobile Phone Dependency

RQ3 aimed to identify predictors of the overall mobile phone dependency and explore whether the significant predictors were different between the American and Chinese data. To address it, parallel multiple hierarchical regressions were run on the U.S. and Taiwan data with the overall mobile phone dependency as the criterion variable. For both samples, entered first in the equation as predictors stepwise were control variables (e.g., age, gender, and cultural values), general mobile phone use (e.g., voice calling, text messaging, and duration of calls), extended use (e.g., playing games, e-mailing, voice mailing, using the mobile phone as a PDA, and symbolic use), consciousnesses of mobile phone advertising, and mobile phone attitudes (e.g., attitudes toward the mobile phone and viewing the mobile phone as projected self).

As Table 20.4 (the first two columns) shows, the two regression models were successful in accounting for the systematic variance in overall mobile phone dependency. The percent of variance accounted for, measured by the adjusted R^2, was 30.9% for the U.S sample and 19.4% for the Taiwan sample.

The regression coefficients show that the two regression results shared three common predictors and at the same time showed some differences. The shared significant predictors between the two data sets were individualism, consciousness of mobile phone advertising, and viewing the mobile phone as projected self. These similarities suggest that the stronger the individualist values the American and Chinese respondents held, the more conscious they were of mobile phone ads, and the more they viewed the mobile phone as a reflection of themselves, the greater their overall dependency on the mobile phone to fulfill the needs of understanding, orientation, and play.

Interestingly, the correlation between consciousness of mobile phone advertising and overall mobile phone dependency was significant and positive ($r = .37$, $p<.001$ for U.S.; $r = .35$, $p<.001$ for Taiwan). It showed as a significant predictor of mobile phone dependency in both the U.S and Taiwan data after controlling for the influence of other predictors. In fact, it was the second strongest predictor in the U.S. data and the strongest predictor in the Taiwan data. Such a result suggests that the more the American and Chinese respondents were conscious of mobile phone advertising, the more dependent they were on the mobile phone to fulfill a variety of needs such as understanding, orientation, and play.

The different predictors of overall mobile phone dependency between the U.S. and Taiwan were text messaging, average minutes of calling, e-mailing via mobile phones, symbolic use of the mobile phone, and mobile phone attitudes. For the American high school students, controlling for the influence of other significant predictors, symbolic use of the

Table 20.4 Between-Country Regression Models Predicting Mobile Phone Dependency

Predictor	Mobile Phone Dependency (Overall)		Mobile Phone Dependency (Social Goals)		Mobile Phone Dependency (Self Goals)	
	U.S.	Taiwan	U.S.	Taiwan	U.S.	Taiwan
Age	−.06	−.06	−.03	-.05	−.08	-.05
Gender	−.03	−.02	−.01	−.01	−.06	-.03
Cultural values	.19***	.13***	.19***	.11*	.16***	.14***
ΔR^2 (%)	10.3***	5.6***	8.4***	4.0***	9.3**	6.6***
Voice calling	.03	.01	.01	.02	.05	.00
Text messaging	−.01	.11**	.02	.08	−.01	.13**
Length of calls	.14**	.06	.13**	.05	.14**	.05
ΔR^2 (%)	5.9**	5.3*	4.6*	3.8*	5.4**	6.3*
Playing games	.03	.01	.04	−.02	.01	.04
E-mailing	.02	.12**	.03	.14***	−.00	.08
Voice mailing	.04	.02	.06	.03	.02	.02
As a PDA	.09	.05	.06	.03	.11*	.06
Symbolic use	.20**	.03	.18***	.06	.15**	.00
ΔR^2 (%)	7.5***	3.3*	6.6***	3.9*	7.9*	2.6*
Ad consciousness	.16***	.20***	.16**	.19***	.15**	.18***
ΔR^2 (%)	3.8***	4.6***	4.0***	4.1***	2.9***	4.6***
Attitudes	.09*	.08	.11*	.05	.06	.10*
Mobile phone as self	.22***	.15***	.23***	.11*	.22***	.16***
ΔR^2 (%)	5.1*	1.8***	5.9*	1.0*	4.0***	3.3**
Total Adj. ^{R2} (%)	30.9	19.4	27.9	15.6	28.7	22.0
F value	19.64	18.99	19.37	14.86	17.76	19.48
Significance level	p <.001	p <.001	p <.001	p <.001	p <.001	p <.001

Notes: The entries are standardized regression coefficients from the final equation. The ΔR^2 indicates the percent of variance accounted by the corresponding bloc with the variables in the previous blocs controlled for. N= 334 for the U.S. sample; N = 525 for the Taiwan sample.
*p <.05; **p <.01; ***p <.001.

mobile phone and length of calls were significantly related to mobile phone dependency. These two predictors were the second and fourth strongest in the U.S., suggesting that using the mobile phone to define oneself and making longer calls played an important role in developing dependency on the mobile phone. Attitudes toward mobile phone use were a significant but weak predictor. For the Chinese high school students, text messaging and e-mailing were significant in predicting the overall mobile phone dependency. These results suggest that extended use of the mobile phone beyond voice calls contributed to the dependency on the mobile phone to satisfy needs to understand the world and themselves, to act and interact with others effectively, and to be entertained.

Based on the R square change, the control block in both samples contributed the most to account for the overall dependency on mobile phone. On the other hand, the role of the extended use block was greater in the U.S. data, but the contribution of the general mobile phone use block (thanks to text messaging) was greater in the Taiwan data.

Predictors of Mobile Phone Dependency for Attaining Social Goals

RQ4 was concerned with identifying predictors of dependency on the mobile phone to attain social vs. self-related goals of understanding, orientation, and play. Four more multiple regressions were performed with mobile phone dependency for social and self-related goal attainment respectively as the criterion variable. Similar to the earlier run, predictors entered in the equation included control variables, general mobile phone use, extended use, symbolic use, consciousness of mobile phone advertising, and attitudinal variables.

As results in Table 20.4 (the middle two columns) show, the two regression models were generally successful in explaining the systematic variance in dependency on the mobile phone for fulfilling social needs. The percent of variance accounted for, measured by the adjusted R^2, was 27.9% for U.S. data and 15.6% for the Taiwan data. Out of the five blocks of predictors, extended use contributed the most to explain mobile phone dependency to attain social goals in both samples after the influence of control variables, mobile phone use, consciousness of mobile phone advertising, and attitudes were taken into consideration.

With regard to the specific predictors of dependency on the mobile phone for social goal attainment, as shown in the two middle columns in Table 20.4, individualism, consciousness of mobile phone advertising, and viewing the mobile phone as projected self played a significant part in accounting for the variance in dependency on the mobile phone to satisfy the needs of social understanding, action orientation, and social play in both the U.S. and Taiwan samples. The more individualistic the respondents were, the more conscious they were of mobile phone ads, and the more they considered the mobile phone as who they were, the higher their dependency on the mobile phone for attaining these social goals. In terms of beta size, consciousness of mobile phone advertising was the strongest in Taiwan, and it was the third strongest in the U.S.

For the American high school students, the unique factors that showed predictive power were symbolic use of the mobile phone, length of calls, and attitudes toward the mobile phone. These results were similar to the predictors of overall mobile phone dependency among American high school students. In comparison, for the Chinese high school students, e-mailing played a significant role in shaping their mobile phone dependency for attaining social goals. This particular result underscores the importance of extended use. The more often Chinese youth used the mobile phone for communication, the more they became dependent on it to know what was going on in the world, to coordinate daily routines with peers, and to be entertained with their peers.

Predictors of Mobile Phone Dependency for Attaining Self-related Goals

The number of significant predictors and their contributions to explain the variance in mobile phone dependency for self-related goals was strikingly similar to those predictors of mobile phone dependency for social goals. As Table 20.4 (the last two columns) shows, individualism, mobile phone advertising consciousness, and viewing the mobile phone as projected self were significantly related to dependency on the mobile phone to satisfy the needs of self understanding, interaction orientation, and solitary play in both the U.S. and Taiwan data. The relationships were positive, indicating the more the respondents were individualistic in cultural orientation, the more symbolically, and the more conscious they were of mobile phone advertising, the more they were dependent on the mobile phone to make sense of themselves and to entertain themselves alone.

On the other hand, a number of differences in significant predictors existed between the U.S. and Taiwan. The predictors that were significant only in the U.S. were duration of calls, use of the mobile phone as a PDA, and use of the mobile phone symbolically. They all contributed to the dependency on the mobile phone for self-related goals among American high school students. This result was similar to earlier findings of predictors of mobile phone dependency to attain social goals. For the Chinese high school students, the uniquely significant predictors were text messaging and mobile phone attitudes. Chinese respondents in Taiwan who texted more and held a positive attitude toward the mobile phone had a greater mobile phone dependency for self-understanding, interaction orientation, and solitary play.

Discussion

By applying media dependency theory in examining the habitual and symbolic use of the globally popular mobile phone, this study contributes to research on media dependency. Furthermore, the globalization of a personal communication technology—the mobile phone—in the past 10 years has raised new questions about the consequence of increasing dependency on the mobile phone and the impact of this globally popular mobile communication technology on individuals, society, and culture. Mobile phone dependency refers to a relationship in which the satisfaction of needs of orientation, understanding, and play is contingent upon the high-tech mobile phone. An earlier cross-cultural survey (Katz, Aakus, Kim, & Turner, 2003) of views on the mobile phone among Korean, European, African, and U.S. college students found a convergence in views toward information technologies in general and the mobile phone in particular. Findings of this cross-cultural study of dependency on the mobile phone among American and Chinese youth suggest that the mobile phone may have flattened the influence of culture in the process of globalization.

First, set in the context of two culturally different countries, the United States (an individualistic culture) and Taiwan (a collectivist culture), any difference in mobile phone dependency between American and Chinese youth would be attributable to the difference in their home culture (this is the logical outcome of the cultural influence model proposed by Hofstede, 1980). Findings of this study show that the overall mobile phone dependency of Chinese youth was higher than American youth. Moreover, given the cultural difference between the two countries, one would expect that Chinese high school students in Taiwan would be less dependent on the mobile phone for self-understanding, interaction orientation, and solitary play than American high school students. The result, however, is the opposite. The Chinese adolescents surveyed in this study were found to be more dependent on the mobile phone for attaining those self-related goals than the American adolescents. Culturally, Chinese youth who grew up and live in a collectivist society like Taiwan would be expected to less egoistic. However, Taiwanese high-school students were found to use the mobile phone as an indispensable means to seek a self-identify. By personalizing their phone, they sought to present themselves as individuals with personality, to manage their lives, and for solitary entertainment.

What are the plausible explanations for this surprising finding? One is the impact of a personal communication and entertainment medium— the mobile phone. Its influence has seemingly prevailed with teens over that of Chinese culture. In using the globally popular mobile phone as self, Chinese youth were found to be individualistic, a departure from the dominant collectivist values in Taiwan. An alternative explanation is that Chinese culture has changed and become individualist. But this explanation does not hold because cultures of a society are stable; in addition, the individualist–collectivist difference between the two samples was statistically significant in this study.

Theoretically speaking, findings of this study provide insights into the debate on the role of new media technologies in globalization: the globalization model (Levitt, 1983) vs. the cultural influence model (Hofstede, 1980). The evidence supports the proposition of new communication technologies as a driving force for globalization. New media play a key role in changing an individual's cultural values. As a personal information and communication technology, the mobile phone is a phenomenon of globalization. Thanks to upgrades to 3G worldwide, global roaming is now closer to seamless than at any other time. Users of popular phones such as Blackberry (12 million in 2007) and iPhone (2 million in America alone in 2007; Wei & Lee, 2008) roam the main streets all over the world. At the same time, as an agent of globalization, it is at the forefront of advancing globalization. For example, a teen culture has emerged around text messaging with a global vocabulary (b2u, xoxo, L8, etc).

Second, this study identified a number of common significant predictors of mobile phone dependency between the U.S. and Taiwan: cultural values, consciousness of mobile phone advertising, and viewing the mobile phone as projected self. Therefore, individualist cultural values, being conscious of ads promoting the mobile phone, and a mobile phone derived identity all play an important role in developing the mobile phone dependency. These findings make theoretical sense in that the mobile phone enables teenagers' presentation of self (Oksman & Turtiainen, 2004).

Third, this study on the role of advertising in developing mobile phone dependency revealed that advertising is influential in developing a dependency relationship with the mobile phone. The more conscious the respondents (both American and Chinese) are of mobile phone advertising, the stronger are their dependency relationships with the wireless device. This particular result indicates that advertising cultivates and validates a consumption culture around the mobile phone because its ubiquitous presence provides social cues to youth. Theoretically, in the words of Bogart (1967), "The real significance of advertising is its total cumulative weight as part of the culture—in the way in which it contributes to the popular lore of ideas and attitudes towards consumer products" (p. 78).

Different predictors between the two countries exist. Lengths of call, use of the mobile phone as a PDA, symbolic use, and mobile phone attitudes are significantly related to mobile phone dependency only in the United States. This pattern makes sense because Americans who grew up with the mobile phone are likely to be dependent on it for staying connected and as a means to project personality. On the other hand, predictors unique in Taiwan include text messaging and e-mailing, although American high school students texted more than Taiwan high school students (the large number of females in the U.S. sample may account for the difference). The results provide some insights into the consequence of a youth culture in which text messaging has been extremely popular in Asia. The more Chinese high school students use text messaging, the more dependent they have become on the mobile phone for meeting information and entertainment needs. In spite of these differences, there are more similarities than differences in the predictors of mobile phone dependency, overall and specific goals, between the U.S. and Taiwan. This means a set of common factors is more dominant than the few different predictors in affecting the dependency relations that American and Chinese youth have developed with the mobile phone.

This conclusion, however, needs to be further tested using samples from more countries. This is a direction for future research. Another limitation of this study is the U.S. sample, which was a convenience sample skewed toward females. In addition, measures of advertising consciousness were limited. More items can be used in future studies to strengthen the measure. Finally, future studies should consider collecting longitudinal data to document more evidence on the role of the massively popular mobile phone in changing cultural values in society.

References

Ball-Rokeach, S. J. (1985). The origins of individual media-system dependency: A sociological framework. *Communication Research, 12*, 485–510.

Ball-Rokeach, S. J. (1998). A theory of media power and a theory of media use: Different stories, questions, and ways of things. *Mass Communication & Society, 1*(1–2), 5–40.

Ball-Rokeach, S. J., & DeFleur, M. L. (1976). A dependency model or mass-media effects. *Communication Research, 3*, 3–21.

Ball-Rokeach, S. J., Rokeach, M., & Grube, J. W. (1984). *The great American value test: Influencing behavior and belief through television.* London: Collier Macmillan.

Bandura, A. (1969). *Principles of behavioral modification,* New York: Holt, Rinehart & Winston.

Berger, P., Berger, B., & Kellner, H. (1974). *The homeless mind: Modernization and consciousness.* New York: Vintage.

Bogart, L. (1967). *Strategy in advertising.* New York: Harcourt Brace.

Briley, D., & Wyer, R. (2001). Transitory determinants of values and decisions: The utility (or non-utility) of individualism and collectivism in understanding cultural differences. *Social Cognition, 19*(3), 197–227.

Bush, A., Smith, R., & Martin, C. (1999). The influence of consumer socialization variables on African-Americans and Caucasians. *Journal of Advertising, 28* (3), 13–24.

Charlton, A., & Bates, C. (2000). Decline in teenage smoking with rise in mobile phone ownership, hypothesis. *British Medical Journal, 321*(4), 1155.

de Boer, C., &Velthuijsen, A. (2001). Participation in conversations about the news. *International Journal of Public Opinion Research, 13*, 140–158

DeFleur, M., & Ball-Rokeach, S. J. (1989). *Theories of mass communication* (5th ed.). New York: Longman.

Ewen, S. (2001). *Captains of consciousness: Advertising and the social roots of the consumer culture.* New York: Basic Books.

Grant, A. (1996). Media dependency and multiple media sources. In A. Crigler

(Ed.), *The psychology of political communication* (pp. 199–248). Ann Arbor, MI: University of Michigan Press.

Grant, A., Kendall, G., & Ball-Rokeach, S. (1991). Television shopping: Media system dependency perspective. *Communication Research, 18*(6), 773–798.

Hofstede, G. (1980). *Culture's consequences: International differences in working-related values.* Beverly Hills, CA: Sage.

Hofstede, G. (1991). *Culture and organizations: Software of the mind.* London: McGraw-Hill.

International Telecommunications Union. (2008). ICT statistics database. Retrieved April 17, 2008, from http://www.itu.int/ITU-D/icteye/Indicators/Indicators.aspx#

Katz, J., & Aakhus, M. (2002). *Perpetual contact: Mobile communication, private talk, public performance.* Cambridge, England: Cambridge University Press.

Katz, J., Aakhus, M., Kim, H., & Turner, M. (2003). Cross-cultural comparisons of ICTs. In L. Fortunati, J. Katz, & R. Riccini (Eds.), *Mediating the human body* (pp 75–86). Mahwah, NJ: Erlbaum.

Katz, J., & Sugiyama, S. (2006). Mobile phones as fashion statements: Evidence from student surveys in the US and Japan. *New Media & Society, 8*(2), 321–337.

Kilbourne, J., & Pipher, M. (2000). *Can't buy my love: How advertising changes the way we think and feel.* New York: Prentice-Hall & IBD.

Lee, J. (May 30, 2002). Tailoring mobile phones for teenagers. *The New York Times.* Retrieved April 5, 2006, from http://www.ntytimes.com/2002/05/30/techn.../30Teen.html

Leung, L., & Wei, R. (2000). More than just talk on the move: A use-and-gratification study of the cellular phone. *Journalism & Mass Communication Quarterly, 77*(2), 308–320.

Levitt, T. (1983, May-June). The globalization of markets. *Harvard Business Review,* 92–113.

Ling, R. (2001). *Adolescent girls and young adult men: Two sub-cultures of the mobile telephone.* Kjeller, Norway: Telenor Research and Development.

Loges, W., & Ball-Rokeach, S. (1993). Dependency relations and newspaper readership. *Journalism & Mass Communication Quarterly, 70*(3), 602–614.

Loges, W., & Jung, J. (2001). Exploring the digital divide: Internet connectedness and age. *Communication Research, 28*(4), 538–564.

Markus, H., & Kitayama, S. (1991). Culture and the self: Implications for cognition, emotion and motivation. *Psychological Review, 98,* 224–253.

McLuhan, M. (1964). *Understanding media: The extensions of man.* New York: McGraw-Hill.

Mobile Marketing Association. (2007). Mobile attitude and usage study: 2007. Retrieved April 5, 2008, from http://www.mmaglobal.com/modules/newbb/viewtopic.php?topic_id=1417&forum=4

Morton, T. A., & Duck, J. M. (2000). Social identity and media dependency in the gay community: The prediction of safe sex attitudes. *Communication Research, 27*(4), 438–460.

Myers, P., & Biocca, F. (1992). The elastic body image: The effect of television advertising and programming on body image distortions in young women. *Journal of Communication, 42,* 108–133.

Nielsen Monitor-Plus Reports. (2005, December 5) U.S. Ad spending rose 2.4% in the first quarter of 2005. Retrieved June 1, 2006, from http://www. nielsenmedia.com/newsreleases/2005/M+Q12005Ad%20Spending.htm

Oksman, V., & J. Turtiainen. (2004). Mobile communication as a social stage: Meanings of mobile communication in everyday life among teenagers in Finland. *New Media & Society, 6*(3), 319–339.

Osgerby, B. (2004). *Youth media.* New York: Routledge.

Patwardhan, P., & Ramaprasad, J. (2004, August). *Internet dependency relations in cross national contexts: A study of American and Indiana Internet Users.* Paper presented at the AEJMC conference, Toronto, Canada.

Patwardhan, P., & Yang, J. (2003). Internet dependency relations and online consumer behavior: A media system dependency perspective on why people shop, chat, and read news online. *Journal of Interactive Advertising, 3*(2), 1–21.

Pollay, R. (1986). The distorted mirror: Reflections on the unintended consequences of advertising. *Journal of Marketing, 50,* 18–93.

Scholte, J. A. (2000) *Globalization. A critical introduction.* London: Palgrave.

Schudson, M. (1984). *Advertising, the uneasy persuasion: Its dubious impact on American society.* New York: Basic Books.

Triandis, H. C. (1995). *Individualism and collectivism.* Boulder, CO: Westview Press.

Tussman, J. (1977). *Government and the mind.* New York: Oxford University Press.

Wackman, D., Wartella, E., & Ward, S. (1977). Learning to be consumers: The role of family. *Journal of Communication, 27*(1), 138–151.

Wei, R. (2006). Lifestyles and new media: Adoption and use of wireless communication technology in China. *New Media & Society, 8*(6), 991–1008.

Wei, R. (2008). Motivations for use of the mobile phone for mass communications and entertainment. *Telematics & Informatics, 25*(1), 36–46.

Wei, R., & Lee, Y. (2008). Telephony. In A. Grant & J. Meadows (Eds.), *Technology update* (11th ed.). Boston: Focal Press.

Williams, R. (1980). *Problems in materialism and culture.* London: Verso.

Yu, L., Loudoen, G., & Sacher, H. (2002). BuddySync: Thinking beyond cell phones to create a third-generation wireless application for U.S. teenagers. Retrieved April 14, 2006, from http://www.pointforward.com/articles/news_items_buddy.html

Chapter 21

Fractured Images

Disability Advertising Effects on Filipino Audiences

Zeny Sarabia-Panol

Societies around the world are striving to be more inclusive of histori-cally underrepresented and disadvantaged minorities and that includes the handicapped. These global efforts on the disability front are seen in recent legislation, nongovernmental initiatives, as well as mass media's attempts, including international advertising, to portray these groups in more responsible and realistic terms.

The United Nations, for instance, has sponsored many programs to examine and improve the status of disabled persons worldwide. Such initiatives include the International Year of Disabled Persons (1981), the United Nations Decade of Disabled Persons (1983–1992), and the Asian and Pacific Decade of Disabled Persons (1993–2002). In May 2002, the Economic and Social Commission for Asia and the Pacific (ESCAP) extended the latter for another decade, 2003–2012.

In terms of legislation, the United States passed the 1990 Americans with Disabilities Act (ADA) that gave civil rights protection to individu-als with disabilities. Similar laws are in place in several other countries such as China, Thailand's 1991 Act, the Philippines' "Magna Carta," and related national laws in Bangladesh, Sri Lanka, and Vietnam (UN, 2003).

With universal focus on the plight of handicapped populations came scholarly attention to the disability culture as a contemporary mass media issue. Most of the research is sparked by the generally accepted notion that the media are powerful in creating awareness and in shaping, reinforcing, or even changing public attitudes (Farnall & Smith, 2000; Nelson, 1996).

Enormous progress has been recorded in the diversity sector as shown by the growing public acceptance or tolerance of individuals with dis-abilities. Several factors can account for this. One, the public has become increasingly more familiar with disabled people as their numbers have grown in the workplace and in educational institutions (Taylor, 1994). Two, depictions of the disabled in the media have improved. Both enter-tainment and news programs in print and broadcast media as well as movies and advertising no longer stigmatize handicapped persons (Burnett & Paul, 1996).

Corporate Interest and International Advertising

Corporations likewise realize that appealing to the disabled population has financial rewards. Aside from attracting new customers, disability advertising can be the company's vehicle to meet social responsibilities and thereby contribute to the mainstreaming of handicapped people (Haller & Ralph, 2001).

Businesses recognize that millions of consumers with disabilities have not been targeted with the same rigor and sophistication as other ethnic and gender groups. As a result, 100 high-profile companies, including the world's leading advertiser Procter and Gamble, have moved into this market frontier over the past 10 years (Williams, 1999).

There are at least two good reasons to look into the international aspects of the disability issue, including international advertising that contains disability messages or characters: (1) the continued globalization of business, and (2) advances in communication technology that have made national boundaries porous.

As corporations increase their offshore operations and are tapping worldwide markets for their products, the need to understand international audiences and subcultures such as those to which the disabled belong, gains more primacy. But while there is consensus on the importance of market and audience studies, very little research has been done to empirically test the impact on public attitudes of advertising messages that incorporate images of diversity such as those featuring the disabled. This study investigates the perceptual effects on Filipino audiences of ads containing images of people with disabilities.

Disability Advertising: Mixed Results

Even in the United States, the use of handicapped individuals in advertising has received mixed reactions. Nike's use of paraplegic athletes in their campaign, for example, drew criticism for perpetuating the "super crip" syndrome where a disabled individual defies all odds through sheer heroic determination (Bainbridge, 1997). Other advertisements such as those of Dow Chemical and Burger King, where persons with Down syndrome took center stage, stirred public controversy as well. Critics said the ads were exploitative and condescending. Supporters insist that the ads are a significant breakthrough in depicting the mentally handicapped, perhaps the last untapped group in the new genre of disability advertising (Goldman, 1993).

Overall, global companies that took a proactive approach by showing physically impaired people in their ads, have had positive experiences as a result. McDonald's, one of the first companies to do so, reported a marked increase in business from blind, deaf, and mobility-impaired customers. The same is true for Levi's, IBM, General Motors, and others (Williams, 1999). Still, many corporations remain cautious. Many do not want to alienate the larger market of able-bodied consumers in their attempts to appeal to disabled people. Nor do they want to enrage the disabled community by insensitive or inappropriate depictions.

All told, embracing diversity has its costs and benefits, reasons that would make a persuasive case for careful research on advertising effectiveness, particularly in relation to the use of disability portrayals geared toward domestic and international audiences. Using the experimental design, this study will attempt to measure the effects of advertising that contains disability images on the Filipino public's attitudes. As an initial attempt, the investigation hopes to provide a glimpse, albeit small and preliminary, to Philippine attitudes toward mediated disability messages. By exploring the relationship between advertising and disability-related attitudes, the research aims to produce useful/practical information for communication practitioners in the United States and abroad as well as add to the growing body of media and disability research.

Filipinos are in general an understudied group. Yet as consumers they have been consistently targeted by both domestic and international advertisers (DeMooij, 2005; Nelson, 1994). Over the past decade or so there also has been a growing public awareness of the plight of people with disabilities not just in the Philippines but throughout Asia (Fermin, 2003). A compelling case can be made therefore for assessing Filipino perceptions of mediated disability portrayals, not simply to fill the void in the academic literature but also because commercial institutions have slowly begun to pay attention to this consumer group in the Philippines.

Literature Review

The term *international advertising* refers to "advertising from another country or to global advertising, or to the international dimension of the advertising agency business" (Banerjee, 2000, p. 22). The classic debate whether to standardize or specialize international advertising has continued to occupy the attention of both academics and practitioners alike.

The diversity of markets and cultural differences has been used to justify specialization. De Mooij (2005) has argued that "it is the culture of the consumer that should be reflected in advertising" (p. 7). Furthermore, culture was found to impact execution more than creative strategy in international advertising. This suggests that a single creative strategy may work globally as long as its execution accounts for culture (Wei & Jiang, 2005). This paper is making the case that a disability culture exists and international advertisers need to be in touch with the sensibilities of both the able-bodied and handicapped audiences.

There are three major streams of research on disability and the mass media:

1. Research that looked at content and media portrayals (Elliott, Byrd, & Byrd, 1983; Haller & Ralph, 2001; Longmore, 1987; Nelson, 1996; Parker, 2001; Thompson & Wassmuth, 2001; Zola, 1995).
2. Research that identified public attitudes and the direction of media-mediated changes in these attitudes (Donaldson, 1981; Farnall, 1996; Haefner, 1976; Panol & McBride, 1999);
3. Research that assessed the media habits of disabled persons (Burnett & Paul, 1996; Ganahl & Kallem, 1998).

Earlier studies of media content and portrayals of the ability-impaired have indicated the absence or minimal presence of the disabled in various media, and where depictions existed, these were stereotypical and negative (Elliott et al, 1983). Marked improvements, however, were noted in later studies: greater numbers of handicapped people appeared in the media and the portrayals were becoming positive and realistic. Still, the proportion of disability advertisements on prime time television is abysmally low compared with the actual handicapped population in the United States (Ganahl & Arbuckle, 2001). With the advent of the Web, at least one study analyzed banner ad images of the disabled. Thompson and Wassmuth (2001) found that banner ads in 67 online newspapers failed to use accessible content.

Farnall (1996) examined the influence of positive television advertising images on previously held attitudes toward the disabled. The independent variables tested were varied exposure levels of positive stereotypes of disabled characters in the commercials, time lag, and amount of elaboration. The research also looked at gender and personal familiarity with disability. No significant changes overall were indicated, although differences were determined based on degree of familiarity and previous exposure to television and film portrayals.

The differences can be explained in part by the results of the 1991 U.S. survey commissioned by the National Organization on Disability (1991) which highlighted the fact that one in three Americans are personally familiar with a handicapped person. The survey also found that a significant percentage of Americans who have seen at least two television programs or movies reported a change of attitude toward the disabled.

In a much earlier study that attempted to directly measure the impact of advertising messages about the disabled on public attitudes, Haefner (1976) found that 10 different prime time television spots did encourage employers to hire and train persons with disabilities. Not only were there higher recall and comprehension rates than are usual for information campaigns, the treatment groups indicated positive behavioral intentions to hire handicapped applicants.

The Disability Issue in Asia

The United Nations estimates that in the Asian and Pacific region there are about 400 million people with disabilities, by far the largest population of handicapped persons in the world. The UN Economic and Social Commission for Asia and the Pacific (UNESCAP; 2003) notes that despite recent achievements, most of these people "are poor, their concerns unknown and their rights overlooked."

Lewis (1994) wrote that East Asian norms would view a disabled person as one needing a caretaker, typically a family member. While the willingness of Asian families to care for the handicapped is admirable, this strong caretaker model perpetuates a lifestyle of helplessness and dependence.

According to Kaufman-Scarborough (2002),

> culturally-determined mindsets of therapeutic, medical, sympathetic, and philanthropic views of disability affect the expectation that many disabled persons have the potential to participate significantly, if not fully, in society. That mindset, which can be used to legislate fair access, while creating more access, also tends to reinforce the view that disabled persons need to be helped rather than to be viewed as peers. (p. 390)

Central to the disability discussion in Asia, as in many countries in the developing world, are the issues of attitude and access, which are shaped by culture, education, and the mass media. Access to technology such as wheelchairs that allow disabled individuals in the United States to live independent lives is often problematic in Asia. For developing nations in that geographical area, the cost of owning and maintaining wheelchairs can be prohibitive. In areas where the technology is available at reasonable cost, prevailing cultural attitudes that mandate the permanently disabled to remain in the family system often discourage the use of such tools to develop independent lifestyles (Lewis, 1994).

Another obstacle that is particularly found among developing nations on the macrolevel is economic in nature. Komardjaja (2001) wrote,

"Marginalization of people with disabilities is not deemed a significant problem in contemporary Indonesia.... Only when basic human needs have been met and social justice and equity are assured can people with disabilities demand access" (p. 102). Thus, in the case of conflicting priorities, the handicapped receive lower consideration than other groups.

Asian Media

International organizations such as the UN, which work primarily with governments, and the Canada-based Disabled Peoples International, which has collaborative arrangements with nongovernmental institutions, have both used the mass media to raise social awareness and improve conditions of the world's disabled population. Coverage of disability issues by international media, however, is best described as scant and often tends to perpetuate the charity model with a preponderance of news about fund-raising events (Haller & Ralph, 2001; Lewis, 1994).

In Asia, as in other parts of the globe, attitudes toward the disabled that range from pity to ridicule are a major barrier to full integration. Moreover, in certain Asian societies, a disability is often associated with an earlier misbehavior, a kind of "punishment" for a transgression or bad conduct; hence the handicapped person deserves his or her fate. Parker (2001) added that "...in some instances, a family member with a disability is perceived as a disgrace to the family" (p. 105). These stereotypical images and negative attitudes can, however, change with education and positive media exposure (Longmore, 1987; Nelson, 1996).

Profile of the Philippine Disability Sector

There is heightened awareness of the condition of people with disabilities in the Philippines. The UN Decade for the Disabled (1983–1992) brought about a sharper focus on the issues that affect the close to a million Filipinos with disabilities. The decade saw stronger government and private sector efforts designed to address needs such as disability prevention, rehabilitation, and promotion of the rights of persons with disabilities (Gumiran, 1999).

Based on the 2000 survey by the National Statistics Office (2005), there are 942,098 handicapped Filipinos or about 1.23% of the country's population. Of this number, there is an almost even split between Filipino men and women with disabilities. The median age is 49. The majority live in rural areas, some 69.43% are literate, and about half are economically active. The types of disability include: blindness, hearing impairment, speech defects, loss of or paralysis of arms or legs, mental retardation, or mental illness (National Statistics Office, 2005).

Role of Government

The 1990s saw significant strides in legislation that promoted the rights and welfare of the disabled in the Philippines. The Magna Carta for Disabled Persons or Republic Act No. 7277 was promulgated to provide rehabilitation and develop self-reliance among disabled Filipinos by ensuring access to training and employment opportunities. Another law *Batas Pambansa Bilang 344,* also known as the Accessibility Law, required public buildings to install facilities that enhance the mobility of handicapped people.

But while these efforts placed disability issues such as employment and other rights on the public agenda, the country still has a long way to go in realizing the goal of fully integrating the handicapped population in the Philippines. As a participant of UNESCAP's Biwako Millennium Framework for Action toward an Inclusive, Barrier-Free and Rights-Based Society for Persons with Disabilities in Asia and the Pacific, the Philippines marked the 21st century with a number of projects that resulted in two milestone documents: the "Manila Declaration on Accessible ICT" and "Manila Accessible ICT Design Recommendations" (Fermin, 2003).

President Gloria Macapagal-Arroyo also issued Proclamation No. 240 declaring the period 2003 to year 2012 as the "Philippine Decade of Persons with Disabilities." The proclamation is touted as "another manifestation of the government's ardent desire for the total development of the sector of disability" (Fermin, 2003).

The National Council for the Welfare of Disabled Persons is the leading Philippine government agency tasked with the promotion and protection of the rights of people with disabilities. Established in 1978, the council instituted programs to improve accessibility, advocacy, interagency coordination, and establish community-based rehabilitation. In its advocacy role, the council has used various Philippine media to provide visibility and a forum for the discussion of disability issues.

Mass Media Portrayals

Philippine media, in general, have shown sensitivity in the portrayal of people with disabilities especially during the 1990s. Companies have begun to show disabled characters in their commercials. Notable among these are a local cell phone company (Globe) that promoted the use of "texting" by featuring mute people courting and proposing marriage via text messages sent on the cell phone. Another multinational corporation used blind models in a Palmolive soap advertisement extolling beautiful skin that was soft to touch because they could tell smoothness of the skin by simply touching. Additionally, one of the public service campaigns of a Manila rehabilitation facility called the *Tahanang Walang Hagdan*, which literally means a "house without stairs," featured handicapped men playing basketball.

These are, of course, a monumental departure from years of negative stereotyping in Philippine media that often depicted the handicapped as criminals, objects of ridicule, pitiful or helpless beings, or superheroes (Borjal, 1988).

Problem and Hypotheses

This research attempts to evaluate the impact of print advertising containing different types of visually detected disabilities on the attitudes of nondisabled Philippine audiences.

Attitudes that are "learned predispositions to respond in a consistently favorable or unfavorable manner with respect to a given object" (Fishbein & Ajzen, 1975, p. 6) have different dimensions. Liebert (1975) proposed that attitudes have three components: cognitive, affective, and behavioral. The cognitive domain consists of beliefs or mental predispositions acquired through information given to the individual. The affective component is based on emotional reactions to a stimulus, while the behavioral element refers to the action prompted by the cognitive and affective spheres of attitudes.

Clearly, past research that investigated the impact of mass media or advertising portrayals of the disabled did not explore all three dimensions of attitudes. Some portrayals dealt with either just the cognitive or affective aspects or both. One assessed behavioral intention (Haefner, 1976), but none covered all attitudinal aspects; most studied television or film, which have strong affective elements as media (Wilcox, Cameron, Ault, & Agee, 2003). Scant attention was given to print, much less print advertising. This study attempts to fill in these research gaps.

The main research interests are: (1) corporate advertising using the print medium; (2) variations in the presentation of disabled characters; and (3) the influence of these stimuli on viewer attitudes.

The primary research question is: What are the effects on Filipino perceptions, feelings, and behavior of print advertisements that depict a disability? Will the impact vary according to the presence or absence of disability images?

This study will test the following hypotheses:

H1. Depending on the nature of the company business and advertising messages, Philippine audiences shown print ads depicting disabled persons will manifest differences in perception, feeling, and behavior compared to those shown ads that portray models with no visually detectable impairments.

H2. A positive relationship exists between perception and try/use intention, purchase intention and feeling, as well as try/use and purchase intention of respondents shown ads with or without persons with disabilities.

H3. A strong positive relationship exists between the cognitive and affective responses of those shown disability and nondisability advertisements.

H4. Subjects that are shown ads that depict models with visually discernible handicaps will respond more negatively than those shown ads that contain both disabled and able-bodied characters.

Method

An experiment using a factorial with completely randomized block design was used to test the hypotheses. The research's primary instrument consisted of print ads featuring blind or mobility-impaired men or women. The experimental variables, that is, attitudinal dimensions (perception, feeling, purchase and use intention), were operationally defined as the score on a 1 to 7 scale measuring positive or negative response, with a score of 1 being most positive and 7 most negative.

This is an instrument replication of a 1999 study done by the author and a colleague. Some modifications, however, were introduced on both the experimental ads and questionnaire to suit the Philippine audience and the additional variables introduced. For instance, translations in Cebuano and Tagalog of certain terms were provided in the questionnaire. A completely new experimental design was used in the present study.

Respondents

Ten groups of 22 students each or a total of 220 respondents compose the sample population. College students were from two major universities in the Philippines (one in the Visayas and the other in Metro Manila).

All subjects in each group were shown institutional ads containing environmental, philanthropic, and employee recognition messages with the experimental ads depicting various disabled characters. Subjects were then asked to complete a questionnaire.

Originally, the 10 groups varied in number from 22 to 33 students. Since the planned statistical evaluation required equal sample sizes, the lowest number of 22 was used as the base. To achieve the necessary balanced data, the other groups exceeding 22 were reduced randomly using computer-generated random numbers. However, it was not possible to obtain ideal gender balance in the sample. Of 220 respondents, 181 or

82% were female and 39 or 18% were male. Mean age is 18.66 years with a narrow age range of 17 to 20 years.

Treatments

Corporate messages included four nondisability ads and six disability ads of fictitious companies. Use of hypothetical companies was intended to control for prior knowledge or opinions of real companies. Four ads were shown to each group. The control group was shown four nondisability ads only. The rest of the groups were shown a mix of disability and nondisability ads. This arrangement enabled two groups to be lumped as one experimental treatment in the analysis, thus providing 44 samples per treatment ad. The companies include an independent distributor, a charitable trust, a hi-tech, and a health-care provider.

In testing the sixth hypothesis on the response differences toward ads that contain only disabled characters versus ads that portrayed both disabled and able-bodied individuals, two ad treatments each were combined for the disabled group and the combined disabled and nondisabled set. This allowed for a total of 88 sample population per group.

Three attitudinal dimensions including perception, feeling, and product purchase or service use intention (behavioral) were measured for all ads.

Statistical Analysis

A two-way analysis of variance (ANOVA) with replication was used to test the equality of treatment means. The assumptions of normally distributed population, equal variances, and independent random samples are satisfied. The balanced data, that is, the same number of respondents in all 10 groups, allowed the use of two-way ANOVA. The focus of the analysis was on the differences in mean values between the treatment ads of the four companies and on the differences in mean values between the disability and nondisability ads of each company.

The existence of relationships between perception and feeling, on the one hand, and purchase and use intentions, on the other, was determined using linear regression analysis. Separate regression analysis for each combination of attitudinal dimensions, that is, purchase intention-perception, purchase-intention feeling, use intention-perception, and use intention-feeling was performed for each type of ad. Purchase or use intentions served as the response variables while perception or feeling were the explanatory variables in each analysis.

Another regression analysis was performed to determine relationships between perception and feeling.

Results and Discussion

Table 21.1 summarizes the overall mean responses and ANOVA for the nondisability and disability ads. The ANOVA indicates the existence of significant differences in mean values between the attitudinal dimensions (sample) and between the company ads (columns). Results support the predicted variation in perception, feeling and behavior of nondisabled audiences that were shown different corporate print ads portraying handicapped characters compared to those who saw ads with nondisabled models. The degree of response differences depended on the type of company and the nature of advertising messages.

The charitable trust company ads with a philanthropic message and featuring a nondisabled child (Ad1) and a child in a wheelchair (Ad2) were rated the most positive overall. This confirms the universal appeal of children in advertising regardless of culture and the presence or absence of a physical impairment (Haller & Ralph, 2001). There was hardly any difference in appeal between the unimpaired child and the one in a wheelchair.

Overall, the least positive ad is the health-care company's Ad2 depicting a medical specialist in a wheelchair, followed by Ad1 of the same company. The mean scores of these ads in two attitudinal levels (feeling and use intention/purchase intention) were statistically significant compared with those of the other corporate ads. The medical-related nature of the message in these ads could have affected the respondents' cognition and negative behavioral response. Although not statistically significant, the perception scores of these two ads are actually high or significantly negative.

The greater resistance toward health-related advertising featuring a mobility-impaired physician can be partly explained by the relative obscurity of such a practitioner in the typical Filipino experience (Gumiran, 1999). This could have created the overwhelming expectation that for a doctor to be competent, he or she should not have any visible disability.

The distributor company's Ad2 has the 3rd least positive overall score, followed by its Ad1. The highest score (most negative) occurred in the purchase intention of this distributor company's Ad2 that conveys an environmental message with a picture of three disabled characters, a blind man and woman together with a woman on crutches. The apparent refusal to purchase a product or use a service is understandable even for an environmentally oriented company because by the nature of the advertisement shown, no direct promotion was made for particular products or services. Moreover, since a hypothetical company was used, no association could be made with any product. It is, therefore, pos-

Table 21.1 Mean Responses and ANOVA: Disability and Non-Disability Ads

	Attitudinal Dimension		Distribution Company		Charitable Trust		Health-care Company		Technology Company		Averge
	Ad1	Ad2	Ad1	Ad2	Ad1	Ad2	Ad1	Ad2	Ad3	Ad4	
Perception	2.77	2.61	1.82	1.82	3.07	3.19	2.32	2.66	2.43	2.11	2.47
Feeling	2.89	2.79	2.84	3.16	3.45*	3.65*	2.84	3	2.73	2.54	2.99
Try/Use Intention	3.2*	3.45*	2.57	2.36	3.52*	3.48*	2.77	3.14	3.11	3.11	3.07
Purchase Intention	3.48*	3.91*	2.64	2.3	3.7*	3.75*	3.16	3.05	3.3*	3.09	3.23
Average	3.09	3.19	2.47	2.41	3.44	3.51	2.77	2.96	2.88	2.72	

* Significant between rows (sample) at 95% confidence level

ANOVA

Source of Variation	SS	Df	MS	F	P-value	F crit
Sample	139.979	3	46.659	32.399	2.27E-20	3.011
Columns (Ads)	219.744	9	24.415	16.923	5.32E-27	1.885
Interaction	75.913	27	2.812	1.9488	0.0025	1.492
Within	2481.568	1720	1.4428			
Total	2917.204	1759				

Notes: Ad1 = Non-disability ads; Ad2, Ad3, Ad4 = Disability ads.

sible that with a company known for certain products, the results may differ.

The hi-tech company's Ad3 that portrays outstanding employees, a female in a wheelchair and a nondisabled male, also had statistically significant negative score for purchase intention. Evidently, even if a company promotes itself as a good place to work, its image is affected if it shows one of the two outstanding employees in the ad as disabled. Perceptions of workplace safety could be a factor here since the advertiser used is in the manufacturing industry. For Ad3, however, sample characteristics specifically that 82% were female may account for the negative purchase intention.

The hypothesized differences in mean response between those shown disability ads and nondisability ads (Ad1 vs. Ad2) of the same company (H2) were not supported based on values in Table 21.1 and as obtained in a separate ANOVA undertaken for each company. The absence of differences points to an emerging integration trend of disabled individuals into the mainstream of Philippine society. Due to efforts by government, the media, and organizations such as the United Nations to put the disability issue on the public agenda, Filipinos have become aware and are slowly accepting of the idea that people with disabilities have rights and can lead independent lives. Where differences occurred, the nature of the advertising message such as the one that was health-related may explain the adverse reactions toward the ad more than the presence or absence of disabled characters.

Perception and Purchase or Use Intention

Table 21.2a presents the degree of relationships between perceptual and behavioral effects such as try/use intention and purchase intention. Based on Table 21.2a, the second hypothesis is supported in 7 out of the 10 use intention-perception regression analyses. The same is true in the 10 purchase intention-perception regression analyses. As a whole, a positive cognitive response directly influenced the desire to use or purchase a company's product or service. The R Square values showed that a range of 17.02 to 46.64% explains the degree of change in use and purchase intentions as a result of positive perception of the corporate advertisement.

Feeling and Purchase or Use Intention

Table 21.2b shows the test results on the degree of relationship between feeling and the two behavioral effects (try/use intention and purchase intention).

The regression equation for Ad2 of the hi-tech firm (Table 21.2b) yielded the highest R Square of 74.43% in the try/use intention-feeling

Table 21.2a Summary Regression Statistics for Relationships Between Perception and Behavior of Respondents Shown Non-disability and Disability Ads

COMPANY/Ad		Try/Use Intention - Perception			Purchase Intention - Perception		
		R Square (%)	P-value	t-Statistics	R Square (%)	P-value	t-Statistics
Distributor	Ad1	19.73	0.0025	3.213	0.56*	0.623	0.495
Co.	Ad2	17.02	0.0054	2.935	23.38	0.0009	3.581
Charitable	Ad1	1.11*	0.4951	-0.688	1.39*	0.4448	-0.771
Trust	Ad2	33.61	9.81E-05	4.304	33.25	4.19E-05	4.574
Health	Ad1	37.27	1.08E-05	4.996	22.45	0.0012	3.4873
Care Co.	Ad2	0.65*	0.6029	0.5241	2.54*	0.3018	1.045
Technology	Ad1	43.20	1.257E-06	5.652	43.21	1.251E-06	5.653
Co.	Ad2	34.31	2.948E-05	4.684	31.95	6.602E-05	4.431
	Ad3	42.34	1.74E-06	5.554	43.75	1.02E-06	5.715
	Ad4	2.02*	0.3574	-0.930	46.64	3.27E-07	6.059

relationship. Ad2 shows two stellar employees of a technology company with a disabled male in a wheelchair and a healthy female. The same Ad2 of this hi-tech company has the highest R Square (49.77%) in the purchase intention-feeling relationship. The other ads have R Square range of 12.68 to 39.82% that are all significant except for three ads each in purchase intention-feeling and use intention-feeling relationships marked by asterisks. Since a positive relationship exists, the fourth hypothesis is supported with the above qualifications.

Table 21.2b Summary Regression Statistics for Relationships Between Feeling and Behavior of Respondents Shown Non-disability and Disability Ads

COMPANY/Ad		Try/Use Intention - Perception			Purchase Intention - Perception		
		R Square (%)	P-value	t-Statistics	R Square (%)	P-value	t-Statistics
Distributor	Ad1	5.72	0.1182	1.595	33.89	4.01E-05	4.5885
Co.	Ad2	17.35	0.0049	2.969	6.51*	0.0945	1.710
Charitable	Ad1	9.73*	0.0393	-2.128	6.35*	0.0989	-1.6881
Trust	Ad2	30.61	0.00021	4.060	8.40*	0.0563	1.962
Health	Ad1	30.73	9.45E-05	4.317	43.53	1.11E-06	5.690
Care Co.	Ad2	32.37	5.59E-05	4.483	28.17	0.00021	4.058
Technology	Ad1	34.07	3.19E-05	4.659	39.82	4.39E-06	5.272
Co.	Ad2	75.43	2.204E-14	11.356	49.77	8.917E-08	6.451
	Ad3	21.74	0.00142	3.416	31.24	8.02E-05	4.369
	Ad4	3.27*	0.23986	-1.192	37.41	1.03E-05	5.011

Ad4 of the technology company had very low R square values for both try/use intention-perception and try/use intention-feeling relationship. This is an anomaly because this disability ad had strong relationship values for both purchase intention-perception and purchase intention-feeling. This result is difficult to explain but may be attributed to sample characteristics such as the age of respondents and the fact that the majority, being students, did not hold full-time jobs, which can affect purchase decisions.

Perception and Feeling

Table 21.3 reveals a strong relationship between perception and feeling of respondents that viewed disability and non-disability ads. The third hypothesis is, therefore, supported. One exception is Ad1 of the distribution company where the R square value was only 0.38%. The highest R square value of 61.90% was obtained in the technology company's Ad1, followed by Ad3 for the same company with a value of 48.87%. Overall, the relationship was strongest with the hi-tech company's ads, followed by those of the health-care company. This finding implies a consistency between the cognitive and affective impact of the ads. In other words, a positive perception of an ad would more likely evoke favorable feelings toward it.

Disability Only Versus Combination of Disability and Nondisability Groups

Table 21.4 does not provide support for the fourth hypothesis that predicted differences in mean response toward the ads portraying disabled

Table 21.3 Summary Regression Statistics for Relationships Between Perception and Feeling of Respondents Shown Non-disability and Disability Ads

COMPANY	Ad	Perception - Feeling		
		R Square (%)	P-value	t-Statistics
Distributor Co.	Ad1	0.38*	0.6919	0.399
	Ad2	29.19	0.0002	4.161
Charitable Trust	Ad1	8.24	0.0589	1.942
	Ad2	12.74	0.0174	2.476
Health-care Co.	Ad1	42.23	1.81E-06	5.541
	Ad2	24.01	0.0007	03.643
Technology Co.	Ad1	61.90	2.43E-10	8.260
	Ad2	48.87	1.3E-07	6.336
	Ad3	55.86	5.59E-09	7.291
	Ad4	45.53	5.09E-07	5.925

persons only (Group I) and ads depicting a mix of disabled and non-disabled individuals (Group II). The *P-value* of 0.6931 for "Columns" source of variation indicates a very high probability of drawing the sample from a population where no differences in response exist. The F and F *critical* values likewise indicate nonsignificance between the columns source of variation. The hypothesis, therefore, is rejected as no significant differences in response were recorded between those shown ads portraying disabled persons only and those exposed to ads with both disabled and nondisabled individuals.

From these results, it would seem that Filipinos don't have problems integrating disabled people with able-bodied individuals in advertisements. This may be attributed to the Filipino culture where people with disabilities are cared for by their families. With an aging population, having partially impaired family members is not uncommon. It is interesting though that such attitudinal integration was carried into a public sphere because normally disabled family members are not often seen in public.

However, as in Table 21.1, there are significant differences in response between the various attitudinal dimensions; that is, increasingly becoming negative from cognitive to behavioral components in both groups. There appears to be a disconnect or inconsistency in respondents' perceptions, true feelings, and behavioral intentions. This finding confirms past observations that awareness does not automatically or easily

Table 21.4 Summary of Mean Responses and ANOVA: Grouped Data

Attitudinal Dimension	Group I	Group II	Average
Perception	2.36	2.55	2.45
Feeling	2.67	2.86	2.77
Try/Use Intention	3.28*	3.13	3.20*
Purchase Intention	3.50*	3.14	3.32*
Average	2.95	2.92	2.92

*Significant between rows (sample) at 95% confidence level
ANOVA

Source of Variation	SS	dF	MS	F	P-value	F crit.
Sample	84.220	3	28.0734	18.2289	2.14E-11	2.6177
Columns	0.2401	1	0.2401	0.1559	0.6931	3.8548
Interaction	9.7884	3	3.2627	2.1186	0.0965	2.6177
Within	1071.87	696	1.5400			
Total	1166.12	703				

Note: Group I is composed of the distributor company's Ad2 and technology company's Ad4 (with-disability group) while Group II included the technology company's Ad2 and Ad3 (mixed group).

translate to favorable feelings, much less positive behavior. To effect behavior change, communication is not a sufficient condition. Rogers (2003) identified at least five factors that affect whether or not people will adopt a new idea or product. These are relative advantage, compatibility, complexity, trialability, and observability.

Conclusion

Conventional knowledge usually indicates that Third World countries such as the Philippines would lag behind the more developed nations in many aspects. In the case of the disability issue, it would seem that the Philippines is catching up. The study suggests that Filipinos, at least those who were sampled, can integrate people with discernible impairments in advertising. They didn't have negative attitudes about advertisements that featured disabled characters separately, nor did they show negative attitudes toward ad images combining able-bodied and disabled persons. The increasing visibility of this minority group in the media and their generally positive portrayals during recent years (i.e., working artists who are disabled) appear to have succeeded in transforming culturally driven values that for centuries impeded the ability of disabled Filipinos to lead relatively independent and economically active lives (Fermin, 2003).

For international advertisers, this research presents additional confirmation of some universal appeals, particularly that of children, regardless of the presence or absence of a visible disability. In terms of message strategy, however, caution must be exercised since there are topics that don't seem to gel harmoniously with disability advertising images. The case of the health message given using a paraplegic physician is a case in point. As in other communication, cultural idiosyncrasies are important variables to consider. But while similarities can be located in advertising audiences regardless of countries, it would be foolhardy to ignore the heterogeneity that seems to account for the increasing fragmentation of markets that include emerging ones such as disabled communities and other minority groups in the international arena.

The study likewise corroborates what scholars have said about the complex relationships between and among attitudinal aspects that are in play when audiences are exposed to mediated commercial messages (Farnall, 1996; Mehta & Davis, 1990; Ostrom, Petty, & Brock, 1981). The complicated nature of information processing that occurs at the perceptual, emotional, and behavioral levels seemed to reverberate, as this study implies, with advertising that is inclusive of disabled individuals as well. Indeed the discrepancies that surfaced between awareness, feelings, and purchase/use intention show that it is not a straight express route to advertising effectiveness.

Some future research directions include: an empirical analysis of Philippine media content to evaluate trends pertaining to disability, a study of media habits of disabled Filipinos, and a larger attitude survey geared toward identifying culturally held perceptions of people with disabilities, changes in Philippine attitudes, and segments of the population holding specific attitudes. These research initiatives will undoubtedly help public policy makers and communication professionals alike.

References

Bainbridge, J. (1997). Overcoming ad disabilities. *Marketing, 8.*

Banerjee, A. (2000). International advertising developments In J. P. Jones (Ed.), *International advertising realities and myths.* Thousand Oaks, CA: Sage.

Borjal, A. A. (1988). *The role of media in disability prevention, rehabilitation and equalisation of opportunities for disabled persons (Philippine experience).* Paper presented at the 16th World Congress of Rehabilitation International, Tokyo.

Burnett, J. J., & Paul, P. (1996). Assessing the media habits and needs of the mobility-disabled consumer. *Journal of Advertising, 25*(3), 47–59.

De Mooij, M. (2005). *Global marketing and advertising.* Thousand Oaks, CA: Sage.

Donaldson, J. (1981). Changing attitudes toward handicapped persons: A review and analysis of research. *Exceptional Children, 46*(7), 504–514.

Elliott, T. R., Byrd, E. K., & Byrd, P. D. (1983). An examination of disability as depicted on prime-time television. *Journal of Rehabilitation, 49,* 39–42.

Farnall, O. (1996). *Positive images of the disabled in television advertising: Effects on attitude toward the disabled.* Paper presented to the Association for Education in Journalism and Mass Communication.

Farnall, O., & Smith, K. A. (2000). Reactions to people with disabilities: Personal contact versus viewing of specific media portrayals. *Journalism and Mass Communication Quarterly, 76*(4). 659–672.

Fermin, C. (2003). *Country paper on the elaboration of the proposed international convention on disability.* Manilla, Philippines: National Council for the Welfare of Disabled Persons.

Fishbein, M. & Azjen, I. (1975). *Belief, attitude, intention, and behavior.* Reading, MA: Addison-Wesley.

Ganahl, D., & Arbuckle, M. (2001, Spring). The exclusion of persons with physical disabilities from prime-time television advertising: A two-year quantitative analysis [Electronic version]. *Disability Studies Quarterly, 21*(2).

Ganahl, D. & Kallem, J. (1998). *Physiographic aggregation and segmentation: Inclusion of visually detected physically impaired role models in advertisements.* Paper presented to the Association for Education in Journalism and Mass Communication.

Goldman, K. (1993, September 3). Ad with disabled child stirs controversy. *Wall Street Journal.* p. B8.

Gumiran, I. (1999). *A communication campaign study of the National Council for the Welfare of Disabled Persons on the issue of equalization of opportunities and employment for persons with disabilities.* Unpublished master's thesis. University of the Philippines, College of Mass Communication. Diliman, Quezon City, Philippines.

Haefner, J. E. (1976). Can TV advertising influence employers to hire or train disadvantaged persons? *Journalism Quarterly, 53*(2), 95–102.

Haller, B. & Ralph, S. (2001). Profitability, diversity, and disability images in advertising in the United States and Great Britain [Electronic version]. *Disability Studies Quarterly, 21*(2).

Kaufman-Scarborough, C. (2002). Disabilities access in cross-cultural settings: The case of the Republic of Korea. In *Conference Proceedings* (Vol. 13, p. 390). Chicago: American Marketing Association.

Komardjaja, I. (2001). The malfunction of barrier-free spaces in Indonesia. *Disability Studies Quarterly, 21*(2), 97–104.

Leonard, B. D. (1978). *Impaired view: Television portrayal of handicapped people.* Unpublished doctoral dissertation, Boston University.

Lewis, C. S. (1994). International aspects of the disability issue. In J. A. Nelson (Ed.), *The disabled, the media, and the information age* (pp. 189–195). Westport, CT: Greenwood Press.

Liebert, R. M. (1975). *Television and attitudes toward the handicapped.* Albany, NY: New York State Education Department.

Longmore, P. K. (1987). Screening stereotypes: Images of disabled people in television and motion pictures. In A. Garner & T. Joe (Eds.), *Images of the disabled, disability images* (pp. 65–78). New York: Praeger.

Mehta, A., & Davis, C. M. (1990). *Celebrity advertising: Perception, persuasion and processing.* Paper presented at AEJMC Annual Conference, Minneapolis, MN.

National Organization on Disability. (1991). *Public attitudes toward persons with disabilities* (Research Report No. 912028). New York: Louis Harris.

National Statistics Office. (2005). *Persons with disability comprised 1.23 percent of the total population* (Special release no. 150). Manila, Philippines. http://www.nso.ph

Nelson, J. (Ed.). (1994). *The disabled, the media, and the information age.* Westport, CT: Greenwood.

Nelson, J. A. (1996). *The invisible cultural group.* In P. M. Lester (Ed.), *Images of disability, images that injure: Pictorial stereotypes in the media* (pp. 114–132). Westport, CT: Praeger.

Panol, Z., & McBride, M. (1999, August 3–8). *Print advertising images of the disabled: Exploring the impact on non-disabled consumer attitudes.* Paper presented at the Association of Educators in Journalism and Mass Communication. New Orleans, Louisiana.

Parker, K. J. (2001). Changing attitudes towards persons with disabilities in Asia. *Disability Studies Quarterly, 21*(4), 105–113).

Preston, I. (1982). The association model of the advertising communication process. *Journal of Advertising, 11*(2), 3–15.

Preston, I., & Thorson, E. (1984). The expanded association model: Keeping the hierarchy concept alive. *Journal of Advertising Research, 24*(1), 59–66.

Rogers, E. (2003). *Diffusion of innovations* (5th ed.). New York: Free Press.

Taylor, H. (1994, May 10). N.O.D. survey of Americans with disabilities. *Business Week.*

Thompson, D., & Wassmuth, B. (2001). Accessibility of online advertising: A content analysis of alternative text for banner ad images in online newspapers [Electronic version]. *Disability Studies Quarterly, 21*(4).

United Nations. (2003). http://www.un.org

UN Economic and Social Commission for Asia and the Pacific (UNESCAP). (2003). Highlights of the Asian and Pacific Decade of Disabled Persons, 1993–2002 (Social Policy Paper No. 13). http://www.unescap.org.

Wei, R., & Jiang, J. (2005). Exploring culture's influence on standardization dynamics of creative strategy and execution in international advertising. *Journalism and Mass Communication Quarterly, 82*(4), 838–856.

Wilcox, D. L., Cameron, G., Ault, P. H., & Agee, W. K. (2003). *Public relations strategies and tactics* (7th ed.). Boston: Pearson Education.

Williams, J. M. (1999). And here's the pitch. Madison Avenue discovers "the invisible consumer." *WE Magazine, 3*(4), 28–31.

Chapter 22

Concentration of Ownership in European Broadcasting

Marius Dragomir

This chapter analyzes the nature of, and problems caused by, concentration of ownership, which is considered as the most negative development affecting the commercial broadcasting sector since the deregulation of the television industry in Europe in the 1980s. The control of large parts of the media by a few owners, sometimes with interests in the political sphere or in other businesses, has proved to be detrimental to political and cultural diversity and pluralism and to hurt editorial independence. Although it is hard to prove systematically the damage that concentrated media ownership has inflicted on diversity, pluralism, and independence, there are numerous researched examples of how badly concentration of ownership can hurt media independence. This demonstrates that concentration of ownership in TV, the most influential medium in Europe, is potentially dangerous, in that it spawns a concentration of influence that can be used for political, personal, ideological, or commercial purposes. This chapter looks into the concentration of ownership in Europe in general, focusing on how this spread to Central and Eastern European media markets after 1990.

In 2002, the French media conglomerate Lagardere, which is a majority owner in the Romanian nationwide radio station Europa FM and used to own 47.5% of Radio XXI, was required by the country's broadcasting regulatory body, the National Audiovisual Council (CNA) to partly divest itself from Radio XXI in order to comply with new legal provisions on media ownership introduced that year, which obliged broadcasters not to own more than 20% of a second radio station in the country. What Lagardere had to do was to sell at least 27.5% of its ownership in Radio XXI. They complied with the rule and sold the stake to a company called Hullenberg Holland Holding. Nothing unusual so far: but further investigation into the deal revealed 2 years later that actually Hullenberg Holland Holding was run by a Czech citizen, Adam Blecha, who owned the company through a company ironically called Hoax. Blecha has been a vice-president of the Lagardere Group since 1994, chairing the Supervisory Board of the radio station Frekvence 1, operated by Lagardere in the Czech Republic. He was also working as an adviser to Lagardere in the Czech Republic (Dragomir, 2004; Preoteasa, 2005). In other words, Lagardere did not want to lose its grip over the shares it owned in Radio XXI and used its multilayered, opaque company structure, built purposely to hide the real owners, to bypass legal requirements on media ownership.

Lagardere is only one example of the lack of transparency in the European media industry where concentration of ownership has continued at a very fast pace over since the 1990s, bringing control over the media into the hands of a small number of entities.

Measuring Concentration

There are three main ways to measure media concentration in Europe: horizontal, vertical, and diagonal. Within horizontal concentration, which means concentration on the same television market, three chief models of measuring concentration have been distinguished. The first is based on audience share, the percentage of all television viewers reached by programs aired by a broadcaster over a period of time. This model is employed, with some local characteristics, by Germany and the United Kingdom (Nikoltchev, 2001, pp. 2–6).

The second model takes into account the license holders in the broadcasting market. Employed in Spain, this model forbids a company from owning a certain number of licenses in a given market. This model has two aspects. On the one hand, it restricts the number of broadcast licenses that a company can own, but at the same time it puts a ceiling on voting rights in a company that owns a broadcast license (Nikoltchev, 2001). Finally, Italy employs a revenue share model whereby a broadcast company has a limit imposed on the revenues that it can take in from the total advertising revenues in a broadcast market. Concentration regulation in France follows a more complex model, combining some characteristics of the three models. Thus, each market player in the French broadcast market has a capital share ceiling imposed and a limit on the number of licenses (Nikoltchev, 2001).

The vertical concentration pattern refers to the players operating in production and distribution markets. There are various regulations at this level in most of the European countries. In Britain, for example, restrictions on ownership are imposed mostly on digital services deliverers such as Electronic Programming Guides (EPG) and multiplexes.[1]

The third pattern, the diagonal concentration or cross-ownership pattern, refers to mutually distinct markets, which have a horizontal character such as print media or radio markets. In most of the European countries, there are legal provisions that forbid ownership of different media, and in particular ownership of print media and television. In countries such as Poland or the Czech Republic where such restrictions do not exist, we have seen cases of media conglomerates controlling print and electronic media. In the Czech Republic, for example, the German-owned publisher Mafra, which owns the second largest daily newspaper in the country *Mlada fronta Dnes*, in the past 5 years has also invested in radio and TV stations.

Besides specific legal provisions contained in the media legislation, the European broadcast market is also governed by competition law, which has different goals from media legislation. The media laws have as their prime goal to ensure pluralism in the media while competition law deals mainly with mechanisms for ensuring competition in the media market. The two laws are applied in parallel in almost all European nations, with the possibility that application of the two will result in different outcomes (Nikoltchev, 2001).

At the pan-European level, the issue of media concentration is only dealt with by the European Commission (EC) competition law, which overrides national legislation. It is worth noting that the European Commission accepts national policies and legislation on the media. The European Parliament stated in a 1990 resolution (European Parliament, 1990) that restrictions on concentration are "essential" in the media sector, not only for economic reasons, but chiefly "as a means of guaranteeing a variety of information and freedom of the press."

The Concentration Saga

The European broadcast media are a market worth more than €74 billion ($102 billion), with commercial TV broadcasters accounting for around a quarter of these revenues (Lange, 2006, p. 10).

Commercial television in Europe is funded from advertising and other commercial revenues, including sponsorship and teleshopping. In most of the European media markets, television still controls the largest part of the advertising revenues compared with other media, with only a few countries, such as France, Italy, the Czech Republic, or Latvia where the television sector enjoys less than 50% of the country's total ad spending (Dragomir, Reljic, Thompson, Reed, Danov, 2005, pp. 66, 69, 70). With few exceptions, such as Bosnia and Herzegovina or Poland, commercial television takes in the largest share of total television advertising, more than the public service broadcasters. Although there is still a large gap between the total amount of advertising spending in Western European countries and the Eastern markets, the advertising growth in the transition countries[2] has been buoyant in recent years.

The concentration of ownership in the media markets has advanced rapidly since the late 1990s, with massive mergers and acquisitions leading to the emergence of a small group of media goliaths across the continent. This trend has appeared despite the existence of antimonopoly legislation in all European countries as companies took advantage of permissive laws, legal loopholes, or tolerant attitudes on the part of the regulators that derived either from a culture of collusion between regulators and broadcast operators, or from weak regulatory mechanisms that did not allow regulators to force broadcasters to comply with ownership ceilings. The methods most used by broadcasters to escape the ownership limitations imposed by media legislation are registering their companies in tax havens that enable them to conceal their identity as owners, or employing sophisticated, multilayered ownership structures that complicate the investigations carried out by regulators (when they are carried out) into finding the real owner(s) of a particular broadcaster (Dragomir et al., 2005).

One of the most notorious examples of ownership concentration in the broadcast sphere is Italy where Berlusconi's Mediaset corporation owns the three largest channels in the country, Canale 5, Italia Uno, and Rete4, which together garner over 40% of the nationwide audience in the country and almost half of the total TV advertising spending in the Italian market (Kirsch, 2006, pp. 231, 237).

Here, a decade of overt control over nearly the entire broadcasting landscape in the country by the Milan businessman and prime minister for 12 years, Silvio Berlusconi,[3] prompted the European Parliament and the Council of Europe to issue two resolutions in 2004 against the "concentration of political, commercial and media power in Italy in the hands of one person" (Council of Europe Parliamentary Assembly, 2004; European Parliament, 2004). In unusually strong language for official documents issued by the European institutions, the European Parliament's resolution denounced "the repeated and documented intrusions, pressure and acts of censorship by the administration in the present corporate chart and organization of the Italian state-controlled television RAI" (Council of Europe Parliamentary Assembly, 2004; European Parliament, 2004). The two resolutions denounced the lack of independence suffered by Italian public service television, expressing serious concerns about freedom of expression and media pluralism.

In a unique example of overwhelming control over the media, Berlusconi was as prime minister able to enjoy decisive influence over public service television and most of the Italian commercial television networks. He understood what the media can do and used them as a useful tool to propel him to the top of political life, and then used them to silence his critics (Mazzoleni & Vigevani, 2005).

With Berlusconi taking the helm of the Italian government back in the mid-1990s, RAI's journalists were forced to employ the "sandwich" news formula whose main trait was that the first political report during the newscasts had to start with the government's point of view, follow with short sound bites from the opposition, and end with a rebuttal from the government (Stille, 2006). On the other hand, Berlusconi's commercial media, the nationwide channels Canale 5, Italia Uno, and Rete4, made relentless and aggressive attacks against the magistrates who were investigating Berlusconi and his cronies (Stille, 2006). "In his time, Berlusconi destroyed not only the notion of journalistic objectivity in Italy, but also journalistic autonomy" (Stille, 2006).

The Italian anomaly (Mazzoleni & Vigevani, 2005) prompted some media experts in other parts of Europe to talk about the *berlusconization* of the media. In Romania, for example, the term is used to define how politicians rush to own television stations and use them as tools for building their own careers and to defend their personal, business, and political interests.

The Berlusconi era was temporarily finished on a political level with his loss in the 2005 Italian elections (although he was reelected in 2008), and has continued to be an extreme example of control over the media. Concentration of media ownership and lack of transparency of the real owners of the large media companies are the main impediments to building independent and trustworthy commercial television broadcasters (Dragomir et al., 2005).

There is a higher concentration of media ownership in Western Europe than in the transition countries of Eastern and Central Europe, which until 1990 had been under the rule of communist regimes (Dragomir et al., 2005). But the consolidation process in these nations is advancing at a very fast pace. Concentration of ownership in the broadcast media is considered one of the most negative developments in the commercial television sector because it jeopardizes the diversity of programming and, in particular, the independence of the stations (Dragomir et al., 2005) and means that a concentration of influence can be easily used for political, personal, ideological, or commercial gains (Dragomir et al., 2005).

In a study on concentration of ownership in Europe, Sandra B. Hrvatin and Brankica Petkovic summarized the perils of this process for the media:

> Media owners are in a position to influence media content, and the mere possibility that they would choose to exert such influence justifies restrictions. Their motives may be political, ideological, personal or commercial, but the outcome is the same. Media owners are those who dictate media content.... Fewer owners means lesser diversity of content. A prerequisite for the diversity of content is a variety of owners, meaning that media pluralism can be guaranteed only by plural ownership. Media concentration has an impact not only on media content but on the manner of reporting as well.... Investigative journalism and investigative articles are increasingly rare.

Media owners tend to see journalists as non-essential items on their cost sheets, so streamlining in the media business is often accompanied by layoffs, salary cuts and widespread disregard for collective agreements. Today, the independence of both the media and journalists rests in the hands of media owners, and, consequently so does the freedom of expression of every individual. (Hrvatin & Petkovic, 2004, p. 12)

In France, as in other large European countries, the conundrum in the broadcast regulation field has long been to find a system that would reconcile the creation of large media conglomerates able to compete internationally (which must allow for a certain degree of concentration) with the preservation of pluralism and diversity in the media (which has to do with establishing anticoncentration rules) (Vedel, 2005).

In Central and Eastern Europe, with the opening of the markets after the wave of anticommunist revolutions in the region, large Western groups set up the first private TV networks in these countries. They had to face strict legal provisions in the early 1990s forbidding foreign ownership, which obliged them to use local partners to be able to invest in the region's media. But within the past decade, the rules on foreign ownership have relaxed and now foreign companies are freely investing in the media in this part of Europe (Dragomir & Thompson, 2008).

The largest investor in television operations in Central and Eastern Europe is the U.S. company Central European Media Enterprises (CME), which over more than a decade has built a network of 11 stations in six countries in the region. The company's founder is the heir to the Estee Lauder fortune, the U.S. billionaire and former diplomat Ronald S. Lauder. In August 2006, he sold nearly 50% of his full stake in the company, saying that he wanted to move part of his investment into new ventures (Fabrikant, 2006).

Another large player operating in the region is the German RTL Group, part of the Bertelsmann media conglomerate, which runs stations in Hungary and Croatia, and which has been eyeing more acquisitions over the past few years. The Swedish Modern Times Group (MTG), which has been a robust investor, has been very proactive in investing in the region's broadcast media, and today operates terrestrial stations in all three Baltic states and the Czech Republic. Finally, two other large players that have investments in the transition countries are Rupert Murdoch's News Corporation, which owns the largest Bulgarian television station, and SBS Broadcasting, which has operations in Hungary (Dragomir et al, 2005; Hrvatin & Petkovic, 2004).

An emerging trend in many European countries is the growth in cross-ownership structures. The regulation of this form of ownership, between various types of media, varies broadly across Europe, but most of the countries have some cross-ownership restrictions in place (Drago-mir et al., 2005). A common legal provision in some European countries is the restriction against joint ownership between print and electronic media (Dragomir et al., 2005). Among Eastern and Central European countries, only Bulgaria, Lithuania, Czech Republic, and Poland have no clear limits on cross-ownership (Dragomir et al., 2005). On the other hand, in Western Europe in recent years there has been a flurry of mul-timedia ventures, a trend that is also reaching the transition countries (Dragomir et al., 2005).

An interesting example of cross-ownership is the Czech market where a print media group has ventured into electronic media. Taking advan-tage of legislation that sees the mass media as a single market, German-owned publisher Mafra, which runs the second largest daily newspaper in the country, *Mlada fronta Dnes*, purchased over several years the local radio stations Classic FM and Expresradio and then the company Stanice O, which operates the music television channel Ocko, which is transmitted via cable and satellite (Rybkova, 2005).

But even in those countries where there are laws forbidding cross-ownership, such concentration has appeared. To do that, local media moguls have built sophisticated ownership structures that make it impos-sible to trace the real ownership of their media groups. An example is Slovakia where, despite strict legal limitations on cross-ownership, the local media mogul Ivan Kmotrik allegedly owned shares in three televi-sion stations plus Mediaprint and Kapa Pressegrosso, which is the larg-est newspaper distribution network in the country (Kuzel & Godarsky, 2005).

On the other hand, some of the smaller European countries are laud-ing concentration of ownership. In Estonia, for example, a country of some 1.3 million inhabitants, media policy-makers argue that media companies operating in such small markets must be allowed to own more media outlets, claiming that otherwise they wouldn't be able to survive. The Norwegian group Schibsted controls the largest media out-lets in Estonia. The outlets include Kanal 2, the second largest TV chan-nel in the country in terms of advertising market share, and the media conglomerate Eesti Meedia (Estonian Media), which publishes the two largest daily newspapers in the country and several local dailies. The company also runs Ajakirjade Kirjastus, the largest magazine publisher in Estonia, and operates the broadcast company Trio LSL Radio Group, which runs six radio stations (Dragomir et al., 2005).

In Poland, there has also been the argument that cross-ownership can be beneficial for the media market. The Polish company Agora, which publishes the largest daily newspaper in the country, *Gazeta Wyborcza*, and operates a network of 29 radio stations, argued also that domestic companies controlling more media outlets are not posing any threat to diversity and pluralism and that this threat is coming from mostly American multinational media corporations (Piechota, 2002).

Transparency of Ownership

A serious deficiency of the commercial television sector is the lack of transparency of the stations' owners. Through sophisticated and Byzantine ownership structures, companies operating commercial television are hiding their tracks by registering their media outlets in offshore countries or countries where confidentiality of ownership is guaranteed, such as Cyprus and Switzerland. By hiding the real owners, media companies aim, on the one hand, to hide possible conflicts of interest from the public eye and their owner's interference with the stations' programs, and, on the other hand, to evade legal provisions that set limits on concentration of ownership. In other words, regulators cannot really enforce legislation against formation of dominant positions or legal provisions against concentration of ownership without knowing the real owners of the TV stations operating in the market (Dragomir et al., 2005).

In Bulgaria, for example, the broadcast market has been marred by lack of transparency on media ownership, capital, and financing. The real owners of broadcast companies are hidden behind ordinary shares or offshore corporations (Popova, 2004, pp. 96–98). Licensed in 2000, the first private nationwide channel in Bulgaria, bTV, was only listed in 2001 as a company fully owned by Rupert Murdoch's News Corporation. Since its very first days on the market, there were speculations that the station's management had close ties with Krassimir Gergov, an advertising businessman, who was officially presented by a station executive as a consultant to bTV. The station remains the largest TV broadcaster in the country, with an average audience share of almost 38% and some 50% of the total TV ad spending (Popova, 2004).

A similar story exists in Romania where until 2 years ago, many of the TV stations were hiding their ownership in foreign jurisdictions. At first glance, the Romanian media market seems vibrant. It boasts numerous media outlets and fierce competition, with the TV sector populated by a large number of players. However, in fact, the entire TV market has been dominated for years by two poles of influence built around aggressive and powerful groups of interests linked with both politicians and businesses. One of these poles was created around the Romanian politician and businessman Dan Voiculescu, and the second around the U.S. media company CME and its Romanian partner Adrian Sarbu (Preoteasa, 2005).

One of the richest families in Romania, with a fortune estimated to hover around €200 million ($272 million), the Voiculescus control, besides their media ventures, a myriad of other businesses, including industrial and trade companies. The pearl of their media business is the nationwide TV channel Antena 1, the third largest channel in the country in terms of audience and advertising revenues. Its license holder is Corporatia pentru cultura si arta Intact (CCAI), which is 40% owned by Dan Voiculescu, with much of the rest of the stake owned by the Cyprus-registered company Crescent Commercial and Maritime.[4] Crescent used to be the company of choice for external trade serving the communist political apparatus during the communist dictatorship of Nicolae Ceausescu, who was toppled in an anticommunist revolution in December 1989. Because this entity was based in Cyprus, it was always hard for the regulators and other parties to find the real owners of the station as they hid behind the company's trustees. Under pressure from civil society and some of the country's media, in 2005 the Romanian broadcast regulator, the National Audiovisual Council (CNA), managed to find more about the company's structure and revealed that Dan Voiculescu was in fact its owner with combined direct and indirect interest of nearly 84%. He became a senator in December 2004 (Preoteasa, 2005).

Another story of blatant lack of transparency in the Romanian broadcast media was linked with the all-news station Realitatea TV, a CNN-type channel, which has been scoring a relatively small (but normal for a niche station) audience share of around 4% in the past 2 years, and which manages to attract almost 8% of the total TV advertising cash in the country, thanks mainly to its predominantly urban, wealthier audience, which is very attractive to advertisers. In 2004, Realitatea TV reported to the Romanian regulator that it was majority-owned by the company Bluelink Comunicazioni, registered in Switzerland, whose main shareholders were two unknown people, Dario Colombo and Anna Croci (Preoteasa, 2005). There have been speculations over the past years that, in fact, the station was controlled by the Romanian businessman Sorin Ovidiu Vintu, who has been for many years under police investigation and is notorious for his alleged involvement in one of the biggest bankruptcies in the country. For more than 2 years, Vintu declined to say whether he had any interest in Realitatea TV. But in the end, the speculations proved to be true. In 2006, Vintu admitted that he owned the station when he announced the purchase of more media outlets, including print media and radio stations. His media empire has been emerging recently as the country's third pole of influence (Preoteasa, 2005).

Serbia is another example of nontransparent ownership structures and practices. Businessman Bogoljub Karic, along with his brothers, owned BK Telecom, a nationwide TV channel, which was known for its support to the now-defunct Slobodan Milosevic regime. BK is the third largest channel in the country in terms of audience share and ad revenues. Karic's company was also suspected for years of having an interest in weeklies and other print media (Dokovic, 2004, pp. 436–438).

Transparency of the financial resources behind the media has also become a hot topic in many European countries. There are four main areas where conflicts arise: state advertising, hidden advertising, state subsidies for the media, and other forms of "assistance" (Dokovic, 2004).

Through advertising granted by state-owned companies to selected media outlets; through paid (but not labeled as such) appearances of political guests or public figures during TV shows; through direct state subsidies granted to some media from special state funds earmarked for the support of certain media; and through privileges offered to some media such as advantageous tariffs for renting state-owned facilities, the state is often directly and blatantly interfering with the media's job. A recent example is Slovenia, the richest market in the entire former communist bloc and the EU's sweetheart after its enlargement to the east in 2004, where the state has tremendously increased its presence and influence over the media in the past 2 years. The center-right government in Slovenia—the country took over the European Union presidency in January 2008—came to power in October 2004 with an "ambitious" plan for reforming the country's media landscape. Its plans were mainly directed to controlling as much as possible the country's electronic and print media (Mekina, 2007).

In some countries such as Romania, civil society and media experts have called recently for more legal steps aimed at forcing media to disclose their financial flows in order to shed more transparency over the connections between owners, the state, politicians, and business. Not knowing such connections exist can at the end of the day seriously damage the independence of media outlets.[5] There are already countries such as Poland where the broadcast regulator is entitled to ask broadcast operators to present them with their annual reports, detailing their source of finances. However, lacking mechanisms to enforce such provisions, the Polish regulator could not effectively supervise the cash flowing into the country's media market (Krajewski, 2005).

Several recent studies[6] have called for a series of steps aimed at ensuring better control over the creation of dominant positions and poles of power in the media landscape. First of all, it was recommended that broadcast regulators must be empowered through legislation to examine all layers of ownership in the broadcast companies. So far, legislation does not entitle regulators to go as far as they need to in order to find the real owners behind electronic media. Another important measure aimed at shedding more light on the ownership of the electronic media is creation of central databases of media owners, which should be publicly available. Such steps were taken by independent media organizations in various European countries. However, such databases should be maintained by regulators entitled to then follow up by implementing media policies and legislation in the country.

It has been noted that in many European countries, the sanctions against broadcasters that do not comply with requirements for transparency over their ownership are not very substantial or are missing completely (Dragomir et al., 2005). Usually, during the license tender, legislation obliges applicants for a broadcast license to present the regulator (which grants these licenses) with a clear structure and financial overview of the company that wants to establish a TV station. Then, once a license is granted, broadcasters are forced by legislation to announce to the regulator any changes in their ownership and to wait for the regulatory body's green light before completing a transaction. However, it has been notably difficult for regulators to follow changes in the deeper structures of ownership and to dig for the real owners who can hide their identity in offshore countries (Dragomir et al., 2005). Therefore, more drastic sanctions have been called for by media freedom advocates and journalists, even to the extent of stripping a broadcaster of its license, especially in the case of those media companies that hide their ownership data or provide false data on their owners (Dragomir et al., 2005).

Even ownership under foreign jurisdictions where confidentiality of owners is ensured should not mean that broadcasters can breach national requirements on full transparency. Media freedom advocates have recommended that regulators force broadcasters to reveal the ownership of TV stations even though they are registered in offshore tax havens (Dragomir et al., 2005).

Ownership and Independence

In order to operate a commercial television station, companies in most European countries must apply for a broadcast license, which is issued for a certain period of time by domestic broadcasting regulators. They are also in charge of monitoring the output of these stations to ensure that they comply with the legislation that governs television content in each country (Dragomir et al., 2005).

Private television stations have total freedom in building their own programming schedules and content (Dragomir et al., 2005). In many Western European countries, which have a much longer tradition of free television markets than their Eastern European peers, commercial TV stations are usually obliged to comply with a set of general obligations to serve the public interest (Dragomir et al., 2005). They are almost inexistent in postauthoritarian countries. Such public service obligations, but not as specific as those imposed on public service broadcasters, are enshrined in broadcasting legislation or the broadcast license contract. In Britain and Germany there are broad public service requirements for commercial channels while in France, commercial broadcasters are obliged to show particular types of programming, chiefly related to preservation of the national cultural heritage (Dragomir et al., 2005).

With some exceptions, in Western European countries the independence of television stations is less endangered than in the transition countries of Central and Eastern Europe. A notably negative Western example remains Italy where Berlusconi used his power and influence, backed up by his control over the majority of the electronic media, to muffle critics. Enzo Biagi, one of the fathers of modern Italian journalism, and host of a news program on the first channel of the Italian public service RAI, was kicked out of the station after the broadcast of one of his programs where his guest, a popular filmmaker mocked Berlusconi (Mazzoleni & Vigevani, 2005).

In general, the arrival of commercial television in the postcommunist countries in Europe meant fundamental changes in the television landscape where former state broadcasters were enjoying a monopoly. Faced with competition, something they had not previously experienced, the former state broadcasters had to rejuvenate their programming and modernize their operations in the course of their transformation to public service stations.

In the early 1990s, many commercial broadcasters pioneered dynamic news and political programs and investigative reporting. But meanwhile, in their struggle for ever-larger ratings and fat bottom lines, the zest for such programming vanished, and commercial television ceased supporting solid investigative journalism and quality news programs. Instead, they resorted to low-quality entertainment and sensationalist news (Dragomir et al., 2005).

Combined with the concentration of ownership and the formation of poles of influence and power, the space for diverse and plural content on commercial broadcasting has been going down (Dragomir et al., 2005). In a market where a few large enterprises control most of the media, it has been becoming increasingly difficult for journalists to maintain their independence (Dragomir et al., 2005). This is also linked with the conditions in which they work. In most of the transition countries, self-regulatory mechanisms in commercial television are few in number, and as a result, journalists working for these stations have to face direct or indirect pressures (Dragomir et al., 2005). In many countries in the region, with limited choice of workplaces, journalists have to accept poorly paid work and sometimes work without clear working contracts (Dragomir et al., 2005).

In such a climate, vitiated also by aggressive pressures from owners and politicians, a culture of self-censorship has been thriving. In Romania, for example, during the Social-Democrat government, which lost political power in the 2004 elections, journalists from the commercial TV station Pro TV were ordered not to present negative coverage of the government. This embargo followed an unofficial pact between the station's owners and the government, according to which the station was not going to report critically on the government while the government would make sure that the station's owners were not prosecuted for failing to pay back taxes (Dragomir, 2002).

Another marked trend in various places is tabloidization of newscasts in an attempt to avoid hard news and investigative reporting (Dragomir et al., 2005). Romania is again an example. Here most of the commercial TV stations have removed their in-depth political and current affairs programs and talk shows from their schedules over the past decade, justifying their move by saying that their programming was dictated by the viewers' tastes. Instead of serious news, commercial TV programming in Romania abounds in "political cabarets," programs mixing political debate with light variety shows. The country has also contributed to the media literature with a new term *non-news*, meaning news reports on isolated cases of domestic violence, parties, cases of pilfering, and so on. Most of the newscasts on Romanian commercial TV stations choose to air such news in order to avoid controversial political and economic issues that could anger influential politicians and businesses because of negative consequences in terms of regulation or advertising contracts (Preoteasa, 2005).

Editorial independence of commercial TV stations is also dramatically encroached upon by the links between the owners of the stations and other businesses and by their attitudes toward the media outlets that they own and control. For many media owners in some countries, the media they run are instruments used for advancing their business interests rather than objective channels of news and information that should serve the viewers (Dragomir et al, 2005). An example of such practices is Turkey where the broadcast market is concentrated in just a few hands, mostly influential businessmen or public figures who use the media primarily to pursue their business interests. The result is that very often commercial broadcasters have taken an editorial line that more or less overtly favored their owners' interests. For example, if the owner of one of these stations wanted to win a privatization tender, then his or her station would air news bulletins that would take a positive stance toward the station's owners or that would praise or criticize the government depending on the interests in the tender (Capli, 2005, p. 1575). Similar situations are found in the broadcast markets of countries such as Romania, Albania, Serbia, and the Republic of Macedonia.

The Digital Factor

These days European broadcasting is seeing a huge leap forward in its evolution as digital television has been rapidly gaining ground and is set to replace analog television in many European countries by 2012. Digitization was given a strong impetus at the Radio-Communication Conference (RRC-06) organized in May-June 2006 by the International Telecommunications Union (ITU) where a new agreement on the redistribution of frequencies was adopted, heralding the development of all-digital terrestrial broadcast services in Europe. In parallel with the work on the new frequency agreement, the European Union has been pushing for several years for a complete switch-off of analog broadcasting by 2012 (European Commission, 2004).

Digitization of broadcasting had a slow start in 2000 when several digital television companies went bust in Western Europe (Dragomir et al., 2005). But over the past few years, it has advanced very rapidly in many European countries (Dragomir & Thompson, 2008). However, there is still a big gap in digital development between Western and Eastern Europe. In some Western European countries, the penetration of digital TV has reached high levels. In Britain it was over 60% in mid-2005 while in some Eastern European countries the digitization barely reached 10% of the households in the same year (Lange, 2007).

Digital broadcasting improves picture and sound quality, and mobile reception. It uses the frequency spectrum more efficiently, and therefore it can offer more television and radio channels on the same frequency, along with enhanced information services, including interactive television services, such as online shopping, multiple viewing angles, and live betting. Because it promises a multiplication of the number of TV channels, digitization is expected to bring more competition on a continent where the media industry is concentrated in the hands of a small number of players (Dragomir et al., 2005). At the same time, digitization is likely to pose numerous new challenges to broadcasting regulation, and to have a significant impact on both public service broadcasting and commercial television (Dragomir et al., 2005). To understand the expected changes in the patterns of media concentration, it is important to put this debate into the larger context of the whole range of consequences that digitization is likely to have on the media market in general.

The EU's regulation of digital broadcasting includes regulation at the transport level through the 2002 Access Directive, which is a uniform and horizontal approach to regulation of technical bottlenecks.[7] In its articles 5 and 6, the directive covers the viewers' access to digital broadcasting services such as Conditional Access (CA) systems[8] or Electronic Programming Guides (EPG). Articles 8 to 13 of the same directive contain rules on competition at service and infrastructure levels, mostly technical facilities such as broadband networks, encoders, or multiplexes. The second level of the EU regulation is on broadcast content through the Television without Frontiers (TVwF) Directive, which establishes rules on the use of advertising, protection of minors in broadcasting, and quotas for European programming. The TVwF Directive has been for almost 2 decades the main instrument regulating broadcasting at the pan-European level. It was reviewed in the past 2 years and a new version of the directive was adopted in December 2007.[9]

At the moment, digitization is being implemented in most European countries, which have adopted policies and legislation on digital broadcasting and, some of them, already grant broadcast licenses to operate digital channels. The process already poses new challenges to regulation. In most of the European countries, there are two regulators: one dealing with the broadcast content (they grant broadcast licenses, monitor TV programming to ensure that stations comply with legislation, impose fines on broadcasters that breach legislation, etc.); and a second regulator managing the frequency spectrum and handling mostly technical issues related to broadcasting (Dragomir et al., 2005). The remit and tasks of the two types of regulators must be clearly distinguished by law because with digitization more operators in the digital chain will have to be licensed. There have already been situations where overlapping of tasks between the two regulators has taken place in countries such as the Czech Republic (Rybkova, 2005).

Although in recent years there has been less politicization of broadcast regulators in many European countries, there are still cases of state interference with the regulators' decisions.

With the broadcast market becoming much more complex, ensuring the independence of regulators is becoming a key issue as the spectrum of interests is also going to expand, requiring adequate and independent regulation (Dragomir et al., 2005). Independence of regulators is guaranteed through clear and objective appointment and termination conditions for the members sitting on these bodies, conditions for their term in office and their legal remit, conflict of interest provisions in legislation, and a model of financing allowing this body to function independently. Some of the countries have improved their regulatory frameworks by adopting legal provisions that fulfill the conditions described above. However, politicization of these bodies has continued apace, especially in Central and Eastern Europe. Politicians have continued to strive to appoint close allies to these bodies who are defending various business and political interests rather than regulating the market independently for the benefit of the citizens.

Digital television is expected to bring major changes in this commercial television landscape characterized by high degrees of concentration of ownership and viewership, with large broadcasting players maintaining their stranglehold on advertising revenues. In most of Europe, the three largest channels in a national market control the bulk of nationwide audience (Dragomir et al., 2005). In the Czech Republic, Bulgaria, and Croatia, the top three channels enjoy together over 80% of the nationwide audience. As a result, the advertising market is also highly concentrated in the hands of a very small number of broadcasters in each country. In France, for example, the three largest stations in the country command over 75% of the total TV advertising revenues (Dragomir et al., 2005).

There is a body of media experts and observers who expect digitization to bring fresh competition to such a concentrated media landscape. But that depends to a large extent on how commercial broadcasting is regulated. Already established broadcasters are aggressively lobbying to seize as many digital licenses as possible to perpetuate their market dominance (Dragomir & Thompson, 2008).

At the same time, digital markets bring a totally new pattern of regulation. Besides the actual broadcasters, the digital chain will see the emergence of new operators at both the service and transport levels. They will include the digital multiplex operators, which will bundle more TV programs and transmit them to the viewer, and Electronic Programming Guides (EPG)—TV schedules incorporated in the TV set guiding the viewers through the available content. Therefore, it is crucial for future regulation to prevent formation of concentrations within the digital chain as many of these operators will have a say in how the content will be accessed by and delivered to the public (Dragomir et al., 2005).

The advent of digitization presents an opportunity for a set of regulatory and policy mechanisms aimed at ensuring independence of regulators and clear regulatory remits; independence and a strong basis for public service broadcasters; and preventing perpetuation of the current dominant positions of commercial broadcasters and formation of new poles of power and influence within the digital chain (Dragomir et al., 2005).

Opinions on how digitization is going to influence the current state of affairs in European broadcasting vary widely. Monica Arino (2004) defined what she called "the multi-channel paradox."

"First, privatization and now digitization have multiplied the number of channels available, and therefore, the number of potential voices. As services are personalized, the power of influence and the ability to control mass viewing habits would appear to be reduced" (Arino, 2004, p. 99). Therefore, the proponents of this opinion argue that strict regulations governing the protection of pluralism are no longer necessary.

But it is not clear whether the expansion of television offerings will necessarily mean more diverse content or that it will guarantee free consumer choice. First, more channels could mean instead an increased variety of content rather more of the same as we have today (Arino, 2004). Second, the crucial factor is how this offering will actually impact on citizens. This is measured by audience reach rather than by the number of channels. Moreover, with the apparently inevitable tendency toward globalization and internationalization of the media, ownership restrictions are likely to be loosened and all the problems explained in this chapter of how concentration of ownership dents the plurality and diversity of voices will worsen.

Digitization of broadcasting coupled with the extraordinary technological convergence is bound to make dramatic changes in the broadcasting markets. It is already having a major impact on the business models employed by broadcast companies, their production flows, and distribution platforms. Mergers and acquisitions in the media market and continual consolidation of print, electronic, and Internet media is changing the face of the media and the patterns of media consumption today. Moreover, with technology players, mostly telecommunications companies and software manufacturers entering these changing media markets (as their products are increasingly used in the distribution and captioning of media content), it will be essential for a healthy and independent media landscape to ensure transparency of ownership and restrict concentration of media ownership that poses dangers to cultural and political pluralism

Conclusions

Concentration of ownership poses numerous dangers to cultural and political pluralism and diversity and independent broadcasting. A number of markets are being dominated by a few powerful media conglomerates, which thereby enjoy the power of opinion formation. The implementation of the European legislation on competition is important for reining in the dominance of such groups and for preventing foreclosure of competitors from national European markets.

At the European Union level, there is no specific legislation on media ownership and it is not likely that such provisions would be adopted in the near future. Under pressures from the European Parliament, the European Commission is preparing a paper on proposed actions for ensuring media pluralism. The Commission, the executive body of the EU, is to publish this paper in 2009. With the ownership of the media, and of broadcasting in particular, becoming increasingly internationalized, there is a need to monitor in more depth the developments in broadcasting ownership at a pan-European level to identify the risks posed by concentration of ownership.

However, the competition legislation cannot replace mechanisms of control preventing concentration of ownership that exist at national levels. Such mechanisms differ widely from country to country. In some places, they are part of the competition legislation that prevents media companies from gaining a dominant position, which is measured based on either audience share, number of broadcast licenses, capital shares, or advertising revenues.

Although concentration of ownership could be dangerous for pluralism, this problem should be treated in a larger context, taking into account the size of the market, the cultural and political environment, and the regulatory systems in place. In smaller markets it is indeed difficult for the advertising industry to support more than a few broadcasters. External media pluralism, meaning a large number of channels, is much more difficult to achieve in such countries. As long as these media outlets comply with a certain set of rules, principles, and standards on programming, concentration of ownership does not lead to dangerous situations where news coverage is slanted toward certain interest groups. Therefore, concentration of ownership should be treated on a case by case basis. More important is for regulators and lawmakers to embrace a set of principles based on avoidable risks to cultural and political pluralism.

Regulation of concentration of ownership should not be relegated exclusively to the competition legislation domain. It has been proven that media is a sector that requires a broader and more complex regulatory approach. To manage to control concentration of ownership in the media, clear mechanisms to ensure transparency of ownership and funding should be in place.

Legislation should contain provisions that would force owners of broadcast companies to disclose their real shareholders. At the same time, broadcast regulators should have more power in investigating cases of nontransparent ownership structures. Legislation should give regulators the authority to impose drastic sanctions against those media outlets that do not comply with transparency rules. Other efforts to boost transparency on the broadcast market should come from civil society and professional journalistic groupings. Publicly available registers of media owners should be encouraged by broadcast regulators.

In general, continuous monitoring of media ownership would boost transparency of the media markets while a set of mechanisms for implementing provisions on ownership would lead to more pluralism and diversity in broadcasting.

Notes

1. Electronic Programming Guide (EPG) is software that allows viewers to browse through TV schedules directly on a digital TV set. A multiplex is a platform bundling several TV programs at once into a digital signal for transmission.
2. The transition countries are the postcommunist countries in Central and Eastern Europe.
3. After losing elections in 2006, Berlusconi returned to power in April 2008 after a political crisis in early 2008.
4. Information from CNA. "Cine sunt proprietarii de radio si televiziune"

(Who are the owners of the television and radio stations), a document published and regularly updated on the Web site of the Romanian broadcast regulator, the National Audiovisual Council (CNA).

5. This was one of the topics debated at the conference "Follow the Money" in Bucharest, May 4, 2007, where the author of this article spoke on "Financing the Media: The More Transparency, the More Independence."

6. Worth mentioning are: Dragomir, Reljic, Thompson, Reed, and Danov (2005) and Hrvatin and Petkovic (2004).

7. Directive 2002/19/EC of the European Parliament and of the Council of 7 March 2002 on access to, and interconnection of, electronic communications networks and associated facilities, L108/7, Brussels, April 24, 2002 (hereafter, Access Directive).

8. CA is any technical measure whereby access to a protected service is made conditional upon prior approval, individual authorization. Broadcasters can do this by encrypting data.

9. Directive 97/36/EC of the European Parliament and of the Council of June 30, 1997 amending Council Directive 89/552/EEC on the coordination of certain provisions laid down by law, regulation, or administrative action in member states concerning the pursuit of television broadcasting activities, *Official Journal*, L 202, July 30, 1997, P. 0060–0070. (The directive was amended last year: Directive 2007/65/EC of the European Parliament and of the Council of December 11, 2007 amending Council Directive 89/552/EEC on the coordination of certain provisions laid down by law, regulation, or administrative action in member states concerning the pursuit of television broadcasting activities, *Official Journal of the European Union*, December 18, 2007, L 332/27.)

References

Arino, M. (2004). Competition law and pluralism. *European Digital Broadcasting: Addressing the Gaps in Communications and Strategies*, 54, 99–100.

Capli, B. (2005). Turkey. In M. Dragomir, D. Reljic, M. Thompson, Q. Reed , & D. Danov (Eds.), *Television across Europe: Regulation, policy and independence* (pp. 1575–1577). Budapest/New York: Open Society Institute.

Council of Europe Parliamentary Assembly. (2004). Resolution 1387 (2004) of 24 June 2004, on Monopolization of the electronic media and possible abuse of power in Italy.

Dokovic, D. (2004) Serbia. In *Media ownership and its impact on media independence and pluralism*. Ljubljana, Serbia: Peace Institute and SEENPM.

Dragomir, M. (2002, June 21) Propping up propaganda. Transitions online. Retrieved June 6, 2007, from http://www.tol.org.

Dragomir, M. (2004, October 4). Avoid media ownership restrictions: Use a Blecha. *Czech Business* Weekly. Retrieved May 6, 2007, from http://www.cbw.cz/phprs/2004100418.html?search=Blecha

Dragomir, M., Reljic, D., Thompson, M., Reed, Q., Danov, D. (Eds.). (2005). *Television across Europe: Regulation, policy and independence*. Budapest/New York: Open Society Institute. 2005.

Dragomir, M., & Thompson, M. (Eds.). (2008). *TV across Europe: Follow-up reports 2008*. Budapest/New York: Open Society Institute. Retrieved June 1, 2008, from http://www.mediapolicy.org/tv-across-europe

European Commission. (2004, September 17). Communication from the Commission to the Council, the European Parliament, the European Economic and Social Committee and the Committee of the Regions on accelerating the transition from analogue to digital broadcasting (from digital "switchover" to analogue "switch-off").

European Parliament. (1990, February 15). Resolution on media takeovers and mergers. OJ C 68/137–138.

European Parliament. (2004). Resolution of 22 April 2004 on the risks of violation, in the EU and especially in Italy, of freedom of expression and information (Article 11(2) of the Charter of Fundamental Rights). 2003/2237(INI), A5-0230/2004.

Fabrikant, G. (2006, October 16). It's not a Klimt, but the Eastern European TV venture is sweet. *The New York Times*, p. C1.

Hrvatin, B. S., & Petkovic, B. (2004). Regional overview. In B. S. Hrvatin & B. Petkovic (Eds.), *Media ownership and its impact on media independence and pluralism* (p. 12). Ljubljana, Serbia: Peace Institute and SEENPM.

Kirsch, T. (2006, October). IP International Marketing Committee (CMI). Television 2006. International Key Facts.

Krajewski, A. (2005). Poland. In M. Dragomir, D. Reljic, M. Thompson, Q. Reed, & D. Danov (Eds.), *Television across Europe: Regulation, policy and independence* (pp. 1077–1152). Budapest/New York: Open Society Institute.

Kuzel, R., & Godarsky, I. (2005). Slovakia. In M. Dragomir, D. Reljic, M. Thompson, Q. Reed , & D. Danov (Eds.), *Television across Europe: Regulation, policy and independence* (pp. 1385–1471). Budapest/New York: Open Society Institute.

Lange, A. (Ed.) (2006). *Trends in European television* (Vol. 2). Strasbourg, France: European Audiovisual Observatory.

Lange, A. (Ed.) (2007). *Trends in European television*. Strasbourg, France: European Audiovisual Observatory.

Mazzoleni, G., Vigevani, G. E. (2005). Italy. In M. Dragomir, D. Reljic, M. Thompson, Q. Reed, & D. Danov (Eds.), *Television across Europe: regulation, policy and independence* (pp. 865–955). Budapest/New York: Open Society Institute.

Mekina, B. (2007). Under my thumb. Transitions online, June 25, 2007. Retrieved May 6, 2008, from http://www.tol.cz/look/TOL/article.tpl?IdLanguage=1&IdPublication=4&NrIssue=223&NrSection=1&NrArticle=18797&search=search&SearchKeywords=Slovenia&SearchMode=on&SearchLevel=0

Nikoltchev, S. (Ed.) (2001). *Television and media concentration: Regulatory models on the national and the European Level*. Strasbourg, France: European Audiovisual Observatory.

Piechota, G. (2002, April 10). Interview with Alfonso Sanchez-Tabernero. Potrzeba czempionow (Need for champions). *Gazeta Wyborcza*.

Popova, V. S. (2004) Bulgaria. In *Media ownership and its impact on media independence and pluralism*. Ljubljana, Serbia: Peace Institute and SEENPM.

Preoteasa, M. (2005). Romania. In M. Dragomir, D. Reljic, M. Thompson, Q. Reed, & D. Danov (Eds.), *Television across Europe: regulation, policy and independence* (p. 1286). Budapest/New York: Open Society Institute.

Rybkova, E. (2005) Czech Republic. In M. Dragomir, D. Reljic, M. Thompson, Q. Reed, & D. Danov (Eds.), *Television across Europe: regulation, policy and independence* (pp. 483–555). Budapest/New York: Open Society Institute.

Stille, A (2006, September/October). Silvio's shadow. *Columbia Journalism Review*. Retrieved June 10, 2007 from http://cjrarchives.org/issues/2006/5/Stille.asp

Vedel, T (2005). France. In M. Dragomir, D. Reljic, M. Thompson, Q. Reed, & D. Danov (Eds.), *Television across Europe: regulation, policy and independence* (pp. 646–727). Budapest/New York: Open Society Institute.

Index

A

ABC, 129–142
  Congo, 149
  Sudan, 149
Advertising standardization, 329
Afghanistan, 148–149
Africa, counterterrorism, U.S. efforts, 220–221
Al-Jazeera English-language Web site credibility, 242–258
  Al-Jazeera television network transference, 244–258, *250, 251, 252, 253*
Al-Jazeera television network credibility, 244–258
  Al-Jazeera English-language Web site transference, 244–258, *250, 251, 252, 253*
American cultural imperialism, *see* Cultural imperialism
Americans with Disabilities Act, 423
Anti-Terrorism Assistance program, 220
Arab newspapers, Iraq War comparisons, 205–215
  methods, 206–209
  results, *209,* 209–215, *210, 211, 212, 213*
Asia, disability, 426–427
  negative attitudes, 427
Atomistic model, 52–53
Australia
  news flow determinants, 261–274
    colonial relations, 266–267, *271,* 271–274
    content analysis, 268–269, *269*
    contextual determinants, 263–264
    defense expenditures, 266–267, *271,* 271–274

GDP, 265–266, 271–274, *274*
    geographic distance, 264, *271,* 271–274
    hypotheses, 264–267
    independent variables, 269–270
    land area, 264, *271,* 271–274
    method, 267–271
    military power, 266, *271,* 271–274
    population, 264–265, *271,* 271–274
    press freedom, 266, 271–274, *274*
    results, *271,* 271–274, *273*
    tourism, 265, 271–274, *274*
    trade, 265, 271–274, *274*
  online media, 261–274
    colonial relations, 266–267, *271,* 271–274
    content analysis, 268–269, *269*
    contextual determinants, 263–264
    defense expenditures, 266–267, *271,* 271–274
    GDP, 265–266, 271–274, *274*
    geographic distance, 264, *271,* 271–274
    hypotheses, 264–267
    independent variables, 269–270
    land area, 264, *271,* 271–274
    method, 267–271
    military power, 266, *271,* 271–274
    population, 264–265, *271,* 271–274
    press freedom, 266, 271–274, *274*
    results, *271,* 271–274, *273*
    tourism, 265, 271–274, *274*
    trade, 265, 271–274, *274*
Autopoiesis, 36

B

Bell's theorem, 36

Blogs
  China, 277–292
    censorship, 279–280
    challenges to, 278–282
    dissent by allusion, 278, 282–292
    Eighteen Touch Dog Newspaper,
      282–292
    metaphors and allusions, 283–285
    perils, 278–282
    self-censorship, 280
    subject matter, 286–289
    victory in weblog contest, 284–
      286, 290–291
  news selection process, 4
  as stealth dissent, 277–292

Brand authenticity, 385–387

Brand revitalization
  Colombia, 380–397
    analysis, 394–397
    brand authenticity, 385–387
    country-of-origin effect, 385
    findings, 390–394
    global brand building, 387–388,
      393–394
    literature review, 382–390
    method, 390
    nation building, 384, 392–393
  Juan Valdez campaign, 380–397
    analysis, 394–397
    brand authenticity, 385–387
    country-of-origin effect, 385
    findings, 390–394
    global brand building, 387–388,
      393–394
    literature review, 382–390
    method, 390
    nation building, 384, 392–393

British newspapers, Iraq War
  comparisons, 205–215
    methods, 206–209
    results, *209*, 209–215, *210, 211,
      212, 213*

Buddhist philosophy
  dependent co-arising paradigm,
    46–49, *47*
  living systems theory, parallels,
    46–50
  Yijing paradigm, 49–50

Bulgaria, media ownership
  transparency, 449

Bystander nonintervention effect,
  international aid, global
  bystander intervention model,
  92–94

C

Case study method
  defined, 349–350
  South Korea, 349–362

CBS, 129–142
  Congo, 149
  Sudan, 149

Celebrity endorsement
  match-up hypothesis, 243
  meaning transference model, 243

Celebrity nude photos
  cell phones, 345
  Korean comfort women, 345

Cell phones, *see* Mobile phones

Censorship, 279–280

Central Europe, media ownership
  concentration, 447–449

Central European Media Enterprises,
  447

Centralization, 331

Chaos theory, 51

China
  blogs, 277–292
    censorship, 279–280
    challenges to, 278–282
    Eighteen Touch Dog Newspaper,
      282–292
    metaphors and allusions, 283–285
    perils, 278–282
    self-censorship, 280
    stealth dissent by allusion, 278,
      282–292
    subject matter, 286–289
    victory in weblog contest, 284–
      286, 290–291
  corporate social responsibility, 305,
    306
  Internet, 277–292
    censorship, 279–280
    challenges to, 278–282
    Eighteen Touch Dog Newspaper,
      282–292
    metaphors and allusions, 283–285
    perils, 278–282
    self-censorship, 280
    stealth dissent by allusion, 278,
      282–292

subject matter, 286–289
   victory in weblog contest, 284–
      286, 290–291
mobile phone, cross-cultural study,
   401–419
multinational corporations, 305,
   306
News Corporation, 13
Circulation size, 73
Closed flow
   Internet, 15–17
   open network, 15–17
CNN, 129–142
   foreign bureaus, 164
Code of Ethics
   International Association of
      Business Communicators, 372
   Public Relations Institute of
      Australia, 372–373
   Public Relations Society of America,
      372
Coffee growing, 380–397
Collectivism, South Korea, 348
Colombia
   brand revitalization, 380–397
      analysis, 394–397
      brand authenticity, 385–387
      country-of-origin effect, 385
      findings, 390–394
      global brand building, 387–388,
         393–394
      literature review, 382–390
      method, 390
      nation building, 384, 392–393
   Juan Valdez campaign, 380–397
      analysis, 394–397
      brand authenticity, 385–387
      country-of-origin effect, 385
      findings, 390–394
      global brand building, 387–388,
         393–394
      literature review, 382–390
      method, 390
      nation building, 384, 392–393
   nation building, 384–385
   political, social, and economic
      background, 382–384
Communication, changes alter
   cultures, 11–12
Communication scholarship, living
   systems theory, 51–52
Complexity, 51

Conflict aggravation, 225, 227–228,
   228, 231
Conflict management
   Cameron's contingency theory,
      346–362
   cell phones, 346–362
      analysis, 358–362
      changing stance, 354–355
      crisis development, 350–352
      crisis ending, 357–358
      crisis maturation, 352–353
      findings, 350–358
      method, 349–350
      reverse turn, 356–357
   contingency theory, 346–362
      analysis, 358–362
      changing stance, 354–355
      crisis development, 350–352
      crisis ending, 357–358
      crisis maturation, 352–353
      findings, 350–358
      method, 349–350
      reverse turn, 356–357
      theoretical background, 346–349
   international public relations,
      346–362
Congo
   ABC, 149
   CBS, 149
   NBC, 149
Content analysis, 73–74, 129–142,
   268–269, 269
   foreign elections, 109–123
      data analysis, 119–120
      hypotheses, 115
      international attributes, 114–115,
         117–118, 119, 121–123
      international interactions, 113–
         114, 117, 119, 121–123
      literature review, 110
      location in world system, 112–
         113, 116–117, 119, 121–123
      method, 116–118
      results, 119, 120
   Lesotho, 335
Contextual selection factors, 263–264
   news frames, 177–195
      cross-national studies, 177–195
      economic factors, 180–182
      hypotheses, 182–185
      influence of contextual factors,
         189–195, 191

Contextual selection factors (*continued*)
    measurement, 186–187
    methods, 185–187
    newspapers, 185–195
    research questions, 182–185
    results, 187–195, *188, 189, 190,
        191*
    sampling, 185
    newspapers, 185–195
Contingency theory, conflict
        management, 346–362
    analysis, 358–362
    changing stance, 354–355
    crisis development, 350–352
    crisis ending, 357–358
    crisis maturation, 352–353
    findings, 350–358
    method, 349–350
    reverse turn, 356–357
    theoretical background, 346–349
Corporate accountability,
        international public relations,
        370–371
Corporate social responsibility
    China, 305, 306
    Japan, 306
Cosmopolitan communication,
        57–58, *See also* International
        communication
Cosmopolitan democracy, 58
Counterterrorism
    Africa, U.S. efforts, 220–221
    media framing
        conceptualizing frame building,
            225–228
        conflict aggravation, 225, 227–
            228, *228, 231*
        data, 229–230
        freedom of information, 228–229
        methods, 229–230
        politics, 228–229
        power persuasion, 225, *226,
            226–227, 231*
        results, *231*, 231–237, *233*
    Uganda, 220–221, 224–237
Country-of-origin effect, 385
Covering laws model, 36
Credibility
    Al-Jazeera English-language Web
        site, 242–258
    Al-Jazeera television network,
        244–258

    transference, 244–258
    cultural factors, 245–247
    expertise, 242–244, 255
    meaning transfer model, 242–258
    transference, 242–258
    dependent measure, 247
    hypotheses, 246–247
    independent measures, 248
    method, 247–248
    predictors, 251–253, *252, 253*
    results, 248–253, *250, 251*
    trustworthiness, 242–244, 255
Crisis life-cycle models, 348–349
Crisis response, 336–337
Cross-cultural research approach,
        international public relations,
        373–374
Cross-national conflict shifts
    conceptualization, 333–335
    international public relations,
        320–340
    advertising standardization, 329
    centralization, 331
    coordination and control choices,
        323–324
    coordination and control
        mechanisms, 320–326
    coordination and control
        structure, 337–340
    coordination by socialization,
        326–328
    crisis response, 336–337
    between global integration and
        local responsiveness, 330
    global public affairs management,
        328–333
    integration, 331–332
    literature review, 320–333
    relationships among units in
        transnational organizations,
        328
    split-control structure, 326
    transnational organizations, 320–
        340
    advertising standardization, 329
    centralization, 331
    coordination and control choices,
        323–324
    coordination and control
        mechanisms, 320–326
    coordination and control
        structure, 337–340

coordination by socialization,
326–328
crisis response, 336–337
between global integration and
local responsiveness, 330
global public affairs management,
328–333
integration, 331–332
literature review, 320–333
relationships among units in
transnational organizations,
328
split-control structure, 326
Cultural affinity, 132
international news coverage,
127–128
Cultural discount, international
communication research, 21,
21
Cultural environments, importance of
understanding, 347–348
Cultural factors, credibility, 245–247
Cultural imperialism, 8–33
analytical weakness, 18
cultural values, relationship, 25–26
digital technologies, 8–33
as dominant paradigm, 9–10
globalization, 14–15
relationship, 10
history, 9
hyperlinks, 14–15
international communication,
default vs. design, 17, 17
international communication
research, 9–33
Internet, 8–33, 14–15
methodological domains, 22
persistence as paradigm, 9
theoretical domains, 22
unequal flow of cultural products,
18
Cultural proximity, 20
film industry, 20–21, 21
international communication
research, 21, 21
Cultural setting, international public
relations, 306
Cultural values, cultural imperialism,
relationship, 25–26
Culture
dimensions, 347–348
news, relationship, 200–215

D
Daoist philosophy
dependent co-arising paradigm,
46–49, 47
living systems theory, parallels,
46–50
Yijing paradigm, 49–50
Dependency, mobile phone, 401–419
analysis, 416–419
between-country differences, 412,
412
individual media dependency,
403–405
literature review, 403–406
measures of key variables, 407–412
method, 406–411, 410, 411
predictors of individual media
dependency, 405–406
predictors of mobile phone
dependency, 413–415, 414
predictors of mobile phone
dependency for attaining self-
related goals, 416
predictors of mobile phone
dependency for attaining social
goals, 415–416
results, 411–416, 412, 414
Dependent co-arising paradigm, 36
Buddhist philosophy, 46–49, 47
Daoist philosophy, 46–49, 47
living systems theory, 46–49, 47
Deviance, 74–75, 77, 131
Diffusion, 25–26
international communication
research, 21, 21
Digital broadcasting, European
broadcasting, 454–458
Digital technologies, see also Specific
type
cultural imperialism, 8–33
Direction of flow, 26–28
Disability, 423–424
Asia, 426–427
negative attitudes, 427
Philippines
characterized, 427–429
government role, 428
mass media portrayals, 428–429
Disability advertising
mixed results, 423–424
multinational corporation, 423–424
Philippines, 423–439

Disability advertising (*continued*)
  analysis, 431–439
  disability only *vs.* combination
    of disability and nondisability
    groups, 436–438, *437*
  feeling and perception, 436, *436*
  feeling *vs.* behavioral effects, *433*,
    434–436, *435*
  hypotheses, 429–430
  literature review, 424–426
  method, 430–431
  purchase intention, *433*, 434, *435*
  results, 431–438, *433, 435, 436,
    437*
  try/use intention, *433*, 434, *435*
Disabled Peoples International, 427
Dissent
  Chinese blogs, 277–292
  types in controlled societies, 278
Dissipative structures theory, 36–37

E
Eastern Europe, media ownership
    concentration, 447–449
Eastern philosophy, 37
Eighteen Touch Dog Newspaper,
    282–292
Embedded journalism, 153–154, 205
Emergence, 37, 50–53
Entropy, 37, 50–53
Environmental challenges
  international public relations, 308
  multinational corporations, 308
Equilibrium, 37, 50–53
Ethical decision checklist,
    international public relations,
    371–372
European broadcasting
  digital broadcasting, 454–458
  ownership concentration, 442–459
    cross-ownership, 443–444,
      447–448
    diagonal concentration, 443–444,
      447–448
    history, 444–449
    horizontal concentration, 443
    vertical concentration, 443
European Union, 13–14
Event-related approaches, media
    frames, 178–180
Expertise, credibility, 242–244, 255
Exports, 133

F
Film industry
  cultural proximity, 20–21, *21*
  France, 8
  India, 25–26
  international communication
    research, 19–21, *21*
  South Korea, U.S. movies, 19–21, *21*
  United Kingdom, U.S. movies,
    19–21, *21*
  U.S., 25–26
Firestone/Bridgestone tires, 368–369
Flat world, 3
  forces, 3
Foreign bureaus
  CNN, 164
  U.S. news media, 163
  U.S. newspapers, 163
  U.S. television news, 163
Foreign elections, content analysis,
    109–123
  data analysis, 119–120
  hypotheses, 115
  international attributes, 114–115,
    117–118, *119*, 121–123
  international interactions, 113–114,
    117, *119*, 121–123
  literature review, 110
  location in world system, 112–113,
    116–117, *119*, 121–123
  method, 116–118
  results, *119*, 120
Framing, 177
  consequences, 203–206
  ideology
    macroattributes, 202
    microattributes, 202
    relationship, 202–203
France
  film industry, 8
  newspapers, Iraq War
    comparison, 205–215
    comparison methods, 206–209
    comparison results, *209*, 209–
      215, *210, 211, 212, 213*
Friedman, Thomas, 3

G
Gatekeepers, 74
General systems theory, 51
Geographic variables, international
    news coverage, 127

size, 134
Global brand building, 387–388,
    393–394
Global bystander intervention model,
    92–94
Global communication, *See*
    International communication
Global ethical standards
    international public relations, 367–
        370, 371–373
    Media Transparency Charter, 367
Globalism, international aid, 91–92
Globalization, 3, 29
    change in belief about reality, 25
    cultural imperialism, 14–15
        relationship, 10
    expansion of viewing and reader
        markets, 4
    imperialism
        contrasted as defining paradigm,
            22–23
        diffusion, 25–26
        direction of flow, 26–28
        effects on culture, 30–31
        major actors, 28–29
        mode of influence, 30
        research locus, 29–30
        underlying process, 25–26
        unit of analysis, 24
    international communication, 3
    international communication
        research, 21, *21*
    media conglomerates, 3–4
    methodological domains, 22
    nation-state, relationship, 13–15
    theoretical domains, 22
Global media, changing landscape,
    10–17
GNP, 133
Google, 24
Gross Domestic Product, *See* GDP
Gross National Product, *See* GNP

H
Homeostasis, 37, 50–53
Hybridization, 29
Hyperlinks, cultural imperialism,
    14–15

I
Idealism, international aid, 91–92
Ideology

framing
    macroattributes, 202
    microattributes, 202
    relationship, 202–203
    news, relationship, 201–202
Imperialism
    globalization
        contrasted as defining paradigm,
            22–23
        diffusion, 25–26
        direction of flow, 26–28
        effects on culture, 30–31
        major actors, 28–29
        mode of influence, 30
        research locus, 29–30
        underlying process, 25–26
        unit of analysis, 24
    international communication
        research, 21, *21*
    terminology, 29
    U.S. no longer dominant, 22–23
Independence
    ownership, 452–454
    television, 452–454
India
    film industry, 25–26
    international public relations,
        308–309
Influential case analysis, 136, *137, 138*
Innovation, 25
Integration–responsiveness grid,
        international public relations,
        300, 310–313, *313*
    multinational corporation, 300,
        310–313, *313*
International advertising, 424
    multinational corporation, 424
International aid
    bystander nonintervention effect,
        global bystander intervention
        model, 92–94
    determinants, 91–92
    globalism, 91–92
    idealism, 91–92
    international news coverage
        aid amount and number of
            donors, *98–100*
        analysis strategy, 97
        control variables relationships,
            95, *95,* 97
        data, 96–97
        GDP per capita, 95, *95,* 97, 104

International aid (*continued*)
  hypotheses, 94, *95*
  international trade, 95, *95*, 97, 104
  method, 96–97
  population, 95, *95*, 97, 104
  relationship, 89–105
  results, 97–103, *98–100, 101, 102*
  national security, 92
  realism, 91–92
International Association of Business
    Communicators, Code of
    Ethics, 372
International communication, *See also*
    Specific type
  characterized, 41
  cultural imperialism, default *vs.*
    design, 17, *17*
  globalization, 3
  living systems theory, 36–64
International communication research
  cultural discount, 21, *21*
  cultural imperialism, 9–33
  cultural proximity, 21, *21*
  diffusion, 21, *21*
  film industry, 19–21, *21*
  globalization, 21, *21*
  imperialism, 21, *21*
  network structure, 10
  paradigm testing, 8–33
  proximity, 20
  structure of offline world
    reproduced in cyberspace, 15
  theoretical orientation
    diffusionist, 18–19
    functionalist, 18–19
  theory cannot be assessed in
    isolation, 19
  theory weakness, 12
International conflicts, media frames,
    178–180
International elections
  news flow model, 112–115
    factors, 112–115, *119*
  U.S. media coverage, 109–123
    data analysis, 119–120
    hypothesis, 115
    international attributes, 114–115,
      117–118, *119*, 121–123
    international interactions, 113–
      114, 117, *119*, 121–123
    literature review, 110

    location in world system, 112–
      113, 116–117, *119*, 121–123
    method, 116–118
    results, *119*, 120
International industry codes,
    international public relations,
    371–373
International journalism, expansion of
    viewing and reader markets, 4
International Monetary Fund, 14
International news coverage
  citizen interest in, 161
  cultural affinity, 127–128
  determinants, 89–91, 125–142
    contextual approach, 125
    event-oriented approach, 125
    hypotheses, 128–129
    literature review, 126–128
  flow model, 109–123
  geographic variables, 127
  importance, 160–161
  international aid
    aid amount and number of
      donors, *98–100*
    analysis strategy, 97
    control variables relationships,
      95, *95*, 97
    data, 96–97
    GDP per capita, 95, *95*, 97, 104
    hypotheses, 94, *95*
    international trade, 95, *95*, 97, 104
    method, 96–97
    population, 95, *95*, 97, 104
    relationship, 89–105
    results, 97–103, *98–100, 101, 102*
  Internet, 164
  post-9/11, 147–158
    American audience interest,
      148–149
    breadth of news, 147
    embedded journalism, 153–154
    foreign correspondent ignorance,
      154–156
    framing news events, 149–150
    gatekeeping, 150–152
    graphicness, 150
    image selection, 154
    increase in audiences following
      international news, 153
    language barrier, 155–156
    misinterpretation of news events,
      153–154

misperceptions regarding Iraq War, 152–153
news professional constructions, 150
overestimating public disinterest in foreign news, 151–152
overload effect, 152–153
patriotic framework, 155–157
perceptions of reality, 149
photo selection, 150–151
quantity *vs.* quality, 147–148
volume of foreign news, 147
structural determinants, 90–105
U.S. news media, 73–86 (*see also* Specific type)
  circulation size, 73
  content analysis, 73–74
  context-oriented approach, 73, 74
  deviance, 74–75
  economic development, 79, 80–86, *81, 82, 83*
  economic system, 79, 80–86, *81, 82, 83*
  event-oriented approach, 73, 74–75
  findings, *80,* 80–86, *81, 82, 83*
  gatekeepers, 74
  hypotheses, 76–77
  international relations approach, 73
  literature review, 73–76
  loss of lives and property, 79–86, *81, 82, 83*
  method, 77–84
  natural disaster, 79–86, *81, 82, 83*
  newshole assignments, 75
  new variables conceptual and operational definitions, 78–80
  nonthreatening event relevant to U.S., 79, 80–86, *81, 82, 83*
  organizational approach, 73
  research questions, 76–77
  sampling procedure, 77
  statistical procedure, 80
  threatening event relevant to U.S., 78, *80,* 80–86, *81, 82, 83*
  trade relations with U.S., 79, 80–86, *81, 82, 83*
  U.S. relevance, 78, *80,* 80–86, *81, 82, 83*
  wire services, 72–73
  Wu's study, 76

U.S. newspapers, 77–86, 161–174
  domestic news, 168–171, *169, 170, 171,* 172–174
  financial cost, 163–164
  hypotheses, 165
  international news, 168–171, *169, 170, 171,* 172–174
  literature review, 161–163
  method, 165–168
  results, 168–171, *169, 170, 171,* 172–174
  story origin, 168–171, *169, 170, 171,* 172–174
U.S. television news, 161–174, 168–171, *169, 170, 171,* 172–174
  analysis method, 134–135
  content analysis, 129–142
  country-based factors, 126–142
  cultural affinity, 132
  dependent variable, 129–130
  determinants, 126–142
  deviance, 131
  domestic news, 168–171, *169, 170, 171,* 172–174
  exports, 133
  financial cost, 163–164
  geographic size, 134
  GNP, 133
  hypotheses, 165
  hypothesis evaluation, 137–141
  independent variables, 130–135
  influential case analysis, 136, *137, 138*
  literature review, 161–163
  main topics, 168–171, *169, 170, 171,* 172–174
  method, 129–135, 165–168
  military expenditure, 133
  multivariate measurements, 126–142
  population, 133
  position in hierarchy of nations, 132–133
  results, *135,* 135–136, 168–171, *169, 170, 171,* 172–174
  story origin, 168–171, *169, 170, 171,* 172–174
  U.S. relevance, 131–132
  world system location, 132–133
Web sites, 164
world system location, 128
world systems theory, 110–112

International public relations
  conflict management, Cameron's
    contingency theory, 346–362
  corporate accountability, 370–371
  cross-cultural research approach,
    373–374
  cross-national conflict shifts,
    320–340
    advertising standardization, 329
    centralization, 331
    coordination and control choices,
      323–324
    coordination and control
      mechanisms, 320–326
    coordination and control
      structure, 337–340
    coordination by socialization,
      326–328
    crisis response, 336–337
    between global integration and
      local responsiveness, 330
    global public affairs management,
      328–333
    integration, 331–332
    literature review, 320–333
    relationships among units in
      transnational organizations,
      328
    split-control structure, 326
  cultural setting, 306
  environmental challenges, 308
  ethical decision checklist, 371–372
  global ethical standards, 367–370,
    371–373
  India, 308–309
  integration–responsiveness grid,
    300, 310–313, 313
    multinational corporation, 300,
      310–313, 313
  international industry codes, 371–373
  multinational corporations, 299–314
    balancing global integration and
      local responsiveness, 309–310
    cases, 300–304
    global integration, 300–304
    integrated communication
      programs, 302–304
    interdependence, 301
    local responsiveness, 304–308
    pooled interdependence, 301
    strategy, 300–304
  paradigm shift, 366
    roles, 368
    social responsibility
      communication, 301
    survey research, 302
    theoretical framework, 366–375
Internet
  China, 277–292
    censorship, 279–280
    challenges to, 278–282
    Eighteen Touch Dog Newspaper,
      282–292
    metaphors and allusions, 283–285
    perils, 278–282
    self-censorship, 280
    stealth dissent by allusion, 278,
      282–292
    subject matter, 286–289
    victory in weblog contest, 284–
      286, 290–291
  closed flow, 15–17
  cultural imperialism, 8–33, 14–15
  economical gains, 11
  history, 10–11
  international news coverage, 164
  local access, 13–15
  nation-state, 13–15
  open network, 15–17
  single communication platform, 11
  size of daily audiences, 11
  who controls, 13
Iraq War, 200–215
  Arab newspapers
    comparison, 205–215
    comparison methods, 206–209
    comparison results, 209, 209–
      215, 210, 211, 212, 213
  British newspapers
    comparison, 205–215
    comparison methods, 206–209
    comparison results, 209, 209–
      215, 210, 211, 212, 213
  coverage, 204–215
  French newspapers
    comparison, 205–215
    comparison methods, 206–209
    comparison results, 209, 209–
      215, 210, 211, 212, 213
  U.S. newspapers
    comparison, 205–215
    comparison methods, 206–209
    comparison results, 209, 209–
      215, 210, 211, 212, 213

Italy, media ownership concentration, 445–446

J

Japan, corporate social responsibility, 306
Joint counterterrorism, media framing, U.S.–Uganda comparison, 220–237
Juan Valdez campaign
brand revitalization, 380–397
analysis, 394–397
brand authenticity, 385–387
country-of-origin effect, 385
findings, 390–394
global brand building, 387–388, 393–394
literature review, 382–390
method, 390
nation building, 384, 392–393
Colombia, 380–397
nation building, 384, 392–393

K

Knowledge-based industries, 3
Korean comfort women, 345
Kuhn, Thomas, 12

L

Language barrier, 155–156
Lesotho, content analysis, 335
Living systems theory
applications, 64
Buddhist philosophy, parallels, 46–50
central thesis, 42
communication applicability, 53–57
communication scholarship, 51–52
critical subsystems of living system, 40
Daoist philosophy, parallels, 46–50
dependent co-arising paradigm, 46–49, 47
essential concepts, 43
hierarchical levels, 38–41, 39, 43–44
international communication, 36–64
limitations, 45
news flow, 54–55
research strategy, 62–63
strengths, 44–45

subsystems, 40, 43–44, 60–62
supranational system, 44
validation, 63–64
world systems analysis, 56–57
Yijing paradigm, 49–50
Local access
Internet, 13–15
nation-state, 13–15
Local cultural factors, South Korea, 348

M

Match-up hypothesis, celebrity endorsement, 243
Meaning transfer model
celebrity endorsement, 243
credibility, 242–258
Media conglomerates, globalization, 3–4
Media framing, 224–237, see also News frames
counterterrorism
conceptualizing frame building, 225–228
conflict aggravation, 225, 227–228, 228, 231
data, 229–230
freedom of information, 228–229
methods, 229–230
politics, 228–229
power persuasion, 225, 226, 226–227, 231
event-related approaches, 178–180
international conflicts, 178–180
joint counterterrorism, U.S.–Uganda comparison, 220–237
results, 231, 231–237, 233
risk communication, 178–180
Mediaset corporation, 445–446
Media Transparency Charter, global ethical standards, 367
Military expenditure, 133
Miller, J.G., 38–65
Mobile phones
celebrity nude photos, 345
China, cross-cultural study, 401–419
conflict management, 346–362
analysis, 358–362
changing stance, 354–355
crisis development, 350–352
crisis ending, 357–358

Mobile phones (*continued*)
   crisis maturation, 352–353
   findings, 350–358
   method, 349–350
   reverse turn, 356–357
  dependency, 401–419
   analysis, 416–419
   between-country differences, 412, *412*
   individual media dependency, 403–405
   literature review, 403–406
   measures of key variables, 407–412
   method, 406–411, *410, 411*
   predictors, 413–415, *414*
   predictors for attaining self-related goals, 416
   predictors for attaining social goals, 415–416
   predictors of individual media dependency, 405–406
   results, 411–416, *412, 414*
  South Korea, 345
  ubiquity, 402
  U.S., cross-cultural study, 401–419
Mode of influence, 30
Multinational corporations, 28
  China, 305, 306
  disability advertising, 423–424
  environmental challenges, 308
  international advertising, 424
  international public relations
   balancing global integration and local responsiveness, 309–310
   cases, 300–304
   global integration, 300–304
   integrated communication programs, 302–304
   interdependence, 301
   local responsiveness, 304–308
   pooled interdependence, 301
   strategy, 300–304
  social responsibility communication, 301

N
National security, international aid, 92
Nation building, 384, 392–393
  Colombia, 384–385
Nation-state
  globalization, relationship, 13–15

  Internet, 13–15
  local access, 13–15
  U.S. government, 13
NBC, 129–142
  Congo, 149
  Sudan, 149
News
  culture, relationship, 200–215
  ideology, relationship, 201–202
  reality construction, 203–206
News Corporation, China, 13
News flow determinants
  Australia, 261–274
   colonial relations, 266–267, *271,* 271–274
   content analysis, 268–269, *269*
   contextual determinants, 263–264
   defense expenditures, 266–267, *271,* 271–274
   GDP, 265–266, 271–274, *274*
   geographic distance, 264, *271,* 271–274
   hypotheses, 264–267
   independent variables, 269–270
   land area, 264, *271,* 271–274
   method, 267–271
   military power, 266, *271,* 271–274
   population, 264–265, *271,* 271–274
   press freedom, 266, 271–274, *274*
   results, *271,* 271–274, *273*
   tourism, 265, 271–274, *274*
   trade, 265, 271–274, *274*
  blogging, 4
  international elections
   factors, 112–115, *119*
   model, 112–115
  literature review, 262–263
  living systems theory, 54–55
  online media, 261–274
   colonial relations, 266–267, *271,* 271–274
   contextual determinants, 263–264
   defense expenditures, 266–267, *271,* 271–274
   GDP, 265–266, 271–274, *274*
   geographic distance, 264, *271,* 271–274
   hypotheses, 264–267
   independent variables, 269–270
   land area, 264, *271,* 271–274

method, 267–271
military power, 266, *271*, 271–
    274
population, 264–265, *271*,
    271–274
press freedom, 266, 271–274,
    274
results, *271*, 271–274, *273*
tourism, 265, 271–274, *274*
trade, 265, 271–274, *274*
user generated content, 4
News frames, *see also* Media framing
contextual selection factors, 177–
    195
    cross-national studies, 177–195
    economic factors, 180–182
    hypotheses, 182–185
    influence of contextual factors,
        189–195, *191*
    measurement, 186–187
    methods, 185–187
    newspapers, 185–195
    political factors, 180–182
    research questions, 182–185
    results, 187–195, *188, 189, 190,
        191*
    sampling, 185
newspapers, 185–195
SARS, 177–195
    cross-national studies, 177–195
    economic factors, 180–182
    hypotheses, 182–185
    influence of contextual factors,
        189–195, *191*
    measurement, 186–187
    methods, 185–187
    newspapers, 185–195
    political factors, 180–182
    research questions, 182–185
    results, 187–195, *188, 189, 190,
        191*
    sampling, 185
News media, proliferation, 23
Newspapers
contextual selection factors, 185–
    195
news frames, 185–195
News quality, patterns, 160–174
Newsworthiness, *See* International
    news coverage
Newtonian–Cartesian paradigm,
    37–38, 52–53

O
Objectivity, media's claim of, 200
Online media, *see also* Specific type
Australia, 261–274
    colonial relations, 266–267, *271*,
        271–274
    content analysis, 268–269, *269*
    contextual determinants, 263–
        264
    defense expenditures, 266–267,
        271, 271–274
    GDP, 265–266, 271–274, *274*
    geographic distance, 264, *271*,
        271–274
    hypotheses, 264–267
    independent variables, 269–270
    land area, 264, *271*, 271–274
    method, 267–271
    military power, 266, *271*, 271–
        274
    population, 264–265, *271*,
        271–274
    press freedom, 266, 271–274,
        274
    results, *271*, 271–274, *273*
    tourism, 265, 271–274, *274*
    trade, 265, 271–274, *274*
news flow determinants, 261–274
    colonial relations, 266–267, *271*,
        271–274
    contextual determinants, 263–264
    defense expenditures, 266–267,
        271, 271–274
    GDP, 265–266, 271–274, *274*
    geographic distance, 264, *271*,
        271–274
    hypotheses, 264–267
    independent variables, 269–270
    land area, 264, *271*, 271–274
    method, 267–271
    military power, 266, *271*, 271–
        274
    population, 264–265, *271*,
        271–274
    press freedom, 266, 271–274, *274*
    results, *271*, 271–274, *273*
    tourism, 265, 271–274, *274*
    trade, 265, 271–274, *274*
Open network
closed flow, 15–17
Internet, 15–17
Ownership, independence, 452–454

Ownership concentration
  Central Europe, 447–449
  Eastern Europe, 447–449
  European broadcasting, 442–459
    cross-ownership, 443–444,
      447–448
    diagonal concentration, 443–444,
      447–448
    history, 444–449
    horizontal concentration, 443
    vertical concentration, 443
  Italy, 445–446
  self-censorship, 453–454
  Western Europe, 446–449
Ownership transparency
  Bulgaria, 449
  Romania, 449–450
  sanctions, 451–452
  Serbia, 449–452

P
Paradigm testing
  characterized, 17–18
  importance, 17–18
  international communication
    research, 8–33
Philippines
  disability
    characterized, 427–429
    government role, 428
    mass media portrayals, 428–429
  disability advertising, 423–439
    analysis, 431–439
    disability only *vs.* combination
      of disability and nondisability
      groups, 436–438, *437*
    feeling and perception, 436, *436*
    feeling *vs.* behavioral effects, *433*,
      434–436, *435*
    hypotheses, 429–430
    literature review, 424–426
    method, 430–431
    purchase intention, *433*, 434, *435*
    results, 431–438, *433*, *435*, *436*,
      437
    try/use intention, *433*, 434, *435*
Population size, 133
Post-9/11
  international news coverage,
    147–158
    American audience interest,
      148–149

    breadth of news, 147
    embedded journalism, 153–154
    foreign correspondent ignorance,
      154–156
    frames news events, 149–150
    gatekeeping, 150–152
    graphicness, 150
    image selection, 154
    increase in audiences following
      international news, 153
    language barrier, 155–156
    misinterpretation of news events,
      153–154
    misperceptions regarding Iraq
      War, 152–153
    news professional constructions,
      150
    overestimating public disinterest
      in foreign news, 151–152
    overload effect, 152–153
    patriotic framework, 155–157
    perceptions of reality, 149
    photo selection, 150–151
    quantity *vs.* quality, 147–148
    volume of foreign news, 147
  U.S. news media
    American audience interest,
      148–149
    breadth of news, 147
    embedded journalism, 153–154
    foreign correspondent ignorance,
      154–156
    frames news events, 149–150
    gatekeeping, 150–152
    graphicness, 150
    image selection, 154
    increase in audiences following
      international news, 153
    language barrier, 155–156
    misinterpretation of news events,
      153–154
    misperceptions regarding Iraq
      War, 152–153
    news professional constructions,
      150
    news selection, 150–152
    overestimating public disinterest
      in foreign news, 151–152
    overload effect, 152–153
    patriotic framework, 155–157
    perceptions of reality, 149
    photo selection, 150–151

quantity *vs.* quality, 147–148
  volume of foreign news, 147
Power-law distribution, 15–17, *16*
  structural attribute common to
    networks, 15–16
Power persuasion, 225, *226*, 226–227,
  231
Professional imperialism, 28
Proximity, international
  communication research, 20
Public Relations Institute of Australia,
  Code of Ethics, 372–373
Public Relations Society of America,
  Code of Ethics, 372

Q
Quantum physics, 38

R
Realism, international aid, 91–92
Reality construction, news, 203–206
Risk communication, media frames,
  178–180
Romania, media ownership
  transparency, 449–450

S
SARS
  impact, 180
  news frames, 177–195
    cross-national studies, 177–195
    economic factors, 180–182
    hypotheses, 182–185
    influence of contextual factors,
      189–195, *191*
    measurement, 186–187
    methods, 185–187
    newspapers, 185–195
    political factors, 180–182
    research questions, 182–185
    results, 187–195, *188, 189, 190,*
      191
    sampling, 185
Self-censorship, ownership
  concentration, 453–454
Serbia, ownership transparency,
  449–452
Severe acute respiratory syndrome,
  See SARS
Socialization, 326–328
Social responsibility communication
  international public relations, 301

multinational corporations, 301
Social science, 38
Sociocybernetic theories, *59*
South Korea
  case study method, 349–362
  cell phones, 345
  collectivism, 348
  film industry, U.S. movies, 19–21, *21*
  foreign imposition of commercial
    products, 14
  Korean comfort women, 345
  local cultural factors, 348
Standardization, 302
Sudan
  ABC, 149
  CBS, 149
  NBC, 149
Survey research
  international public relations, 302
  standardization, 302
Systems theory, three "waves," 50–51

T
Tabloidization, 454
Television, independence, 452–454
Terrorism
  characterized, 221–224
  conceptualizations, 211–212
  definition, 211
  Uganda, 222–224
  U.S., 222
Terrorist Finance Working Group, 220
Timberlands logging scandal, 369
Traditional media, decline, 11
Transference, credibility, 242–258
  dependent measure, 247
  hypotheses, 246–247
  independent measures, 248
  method, 247–248
  predictors, 251–253, *252, 253*
  results, 248–253, *250, 251*
Transnational organizations, cross-
  national conflict shifts, 320–
  340
  advertising standardization, 329
  centralization, 331
  coordination and control choices,
    323–324
  coordination and control
    mechanisms, 320–326
  coordination and control structure,
    337–340

Transnational organizations
    (continued)
  coordination by socialization,
      326–328
  crisis response, 336–337
  between global integration and
      local responsiveness, 330
  global public affairs management,
      328–333
  integration, 331–332
  literature review, 320–333
  relationships among units in
      transnational organizations,
      328
  split-control structure, 326
Trustworthiness, credibility, 242–244,
    255

U
Uganda
  counterterrorism, media framing,
      220–221, 224–237
  terrorism, 222–224
United Kingdom, film industry, 19–21,
    21
Universal interconnectedness, 36
U.S.
  film industry, 25–26
  imperialism, no longer dominates,
      22–23
  mobile phone, cross-cultural study,
      401–419
  terrorism, 222
U.S. government, nation-state, 13
U.S. news media, see also Specific type
  international election coverage,
      109–123
    data analysis, 119–120
    hypothesis, 115
    international attributes, 114–115,
        117–118, 119, 121–123
    international interactions, 113–
        114, 117, 119, 121–123
    literature review, 110
    location in world system, 112–
        113, 116–117, 119, 121–123
    method, 116–118
    results, 119, 120
  internationalnewscoverage,161–174
    determinants, 73–86
    domestic news, 168–171, 169,
        170, 171, 172–174

financial cost, 163–164
    hypotheses, 165
    international news, 168–171,
        169, 170, 171, 172–174
    literature review, 161–163
    main topics, 168–171, 169, 170,
        171, 172–174
    method, 165–168
    post-Cold War, 73–86
    results, 168–171, 169, 170, 171,
        172–174
    story origin, 168–171, 169, 170,
        171, 172–174
  international news coverage
      determinants, 73–86
    circulation size, 73
    content analysis, 73–74
    context-oriented approach, 73,
        74
    deviance, 74–75, 77
    economic development, 79, 80–
        86, 81, 82, 83
    economic system, 79, 80–86, 81,
        82, 83
    event-oriented approach, 73,
        74–75
    findings, 80, 80–86, 81, 82, 83
    gatekeepers, 74
    hypothesis, 76–77
    international relations approach,
        73
    literature review, 73–76
    loss of lives and property, 79–86,
        81, 82, 83
    method, 77–84
    natural disaster, 79–86, 81, 82, 83
    newshole assignments, 75
    new variables conceptual and
        operational definitions, 78–80
    nonthreatening event relevant to
        U.S., 79, 80–86, 81, 82, 83
    organizational approach, 73
    research questions, 76–77
    sampling procedure, 77
    statistical procedure, 80
    threatening event relevant to U.S.,
        78, 80, 80–86, 81, 82, 83
    trade relations with U.S., 79,
        80–86, 81, 82, 83
    U.S. newspapers, 77–86
    U.S. relevance, 78, 80, 80–86, 81,
        82, 83

U.S. television networks, 77–86
wire services, 72–73
Wu's study, 76
post-9/11
American audience interest,
    148–149
breadth of news, 147
embedded journalism, 153–154
foreign correspondent ignorance,
    154–156
frames news events, 149–150
gatekeeping, 150–152
graphicness, 150
image selection, 154
increase in audiences following
    international news, 153
language barrier, 155–156
misinterpretation of news events,
    153–154
misperceptions regarding Iraq
    War, 152–153
news professional constructions,
    150
news selection, 150–152
overestimating public disinterest
    in foreign news, 151–152
overload effect, 152–153
patriotic framework, 155–157
perceptions of reality, 149
photo selection, 150–151
quantity *vs.* quality, 147–148
volume of foreign news, 147
U.S. newspapers, 77–86
foreign bureaus, 163
international news coverage,
    161–174
domestic news, 168–171, *169,*
    170, 171, 172–174
financial cost, 163–164
hypotheses, 165
international news, 168–171,
    169, 170, 171, 172–174
literature review, 161–163
method, 165–168
results, 168–171, *169, 170, 171,*
    172–174
story origin, 168–171, *169, 170,*
    171, 172–174
Iraq War
comparison methods, 206–209
comparison results, *209,* 209–
    215, *210, 211, 212, 213*

comparisons, 205–215
U.S. television networks, 77–86
U.S. television news
foreign bureaus, 163
international news coverage, 161–
    174, 168–171, *169, 170, 171,*
    172–174
analysis method, 134–135
content analysis, 129–142
country-based factors, 126–142
cultural affinity, 132
dependent variable, 129–130
determinants, 126–142
deviance, 131
domestic news, 168–171, *169,*
    170, 171, 172–174
exports, 133
financial cost, 163–164
geographic size, 134
GNP, 133
hypotheses, 165
hypothesis evaluation, 137–141
independent variables, 130–135
influential case analysis, 136,
    137, 138
literature review, 161–163
main topics, 168–171, *169, 170,*
    171, 172–174
method, 129–135, 165–168
military expenditure, 133
multivariate measurements,
    126–142
population, 133
position in hierarchy of nations,
    132–133
results, *135,* 135–136, 168–171,
    169, 170, 171, 172–174
story origin, 168–171, *169, 170,*
    171, 172–174
U.S. relevance, 131–132
world system location, 132–133
networks, 76–85, 129–142
User-generated content, news selection
    process, 4

V
Validation, living systems theory,
    63–64

W
Web sites, international news
    coverage, 164

We-ness, 348
Western Europe, media ownership
    concentration, 446–449
Wire services, 72–73
World Bank, 14
World system location, international
    news coverage, 128
World systems analysis, living systems
    theory, 56–57

World systems theory, international
    news, 110–112

Y
Yijing paradigm, 38
    Buddhist philosophy, 49–50
    Daoist philosophy, 49–50
    living systems theory, 49–50